D1604000

TOFINO and CLAYOQUOT SOUND

A History

Margaret Horsfield and Ian Kennedy

TOFINO and CLAYOQUOT SOUND

A History

Harbour Publishing

Harbour Publishing Co. Ltd.
P.O. Box 219, Madeira Park, BC, V0N 2H0
www.harbourpublishing.com

Edited by Audrey McClelland
Indexed by Stephen Ullstrom
Text design by Lisa Eng-Lodge
Dust jacket design by Anna Comfort O'Keeffe
Maps by Carlos García González
Printed and bound in Canada

Front jacket: Carol Evans' watercolour, "Feather in a Pool," depicts Frank Island and Chesterman's Beach near Tofino, BC. *Courtesy the artist and Dayspring Studio Inc. (carolevans.com).* Front flap and back jacket (detail): This painting, "A Whale Ashore—Klahoquaht," by American artist George Catlin shows a beached whale with Nuu-chah-nulth hunters converging on the scene. For many years Catlin travelled widely in North America to record the appearance and activities of indigenous people. He made one voyage along the Northwest Coast, going as far north as the Aleutians, in the 1850s. Note the sailing vessel near the shore and the steamship on the far horizon. *National Gallery of Art, Washington, DC, Image 1965.16.214.*

Harbour Publishing acknowledges financial support from the Government of Canada through the Canada Book Fund and the Canada Council for the Arts, and from the Province of British Columbia through the BC Arts Council and the Book Publishing Tax Credit.

Cataloguing data available from Library and Archives Canada
ISBN 978-1-55017-681-0 (cloth)
ISBN 978-1-55017-682-7 (ebook)

In memory of Gordon R. Elliott,
teacher and friend.

1920–2006

Contents

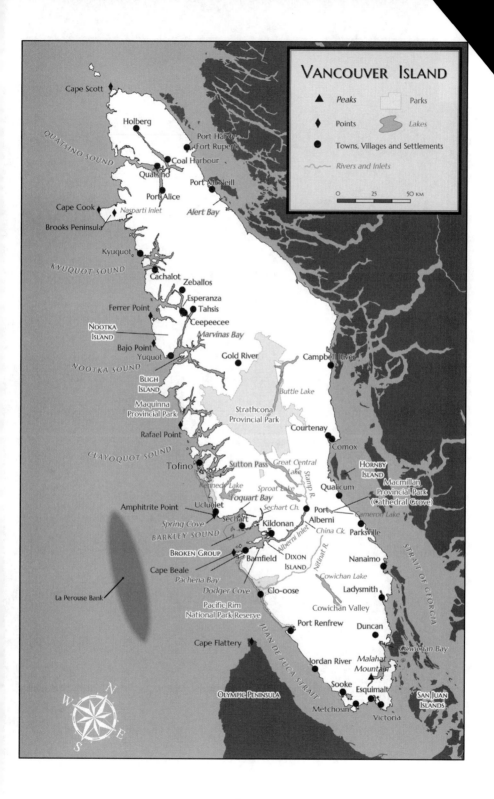

VANCOUVER ISLAND

▲ *Peaks*   *Parks*

◆ *Points*   *Lakes*

● *Towns, Villages and Settlements*

〜 *Rivers and Inlets*

0   25   50 KM

Cape Scott

Holberg

QUATSINO SOUND

Port Hardy
(Fort Rupert)

Coal Harbour

Quatsino

Port McNeill

Port Alice

Alert Bay

Cape Cook

Nasparti Inlet

Brooks Peninsula

Kyuquot

KYUQUOT SOUND

Cachalot

Zeballos

Esperanza

Ferrer Point

Tahsis

NOOTKA
ISLAND

Ceepeecee

Marvinas Bay

Bajo Point

Yuquot

Gold River

Campbell River

NOOTKA SOUND

BLIGH
ISLAND

Buttle Lake

Maquinna
Provincial Park

Strathcona
Provincial Park

Rafael Point

Courtenay

CLAYOQUOT SOUND

Comox

Tofino

Sutton Pass

Great Central
Lake

HORNBY
ISLAND

Kennedy Lake

Qualicum

Macmillan
Provincial Park
(Cathedral Grove)

Amphitrite Point

Ucluelet

Toquart Bay

Sproat Lake

Sechart Ch.

Stamp R.

Spring Cove

Sechart

Kildonan

Port
Alberni

Cameron Lake

BARKLEY SOUND

China Ck.

Parksville

BROKEN GROUP

DIXON
ISLAND

Alberni Inlet

Nitinat R.

Nanaimo

Cape Beale

Bamfield

Pachena Bay

Cowichan Lake

Ladysmith

La Perouse Bank

Dodger Cove

Clo-oose

Pacific Rim
National Park Reserve

Cowichan Valley

Port Renfrew

Duncan

STRAIT OF GEORGIA

Cape Flattery

JUAN DE FUCA STRAIT

Cowichan Bay

Jordan River

Malahat
Mountain

OLYMPIC PENINSULA

Sooke

Esquimalt

SAN JUAN
ISLANDS

Metchosin

Victoria

N
W   E
S

ix

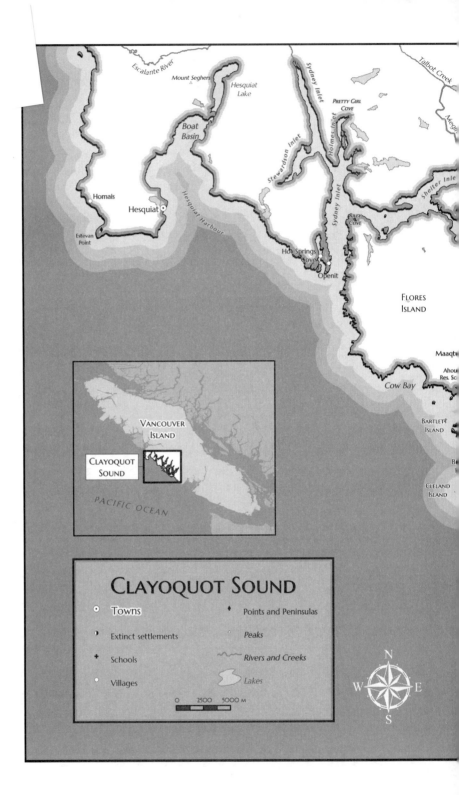

Escalante River

Mount Seghers △

Hesquiat Lake

Sydney Inlet

Talbot Creek

PRETTY GIRL COVE

Holmes Inlet

Megi

Boat Basin

Stewardson Inlet

Sydney Inlet

Shelter Inle

Homais

Hesquiat Harbour

RILEY COVE

Hesquiat ⊙

Estevan Point

Hot Springs Cove

Openit

FLORES ISLAND

Maaqtu

Ahou Res. Sc.

Cow Bay

BARTLETT ISLAND

B

CLELAND ISLAND

VANCOUVER ISLAND

CLAYOQUOT SOUND

PACIFIC OCEAN

CLAYOQUOT SOUND

⊙ Towns

◗ Extinct settlements

✚ Schools

○ Villages

◆ Points and Peninsulas

∴ Peaks

〰 Rivers and Creeks

⬳ Lakes

0   2500   5000 M

N
W   E
S

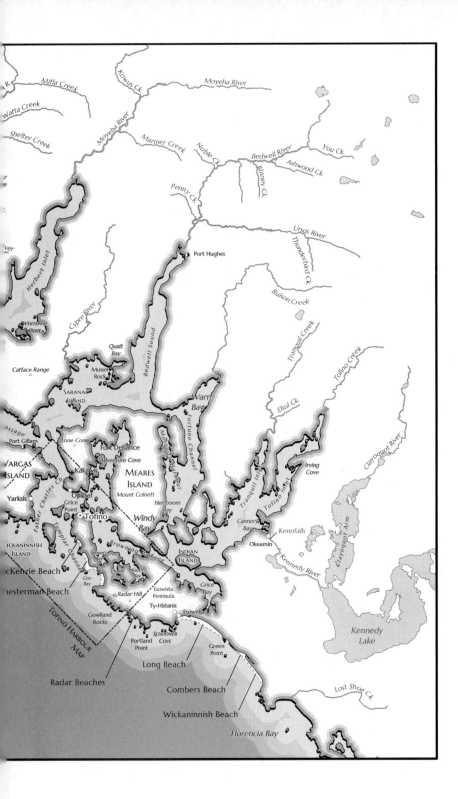

Mitla Creek
Watta Creek
Shelter Creek
Kowus Ck.
Moyeha River
Moyeha River
Mariner Creek
Noble Ck.
Bedwell River
You Ck.
Blaney Ck.
Ashwood Ck.
Penny Ck.
Ursus River
Thunderbird Ck.
Port Hughes
Herbert Inlet
WHITEPINE COVE
VARGAS ISLAND
Cypre River
Bedwell Sound
Bulson Creek
Quait Bay
Mussel Rock
Catface Range
SARANAC ISLAND
Warm Bay
Fortune Channel
Tranquil Creek
Tofino Creek
Elsul Ck.
Clayoquot River
Passage
Port Gillam
Lone Cone
Fort Defiance
Adventure Cove
Matlset Narrows
Irving Cove
VARGAS ISLAND
Yarksis
Father Charles Ch.
Kakawis
MEARES ISLAND
Mount Colnett
Heelboom Bay
Tranquil Inlet
Tofino Inlet
Clayoquot Arm
Opitsat
Grice Point
Tofino
Windy Bay
Cannery Bay
Kennfalls
Kennedy River
Kennedy Lake
WICKANINNISH ISLAND
Templar Channel
Browning Passage
INDIAN ISLAND
Okeamin
McKenzie Beach
Jensen's
Indian South Bay
Cox Bay
Grice Bay
Chesterman Beach
Radar Hill
Esowista Peninsula
Ty-Histanis
Esowista
TOFINO HARBOUR MAP
Gowland Rocks
SCHOONER COVE
Portland Point
Green Point
Long Beach
Radar Beaches
Combers Beach
Lost Shoe Ck.
Wickaninnish Beach
Florencia Bay

xi

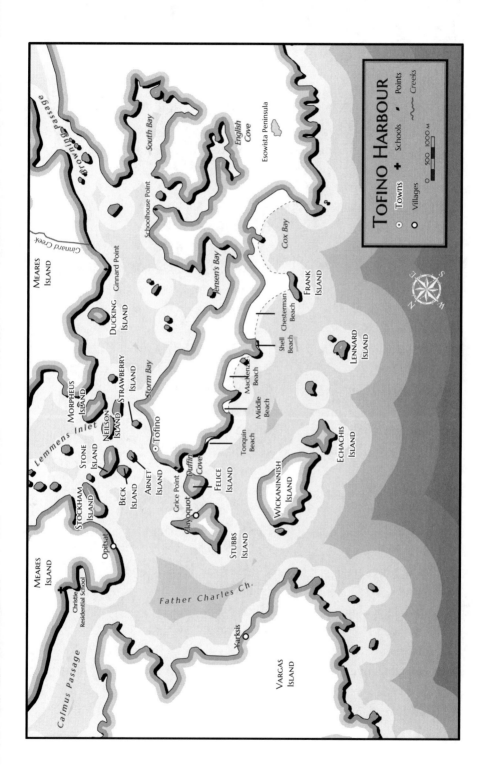

Concerning Place Names

MANY PLACES MENTIONED IN THIS BOOK are known by, or have been known by, more than one name. A selective list of these follows. The official names, listed on the left, are taken from current marine charts, or the Gazetteer of British Columbia.

Official Name	Alternate Name(s)
Cypre River	Trout River
Stubbs Island	Clayoquot Island
Arnet Island	Dream Isle, Castle Island, Tibbs Island
Beck Island	Garden Island
Florencia Bay	Wreck Bay
Neilson Island	Bond Island
Esowista Peninsula	Low Peninsula*
Bedwell River	Bear River
Lemmens Inlet	Disappointment Inlet
Felice Island	Round Island
Strawberry Island	Leach Island
MacKenzie Beach	Garrard's Beach
Cox Bay	False Bay
English Cove	Maltby Slough, Deep Mud Bay
Long Beach	Long Bay, Wickaninnish Bay
Grice Bay	Mud Bay, Mill Bay
Quait Bay	Calm Creek
Haida Gwaii	Queen Charlotte Islands
Yuquot	Friendly Cove
Calmus Passage	Hecate Pass
Heelboom Bay	C'is-a-quis Bay
Hot Springs Cove	Refuge Cove
Kennedy Cove	Back Bay
Kennedy River	Elk River
Marktosis	Maaqtusiis

* Name still in use on 1921 census.

Throughout the book we have generally chosen to use place names as given in the Gazetteer of British Columbia. For this reason, First Nations villages appear as "Hesquiat" or "Ahousat," without the "aht" ending that is increasingly used. However, we use the "aht" ending (meaning "people of") in the names of the aboriginal peoples of Clayoquot Sound.

We do not attempt to provide all of the names traditionally used by First Nations, nor all the names used by the Japanese who lived on the coast prior to World War II.

Place names around the world reflect choices made in previous generations, often for political reasons. Official West Coast place names repeatedly honour explorers, traders, naval vessels, missionaries, and settlers. Writing for the *Daily Victoria Gazette* in 1858, William Banfield questioned the names colonial authorities were giving to places on Vancouver Island's west coast. "Good taste would lead us at the present day to adopt the Indian names," he wrote, "in most instances... much prettier, many of them having a natural beauty of sound...Great Britain's Colonies have enough Royal names, noble names, and titles of our grandfathers and grandmothers." His comments went unheeded. But as time passes, place names in Clayoquot Sound, and all over British Columbia, remain subject to change. In a hundred years, a list of place names in this area could look very different.

The Tla-o-qui-aht village of Okeamin on the east shore of the Kennedy River near the Clayoquot cannery, ca. 1930. *Image AA 00287 courtesy of Royal BC Museum, BC Archives*

INTRODUCTION

FROM ACROSS CANADA AND FAR BEYOND, visitors travel in great numbers to Tofino and Clayoquot Sound at the edge of the Pacific Ocean. Inspired by spectacular images of old-growth rainforest, vast sandy beaches, and abundant wildlife, they flock in the hundreds of thousands to the westerly end of a winding road across the mountains and find themselves in one of the most acclaimed wilderness areas in the world.

Midway up the west coast of Vancouver Island, Clayoquot Sound covers approximately 2,600 square kilometres, measures some fifty kilometres in length and as much as twenty-five kilometres wide. The Sound embraces the land, lakes, rivers, islands, and inlets between Hesquiat Peninsula to the north and Long Beach and Kennedy Lake to the south. It includes nine major watersheds and four major inlets: Sydney Inlet, Shelter Inlet, Herbert Inlet, and Bedwell Sound, also covering Warn Bay and Tofino Inlet. Many rivers and streams flowing westward from the interior mountains of Vancouver Island run into Clayoquot Sound: Tofino, Bulson, and Ursus Creeks, and Bedwell, Moyeha, Megin, and Sydney Rivers, among others. The largest islands of the Sound—Flores, Vargas, and Meares—along with a scattering of seemingly countless smaller islands, Wickaninnish, Echachis, Lennard, Frank, and Stubbs to name only a few, protect much of the shoreline and the inside waters from the open Pacific Ocean. Several small communities are located in Clayoquot Sound: Hot Springs Cove, Ahousat, Opitsat, Esowista, Ty-Histanis, and Tofino; of these, only the last three can be accessed by road.

1

The lush temperate rainforest of Clayoquot Sound supports one of the richest forest ecosystems on earth. Here stand some of the world's most impressive old-growth trees, giant Sitka spruce, Douglas fir, and most particularly the red cedars, some of them up to 100 metres high and between 800 and 1,000 years old, flourishing in the mild climate, dense fogs, and heavy coastal rains. The wealth of marine life in the area includes grey whales, humpbacks, and orca, with porpoises, fur seals, sea lions, and sea otters abounding in the offshore waters. Bird life teems on the expansive tidal mud flats of the Sound, and the annual return of the salmon to the rivers, streams, and lakes continues to be a source of wonder.

Our book focuses on Clayoquot Sound and Tofino, with a few necessary detours taking us farther afield. The early history of European exploration, and the ensuing sea otter trade, inevitably leads us to Nootka Sound, just as the fur seal trade leads to the Bering Sea, the lust for gold to Wreck (Florencia) Bay, and the need to track businesses, bureaucrats, and gunships to Victoria. Despite such geographic departures, we have attempted as much as possible to remain within Clayoquot Sound and its immediate vicinity.

A rich, multi-layered past and a wealth of story have made this area what it is today, beginning with grindingly slow eons of geological upheaval and glacial movement forging the remarkable landscape. Some 4,200 years ago, indigenous peoples established themselves here, living in harmony with the environment, and harvesting the resources of land and sea in a seasonal cycle. Not quite 250 years ago, European explorers arrived—first the Spanish, then the British—vying for territory and power, bringing with them international conflict and hard-bitten, highly competitive fur traders, avid for sea otter pelts. Then ships arrived from the newly fledged United States, their captains fiercely determined to obtain furs and to establish an American presence in the Pacific Northwest. The presence of these early explorers and traders accelerated the spread of deadly diseases along the coast, with catastrophic impact on the aboriginal people. The Nuu-chah-nulth, as the people living along Vancouver Island's west coast have become known, diminished drastically in number throughout the nineteenth century as their contact with traders and newcomers increased.

By the late nineteenth century, immense scene-shifting changes occurred as more, and yet more, outsiders arrived on the coast and left their mark. These included captains of sealing schooners during the intense years of the fur sealing industry; then more traders, followed by missionaries, settlers, prospectors, fisherfolk, and early loggers. Some came to stay, to raise families, and to forge a community; all had an eager interest in the resources of the land and sea.

Many outstanding personalities have contributed to the history of this area over the years. They include such forceful characters as Tla-o-qui-aht Chief Wickaninnish, the duplicitous British captain John Meares, American captains Kendrick and Gray, the wildly eccentric trader Fred Thornberg, the outspoken Ahousaht leader Billy August, the legendary sealing captain Alex MacLean, the self-serving entrepreneur Walter Dawley. They also include the powerful Roman Catholic missionary Father Augustin Brabant and other missionaries who followed him, all ruthlessly determined to convert aboriginal people to Christianity. This process of "conversion" came to mean removing children from their families and placing them in residential schools, where they could not speak their own language. Two such schools existed in Clayoquot Sound: the Catholic school at Kakawis on Meares Island, and the Presbyterian school at Ahousat.

The determined settlers who came, and who remained here, eked out a living through ingenuity and hard work; the community they established became Tofino, a village that from its inception attracted loners, eccentrics, and dreamers. As time passed and the community grew, townsfolk gathered to dance on Saturday nights in the Community Hall, and every ten days they rushed to meet the coastal steamer on Boat Days, delighted to have contact with the outside world. Before World War II, Japanese Canadians made up nearly a third of the town's population, only to face evacuation and internment as enemy aliens in 1942. A large air base at Tofino Airport during the war brought thousands of servicemen to the west coast; because of them, a half-decent gravel road finally extended to Ucluelet, some forty kilometres southeast of Tofino, at the entrance to Barkley Sound.

For decades, west coast residents lobbied energetically for a road across the mountains that would connect them to Port Alberni and the rest of Vancouver Island. When the road finally arrived in 1959, unimagined consequences followed. Residents looked on in baffled amazement as crowds of campers and tourists, thrill-seekers and motorcycle gangs, hippies and surfers followed the road to the coast. Their sheer numbers at times caused chaos on the beaches and contributed to the impetus to create a national park along the west coast.

Meanwhile, fishing off the coast intensified, taking immense, unsustainable hauls of fish, as if the stock could last forever. The multinational logging companies also set to work, hungry for the great trees, careless of how they obtained them, leaving vast clear-cut scars on the land and mountainsides. After years of protests about logging methods, and growing dismay at environmental degradation, the summer of 1993 brought hundreds of not-easily-intimidated people from around the world to stand on the Kennedy Lake Bridge and block the loggers. The largest mass arrests in Canadian history followed, and the fame of Clayoquot Sound spread like wildfire.

Following this intense storm of worldwide publicity, the village of Tofino could never be the same again. The quiet, rain-drenched community at the end of the road found itself transformed into a major international tourist destination. In common with places like Banff, Whistler, or Niagara Falls, the very names "Tofino" and "Clayoquot Sound" conjure up potent images, instantly recognizable across Canada and in countries ranging from Australia to Germany to Japan.

A word of warning about the name "Clayoquot" in the following pages; its many applications can cause confusion. Widely used, it refers to all of Clayoquot Sound, to Clayoquot Arm on Kennedy Lake, and to the Clayoquot River running into that lake. Some people call Stubbs Island, just off Tofino, "Clayoquot Island," because an early trading post and a small townsite, both called Clayoquot, stood here in the late nineteenth and early twentieth century. For a brief period, the rival townsite at the head of the Esowista Peninsula, later named Tofino, also bore the name Clayoquot; and for a time this area had two schools, one on Stubbs Island, one in Tofino, and both named "Clayoquot School."

The Tla-o-qui-aht people, living in the southern reaches of Clayoquot Sound, are sometimes called the "Clayoquots"; the name originated with them. They are one of three Nuu-chah-nulth First Nations inhabiting Clayoquot Sound, the others being the Ahousaht, who occupy the central area of the Sound, and the Hesquiaht, to the north. These First Nations all have ancient connections to their long-inhabited traditional territories, and they are all currently engaged in negotiations with various levels of government to settle land claims, to establish self-governance, and to gain greater control over their lands and resources.

The wealth of natural resources in Clayoquot Sound sustained the First Nations for thousands of years. This abundance also acted as a magnet that drew explorers, traders, and settlers here, followed by industrial-scale fishing and logging. The international protests about clear-cut logging in Clayoquot Sound led to intense popular awareness of the attractions of this area, establishing it firmly as a hot spot for tourism. When visitors arrive now, they expect the best. They walk the beaches, explore the rainforest and soak in the hot springs; they come for surfing and kayaking, for whale and bear and bird watching, and for winter storm watching. All of these activities rely on the natural resources here, on elements sustained and produced by the land and the sea and the temperate climate.

The economic fate and environmental health of this entire region have always been entwined. Past mistakes in resource management along this coast have been epic in scale: sea otters nearly became extinct, salmon and herring and various shellfish have been overharvested, mountainsides and watersheds have been stripped. The people of Tofino and Clayoquot Sound continue to face immensely challenging decisions concerning resource management and land use. Not all agree on the best way forward, but whatever their differences, no one wants to repeat past mistakes. So they work together, many different interest groups and organizations, striving to find consensus on the broad issues that affect the area.

To be in Tofino, or anywhere in Clayoquot Sound, means being on a storied coast with a complex past. As we trace the history in this area from slow geological movements to the fast-paced changes of recent years, we encounter many dramatic shifts and changes in landscape and in population, in resource management and in attitudes. Extraordinary events have shaped the history of Tofino and Clayoquot Sound, and no doubt many more will continue to do so. After all, here on the west coast, at the end of the road, the extraordinary often does seem to be the norm.

Chapter 1:

THE LAY OF THE LAND

Clayoquot Sound has hundreds of small islands made of ancient volcanic rock.
Thousands of years of erosion by glaciers and wave action shaped these islands.
The mud flats, home to thousands of birds and a wealth of marine life, can be seen
to the right. Tofino appears at the bottom of the photo, and Opitsat on the left, on
Meares Island, across the harbour. *Sander Jain photo*

IMMENSE, SLOW, AND COMPLEX FORCES have shaped the
land around Tofino and Clayoquot Sound. The scenery that has drawn
millions of visitors to the west coast took its present form over eons of
time and through cataclysmic geological events. The relentless actions
of plate tectonics, volcanoes, earthquakes, glaciers, rivers, wind, and
ocean waves have produced this landscape, leaving the entire west coast
of Vancouver Island with a beautiful, bewildering array of geologic and
geographic features.

The formation of the land around Tofino and Clayoquot Sound
began in the tropical regions of the South Pacific some 200 million

years ago, when the landmass that would become British Columbia did not even exist. Then, as now, massive tectonic plates that make up the earth's crust and range in depth from thirty to one hundred kilometres moved very slowly on top of the earth's molten mantle. The constant movement of these plates, resembling huge industrial conveyor belts driven by convection currents in the mantle, caused earthquakes to occur, volcanoes to erupt, mountains to form and portions of the earth's crust to appear and disappear. What is now the West Coast of Canada lay east of today's Rocky Mountains, with Pacific Ocean waves sweeping ashore where the foothills of Alberta now meet the prairies. These ancient Pacific waves crashed against the western edge of a large tectonic plate called Laurentia, which comprised the Canadian Shield and most of what would later become Canada. After moving slowly eastward for millennia, for some unknown reason Laurentia quietly changed direction and began moving westward at a rate of two to ten centimetres a year, bumping into offshore island chains and reef-like landmasses called *terranes* lying in its path. This slow collision caused the soft sea bed between the colliding landmasses to buckle and fold upward, forming the Rocky Mountains. This young fold mountain range, as geologists call it, thrust upward in exactly the same way as the Himalayas, the Alps, and the Andes, which explains why climbers and geologists find marine fossils in the layers of sedimentary rock as they ascend these ranges. This also explains why limestone—formed from coral and other living sea creatures—is still being mined on the western side of the Rockies.

Laurentia's slow movement continued crumpling the sea bed for the succeeding 200 million years, incorporating other terranes into Canada's western landmass. Sometimes this tectonic movement caused new volcanic activity to occur as plates forced their way over other plates along North America's West Coast. Consider the string of volcanoes between Alaska and California: California's Mount Shasta; Oregon's Mount Rainier; Washington's Mount St. Helens and Mount Baker; British Columbia's Whistler Mountain and Mount Edziza; and Mount McKinley in Alaska—all the result of volcanic action brought about by plate tectonic movement.

A mere hundred million years ago, after five separate terranes slowly collided with the west coast of Laurentia to form most of British Columbia, the Wrangellia terrane showed up. Having begun its millennia-long journey somewhere in the eastern South Pacific near the island of Tonga, Wrangellia arrived off Laurentia, and slowly the two welded together. Wrangellia came equipped with ready-made volcanic mountains, which today make up the Vancouver Island Ranges, Haida Gwaii, and parts of southeastern Alaska. Formed of igneous rocks produced by volcanic activity, these Wrangellian mountains differ entirely from the sedimentary formations of the Rocky Mountains.

In geological terms, the West Coast's Wrangellian mountains make the Rockies look like infants. Some of the rock in Wrangellia's mountains dates back as far as 400 million years before Wrangellia hit the BC coast. This means that 200 million years before Laurentia collided with its very first terrane to begin to form the Rockies, the earliest signs of Wrangellia began emerging above the ancient South Pacific ocean floor near Tonga. Volcanoes erupted under the sea, pouring lava and ash upward to form islands. After the volcanoes stopped erupting and the lava cooled, coral and other tropical sea life began living on the cooled rock along the shorelines, forming coral reefs. River-borne sediments from these newly formed islands began washing down rivers to form deltas and broad coastal plains. Then, about 160 million years ago, volcanic action restarted the island-building process. Unlike the first undersea volcanic activity, this time the volcanic material, or lava, cooled in the air, forming rock that looked entirely different from that formed under water. When Wrangellia crossed the equator into more temperate climates, advancing at a speed of seven or eight centimetres a year, deposits of land-formed rock like shale and sandstone began to adhere to the moving platform of islands, increasing its size. This massive rock mass evolved as it moved; a lot can happen in a million years of travel.

By the time Wrangellia arrived off the coast of Canada, it had incorporated many newer forms of rock on its surface, but it still consisted largely of ancient igneous rock formed under the sea. Some of this 270-million-year-old rock, the oldest on Vancouver Island, can be found near Buttle Lake, about fifty kilometres east of Clayoquot Sound. A rock sample found at Grice Bay near Tofino is believed to be 260 million years old, and the bedrock of Lemmens Inlet also derives from the Wrangellia terrane. Lone Cone and Catface Mountain arrived in Clayoquot Sound on the Wrangellia terrane; their age, some 41 million years. Contrary to a widespread local belief, Lone Cone is not a volcano. According to Melanie Kelman, a volcanologist with the Geological Survey of Canada, "Lone Cone is one of the Catface Intrusions, masses of quartz diorite that intruded the Westcoast Crystalline complex about 41 million years ago. So Lone Cone is definitely made of igneous rock but it is intrusive, not volcanic." In lay terms, the rock that formed Lone Cone solidified deep underground.

When this mixed-up mass of geology named Wrangellia slowly collided with Laurentia, the collision caused earthquakes that crushed, folded, and fractured the rock. The sea bed between the two plates rose up with pressure so great that Wrangellia eventually split in two. The western section continued on its slow way 2,000 kilometres northward to form parts of Alaska; the rest remained in what is now southern British Columbia.

The story does not end there. Far from it. The most important part of Clayoquot Sound's geological drama still lay in the future. After Wrangellia had adhered to what became British Columbia, huge submarine landslides, caused by the collision of tectonic plates, occurred in the area of the San Juan Islands, south of Victoria in Washington State. A mass of underwater rock and other material released by these landslides began moving northward, attaching itself to the western edge of Wrangellia about 55 million years ago. This Pacific Rim terrane, as geologists call it, includes material underlying Vargas Island and extending down to Port Renfrew. Highly visible outcroppings of this terrane appear along the Esowista Peninsula, on the stretch of land running past Long Beach down to Ucluelet, including Radar Hill, and also on various islands offshore, including Frank and Lennard Islands. About 42 million years ago the Crescent terrane, the last of the terranes making up Vancouver Island, and the smallest one, arrived to complete the puzzle; this now makes up the Metchosin area near

Victoria. With these terranes in place, water, wind, waves, and, later, ice began attacking the land and busily wore away masses of rock and other material over the next 40 million years. A great deal of this eroded material settled on top of the Pacific Rim and Crescent terranes and piled up on the original bedrock surrounding places like Radar Hill.

The greatest transformation of Vancouver Island occurred in fairly recent geologic time. During the Pleistocene era, which lasted 200,000 years and ended only 10,000 years ago, four separate continental ice sheets covered almost the whole landscape of what is now Canada. Imagine ice up to 3,000 metres thick covering Canada from Newfoundland to Vancouver Island, and as far south as the mid-United States. The weight of such a mass of ice caused Vancouver Island to sink under the pressure, and as that immensely deep ice shifted back and forth it sculpted the land beneath. At one time the ice extended as much as ten to fifteen kilometres off the west coast of Vancouver Island. When it melted, as it did from time to time, contemplate the amount of water released, and how the land would have rebounded—a geological process called *isostasy*—as the weight of the ice lifted. During this melting process, sea levels stood an estimated ninety metres above today's sea level, leaving only the highest points, such as Mount Colnett, Lone Cone, and Catface Mountain, emerging above the sea as small islands. The deep valleys and inlets of Clayoquot Sound; the huge boulders found on some beaches, called glacial erratics; the gouges, or striations, seen on some bedrock; the glacier-formed lakes such as Kennedy Lake; and the rocky soils all attest to the last ice age.

The flat land lying at the foot of the mountains and along the shore between Tofino and Ucluelet consists of glacial till, a mix of jagged rocks, sand, and silt making up what geologists call the Estevan Coastal Plain. Rivers flowing across that plain in front of the glaciers sorted some of the glacial material into rounded rocks and pebbles, as well as silt and sand, depositing it in deltas. Then the sea and the waves lashed the shore, further grinding the river deposits and creating long sandy beaches such as those at Wreck (Florencia) Bay, Long Beach, Cox Bay, Chesterman Beach, and MacKenzie Beach. Within Clayoquot Sound, away from the pounding waves, at low tide massive mud flats

The beaches of Clayoquot Sound, including Long Beach, seen here with the Estevan Coastal Plain lying behind, consist of debris from the last ice age 10,000 to 12,000 years ago. Waves ground the material into long, sandy beaches. *Sander Jain photo*

reveal an abundance of the finely ground material created during the post-glacial period.

Once the ice receded for the last time about 10,000 to 12,000 years ago, the newly uplifted land began basking in warmer temperatures, and plant life and animals began to reappear, eventually drawing the first human settlement to Clayoquot Sound. The earliest people may have migrated along the *Beringia* land bridge, a stretch of land across the present-day Bering Strait that once connected Asia and North America. They then could have made their way slowly down the coast and through North, Central, and South America on what anthropologists call the Coastal Migration Route. Other theories suggest the first inhabitants of North America arrived by sea via an ice-free coastal corridor along the edge of the Bering Sea about 17,000 years ago. Anthropologist Alexander Mackie argues this means "that all early period sites could be accommodated by people immigrating along the edge of the Bering Sea—previously thought by naysayers to be so inhospitable an edge of ice that no one could pass that way."

Archaeological evidence suggests that aboriginals lived at Yuquot in Nootka Sound 4,300 years ago, in Barkley Sound 5,000 years ago, and in Bear Cove near Port Hardy 6,000 years ago. Others likely lived on the mainland coast of BC near Namu as long as 10,000 years ago. The village of Opitsat, visible across Tofino Harbour, is believed to have been continuously inhabited for at least the past 2,000 years and possibly longer, given that aboriginal people have lived in Clayoquot Sound for some 4,200 years. Before the first contact with Europeans, the indigenous population in what is now British Columbia is estimated to have been anywhere from 100,000 to 250,000, though more conservative estimates suggest only around 80,000. Of these people, an estimated 15,000 lived along the west coast of Vancouver Island.

One of the most important natural resources on the West Coast, enabling aboriginal people to live and settle here in such numbers, is the versatile red cedar (*Thuja plicata*), sometimes referred to as the "tree of life." Massive red cedars thrive on this coast because of the moist climate, and for the aboriginals, truly "people of the cedar," these trees came to have great spiritual significance, as well as countless practical uses. Cedars provided material for dugout canoes, housing, paddles, clothing, baskets, rope; for many household implements; for medicine; and for ceremonial purposes. Planks of cedar could be cut from living trees, and the trees would survive; similarly, areas of bark could be stripped from standing trees with no harm done. Such "culturally modified trees"—or CMTs—can be found, still thriving, in the great forests of Clayoquot Sound, evidence of how a resource could be used wisely and well.

These immense cedars require an equally immense amount of rain, an inescapable fact of life here, especially in the winter. In this temperate rainforest, where the great cedars can grow to heights of sixty metres, heavy rains *must* fall, and they do. Tofino averages 202 days

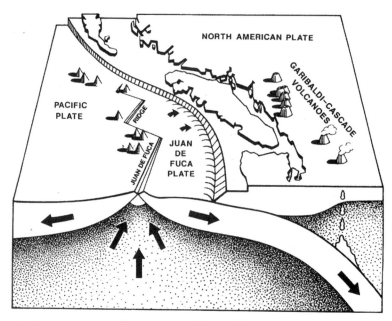

Tectonic plates are constantly in motion off Canada's west coast. The Juan de Fuca plate is forced under the North American plate, less than 500 kilometres off Clayoquot Sound, creating an ever-present danger of earthquakes. *Courtesy of Chris Yorath*

of precipitation a year and an annual rainfall of 3.3 metres—over ten feet. The maximum precipitation recorded at the Tofino Airport weather station for one day stands at 18.4 centimetres and on October 6, 1967, a record-breaking rainfall of 48.9 centimetres was recorded by the former weather station at the now defunct Brynnor Mine near Maggie Lake. By comparison, Vancouver receives a paltry one metre of rain a year and only averages 166 days of precipitation. As for the temperature, freezing temperatures and snow rarely occur at sea level, and the Tofino Airport weather station records an average of 364 days per year when the thermometer stands above freezing. January boasts a daily average minimum temperature of 1.2°C, while the summertime average stands at only 14.4°C.

The location and geography of the West Coast present another drawback to people here, a potentially deadly hazard. Vancouver Island's outer coast is located toward the northern end of the 1,100-kilometre-long

Cascadia subduction zone, which extends up the coast from Cape Mendocino, California. Within this suboceanic zone, tectonic plates are constantly on the move, grinding past one another. The Juan de Fuca Plate, moving eastward, slips under, or *subducts*, the North American Plate, heading west. The continual slow-motion collision causes minor earth tremors, only detectable by delicate seismographs, almost every day. But the action taking place at the Cascadia subduction zone can, from time to time, cause calamitous natural disasters.

The danger occurs when the two plates become "locked," causing pressure to build to the point where it must be released as a massive "megathrust" earthquake. Seismologists estimate that plate locking takes place every 400 to 500 years, meaning that the West Coast is constantly under threat from a "Big One." Paleoseismic research has determined that thirty-nine megathrust earthquakes have occurred along the Cascadia fault in the past 10,000 years. Nineteen of these quakes ranged from 8.7 to 9.2 in magnitude on the Richter scale. Some of them took place 800 years apart, others less than 200 years apart. In geologic time, the last one occurred fairly recently, just over three centuries ago.

At about 9 p.m. on Tuesday, January 26, 1700, a massive earthquake shook the West Coast. The tremors lasted for several minutes, throwing people to the ground and continuing long enough for survivors to experience nausea and vomiting. First Nations oral history tells of whole villages being swept inland by a massive *tsunami*, or tidal wave, fifteen to twenty metres high, before the backwash took them out to sea. At Pachena Bay, just south of Barkley Sound and 130 kilometres south of Tofino, the wave swept the heavily populated Huu-ay-aht winter village of Clutus entirely out to sea. There were no survivors. Huge trees snapped like matches, landslides rained rocks and debris down slopes, and to the south a massive landslide completely blocked the mighty Columbia River, causing it to carve a new route for itself. In what is now Washington State, red cedar and spruce trees far inland died when sea water driven by the tsunami inundated their roots, leaving "ghost forests." Destruction swept the land.

Ten to twelve hours later, the tsunami caused by this earthquake hit the shores of Japan, sending a five-metre wave crashing inland, killing thousands of people and causing widespread damage. Because no local earthquake had forewarned of the danger, the wave swept in unannounced. This has become known as the Orphan Tsunami.

The Japanese keep written records of earthquakes and tsunamis as far back as the 1500s, so seismologists have been able to calculate the time of the Cascadia Earthquake. By studying the cedar trees in the "ghost forests" in Washington state, researchers determined that their last growth ring dates back to 1699, the year before the earthquake. These findings coincide exactly with the First Nations oral traditions. A Cowichan tale recorded at the turn of the twentieth century and cited in the journal *Seismological Research Letters* describes the event. "In the days before the white man there was a great earthquake. It began about the middle of one night...threw down...houses and brought great masses of rock down from the mountains. One village was completely buried beneath a landslide. It was a terrible experience: the people could neither stand nor sit for the motion of the earth." Another account, which appears in Kathryn Bridge's book *Extraordinary Accounts of Native Life on the West Coast*, tells of the eradication of Clutus village near the mouth of Pachena Bay. "They had gone to bed, it was just like any other normal night. They were awoken during the night when the earth began to shake. The earth shook. Startled the people. They woke up. Thinking everything was over, they just relaxed. A little while later, the water came in real fast. Swept their homes away. Swept everything away. The water just came too fast. They didn't have time to go to their canoes, so all the people that were living there were drowned. They were all wiped out."

Brian Atwater's book *The Orphan Tsunami* passes on information from James Swan, the first schoolteacher on the Makah Reserve on the Olympic Peninsula. On January 12, 1864, Swan recorded in his diary a conversation with Billy Balch, a Makah leader who lived near Neah Bay. Balch spoke of how all the lowland areas on the west coast of the Olympic Peninsula and Vancouver Island sank following the earthquake, with sea water inundating these areas after the tsunami. "That water receded and left Neah Bay dry for four days and became very warm. It then rose again without any swell or waves and submerged the whole cape and in fact the whole country except the mountains back of Clayoquot. As the water rose, those who had canoes put their effects into them and floated off with the current that took them north. Some drifted one way then the other and when the waters again resumed their accustomed level a portion of the tribe found themselves beyond Nootka where their descendants now reside and are known by the same name as the Makahs—or Quinaitshechat."

At 5:36 p.m. on Good Friday, March 27, 1964, the largest earthquake ever to be recorded in North America shook Anchorage, Alaska, for four minutes. Measuring 9.2 on the Richter scale, the intensity of this quake is exceeded only by the Chilean earthquake of 1960, which measured 9.5. The Anchorage earthquake set off a tsunami that rushed south and west across the Pacific Ocean at speeds of up to 640 kilometres (400 miles) per hour. Of the 131 people killed by the quake, 122 drowned, not only in Alaska, but also in Oregon, where four people died, and California, where thirteen lost their lives. Though no deaths occurred in British Columbia, the tsunami hit Prince Rupert with a 1.4-metre wave just over three hours after the quake. Moving south it caused damage at Amai Indian Reserve at the head of Kyuquot Sound, at Zeballos, Hot Springs Cove, Tofino, and Ucluelet before surging up the Alberni Canal. There it washed away 55 houses, damaged 375 others, and left a swath of destruction. The cost to British Columbia is estimated to have been the current equivalent of $65 million.

Neil Buckle lived at Long Beach in 1964, and he recalled the tsunami in an interview with Joanna Streetly for her book *Salt in Our Blood*.

> A rumbling roar woke me up...The salal was completely still. Then I looked and saw that the water was right level with the bank and there were logs banging around it..."Oh for Christ's sake, it's a tidal wave!" I realized, because the water never came that high, normally. It was absolutely mesmerizing. These big spruce trees were snapping in two or three pieces and the logs were banging and clunking around. They caused a log jam that lasted for years and years. It went a good mile

[over 1.5 kilometres] up Sandhill Creek. Then all of
a sudden the water seemed to go. It just—left! And as
it did, the logs that were in the creek came tumbling
down, end over end. These huge logs being tossed like
match sticks and the water raging out toward the ocean.
I was totally stunned.

The slow grind of plate tectonic action remorselessly continues.
Countries surrounding the Pacific Ocean and its so-called Ring of Fire
keenly realize that any earthquake, anywhere in the Pacific Ocean,
has the potential to create multiple tsunamis that could send waves
from ten to fifteen metres high travelling at high speed right around
the Pacific basin. Governments have established coordinated tsunami
warning systems to alert people to potential danger in time for them
to make for higher ground. Everyone living along the Pacific coast
has now become aware that they must proceed to the highest available
ground following an earthquake, in expectation of a tsunami. Nothing
has made this clearer than the catastrophic earthquake of December
27, 2004, with its epicentre just off the coast of Sumatra. The subsequent tsunami, with waves up to thirty metres high, swept around the
Indian Ocean, killing 230,000 people in fourteen countries. Most had
no idea it was coming; at the time, no tsunami warning systems were
in place in countries bordering the Indian Ocean.

In common with many communities along the outer coast of Vancouver
Island, Washington, Oregon, and California, Tofino now has a highly
sensitive tsunami warning system. Tofino's system is recognized as a
key "alarm bell" on the West Coast for detecting what experts term
"tsunami events." Once a tsunami hazard has been identified, sirens
wail out, and residents should have at least fifteen to twenty minutes
to get to higher ground, following the evacuation route signs along
the roads. This system has evolved over a number of years, along
with awareness among locals of the nature of the risk. On Vancouver

The threat of tsunamis around the Pacific Rim's Ring of Fire has led communities like Tofino to establish detailed emergency response plans, including sirens near beaches to warn of potential threats. Signs identify hazard zones and evacuation routes to follow in the event of a tsunami alert. *Ian Kennedy photo*

Island's west coast, tsunami warnings have been issued frequently enough in the past decades that people know the drill. Some take it more seriously than others, and every tsunami warning leaves a host of stories in its wake.

On May 9, 1986, an earthquake in the Aleutian Islands off Alaska prompted a tsunami warning for Hawaii and the Pacific coast of North America. When the warning came, four hours before the impending tidal wave, Tofino boat owners began taking their smaller boats out of the water and anchoring their larger ones in Browning Passage, aiming them toward the open ocean and hoping they would ride out the wave. RCMP cruisers and a helicopter, all with loud-hailers, ordered people to make their way to Radar Hill. Some patrons of the Maquinna Hotel beer parlour, choosing not to go, carried their drinks up to the roof

Following the 2011 earthquake in Japan and the subsequent tsunami, this motorcycle came ashore on Haida Gwaii, inside a container. When contacted, the owner chose to donate the motorbike to the Harley-Davidson Museum in Milwaukee, Wisconsin. *Harley-Davidson Museum*

and set up chairs to watch the excitement. About 600 Tofino residents eventually did make it to Radar Hill where, according to Frank Harper in his book *Journeys*, "a huge bonfire was crackling. Many car trunks were open and out of them had come the beer, the chips, the sandwiches, the juice, the blankets. Music was blaring from Sue Kimola's fine speaker system and the people, even kids, were dancing, some frenzied, some mellow, all happy...

At five minutes after ten, the great, bogus, two-inch tsunami warning was officially cancelled." Following Russia's Kuril Islands earthquake of October 4, 1994, Frank Harper related how Tofino handled the third tsunami warning in eight years. Even though rumours circulated about potential fourteen-metre waves, no one seemed unduly troubled. Tourists evacuated from their hotels milled around the Wickaninnish School, but few local people paid much heed to the warning.

More recently, on March 11, 2011, the 9.0 magnitude Tohoku earthquake, the world's fifth most powerful since 1900, detonated seventy kilometres underwater off the northeast coast of Japan. The savage tsunami that followed sent forty-metre waves sweeping ashore, extending up to ten kilometres inland over the Tohoku area of coastal Japan. More than 25,000 people were killed or injured. Seconds after the quake, authorities issued tsunami warnings for the whole Pacific Rim region. Although some areas of the US West Coast suffered damage, Vancouver Island's west coast escaped; a wave of only one metre came ashore.

The tsunami in Japan swept enormous amounts of debris out to sea, estimated at 1.5 million tonnes. It travelled slowly eastward on the Kuro Siwo current, and within months some of this flotsam began to appear on West Coast beaches, prompting the Japanese government to give Canada $1 million to help with the cleanup. Community groups along the West Coast began collecting the plastic bottles, Styrofoam, rope, fishing nets, and buoys that washed up. Everyone finding debris was required to report it to the appropriate authorities, but stories have eddied up and down the coast on the "kelp telegraph" of fascinating objects both large and small discovered and quietly retained. A small boat washed up on Long Beach, another near Hesquiat Harbour, but the object most discussed in the media proved to be a motorcycle. A year after the tsunami, a Japanese shipping container turned up on an island in Haida Gwaii, containing a Harley-Davidson. The company managed to locate the owner, Mr. Yokoyama, in Japan; he had survived the quake but lost three members of his family. He declined the company's offer to restore the bike and ship it back to him, and instead donated it to Harley-Davidson to be placed, just as it was found, in the company's Milwaukee museum. Experts suggest that detritus from the tsunami will continue to land on West Coast beaches for years to come; so far, less has arrived than many people anticipated.

Knowing that a "Big One" could shake the West Coast one day, and that a tsunami could engulf the low-lying land along the shore, has become an accepted fact of life in the Tofino area. The seismological threat will never fade away. Immense geological upheavals shaped this landscape, the movements continue under the surface of the earth, and the people living here choose different ways of handling this reality. Some simply try to ignore the geological time bomb, others hope the "Big One" will be deferred indefinitely, while many spend time and effort educating themselves and their children and putting complex disaster plans in place for the public good. Whatever their attitude, everyone living here has an awareness of what could happen, and in a very special way they all know what it means to live on the edge.

Hesquiat village around 1900. The Nuu-chah-nulth people built their villages on gradually sloping beaches of sand or light gravel, with fresh water nearby. In such locations, they could easily land and launch their canoes. Note the sizes and variety of canoes. These dugout canoes could be up to eleven metres long and carry a dozen or more men on whale hunts. *Mount Angel Abbey Library*

Chapter 2:

THE PEOPLE OF THE SOUND

The entire story of our people exists as a large body of information carried

in our memories...It is an ongoing conversation among the people.

— Ahousaht Hereditary Chief Earl Maquinna George

THREE NUU-CHAH-NULTH FIRST NATIONS call Clayoquot Sound their home: the Hesquiaht, Ahousaht, and Tla-o-qui-aht. Their traditional territories, or *ha'houlthee*, extend from Hesquiat Peninsula in the north to Kennedy River and Long Beach in the south, and each nation recognizes a number of hereditary chiefs, or *ha'wiih*, within its territory. Other tribal groups inhabited the area in earlier times, each with its own territory and chiefs, among them the Otsosaht, the Kelsemaht, the Manhousaht, the Owinmitisaht, the Quatsweaht, and the Puneetlaht. Over time, these various groups either amalgamated with larger groups or were conquered by them in wars.

The traditional territory of the Hesquiaht, a name that comes from the word *hiishhiisha*, meaning "the sound made by eating herring eggs off eelgrass," covers the northern reaches of Clayoquot Sound around Hesquiat Peninsula, Hesquiat Harbour, and Hesquiat Lake. The Hesquiaht First Nation formed when five smaller tribes from around the harbour amalgamated, making for a combined population numbering in the thousands in the years before European contact. The traditional winter village of the Hesquiaht stands at the mouth of the harbour; home to over 200 people in the late nineteenth century, now very few people live there. Since the mid-twentieth century, Hot Springs Cove, near the entrance to Sydney Inlet, has served as the principal village of the Hesquiaht. Their five reserves comprise a total of 323.5 hectares. In total, their present-day population numbers around 700, with fewer than 100 living in Hesquiaht territory.

The Ahousaht, meaning "people living with their backs to the land and mountains on a beach along the open sea," traditionally occupied the western side of Vargas Island, along Ahous Bay, and a small area of land across Calmus (Hecate) Passage below Catface Mountain. Through warfare and amalgamation with other groups, including the Otsosaht, Kelsemaht, and Manhousaht, their traditional territory now encompasses a large area in the heart of Clayoquot Sound covering Vargas and Flores Islands and up Herbert, Shelter, and Sydney Inlets. Early in the nineteenth century, the Ahousahts established their main village, Maaqtusiis (Marktosis), on the east side of Flores Island. Their twenty-four reserves, ranging in size from 2 to 116 hectares, make up a total of 565.6 hectares. The Ahousaht are the largest Nuu-chah-nulth tribe on the west coast, with a current population of some 2,000; approximately 800 live within Ahousaht territory.

The Tla-o-qui-aht (Clayoquot) First Nation, located in the southern end of Clayoquot Sound, took shape from an alliance of smaller groups, many originally living around Kennedy Lake. The word "Tla-o-qui-aht" translates as "people of different tribes" and also as "people of Clayoqua (Tla-o-qua)," an area of the Kennedy Lake system. Their traditional territory covers the land around Kennedy Lake and Kennedy River, as well as Tofino Inlet, Esowista Peninsula, the islands offshore, and Meares Island. Centuries ago, the Esowistaht tribe controlled the Esowista Peninsula, keeping a tight hold on ocean resources and occasionally raiding the settlements at Kennedy Lake. The Tla-o-qui-aht banded together with other smaller tribes, and together they fought back, killed all the Esowistaht, and seized their territory. "Esowista" means "clubbed to death." Esowista village lies alongside the road north of Long Beach, adjacent to the recently constructed Ty-Histanis development. The principal Tla-o-qui-aht village is Opitsat, located directly across the harbour from Tofino. Their twelve reserves comprise a total of 347.8 hectares, and their population now numbers around 1,000, with over 400 living in Tla-o-qui-aht territory.

These three First Nations belong to the Nuu-chah-nulth people, formerly called the Nootka. The West Coast Tribal Council adopted the name Nuu-chah-nulth, meaning "all along the mountains and sea," in 1978. This group includes all of the First Nations along Vancouver Island's west coast between Cape Cook on the Brooks Peninsula in the north and Jordan River in the south, extending inland about halfway across Vancouver Island, taking in Port Alberni and Gold River. The fourteen Nuu-chah-nulth First Nations in this territory share the same language and the same "aht'" suffix on their names, meaning "people of." Their most dense areas of settlement lie in Nootka, Barkley, and Clayoquot Sounds.

Estimates vary enormously about the size of aboriginal populations in British Columbia prior to contact with Europeans. Recent estimates run to 100,000 and above, although others put the figure at just above 80,000. One undisputed point does emerge: the Pacific Northwest supported one of the most densely populated areas in North America, with at least 15,000 Nuu-chah-nulth living on the west coast of Vancouver Island prior to European contact.

The mild climate and the abundance of food made the location ideal for supporting a large population, and the Nuu-chah-nulth survived and prospered. Two extraordinary resources enabled this: the red cedar trees, which provided housing, transport, and clothing; and salmon, the aboriginal people's main food source. Many other readily accessible seafoods also ensured their well-being.

Over countless generations, the people on the coast structured their lives in harmony with the seasonal changes of each passing year. The arrival of the herring to spawn in the inlets and bays of the west coast in late February and early March saw the beginning of the Nuu-chah-nulth seasonal cycle. The people raked and dip-netted the massive schools of spawning herring for their oil, roe, and flesh. They also gathered the herring roe when it had been deposited on kelp or eelgrass, and they submerged boughs of hemlock in areas where herring spawned to attract the roe. In his book *As Far As I Know*, Ahousaht elder Peter Webster recalled the excitement of herring season when he was a boy.

The canoes were hurriedly pulled into the water and paddled to the area of activity. Many tons of fish could be seen circling near the surface. These were hauled into the canoes by means of dip nets. Each of these was about two and a half feet [0.75 metres] in length and the same measurement in width at the top and about three or four feet [1 or 1.25 metres] in depth. Each had a handle about twenty feet [6 metres] long. Three loads of the dip net would fill a canoe.

Once the canoe was loaded it was paddled to shore. The fish were transferred to baskets woven from spruce roots...The herring were then dumped into a bin of logs and boards that had been made especially for the catch. Each of these bins held the contents of several canoes.

My mother and grandmother cleaned the herring one at a time. My father cut the sticks on which the herring were hung to be smoked. My grandfather would get the wood ready for the smoke house which would be in use day and night for a week.

After this the herring were packed into large containers made of cedar bark. Each of these was three feet by three feet [1 metre] with a separate cover tied to the top.

Revitalized from feasting on the herring, and encouraged by the warmer weather, people loaded their canoes with whatever they needed and paddled from their winter villages to their summer fishing villages and camps on the outer coast. Many of the Tla-o-qui-aht, who wintered at Opitsat, moved round into Templar Channel to their village on Echachis Island, while the Ahousaht moved to summer settlements on various small islands and on the outer coasts of Flores and Vargas Islands.

Upon arriving at their summer homes, the people began trolling for spring salmon—the first of five runs of salmon appearing each summer and fall: spring, sockeye, coho, pink (or humpback), and chum (or dog salmon). They dried or smoked their catch immediately to

The arrival of shoals of herring to spawn into Clayoquot Sound each spring started the seasonal cycle of food harvesting. The Nuu-chah-nulth anchored hemlock boughs in the bays and inlets during a herring spawn. When heavily coated with herring roe, the boughs were collected and dried on racks, for use in the winter. *Mount Angel Abbey Library*

preserve their seasonal overabundance of fish for the lean winter months. By April, a time known as *Ho'ukamil*, meaning "flying flocks," migrating ducks and geese fell to the arrows and nets of these skilled hunters. April was also the month the Nuu-chah-nulth fished for halibut and cod using a variety of methods where four men in a big canoe could catch as many as a hundred halibut in a morning's fishing. These they dried for later consumption. Low spring tides allowed the women to gather clams, urchins, chitons, and black turban snails on the beaches, and they would continue to harvest barnacles, butter clams, and razor clams throughout the summer. In early spring they harvested the young shoots of salmonberries, thimbleberries, horsetail, and cow parsnips, and the roots of eelgrass and other plants that could be dried and stored away for winter. As the season progressed, they picked many types of berries: salmonberries, huckleberries, and salal, to name a few. These would be cooked to a paste-like consistency, formed into small cakes, placed on skunk cabbage leaves, then set on racks to dry.

One of the last traditional Tla-o-qui-aht whale hunts brought this whale ashore to the beach at Echachis. "Indians caught a whale. A big monster of a humpback," wrote Father Charles Moser in his diary on April 21, 1905. Father Charles took many photographs, including this one, during his years as a missionary on the coast.
Mount Angel Abbey Library

From late February onward, throughout the springtime, the migrating California grey whales would appear in Clayoquot Sound on their journey north from their winter breeding and calving grounds in Baja, California, to their rich feeding grounds in the Bering Sea. Their timing coincided with the arrival of the herring, for like so many other creatures, the whales feasted on herring roe, straining it through their baleen or scraping it loose near shore from the eelgrass and kelp. By April, the season of the whale hunt would begin, lasting two or three months.

The hunting of these grey whales, as well as humpback whales, set the Nuu-chah-nulth apart from other First Nations. Only they and the Makah people, farther to the south on the Olympic Peninsula, were "the people of the whale." To participate in a whale hunt carried immense spiritual significance, as well as considerable danger. Hunters had to be carefully trained and ritually prepared; they abstained from sexual activity, cleansing themselves with elaborate cold-water bathing ceremonies before the hunt. The head harpooner underwent lengthier and far more rigorous preparations extending from November until

April, cleansing and scouring his body and sea bathing in a highly ritualized manner, following intricate ceremonies and adhering to complex taboos. Toward the end, he retired to a powerful and secret shrine containing totems, skulls, masks, and other talismans, where he prayed and invoked the spirits to aid him in the upcoming challenge. A chief who inherited the role of head harpooner held a revered position within the tribe.

The whale hunt set forth in magnificent extra-large dugout canoes measuring from nine to eleven metres in length and up to two metres wide, carrying crews of between six and twelve: the harpooner, a steersman, and paddlers. One or more whaling canoes with a similar crew, each with a harpooner of lower rank, would accompany the main canoe carrying the head harpooner. Once they were out to sea and the hunters sighted a whale, the canoes positioned themselves so that when the whale came to the surface for air, the head harpooner, standing on the prow of the canoe, could thrust his three-metre-long harpoon just behind the whale's front flipper. The head of the harpoon, attached to line made of whale sinew and cedar withes, embedded in the whale, and the yew-wood harpoon shaft came free. When the whale sounded, the line played out, and the crew ensured the smooth exit from the canoe of the four sealskin floats attached at intervals to the line. In 1858, William Banfield, the first settler and government agent who lived on the west coast of Vancouver Island, witnessed a traditional whale hunt. His colourful description, published in the *Daily Victoria Gazette*, noted how the whale sounded "at a great rate," and that "the seal skins attached to him [tended] to impede and cramp his movements much."

After the first harpoon thrust, the harpooners in the accompanying canoes joined the hunt. Each time the whale surfaced, a harpooner would be waiting to spear him, while paddlers and steersmen worked hard to keep the canoes out of reach of the whale's violent struggle. Eventually, according to Banfield, the harpoons attached as many as forty or fifty sealskin bladders to the stricken whale, as it "beats and plunges in a fearful manner, overturning and breaking canoes." As the whale lost strength, it dove less deeply each time it sounded, eventually staying at the surface, at which point the hunters "surround him...

and goad him with their short spears until he becomes exhausted and dies." A whale still capable of heading far out to sea could sometimes tow the canoe great distances, weakening all the time, before finally succumbing. If all went well, the whalers made their final kill without that happening. Then came the most gruelling challenge of all: towing a carcass the size of a semi-trailer back to their village—an extraordinarily arduous feat, accompanied by loud, rhythmic singing of "a song that would paralyze a strange white man," in Banfield's estimation. Peter Webster related how on one hunt his father and his crew harpooned a whale that towed them so far out to sea that "only the snow capped mountains were visible on the horizon." The men, out of food, had to leave the whale and return to land to replenish their supplies before returning to tow it to land. "It would appear that the entire pursuit took two weeks from the beginning to the end."

Having beached the whale at high tide in front of their village, the men flensed the whale, removing its blubber and meat, and distributed the pieces according to a strict protocol reflecting status and custom within the tribe. "The piece which is considered the most desirable," stated Banfield, "is cut off for the chief and generally weighs about 100 pounds [45 kilograms]. The next in priority is the individual who first harpooned the whale." Nothing went to waste. A successful whale hunt led to intense jubilation, and the hunters, hailed with traditional songs, dances, and ceremonies, gained great prestige. If they returned without a whale, or if accidents occurred during the extremely high-risk hunt, the people believed some taboo had been violated or one of the crew had not properly followed the purification rituals.

In July, sockeye salmon began migrating into the inlets and bays of Clayoquot Sound, heading toward their spawning rivers and streams. The aboriginal people followed, heading to their traditional inshore fishing territories. For the Tla-o-qui-aht, this included the mouth of the Kennedy River. There they caught the fish, mostly by using weirs and salmon traps, and either dried or smoked them. As the successive runs of salmon arrived in the inlets, the people would move with the fish from one area to another within their territory, collecting their harvest. By September, with the weather changing, the outer shore summer encampments stood mostly empty. The fishing activity now centred on the salmon streams. The final run of chum, or dog salmon, had very high value because the fish had less fat than other salmon so dried better for storage over the winter.

The Nuu-chah-nulth hunkered down for the winter months as the rain and storms restricted outdoor activity. Their winter villages varied considerably in size but generally had at least twenty longhouses, each housing several families. These structures stood at the tops of sloping sandy beaches adjacent to a supply of fresh water. The fragility of the cedar canoes made a sand or light gravel foreshore an essential feature for a village site. Huge cedar timbers and beams formed the permanent frame of the longhouses, with removable split cedar planks cladding the outside and the roof. Captain Cook described the Nuu-chah-nulth longhouses as resembling "a long English stable with a range of double stalls, and a pathway in the middle." Totem poles sometimes graced the fronts of the longhouses, and carved house poles stood inside.

In 1791, John Boit, a sixteen-year-old officer aboard the American trading vessel *Columbia Rediviva*, wrote of the Tla-o-qui-aht chief's house in his diary: "The house was large and commodious and wou'd hold fifty Indians very comfortably. All around were packages of fish in boxes decorated with pearl shell. The furniture consisted chiefly of matts and wooden boxes, which last serve to boil their fish in, which they easily do by applying red hot stones, till it boils. There were severall fires about the house but there were no chimnies and the smoke was too mighty for my eyes. They sleep on boards, rais'd about a foot from the ground and covered with matts, rolling themselves up in furs."

Some of these large structures housing many families remained central to village life well into the twentieth century, only very gradually being replaced by individual dwellings for families. Peter Webster recalled his grandfather's big house at Yarksis on Vargas Island: "It must have measured sixty feet by forty feet [eighteen by twelve metres]... constructed of boards on the outside and lined on the inside...with a big iron stove that was used for heating and cooking...I recall on many occasions falling asleep beside my grandfather while listening to his stories of the past and to the songs that were handed down."

These songs, so central in the cultural memory of the people, passed down from generation to generation: prayer and lullaby songs; others for dances, potlatches, and marriages; songs for bad weather and for funerals.

The storytelling and oratory that played an equally vital role in Nuu-chah-nulth culture also passed down from generation to generation. Great orators, respected as highly as great singers and dancers, inherited their stories, learning them from their fathers and grandfathers. Writing in 1868, Gilbert Sproat, one of the earliest colonial administrators on the West Coast, commented on the outstanding quality of oratory at large Nuu-chah-nulth gatherings. "The Clayoquot excel at public speaking... The voices of one or two noted chiefs are very powerful, yet clear and musical, the lower tones remarkably so; their articulation is distinct and their gestures and attitudes are singularly expressive...An actor or artist who wished to know what natural earnest manner in public speaking really is, should visit Clayoquot Sound...There is nothing to be seen in England like it."

At all traditional gatherings, often with large numbers of people present, the songs, the oratory, and the dances expressed the accumulated wisdom and the history of the people. Recalling his grandfather Keesto, an Ahousaht hereditary chief, Dr. E. Richard Atleo (Umeek) wrote in his book *Tsawalk: A Nuu-chah-nulth Worldview*: "From his mother's womb, according to ancient custom, he heard the songs and teachings about his ancestors, his identity, and his future promise as a chief. Through story and song, he heard and understood the meaning of his people, the meaning of his land, and the connection between spiritual power and the acquisition of resources for the wellbeing of his people."

In the villages, with everyone gathered together, the winter season was a time for feasts, ceremonial dances, and for potlatches. "Potlatch" originates from the Nuu-chah-nulth verb *pachitle*, meaning "to give." Generally potlatches took place during the winter to mark a significant event: the assumption of a chief; the official naming of a child; the maturing of a chief's daughter; the eradication of a debt; and other landmark events. These lengthy ceremonies saw a leading member of a tribe inviting all of his people and often neighbouring tribes to feast,

Potlatch at Opitsat in 1916. Though banned by the government in 1884, potlatches continued. Here Tla-o-qui-aht people carry guests in their large canoe up the beach at Opitsat, while drummers beat out a welcome. Potlatches took place during the winter months to celebrate important events with feasting, storytelling and gift-giving.
PN 02077, Alberni Valley Museum

dance, sing, play games, and listen to long orations—and to receive gifts from the host. At potlatches, the host could part with everything but his house, and in doing so heightened his social status and reputation. Traditionally only the principal chief and the *ha'wiih*, hereditary chiefs, could afford to hold potlatches, but with the arrival of the Europeans, who brought with them a wide array of material goods and a cash economy, potlatching became more widespread. Believing potlatches to be heathen and wasteful, and fearing that large gatherings of aboriginals encouraged the spread of disease, the Canadian government outlawed the ceremony in 1884.

In the initial years of the ban, authorities tended to turn a blind eye. Harry Guillod of the West Coast Indian Agency proved to be one of the most sympathetic of all Indian agents, writing in 1885, "No doubt there is some waste at these meetings, where a canoe full of cooked rice and several sacks of sugar, or six or eight boxes of biscuits are distributed, but the poorer Indians reap some benefit from it, and all carry away what they cannot eat." The Presbyterian missionary John Ross, for many years based at various West Coast locations, including Ahousat and Ucluelet, left a vivid description of a potlatch he attended in the early 1900s. Ross described the vast quantities of rice being cooked in huge iron kettles, stirred by canoe paddles, and later served with fish, apples, and biscuits to the assembled guests. Looking around, Ross noted the timeless quality of the event, the size of the longhouse with its "huge posts supporting the beams [which] were carved totems," and the convivial atmosphere. "The Indians were all decked out in paint and feathers," he wrote, "their heads covered with white down which is always a sign of peace...Two large fires were burning brightly and with the light of the fires and lanterns hung here and there around the building there was a feeling of comfort also as the rain was pouring down outside and the wind blowing a south-easter. We could hear the waves rolling up on the beach which all added to a sense of cosy comfort and real interest as we watched the natives enjoying themselves in one of their ancient customs."

The Nuu-chah-nulth First Nations all shared a similar social and political structure, a hierarchical system based on inheritance that conferred status within the tribe. The hereditary chiefs, or *ha'wiih*, each with a fixed rank and responsibilities and privileges, came under the leadership of a principal chief, the *taises* or *tyee*. Each *ha'wiih* had his own *ha'houlthee*, or chiefly territories, and taken all together these formed the *ha'houlthee* of the tribe. The *taises*, like the others, inherited his position from his father; his role required consultation with the *ha'wiih*, elders, and heads of families to reach consensus on important matters.

At the time of European contact, the *taises* held great power, claiming ownership of all the tribal territory as well as its resources: the village sites and houses, the salmon streams, clam beds, herring spawning grounds. The principal chief's younger brothers served as minor or sub-chiefs, acting as war leaders, ambassadors, or orators. Each First Nation operated somewhat differently; the numbers of hereditary chiefs and their designated roles varied from one territory to another. Consistently, though, the clear hierarchy among the chiefs and within families played a crucial role in the daily lives of all Nuu-chah-nulth people. This hierarchy determined status, ceremonial roles, responsibilities, and place in line when riches like whale meat and blubber were distributed.

Up to a quarter of any given tribe could be made up of slaves, usually taken in wars with nearby tribes. The slaves did much of the work and lived as part of the family group that owned them. They could be well treated or shamefully treated; their lives rested on the whim of their owners, who could sell, ransom, trade, or kill them as they saw fit. To become a slave brought disgrace, especially if the victim had to serve someone of lower rank. Many tried to escape; if caught, the penalties could be dire.

Intertribal warfare pervaded northwest coast society; slave raids, revenge, or territorial raids being the main motivators. Using the element of surprise, attacks took place at night or at dawn; the attackers could be few or number in the hundreds. Once in the enemy's camp, they killed as many men as possible, sometimes decapitating them. Women and children fled or were taken as slaves.

The most significant war in Clayoquot Sound occurred only decades before Europeans arrived on the coast. As mentioned earlier, in this war the Tla-o-qui-aht, allied with three or four other tribes, wiped out the Esowistaht on the Esowista Peninsula. Afterward, the Tla-o-qui-aht chief Ya'aihlstohsmahhlneh (who later took the name Wickaninnish) redistributed Esowistaht territories and possessions to his relatives and allies, whom he urged to come and live with him at Opitsat. This war consolidated Wickaninnish's position as the dominant chief in the Clayoquot Sound area.

Following European contact, Wickaninnish continued to expand his influence over neighbouring tribes through warfare, and he monopolized commerce with traders who visited Clayoquot Sound. Once he had access to firearms, he used them to control trade and subjugate tribes to the south in Barkley Sound. Around 1792, a member of the Hatc'a'atHa tribe in Barkley Sound killed a Tla-o-qui-aht, and Wickaninnish retaliated by attacking the tribe. Even though the Tla-o-qui-ahts had guns, the Hatc'a'atHa laughed at them, believing such objects were only for frightening, and that they could not kill. According to Daniel Clayton in *The Imperial Fashioning of Vancouver Island:* "The Tla-o-qui-aht never raided twice, but always wiped out the enemy in a single raid, because they knew how to fight"; after the raid "no one was left of the Hatc'a'atHa."

Up to the early nineteenth century, the Ahousaht had been a relatively small tribe and not wealthy. Crucially, their limited territory on the western side of Vargas and beneath Catface Mountain held no salmon streams. Despite intermarriage with the Otsosaht, who had rich fishing grounds on Flores Island and up Herbert, Shelter, and Sydney Inlets, the Otsosaht would not allow the Ahousaht to fish there. Tensions mounted gradually between the two tribes. Several ugly clashes and skirmishes led to a number of grisly deaths on both sides, and eventually to a major attack in which the Ahousaht killed and decapitated eighty Otsosaht. This occurred at night, when the Otsosaht were asleep at their summer fishing camp on the northwest tip of Bartlett Island. The blood-soaked hostilities dragged on for many years in a series of raids on villages and attacks on fishermen, with the smaller Ahousaht group gradually gaining dominance as they killed ever more Otsosahts. In all likelihood, the Ahousaht's strength lay in their firepower; they had acquired firearms and ammunition through their allies the Mowachaht and Nuchatlaht, farther up the coast. In the end, the few remaining Otsosaht moved permanently out of Clayoquot Sound, taking up residence along the coast of Washington and Oregon. Following their departure, the Ahousahts divided the rights to the eighteen salmon rivers in Otsosaht territory among themselves and their allies, including the Kelsemaht, the Owinmitisaht, the Quatsweaht. The Ahousaht took over the Otsosaht winter village Maaqtusiis, making it their principal village.

In 1855, war erupted between the Tla-o-qui-aht and the Kyuquot, farther up the coast beyond Nootka Sound. The killing of a half-Kyuquot and half-Tla-o-qui-aht woman precipitated the conflict. The murderer confessed to the crime, and the Tla-o-qui-aht used this as a reason to attack the whole Kyuquot tribe, building on former hostilities.

Tla-o-qui-aht chief Sitakanim united the Hesquiaht, Mowachaht, Ehat-tesaht, and Cheklesaht in this enterprise, and they all assembled on an island near the two Kyuquot villages. Leaving some men to guard the canoes, at midnight the attackers crossed a spit to where the Kyuquots lived. Sitakanim and his men surprised the sleeping Kyuquots, killing them on their mats and setting fire to their longhouses. Accounts of the number killed vary considerably. Father Augustin Brabant later reported as many as seventy Kyuquots lay dead after the raid, many with their heads removed. Gilbert Sproat put the number at about half that. The Tla-o-qui-aht took the heads of the slain Kyuquot back to Clayoquot Sound, along with some twenty slaves; the heads, displayed on poles on the Stubbs Island sandspit, remained there for years afterward.

The first permanent European resident at the Clayoquot trading post on Stubbs Island, trader Fred Thornberg, wrote of finding skulls on the sandspit when he arrived there in 1874. According to Thornberg, who revelled in dramatic storytelling, the beheadings had continued right there on Stubbs Island, with Chief Sitakanim decapitating all the prisoners he had taken: "Chief Ceadarcanin [sic] alone went on the Spit and finding a suitable place for what this Devil was going to doe, he comandet his men to bring one by one these prisoners on shore to him & they done so. And Ceadercanin alone cut the Head off these 18 Ind. And there head was then stuck on to a small poles & they were stuck in the Sand." Thornberg claimed that the chief bragged to him about decapitating his enemies, saying he used a large mussel shell about seven inches [17.5 centimetres] long, honed on a rock to razor sharpness.

The days of tribal warfare in Clayoquot Sound waned, disappearing altogether following the mid-nineteenth century. Broader social and economic upheavals eclipsed intertribal conflicts after that. The emerging settlement of Fort Victoria swelled in importance and size, its influence rippling up the West Coast. More and more trading vessels visited the coast, seeking furs and dogfish oil, and in scattered coastal locations permanent trading posts came to stay. Gunboats of the Royal Navy appeared along the West Coast, occasionally engaging in fearsome displays of power and authority. And as ever more Europeans drifted in and out of Clayoquot Sound, they brought with them more change, more trade goods, and more alcohol. They also brought more disease.

In 1856, the combined European population of the settlements of the Victoria district, Nanaimo, and Fort Rupert (Port Hardy) stood at 774. The estimated aboriginal population of the whole of Vancouver Island was nearly 26,000. With the introduction of venereal diseases, measles, whooping cough, typhus, typhoid fever, tuberculosis, and the worst scourge of all, smallpox, the indigenous population would be reduced by almost 90 percent by the end of the nineteenth century. Most died of smallpox.

Smallpox had already laid waste to millions of lives in the Americas. It arrived with the first explorers and immediately began devastating the indigenous populations of Mexico, Peru, Cuba, Hispaniola, and Puerto Rico, wiping out an estimated 50 to 90 percent of the locals. That first epidemic, at least in part, made it possible for Hernán Cortés and his 300 conquistadores to conquer the Aztecs in 1520. It killed an estimated 15 million Mexicans, half of the population, and claimed an estimated one-third of the indigenous peoples of North and South America. In the 1770s, smallpox struck again, this time in the Missouri River Basin, spreading westward along aboriginal trading routes to the Pacific coast, hitting the northwest coast in 1775–1782. Captain George Vancouver, on his voyage in 1792, found many deserted villages in Puget Sound and the Strait of Georgia. A third epidemic, from 1835 to 1838, cut a swath from California up the Pacific coast as far as the Aleutian Islands, killing about one-third of the population of northern tribes, including the Haida, Tlingit, and Tsimshian, as well as affecting the population of Clayoquot Sound.

The most recent and, for British Columbia, the worst smallpox epidemic began in New Westminster in March 1862, brought by a steamer passenger from San Francisco. Victoria's *British Colonist* misleadingly stated in its March 22 edition: "The case is not considered serious." By the 1850s, early forms of immunization against the disease existed, but with no effective means of quarantine among aboriginal people, the disease rapidly escalated out of control. Within a year it killed some 32,000, or over 60 percent, of BC's aboriginal population.

When smallpox reached Victoria in April 1862, the nearby aboriginal encampments bore the brunt of the affliction. Because many people from North Coast First Nations migrated down to Victoria each spring seeking trade and employment, an estimated 2,000 or more Natives from up the coast could be found living near Victoria, including large groups of Haida, Tlingit, and Tsimshians. As the infection rapidly spread among them, fear escalated in the settler population, fuelled by commentary in the *British Colonist*, then edited by future provincial premier Amor de Cosmos. On April 28, 1862, an editorial demanded that in order to protect whites "from the pestilential scourge that is hovering among the savages on the out skirts of the town," all aboriginals be removed "to a place remote from communication with the whites, whilst the infected [Indian] houses with all their trumpery should be burned to ashes." Commissioner of Police, Joseph Pemberton, took action. Within days, the authorities burned the villages and encampments around Victoria, forcing the northern aboriginals to leave. The gunboats *Grappler* and *Forward* implacably assisted in the exodus, with *Forward* towing twenty-six canoes full of infected people back to their home villages.

This enforced departure spread the disease to villages up the coast from Victoria to Alaska, and before long infection spread to First Nations along the Skeena, Fraser, and Nass Rivers and into the province's interior. The death toll rose relentlessly, wiping out whole villages, leaving many abandoned, and causing some bands to amalgamate in order to survive. On June 21, 1862, the *British Colonist* foresaw this outcome, and showed no compunction, particularly in relation to the warlike Haida: "How have the mighty fallen! Four short years ago, numbering their braves by thousands, they were the scourge and terror of the coast; today, broken-spirited and effeminate, with scarce a corporal's guard of warriors remaining alive, they are proceeding northward, bearing with them the seeds of a loathsome disease that will take root and bring both a plentiful crop of ruin and destruction."

"These mass deaths [from the 1862–63 epidemic] tore irreparable holes in the cultural fabric of societies in which oral traditions were the custodians of the genealogies, laws, histories and literature of entire peoples," wrote Stephen Hume in the *Vancouver Sun* on the 150th anniversary of the epidemic. On Vancouver Island's once densely populated west coast, First Nations faced near annihilation of their structured, long-established way of life. And yet, cataclysmic though they were, the various smallpox epidemics represented only one of the disasters unleashed on the people. Simultaneously, into their world came heavily armed strangers determined to impose their mores, institutions, and religion on the local people. All too often these strangers assumed that the land, with its complex traditional territories and its hierarchical, deeply rooted patterns of ownership and use, could be theirs for the taking. Today, nearly 250 years after the initial contact between the First Nations and Europeans, the consequences of such assumptions and such actions continue to be played out in Clayoquot Sound and elsewhere. The processes of recovery and reconciliation still have a long road to travel.

Chapter 3:

THE KING GEORGE MEN

FOR EUROPEAN EXPLORERS, the northwest coast of North America remained *terra incognita* for a very long time. Their voyages of exploration took them far and wide around the globe, yet not into the uncharted North Pacific, so distant and difficult to reach. To travel there from Europe meant braving a six-month voyage over vast and dangerous distances, sailing into the South Atlantic, around Cape Horn at the southern tip of South America, then up the west coast of South and North America. Russian explorers and traders approached from a different direction, making a three-year journey across Europe and Asia, then a sea voyage across the Bering Strait to the coast of Alaska.

Before the mid-eighteenth century, few dared consider such journeys, but by the end of that century, five maritime nations—Russia, Spain, Britain, France, and the newly formed United States of America—vied for control of the Pacific Northwest. They pursued a high-stakes trade in sea otter pelts there, and in some cases established permanent trading posts.

In the late 1700s, as early Canadian settlers struggled to gain a foothold in the eastern provinces, the lands west of what is now Manitoba lay virtually unexplored by newcomers, save for a limited number of isolated fur trading posts. The exploration and settlement pattern common to most of North America, with settlers steadily moving by land from east to west, did not hold true on the northwest coast of Canada. By the time Alexander Mackenzie famously crossed the continent from east to west in 1793, emerging near Bella Coola, the coast was already internationally renowned, and trade vessels from several nations visited regularly. With the frenzied trade in sea otter pelts underway, the coast became part of a territorial tug of war and an economic boom so lucrative it nearly precipitated a war between European powers. All this occurred before the Rockies had been mapped; before the great rivers of the Canadian west, the Skeena, Peace, Fraser, Thompson, and Columbia had been navigated by European explorers; before even one-quarter of North America had been mapped.

The first Europeans to arrive on the west coast of Vancouver Island and to make contact with aboriginal people appeared in 1774 aboard the twenty-five-metre frigate *Santiago*, sailing under the Spanish flag. Captain Juan Josef Pérez Hernández had been sent north by his superiors at San Blas, the Spanish naval base on the west coast of Mexico established by Spain in 1768. Pérez had instructions to explore the uncharted northern waters, to investigate reports of Russian activity in Alaska, and to lay claim to what Spain considered its territory. After sailing to the northern end of Haida Gwaii, Pérez returned along the coast of Vancouver Island. He anchored off what are now called Perez Rocks near Estevan Point on August 7, 1774, the sight of his ship exciting astonishment and fear among the witnesses on shore. Many who saw the strangers fled or hid, but a number of Hesquiaht warriors approached cautiously in their canoes, and the first coastal trading took place; Pérez and his crew obtained otter skins and conical hats in return for knives, cloth, and abalone shells from California beaches. Increasing winds prevented Pérez from going ashore with the large 4.2-metre-high cross his crew had made, intending to plant it as a formal Spanish claim to the area. The winds continued to increase overnight, and Pérez found himself in danger of going onto the rocks. Unable to hoist his anchor, he was forced to cut the cable and put out to sea. Before leaving, he named the head of the peninsula at Hesquiat Harbour Punta San Esteban—Estevan Point—for officer Esteban José Martínez, who later played a leading role in Nootka Sound when the Spanish returned.

Spanish authorities found Pérez's voyage a disappointment: he had not formally claimed territory, he had not gone far enough north to encounter the Russians in Alaska, nor had he produced a detailed chart. His pilot did, however, draw a coastline map of British Columbia, the first ever made, showing Nootka Sound and part of Haida Gwaii. Because Pérez and his men did not actually go ashore and ceremonially lay claim to the land, the British would later refuse to acknowledge

Spanish sovereignty over the area. This lack of foresight on Pérez's part would prove costly to Spain.

Four years after Pérez's voyage, on March 29, 1778, British captain James Cook landed at Nootka Sound, which he named King George's Sound. Although the extraordinary navigator Cook is widely acknowledged as the first explorer to set foot on the coast of British Columbia, theories of other, earlier explorers reaching the coast have surfaced over the years. Some archaeologists speculate that a Chinese Buddhist priest named Hui-shen, may have visited the North America continent, which the Chinese called Fusang, in 458 A.D. Many centuries later, further Chinese contact may have occurred. According to Gavin Menzies in his book *1421: The Year China Discovered America*, Chinese junks could have sailed in BC waters in 1423. Menzies also points out that Vancouver Island appears on the Waldseemüller map, published in 1507, 250 years before Europeans "discovered" coastal BC. A later chart, published by Venetian Antonio Zatta in 1778, the same year Cook arrived at Nootka, names Haida Gwaii as *Colonia dei Cinesi*. Another notion suggesting a possible early arrival appears in Sam Bawlf's book *The Secret Voyage of Sir Francis Drake*. Bawlf maintains that the explorer Sir Francis Drake secretly sailed his *Golden Hinde* along the coast of BC in 1579, 200 years before Cook. He claims Drake circumnavigated Vancouver Island, sailed through Juan de Fuca Strait, and identified the area around Comox and Courtenay as a possible site for a future English colony, to be named New Albion. All of these "earliest" explorer theories and claims remain contentious.

No one disputes the arrival of Captain James Cook. On his third circumnavigation of the world and in search of the Northwest Passage, Cook and his men sailed their two ships, the *Resolution* and the *Discovery*, into Nootka Sound seeking a sheltered bay in which to make repairs to the storm-battered vessels. After finding a temporary anchorage for the first night, Cook navigated a short distance into the Sound and dropped anchor in Resolution Cove (Ship Cove), off Bligh Island. Cook named the island after his midshipman William Bligh, later to become famous as captain of HMS *Bounty*.

The braver among the local Mowachaht approached in several canoes and remained nearby, standing off the ship in complete silence for many hours. "My forefathers, on seeing [the white men] thought they were the dead returning," wrote August Murphy of the Mowachaht First Nation. "The hunters returned to the village with the astonishing news that they had seen a floating house on which a strange people lived and moved around on the waters. They expressed it in a single word that to this day describes the people who have come after them, 'Mamuthlne.'" In an interview for the *Sound Heritage* series, Peter Webster of Ahousat explained further, stating that the Nuu-chah-nulth word, sometimes written as *mamalth'ni*, "means that you are living on the water and floating around, you have no land." According to Webster, right after seeing the ships and the strangers on board, "somebody composed a song...while they were still on the ocean. The song says: 'I got my walls of a house floating on the water.'"

Once Cook and his men had anchored in Resolution Cove, the Mowachaht came near their vessels again and called out *"Itchme nutka! Itchme nutka!"* urging them to go around Bligh Island and anchor at Yuquot, later known as Friendly Cove. Not knowing that the word *nutka* means "go around," Cook assumed the men were indicating their name or the name of the place. Both became known as "Nootka" in subsequent years, and for many years the term "Nootka" came to include all of Vancouver Island's west coast peoples, as well as their linguistic group.

For the following month Cook's men cut trees for masts, brewed spruce beer, and traded with the indigenous people and their powerful chief, Maquinna, who would later exert immense influence on the sea otter trade. The Mowachaht offered the British various furs for trade, including sea otter pelts, and also carvings, spears, and fish hooks. In exchange they gladly accepted knives, chisels, nails, buttons, and any kind of metal. While repairs continued, Cook explored the rest of Nootka Sound by longboat, stopping at Yuquot where John Webber, his shipboard draughtsman, produced many sketches and watercolours depicting the dwellings, the way of life, and the people.

After almost a month in Nootka Sound, Cook and his men left the area on April 26 and sailed north to Alaska and into the Bering

On his third voyage of discovery, Captain James Cook had artist John Webber aboard. Webber sketched this scene of Yuquot in Nootka Sound in 1778. Members of Cook's crew are on the beach talking to and trading with Mowachaht people. Above them, longhouses dot the shore. *Image PDP00234 courtesy of Royal BC Museum, BC Archives*

Strait, seeking the elusive Northwest Passage, before heading home via Hawaii. On February 14, 1779, Cook met his death there, on the beach of Kealakekua Bay on the Big Island of Hawaii, while investigating the theft of one of his ship's boats by Hawaiians. His crew later returned to the beach, collected his dismembered body parts, and, after placing them in a coffin made by the *Resolution*'s carpenter, consigned him to the deep. The *Resolution* continued across the Pacific to Canton in China, and there the crew traded 300 sea otter pelts they had acquired at Nootka. These pelts, which the crew had been using as bedding in their hammocks, fetched the staggering sum of 120 Spanish dollars each, more than double the yearly wages for a seaman. They loaded up with porcelain, silks, and spices, and the *Resolution* continued its circumnavigation of the globe by sailing across the Indian Ocean, round the Cape of Good Hope, and north to Britain. Back in England, they sold the trade items they had purchased in China for profits ranging as high as 1,800 percent. News of such vast profits spread rapidly.

John Webber's depiction of the inside of a longhouse in 1778, with house totems in the background, raised sleeping platforms along the sides and a central firepit. Fish hang from racks on the ceiling. The people wear capes made of cedar bark, and the man in the lower left corner wears a typical "conical" hat. *Image PDP02192 courtesy of Royal BC Museum, BC Archives*

In 1783, John Ledyard, one of the two Americans in Cook's crew, published his memoir entitled *A Journal of Captain Cook's Last Voyage to the Pacific Ocean, and in Quest of a North-West Passage between Asia and America*. In his book, Ledyard described how sea otter pelts, "which did not cost the purchaser six pence sterling, sold in China for one hundred dollars." The following year the British Admiralty published a heavily edited account of Cook's voyages in three volumes; the books sold out within days and went into several more editions, followed by translations. As word of Cook's voyages spread, avid interest in the North Pacific fur trade escalated, spurring British investors to sponsor trading ventures on the Pacific Coast, using Cook's precise maps and observations. Some of Cook's officers, Nathaniel Portlock, George Dixon, and James Colnett, recognizing the commercial opportunity in the sea otter fur trade, quit the Royal Navy and formed their own trading company, the King George's Sound Company, to engage in fur trading in the Pacific Northwest.

The rush for "soft gold" was on. Because sea otters only live in the Pacific Northwest, traders and adventurers targeted this area for decades to come, in a frenzy of trade for the glossy, luxurious furs. With 600,000 hairs per square inch, sea otter pelts have the thickest fur of any mammal. Their unparalleled softness, near-luminous sheen, and immense warmth made them an invaluable commodity. In the peak years of the sea otter trade, from 1790 to 1812, up to two dozen trading vessels plied the coast of what is now British Columbia, taking tens of thousands of sea otter pelts. Farther north, the Russians generally confined their territorial and trade interests to Alaska, where they had first landed in the early 1740s. They established a permanent settlement on Kodiak Island in 1784. In all locations along the coast, as the trade increased, the various First Nations became more experienced at driving hard bargains and more accustomed to European goods, including firearms, alcohol, and foods like molasses and beans. They also became more exposed to disease, particularly syphilis and tuberculosis.

The sea otter trade began in earnest with the voyage of Captain James Hanna. On August 18, 1775, Hanna became the first British commercial trader to reach the West Coast, arriving at Nootka aboard his sixty-ton brig *Sea Otter*. He had set sail four months earlier with a crew of thirty, leaving from the Portuguese colony of Macao, just south of Hong Kong. Hanna's voyage received backing from John Henry Cox, a British trader in China, and though he never set foot in BC, Cox Bay near Tofino, and Cox Island, off Cape Scott, bear his name. Hanna traded iron bars for furs at Nootka, returning to China at the end of September with 560 sea otter pelts, which sold in Canton for 20,600 Spanish dollars.

Although Hanna's trip proved highly successful in commercial terms, it introduced the first bitter note of conflict in relations between traders and aboriginals on the West Coast. During Hanna's time in Nootka Sound, he and his crew killed twenty Mowachaht men and a chief as they tried to board the *Sea Otter* in broad daylight. This confrontation arose either because of a practical joke in which gunpowder exploded under Chief Maquinna's chair, or because of the theft of a chisel from the *Sea Otter*. Despite the killings, and possibly because Hanna and his crew took care of the Mowachaht whom they had wounded, he was able to complete his trading and leave with his ship and crew intact.

Different notions of property ownership repeatedly fuelled disagreements between local people and the visiting traders, sometimes with fatal results. Aboriginals generally held to the idea of universal ownership of property, seeing nothing wrong in taking whatever the owner could not protect. Nails, rowboats, tools, and clothing proved fair game, but the traders saw this as theft deserving severe punishment. The coastal people never forgot violent responses, such as the *Sea Otter* incident, and they could wait a long time for revenge. Nearly twenty years after the unhappy confrontation with Hanna and the loss of so many of his people, Chief Maquinna achieved his revenge when he and his tribe seized the American trading vessel *Boston* and killed all but two of that ship's crew.

In 1786, Hanna returned in a larger 120-ton ship, also named *Sea Otter*, on a voyage financed by the Bengal Fur Society. He found that other traders had already bought most of the available skins at Nootka, so after two weeks there, during which he obtained only fifty pelts, he sailed north to the top of Vancouver Island and then south again into Clayoquot Sound, seeking more furs. At the principal Ahousaht village, then on Vargas Island, he befriended Ahousaht chief Cleaskinah, who subsequently became known as "Captain Hanna" following an exchange of names in accordance with local custom. With this visit, Hanna and his crew became the first Europeans to enter Clayoquot Sound and to trade there. Hanna acquired some furs, although far fewer than on his first voyage, and netted only 8,000 Spanish dollars for his cargo when he returned to Macao in February 1787.

Another private trader arrived on the coast in 1786; Captain James Strange, son of the eminent engraver Sir Robert Strange and godson of James, the Pretender to the Scottish throne. With his crew suffering from scurvy, Strange arrived at Nootka Sound aboard the vessels *Captain Cook* and *Experiment*. He remained at Nootka long enough to plant a vegetable garden, and on departing he left his surgeon's assistant, Irishman John Mackay, with Chief Maquinna. Before joining Strange's ship, Mackay had served in the British Army in Bombay, and when in Nootka he contracted an illness described as "purple fever," forcing Strange to leave him at Nootka with a promise to return for him at a later date. Maquinna assured Strange that his doctor "should eat the Choicest Fish the Sound produced; and that on my return, I should find him, as fat as a Whale." Having equipped Mackay with two goats, some seeds, and a gun, Strange departed, leaving Mackay to become the first European resident of British Columbia. In mid-November 1786, when Strange reached China, he sold his cargo of 600 pelts for 24,000 Spanish dollars.

At Nootka, Mackay endeared himself to Maquinna by curing the chief's daughter Apenas of a "scabby disease." Having recovered from his own malady, he settled into life among the Mowachaht, and all went well until he unwittingly broke a local taboo by stepping over a cradle bearing Maquinna's child, for which he was beaten and banished. Later, when the child died, Maquinna exiled Mackay from his house, forcing him to live on his own. He barely managed to survive, but he did discover the place he resided was not on the continent of America but on a sizable island, something not reliably acknowledged until a decade or more later when Captain Vancouver circumnavigated Vancouver Island in 1792.

As Strange sailed for China, the fourth European nation to take an interest in the Pacific Northwest arrived on the coast, not seeking sea otters, but bent on finding the Northwest Passage. Eager to keep pace with Britain, in 1785 King Louis XVI of France sent Jean-François de La Pérouse with the vessels *Boussole* and *L'Astrolabe* on a scientific expedition of discovery in the Pacific Ocean. After visiting Easter Island and Hawaii, La Pérouse arrived off the coast of Alaska on June 23, 1786, and then sailed south, mapping the coast of Haida Gwaii and the west coast of Vancouver Island, continuing until he finally reached Monterey, California. Neither La Pérouse, nor any of his 114-man crew, set foot on British Columbia soil. La Pérouse continued to explore in the Pacific for the next two years. In December 1787, his expedition lost eleven crew and the commander of the *Astrolabe*, killed by Samoan Islanders, before landing near Botany Bay, Australia, in 1788. After leaving Australia, all members of the expedition died when both ships sank during a violent storm off Vanikoro Island in the Solomon Islands. Offshore from Vancouver Island, La Perouse Bank, famed as the feeding grounds for migrating fur seal, bears the name of this explorer.

In June 1787, Captain Charles William Barkley, aboard the 400-ton *Imperial Eagle*, arrived at Nootka with his wife, eighteen-year-old Frances Hornby Barkley, the first European woman to visit British Columbia. *Imperial Eagle* was the largest ship ever to enter Nootka Sound. The size of the ship, along with Frances Barkley's impressive red-gold hair, left a lasting impression. Barkley sailed under the flag of the Austrian East India Company, trying to avoid the high fees demanded by the large English trading monopolies, the East India Company and the South Sea Company. During their month-long stay at Nootka, the Barkleys met John Mackay, whose facility with the language greatly assisted Barkley in negotiating for pelts. They took Mackay aboard and eventually returned him to the Orient; fortunately for him, as Captain Strange had not returned to pick up Mackay as promised.

The summer of 1787 also saw the arrival of the *Prince of Wales* and *Princess Royal* in Nootka Sound at the same time Barkley's *Imperial Eagle* was moored there. The arrival of these ships, belonging to the authorized King George's Sound Company and commanded by Captains James Colnett and Charles Duncan, forced Barkley to leave because he did not possess proper trading credentials. He sailed south on July 24, 1787, in search of more pelts in less conspicuous territory. Entering Clayoquot Sound, he named it Wickaninnish Sound, after the Tla-o-qui-aht chief. Frances Barkley described the chief vividly in her journal, writing that he "seemed to be quite as powerful as the potentate Maquilla [Maquinna]. Wickaninnish has great authority and this part of the coast proved a rich harvest of furs for us. Likewise, close to the southward of this sound, to which Captain Barkley gave his own name. Several coves and bays and also islands in this sound we named. There was Frances Island, after myself; Hornby peak, also after myself; Cape Beal after our purser." This visit made Barkley and his crew the second shipload of Europeans to visit Clayoquot Sound.

The *Imperial Eagle* continued south to Washington State, where a tragic confrontation with aboriginals left six crew members dead. The ship continued across the Pacific to Macao, where Barkley sold his 800 sea otter pelts for 30,000 Spanish dollars. Barkley then sailed on to Calcutta to outfit the *Imperial Eagle* for a second voyage to the northwest coast, but his promoters sold his ship and cancelled their contract with the captain. Former Royal Navy lieutenant John Meares acquired Barkley's navigational instruments and charts from the *Imperial Eagle*, which he would later use to advantage. According to Frances Barkley, Meares also "with the greatest effrontery" took possession of Barkley's valuable seafaring journal, later taking credit for and publishing many of Barkley's achievements as his own.

In 1786, Meares had ventured across the Pacific on his first voyage as a commercial fur trader sponsored by John Henry Cox and the Bengal Fur Society, earlier sponsors of James Hanna. On that voyage, Meares lost twenty of his twenty-nine crew to scurvy and nearly froze to death in Prince William Sound, Alaska. Undaunted by the ravages of his first adventure, Meares once again set out for the northwest coast, now armed with Barkley's charts and journals, and under the auspices of a new sponsor, the Company of Free Commerce of London. He arrived at Nootka in May 1788, following a nearly four-month voyage from China in the Portuguese-registered *Felice Adventurer*. On board with him, Meares had twenty-nine Chinese workers, including "seven carpenters, five blacksmiths, five masons, four tailors, four shoemakers, three sailors and one cook." A handsome, controversial figure, Meares has been variously described as a liar, scallywag, scoundrel, and conniver, the Machiavelli of the maritime fur trade. Historians concur that Meares rarely acted honourably, and Chief Maquinna called the wily trader

The "scallywag" British trader, Captain John Meares, renowned for his duplicity and lies in his time on the West Coast. He wrote vivid descriptions of his visits to Clayoquot Sound in the late 1780s. The large island named for him stands opposite Tofino.
Image PDP05179 courtesy of Royal BC Museum, BC Archives

Echachis village, around 1905. An important summer village of the Tla-o-qui-aht people who migrated here for the spring and summer fishing season. From here, hunters had easy access to the open ocean to hunt whales and northern fur seals. In June 1788, John Meares described attending a feast in a longhouse at Echachis, hosted by Chief Wickaninnish, with some 800 men present. *Mount Angel Abbey Library*

Aita–aita Meares, meaning "the lying Meares." During the month of May 1788, which he spent at Friendly Cove, Meares purchased land from Maquinna for "8 to 10 sheets of copper and several other trifling articles." At this site, he instructed his Chinese workers to build a house, a storehouse, and a ship. When completed, the 40-ton *North West America* would become the first ship built in British Columbia. Meares intended the ship as a coastal trader, to scour the coast for furs, winter in Hawaii during the stormy months, and return each summer to operate out of a permanent base he planned to establish at Nootka. Leaving his compatriot Captain William Douglas of the *Iphigenia Nubiana* at Nootka to supervise construction, he set sail in the *Felice Adventurer* to explore the area to the south.

On June 13, 1788, Meares arrived at Echachis, Chief Wickaninnish's main summer village. Located on a small island in Templar Channel near Wickaninnish Island and just west of MacKenzie Beach, Echachis at the time was a hubbub of activity, as the Tla-o-qui-aht gathered for a special feast. Meares and his men joined 800 other men in

Wickaninnish's longhouse for a welcome feast of boiled whale, while the women watched from the outer fringes.

Meares left behind detailed descriptions of Chief Wickaninnish and of life among the Nuu-chah-nulth, the Tla-o-qui-aht in particular. According to Meares, Wickaninnish held sway over a vast area between the Strait of Juan de Fuca and Woody Point, and although Wickaninnish estimated he had 13,000 subjects, Meares remarked that "we rather think that the chief, either from modesty or ignorance, under-rated the population of his country." Meares visited Chief Wickaninnish's principal village of Opitsat, naming it and the nearby waters Port Cox after his backer. He estimated Opitsat to be "three times the size of Maquinna's Yuquot, with a population of about four thousand inhabitants." There lived the chief "in a state of magnificence much superior to any of his neighbours, both loved and dreaded by other chiefs." Meares described Wickaninnish to be in his early forties, reputedly with ten wives, and "rather inclined to be corpulent...athletic and active." In Meares's estimation, Wickaninnish equalled Chief Maquinna in power, and only the fact that Maquinna's favourite wife came from Wickaninnish's family kept the two tribes in a state of relative peace.

Having noted that the Tla-o-qui-aht women were "very superior in personal charm to the ladies of Nootka," Meares traded for 150 otter skins and presented Wickaninnish with many gifts, including "six brass-hilted swords, a pair of pistols, and a musket and powder." He then set off south as far as Juan de Fuca Strait before returning north again. As he neared Nootka, Meares encountered Captain Charles Duncan and his fifteen-man crew on the 65-ton *Princess Royal* sailing southward into Clayoquot Sound. Duncan and his companion James Colnett had spent the spring and summer exploring and trading in and around Haida Gwaii, and now Duncan intended to visit Ahousat to top up his cargo of furs before sailing on to Hawaii to winter. Meares stayed at Nootka until September 24, 1788. By then he had squelched the second mutiny of this voyage among his men, launched the *North West America* on September 20, and loaded his ships with furs, spars, and masts. Meares well realized the vast potential of the coastal timber, knowing Europe's shipbuilding timber to be all but depleted.

"The woods of this part of America are capable of supplying...all the navies of Europe," he wrote.

Just a week prior to Meares's departure, on September 16, American captain Robert Gray, in the 90-ton sloop *Lady Washington* with a crew of nine, arrived at Nootka. Seven days later his compatriot and commander, Captain John Kendrick, arrived in the 212-ton *Columbia Rediviva* with a crew of thirty-nine. While rounding Cape Horn the two ships became separated but they eventually reunited, and their arrival on the West Coast opened a new chapter in the Pacific maritime fur trade. The introduction of the Americans into this highly controlled and jealously monitored trade ultimately broke the monopoly held by the East India Company and other British-owned companies. The Americans, or "Boston Men" as the aboriginals on the coast called them, would become the dominant players in the sea otter trade on the coast.

During this early period of exploration and trade on the northwest coast, most of the explorers and traders dealt with the local people in a fair and respectful manner. "King George's" captains, such as James Cook and later George Vancouver, were under orders to explore this territory and negotiate with the aboriginal people in a decorous manner. Not so the Americans. Motivated by quick profit, they treated the local people in an entirely different way, leading to dire consequences for both sides.

Chapter 4:

The Boston Men

THE END OF THE AMERICAN WAR of Independence in 1783 saw the newly fledged United States setting out to establish a triangular trade route linking the eastern seaboard of the United States with the Pacific Northwest and China. At the time, the young country had few trade goods of its own, so it sought goods elsewhere to trade in China for tea, spices, and other exotic luxuries. This triangular trade route played a key role in establishing America as a trading nation, a century later evolving into the era of the legendary Clipper Ships, which raced across the Pacific, round the Horn, and up to New England carrying tea and spices, just as the age of sail ended and the age of steam began.

Captain John Kendrick and Captain Robert Gray became the first Americans attempting this new trade route and, in the process, the first American traders to enter Clayoquot Sound. Kendrick and Gray both hailed from Massachusetts, where a consortium of merchants invested $47,000 to outfit their two vessels, the *Columbia Rediviva* and the *Lady Washington*. On September 28, 1787, they departed Hancock's Wharf in Boston, setting off for the Pacific Northwest coast to acquire furs for sale in China, where they would load up with tea, spices, and luxury items and make the long journey back around the Horn to the eastern ports of the United States.

Before Robert Gray, aboard the *Lady Washington*, arrived at Nootka to begin trading, he suffered a personal loss that angered him deeply. Aboriginals at Tillamook Bay in Oregon killed his black manservant, Marcus Lopius. Gray named the location "Murderers' Harbour." This episode soured Gray's dealings with, and attitude toward, all aboriginals of the Pacific Northwest, including those in Clayoquot Sound, dubbed "Hancock Harbour" by the Americans.

Gray first entered the Sound in early September 1788, and Robert Haswell, Gray's third mate, kept a diary that reveals how the "Boston Men," as the indigenous people called the Americans, encountered the Tla-o-qui-aht. The entry also shows the paucity of trade goods brought by the Americans:

> a great maney of the inhabitants came bringing with them an abundance of skins but greatly to our mortification there was nothing in our vessell except muskets would perchace one of them but that was an article of commerce we were not supplied with having scarce armes enough for our defence copper was all there cry and we had none for them, the principal or superior chief of this tribe's name is Wickaninish he visited us accompaneyed by one of his brothers completely dressed in a genteel sute of cloths which he said Capt. Mears had given him. Capt. Mears name was not the only one they mentioned for they spoke of Capt. Barkley Capt. Hannah Capt. Dunkiin and Capt. Duglas what they said of them we now know so little of there language we could not comprehend.

After his short stop in Clayoquot Sound, Gray sailed the *Lady Washington* up to Nootka Sound, arriving on September 16, 1788. There he met the duplicitous John Meares, who did all in his power to dissuade the Americans from cutting in on his territory. Haswell wrote: "All the time these gentlemen were on board they fully employed themselves falsicating and rehursing vague and improvable tales relative to the coast and the vast danger attending its navigation of the monsterous savage disposition of its inhabitants adding it would be madness in us so week as we were to stay a winter among them...The fact was they wished to frighten us off the coast that they alone might menopolise the trade but the debth of there design would be easily fathomed."

After Meares departed for China, the American traders settled in for the winter in Nootka Sound. Kendrick built an outpost, which he named Fort Washington, at Mowina, now called Marvinas Bay, seven kilometres north of Yuquot, on land he "purchased" from Chief Maquinna for ten guns and a little gunpowder. In their dealings with local people, the British had usually avoided trading firearms for furs, bringing with them from China specific trade items such as iron, copper, tin, metal knives, frying pans, axes, adzes, a variety of tools, cloth, buttons, and the like. The Americans, with limited trade items, had no compunction in trading firearms for furs. In his book *The Golden Spruce*, John Vaillant commented on Kendrick's subsequent visit to Haida Gwaii: "[He] will go down as one of the most destructive trade ambassadors in early American history. Kendrick was, among other things, the first man to sell large quantities of arms to West Coast tribes, including the Haida, and it is thanks in part to him that the Queen Charlotte Islands have the bloodiest history of any place on the coast."

In the spring of 1789, on Kendrick's orders, Gray set sail south from Nootka Sound in the *Lady Washington* in search of sea otter pelts, making several stops in Clayoquot Sound to trade with Chief Wickaninnish. Haswell noted in his diary that the villages in Clayoquot Sound were larger and more populous than those at Nootka, estimating Opitsat to have 2,500 inhabitants. He also commented that the people seemed taller and better proportioned than the Mowachaht, describing Wickaninnish as a handsome man over six feet tall. On March 28, following ten days of trading in Clayoquot Sound, Gray sailed farther south and eventually entered Juan de Fuca Strait. Because of poor weather he did not venture far inside this passage, which some mariners hoped could lead to the Northwest Passage.

While on this trading mission, Gray encountered Spanish captain Esteban José Martínez in the *Princesca* making his way to Nootka Sound. Viceroy Manuel Antonio Flores Maldonado, commander of the Spanish naval base at San Blas on the Baja Peninsula in the Gulf of California, had sent Martínez north in a further attempt to assert Spanish sovereignty over the entire Pacific Northwest coast. Martínez demanded to know why Gray was sailing and trading in Spanish waters. After Gray convinced Martínez that he posed no threat, Gray continued trading while Martínez headed on to Nootka, arriving there on May 5, 1789. Accompanying him were Captain Gonzales López de Haro in the *San Carlos* and José María Narváez in the *Santa Gertrudis*. Over the next month all remained calm as the Spaniards built a small fort on Hog Island, now Lighthouse Island, in Nootka Sound. They set up two batteries of cannons and claimed Yuquot, which they called Santa Cruz. Martínez hosted banquets for the British and Americans whose ships sat at anchor, but on May 12 this conviviality ended. Martínez seized the British ship *Iphigenia Nubiana*, along with her captain, William Douglas, and crew, accusing them of anchoring in Spanish waters without a permit from the Spanish king. Two weeks later, with the captive crew of the *Iphigenia* rapidly consuming his limited provisions, Martínez chose to release Douglas and his ship after Douglas signed a bond that he would not trade for furs and would sail to Hawaii. Once out of Nootka harbour, Douglas ignored Martínez's warnings and sailed north to continue trading. Unfortunately, Douglas failed to connect with Captain Robert Funter, who had taken charge of the *North West America*, and had been trading to the north. Entirely unaware of the recent Spanish hostility toward Douglas and his men, Funter returned to Nootka, and on June 8 Martínez seized his ship.

Tensions escalated when British captain James Colnett arrived from China on July 3 aboard his *Argonaut*. The hot-headed Colnett flatly declared his intention, like Meares before him, of building a trading fort. The Associated Merchants of London and India, a company owned by John Meares and John Etches, had sent Colnett from Macao to establish a permanent base in Nootka Sound, and he was not pleased to find the Spanish already there, embarking on a similar venture. Colnett, who had sailed as a midshipman with Cook from 1772 to 1775 on Cook's second circumnavigation, and who had seen action during the American War of Independence, adamantly refused to concede that Martínez and the Spanish had any right to Nootka. He declared that Captain Cook had laid claim to the area in 1778 and that Pérez and Martínez, who had sailed with Pérez on his voyage in 1774, had not landed nor had they officially claimed the area for Spain. He also pointed out that John Meares had "purchased" land from Chief Maquinna and had built an outpost in Nootka Sound a year before Martínez arrived.

Losing patience with these arguments, Martínez seized Colnett, confined him, imprisoned his officers, and clapped his men in irons. He took possession of the *Argonaut* and seized Thomas Hudson's *Princess Royal*, to add to the *North West America* he already held. This aggressive action became known, famously and infamously, as the Nootka Incident; major repercussions followed. To make matters worse, after Martínez had boarded one of the British ships, an angry argument broke out when the unarmed Chief Callicum, a kinsman of Maquinna, came alongside in his canoe, accusing Martínez of being a thief. Martínez shot and killed Callicum, an action that blackened the reputation of the Spanish in the eyes of the Mowachaht for years to come.

Martínez sent the *Argonaut* and *Princess Royal* as prizes to the naval base at San Blas, with their captains and crews as prisoners. Surprisingly, he allowed the American captains Gray and Kendrick to continue trading from Nootka Sound and even solicited Kendrick's help to transport the captive crew of the *North West America* to Macao. Kendrick gave command of his larger ship, the *Columbia Rediviva*, to Gray, loaded it with the prisoners and the sea otter pelts he had accumulated, and sent Gray off to China, while he sailed north aboard the *Lady Washington* in search of furs in Haida Gwaii.

Meanwhile, Martínez began fortifying the Spanish *presidio*, their small fort, at Yuquot. Combined with the shooting of Chief Callicum, this intensified Chief Maquinna's suspicion of and animosity toward the Spanish. The Mowachaht chief then chose to leave his own village and go and stay with his brother-in-law Chief Wickaninnish in Clayoquot Sound. The rest of the tribe moved five kilometres north, from Yuquot to the other side of Nootka Island, where they established a new village.

Martínez had turned his original mission into a diplomatic mess. The arrests and seizures he made at Nootka Sound sparked serious diplomatic squabbles between Britain and Spain. He received orders from his viceroy in Mexico to vacate Yuquot and return to San Blas, commanded since 1789 by Captain Juan Francisco de la Bodega y Quadra. The following spring Francisco de Eliza y Reventa sailed north to replace Martínez and take command at Yuquot. In June 1790, Eliza sent one of his officers, Manuel Quimper Benítez del Pino, to explore

Juan de Fuca Strait. As he passed Clayoquot Sound, Quimper stopped in to visit Chief Maquinna and assured him that the loathed Martínez no longer commanded the Spanish fort at Yuquot. He suggested that Maquinna return to his home territory. On making further inquiries, and after Quimper gave him a sheet of copper and a sail for his canoe, Maquinna returned to his village. In a further attempt to improve relations between the Spanish and the local people, Commander Eliza visited Clayoquot Sound in March 1791 to meet with Wickaninnish and the Tla-o-qui-aht. Fifty canoes came to greet him, and the following day Wickaninnish invited Eliza and his men to his longhouse, where 600 guests gathered for a welcoming feast. From his visits to Clayoquot Sound in 1790 and 1791, Commander Eliza estimated that the Tla-o-qui-aht had four large settlements, each with some 1,500 people. For the most part, his efforts at restoring goodwill led to friendlier relations between the Spanish and the Nuu-chah-nulth. Not so between the British and the Spanish.

John Meares, whose Associated Merchants of London and India owned the three ships seized by Martínez, pressed the government of Prime Minister William Pitt in London to seek reparations from the Spanish government for his losses, stirring up anti-Spanish public opinion with inflammatory reports of the incidents at Nootka. The British government acted quickly, appropriating one million pounds from the Treasury in case it was needed should an armed conflict occur. Pitt threatened war with Spain, asserting that Britain had the right to trade in areas with no Spanish settlement. With the French Revolution then underway, the Spanish could not rely on their traditional ally and decided that maintaining friendship with Britain might be a prudent policy. Following months of posturing and negotiations, on October 28, 1790, the two nations signed the Nootka Convention, which required the Spanish to release Meares's captured ships and men, and for Meares to receive 210,000 Spanish dollars in compensation. The two countries eventually reached a territorial agreement allowing for mutual access to the Pacific Northwest, naming Captain Bodega y Quadra and Captain George Vancouver to oversee the details of this truce.

In October 1790, following his release from the fetid San Blas prison, where eighteen of his thirty-one crew had died, Captain James Colnett hove into Clayoquot Sound in his unseaworthy *Argonaut*, now released by the Spanish and once again under his command. He was in no mood to suffer any further indignities. However, after he arrived in Clayoquot Sound, a longboat with several of his crew failed to return to the ship, and Colnett sent some of his men in a small jolly boat to look for it. Within a few days the longboat arrived back safely, but the search party on the jolly boat failed to return. Colnett sent the longboat out, seeking the others, and a month passed with no sign of either vessel. On November 21, Chief Tooteescosettle, Wickaninnish's brother, informed the anxious captain that the jolly boat had foundered at the entrance to Nootka Sound and that high winds had prevented the longboat from returning to Clayoquot. Another aboriginal man told a somewhat different story, so Colnett decided to hold Chief Tooteescosettle and another chief as hostages until he learned from the Spanish at Nootka what had happened to his men.

When Colnett informed Wickaninnish that he was holding the two hostages, the chief became furiously angry. Wickaninnish's sister offered to defuse the situation by taking a letter to the Spanish commander at Nootka, Francisco de Eliza, asking for information. Four days later she returned with news that Tooteescosettle had spoken the truth. The jolly boat had indeed foundered; no one survived, the crew disappeared, and none were seen again. With that, Colnett released his hostages and set about repairing his ship. Bad feelings continued to fester, and on December 31 the Tla-o-qui-aht attacked the *Argonaut*. The English retaliated, firing the ship's cannons on the village of Opitsat. With no trust remaining between the Tla-o-qui-aht and Colnett, he set sail for Macao in 1791 after wintering in Clayoquot Sound. Colnett's name and that of John Meares remain well known in Clayoquot Sound, with Mount Colnett and Meares Island named after them.

On August 29, 1791, American captain Robert Gray sailed into Clayoquot Sound following his circumnavigation of the globe in the *Columbia Rediviva*. He returned with the intention of establishing a winter base there, well away from the site of the previous tension between the British and Spanish at Nootka. While Gray had been travelling, his commander John Kendrick had "purchased" from Chief Wickaninnish 840 square kilometres of Clayoquot Sound, centred on Opitsat, for four muskets, a large sail, and a quantity of powder. After acquiring this land, Kendrick built a small trading outpost on an island in "Fair Harbor" near Opitsat which, like his base in Nootka Sound, he named Fort Washington. This island has never been identified.

In a location he called "Adventure Cove" in Lemmens Inlet on Meares Island, Gray and the fifty men under his command cleared land and built a ten-by-six-metre, two-storey log structure complete with two chimneys, built with some of the 5,000 or more bricks he brought from Boston as ballast. Wary of the Tla-o-qui-aht, Gray mounted two of the ship's guns and cut musket loopholes in the walls of the building he called Fort Defiance. The Americans also constructed several cabins, a blacksmith shop, and a boat-building shed outside the fort, as well as two saw pits. They began building a forty-five-ton sloop using timbers, stern post, and stem that Gray had brought with him from Boston. They purchased some boards, "which we procured from the natives for a trifling consideration of iron," according to John Hoskins, the *Columbia*'s supercargo (clerk), and also felled fir and cedar trees that they whipsawed into planks; others they fashioned into masts and spars.

On Christmas Day 1791 the "Boston men" decorated their fort and ship with evergreens, bunting, and flags, and cooked twenty geese and "whortleberry" (huckleberry) pudding. They invited Chief Wickaninnish and some of the Tla-o-qui-aht hierarchy to join them for Christmas dinner, at which they proffered toasts to one another, played games, and sang songs. Before Wickaninnish and his party paddled off after midnight, Gray fired a salute from the *Columbia*'s guns. Wickaninnish reciprocated with a feast to which he invited some of the Americans from Fort Defiance. By February 1792, all of this conviviality and friendship came to an end. The Tla-o-qui-aht appeared to be making preparations for a war against neighbouring tribes, and Gray feared they might attack him and his men in order to capture his ship and acquire guns, which Wickaninnish coveted.

Gray's cabin boy, a Hawaiian lad named Atoo, who had earlier tried to defect from Gray's crew to join the Tla-o-qui-ahts, found himself

WINTER QUARTERS.

Winter Quarters, an engraving of Fort Defiance in Adventure Cove, on Meares Island. American captain Robert Gray and the crew of the *Columbia Rediviva* built this fort and lived here in 1791–92. They built the trading vessel *Adventure* here—seen in front of the main building. Tofino resident Ken Gibson discovered the location of Fort Defiance in 1966. *Image C06375 courtesy of Royal BC Museum, BC Archives*

embroiled in the mounting tensions. One of Wickaninnish's brothers told Atoo to wet the crew's priming powder in order to weaken their defences. Under pressure from Gray, Atoo confessed the proposed plot and the captain hastily posted more guards. Several canoes loaded with warriors paddled near the fort one night shortly after. Hoskins wrote: "It was a beautiful starlit night...the natives gave a most dismal whoop. This was between one and two o'clock in the morning. The people who belonged to the Fort flew to their arms and those who belonged to the ship was by no means behind them. In less than five minutes every man was to his quarters with arms and ammunition ready for action...We continued to hear the most dreadful shrieks and whoops till day began to dawn."

Angered by this threatening display, Gray reached a fateful decision. He decided to leave, but not before wreaking havoc. He hurriedly launched his new ship, the *Adventure*; tore down Fort Defiance; and, using the chimney bricks as ballast for his new ship, sailed out of the Sound. As he left, he sent three boatloads of his crew into the largely deserted village of Opitsat, ordering them to burn all of the houses there. John Boit, the ship's sixteen-year-old fifth mate, recorded in his diary: "I'm very sorry to be under the necessity of remarking that this day I was sent with three boats all well manned & armed to destroy the village of Opitsatah; it was a command I was in no way tenacious of & am griev'd to think that Capt Gray should let his passions go so far. This village was about half a mile in Diameter, and Contained upwards of 200 Houses...This fine Village, the Work of Ages, was in a short time totally destroy'd." The exact location of the American Fort Defiance remained a mystery for over 150 years until, in 1966, local historian Ken Gibson, after much searching, confirmed its location in Lemmens Inlet on Meares Island.

Gray sailed north and anchored in Nasparti Inlet, north of Kyuquot and just below the Brooks Peninsula. A war canoe manned with twenty-five aboriginals, followed by others in a number of canoes, approached the *Columbia* in what seemed a suspicious and hostile manner. Gray ordered the crew to battle stations and armed all hands. John Boit recounted what happened next: "Capt. Gray order'd us to fire, which we did so effectually as to kill or wound every soul in the canoe. She drifted along the side, but we push'd her clear, and she drove to the north side of the Cove, under the shade of the trees. 'Twas bright moon light and the woods echoed with the dying groans of these unfortunate Savages."

Following this incident, Gray sailed south and for nine days attempted to find a way across the dangerous bar at the mouth of the vast Columbia River. Failing to find a way upriver, he returned northward again and on April 28 met at sea with Captain George Vancouver aboard the *Discovery*. Vancouver had been sent by Britain to re-establish his country's claim at Nootka; he was heading there to meet and negotiate with the Spanish commander Bodega y Quadra and had sailed right past the mouth of the Columbia without realizing its existence. Even after conversing with Gray, Vancouver remained skeptical about the river's presence.

With that, Gray again turned south and this time, on May 11, he found a way over the treacherous sandbars that guard the Columbia River, which he named after his ship, the *Columbia Rediviva*. He traded with the Natives at the mouth of the river and on May 20 exited the river, then set sail once again for China. In 1981, nearly two centuries later, in recognition of Gray's exploration of the Columbia River, and in honour of his circumnavigation of the globe in 1789–90, NASA named its space shuttle *Columbia* after his ship. In 1858, when asked to provide a name for the latest Crown colony of her Canadian dominion, Queen Victoria chose the name British Columbia. By then, the Hudson's Bay Company had long used the name "Columbia" to describe what is now southern BC and northern Washington State. To distinguish the area north of the 49th parallel, established in 1846 as the international boundary, the queen added "British" to the name.

Captain Bodega y Quadra arrived in Nootka Sound with three ships in April 1792 and spent four months there awaiting the arrival of Captain George Vancouver. He used his time well, learning about the area and the people. The diplomatic and well-liked Quadra went to great pains to improve relations with the Mowachaht people, paying special attention to Chief Maquinna, always giving him the honoured place at table and serving him personally. His negotiating skills smoothed over many local disputes, and his support of Maquinna helped prevent a war planned against him by the Ahousaht and Tla-o-qui-aht.

Captain George Vancouver arrived at Nootka in August 1792. He and Quadra, representing their respective countries in diplomatic capacities, came to like and respect each other, despite communicating through interpreters, and often in writing. Strongly impressed by Quadra's diplomacy and politeness toward the local people, Vancouver noted "with a mixture of surprise and pleasure how much the Spaniards had succeeded in gaining the good opinion and confidence of the people." In their amicable but inconclusive meetings, Vancouver and Quadra agreed to call what is now Vancouver Island "The Island of Quadra and

Vancouver," but did not achieve much toward clarifying the terms of the Nootka Convention. They decided to let their respective governments do the negotiations. As time passed, the urgency of the English/Spanish dispute over the territory faded away. Sea otter prices fell due to an oversupplied market, the expectation of finding a Northwest Passage abated, and the Spanish finally relinquished their claim on the Pacific Northwest. On October 15, 1795, they tore down their *presidio* at Yuquot and returned to Mexico, leaving Nootka as a free port.

Following negotiations at Nootka, Captain Vancouver sailed south to California, and after wintering in Hawaii, in the spring of 1793 he returned to continue his surveying work on the northwest coast. In early June, when mapping Dean Channel, on the mainland just north of Vancouver Island, some members of his crew rested in Elcho Harbour near what is now Bella Coola. Six weeks later, fur trader and explorer Alexander Mackenzie arrived in that same bay by an entirely different route. He and his party had reached the coast by crossing the North American continent by land, the first Europeans to do so. On a rock in Dean Channel, Mackenzie famously inscribed "Alex Mackenzie from Canada by land 22nd July 1793." He related in his diary that aboriginals told him of the recent activities of longboats and surveying crews in their area. Mackenzie and Vancouver very nearly met, missing each other by only a matter of weeks.

Captain Robert Gray's destruction of Opitsat on his departure from Clayoquot Sound in April 1792 put intense strain on relations between the Nuu-chah-nulth and the fur traders. At the same time, competition mounted between British and American traders. John Kendrick had taken trading to a new level by pre-purchasing skins from the local tribes, thwarting attempts by British traders to buy skins. In June 1792, when William Brown, a British trader on board the *Butterworth*, arrived at what remained of the village of Opitsat, the Tla-o-qui-aht refused all his offers. His frustration growing, Brown sent sailors ashore at another unnamed village to acquire what furs they could.

His crew resorted to violence, cutting the otter skins from the backs of local people, and killing four. Wickaninnish's musket-armed warriors retaliated, killing one sailor and wounding four others. Infuriated, Brown took revenge when sailing out of the area. He seized nine Tla-o-qui-ahts from their fishing canoes, whipped them, and threw them into the sea. His accompanying ship, *Jenny*, then used the swimming men as target practice for its cannons. Of the nine men, four were chiefs, and one a brother of Wickaninnish.

Year by year, Wickaninnish held greater control over trade with the Europeans, and suspicion and mistrust grew on both sides. With the Tla-o-qui-aht chief now in possession of over 200 muskets and two barrels of powder, the potential for violence also increased steadily. In May 1793, when American trader Josiah Roberts arrived in Clayoquot Sound on his *Jefferson*, Wickaninnish would only agree to trade with the Americans if two of the ship's officers remained ashore as hostages while trading took place aboard ship. If trade took place on land, one of the chief's brothers would remain on the ship as hostage. The following winter found Roberts and the *Jefferson* in Barkley Sound. After one of his men was killed while hunting, Roberts took his revenge. Imitating Gray's actions at Opitsat, he destroyed the village of Sechart in March 1794, his armed boats firing their swivel guns, smashing houses and canoes. "After having sufficient satisfaction for their depravations on us," as first officer Bernard Magee put it, the *Jefferson* sailed from Barkley Sound. In 1795 another American ship, the *Ruby*, commanded by Charles Bishop, successfully traded with Wickaninnish, but this appears to have been the last ship to conduct any peaceful trade for sea otter skins in Clayoquot Sound.

By 1800 the fur trade on the Pacific Northwest coast saw the Americans in the ascendency; they had eight ships plying the area for furs that year, while the British had only one. In 1801, twenty American and three British ships sailed the coast, all seeking the dwindling supply of "soft gold." According to records compiled by early British Columbian historian F.W. Howay, about 450 fur trading vessels visited the North Pacific coast between 1774 and 1820. More than half flew the Stars and Stripes; ninety-three the Union Jack; and the red-and yellow-striped flag of Spain flew on forty-three ships. Between 1790 and 1818, traders carried some 300,000 sea otter pelts to China from the northwest coast. With the price of a pelt over the same period averaging between twenty-five and thirty dollars, overall the trade netted somewhere between $7.5 and $9 million. By the turn of the century, with the sea otter population dramatically reduced, and because of the establishment of land-based trading posts west of the Rockies by the Hudson's Bay Company, the Northwest Company, and John Jacob Astor's Pacific Fur Company, the maritime fur trade began to die out. As it faded, the pent-up indignities of the past decades led to yet more tragic incidents.

In March 1803, following an affront to Chief Maquinna by Captain John Slater, and after years of insults perpetrated on Maquinna and his people by British and American traders, the Mowachahts attacked and beheaded all but two of the twenty-six-man crew of the American ship *Boston* near Yuquot. John Jewitt and John Thompson, the only survivors of the *Boston*, became slaves of Chief Maquinna for two years. Jewitt's highly prized talents as a blacksmith may explain their survival, and on the whole they received good treatment. Chief Wickaninnish attempted on several occasions to purchase Jewitt from Maquinna. In 1805 another trader rescued the two men, and on his return to New England Jewitt published the daily journal he had written during his time in captivity as *A Journal Kept at Nootka Sound*. In 1815, in collaboration with Richard Alsop, a much expanded version of the diary appeared under the title *A Narrative of the Adventures and Sufferings of John T. Jewitt*. Because Jewitt had been highly observant and an active participant in the daily life of the local people, his account provides an invaluable early record of Nuu-chah-nulth life. Published and reprinted many times, it made Jewitt into a minor celebrity, although he sank into obscurity in later life. Tellingly, a passage in the *Narrative* reveals that he understood why his ship and fellow sailors fell victim to an attack. "Many of the melancholy disasters have principally arisen," he wrote, "from the imprudent conduct of some of the captains and crews...insulting, plundering and even killing [the local people] on slight grounds. This, as nothing is more sacred with a savage than the principle of revenge...induces them to wreak their vengeance upon the first vessel or boat's crew that offers, making the innocent too frequently suffer for the wrongs of the guilty."

The downward spiral of relations between fur traders and aboriginals continued, becoming ever more disturbing. In 1810, Captain George Washington Ayers of the American ship *Mercury* took a dozen Tla-o-qui-aht sea otter hunters to California's Farallon Islands where, having promised to return them home after the hunt, he abandoned them. Only two managed to make their way back, and the Tla-o-qui-aht resolved to exact revenge on the next ship that arrived in Clayoquot Sound. Enter the *Tonquin*, owned by John Jacob Astor's Pacific Fur Company, based at Fort Astoria, Oregon. In June 1811, with a crew of twenty-three men, and captained by the quick-tempered Jonathan Thorn, this ship arrived in Clayoquot Sound, anchoring in Templar Channel opposite Wickaninnish's summer village of Echachis.

Trading progressed well for a few days, but Thorn's harsh and un-compromising manner and his open insults in dealing with Nookmis (also spelled Nokamis), Chief Wickaninnish's trade representative, in-flamed the Tla-o-qui-aht. Thorn rejected the advice of his experienced supercargo Alexander McKay, and relations soured. McKay had travelled with Alexander Mackenzie on his famous journey across the continent, arriving with him at Bella Coola in July 1793. He had considerable experience as a trader, but to no avail. Under Thorn, relations with the Tla-o-qui-aht reached crisis point during trade negotiations aboard the *Tonquin*. The Tla-o-qui-aht attacked, killing the captain and all but six of the crew. That night, five of the survivors escaped in a ship's boat under cover of darkness, leaving the badly wounded ship's clerk, a man named Lewis, on the *Tonquin*. The following day an estimated 200 Tla-o-qui-ahts boarded the seemingly deserted *Tonquin*, bent on plunder. With the decks crowded, a tremendous explosion suddenly tore the ship apart. Apparently Lewis had managed to crawl into the bowels of the ship to ignite the large supply of gunpowder; in effect, he became a suicide bomber. Over eighty bodies were blown all over the bay, with debris, including canoes and trading blankets, strewn across the water. The surviving Tla-o-qui-aht later captured the five crew members who had escaped, killing all of them and leaving alive only the aboriginal interpreter, Joseachal, who had boarded in Astoria. He witnessed the destruction of the *Tonquin* from shore.

William Banfield wrote an account of the Tonquin's dramatic end based on what he heard from the Tla-o-qui-aht. His article appeared in the *Victoria Daily Gazette* of September 9, 1858.

> The whole of the tribe were assembled, either on board or alongside in canoes, taking and receiving plunder, when a fearful explosion took place, and the whole top works of the ship blew off with a fearful crash. The Indians were scattered in all directions, and mangled and mutilated bodies covered the face of the water. The Indians were nearly all more or less hurt, but the greatest number that were killed were those in the canoes struck by broken fragments of the ship; most of the Indians on deck were comparatively little hurt. McKay and Lewis' names are frequently talked of to this day. McKay was, before this tragedy, a great favorite with them.

The story of the *Tonquin*, possessing all the tragic drama of frontier violence, a massacre, and individual heroism, eventually inspired a Hollywood movie. Filmed in the Philippines in 1941 and directed by Frank Lloyd, who also directed Charles Laughton in the 1935 classic *Mutiny on the Bounty*, this film embellished the story of the *Tonquin* with a love interest, featuring Carol Bruce as a beautiful stowaway. Cast members included Walter Brennan as Captain Thorn; Canadian aboriginal actor Jay Silverheels, later famed as the Lone Ranger's sidekick, Tonto; Nigel Bruce, later to play Dr. Watson alongside Basil Rathbone's Sherlock Holmes; and Leo G. Carroll as Sandy McKay, one of Carol Bruce's admirers. Entitled *This Woman Is Mine* and later renamed *Fury of the Sea*, the Hollywood version of the *Tonquin*'s terrible end never became a classic of the silver screen. It did receive a nomination in the 1942 Academy Awards for Best Musical Score (Richard Hageman), along with nineteen others. It did not win.

ATTACK AND MASSACRE OF CREW OF SHIP TONQUIN BY THE SAVAGES OF THE N.W. COAST

An artist's rendering of the trading vessel *Tonquin* being attacked by Tla-o-qui-aht warriors in 1811 in Templar Channel. The Tla-o-qui-aht killed most of the crew. A wounded crewman ignited explosives that blew the ship apart, killing scores of Tla-o-qui-ahts. The *Tonquin* sank off MacKenzie Beach, and divers still hope to find the wreck. *Image D04334 courtesy of Royal BC Museum, BC Archives*

Tla-o-qui-aht oral history, and the account of the aboriginal inter-preter, Joseachal, indicate that following the explosion the *Tonquin* did not sink immediately, and only the stern had been blown off. The Tla-o-qui-aht attempted to tow the hulk westward toward Echachis Island, but southeast winds prevented progress. They began towing it eastward, with the wind, toward Tin Wis Bay (MacKenzie Beach) on the Esowista Peninsula, hoping to beach it there. Before they could do so, the badly damaged ship sank. Nearly a century later, in 2003, a local fisherman snagged an old anchor on the bottom of Tin Wis Bay. Local diver and underwater explorer Rod Palm retrieved the anchor, with the help of several others. It is widely held to be the anchor of the *Tonquin*. On a coast littered with wrecks and maritime disasters, the *Tonquin* has attracted more interest than almost any other. Some-times called the Holy Grail of wrecks, the *Tonquin* has proved endlessly fascinating for underwater archaeology enthusiasts.

The *Tonquin* incident marked the end, in any meaningful sense, of the maritime fur trade in the Pacific Northwest. By the time this ship sank, much profit had been made: mostly by international interests in the fur trade, some by individual traders, and a very limited amount by the Nuu-chah-nulth people of Vancouver Island's west coast. Certainly this trade introduced the coastal people to the often harsh reality of doing business with outsiders, and to the sometimes—by no means always—useful benefits of acquiring goods. The sea otter trade opened the way for future trade and for later settlement, which would bring unimagined consequences to the Nuu-chah-nulth. Chief Wickaninnish, one of the most powerful figures in this initial fur trade, did not live to see its ongoing impact on his people. He died sometime between 1817 and 1825.

Chapter 5:

"OUTRAGES AND DISORDERS"

WITH THE SEA OTTER POPULATION depleted to the point of near extinction, few fur trading ships entered Clayoquot Sound in the decades following the *Tonquin* incident of 1811. The incentive to trade for furs on the hazardous West Coast largely disappeared, as events to the south and east took precedence.

In order to secure British claims to Vancouver Island, in 1843 the Hudson's Bay Company founded Fort Victoria on the southern tip of the Island. James Douglas, then the company's chief factor in Fort Vancouver, at the mouth of the Columbia River, selected the site, surveyed the land, and supervised construction of this new outpost. Six years later, in 1849, Douglas moved to Fort Victoria to take charge when Victoria replaced Fort Vancouver as the headquarters of the fur trade on the Pacific coast. That same year, the British government established Vancouver Island as a Crown colony, ceding it to the Hudson's Bay Company for seven shillings a year, on the understanding that the HBC would administer affairs in the colony and encourage settlement.

Throughout the 1850s, the settlement of Fort Victoria, and indeed the entire Colony of Vancouver Island, failed to amount to much. Few settlers arrived, partly because land cost one pound an acre (half a hectare) in the colony, whereas in America land could be had for free, and also because many would-be settlers followed the lure of gold to California after the first exciting discovery there in 1848. Even employees of the Hudson's Bay Company abandoned the new colony and went south. Vancouver Island could not compete. "It is in my view worthless as a seat for a colony," Archibald Barclay, the HBC secretary, declared, adding that Vancouver Island was the "last place on the globe" he would select as an abode.

By early 1851, only twenty settlers had taken the rash step of purchasing land in the colony, and four years later the entire European population on Vancouver Island came to only 774, of whom nearly half were children. These settlers clustered around four locales on the east coast of the Island: Fort Victoria (now the City of Victoria), the Cowichan valley, Fort Rupert (Port Hardy), and Nanaimo. At that time, no one even imagined settling on the remote west coast of Vancouver Island.

After Britain declared war on Russia in 1854, involving itself in the Crimean War, gunboats of the Royal Navy's Pacific fleet, then headquartered at Valparaíso, Chile, began to make use of Esquimalt Harbour near Victoria as a strategic supply base for their excursions into the North Pacific. Following a British naval attack on Russian fortifications on the Kamchatka Peninsula, three Royal Navy ships carrying eighty wounded men entered Esquimalt Harbour seeking assistance. Fort Victoria could not provide the required medical aid, and the ships continued on to San Francisco. Anticipating more casualties, in 1855 James Douglas ordered the construction of three rough little hospital buildings at Esquimalt Harbour. No further casualties showed up, so these buildings never served their original purpose, but from that time forward, naval vessels regularly appeared in the harbour. A decade later, in 1865, Esquimalt officially became the new headquarters of the Pacific fleet, and by then Victoria had changed beyond recognition.

Gold fever had transformed the place. In 1858, the discovery of gold along the Fraser River saw Victoria explode in size. Some 30,000 prospectors, mostly Americans, flocked up the river after first going through Victoria because the colonial government required them to obtain their licences there. Within a couple of years, many of them had continued north along the Fraser into the interior of British Columbia, discovering more gold in the Cariboo region. By 1862 the gold discovered near Barkerville set off another stampede, attracting tens of thousands more prospectors through Victoria. From a quiet backwater of about 800 people in 1858, for a few mad years Victoria became "a rowdy boisterous, transient settlement," according to historian Terry Reksten, with "saloons and hotels and shanties [crowding] the palisades of the fort." Prices soared, a city of grey canvas tents sprang up, and at times during the dry summer months, "liquor was cheaper than water." The Cariboo gold rush alone extracted an estimated $30 million in gold during the 1860s—an exceptional return considering that gold then sold for around $20 an ounce.

On the west coast of Vancouver Island, the middle years of the nineteenth century saw far less European activity than the decades immediately following first contact. By the early 1850s, a few independent coastal traders cruised the coast in small schooners, reviving trade with the aboriginal peoples. These traders undertook annual and semi-annual tours, usually each autumn when the Natives had completed their year's hunting, fishing, and gathering. They would stop at various villages along the coast, exchanging trade goods for dogfish oil, whale and seal oil, fresh and dried fish, berries, and furs. They carried out business in much the same way the earlier sea otter traders had done, negotiating with the chief of each tribe after the appropriate ceremonies and exchanges of gifts had taken place.

Once the trading parties negotiated a price, the close personal and economic ties among the aboriginal people in their far-flung communities meant that the established price would be maintained all along the coast. In his book *The Nootka: Scenes and Studies of Savage Life*, first published in 1868, Gilbert Sproat noted, "News about prices...travels quickly to distant places from one tribe to another. If a trading schooner appeared at one point on the shore and offered a higher price than one usually gives, the Indians would know the fact along the whole coast." Sproat described the Nuu-chah-nulth as "astute, and rather too sharp at bargaining."

During the 1850s a vigorous trade emerged along the coast with the growing demand for dogfish *(Squalus acanthias)* liver oil. The developing resource industries throughout the Pacific Northwest began to require immense amounts of it. Loggers used dogfish oil to grease their corduroy skid roads and to lubricate machinery, and miners to light their lamps in the coal mines opening at Fort Rupert and at Nanaimo. Two early lighthouses even used dogfish oil to fuel their beacons.

Governor Douglas commended this new enterprise in 1855: "The oil procured from this colony is procured from Native tribes inhabiting the west coast of Vancouver Island. It is of excellent quality, and has a high character in California where it brings from three to four dollars a gallon [4.5 litres]." That same year Douglas estimated that 10,000 gallons (45,460 litres) of dogfish oil had been purchased along the west coast of Vancouver Island.

The demand for dogfish oil increased yearly, resulting in a profitable trade for aboriginal people along the coast. In July 1864, Robert Brown visited the west coast as commander of the Vancouver Island Exploring Expedition, and noted in his diary: "The dog-fish season is just commencing. Laughton [coastal trader Thomas Laughton] calculates that from Pachena to Woody Point [Cape Cook] there is about 15,000 gallons [68,000 litres] of Dog-fish oil traded every year...This does not include what is...traded by the Indians to the Americans...The Clay-o-quot Chief is a great trader & collects oil of the neighbouring tribes; he then goes over to Cape Flattery and sells it for American goods, and perhaps a little 'fire-water.'"

Entire tribes went to work rendering the oil. William Banfield, the Colonial Secretary's agent in Barkley Sound, reported in 1858 that in the previous four years the Port San Juan band, the Pacheedaht, living just south of Barkley Sound on the coast and comprising only forty adults, processed between 22,000 and 28,000 litres of dogfish oil per year. By 1874, the aboriginal communities in Barkley Sound alone produced between 91,000 and 114,000 litres of oil. Because it took ten dogfish livers to produce 4.5 litres of oil, this meant catching and processing a quarter of a million dogfish from the immense shoals of these fish along the coast. Using multiple hooks, some aboriginals could catch as many as 400 in one day. They baited the hooks and tied rocks to the line as weights to catch these bottom-dwelling spiny sharks, ranging from 0.75 metres to two metres in length. According to Robert Brown, the process of extracting oil from the dogfish livers involved a simple apparatus, "merely a box of water into which hot stones are thrown and the oil skimmed off."

Dogfish oil attracted a growing number of independent traders to venture up the west coast in their small sailing vessels. They would purchase the oil from tribes all along the coast, paying from twenty-five to forty cents for about four litres, and later resell the same quantity of oil to the HBC in Victoria for fifty cents to a dollar. The trade encouraged the establishment of seasonal, and later permanent, trading posts at various locations along the outer coast. Storekeepers at these posts would purchase the oil and collect it in 180-litre wooden barrels, shipping as many as fifteen barrels at a time to Victoria. Decade after decade, this trade continued.

Fred Thornberg managed the trading post at Clayoquot on Stubbs Island from 1874 until 1889; in his memoirs he noted "the Dogfish that in those days swarmed by the millions on the W. coast." Later, as the trader based at Ahousat, Thornberg complained bitterly about having to manhandle heavy barrels of dogfish oil in and out of his canoe, often at night and in inclement weather. He would paddle to meet a Victoria-bound schooner or coastal steamer, load the full barrels onto the vessel, and offload empty barrels for future oil purchases. Sometimes in summer the barrels of oil burst in the heat, and on dark and stormy nights the cumbersome barrels occasionally disappeared overboard.

The dogfish oil trade continued well into the twentieth century. Ahousaht elder Peter Webster, in his book *As Far as I Know*, described how his grandmother processed the oil when he was a child in the 1910s. "She would cut off the heads and tails and remove their livers... The remainder of the dogfish was placed in a big brass pot and boiled." After boiling,

> she would remove the oil from the surface with large shells of the horse clam. She would then transfer the fish to a large saucepan. Once there the skin was removed and the white meat cleaned and stirred into a consistency like mush or cream of wheat. This was served in soup bowls...The dogfish oil was stored in a bag made from the stomach of a seal. This oil would be used for cooking purposes throughout the following year. In this way it could be stored for a long time...

The oil obtained by boiling the livers was placed in four-gallon [18-litre] cans.

In the early years of the dogfish oil trade, the lot of the independent trader on the coast proved lonely, precarious, and at times dangerous. In 1854 a Maltese trader named Barney, employed by William Banfield and Peter Francis at their Kyuquot trading post, had amassed 13,600 litres of dogfish oil. He needed the company schooner to come and collect the oil, but he decided not to wait for Peter Francis, who was likely on one of his drinking sprees in Victoria. Barney left the oil with trustworthy Kyuquot chief Ca-ca-hammes and headed south with a number of Kyuquots to confer with Banfield, then in charge of the seasonal trading post at Clayoquot. Neither he nor his companions were seen alive again. Three weeks later, alarmed by rumours of Barney's murder, Banfield sent Francis up to Kyuquot in the *San Diego*. Upon arriving, Francis strongly suspected Chief Ca-ca-hammes of murdering Barney for the dogfish oil, which the chief refused to hand over. Protesting that Barney had told him to keep it until his safe return, the chief volunteered to go with Francis to Victoria to clear his name in front of Governor Douglas.

On the return journey to Victoria, the *San Diego* stopped at Clayoquot, where Tla-o-qui-aht warriors surrounded the ship in their canoes, demanding Francis hand over the enemy Kyuquot chief. Fearing for his life, the chief escaped under cover of darkness, hoping to find his way back to Kyuquot, but the Tla-o-qui-ahts pursued him. After killing and decapitating him, they headed north to attack the unsuspecting and leaderless Kyuquot. They killed thirty of them before being routed. Two years later, Banfield and Francis sailed into Kyuquot to retrieve their dogfish oil only to find that the chief's son had sold it to rival traders Hugh McKay and William Spring.

In March 1863, word reached Victoria that the schooner *Trader*, owned by Hugh McKay, had been attacked at Yuquot in Nootka Sound. The captain and a young Tla-o-qui-aht crewman had been murdered. The perpetrators punctured all of the dogfish oil barrels and chopped the *Trader* into pieces to make it seem she had been lost in a storm, then distributed items of value from the ship among their tribe. When the Tla-o-qui-ahts learned their tribesman had been killed by the Mowa-chahts, they prepared an attack to avenge the loss. In September, the naval gunboat HMS *Cameleon* visited Nootka but did not find enough concrete evidence to arrest anyone for the crime. Nevertheless, Captain Edward Hardinge ordered his crew to put on a display of firepower, using the ship's cannons to "give a foretaste of what they were to expect," according to the *British Colonist* on September 21, 1863.

Elsewhere on Vancouver Island, over a decade before the loss of the *Trader*, naval gunboats had responded vigorously to another inflam-matory incident. In 1849 the Hudson's Bay Company started a small coal-mining operation on the northeast coast of Vancouver Island at Fort Rupert (Port Hardy) amid what visiting naturalist John Keast Lord described as "a sea of savagery." Three HBC sailors, hoping to make their fortunes on the goldfields, had deserted their posts on the company barque *Norman Morison*, escaping from Victoria aboard the *England*, which headed toward Fort Rupert. The three men were mur-dered by the Newitty band of the Kwakwaka'wakw, apparently because the Newitty believed the deserters were wanted "dead or alive." The newly appointed governor of the Colony of Vancouver Island, Richard Blanshard, decided to mete out his form of justice, following an initial investigation by the HBC's surgeon, Dr. John Helmcken, who also served as a magistrate. Blanshard sailed north in the Royal Navy corvette *Daedalus*, with a crew of sixty, to confront the Newitty, and he demanded the suspected murderers be handed over. The chief refused, whereupon Blanshard ordered the crew of the *Daedalus* to destroy two nearby Newitty villages, standing vacant at the time. The following year Blanshard returned in the sloop *Daphne*, once again trying to apprehend the suspects. This time the Newitty fired shots at a party of sailors, wounding some of them. Blanshard then ordered the *Daphne's* crew to destroy yet more villages. This action led to the Newitty turning over three dead bodies, reputedly those of the murderers, thus ending "this miserable affair," as Dr. Helmcken described the episode.

Blanshard's actions at Fort Rupert marked the first time the co-lonial authorities used gunboat diplomacy—or lack of diplomacy—to deal with aboriginal people on Vancouver Island. It was not the last. Summing up the situation, the *1901 Year Book of British Columbia* says of the First Nations along the coast that "they had ever in their hearts the wholesome dread of a Hudson's Bay Company gun-boat or man-of-war." Richard Blanshard's eighteen-month tenure at Fort Victoria as governor of the colony ended with him leaving in disgust, returning to England in September 1851. He had loathed life in the colony and did considerable harm, seeing it as his duty to "repress and over-awe the natives." As chief factor of the HBC at Victoria, James Douglas argued against Blanshard's high-handed actions, maintaining that "it is expedient and unjust to hold *tribes* responsible for the acts of *individuals*." Yet even with his more enlightened attitude, when he succeeded Blanshard as governor, Douglas found himself deploying gunships to quell trouble with aboriginals.

On November 5, 1852, two aboriginal men murdered Peter Brown, a Scottish shepherd working for the Hudson's Bay Company at Lake Hill, eight kilometres from Fort Victoria. Surmising that the culprits had fled to Cowichan, Governor Douglas set off in January 1853 with a force of 150 naval crew and Royal Marines. They travelled aboard the frigate HMS *Thetis* and the HBC's brig *Recovery*, towed by the HBC paddlewheeler *Beaver* to ensure safe passage through the uncharted and narrow waterways off southeastern Vancouver Island. Surrounded by the armed sailors and marines, and under the protection of the ships' guns, Douglas met with 200 Cowichans at the mouth of the Cowichan River and negotiated the surrender of one of the suspects. Hearing that the other suspect had fled north, Douglas and his force later apprehended the second man, a member of the Snuneymuxw band, near Nanaimo. After a trial on the deck of the *Beaver* in Nanaimo Harbour in front of a jury made up entirely of naval officers, and with all of the Snuneymuxw in attendance to witness the event, the authorities hanged the two condemned men at Gallows Point on Protection Island. Douglas described his handling of this event as "a fist of iron in a glove of velvet."

The attempted murder of British subject Thomas Williams in 1856 in the Cowichan Valley provoked another strong response from

Douglas. With the Crimean War over and more Royal Navy ships and men at his disposal, Douglas dispatched a force of over 400 aboard HMS *Trincomalee* (twenty-six guns), towed by the HBC steamer *Otter*, to the mouth of the Cowichan River. This time the massive show of force produced a suspect, whom the authorities tried, found guilty, and executed in front of his assembled Cowichan people the following day.

In January 1859, the American brig *Swiss Boy*, outward bound and loaded with lumber from Port Orchard in Washington State, sprang a leak and put in to Barkley Sound. The master beached the vessel in order to make repairs, only to be boarded by hundreds of Huu-ay-ahts. They sawed off the main mast, pillaged the vessel, and robbed the crew of nine, but did them no other harm. Coastal trader Hugh McKay, passing in his *Morning Star*, conveyed the captain and crew to Victoria. Governor Douglas sent the twenty-one-gun, steam-powered corvette HMS *Satellite* to investigate. Captain Prevost convened an inquiry, attended by the Huu-ay-aht chiefs, on the deck of his ship. The Huu-ay-ahts readily admitted their actions, claiming they had boarded a foreign ship in "King George's" waters, expecting commendation, not censure. Taken aback, Prevost took one chief to Victoria with him and reported to Douglas that auger test samples showed the hull and mast of *Swiss Boy* had rotted throughout, and that *Swiss Boy* should never have been at sea in the first place. In the end, another ship recovered the cargo of lumber, and the chief who had been taken to Victoria returned home after a few weeks.

Incongruously, two energetic Englishmen in search of adventure showed up on the west coast at this juncture. Classic adventure-seekers of the Victorian age, these men proved themselves cheerfully oblivious to the risks on the coast, and like other eccentric explorers of the era they arrived in territory entirely unknown to them with an unlikely aim. They wished to circumnavigate Vancouver Island—apparently just for the fun of it. Captain Charles Edward Barrett-Lennard, a Crimean cavalry veteran, and Captain Napoleon Fitzstubbs—whose name often appears as Fitz Stubbs—arrived in Victoria in 1860 aboard the *Athelstan*. As deck cargo, the two brought with them Barrett-Lennard's twenty-ton cutter *Templar*, which he had sailed in British waters as a member of the Royal Thames Yacht Club. Barrett-Lennard also brought his dogs; one a purebred bulldog.

The two set off aboard the *Templar* in the autumn of 1860 "to re-create," as the *British Colonist* put it. This recreation took them on a two-and-a-half-month voyage around Vancouver Island. Flying the blue burgee of the Royal Thames Yacht Club, and wearing the club's brass-buttoned jacket, Barrett-Lennard appeared to be a high-ranking officer in the eyes of the First Nations chiefs he visited. His bulldog also made quite an impression; at Yuquot the local chief offered to exchange one of his own dogs, "a vile mongrel," for the bulldog. Barrett-Lennard instead offered the chief a pair of his own trousers, which the chief did not care for, despite the trousers "having been cut by Hill, of Bond Street." In Clayoquot Sound, the two Englishmen marvelled at the size of the timbers supporting the big houses they visited in the villages, estimating the timbers to be a hundred feet long by three or four feet in diameter (30.5 metres by 1 metre), and baffled by how "these savages" could raise such beams. "The sight of these buildings," Barrett-Lennard wrote in his colourful account of their travels, "produced the same effect of wonder on my mind as did the first visit to Stonehenge."

Following their adventure, they sailed the *Templar* to Clayoquot where they briefly took over the trading post. "Trading for oil and furs with the Indian offers a remunerative field for energetic men with small capital," commented the *British Colonist* approvingly. After he returned to Britain in 1862, Barrett-Lennard published an account of their cruise, *Travels in British Columbia: With a Narrative of a Yacht Voyage Around Vancouver's Island.* He later became a baronet following the death of his father. Before leaving Victoria, Barrett-Lennard sold the *Templar* to Robert Burnaby; it foundered in 1862 in a southeast gale off Foul Bay. Fitzstubbs stayed on in British Columbia, serving as government agent, stipendiary magistrate, and gold commissioner at Hazelton and later at Nelson. Their names, and that of their boat, are commemorated in Clayoquot Sound: Stubbs and Lennard Islands and Templar Channel.

These various traders and early settlers on the west coast all lived a risky existence. On October 20, 1862, William Banfield lost his life.

First reports claimed he had drowned while going out in his canoe to meet the schooner *Alberni*, but later the *British Colonist* reported that he had been killed on shore. A wave of alarm ran along the coast following Banfield's death, and the naval vessel *Devastation* headed out to investigate. Authorities charged a Huu-ay-aht named Klatsmick with the murder, but after being tried in Victoria, he was acquitted. On his return to Barkley Sound, Klatsmick boasted of killing Banfield. Rumours about the murder continued to circulate on the coast for a long time. As the Colonial Secretary's agent at Barkley Sound, and well known as a coastal trader, Banfield had lived for many years on Vancouver Island. He arrived at Fort Victoria in 1844 as a ship's carpenter aboard HMS *Constance* and soon realized the area's potential for trading when he sailed off the coast with the Royal Navy. Upon his discharge in 1849, he began trading at various locations, including Clayoquot, in partnership with Captain Peter Francis and Thomas Laughton. He wrote a series of articles about the Barkley Sound area for the *Daily Victoria Gazette* in 1858 and moved to live there permanently in 1859.

In August of 1864, Captain James Stevenson anchored his sixteen-ton trading vessel *Kingfisher* at Matilda Creek, Flores Island, in the heart of Ahousaht territory. The previous year Stevenson had been convicted and fined $500 at New Westminster for selling liquor to aboriginals. Accounts vary concerning what occurred next at Matilda Creek, but unquestionably the *Kingfisher* incident and its aftermath represent the most aggressive gunboat action on the West Coast.

The Ahousaht chief Cap-chah may have told Stevenson he had dogfish oil to sell and then, possibly due to alcohol-related incidents and the abduction of Native women by the traders, the Ahousahts' anger ignited. Chief Cap-chah and twelve Ahousahts attacked and killed Stevenson and his two-man crew, a European named Wilson and a Fort Rupert Native. Weighting the bodies with stones, they sank them in the sea and afterward plundered, set fire to, and scuttled the *Kingfisher*. On September 10, 1864, when word of the incident reached Victoria, the *British Colonist* declared: "It behooves the government to institute prompt enquiries into this matter, and if the outrage has been committed as represented to inflict prompt punishment. The tribes involved had their habitation on the sea coast and can, therefore, be reached at all times by a ship of war. It has been for some time the boast of the Indians on the west coast that murders have been committed by their tribes without any attempt at retribution."

With the pressure of public opinion mounting, in late September 1864 Rear Admiral Joseph Denman sent the gunboat HMS *Devastation* to Clayoquot Sound, under the command of Captain J.W. Pike, to demand the murderers be given up. Finding Matilda Creek deserted, Pike headed to Herbert Inlet, where "a large body of Indians in their fighting paint fired upon the boat and ship," according to Denman's account. Pike retreated to report to Denman, and in short order he returned to the area on the *Devastation*, this time accompanied by the *Sutlej*, commanded by Admiral Denman himself. Denman's wife accompanied her husband aboard the *Sutlej*. They found the Ahousahts still defiant, refusing to surrender any of the suspects.

The two vessels opened fire, systematically destroying villages and encampments in several locations over several days. In all, the *Sutlej* and *Devastation* shelled nine Ahousaht settlements in Herbert Inlet, Shelter Inlet, and elsewhere. Still the Ahousahts refused to co-operate. A lengthy attempt to negotiate through an interpreter led to Denman receiving "a message from the Indians saying that if I wanted the men I might come and take them, if I destroyed the village they would soon build it up again and if I attempted to touch the canoes they would shoot every man who came near the shore. I then ordered heavy fire to be opened on the village." To ensure the complete destruction of this village, Denman sent boats ashore to set the place alight. Feeling "obliged to strike a yet more severe blow," Denman then ordered an attack over land. "On the morning of the 7th October, forty seamen and thirty marines (with seven aboriginal guides) were landed at White Pine Cove in Herbert Inlet...[and] ordered to march across the trail to Trout River...to seize Cap-chah and any of his people." Taken by surprise, the Ahousahts attempted to fire back at their heavily armed

Officers and crew posing aboard the HMS *Sutlej* in the mid-1860s, displaying the gunship power of the Royal Navy on the BC coast. The *Sutlej* along with HMS *Devastation* conducted a punitive strike against the Ahousahts in Clayoquot Sound in 1864, under Admiral Joseph Denman. The cannons used in the attacks can be seen at the right. *Image A00268 courtesy of Royal BC Museum, BC Archives*

attackers, but in the end they fled. At least ten of their people lay dead. Chief Cap-chah, although wounded, managed to escape.

In all, the firepower let loose by the gunboats and the land attack killed fifteen Ahousahts, said to include three of the culprits, and destroyed scores of canoes. The Navy took eleven prisoners, including Chief Cap-chah's wife and child as hostages, and five large war canoes to Victoria. In his official dispatch to Governor Arthur Kennedy, Denman wrote: "It is with great pleasure that I inform you that the service in which 69 canoes have been destroyed and about 15 men killed, has been performed with the slightest injury on our side."

When the Ahousahts who stood accused of murdering the crew of the *Kingfisher* were tried in the Supreme Court in Victoria, Chief

In December 1864 the *Illustrated London News* contained this engraving of the attacks by Royal Navy vessels on the Ahousaht. Two gunships shelled nine villages, killed fifteen men and destroyed sixty-nine canoes. The men seen rowing ashore here would set fire to the remains of this village. The two vessels on the right are firing rockets. The Hale rocket was a standard British naval armament during the Victorian era.
Image PDP00084 courtesy of Royal BC Museum, BC Archives

Justice David Cameron acquitted them on the grounds that he could not accept evidence from non-Christians: "These people do not believe in the existence of a Supreme Being and therefore they are not competent to take an oath." This prompted Rear Admiral Phipps Hornby to pronounce, "From the refusal to admit Indian testimony, it follows that as long as the Natives, in attacks upon British traders, take care to leave no survivors to give evidence they are secure from conviction and punishment in the Supreme Court at Victoria."

Many years after the event, in 1910, the *British Colonist* ran an article by J. Gordon Smith, retelling a story he had heard from a prospector of how the *Kingfisher* came into Clayoquot Sound. The article provides an eyewitness account of the destruction of one of the Ahousaht villages, told to the prospector by a man named Skundo, who acted as pilot aboard one of the gunships. His people blamed Skundo for having guided the gunship to this village and banished him. The man had been living alone as an outcast for twenty years when he met the prospector.

> The men on board took me from my canoe. I was stiff with fright. They asked me where the deep waters lay, and, fearing death, I told them. As we came to the village I saw my people running to the forest as the ship threw fireballs on the lodges. When the balls broke they made noises like the whirring of the wings of the Thunder Bird himself. The Lodges fell; their timbers piled up like the fallen pines after the winds of winter. Totems broke in the middle, canoes were broken, and when the smoke was gone some of the *illahees* [big houses] were burning...I was filled with sadness, and when the King George's men put me on the shore I wailed with sorrow.

On October 17, 1864, the *British Colonist* stated that the shelling of the Ahousaht villages had been "conducted according to the strict rules of civilized warfare." Many would dispute that. "This was not a war," declared Ahousaht hereditary chief Earl Maquinna George in his 2003 book *Living on the Edge*. "We consider it punishment for the Ahousaht Nation...According to our history they killed over 100 people...They wrecked the houses and canoes and took as hostage a chief, or *Ha'wiih* youngster, called Keitlah Mukum." Nonetheless, according to Father Augustin Brabant, the Roman Catholic missionary who lived on the west coast for nearly thirty years in the late nineteenth century, some Ahousahts came to view the *Kingfisher* episode with a degree of pride. "They had not given up their chief to the white man: they had lost houses, canoes and *iktas* [things], but these they could and would build again; some of their number were taken prisoner, but were afterwards returned to them...therefore they claimed a big victory over the man-of-war and big guns."

The *Kingfisher* incident and its aftermath attracted international attention. A lengthy and detailed article appeared on December 31, 1864, in the pages of the *Illustrated London News*, complete with drawings by Lieutenant Edward Hall of the *Sutlej*. Entitled "Conflict with the Indians of Vancouver Island," the article ends by reproaching the action of the gunboats. "The frequency of outrages and disorders on this coast," it states, "is a subject of the more regret, as it is notorious that the white man himself is often to blame when the Indian takes the law into his own hands. The appointment of a government agent, a man of character and intelligence, well acquainted with the Indian language and customs, to whom they might appeal in disputed cases would perhaps obviate the necessity for any hostile action in future."

A particularly strange twist of fate arising from the *Kingfisher* incident involved a very young child. Mrs. Denman, the admiral's wife, decided to adopt a little aboriginal girl, possibly an orphan, who had been brought aboard the *Sutlej* during the hostilities. She named the child Maggie Sutlej and dressed her in the latest fashions. The crew of the *Sutlej* made much of the child, spoiling her outrageously. The little girl lived less than two years after being taken from Clayoquot Sound. She died aboard the *Sutlej* as it sailed off South America. Her name appears on a memorial marker erected to commemorate crew members of the *Sutlej* who died while serving on the vessel. The marker still stands in the Old Burying Ground in Pioneer Square in Victoria, where the inscription recalls "The Little Indian Girl Maggie Sutlej who was Captured During the Indian Outbreak on the West Coast in 1864... who Afterwards Died at Sea."

Named "Maggie Sutlej" by Admiral Denman's wife, this young Nuu-chah-nulth girl was brought aboard the HMS *Sutlej* following the attacks on Ahousaht villages in 1864. Mrs. Denman "adopted" her, and Maggie became a favourite of ship's crew. She died after two years of voyaging far and wide aboard the gunship and was buried at sea. *Image B06641 courtesy of Royal BC Museum, BC Archives*

88

What the *Illustrated London News* termed the "outrages and disorders" of gunboat diplomacy did not end with the *Kingfisher*. Five years later the shipwreck of the *John Bright* near Hesquiat proved to be not only a maritime tragedy, but also a tragedy of Victorian attitudes and of relations between European and aboriginal peoples. In February 1869 the *John Bright*, a 126-foot (38.5-metre) barque with twenty years of worldwide lumber trading, set sail from Port Gamble in Puget Sound, bound for Valparaíso, Chile. Captain Burgess had charge of the ship, accompanied by his Chilean wife and children, as well as an English nursemaid, seventeen-year-old Beatrice Holden. Once clear of Puget Sound, the ship found itself in the teeth of a vicious winter gale. The ship rode with the southeast wind, struggling to stay offshore, but the storm bore the *John Bright* too close to land. She struck at Hesquiat Peninsula, near Estevan Point, about three kilometres from Hesquiat village. No one survived, and news of the wreck did not reach Victoria until early March, when sealing captain James Christensen brought a sensational story to government officials and to the newspapers.

Christensen, whose previous trading along the coast had earned him an unsavoury reputation, reported that because some of the bodies had been found disfigured and above the tide line, and since some Hesquiahts were seen wearing clothes belonging to some of the victims, foul play looked likely. He also reported that he had purchased three rings from the Hesquiaht, which he believed had been stripped from the victims. *British Colonist* newspaper owner and columnist David William Higgins took up the story. He concluded his article of March 16: "All have undeniably found either a watery grave, or have fallen by the hands of the West Coast savages." Governor Frederick Seymour, a long-serving colonial administrator, took a more skeptical view and hesitated to send warships to the area.

Wild speculation based on very little sound evidence continued, fed by Christensen and Higgins, blowing the story out of all proportion. By April 23 the headline in the *British Colonist* read: "Six more bodies of the Bark *John Bright* found with their heads cut off? They were without doubt murdered by the Indians." Then followed more of

Higgins's speculative hyperbole: "It was shown that the captain had been shot through the back while in the act of running away in the vain hope of escaping from the cruel savages, who had proved themselves to be less merciful than the wild waves. The other prisoners were thrown down and their heads removed while they piteously begged for mercy." As for the nursemaid, Beatrice Holden: "The pretty English maid was delivered up to the young men of the tribe, who dragged her into the bush. Her cries filled the air for hours, and when she was seen again by one of the native witnesses some hours later, the poor girl was dead, and her head had disappeared." On April 26, Higgins castigated Governor Seymour for his inaction: "Gov. Seymour has allowed the British flag to be insulted and trampled by the savages of the West Coast...We are exposed to the attacks of savages, who are allowed to rob and murder white men trading upcoast, with impunity."

Forced into action, Seymour sent the steam-driven HMS *Sparrowhawk* north from Victoria on May 1, bound for Hesquiat. Her mission: to investigate the sinking of the *John Bright* and subsequent events, nearly three months after the shipwreck. On board were a group of Royal Marines; Henry Pellew Crease, the Attorney General of BC; the Honourable Henry Maynard Ball, magistrate of Cariboo West; as well as Captain James Christensen, who had advanced the story of massacre, to act as interpreter. When his ship arrived off Hesquiat village, *Sparrowhawk*'s commander, Henry Wentworth Mist, noted in his log that despite the strong military force the locals "seemed utterly unconcerned with our arrival, or at the landing of so large a force."

Surgeon-Lieutenant Peter Comrie supervised the exhumation of the eleven bodies, buried by Christensen on his second visit to Hesquiat following the sinking. After examining the remains, and after summoning witnesses, a coroner's inquest began on board the *Sparrowhawk*. The inquest continued for three days, and in his testimony Dr. Comrie asserted that "he could find no medical evidence that indicated that the bodies had been decapitated by human hands." In the medical journal of the *Sparrowhawk*, Comrie wrote that "he believed that the gnawing of wild animals and the terrible pounding of the bodies in the surf on that rocky coast sufficiently accounted for their mutilated conditions." Despite this testimony, the inquest ruled that murder had indeed taken place and demanded the Hesquiaht chiefs turn over the perpetrators. They failed to do so, perhaps not knowing who to produce, and Commander Mist ordered the Royal Marines to set fire to the village houses, and to fire salvoes from the *Sparrowhawk*'s cannons into the canoes drawn up on the foreshore. That done, Commander Mist ordered seven Hesquiahts—five witnesses and two accused—seized and taken aboard the *Sparrowhawk* to be bound over for trial in Victoria.

In Victoria, in proceedings that by today's standards would be declared a mistrial, the two accused, Katkinna and John Anietsachist, had little chance of acquittal. Higgins kept up his relentless stream of alarmist reporting in the *British Colonist*, so the people of Victoria wanted nothing less than for the jury to find the two men guilty and hang them. With James Christensen acting as Chinook interpreter and his friend Gwiar, a Tla-o-qui-aht chief who had no love for the Hesquiaht, acting as Nuu-chah-nulth interpreter, the two accused—without legal representation—faced a twenty-man, all-white jury. In the middle of the first trial, of Katkinna, the judge ordered a recess for a week for the funeral of Governor Seymour, and further postponed the trial while awaiting the return of Surgeon-Lieutenant Comrie, who was away on duty. During these adjournments the jury roamed Victoria and talked to the press. The *British Colonist* even published a letter from Robert Burnaby, foreman of the jury, who took the government to task for its inaction and mentioned the "praiseworthy conduct" of Captain Christensen. In the end, with Christensen acting not only as interpreter but also as a witness, Katkinna admitted: "I shot the man, as he was coming ashore from the wreck." Condemned from his own mouth, the jury found him guilty.

In the second trial, John Anietsachist stood accused of the murder of Beatrice Holden. Despite assertions from Surgeon-Lieutenant Comrie that the injuries to the body were "very likely to have occurred from a fall on the boulders or having washed backwards and forwards against the boulders by the tide," and relying heavily on interpreted statements from the five Hesquiaht witnesses, the jury took only five minutes to find Anietsachist guilty.

With both men sentenced to be hanged, the authorities placed them in irons aboard the *Sparrowhawk*, which steamed back to Hesquiat carrying the High Sheriff of Victoria, fifteen police constables, twenty Royal Marines, and a few carpenters, as well as the prisoners. Ironically, the *Sparrowhawk* nearly ran aground in fog at the location where the *John Bright* had foundered. Once the gunship reached Hesquiat, the carpenters, protected by Royal Marines, set about building gallows on the shore.

Father Charles Seghers, a parish priest in Victoria, also travelled aboard the *Sparrowhawk*, his task being to accompany the two condemned men and to proffer Christian comfort. Originally from Belgium, Seghers had been in Victoria since 1863 and had long yearned to work as a missionary on the west coast, but the bishop of Victoria, Modeste Demers, believed the priest's health to be too frail to take on such work. Until this highly charged trip to Hesquiat, Seghers had never seen the vast *terra incognita* of Vancouver Island's west coast, an area he believed to be peopled with savage tribes in desperate need of Roman Catholic missionaries.

Having done his best to console the two condemned men, Seghers baptized them both. The entire Hesquiaht tribe stood, perplexed and fearful, in front of the gallows to witness what ensued. As the cannons of the *Sparrowhawk* boomed out, the two men were hanged. Deeply affected by everything he witnessed, Seghers found this trip up the coast to be a decisive turning point in his life. "Then and there," according to Father Maurus Snyder, a later missionary on the coast, "[Seghers] resolved to return soon...that he might bring the blessings of Christianity to the benighted natives."

Five years later, Seghers did indeed return to the Hesquiaht, bringing with him Father Augustin Brabant. When the two men arrived in the spring of 1874, the gallows on which the two aboriginal men had been hanged still stood on the shore, a reminder to the local people of the nature of British justice, and an example of the outrages and disorders afflicting the coast.

Chapter 6:

ENTER THE MISSIONARIES

BY THE TIME CHARLES SEGHERS RETURNED TO HESQUIAT, he had a new role and a clear purpose. Now bishop of Victoria, Seghers had decided to establish a permanent Roman Catholic mission on the west coast of Vancouver Island, and he had chosen the powerful and dynamic Father Augustin Brabant to be the first resident missionary. The two men set out from Victoria in April 1874 on the sealing schooner *Surprise* with one goal in mind—to determine the location of this future mission.

Like Seghers, Brabant had been born and educated in Belgium. Since arriving in Victoria in 1870 he had served as a parish priest, all the while yearning for greater challenges. Buoyed by his impressive physical strength, and inspired by the ascetic and stubborn Seghers, Brabant, from the outset, proved himself dedicated, tireless, and ruthlessly determined. In his world view and that of his bishop, the Native peoples of the coast lived as pagan savages, doomed to an eternity in hell unless saved by the one true religion. Propelled by their immense force of will and by an absolute certainty that their religion must be imposed on the Nuu-chah-nulth, the two men never for one instant doubted their actions.

Their initial missionary voyage lasted a month. They travelled hundreds of kilometres, stopping in as many villages as possible, all the while expanding their

Father Charles Seghers as a young man. Later bishop of Victoria, his determination to establish a Roman Catholic mission on the west coast of Vancouver Island had far-reaching consequences. With Father Augustin Brabant, Seghers selected Hesquiat as the site of this mission in 1874, after two arduous voyages along the coast, seeking a location. *Image A01764 courtesy of Royal BC Museum, BC Archives*

Father Augustin Brabant in the late 1870s. His right hand was disfigured when Hesquiaht Chief Matlahaw shot him in 1875, following a devastating outbreak of smallpox along the coast. *Image A01432 courtesy of Royal BC Museum, BC Archives*

religious ambitions. Despite a few setbacks, and despite a decidedly lukewarm response from some of the Natives they met, they judged that, on balance, they had been welcomed. On more than one occasion the local people had gathered in considerable numbers to hear the priests speak, which they did through interpreters and also by using what they had learned of the language. In several locations, the Natives greeted them with ceremony and civility, even with enthusiasm. At Kyuquot, they erected a seven-metre-high cross on a small island to mark the arrival of Christianity. Everywhere they went, the two spoke vehemently against traditional beliefs; they taught people to make the sign of the cross and to repeat prayers and hymns in their own language. On this first trip, according to Brabant, he and Seghers succeeded in baptizing nearly 800 people in total: 80 children in Barkley Sound, 93 at Clayoquot (Opitsat), 135 at Ahousat, 177 at Kyuquot—and more. Heartened by these numbers, Brabant and Seghers resolved to return as soon as they could, and five months later they headed up the coast again.

The second missionary trip proved challenging from the outset. Having left Victoria on September 1, 1874, aboard the schooner *Surprise*, they soon realized that the captain, Peter Francis, was drinking heavily. With the help of the mate they attempted to confiscate the captain's liquor, but he still managed to hit a sandbar at full tilt when they entered Pachena Bay seeking anchorage. A short while later they encountered, according to Brabant, "a canoe from Victoria with a supply of whisky," and hard on its heels the gunship HMS *Boxer* heading into Pachena village, where one of Captain William Spring's trading posts was located. On board the *Boxer*, the newly appointed superintendent of Indian Affairs, Dr. Israel Powell, on his first tour of the west coast, discovered everyone in the village "beastly drunk." Reporting this event, the *Colonist* stated, "The Indian Commissioner expressed his grief, and they promised to amend."

Brabant and Seghers parted company with Captain Francis and the *Surprise* at Ucluelet, continuing their journey north by canoe, three aboriginal men paddling. With heavy seas breaking over the bow, soaking their provisions of flour and biscuit, they made their way to Opitsat. There they discovered that HMS *Boxer* stood at anchor just ahead of them in the lee of Vargas Island, but paying it no heed they finally made camp on Flores Island. Twice in the night they were awakened, first by some Ahousahts inviting them over to the village and secondly by a group of Hesquiahts, en route to Ahousat, wondering who these strangers were. Waking in the morning rain, they paddled drearily on toward Refuge Cove (Hot Springs Cove), arriving late that afternoon. Again they found HMS *Boxer* ahead of them and at anchor, and with many visitors from neighbouring tribes "the place presented quite a lively appearance. A number of junior officers and blue-jackets were on shore." Despite being warned by the *Boxer*'s steward against travelling further by canoe, the two clerics refused assistance—though they did accept provisions—insisting they would continue. The following day, through heavy seas and with a dismally seasick crew, they came ashore for lunch at Home-is, an encampment on the outer shore just north of Estevan Point, before doggedly continuing toward Friendly Cove in Nootka Sound.

"There, to our horror," wrote Brabant, "we again found the *Boxer* at anchor." Travelling in tandem with government authorities aboard a gunboat had not been part of their original plan. But the steward of the vessel again approached them with an invitation to come aboard, and this time Brabant and Seghers decided to continue their journey on the gunship. The *Boxer*'s crew hoisted their canoe on board, accommodated their paddlers, and for two days the missionaries travelled in comparative comfort. Reaching Kyuquot, the paddlers and the priests headed for shore and set up camp in an unoccupied store belonging to Captain Spring.

Over the next few days, Brabant and Seghers travelled to scattered encampments and villages around Kyuquot Sound. A dead whale upstaged their arrival at Nuchatlat; the carcass had drifted ashore and no one had a moment for these cassocked visitors. With their "houses full of blubber" being rendered to oil, "the whale was uppermost in [the people's] minds." They found better reception a day or so later when the Mowachaht tribe greeted them "with fervor and zeal." Following this, they headed down the coast to Hesquiat in a canoe manned by the Mowachaht chief and eleven of his men, the most exciting ocean voyage yet, described by Brabant in his classic phrase "the sea ran mountains high." Off Perez Rocks, they met a Hesquiaht canoe "crowded with young men" coming to greet them, and "a regular race between the canoes took place," with the two large dugouts continually losing sight of each other, rising on huge crests only to descend to "the abyss of the ocean."

At Hesquiat, according to Brabant, "The Indians were full of joy to see us once again." Their previous visit to Hesquiat in the spring had been similarly positive, despite the disturbing presence of the scaffolds where John Anietsachist and Katkinna had been hanged five years earlier, following the *John Bright* incident. Brabant later recalled seeing more evidence of the *John Bright* at Hesquiat: a signboard from the vessel mounted above one of the houses. It read *Neminem Time—Neminem Laede*, meaning "Be afraid of nobody—hurt no one." Brabant and Seghers stayed several days at Hesquiat, busying themselves teaching "the Lord's Prayer, Hail Mary, the Creed, Ten Commandments and Seven Sacraments, all of which the Indians learned with much zeal." The evident goodwill in the village led the decisive Bishop Seghers to conclude then and there that Hesquiat would be the location for the first coastal mission. Not only had the people warmly welcomed the priests, but this central location seemed ideal for reaching out to other tribes on the coast. Having proposed this notion to the assembled chiefs of the tribe, the missionaries began negotiating for land where mission buildings would be erected. "We were informed, in the presence of the whole tribe, that land would be given for Mission buildings and other purposes and that we could have our choice as to locality."

The Hesquiaht chief and "a large crew of young men" escorted them to Ahousat, but Brabant and Seghers found their reception at this next stop less positive. The Ahousaht chief refused to meet them, and most of the local people were busily employed at their various salmon rivers, laying in fish for the winter supply. At the bishop's insistence, many of these Ahousahts were ordered back to listen to his religious instruction, only to face "a sharp reprimand" from him when they tried to leave that same evening. The following day found Seghers and Brabant at Opitsat, where, to their chagrin, the chief kept them waiting. "His Lordship, the Bishop of Vancouver Island, and one of his priests were told to go outside," Brabant wrote in astonishment. "The Chief of the Clayoquots could not transact any business with them till he had finished eating his breakfast!" Having eventually granted the missionaries an audience, the chief agreed to assemble his people to listen to them preach, and afterward they baptized four children. The priests then asked the chief to provide an escort for them down the coast to Ucluelet, but he deflected this request, suggesting instead that they go up Tofino Inlet to his salmon station. From there he would escort them across the peninsula to Long Beach, where they could find a canoe at one of the outer fishing camps and travel to Ucluelet.

Having agreed to this, Brabant and Seghers initially found themselves marooned at the Tla-o-qui-aht chief's salmon fishing encampment, a low and smoky dwelling dominated by the powerful smell of fish, where they "could not put a foot except on or over dissected salmon or salmon roe!" Their discomfort and impatience grew, and eventually they convinced the chief to escort them across the peninsula to Long Beach. Once on the outer coast, they found the sea running very high and no canoe could be launched. The chief returned to his home on the inlet, promising to return the following day, and the two missionaries pitched a tent and determined to wait. The following day, the easterly wind and high surf made travel impossible. Another day passed, another night, and still the wind did not abate.

Perhaps unnerved by the visit of a bear to their encampment, and certainly tired of waiting, Seghers imperiously declared they must abandon the idea of travel by water; they would walk the length of the beach and then find the aboriginal trail to Ucluelet. "The Clayoquots hardly approved of the idea, but promised to take our baggage to Captain Francis' house as soon as the weather would permit." Even Brabant inwardly questioned the wisdom of this decision, recording that the bishop "ordered me to prepare some provisions, which I did with reluctance." Two Kyuquots, likely slaves of the Tla-o-qui-aht chief, accompanied them and carried the provisions. That first night the rain poured down, and the following morning they set out again. As the earliest chronicle of Europeans hiking through the bush near Long Beach, Father Brabant's account of what ensued would never qualify as promotional material for wilderness adventure in and around Tofino. "We took to the bush," Brabant wrote, "intending to make a short cut of a projecting point. After struggling about a couple of hours through the thick salal, we came to the Indian trail." Hours later, their trail emerged on the beach they had left that morning. Brabant's account continues, describing how he and Seghers, with woefully inadequate supplies, spent another day stubbornly thrashing through dense forest in the pouring rain, trying to find the trail. "The two Kyuquots," Brabant recorded, "began to show bad will, and insisted on going back to the beach, which we did." They camped out, miserably wet and cold, and their large campfire spread to nearby trees, burning holes in Brabant's boots and clothing. The following day, with no provisions left, Seghers collapsed in exhaustion. Finally the two missionaries followed the example of the Kyuquots, gathering mussels and berries to eat. They staggered on, eventually reaching Ucluelet, where they sought refuge at Captain Francis's trading post. He provided them with food and also new shoes and pants because "our clothes had been reduced to rags in our attempt to travel through the brushwood." Brabant reported that two full weeks passed before they regained their strength.

When they recovered, they arranged canoe transport up the Alberni Canal, then travelled on foot and by canoe to Qualicum, on the east side of Vancouver Island; from there by canoe to Nanaimo, and finally by steamer back to Victoria. Through all this, their zeal never faltered. According to Bishop Seghers's calculations, over the course of their two west coast visits in 1874 they had baptized 960 people, most of them children. This statistic grew to 1,000 in later reports. Given that the population of Native people on the coast at the time probably totalled no more than 5,000, this figure could well be exaggerated, but whatever the number, the two missionaries felt they had accomplished a great deal.

Several months passed before Father Brabant received his marching orders, but finally, in February 1875, Bishop Seghers directed him to go to Hesquiat to "take charge of the West Coast Indians." Formal instructions for the mission at Hesquiat, written in Latin and dated March 22, 1875, stress that the missionary should "encourage labour and growth of industry, and...inspire the love of agriculture," as well as devoting himself to the "salvation and spiritual progress of the Indians." In selecting Brabant to become the first missionary on the west coast, Bishop Seghers had found the perfect man for the job. A man of uncompromising commitment and great physical endurance, Brabant never hesitated to exert himself to any extreme in his work as missionary to the First Nations of the west coast.

On May 6, 1875, just over a year after his first visit to the area, Brabant set sail for his new home on board the sloop *Thornton*. With him travelled Father Rondeault, a Belgian priest stationed at Quamichan, and a carpenter, Noel Leclaire, who came along to help construct the first mission buildings. They were also accompanied by "three small calves, one bull and two heifers," destined to become the pioneer cattle of Hesquiat Peninsula. Father Brabant's Newfoundland dog completed the crew. They set to work at once, as Brabant explained, "to put up a church of 60 X 26 feet [18 X 7 metres] and a small residence for the priest. Everything was to be done as cheaply as possible."

Some building materials used in the construction came from the shipwrecked American barque *Edwin*. In December 1874, loaded with lumber at Puget Sound and bound for Australia, the *Edwin* took on water after the cargo shifted. Despite the best efforts of Captain Hughes, the ship's master, the barque ran aground near the entrance to Hesquiat Harbour, prompting a heroic rescue effort on the part of Chief Matlahaw and his men. They managed to save most of the

The mission church of St. Antonine at Hesquiat, around 1910. The original
church built in 1875 burned down, replaced by this imposing structure in 1891.
Mount Angel Abbey Library

crew, but the captain's two little boys and the Chinese cook drowned, and the captain's wife died when the ship broke up. The Canadian government later awarded Chief Matlahaw and his people a silver medal. "On the one side is a beautifully executed profile of the Queen, and on the other the following inscription: 'To Ma-ha-clow, Chief of the Hesquiakis, for bravery and subsequent kindness in rescuing the Captain and crew...December 1874,'" reported the *British Colonist*. The United States government also acknowledged the rescue by presenting a cash reward to the Hesquiahts.

On July 5, 1875, the first Mass took place in the newly constructed, newly dedicated, St. Antonine Church at Hesquiat. Brabant reported: "All the Hesquiats were present; also, the Chief and a crowd of Muchalat Indians." The following morning, Rondeault and Leclaire left for Victoria, and the priest found himself alone and, in his own words, "in charge of all the Indians from Pachena to Cape Cook." Within a month, Brabant set out on a missionary trip to Nootka and Kyuquot, setting a precedent he would follow for all his years on the coast. Although based at Hesquiat, he continually travelled along the coast from village to village, seemingly indifferent to personal discomfort and danger. His constant travels proved essential in establishing his authority, inspiring respect for his personal endurance, and enabling him to learn about the local hierarchies, family connections, jealousies, and rivalries on the coast. He established local alliances, befriended important people, and as time passed he imprinted himself on the local people as the first European in the area who had come to stay, who would not be deterred, and who, on occasion, spoke up strongly on their behalf to figures of authority.

By late September 1875, a terrible shadow hung over Hesquiat. Smallpox broke out, having spread from Nootka Sound. Many people died, and soon dead bodies lay untended; no one dared approach them. Brabant took charge, administering vaccinations, issuing instructions for the dead to be buried and for the sick to remain isolated, fully realizing the gravity of the situation, and trying to calm the panicky fear that dominated the village. The journal he kept at the time, parts of which appeared in the *Colonist*, tells a sobering story.

Oct 16—Friday. I had made up my mind to visit all the houses on Sat morning...[the] Hesquiot's chief's wife is dead. I go to the ranch to tell the Indians to leave the Tyhee's [chief's] house. Exhort them to wear clean clothing and to clean their houses. I vaccinate all the tribe.
Oct 17—All at Church. After Mass three cases of smallpox. I baptize Charley's mother and aunt. Touchingly good dispositions of both dying Christians.
Oct 18—The two Indians (Christians) are dead...No one is willing to bury them. Shouting in my house!
Oct 19—Universal silence. Towards evening baptize Chief's sister. Sad spectacle, dogs where the dead bodies lay, and cats licking the blood.
Oct 20—Chief's sister is dead. No one willing to bury her...Horrible sight of the deceased, roll her into a canoe and drag it into the bush...No possibility of having any funeral service.

Brabant's memoirs describe one occasion during this crisis when everyone wanted medicine and, having none to give them, he "boiled water, broke some biscuits in it, sweetened the whole with sugar, and insisted that this would be the very best preservative in the world against smallpox." He vividly recalled attending one of the chief's daughters as she died, "a courageous woman [who] did not give up till she was quite blind and her head as black and thick as a large iron pot...The sight of the corpse was simply horrible." As the smallpox outbreak progressed, he "passed most of [his] time in vaccinating the Indians and in trying to cheer them up."

According to the *Colonist*, Chief Matlahaw's family suffered great losses in this outbreak of smallpox. Two of his children died, as well as his sister and his wife. Matlahaw himself fell victim to the smallpox; he came to stay in the priest's house and received two vaccinations, but according to Brabant the vaccine had no effect, and the chief "became morose and avoided the company of his friends." What next occurred nearly cost Brabant his life. On October 27, just as Brabant began hoping that the worst was over, Chief Matlahaw asked to borrow his gun to shoot some jays. When Brabant asked for the gun later in the day, Matlahaw shot Brabant, first in the hand and then in the back. Chaos erupted in the village, and Matlahaw fled—perhaps crazed by the smallpox he carried, perhaps bitterly angry with Brabant and holding him responsible for the plague that had struck the village, but certainly aware that shooting this powerful outsider would have serious consequences.

Convinced he would die, and in great pain, Brabant could do nothing but wait helplessly while being anxiously tended at his house by several Hesquiahts. Incapable of moving, he instructed his supporters to place cold-water compresses on his hand. The Hesquiahts sent word to Refuge Cove and to Clayoquot, seeking assistance; none arrived. The Clayoquot storekeeper, Fred Thornberg, always suspicious of aboriginals and fearing infection and reprisals, responded to the request for help by sending several yards of white cotton back to Hesquiat, to wrap Brabant's corpse. In later years, Thornberg and Brabant laughed at this memory; Brabant eventually used the fabric for dishcloths. At the time, with his wounds feverish and inflamed, this lack of help must have been a terrible blow. Eventually a deputation from Hesquiat reached Victoria by canoe to report the attack to the bishop and to the police. Brabant sent with them "a paper on which I had written a few words every morning."

"My Lord," he wrote to the bishop, "I am dying, I am shot in the right hand and back by Matlahow the Hesquiot chief...Adieu! Pray for me." He added: "The Indians are very kind. The whole tribe is crying day and night. At least three are taking care of me. Do not blame them. Praise for their kindness, and may another priest be soon here to take my place is the wish of your lordship's dying servant." Brabant also sent to the bishop his daily journal of what had happened during the outbreak of smallpox leading up to his attack. On November 7, 1875, the *Colonist* printed some of this material.

Two days later, the naval gunship HMS *Rocket* came to the rescue at Hesquiat, bringing two doctors, Bishop Seghers, and the chief of police. Within two more days, Father Brabant had been transported to Victoria and was receiving medical care. Fears for his life abated, but doctors told him his hand would have to be amputated, an operation he refused to consider, against all advice. Eventually the hand recovered, but he had to remain in Victoria for five months. Determined he would return to Hesquiat, in late March Brabant boarded a sealing schooner heading up the coast. Stopping overnight at Ahousat he wrote, "The Ahousath chief seemed happy to see me, and his Indians were immediately summoned to his house. The Ahousaths astonished me by their good conduct. I baptised all their newly-born children, 8 in number. Altogether I had 25 baptisms on my way to Hesquiat; no objections were made anywhere. Upon landing, every man of the tribe was on the beach to welcome me home." Arriving at Hesquiat on April 5, Brabant found his house as he had left it; the floor was still covered with dried blood and littered with dressings. The Hesquiahts welcomed him back and gave a feast in his honour, with "dancing and gesticulations, and many other extravagant things."

Brabant never considered not returning to Hesquiat following the attempt on his life. If anything, this drama heightened his determination to carry on, and to outface any future attempts to scare him off. Within months of his return, while on a visit to one of the dwellings of Chief Maquinna of the Mowachaht tribe, he discovered a plot on the part of Maquinna to kill him. He narrowly escaped with his Hesquiaht companions in the early morning. Later, discovering that Maquinna's animosity arose from false accusations against him and his companions, he simply shrugged it off. "I was told that such a practice is very common with savages of this coast," his memoirs state. When rumours circulated in the villages on the coast that Father Brabant planned to kill all the Hesquiahts, he remained unperturbed, convinced he was among friends who would stand by him and never turn on him en masse. Later, in a letter to his bishop, he wrote: "The Indians are so very kind and obliging that I am quite happy in their midst; there may be another traitor in the crowd, but traitors you will find everywhere among the whites as well as among the natives...I came here with my full consent, and...there is no more danger in Hesquiath than of an evening in the streets of Victoria."

"The Indians feared Father Brabant and called him the 'Big Chief,'" wrote Charles Morin in his unpublished memoirs, recalling a time shortly after the attempt on Brabant's life. Morin, a carpenter from Quebec, worked alongside Brabant constructing a church in Barkley Sound. Seeing Father Brabant in action among the people he called "his" Indians, Morin noted that, following Brabant's return to Hesquiat in 1876, "the...Indians on seeing him back alive thought he could not be an ordinary man so it gave him greater power among this tribe." One of many contemporary observers who commented on Brabant's physical appearance, Morin observed that "he was a man of massive build, six feet tall and weighing around 200 pounds. He had a very young and handsome face, very interesting to talk to and with health to match. He could survive on dry fish and biscuits, could sleep outdoors and could pass days out in the open, rain or shine, as nothing seemed to bother him."

In the summer of 1876, two new enthusiasts joined the ranks of the Roman Catholic missionaries on Vancouver Island, swelling the number of clergy in the diocese to nine. Fathers Jean Lemmens and Joseph Nicolaye had been nearly two months in transit to Victoria from their native Belgium. They spent time en route in New York and then Philadelphia, where they spent four days marvelling at the Centennial Exposition there, the first World's Fair. This massive show featured industrial and ethnographic displays from around the world, including an eighteen-metre-long canoe from Nootka. Then on to San Francisco and Portland, and finally Victoria, described by Father Nicolaye as "already a city of great prestige, with a great future in store." Within weeks the two young men set forth to their respective mission fields: Father Lemmens to become the first incumbent in Nanaimo, until then visited once a month by a priest; while Father Nicolaye, accompanied by Bishop Seghers, boarded the schooner *Alert*, bound for Hesquiat. There he would become a novice missionary under Father Brabant's guidance. Describing his first voyage up the coast, Father Nicolaye mentions rivalling the bishop to see who would be the more seasick, and also, incongruously, the fun they had with a "cute little black bear on board." "He was not very vicious," Nicolaye wrote. "...He liked to play, as puppies sometimes do...yet it was deemed necessary to chain him up."

Shortly after arriving at Hesquiat, Father Nicolaye came upon the remains of Chief Matlahaw at the foot of a hollow tree not far from the church. Little remained but his bones, his clothing, and Brabant's gun. "Having shot Father Brabant...he fled into the woods and was never seen or heard of till we found his remains," wrote Nicolaye, carrying on to speculate: "He must have felt unsafe among his own people." The Hesquiahts knew about the body; Brabant learned they had discovered it shortly after his departure for Victoria aboard the *Rocket*. In a letter to Bishop Seghers about Chief Matlahaw's body, Father Brabant wrote: "[The Indians] look upon the spot where his remains rest as a cursed spot. His child is taken care of by his wife's mother and father, and they bring him almost every day to my house; I told them to take care of the child as if he were their own."

Father Nicolaye settled in at Hesquiat, learning from Brabant the evolving plan for the west coast mission. Soon it would be split in two sections, with Brabant in charge of the northern section and Nicolaye based farther south, in Barkley Sound. First he had to learn the language. The two priests diligently studied the Chinook trading jargon, but Brabant took his studies much further, focusing in detail on the local Hesquiaht language. Led by the example of Charles Seghers, Brabant already was proving himself a gifted linguist, and in later years he spent considerable time assembling a meticulously detailed dictionary of the Hesquiaht language, totalling some 134 pages, a document that remains to this day in the archives of the Roman Catholic diocese in Victoria.

In learning the language, the priests at first concentrated on religious concepts and vocabulary, not entirely trusting the local interpreters to convey their meaning correctly. Misunderstandings inevitably arose. According to Nicolaye, when Brabant told his interpreter to explain that everyone should bless him or herself with the holy water at the church door, the translator announced, "In future there will be at the church door a tub of water, soap and towel, and everyone is to have a good wash before entering the church." By early July 1876, Brabant reported with satisfaction that "[the Hesquiahts] all know the first lesson of Catechism in their language...I expect to have High Mass in about two weeks; the Indians being able to sing to perfection the Kyrie, Credo Sanctus, and Agnus Dei." Before long, Brabant was delivering his sermons in the Hesquiaht language.

From the outset, Brabant asserted his authority over secular life in the village. He insisted that "Christian" clothing be worn, initially decreeing that men, women, and children should at least wear a shirt in church, and later that men should wear pants to cover their "naked lower limbs." If they did not comply with this dress code, people could not enter his house or the church. He appointed local "policemen" to be his representatives and spoke out forcefully against tribal practices. He realized, especially in the early years, he had very little impact, despite the apparent "conversions" to Christianity. "They laugh at the doctrine I teach," he admitted once. Never deterred by negative reactions, he thundered on against adultery, "pagan" dances, medicine men, and traditional ceremonies.

During the late 1870s, Fathers Brabant and Nicolaye remained the only two Catholic priests on the west coast. Their isolation at Hesquiat proved trying at times. "We have not seen a white man since October," Brabant wrote in March 1877, "and we have not received any mail for several months. Our provisions are nearly all gone...and our Indians are as bad and as much attached to their pagan ideas as before we commenced our work here." By Christmas of 1877, the second church on the coast, at Numukamis in Barkley Sound, neared completion. The first Mass at this mission took place on Christmas Day in the small house built for Father Nicolaye. Some 150 people of the local Huu-ay-aht tribe squeezed into the small space, perching on blocks of wood. The carpenter, Charles Morin, described the event with some amazement in his diary: "Some...were leaning on their elbows, other sitting cross-legged, some had climbed up near the ceiling and were looking down, others had their back ends up and heads on the ground." After the Mass, the chief spoke at length, gesticulating toward Father Brabant: "I say no more wars against other tribes, no more disputes in camp, no more women beating and no more women stealing. We will keep our own women and I will support this priest in what he says...I want to believe the story he has just told us of the Great God...He will listen to us and help us."

Following this encouraging start, Father Nicolaye took up permanent residence in Barkley Sound and almost immediately found himself entirely on his own at the newly constructed mission. Everyone in the village left to go fishing and sealing; he rarely saw another soul for four months. Nicolaye remained there for two years, serving the fluctuating population as best he could before going up to Kyuquot in 1880 to establish another mission and church. He remained at Kyuquot for ten years.

At Hesquiat, on October 9, 1882, another ship came to grief on Perez Rocks, near where the *John Bright* met its fate. Under the command of Captain Edward Harlow, with a crew of eighteen, his wife, Abbie, and their two children aboard, the 924-ton American barque *Malleville* was dashed on the rocks. Local Hesquiahts soon found evidence of the wreck, and one of the bodies, at their fishing camp at Home-is. They alerted Father Brabant, who took a crew of men and went to investigate. They found many items washed ashore, including a trunk full of clothing, the letter-blocks and toys of the little Harlow boys, and the body of their pet pig. They also located the body of Mrs. Harlow. Brabant explained in his diary how "the Indian who discovered Mrs. Harlow's body and brought it ashore, had taken from her hand two diamond and gold rings—wedding and engagement rings; also two diamond earrings, a gold pin and a piece of gold chain...This man afterwards gave me these articles and asked me to take them in charge." Seven other bodies were also recovered. Brabant noted the "noble and heroic" efforts of the Hesquiahts to recover the bodies, "up to their necks in the surf dragging the bodies to shore."

Word reached naval authorities at Esquimalt, and on November 22, HMS *Kingfisher* arrived at Hesquiat. Captain Thornton conducted his investigation and left two days later. Entrusted to him was a parcel containing Mrs. Harlow's recovered jewellery, together with her Bible and sealskin coat, to be sent to her parents in Maine. Later, the United States government awarded the Hesquiaht chief a gold medal as "a souvenir of the kindness and humane conduct of the tribe," as well as $200 to be distributed among his men in recognition of their bravery.

In 1883, Father Jean Lemmens joined the ranks of the west coast missionaries, delighted to leave his parish at Nanaimo to go to "this part of the island [which] was the most desired part for the missionaries." He initially joined Father Nicolaye at Kyuquot, while Nicolaye started to do mission work at Ehattisat and Nuchatlat. Following the example of Father Brabant, these priests asserted temporal as well as religious authority wherever they found themselves. They organized local "policemen" to be their supporters in the villages, they meted out punishments for perceived wrongdoings, in some locations they even established "jails" where they could confine people who had, in their view, done wrong. In his diary of 1884, Father Lemmens wrote: "Mar 3: Put the pock-marked Kyuquot man in irons, and his wife in jail; cause 'katpathl' [they had a fight]." The following day, March 4: "Put a woman doctor in jail for doctoring her old mother. Gave the old woman baptism and Extreme Unction. Had her corpse taken into jail till next morning."

Later, when Father Lemmens became established as the missionary at Opitsat, he again operated a jail. A memoir of his life, assembled by family members following his death, states that when he was at Opitsat, "even for small offences, jail was one solution to keep the peace. One Indian set up a party during Mass, only after payment of three blankets was he released from jail." The offences most often noted by the priests included adultery, bigamy, fighting, drunkenness, holding to old beliefs, and "witch-doctoring"—as well as missing Mass.

Following his time in Kyuquot, and before going to his next mission at Alberni, Father Lemmens travelled to the Council of Baltimore, a large gathering of American clerics, and from there to Europe. His diary entry about this long voyage, foreseen while still at Kyuquot, states: "Went to Alberni, via Baltimore, Antwerp, Shimmert, [Schimmert, in Holland] Victoria and Dodger's Cove." At Alberni he built a church and tried to settle in to his new mission, but he badly wanted to be on the outer coast. On a return visit to Kyuquot, he met with Bishop Seghers—now archbishop of Oregon—and Father Brabant, and they set in motion a plan to establish another permanent mission, this one at Ahousat. Brabant had already built a small church there in 1881, but they now decided a priest should take up residence in the village. Fred Thornberg, the trader at Clayoquot, built a house at Ahousat for Lemmens in 1885; later, Thornberg occupied this house himself during his years as a trader at the village.

"There were days," Father Lemmens's family memoir states, "that he was doing nothing else than provide medical advice." Like all the priests, Lemmens became, de facto, the resident medic wherever he found himself on the west coast. With disease rampant among aboriginal people, this medical role became central in priests' lives, establishing them as authority figures in the lives of people on the coast. In many instances, government agencies provided mission priests with medicines to dispense. Another means of asserting authority involved schools: all of the priests, from time to time, attempted to open small day schools in the villages, teaching reading and writing to the few children who could be convinced, bribed, or coerced to attend.

Father Lemmens did not remain long at Ahousat, but he described the place vividly in letters home. The Ahousahts, he reported to his family, "had tendencies to dispute during Mass, and after Mass they argue about the homily with all the noise they could make." He tried very hard to stop that, but they said "You take us as we are, otherwise you will have to say Mass in an empty church!" By 1887, Lemmens divided his time between Ahousat and Opitsat, likely spending more time at Opitsat, where he had assisted in constructing a new church and priest's house, and where he attempted to run a school. Opitsat generally proved more appealing to the missionaries than Ahousat, being a busier place, less isolated, and within sight of the trading post at Clayoquot. Like Brabant, Lemmens proved to be an outstanding linguist, and like Brabant he spent considerable time and effort compiling a dictionary of the local language.

In July 1886, Archbishop Charles Seghers was murdered on a mission trip to Alaska. With considerable reluctance, Father Lemmens agreed to be nominated as the next bishop of Victoria, and found himself bishop-elect. He remained as long as possible at Opitsat, delaying his consecration as bishop until August 5, 1888. He served in his new office for nearly ten years, frequently visiting the west coast.

With his old friend Charles Seghers dead, and with so many of the aboriginal people on the coast dying all around him, Father Brabant came near despair. Disease spread rampantly along the coast as the local people moved to canneries, to potlatches in other villages, to take up seasonal employment on the hop farms of Puget Sound, or simply to and from their summer encampments. Measles and whooping cough took their deadly toll, smallpox continued to be a major concern, and the terrible scourge of consumption became increasingly prevalent. "Before long," wrote Brabant at the end of 1886, "I counted over forty children of Hesquiat alone who had become victims of the disease. With my bishop murdered and my young people dying around me, I closed this year with many, many sad feelings."

By 1888, four Roman Catholic churches could be found on the west coast, at Hesquiat, Kyuquot, Ahousat, and in Barkley Sound. At the end of that year, Father Brabant occupied himself building the fifth, at Yuquot in Nootka Sound. He attempted to run this mission himself, from Hesquiat, although in later years Yuquot would be served by various resident priests. The missions at Ahousat and in Barkley Sound never thrived. Brabant bitterly regretted the failure of the one at Ahousat; he blamed Father John Van Nevel, who succeeded Father Lemmens as missionary both at Opitsat and Ahousat. Van Nevel favoured Opitsat, leaving Ahousat "abandoned and neglected," according to Brabant.

Given the expansion of the fur sealing trade from the 1870s onward, and the central role played in that trade by aboriginal hunters from the west coast, the early Catholic missionaries found themselves involved on the sidelines of the seal hunt. In 1876 Brabant observed "a dozen or more sealing schooners" calling at Hesquiat; he came to know all the schooners and their captains, sometimes travelling up and down the coast with them. Brabant robustly supported the fur seal trade, occasionally intervening to make sure that sealing captains did not cheat "his Indians," and that they received appropriate pay and treatment. He encouraged aboriginal hunters to hire out on the sealing schooners, not least because the money they brought back would enable people in the villages to acquire what he termed "the accoutrements of Christian civilization." He wholeheartedly approved of the influx of trade goods and the growth of a cash economy among First Nations people: on his very first trip to Kyuquot in 1874, Brabant noted with pleasure the "women in white calico robes and the men with pants and coats." Seeing how the villagers adopted European clothing and household goods, he encouraged the construction of small individual houses to replace the traditional big houses, rejoicing when curtains appeared on windows, when the villagers began to use furniture rather than sitting on the floor, when Singer sewing machines and musical instruments became popular consumer items on the coast. All of this, for Brabant, indicated rejection of traditional "pagan" ways and acceptance of Christian values. Subsequent missionaries on the coast concurred, frequently using goods like hair ribbons, grapes, oranges, and candy to buy goodwill from the people they were trying to convert. Traders on the coast all benefited from this unspoken collusion, as the missionaries tacitly and sometimes overtly promoted sales of various goods.

Nonetheless, during his many long years on the coast, Father Brabant kept a keen eye on the actions of all traders and storekeepers, quick to comment on any hint of dishonest or immoral behaviour. He would thunder condemnation if any trader sold liquor to aboriginals, and he was quick to report any such infraction. Outraged at the evils brought on by alcohol, by disease, by the "vicious" behaviour of some white men, particularly toward aboriginal women, Brabant well knew the consequences suffered by the indigenous population. Writing for the *American College Bulletin* in July 1893, he commented, "On our first visit to this coast, nineteen years ago, we roughly estimated the Indian population in my mission at 4,500 souls. Now I doubt whether there are more than 3,000."

In October 1891, Brabant noted a dire new development on the coast: "I understand that a young man representing the Presbyterian Church of Canada has taken up his residence at Alberni." This young man, the Reverend Melvin Swartout, later moved to Ucluelet, where the first west coast Presbyterian mission had been established in 1890. The Protestants had arrived; more soon followed. Brabant tracked their progress closely. In 1895 he wrote contemptuously: "A monthly steamer now visits the coast...When a man's life was in danger and when the only means of travelling was an Indian canoe, when the mails reached us only once or twice a year...we were welcome to do alone the work of converting the natives. Now with the...absence of danger, the ministers come in sight." By 1896, these encroaching "heretics," as Brabant called all Protestants, had come to stay in the territory Brabant considered his personal fiefdom, audaciously positioning themselves smack in the middle of Clayoquot Sound. "A young man representing the Presbyterian Church is now stationed in Ahousaht," Brabant wrote angrily. "He is a school teacher by profession, but he holds divine service on Sunday...the poor little children so anxious to learn to read and write will be perverted without noticing it." This first Protestant missionary at Ahousat, John Russell, quickly established a small day school there, funded by the Women's Missionary Society.

Over subsequent years, Brabant raged continually, and at length, about the carryings-on of Protestants. He could not express himself too strongly about what he judged to be Protestant perversions of the faith, their corrupt tactics, and the stealing of souls of the people he considered "my Indians." Yet in a moment of sober reflection, writing to a fellow priest in Belgium in 1903, Brabant did admit that Protestants were not altogether evil, and also, most unusually, he admitted that his fellow Catholics had not been without fault in their early mission work on the west coast. "[The Protestants] came with tons of clothing and dress goods for old people and children and set to work with a zeal, an energy, and a spirit of self-sacrifice worthy of a better cause...[They] are well-behaved... hard-working men and women, putting up with all kinds of hardships and privations, and, by their zeal and perseverance, they put to shame some of our priests, who abandoned their Indian charges to do work in white congregations...The Protestant preachers have taken possession of quite an extent of our Coast. The trouble is—our Bishop has no priests to occupy the field...Several strangers, having learned of the need of priests, offered themselves. They were well recommended, came here, stayed a time, got drunk or did worse, and went away to parts unknown, leaving behind them scandal and damage to the cause of religion."

Brabant never again alluded to such problems among the early Catholic priests on the coast. Whatever the misdemeanours in question, he named no names, gave no specifics, and the subject never recurred. From the late 1880s through the 1890s, a number of different priests came and went on the west coast, Father Van Nevel among them; also Father Eussen and Father Verbeke, who briefly served in Barkley Sound and in Opitsat. Verbeke, who had never been in a canoe before he took his first trip across Barkley Sound, astonished his aboriginal paddlers by insisting on taking his caged canary with him. Other priests of the period included Father Meuleman at Kyuquot Sound in the 1890s, Father Heynen at Opitsat, and Father Sobry, who stayed over two decades on the coast, first at Kyuquot and latterly at Yuquot.

In Father Brabant's opinion, this scattershot of priests was inadequate, given the Protestant invasion. He demanded more Catholic action. By the mid-1890s, he had decided the west coast must have a residential Catholic school for aboriginal children, drawing them from villages up and down the coast. With his customary energy and determination, he began lobbying the authorities with this in mind.

Chapter 7:

THE SEALING YEARS

THE NUU-CHAH-NULTH ALWAYS KNEW of the vast numbers of northern fur seals *(Callorhinus ursinus)* migrating offshore every spring as they travelled north from California to their breeding grounds in the Pribilof Islands in the Bering Sea. Highly skilled seal hunters all along the coast prided themselves on their prowess at locating and harpooning these seals, and because these northern fur seals never approached the shore, the hunters paddled far out to sea to find them. For Nuu-chah-nulth hunters, the shallow waters of La Pérouse Bank, some sixty kilometres offshore from Barkley Sound, always provided the best hunting ground. In this area, rich in marine life, the seals stopped to feed and rest.

This seal hunt had been significant for centuries; recent evidence from middens at Hesquiat and elsewhere on the west coast indicates that the Nuu-chah-nulth harvested far more northern fur seals than other mammals such as sea lions, porpoises, or harbour seals. As William Banfield noted in 1858, "The flesh they eat, and deem it quite a luxury." Yet despite this long history of traditional use, no significant trade in seal skins existed on the west coast of Vancouver Island until the mid-nineteenth century. European traders in this area focused on the immensely valuable sea otter pelts, but after the sea otter population dwindled to almost nothing, the fur seal hunt off Vancouver Island's west coast gradually gained momentum. By the 1860s these seals had dramatically increased in number, the population having been seriously threatened in earlier years by the Russians' extensive fur seal hunt off Alaska.

In 1786, Russian captain Gerassim Pribilof, working for an early Russian fur trading company in the Aleutians, discovered the location of the northern fur seal rookeries on the islands in the Bering Sea that now bear his name. For nearly two decades following his discovery,

Russian hunters indiscriminately slaughtered untold millions of these animals in their rookeries. Eventually the Russian government realized that the uncontrolled hunt could destroy the lucrative sealing industry and took action to protect the seals from extinction. It banned sealing entirely for four years, from 1804 to 1808, and imposed rigorous quotas for many years following the ban. These closely enforced restrictions allowed the fur seal population to recover to the point that by 1867, when Russia sold Alaska to the United States for $7.2 million, the Pribilof Islands hosted an estimated two million seals on a total land area of under 260 square kilometres. The increased numbers of fur seals at the rookeries meant they reappeared in great numbers off the coast of Vancouver Island on their migration north. Beginning in December, and for the following five or six months, year after year, a massive host of fur seals journeyed along the outer coast, past Clayoquot Sound and beyond Haida Gwaii, heading for the Pribilof Islands.

Independent traders making their way up and down the outer coast of Vancouver Island became increasingly aware of this immense migration and of the expanding potential of the sealskin trade. The trade developed gradually, with the Haida starting to hunt seal for their pelts, rather than only for meat, in the late 1840s. By 1858, William Banfield observed that the Tseshahts of Barkley Sound had "developed a healthy trade in seal skins." The skins were avidly sought for making sealskin coats; with 300,000 hairs per square inch (half that of the sea otter), they provided one of the richest pelts available.

Coastal trader Captain William Spring, highly influential in the fur seal industry, began trading at Kyuquot, taking over from William Banfield, who had been mysteriously murdered in 1862 in Barkley Sound. Spring worked in partnership with Scottish cooper Hugh McKay, and they traded for seal skins, which, along with dogfish oil, they took to Victoria and sold to the Hudson's Bay Company. Spring and McKay also cured salmon for sale to Hawaii. Within a few years, Spring's interest in the fur seal hunt on the coast of Vancouver Island led to an innovative practice that transformed the hunt completely.

Born in Russia in 1831 to a Scottish engineer and his Russian wife, Spring had arrived in Victoria in 1853, aged twenty-two. He entered

116

the partnership with Hugh McKay, who had arrived in Victoria five years earlier, and together they started in business in 1856 with their vessels *Ino* and *Morning Star*, running freight to the Olympic Peninsula and trading around southern Vancouver Island. *Morning Star* foundered off Discovery Island in 1859, to be replaced by the schooner *Surprise*. By 1864 another schooner, *Alert*, had joined their small fleet, later followed by the stalwart *Favorite*. For many years these vessels plied the coastal waters from Washington State up to Alaska, becoming especially known for their role in sealing.

Through his trading ventures, Spring began to consider how best to maximize the potential profit of the fur seal trade. In 1868 he came up with a new idea. Knowing the dangers faced by aboriginal hunters who paddled up to fifty or sixty kilometres offshore in their small canoes to hunt the fur seals in their feeding grounds, he decided to take the hunters to the seals. He ordered Captain James Christensen of the *Surprise* to take twelve Tla-o-qui-aht hunters and four canoes out to La Pérouse Bank. After three days of hunting, the expedition netted only twenty-seven skins; Spring's schooner kept nine pelts, and the Tla-o-qui-ahts eighteen. Two of their canoes and six hunters were lost in fog, but when *Surprise* returned to Clayoquot Sound the crew discovered the lost hunters had made their way safely back to shore on their own.

This voyage, unpromising though it seemed at the time, marked the beginning of the Victoria-based pelagic, or open ocean, seal hunt. Over the next forty-seven years, this became a massive international business involving Russia, Japan, Great Britain, Canada, and the United States. The industry made the city of Victoria and the province of British Columbia economically stable; transformed the First Nations economy on the west coast, changing it from a system based on trade to one based on currency; and eventually reduced the fur seal populations from an estimated five million in 1864 to 123,000 by 1911.

In 1869, despite the meagre catch on that first pelagic sealing venture, Spring sent Captain Peter Francis out to La Pérouse Bank to try again. With him aboard the schooner *Alert*, Francis had twelve Ucluelet hunters and their canoes. This time the returns could not have been

Victoria harbour with five sealing schooners at anchor: *Wanderer, Favorite, Penelope, W.P. Sayward* and *Venture*. The local economy thrived during the sealing era, and often scores of sealing schooners could be found in the harbour provisioning for voyages, or offloading skins at the end of the sealing season.
Image C06120 courtesy of Royal BC Museum, BC Archives

better, and the crew salted down 900 skins for Francis to take back to Victoria. The west coast fur seal industry suddenly became viable.

By 1876, nine sealing schooners based out of Victoria took Nuu-chah-nulth hunters and their canoes to the sealing grounds. Five of these ships were owned by Captain Spring and his growing number of partners. By 1882, fourteen schooners engaged in this pelagic hunt. That year, sealing captains spent $200,000 on wages and supplies in Victoria, hired as many as 400 aboriginal hunters in a season, and paid them from $2 to $4 a pelt, good money in those times. The numbers of schooners continued to rise, and by the end of the nineteenth century, over seventy sealing schooners, many from San Francisco, could be found anchored in Victoria.

Typical of these schooners, the 120-ton, 27-metre-long, 7-metre-wide, double-masted *Favorite* often frequented Clayoquot Sound during the sealing era. Like so many other schooners, she sailed into the Sound to recruit Tla-o-qui-aht, Ahousaht, and Hesquiaht seal hunters, known to be the best on the coast. Built in 1868 at Sooke for Captain Hugh McKay from Douglas fir cut in the Sooke hills, the *Favorite* could carry a massive 400 square metres of sail.

One of the best known sealing schooners, *Favorite* often sailed into Clayoquot Sound to find aboriginal hunters to sign on for the fur seal hunt. Note the dugout canoes on her deck, belonging to the hunters. The schooner would travel great distances to the sealing grounds, and seals were hunted from the canoes. Built in Sooke in 1868 and first used as a coastal trader, *Favorite* ended her days in Clayoquot Sound, finally sinking in Pretty Girl Cove in 1919. *Mount Angel Abbey Library*

In July 1868, McKay, then in partnership with Captain William Spring, sailed the *Favorite* to Hawaii with 120 tons of mixed cargo. Upon his return two months later, he began using the schooner on the west coast as a trading vessel. After seven years at the helm, McKay sold the ship to Spring and his new partner, Peter Francis, and *Favorite* became more heavily involved in the sealing trade. Father Augustin Brabant frequently found himself a passenger aboard the ship on his trips to Victoria and around the Sound. In 1885 she carried much-needed medicine to Hesquiat during an outbreak of measles and smallpox. On another trip she carried a new bell for the Hesquiat church, which the crew helped install; legendary sealing captain Alex MacLean rang this bell for the first time. In 1888, on a government contract, she carried lumber to build housing in First Nations settlements. The bricks found today in the church at Friendly Cove arrived, along with the lumber, aboard *Favorite*. This schooner lived out her days in Clayoquot Sound; today her hulk lies at the bottom of a small cove at the head of Holmes Inlet.

When schooners such as *Favorite* arrived in Clayoquot Sound, their captains sought out the best aboriginal hunters and, with the help of local middlemen like Fred Thornberg, Walter Dawley, and John Grice, signed them on for the hunt. Hiring took place only after their chief had negotiated a price for each seal caught. Then the hunters loaded their dugout canoes onto the schooner; a dozen and more canoes could be stacked on the decks of the larger vessels, which could carry up to thirty hunters. Sometimes women accompanied their husbands on the seal hunt, handling the canoes and participating skillfully in the hunt. Once at the sealing grounds, the chief hunter, who acted as "boss" for the others on board, would judge the weather and the wind, deciding when to launch the canoes. Crewed by a harpooner and a paddler or steersman, the canoes would be dropped from the mother ship at daybreak to begin searching for and hunting seals.

The fur seals fed at night and slept at the surface during the day. Their keen sense of smell meant they could detect predators from two kilometres away, so the hunters cautiously approached the seals downwind. The steerer brought the canoe to within ten metres of a seal, and the harpooner grasped his weapon, a wooden shaft with two detachable spearheads attached to prongs at the leading edge. Holding the harpoon in two hands, he hurled it at the seal's head. The hunters always aimed near the head to avoid putting a hole in the skin, hoping for an unblemished pelt.

Once the seal had been harpooned, the shaft of the harpoon detached from the spearheads and floated on the surface; tied to the canoe by a four-metre-long cod-line, it was easily recovered later. Without the heavy wooden shaft, the harpooner was more easily able to play the seal, just as a fisherman would play a large fish. After the fight, which might take from five minutes to several hours depending on the size and strength of the seal and on how well, and where, the spearheads had embedded, the harpooner drew the seal to the side of the canoe, where he dispatched it with a blow to the head.

Using this method, hunters rarely lost a seal because the harpooned animal remained attached to the canoe by lines and floats. When both aboriginal and European hunters began to use guns, many seals were lost, their bodies sinking before they could be recovered. Estimates reveal that three seals were often lost for every one collected, and sometimes the ratio was far higher; in 1882, 100,000 seals were killed in order to obtain only 15,000.

Sometimes two or more canoes would raft together for stability, and the steerers would pull the dead seals aboard and skin them on the spot, allowing the carcasses to drop into the sea. Sometimes, if the kill happened near the mother ship, they would skin the seals on the schooner and retain the meat and blubber. Manhandling these carcasses required strength and good balance: a large male could measure over two metres long and weigh over 360 kilograms; the much smaller females weighed only around 50 kilograms. The hunting and skinning continued until nightfall, when the canoes returned to the mother ship, where the crew laid the skins flat and salted them down in the ship's hold. When the skins eventually reached Victoria, where servicing the sealing industry played a major part in the economy of the young city, handlers rolled them in salt and packed them into barrels for shipment to C.M. Lampson, the company in London, England, that processed the fur seal pelts. There, processors dyed the skins—if it was not dyed, the skin looked decidedly unappealing—and cured them. Following processing, Lampson auctioned off the skins, most of which became coats. Five skins made one coat, which sold for a little over $100. At the height of the industry, more than 10,000 people in England found employment processing fur seal pelts.

Pelagic sealing off the coast of Vancouver Island served both the Nuu-chah-nulth hunters and the early schooner owners well. The hunt took place within the aboriginal people's traditional seal hunting season, before the halibut fishing season began, and during a slack time for the schooners, which usually did their trading cruises to collect dogfish oil in the autumn months. The aboriginal "boss," who received a bonus for his role on the schooner, worked collaboratively with the captain on daily decision making. The schooners returned to the hunters' home villages every five or so days to dry the seal meat, a delicacy the aboriginals coveted more than the skins. They would also return to shore when storms made hunting dangerous.

Even while this offshore, schooner-based sealing took place, aboriginals continued hunting seals on their own, selling the skins to nearby trading posts or taking them to Victoria by canoe for sale. According to Peter Murray in his book *The Vagabond Fleet*, in 1880 a total of 900 pelts from shore-based seal hunters at Hesquiat netted $30,000, making some hunters as much as $120 a day. With returns of this magnitude, the once lucrative dogfish oil trade suffered. Father Brabant wrote in 1882: "Two years ago I persuaded the young men to try their luck as fur seal hunters. From the beginning, their success was such that they now seem to be determined to prosecute this lucrative work and leave the dog fish business to the old people."

In 1882, sealing schooner captains began following the fur seals up to Alaska and to the Pribilof Islands, taking their crews much further afield. Many more problems and dangers now presented themselves to the schooners and to their hunters. Until this point, the seal hunt had taken place between January and June, within reasonable distance of Vancouver Island—never more than a couple of days away. When the hunt extended up to the Bering Sea, it began in July and ended in October, taking hunters away from their villages for months at a time, cutting into the fall salmon fishing season, and interfering with the centuries-old rhythm of the Nuu-chah-nulth calendar.

In 1884, Brabant wrote of the first Hesquiaht crews going up to the Bering Sea. "Last June seventy young men went on the sealing expedition to the Bering Sea. They did very well and arrived home highly delighted with the success of their long voyage. They killed 1400 animals, receiving two dollars per animal." By 1885, the harpooners from Kyuquot thought that they had become so indispensible that they demanded $5 a skin from the schooner owners, refusing to sign on until they got their price. Unable to find crews, the owners eventually settled on $4 a skin. As time passed, prices mounted; by 1907, traders were paying hunters $8 a skin as the price of seal skins increased on the international market.

The rising prices of seal skins encouraged aboriginal hunters to take up shore-based sealing, making it more difficult for the captains of pelagic schooners to sign the best hunters. Agents and middlemen, often traders along the coast, took an ever more active role on behalf of the schooner owners, trying to secure the best hunters. These middlemen would start bargaining months before the sealing season began, at a time when hunters needed money, paying them advances on their potential earnings as early as January, well ahead of the Bering Sea hunt that began in June. But by the late 1870s, salmon canneries along the coast, along with hop farms in the Fraser Valley, also vied to attract aboriginal workers, and those industries provided accommodation for entire families. Many aboriginals chose these forms of employment because they could preserve the family structure, rather than having men leave their villages and families for months at a time to go sealing.

In 1897, some of the sealing captains became so frustrated dealing with the hard-bargaining Nuu-chah-nulth hunters that Captain Sprott Balcom, later a prominent figure in the West Coast whaling industry, floated the idea of bringing Micmac hunters from Nova Scotia to take their place. "The Indians of the West Coast will not be so independent in their dealings with the white skippers; incentives for good work will be developed; and our own Siwashes will find in the Micmac's industry an object lesson," observed the *British Colonist* on January 16, 1897. Balcom proposed locating the Micmacs on an unnamed island comprising "5 to 600 acres [200 to 245 hectares] of arable land somewhere between Clayoquot and Ahousaht," suggesting "the Indians [Micmacs] be hired at wages that would astonish the west coasters." The unlikely idea also recommended that the Micmacs bring birchbark with them so they could construct canoes and dwelling huts when they arrived. Nothing came of this scheme.

In many of his letters, Ahousat trader Fred Thornberg described striking bargains with seal hunters on behalf of schooner captains. Always a contrarian business, this became far more complex when several schooners showed up at the same time in the villages, squaring off to obtain hunters. Walter Dawley, at the Clayoquot trading post, received a constant stream of letters from anxious sealing captains, who

Frederick Thornberg, long-time store-keeper at Clayoquot and Ahousat, with his daughter and two of his sons aboard the sealing schooner *Libbie*. One of the first Europeans to live permanently on the west coast of Vancouver Island, Thornberg arrived at Clayoquot in 1874, trading furs and hiring aboriginal crews for sealing vessels. *Ken Gibson Collection*

wrote to ask for advice, inter-vention, or special treatment in finding hunters. In 1899, Cap-tain H.F. Sieward announced, "I have secured 13 canoes try and secure me Kelsamat Jack... get him somehow but get him... clinch him with an advance." In another letter, Sieward foresaw trouble, writing, "I am afraid that with 3 schooners...there will be a hot time in Ahousat," while Cap-tain J.W. Peppett braced himself for an enjoyable scrap at the vil-lage: "If I am obliged to make a fight for hunters, I want to be in the hottest part of the fight." The scene of the fiercest competition always tended to be Ahousat, but all along the coast small conspiracies and shifting allegiances among the captains, hunters, and middlemen made for continual deal making and breaking. The more determined of the seal hunters would head down to Victoria to bargain directly with the captains, cutting out the middlemen and striking deals on behalf of a group of hunters, much to the chagrin of the sealing companies. William Munsie, head of the Victoria Sealing Company, wrote angrily to Walter Dawley more than once, reporting that hunters had been striking their own deals in the city and demanding that Dawley keep them in their villages.

By no means all of the Nuu-chah-nulth seal hunters attempted such assertive bargaining, most being content to let the "boss" of their crew negotiate. The type of conflict experienced at Ahousat did not arise to the same extent in other locations in Clayoquot Sound. At Opitsat, Chief Joseph appears to have been influential in keeping the peace between his Tla-o-qui-aht hunters and the sealing captains. Renowned as a whaler in his youth and as an extraordinary canoeman, Chief Joseph made several trips to the Bering Sea aboard schooners, and the sealing captains "bid high for his services," according to George Nicholson in a *Daily Colonist* article. Held in high esteem by his own people and by the white community, Chief Joseph arbitrated disputes of any kind with a firm hand. His wife, who spent several seasons on sealing vessels as a cook, became known as "Queen Mary," a name probably given to her by a sealing captain. The couple lived to a great age, in later years easily spotted paddling every day from Opitsat to Clayoquot, where they found a warm welcome from the storekeeper.

Tla-o-qui-aht chief Joseph and his wife "Queen Mary," around 1900. As a young man, Chief Joseph was renowned as a whaler and seal hunter, and his wife worked aboard sealing schooners as a cook. *Mount Angel Abbey Library*

Whether shore-based or pelagic, sealing presented many dangers and at times led to loss of life. In May 1875, over a hundred shore-based Nuu-chah-nulth seal hunters, in seventy canoes, died in a sudden storm that carried some of them as far southwest as the Washington coast; this incident made it easier for the schooners to recruit hunters. The single most tragic event affecting hunters from Clayoquot Sound occurred twelve years later, on April 1, 1887. The schooner *Active* sank in a storm off Cape Flattery, claiming the lives of twenty-four Kelsemaht hunters from Yarksis on Vargas Island. The tragedy left nineteen widows and forty-two orphans destitute, and it devastated the relatively small Kelsemaht band, nearly wiping out its male population. Five others also died aboard the *Active*, including one of the vessel's owners,

Jacob Gutman, at the time co-owner of the Clayoquot trading post along with partner Alexander Frank. Gutman had employed Fred Thornberg to run the operation there, and because Thornberg had hired their fellow tribesmen to go on board, many Kelsemahts blamed him for all the deaths. Seeking vengeance, two Kelsemahts broke into the Clayoquot trading post; "bothe had a very wild look on their face...they could hardly speak," Fred Thornberg wrote. He managed to appease the men with tobacco and matches, promising that with the help of the Indian Department and the Catholic priest he would arrange relief for the families of the lost men. Thornberg later wrote, rather sadly, "If I had not askt them to goe sealing they would not be drownet & lost."

As the Bering Sea fur seal hunt continued, serious and lengthy jurisdictional disputes surfaced. In 1867, the United States had purchased Alaska from Russia, partly to secure the fur seal rookeries of the Pribilof Islands. The United States did not want foreign competition in this area, and in 1881 it declared that all fisheries, including the one for fur seals, whether on land or sea, stretching from the coast of Alaska to the International Date Line, were American property. To enforce this edict, the United States dispatched gunboats to the North Pacific to protect its interests. Before long, those gunboats began seizing any foreign schooner in the Bering Sea that had guns, harpoons, or seal skins aboard. The seizures occurred up to a hundred kilometres offshore, at a time when five kilometres (three miles) was considered the limit of a country's territorial waters. The gunboats arrested crews and escorted them to Alaskan ports, where their harvest of pelts, and the schooners themselves, faced impoundment. The aboriginal hunters on board sometimes suffered a worse fate, with the Americans seizing their canoes and gear and often marooning them on islands, or setting them adrift in their canoes. Many died of exposure. The Russians and the Japanese, who also controlled islands in the North Pacific where fur seals bred, conducted similar seizures and arrests. The hunt became an international jousting match.

Right from the beginning of fur sealing on the west coast, the schooner *Favorite* played a role. In 1883, then still owned by William Spring, *Favorite* came under the command of a new captain, Cape Breton-born Alex MacLean. Mac-Lean's fame, and that of his brother Dan, also a sealing captain, reached legendary proportions all along the Pacific Coast from Alaska to Mexico. In his 1904 novel *The Sea-Wolf*, novelist Jack London based his villainous character Captain Wolf Larsen on the larger-than-life exploits of Alex MacLean, while Dan served as the model for Wolf's fearsome brother Death Larsen. This brought them even greater renown, but the MacLeans resented the comparison, for although hard men at sea, and harsh with their crews, their behaviour had nothing in common with the murderous, half-mad Larsens.

In 1885 the two brothers launched "the MacLean experiment." Dan captained the schooner *Mary Ellen* with a European crew on board, and Alex went out in *Favorite* with seventeen Hesquiahts and three Tla-o-qui-ahts. They set out to determine whether Europeans using guns or Nuu-chah-nulth using harpoons would prove the most profitable. From January until August the two schooners plied the waters of the Bering Sea, hunting seals. Dan's *Mary Ellen* acquired 2,309 skins and Alex's *Favorite* 2,073. Yet while Dan MacLean may have beaten his younger brother, he needed the extra profit of *Mary Ellen's* catch to offset the higher costs of his European crew: feeding a white crew doubled the cost of provisioning a schooner. The aboriginal crew lived chiefly on seal meat and hard biscuit. In the end, the MacLean experiment proved inconclusive.

Captain Alex MacLean from Cape Breton, Nova Scotia, was one of the most successful sealing captains. He and his equally canny brother, Dan, could return at season's end with 3,000 to 4,000 skins. Both MacLeans sported grand moustaches, rumoured to be long enough to tie behind their necks.

Image B00067 courtesy of Royal BC Museum, BC Archives

On that same voyage, two hunters on the *Favorite* arrived home in Clayoquot Sound by a curious route. Separated from the mother ship while hunting in the treacherous and foggy seas off the Aleutians, the two men eventually reached a local trading post. The storekeeper provided them with food and directed them to a nearby settlement, where they were put aboard a steamer bound for San Francisco. After being treated well by the captain and crew, they arrived at San Francisco, where the British consul paid their passage back to Hesquiat, via Victoria. Father Brabant reported that "they arrived home last Sunday, just in time to attend Mass. They now excite the wonder of all the Indians."

In 1886, Dan MacLean returned from the Bering Sea with a record 4,256 skins on the *Mary Ellen*, allowing him to affix a broom to his masthead signifying a "clean sweep" of honour for the season. Alex MacLean in *Favorite* returned to Victoria with 3,325 skins. The brothers' joint earnings that season exceeded $60,000; in today's terms this would amount to around $1.5 million. Between them, the MacLeans dominated the sealing industry, renowned not only for the number of skins they caught, but also for their cunning avoidance of authorities in the Bering Sea. In 1886, American authorities seized several Canadian schooners—but not those of the wily MacLeans.

Much of the success or failure of sealing depended on the skill and guile of the sealing captain, and on his ability to keep out of harm's way. Dodging international patrol vessels in the North Pacific waters became an essential skill, and luck also played a part. In 1893, storms in the Bering Sea blew Captain George Heater's sailing schooner, *Ainoko*, into restricted Japanese–Russian sealing grounds. While he was trying to leave the area, a Russian gunship overtook the schooner and arrested Heater, seizing his ship, his papers, and his navigation instruments, and ordering him to follow the gunship into Yokohama to face trial. When his fifteen Hesquiaht hunters noticed the schooner was heading west instead of east, they threatened to mutiny. Heater, realizing they outnumbered him and his crew three to one, chose to make a run from the Russians rather than risk an uprising from the Hesquiahts. The *Ainoko* escaped under cover of fog, and once out of sight of the Russians sailed 4,800 kilometres back to Vancouver Island, without navigational instruments. Heater dropped his Hesquiaht crew at their village and sailed on to Victoria. A court later cleared Heater of hunting within the restricted territory.

Captain Alex MacLean managed to avoid capture by American authorities for many years, but in 1894 his luck ran out. Men from the US revenue cutter *Mohican* boarded the *Favorite* and, after finding an innocuous flare gun, seized the schooner and its 1,247 pelts. This seizure led the British government, representing Canada, to protest to the United States, defending the *Favorite* and other Victoria-based schooners faced with similar problems. In 1897, that protest ended with the American government paying just over $250,000 compensation to Canadian owners of sealing schooners for loss of livelihood and illegal arrest.

The year of MacLean's capture proved to be a turning point in the industry and in the fortunes of the Nuu-chah-nulth hunters. Tensions between the pelagic sealers and the American, Japanese, and Russian rookery owners led to the closure of the Bering Sea hunt during the 1892 and 1893 seasons. Following arbitration hearings involving the British and American governments, new restrictions banned the use of guns in Alaskan waters. This edict made the Nuu-chah-nulth hunters, because of their harpooning skills, even more important. By 1899 the Nuu-chah-nulth comprised fully 88 percent of the hunters in the fur seal industry.

All the while, as the hunt accelerated, the seal population shrank. Alarm bells sounded about this for many years, from the mid-1880s onward, with fisheries inspectors, scientists, and politicians all asking how the seal population could survive. Between 1872 and 1891 an estimated million and a half seals were killed, including unborn seals in slaughtered females and abandoned pups in the rookeries. By 1910 the fur seal population had been reduced to fewer than 125,000 animals from its former millions. Urgent questions arose about the future of the seal population even as complex attempts to regulate the hunt failed and international bickering became ever more acrimonious. For many years, rumours about the imminent collapse of the entire industry circulated, and wily investors began buying up disused sealing schooners in hopes of receiving future compensation from the government

for loss of livelihood. In 1909, negotiations to preserve the seal population began in earnest among the four sealing nations, with a view
to establishing an international moratorium on pelagic sealing in the
Bering Sea.

In the years leading up to this, a diehard coterie of schooner captains
refused to believe their industry would ever cease. Despite their diminished catches, they continued doggedly heading up to the Bering Sea in
search of a disappearing species. But fewer and fewer schooners made
the journey, the number dropping every year during the first decade of
the twentieth century. Embittered and threatened, the captains rancor-
ously blamed their crews, each other, or the government for the hard
times facing the industry, and they seized hopefully on scraps of good
news. Hearts lifted briefly in 1908 when Thomas Stockham's schooner
Thomas Bayard returned from the Bering Sea with over 600 seal skins
and 28 sea otter pelts. Nonetheless, only a handful of schooners went
out from Victoria in 1909, and even fewer the next year. Against all
odds, veteran captain George Heater managed to obtain 878 seal skins
in 1910, and Captain Peppett made his final trip that year also.

In 1911, after prolonged discussions, Japan, Russia, Britain, and the
United States signed the North Pacific Fur Seal Convention on July 7,
halting commercial pelagic sealing for fifteen years. Victoria schooner
owners and their crews, including 861 aboriginal hunters, responded
by making individual claims to a royal commission established by the
Canadian government, seeking compensation for loss of income. Some
of the aboriginal hunters claimed they had made up to $500 per season.
In 1916, after sitting for 120 days, the commission presented its report,
awarding the 1,605 claimants a total of $60,663. Collectively, they had
sought a little over $9 million. The Nuu-chah-nulth received a total
of $15,240, the largest single award being $230. As a concession, the
North Pacific Fur Seal Convention allowed aboriginal sealers to continue hunting seals using their traditional harpooning methods from
canoes, but even that privilege ended in the 1940s.

Most of the Canadian-based sealing fleet was sold for a pittance,
some schooners bringing as little as $150 to $200. Many spent their last
days slowly rotting at anchor in Victoria harbour; a few were refitted

and became rum-runners in the 1920s, carrying liquor from Canada to the United States during prohibition. According to Patrick Lane in his article "The Great Pacific Sealhunt" (published in *Raincoast Chronicles 4*), the pelagic sealing industry employed 1,400 Caucasians and 1,700 aboriginals on 122 schooners; 15,000 people depended on this industry all along the coast from California to Alaska, and it played a crucial role in the history and economy of northwest North America. The Victoria-based sealing industry earned $1.5 million a year, a huge economic boon to the city, and in 1894, at the height of the industry, Victoria's harbour bristled with the masts of over 100 schooners, comprising four-fifths of the entire northwest sealing fleet.

For many years these vessels brought trade, excitement, employment, and a great deal of money into villages and trading posts along Vancouver Island's west coast. Each ship calling at the villages of Clayoquot Sound—*Favorite, Surprise, Alert, Umbrina, Mary Ellen*, to name only a few—had its own personality, and most had colourful characters at the helm. In their heyday, these schooners carried with them a sense of adventure and potential danger, as well as the possibility of large gains for everyone involved. When the west coast of Vancouver Island started to open up for business in the late nineteenth century, the sealing schooners, more than anything else, made that happen.

The first hotel in Clayoquot Sound, built on Stockham Island in 1898 by store-keepers Walter Dawley and Thomas Stockham, who originally set up shop on the island in 1893–94. Within months, Thomas Earle opened another hotel across Tofino Harbour at Clayoquot on Stubbs Island. In 1902, Stockham and Dawley left their establishment, and took over Earle's store and hotel at Clayoquot. *Courtesy of Leona Taylor*

Chapter 8:

SETTING UP SHOP

OF ALL TRADING POSTS on Vancouver Island's west coast, the one at Clayoquot on Stubbs Island emerged as the most significant. First established in 1854, and important for its central location on the coast, Clayoquot offered protected anchorage for trading schooners, an easy landing for canoes on the sandy beach on the lee side of the island, and rich potential for trade with nearby First Nations. Its early years saw only sporadic activity, with periods of seasonal trading followed by long stretches when not much occurred, but as the dogfish oil trade and later the fur seal industry gathered momentum, Clayoquot drew increasing business. By the mid–1890s, it had become a vital centre for commerce and communication on the coast.

Back in 1854, William Banfield set up this pioneer trading post in partnership with Captain Peter Francis and Thomas Laughton. During the mid-1850s, Banfield and Francis came and went at Clayoquot in their trading vessel *Jibo*, doing most of their trading in the late summer and early fall, when aboriginals traded their dogfish oil and a variety of furs, including seal skins. Like other early trading posts, the buildings at Clayoquot consisted of little more than storage sheds with crude living quarters attached. At the end of the season, the traders would empty the rudimentary buildings, load their furs and barrels of oil onto their schooners, and sail to Victoria to sell their stock to the Hudson's Bay Company. The rest of the year the buildings on Stubbs Island stood empty, facing blankly over the water toward the site of present-day Tofino on the Esowista Peninsula. No one lived there; the nearest settlement to Clayoquot lay at the Tla-o-qui-aht village of Opitsat, on Meares Island.

Banfield and his partners set up other trading posts on the west coast at about the same time as the one at Clayoquot. Thomas Laughton ran one to the south, at Port San Juan, near present-day Port Renfrew, and the ill-fated Maltese trader Barney had charge of the Kyuquot trading post. In 1859, Banfield left his partnership with Francis and Laughton and bought land at the head of Barkley Sound from the Huu-ay-ahts for the price of several blankets, some beans and molasses. He extensively explored the area around Barkley Sound and up the Alberni Canal, as well as Clayoquot Sound. In 1860, in his capacity as government agent, Banfield assisted Captain Edward Stamp when he established the first west coast sawmill at Alberni.

Banfield was the first settler in Barkley Sound, and his name still endures there. The town of Bamfield—despite the spelling corruption—is named for him, and also Banfield Creek. Such a legacy would have dismayed Banfield. In 1858, having observed how the explorers, traders, and government mapmakers named the features of the coast after themselves and their cohort, he wrote protestingly, "However much the old navigators' names are entitled to respect, good taste would lead us at the present day to adopt the Indian names [which] in most instances are much prettier, many of them having a natural beauty of sound... Great Britain's Colonies have enough Royal names, noble names, and titles of our grandfathers and grandmothers and birthplace names... let us differ a little from our neighbors of Washington Territory, with their Websters, Pierces, Madisons and Monroes and Jeffersons attached to every little group of log shanties that rises out of the bush." Any quick glance at a map of the coast reveals how Banfield's words went unheeded.

A keen observer of coastal geography and resources, Banfield extolled the rich potential of the west coast of Vancouver Island in a series of articles for the *Daily Victoria Gazette* in 1858, focusing particularly on Barkley Sound and the Alberni Canal, but also describing a trip to Clayoquot Sound. Noting the Tla-o-qui-aht to be "the most intelligent tribe I have met with," he wrote of their territory as "the great canoe mart of the west coast...canoes varying from three to 10 to 60 feet [1 to 3 to 18.75 metres] in length, of the most accurate workmanship and perfect design." Banfield reserved his best descriptive skills for a Tla-o-qui-aht potato feast he attended. "Immense quantities of potatoes are purchased every year by this tribe from white traders and the

Macaws [Makahs]," he wrote. "I have seen 70 bushels of potatoes cooked at once, in two piles on hot stones. They eat whale oil in quantities with potatoes. At these feasts, probably 200 or 300 guests are invited. The females are never asked. Much decorum prevails and positive urbanity is shown to every guest, rich or poor." He continued, describing the strictly observed rituals of cleanliness and eating, and, following the meal, the recitation from memory, by the chief's children, of celebrated stories and speeches.

Banfield's conviction that settlers would soon venture to the west coast proved correct. Early in 1860 he reported to Governor Douglas that Captain Charles Stuart was building a house and planning to settle in the Ucluelet area, the first European to do so. A bay in Ucluelet Inlet bears Stuart's name. He had joined the Hudson's Bay Company in 1842, serving on many of the company's ships until appointed officer-in-charge at Nanaimo in 1855. Later discharged for chronic drunkenness, Stuart briefly operated a trading post at Ucluelet but did not remain there long. He died in 1863. Captain Peter Francis succeeded Stuart in 1862 at the Ucluelet trading post, which he ran for several years. Francis Island in Ucluelet Inlet bears his name.

In 1869 Captain William Spring opened a trading post at Spring Cove in Barkley Sound, on land acquired from the local tribe for a barrel of molasses. By this time the partnership of Spring and Hugh McKay dominated trade on the west coast, with their fleet of schooners and trading posts at Kyuquot, Clayoquot, Spring Cove, Port San Juan, and Ucluelet. Peter Francis continued trading on the coast for years, often working with or for Spring and McKay, operating their schooners *Alert* and *Surprise*, and running their trading posts. At various times Francis took charge of trading posts ranging from Port San Juan to Spring Cove or Clayoquot, where he likely used Banfield's original buildings as his store and living quarters.

Francis's earliest experience as a trader at Clayoquot occurred in June 1861, working with Charles Edward Barrett-Lennard and Napoleon Fitzstubbs, the two English adventurers who briefly dabbled in west coast trade after circumnavigating Vancouver Island in 1860 in their yacht *Templar*. For a short while, *Templar* served the Clayoquot trading station, but Barrett-Lennard soon found trading with the Nuu-chah-nulth not to his liking. Safely back in England in 1862, he wrote that he generally found every aboriginal "treacherous and deceitful...and more or less a thief at heart." Probably the local people got the better of him in trade.

A chart dated 1861, drawn up by Royal Navy surveyor Captain George Henry Richards, notes the presence of the store at Clayoquot and also pinpoints another to the north, at Ahousat. This "store" at Ahousat probably served as little more than an occasional trading facility, operated by Spring and McKay, using their schooner *Surprise* to visit it. Puzzlingly, on this map the letters "PO" appear beside the word "store" at both Clayoquot and Ahousat, indicating a post office. However, in 1861 only two post offices existed on Vancouver Island, at Nanaimo and Victoria. This "PO" notation may simply mean that, on occasion, when a trader showed up, mail might be on board for any fellow trader in the vicinity, or could be taken out from there; such postal service would have been chancy and unofficial.

The detailed surveys carried out by Captain Richards and his crew of over a hundred men created the baseline of information for nautical charts still in use today. Between 1857 and 1862 they charted the entire coastline around Vancouver Island, for the final two years travelling aboard the imposingly large, 810-ton HMS *Hecate*. Richards's officers included Lieutenant Daniel Pender, Edward Parker Bedwell, John Thomas Gowlland, George Alexander Browning and Edward Blunden, all of whose names appear on BC coastal maps. They came prepared to trade with the aboriginals for food and information about the coast, bearing goods such as blankets, molasses, rice, flannel, and blue serge, as well as looking glasses, beads, soap, and tobacco. Captain Richards had been on the west coast before, in 1838–39, when he served aboard the British Navy's survey vessel HMS *Sulphur*, from which Sulphur Passage in Clayoquot Sound takes its name. He had met Chief Maquinna at Nootka, and on this 1861 voyage his "old friend Chief Maquinna" greeted him again, "dressed in a blue frock coat with 3 rows of buttons one row American Eagles the other Royal Marines. A pair of black cloth trousers and over all a long black beaver hat."

In the early 1860s, James Douglas Warren, with his sloop *Thornton*, began trading on the West Coast. By 1864 Warren had taken charge of the trading post at Clayoquot, and within a few years, following Spring's example, *Thornton* was carrying Tla-o-qui-aht hunters out to the sealing grounds in search of fur seals. In 1871, Warren entered into a partnership with Joseph and Jacob Boscowitz, who went on to become the most successful fur buyers in Victoria. Four years later, Warren became the first person to pre-empt land in Clayoquot Sound. He applied to purchase a large portion of Stubbs Island in 1875, paying $62.50 for "Section One," the northern 25 hectares of the island.

Years later, when settler John Grice arrived to stay permanently in the area, he noted Warren's early pre-emption: "I remember being at the Lands Office in 1891 and found his name registered for Stubbs Island." Grice also stated that Captain Hugh McKay had set up a station for the sealing trade where Tofino now stands, adding that McKay "evidently was greatly respected by the Indians, as I learned from Old Indians who had been in his Employ." So by the late 1860s, and certainly through the 1870s, when Warren was at Clayoquot and McKay based at the site of present-day Tofino, the local trading scene gained momentum.

Without question, as trade picked up on the coast, more and more alcohol began to be introduced to the Nuu-chah-nulth. As Captain George Henry Richards observed:

> The west coast was almost free from the Curse until Europeans began to frequent it...Now small vessels frequent all the native places and whisky I believe is their principal article of exchange. The *Surprise* is I believe the keenest trader on the Coast commanded by a well known Cooper named McKay. He gets oil and Skins from the natives and is much liked by them. I believe he treats them always well and fairly—and finds it the best policy. As regards his providing them with whisky, I imagine it is no more than can be expected from a man of his pursuits.

Richards further commented that "it is not difficult to see which way [the aboriginals'] morals are tending—as their communications with ourselves increase." In a letter to his commanding officer, Rear Admiral Robert Baynes, Richards clearly held European traders on the coast responsible for many wrongs, particularly for trafficking in liquor and for demanding and sometimes seizing aboriginal women. When conflicts arose, he firmly stated, "My opinion is that the Natives in most instances are the oppressed and injured parties." In his own travels on the coast, Richards experienced nothing but helpful co-operation from the local people.

In 1874, Captain Warren introduced one of Clayoquot Sound's most memorable characters to the area. He hired Frederick Christian Thornberg to run his Clayoquot trading post, making Thornberg the first year-round European resident of the Tofino area. Over the next three decades, Thornberg became a notable chronicler of events in Clayoquot Sound. Unpredictable, quick-tempered, and mentally unstable, Thornberg wrote volubly about the west coast and his own experiences. His many long, rambling letters and his brief personal memoirs provide a wealth of detail about life in the Sound. He wrote about schooners, storekeepers, and sealing captains, aboriginals, settlers and missionaries, never hesitating to complain, to find fault, or to accuse others—never mind who—of being wrong. Yet even though Thornberg's writings sometimes degenerate into personal tirades, his colourful descriptions, filled with wild misspellings and abbreviations, bring a whole era alive in a way no other documents can match.

Born at Stege, on Mooen Island, Denmark, on December 31, 1841, Thornberg went to sea aged fifteen. After serving six years before the mast, he arrived in Esquimalt on February 22, 1862, aboard the *Black Knight*, carrying a cargo of Welsh coal round Cape Horn for Royal Navy ships based on the West Coast. Luckily for Thornberg, he jumped ship in Victoria; on its homeward journey, *Black Knight*, loaded with ship's spars, foundered and disappeared. At Victoria, Thornberg landed a job as a servant for the Honourable David Cameron, Chief Justice of Vancouver Island. He married Cecily Harthylia, a Songhees woman, in June 1867; she bore him three children. "We had one child live [Johanne]," Thornberg related in his memoirs. "Second Child was O.K. but orders came to have Children vacinadet [vaccinated] and she got sick and died. Third Child was still born in Victoria." Thornberg later tended sheep in the San Juan Islands for some time, and eventually his experience as a seaman and his facility with languages brought him to the attention of west coast traders. Captain Spring signed him on to the schooner *Favorite*, and Thornberg found himself sailing up and down the outer coast of Vancouver Island. In 1874 Captain Warren engaged him to work at the Clayoquot trading post.

When Thornberg and his family arrived at Clayoquot that year, Peter Francis then operated the trading post at Spring Cove in Ucluelet, Andrew Laing had charge of a trading post at Dodger's Cove in Barkley Sound, and Neils Moos ran Spring and McKay's store at Port San Juan. These four traders constituted the only Europeans then living on the west coast of Vancouver Island northwest of Juan de Fuca Strait. The following year the number rose to five when Father Augustin Brabant began building his mission at Hesquiat. "This coast, at the time of our taking possession of it," Brabant wrote, "was exclusively inhabited by Indians. Four trading posts had, however, been established and were each in the charge of one white man. But besides these four men there were absolutely no white settlers to be found on this extensive coast of nearly two hundred miles [325 kilometres]."

In 1874, the trading post on Stubbs Island consisted of a small store with living quarters attached, surrounded by a large fenced garden. Three shacks stood nearby on the long curving sandspit near the trading post, one of them inhabited by a local man named Gwiar, who acted as Thornberg's interpreter and tutor while he learned the local language. This may have been the same Gwiar who acted as interpreter a few years earlier during the trial of the two Hesquiaht men found guilty of murder following the *John Bright* incident. The two other shacks on Stubbs Island, according to Thornberg, "each had an old Man and his Wife. They only came there in the time the Herrings & Salmon run in the harbour—fishing and drying the fish." Two years later Thornberg built a bigger store with separate living quarters, using wood from a shipment of lumber that washed up near Hesquiat when the cargo vessel *Edwin* foundered. Salvaged by Captain Warren, this lumber provided enough material to enclose the new buildings behind "a 6 foot [2 metre] strong Board fence & a strong (double) gate...with a strong wooden barr across."

Thornberg constantly feared for his life during his many years as a trader. He took no chances at Clayoquot while trading with his customers for furs and dogfish oil. "I traded for years through a hole in the End of the Building it was two feet high & about a foot 6 inches wide [60 by 45 centimetres] & two Ind. could just stand & look in with there elbows & breasts leaning on the bottom part of the hole...On the outside was a small veranda so that the Ind. would be out of the rain when he came to trade." Despite being married to an aboriginal woman, Thornberg always suspected treachery and murderous intent from the local people, whom he generally called "savages." He carried his Winchester .44 with him at all times.

When the American barque *General Cobb* foundered at Long Beach in February 1880, the entire crew, rescued by Tla-o-qui-ahts after being stranded on an offshore islet for two days, eventually found themselves at the Clayoquot trading post. "They received every hospitality..," reported the *Colonist*, "in charge of Mr Robert Turnbull." No mention of Fred Thornberg; possibly Turnbull replaced him at Clayoquot for a while, or took charge during that particular crisis. The *General Cobb* crew, laden with gifts from their aboriginal rescuers, travelled with them by canoe to Barkley Sound, where they boarded Peter Francis's *Alert*, heading for Victoria.

One night that same year, two men climbed over Thornberg's fence at Clayoquot and fired a shot through his lighted window. Their flintlock gun misfired, and Thornberg suffered no harm. The attackers came from Nootka, where their people had suffered an outbreak of smallpox earlier in the year, killing ninety people. They blamed all European incomers for their plight, claiming their rivers and drinking water had been purposely infected with the disease in order to eliminate them.

Incidents such as this further excited Thornberg's fears. On July 1, 1882, the *British Colonist* reported Thornberg taking the law into his own hands during a dispute: "At Clayoquot there was much excitement owing to a shooting affray which had taken place a few days ago, and in which a trader employed at one of Captain Warren's stations in Clayoquot Sound had fired at and wounded (though not fatally) a Clayoquot Indian." Thornberg appeared in court in Victoria in November 1883 to answer charges; no further reports appear regarding this incident.

Thornberg's memoirs indicate that in February 1885 he took charge of the small trading post at Ahousat. His wife Cecily having died in 1883, in April 1885 he married, "Indian fashion," Lucy Harbess, an Ahousaht woman. Thornberg appears to have continued running the Clayoquot store, perhaps in rotation with the trading post at Ahousat, for records show that in 1886, when Warren and Boscowitz sold the Clayoquot trading post to Jacob Gutman and Alexander Frank, Thornberg remained as manager. When Harry Guillod and his wife Kate journeyed to Clayoquot at Christmas 1886, they visited Thornberg and his wife and children, and Thornberg certainly lived there when the sealing schooner *Active* sank in 1887 during what he described as "one of the worst gales I ever seen in my meny years on the W Coast." His first child by his wife Lucy, daughter Hilda, was born at Clayoquot in 1889. Thornberg and Lucy had six children together: Hilda, Andreas, William, John, Fred, and a girl who died in infancy. Lucy died of poisoning in 1901 from eating tainted mussels. "I was too late to save her," lamented Thornberg.

In October 1889, two years after the death of Jacob Gutman and twenty-four Kelsemaht hunters on the *Active*, Alexander Frank sold the Clayoquot trading post to "two wealthy Englishmen Penney and Brown," who had recently purchased the sealing schooner *Black Diamond*, which they renamed *Katherine*. According to the *British Colonist* of October 18, 1889, the two intended "not only to engage in the fishing and sealing industries, but also to establish a ship chandlery and general store at which the sealing schooners can refit without having to return to the city." Four days later, the newspaper reported that *Katherine* "sailed yesterday afternoon for Clayoquot Sound, having on board the new owners, Messrs Penny and Brown, and a cargo valued at $3000 and consisting of general stores." To begin the New Year and the new decade, John Lambert Penney inserted a newspaper advertisement about Clayoquot on January 1, 1890, entitled "Notice to Owners of Sealing Schooners." It declared: "The proprietor begs to announce those interested that the above station carries a complete stock of supplies, etc. to meet the requirements for the coming sealing season...Also to meet the requirements of sealers and others a bi-weekly mail service has been instituted between Victoria and Clayoquot via Alberni." At the end of the ad, one further detail: "NB Seal skins stored and shipped free of all commission."

After taking over the Clayoquot store in 1889, John Penney put his stamp on the new enterprise he and Brown had acquired. They released Thornberg, who had by then served fifteen years at Clayoquot, and he moved permanently to Ahousat. To replace him, Penney brought in one Mr. Smith from Victoria to manage the Clayoquot venture, and shortly afterward, in November 1890, Ralph Smailes, accompanied by his wife, Mary, and their two children, arrived to take charge. On January 7, 1891, the *British Colonist* reported that Penney had "erected a powerful red light 50' high" to aid navigation; this consisted of a metal scaffolding on the northwest sandspit of the island, on which he lit bonfires when expecting a schooner. That year he also became the first postmaster of the proudly acquired Clayoquot Post Office. "Clayoquot Station is the West Coast Post Office," announced the *British Colonist*, "the most westerly in the Dominion, [receiving] mail from Victoria bi-weekly." In 1891, Penney produced a "neat and reliable chart of Clayoquot Sound," according to the newspaper, and the following year he became the first magistrate and Justice of the Peace in the district. With each of these official appointments, Clayoquot became more firmly established as an emerging settlement. The era of the rough and ready trading post was drawing to a close.

As the first postmaster at Clayoquot, Penney faced stiff challenges. Initially he arranged for mail to come via Ucluelet, then overland to Tofino Inlet, and then by boat to Clayoquot. The April 26, 1890, issue of the *British Colonist* described the difficulties:

The present mail route is rather difficult—especially the portion of it between Ucluelet and Clayoquot Sound, which crosses the peninsula through a bad trail. Mr. Penney has men at work on this portion of the trail, but it will require considerable labor expended on it before it is fairly passable. The mail carrier, Tatouche, which means "thunder and lighting," is an energetic Indian. His contract is no sinecure. On his last trip he had to drag his canoe over 2 miles [3.2 kilometres], along a mud flat in a small stream when the tide was out, and his one passenger, Alexander Begg, had to walk through the mud and water, knee deep, to reach the canoe.

In later years, mail arrived at Clayoquot aboard the regular coastal steamers, a much simpler method.

Although the census of 1891 indicates only a handful of people living at Clayoquot—the Smailes family accounting for four—settlers gradually began to trickle into the region after that date. The earliest settlers who came and stayed in the Tofino area pre-empted land in scattered locations up Tofino Inlet and in various bays; a few pre-empted land out at Schooner Cove and Long Bay (Long Beach). By 1894 these settlers included several whose names continue to be reflected in the area, commemorated in place and street names, and acknowledged as leading pioneers. At the time, all faced the same daunting challenges of raw land, dark forests, endless rain; their lives revolved around clearing land, trying to establish productive gardens, and eking out a living as best they could. Several did some prospecting for minerals. Among these earliest settlers: John Grice, Jacob Arnet, John Eik, George Maltby, William Kershaw, Thomas Wingen, Haray Quisenberry, John Chesterman, Jens Jensen, Bernt Auseth, Ole Jacobsen. Yet none of these could claim to be the first Europeans to try to settle permanently on the Esowista Peninsula; the Evans family had been first.

The previous decade, in the fall of 1881, David Evans, his wife, Hannah, their four young daughters, and three-month-old baby, Virgil, travelled up the coast by sealing schooner and set up home in a rough little cabin somewhere near the site of the present-day government dock in Tofino. In all likelihood, Evans worked in conjunction with Hugh McKay at least part of the time, or he attempted to build on trade relations McKay had earlier established in that location. He tried to operate a small trading business, but he evidently lacked McKay's experience and proven ability to deal with aboriginals, even though he spoke the trading jargon fluently. According to family lore, two shipwrecked sailors, rescued by Evans in Tofino harbour, came to live with the family. Only sketchy information survives, but the Evans family, despite assistance from these two men, clearly had a difficult time. Hannah found the life extremely challenging, being the only European woman in the entire area, and David Evans did not draw back from confrontation. Several frightening faceoffs with aboriginals resulted. The worst occurred when the Evans children, who liked to play in the nearby Native burial ground, took beads and trinkets from the burial boxes. Fearing infection from this contact, Evans burned the burial ground, an outrageous sacrilege in the eyes of the aboriginals. The Evans family lasted only two years before giving up; they traded cedar shakes for a large dugout canoe and left for the Alberni area, later moving near Seattle. In 1904, their son Virgil and his wife, Mary, returned and settled in the emerging community of Tofino, where they remained for many years.

At the Clayoquot trading post, Penney and his partner Brown, who appears to have played only a minor role in the enterprise, continued in charge until the spring of 1893. They sold out that year to Victoria merchant Thomas Earle, by then a man of considerable property. The Fraser River gold rush had lured Earle west from his native Ontario, but having little success as a miner, he moved to Victoria in 1862. There he found work as a bookkeeper in J. Rueff's grocery business. In 1867 he set out for the Big Bend gold rush on the upper Columbia River, where he ran a successful general store at French Creek, supplying miners. Returning to Victoria, he bought into Rueff's business, and following Rueff's death in 1873, Earle took over the business. By 1881, Earle's Victoria Coffee and Spice Store on Wharf Street at the foot of Johnson Street was prospering nicely. That year Earle branched out and invested in railways in Washington and Oregon as well as on Vancouver Island, and two years later he also became a founding shareholder and board member of the Canadian Pacific Navigation Company, working alongside many prominent businesspeople. In the 1880s, Earle also became interested in the salmon canning industry, investing in the Alert Bay Canning Company on Vancouver Island's east coast, the first cannery between the Skeena and the Fraser Rivers. In 1888 he became part owner of the cannery, joining forces with Stephen Allen Spencer, a Victoria studio photographer of some note, who had helped found the operation in 1881, producing canned salmon under the Nimpkish brand name.

In order to serve his Alert Bay cannery and his dry goods business, the energetic Earle acquired seven boats "of about 100 tons each," including the steamer *Mystery*, which he had built in 1890 at the cost of $20,000. In 1900, flush with his commercial success, he hired Victoria architect Thomas Hooper to build a modern office and warehouse on Yates Street in Victoria. This building still stands, now designated a heritage building. In addition to his widespread commercial interests, Earle involved himself in federal politics; Victorians elected him as their Conservative Member of Parliament in 1891 and twice more, in 1896 and 1900.

By the time Earle acquired the Clayoquot store in 1893, this establishment had become the most important settlement on the west coast north of Victoria. J.C. Brocklehurst served as its second postmaster, remaining there just over a year, and then Earle appointed Filip Jacobsen to manage the store; in 1895 Jacobsen became postmaster. Described by Cliff Kopas in his book *Bella Coola* as "long, lean, learned and loquacious," Jacobsen had been living on the coast of British Columbia for some time. His facility in the Chinook trading jargon, and his experience and ease in trading with aboriginals, made him an ideal employee. Some years before, in 1888, Jacobsen pre-empted 65 hectares of land in the Bella Coola region, and he had been involved in promoting the area for settlement. Later a large number of Norwegians would settle there, encouraged by Jacobsen. In his travels on the coast, Jacobsen often visited Alert Bay, where he came to know

Stephen Spencer, Earle's partner in the cannery.

Jacobsen had first arrived in British Columbia in 1885 to acquire First Nations artifacts for the Berlin Royal Ethnological Museum, working alongside his elder brother Adrian. The two brothers scoured the coast, collecting artifacts, and later that year returned to Germany with a group of nine Bella Coolas (Nuxalk). This aboriginal group spent thirteen months in Europe, appearing at various zoological gardens as living ethnographic displays. They demonstrated their hunting skills, their gambling games, and their dances, including elements of the exotic cannibalistic ritual called the *hamatsa*. Huge audiences gathered to see them, up to 3,000 people at a time. The Bella Coolas wore European clothes, learned some German, and came home unscathed, escorted by Filip Jacobsen.

Meeting these Bella Coolas in Germany proved to be a turning point for the young German ethnologist Franz Boas, introducing him to First Nations culture of the West Coast. The following year Boas visited the coast for the first time and started his ethnographic work, collecting bones and skeletons. By 1890 he had some 200 skulls from all over Vancouver Island. From the outset, this type of collecting stirred up resentment and protest, and it also required the collaboration of knowledgeable agents in the field, among them the Jacobsen brothers.

The Jacobsens and others, including, to varying degrees, most of the storekeepers and traders on the coast, played an essential role in another form of collectors' mania that struck the Pacific Northwest. Throughout Europe and North America, northwest coast cultural artifacts of every description had become objects of desire: potlatch paraphernalia, masks, hats, carvings, totems, cedar implements. Museums and private collectors scrambled to obtain this material, particularly from the mid-1870s to the end of the century. With the active participation of experienced local traders from Vancouver Island and Haida Gwaii to the central BC coast and up to Alaska, hundreds of thousands of items left the northwest coast in crates, loaded on board schooners and steamers. Entire boxcars filled with such material then travelled by train across North America.

Ever since the first European contact on the West Coast in the

1770s, the highly crafted artifacts and cultural items of First Nations people attracted avid attention from the newcomers. No fewer than twelve members of Captain Cook's crew gathered material, including both domestic and ceremonial items, that ended up in the British Museum or in private collections. Alejandro Malaspina for Spain and George Vancouver for England had specific instructions to gather "artificial curiosities" and exotic items to bring home. Malaspina spent fifteen days collecting materials in Nootka Sound, destined for the Royal Museum in Madrid. Much of the material amassed by these early visitors in the eighteenth century eventually found its way into collections and museums ranging from Cambridge to Florence, from Vienna to Helsinki, exciting further interest. By the latter decades of the nineteenth century, major American museums aggressively led a renewed hunt for artifacts, the first hint evidenced in 1863 when the Smithsonian Museum circulated a request to interested parties all over the West Coast, including Vancouver Island and British Columbia, indicating it wanted to extend "its collections of facts and materials" about northwest coast peoples, stressing immediacy because "the tribes themselves are passing away or exchanging their own manufactures for those of the white race."

According to Douglas Cole in his book *Captured Heritage*, a perfect storm of events conspired in favour of the collectors, with rapid expansion of museums all over the world being funded by burgeoning industrial capital at a time of expanding colonialism and settlement. Simultaneously, the "calamitous decline of the native population... must have created a surplus of many objects at precisely the period of the most intense organized collecting." Put starkly, in some coastal communities, more ceremonial artifacts may have existed than people able to use the items. The diminishing population of aboriginals had little defence, with their increasing dependence on a cash economy, local middlemen pressuring them to sell, and priests and politicians undermining the value of their traditions.

At Clayoquot and other coastal trading posts, the traders and storekeepers handled special requests from collectors seeking large items like totem poles and dugout canoes, and they also began to supply the

From Frederick Landsberg's collection of northwest coast artifacts. Landsberg was the largest of five "curio dealers" in Victoria, shipping large collections of carvings, baskets, masks and totems to museums in the United States. The Empress Hotel in Victoria purchased two totem poles from him. Like the other dealers, Landsberg purchased material from middlemen all along the coast.
Image AA00037 courtesy of Royal BC Museum, BC Archives

busy handful of "Indian curio" shops that sprang up in Victoria. The early tourist trade emerging in that city in the 1870s displayed a keen appetite for carvings, baskets, and totems, an appetite that grew over time. Between 1880 and 1912, five different curio businesses operated in Victoria. While they serviced the special needs and requests of collectors and curators, these curio dealers also supplied the hungry and less discerning tourist market. Aaronson's Indian Curio Bazaar on Government Street claimed to be "the cheapest place on the Pacific Coast to buy all kinds of Indian Baskets, Pow-Wow Bags, Wood and Stone Totems, Pipes, Carved Horn and Silver Spoons, Rattles, Souvenirs, Novelties, Etc." Over on Johnson Street, Hart's Indian Bazaar respectfully invited the public, "especially tourists," to visit this shop with the "largest and finest assortment of curios on the Pacific coast." At Stadthagen's Indian Trader, 79 Johnson Street, collectors could buy not only trinkets and baskets, but also large totem poles.

Aboriginal carvers and weavers on the West Coast began producing goods specifically for the tourist trade, often selling through middlemen like Filip Jacobsen and later Walter Dawley at Clayoquot. A steady market developed for baskets, mats, carvings, totem poles, silver jewellery, spoons, plates, and ceremonial gear. As time passed, collectors and dealers became increasingly particular, alarmed by the influx of "tourist-quality" curios and artifacts. Walter Dawley's correspondence contains a number of insistent requests for fine-quality carvings and baskets, specifically rejecting the items made for tourists, or those using European dyes. Nonetheless, this tourist trade material found, or perhaps even created, its own thriving market that continued to grow. Years later, in the mid-1940s, biologist Ed Ricketts commented on this when visiting Clayoquot. Admiring the "old, dull colours" of older artifacts and totems, and seeing the art teacher at Christie Indian Residential School trying to encourage students to study and practise their own traditional art, he wrote, "It does only limited good for us to encourage them...in their own sturdy primitive art [for] when they get back out, what tourists they see will search out and buy the shoddy, gaudy, highly coloured things."

Once established at Clayoquot as store manager and postmaster, Filip Jacobsen proved himself an energetic leader in the emerging settlement. He encouraged other Norwegians to come to Clayoquot, just as he had done in the Bella Coola district. In November 1894 he wrote to the Chief Commissioner of Lands and Works for British Columbia, asking him to set aside land for his fellow countrymen. "I have been out here on the West Coast round Clayoquot Sound specially and I have come to the conclusion that there is an opportunity to have another Norwegian settlement...I will try to get another settlement of honest and sober men...a lot of fishing could be done." Jacobsen's letter prompted the commissioner to write back that the government would survey the land around Clayoquot as soon as possible.

The first of many Norwegian settlers who settled in the Tofino area

Norwegian Filip Jacobsen first came to the West Coast in 1885 to collect northwest coast artifacts for the Berlin Royal Ethnological Museum. In 1893 he became storekeeper at Clayoquot. He campaigned enthusiastically for more Norwegians to settle on the BC coast. *Image F09823 courtesy of Royal BC Museum, BC Archives*

had already arrived by the time Jacobsen wrote this letter, and they had already scouted out the land they wanted. By the end of 1894, Jacob Arnet, Thomas Wingen, Jens Jensen, and Bernt Auseth, all in their early twenties, had registered their land pre-emptions: Arnet, Wingen, and Auseth in Mud Bay (Grice Bay), and Jensen in Jensen Bay, nearer to what would become Tofino. Other Norwegians soon followed, including John Eik, who left Norway in 1891, eventually finding work on a halibut schooner working out of Seattle. His boat put in to Clayoquot Sound during a storm, and the area reminded him so strongly of Norway that Eik vowed to return. He sailed his own sloop up the coast in 1895, accompanied by Ole Jacobsen. The following year, Eik pre-empted 60.7 hectares where Tofino now stands and put up a simple cabin, later building a float house to live in. In 1903, Eik returned to Seattle to marry Serianna Flovik, recently arrived from Norway, and they came back to Clayoquot together. Anton and John Hansen joined the Norwegian settlers in the early 1900s; their sister Julie had already preceded them to Clayoquot, having married Tom Wingen in 1894. Other Norwegians arriving in the area included John Engvik, Michael Haugen, Jacob Knudsen, Ole Larsen, and S. Torgesen.

Jacob Arnet became a leader of the emerging settlement, establishing himself on his 53.4 hectares fronting on Mud Bay. He had worked his way west from Minnesota, eventually gill-netting for the Fraser River canneries in a rented boat, saving to buy his first boat, a robust 6.7-metre sailing vessel. According to his son Trygve Arnet, interviewed in 1981 for *Settling Clayoquot,* "[Jacob] sailed up the west coast and fished in Nootka Sound...They sent the Scandinavians up there because they knew the process. A firm in Victoria would hire a gang of them and send them out." In 1896, having cleared some land and built a small house, Jacob sent for his sweetheart Johanne to join him; they had not seen each other since he left Norway in 1892. She travelled to Victoria in the company of Jacob's brother August, and on May 27, 1896, she and Jacob were married. Their first child, Alma, was born at Clayoquot the following year; six sons followed. A dynasty of west coast Arnets had begun, assisted by the arrival of Jacob's brothers August, Sofus, and Kristoffer, who all followed his lead and settled in the area. When Jacob's grandson, Edward Arnet, arranged a centenary family reunion in Tofino in 1994, some 175 Arnet descendants attended.

John Grice of Newcastle-upon-Tyne became the earliest British settler in the area. Grice arrived in Victoria with his son Arthur in 1891, and he quickly found work aboard the sealing schooner *Mascot*. He does not appear on the Clayoquot census for 1891, but he showed up there that year, scouting for land. On May 1, 1893, he pre-empted 83.3 hectares at the head of the Esowista Peninsula, where much of Tofino now stands. Initially, few settlers were interested in this area of land on the peninsula: the Norwegians clustered around Grice Bay; James Goldstraw, George Maltby, and William Kershaw took up land in Schooner Cove; John Chesterman chose a wide swath of land spanning the narrow neck of the peninsula, extending from the beach that now bears his name over to Jensen Bay; and Haray Quisenberry and his wife settled near Cox Bay.

Some of these new arrivals hoped to farm on their clearings in the bush, bringing with them cows or chickens; some wanted only a shack to use as a base camp when they went out prospecting and trapping. Many were unmarried, or if married, their wives tended to join them later. For all of these settlers, Earle's establishment at Clayoquot served as their "town," with its post office, store, and the visiting traffic of sealing schooners and coastal steamers.

From the early 1890s, potential customers looking to buy goods, trade furs, or exchange local news had another option. Across the harbour from Clayoquot, on an island near Opitsat, Thomas Stockham and Walter Dawley set up shop as general traders in direct competition with Thomas Earle. Stockham had arrived in Canada from his native

From the mid-1890s onward, Walter Dawley dominated commercial activity around Clayoquot Sound. Having first established his store on Stockham Island, he opened two satellite stores at Nootka and Ahousat. His stores became gathering places for miners, sealers and aboriginals. He became a Justice of the Peace and Mining Recorder and he kept a watchful eye on Thomas Earle's store at Clayoquot on Stubbs Island, hoping one day to hold a monopoly on all trade in the area.

Courtesy of Joan Nicholson

England in 1879, and by 1890 he turned up in Victoria, finding employment with a surveying crew. Dynamic and energetic, always keen to try new ventures, Stockham developed a liking for the west coast during his season of surveying. His name pops up on the 1891 census for Kyuquot, giving his occupation as "farmer," an unlikely description for a man destined to be a wheeler-dealer. Stockham found his way down to Clayoquot and by February 1894 had pre-empted the fourteen-hectare island that still bears his name; two years later he received a Crown grant to the island. He had established himself on the island before 1894, because by then he had already opened the store that became known as Stockham and Dawley's. How Stockham met his business partner, Walter Dawley, remains uncertain. Possibly they met over a drink in Victoria during the brief period in 1892 when Dawley worked in the city as a bartender. Hailing originally from Morrisburg, Ontario, Dawley had come west to Victoria in his early thirties, perhaps to get away from the family farm, perhaps to seek his fortune in new surroundings. In 1894, Dawley pre-empted land out at Schooner Cove, his first acquisition of many.

To build their store, Stockham and Dawley used "shipwrecked lumber from Schooner Cove on Long Beach, rafted it and towed it down with a canoe nine miles [14.5 kilometres], not even a row boat available," according to a scrap of memoir left by Dawley. This lumber came ashore near Dawley's land, the event reported in the *Colonist* in May 1893. "A big load of lumber...drifted on to the beach at Long Beach...Some settlers are at work trying to save the lumber, the place where it drifted ashore being very shoaly, where an immense surf breaks in from the ocean. Owing to its position no steamer could pick it up conveniently, and as there is such a large quantity there Captain Foote thinks the settlers can only save a comparatively small portion of the cargo." Enough, however, to build a store.

Through the mid- to late 1890s, Stockham and Dawley went from strength to strength as traders on Stockham Island, pursuing all possible means of gaining influence in local commerce and politics. They took out a number of mining claims and continued to pre-empt more land. Before the end of 1896, Stockham had acquired not only his island but also land at Long Bay, at Mud Bay, and in Sydney Inlet. Dawley eventually owned seven parcels of land, taken out either in his or, following his marriage in 1908, his wife Rose's name. His brother Clarence, who joined him on the coast in 1900, staked many mineral claims around Clayoquot Sound and up at Nootka, and he also acquired several tracts of land.

Having a taste for influential positions, by 1895 Walter Dawley had become a Justice of the Peace for Clayoquot. In 1898 he became the first mining recorder in Clayoquot Sound, a shrewd move that ensured all prospectors and miners passed through the Stockham Island store to record mining claims. Critically for their business, Stockham and Dawley fostered close relationships with the sealing captains, always striving for a monopoly on their trade. Dawley became a powerful middleman in recruiting aboriginal crews for the sealing schooners, and because Stockham Island lay so near the village of Opitsat, the two storekeepers became well acquainted with the Tla-o-qui-aht people living there. According to George Nicholson in his book *Vancouver Island's West Coast*, particularly good relations existed between Dawley and the Tla-o-qui-aht's Chief Joseph and his wife, Queen Mary. Yet although business seemed set to prosper on Stockham Island, the two traders knew their location to be flawed. The place did not offer a good anchorage or anywhere to build a substantial dock, and the small, rocky island offered few opportunities for future development and little space for expansion. Earle's establishment at Clayoquot, in that respect, definitely held the upper hand.

Clayoquot gained an even higher profile in the mid-1890s with the appointment of a resident policeman. Constable Frederick Stanley Spain first showed up there in 1894; provincial police records reveal that he received a total of four months' pay ($60 per month) that year for policing great stretches of Clayoquot Sound from Stubbs Island. The following year he took up his position there full time, patrolling his domain mostly by rowboat, doing his utmost to stop sealing captains selling liquor to aboriginals, among other challenges. He would travel by steamer to far-flung locations to carry out his work, ranging as far as Kyuquot. Spain pre-empted 28 hectares on Stubbs Island in 1896, the entire southern section of the island.

Several years after his arrival, Spain's cousin, Dr. P.W. Rolston, arrived at Clayoquot, the first resident doctor on the west coast. With his wife and young family, Rolston disembarked from the steamer *Willapa* in September 1898; they remained on Stubbs Island for over two years. Probably to her relief, Mrs. Rolston discovered she had female company there: Helga Jacobsen, who married Filip in 1894; Marion Spain, who married her policeman husband in 1895; and from 1899, Annie Brewster, who lived there with her family and husband, Harlan, at least some of the time. Harlan Brewster succeeded Jacobsen as store manager and postmaster in 1899, living at Clayoquot for several years. Better known locally for his later work as cannery owner and manager at Kennfalls, Brewster eventually took up a career in politics that culminated in a brief stretch as provincial premier.

Recollecting her time at Clayoquot, Mrs. Rolston wrote of "the long low line of buildings...in the trading establishment," and the comforts of eating "excellently cooked meals as a good Chinese cook can produce" in the large dining room in the Jacobsens' home. Her vivid recollections of how "every day brings fresh miners and prospectors... with a feverish desire to get gold and other precious metals" led her to conclude that, "by and by, no doubt there will be men and means to make this a western port of great importance."

With the growing numbers of prospectors and settlers on the coast and the increasing maritime traffic, Thomas Earle decided in 1898 to

The hotel at Clayoquot on Stubbs Island built by Thomas Earle in 1898. In 1902 Thomas Stockham and Walter Dawley took over the establishment and for many years their hotel, restaurant and bar attracted locals and travellers in the area. This hotel burned down in 1908 and was rebuilt, only to go up in flames in 1922 and be rebuilt yet again. *Ken Gibson collection*

improve his dock. An upgrade was badly needed, for according to Mrs. Rolston "the storekeeper's wharf [was] not...serviceable at low tide." Earle built an ambitious structure, a long curving dock, extending far out from shore with a trolley running on narrow steel tracks from the store to the end of the dock. This would facilitate the loading and unloading of goods from the Canadian Pacific Navigation Company's new steamer *Queen City*. This 36-metre-long passenger and cargo steamer, resplendent with electric lights, began making twice-monthly runs up and down the coast beginning in December 1898, largely replacing the much-derided old "washtub" *Willapa* that had doggedly plied the coast for some years. Also in 1898, Earle built a hotel to accommodate visitors, prospectors, sealing captains, would-be settlers, and those awaiting passage on the steamer.

Given the comings and goings at Clayoquot, and with the perpetual problem of trying to control the sale of liquor to aboriginals, the harassed Constable Spain faced constant challenges in performing his duties. The constable's job, extending as it did throughout Clayoquot

At Clayoquot, around 1907. Walter Dawley stands in the doorway; Reece Riley is seated to the right of Dawley; Ewen MacLeod, Clayoquot's policeman, is seated to the right of Riley; and Arthur Grice, in the hat, is standing behind him.
Image PN13829 courtesy of Port Alberni Museum

Sound, never promised to be easy, but he found his duties rendered even more difficult by the lack of co-operation from the Justices of the Peace along the coast. These JPs generally included the better-known and more influential settlers. According to a letter of complaint Spain wrote to the Attorney General on November 22, 1900, all of these JPs, everywhere on the west coast from Clo-oose to Quatsino, failed to do their duty properly. He reserved his most severe criticisms for the four JPs at Clayoquot. In his estimation, the "administration of the law has been most glaringly miscarried on many occasions" thanks to the local JPs: Walter Dawley, because he would never sit in judgment on any case that might be against his commercial interests; Dr. Rolston, because he would not prejudice his medical practice; George Maltby, because he lived at Long Bay and found it difficult to come to Clayoquot to hear cases; and John Grice, "the oldest and most unfit," being "under the thumb of Mr Dawley." Quite possibly this condemnation arose in part because Grice had lively sympathies with the aboriginals; as shipping master at Clayoquot he saw a great deal of their interaction with the wily sealing captains, including the bribing of hunters with liquor and the encouragement of gambling on board. Yet clearly, with most JPs unwilling to hear cases, or having strong personal prejudices about each and every local misdemeanour, Constable Spain faced an uphill battle. He remained at Clayoquot, coping as best he could, until 1902, when he moved to New Westminster.

One of the more notable events during Constable Spain's tenure as police constable at Clayoquot occurred when the three-masted American brigantine *Hera* foundered right in Tofino Harbour. On November 25, 1899, Clayoquot settlers found themselves in the thick of the excitement when this stricken ship, on fire and utterly doomed, drifted in sight of their homes on Stubbs Island. Harlan Brewster, busy unravelling Filip Jacobsen's account books, happened to be at Clayoquot that day during the cannery's off-season. Along with Jacobsen, Constable Spain, and three other men—Nigel Campbell, Thomas Carr, and S. Torgesen—Brewster took part in a remarkable rescue mission, observed anxiously by the ladies on shore, including Mrs. Rolston, whose description of the shipwreck and rescue was published in the *Colonist*. With great misgivings, she witnessed her husband's cousin, Constable Spain, embarking on this hazardous venture, going to the aid of a ship they initially believed had struck a rock. "I think you can imagine...my anxiety, as well as Mrs. Jacobsen's and Mrs. Brewster's whose husbands went also. It was a very brave act as they encountered a great deal of danger."

Hera had sailed from Seattle on November 18, fully loaded and heading to Honolulu in the charge of Captain J.J. Warren. Her 700-ton cargo included 1,800 barrels of lime; 1,000 cases of bottled Rainier beer; 2 carloads of tinware; a carload of tinned corn; 10 pianos; 50,000 board feet of lumber; and a quantity of wheat, oats and bran, not to mention part of a church that had been built in Wisconsin, which was carried as deck cargo. After sheltering for several days at Clallam Bay, WA, to escape the stormy weather, *Hera* had ventured out, running into a terrific southeaster that drove her northward up the coast of Vancouver Island. Off Clayoquot, the incoming sea water made contact with *Hera*'s cargo of lime, setting it and the ship on fire. The captain ordered a distress flag, a red tablecloth, be hoisted, and he aimed for the nearest land. By the time *Hera* approached the entrance to Tofino Harbour, she had been burning for twenty-four hours, with the frenzied crew trying to contain the fire below decks. With her sails blown out and smoke pouring from nearly every seam, the ship wallowed helplessly. The captain loaded himself, his daughter (the only female passenger), and three others into *Hera*'s lone lifeboat and set out for shore.

The six rescuers from Clayoquot battled through the heavy seas in their rowboat toward the burning ship. As they passed *Hera*'s lifeboat carrying the ship's captain and his passengers, they shouted back and forth, trying to get a picture of the situation. When the rescuers arrived beside the fully engulfed ship, according to Mrs. Rolston they found "desperate men ready to jump into the boat as soon as she came near enough. Of course if they had done this the boat would have been swamped and all drowned, and it was only by standing up with axes in hand and calling out that the first man who jumped in would be killed that this was prevented. Then one by one they were safely got on board. By this time the whole ship was red hot." The five crewmen, and their rescuers, made it safely ashore.

The abandoned *Hera* continued drifting toward shore, observed with fascination by Mrs. Rolston:

> The wind was blowing very strong, and the tide was coming in, and she came along with it just as though she had had Captain and crew on board steering her. As I write, she is just in front of the house, on a sand bar, one of the grandest and yet one of the most awful sights I have ever seen. The whole room is lit up with the light from her, and I have only to turn my head to see her. She is one mass of raging flame, and as it is a very black night, the entire harbour is lit up.

The ship burned to the waterline, with only her masts left visible. Remarkably, much of her cargo, including the beer, remained intact, as later salvage efforts revealed.

Captain Warren faced stern criticism for taking the only lifeboat and abandoning his ship with men aboard. "The Captain of the burning ship acted like a brute," wrote Mrs. Rolston indignantly. "There was only one boat, and he and the owner of the vessel, with his daughter and 2 men, got into it and left the others to perish. [Those left aboard] had built themselves a raft, but it would have been worse than useless in such a sea." The Royal Humane Society awarded each of the Clayoquot rescuers its bronze medal, and the US State Department acknowledged its "keen appreciation of the gallantry and heroism displayed" by the Clayoquot men, authorizing the American consul in Victoria to present each of the six men with a gold lifesaving medal on behalf of the US president. In 2012, the gold medal presented to Nigel Campbell showed up in the hands of a coin dealer in the United Kingdom; through the efforts of David Griffiths of the Tonquin Foundation in Tofino, the coin has been returned to the west coast.

In 1974, John Svoboda, a local crab fisherman, hooked the sunken remains of the *Hera* off Felice Island, and local diver Rod Palm went down to investigate, finding a world of shipwrecked wonders half buried in the sand: "deck knees, ship's rigging, deadeyes and bottles everywhere," as David Griffiths enthused in his 2002 *Tofino Time* article about the find. Thanks to the efforts of Rod Palm and others, the wreck of the *Hera* became British Columbia's first protected underwater heritage site.

Over on Stockham Island, Walter Dawley and Thomas Stockham had been thoroughly upstaged by Earle's new dock and hotel at Clayoquot. They must have been infuriated, for earlier in 1898 they too had opened a hotel, the very first on the west coast. Catering largely to prospectors and sealing captains, their six-bedroom establishment lacked the graces of the sixteen-room hotel at Clayoquot. There, visitors could find a private ladies' dining room and refinements such as potted plants in the dining room, framed pictures on the wall, and even looking glasses and rugs in several of the bedrooms. The hotel on Stockham Island had few of the finer things of life, apart from a stuffed pelican decorating the saloon, although it was liberally supplied with spittoons. As for the fancy new dock at Clayoquot, it could only remind Stockham and Dawley of the sketchy facilities at their own establishment. Described by the *Colonist* in April 1900 as "a flimsy and dilapidated structure," their dock eventually collapsed completely under the weight of cargo from the steamer *Willapa*. So Clayoquot held all the cards: excellent dock, good moorage, better hotel, regular visits from *Queen City*, large expanse of flat, easily accessible beach waterfront. Still, the two traders on Stockham Island persevered, building powerful trading relationships on the coast, biding their time, keenly alert to future opportunities, and always keeping a close and suspicious eye on developments over at Clayoquot.

Stockham and Dawley did have one potent advantage over Earle's enterprise at Clayoquot; their strong influence up the coast through their satellite stores. In 1894 they opened a store at Yuquot, employing John Goss as manager, and in 1895–96 they opened a store at Ahousat, with Fred Thornberg in charge. These stores gave them a firm hold on aboriginal trade in goods and furs, and a powerful role in provisioning and assisting the sealing schooners. Brokering deals between sealing captains and aboriginal sealing crews became central to their business. The best seal hunters on the coast came from Opitsat and Ahousat; to organize their employment and to corner their custom translated into a lot of money. Stockham and Dawley would offer advances on wages during the sealing season, which all too often meant that local hunters, having equipped themselves at Stockham and Dawley's stores, went hunting while their families lived on credit; the hunters often returned to find themselves more in debt than when they left.

Because most of Stockham and Dawley's inbound correspondence has survived, a vivid picture of their commercial world can be pieced together. Their correspondents ranged from prospectors to sealing captains to earnest settlers requiring information or credit. From up the coast, the storekeepers in Nootka and Ahousat—particularly Fred Thornberg—bombarded their employers with letters about everything imaginable: dogfish oil, damp flour, aggrieved descriptions of unloading goods from coastal steamers in the pouring rain. Everyone who owned pen or pencil on the west coast seems to have written to Stockham and Dawley at some point: politicians, prospectors, missionaries, Indian agents, curio collectors, aboriginal customers—even the rival storekeeper at Clayoquot on Stubbs Island. At one point, Harlan Brewster wrote to ask to borrow Stockham and Dawley's piledriver, and letters survive showing Brewster and Dawley united in opposition to their common foe, "the Chinaman." In one letter, Brewster suggested to Dawley that they "load the Chinaman to his destruction financially with furs at high prices."

Around 1901 this "Chinaman," Sing Lee, had established his store over on the Esowista Peninsula, near the present site of the government dock in Tofino. Initially, Sing Lee probably worked on a small scale, selling and buying furs from aboriginals, and stocking only basic provisions for early Chinese gold prospectors. With increasing traffic in the area, and with a growing number of Chinese gold seekers and itinerant workers coming and going, Sing Lee's trade escalated, becoming ever more of an irritant to the other traders. Dawley repeatedly demanded that his suppliers refuse to deal with Sing Lee; some suppliers cravenly complied, but the feisty Victoria wholesaler Simon Leiser retorted, "You are getting the goods cheaper than the chinaman or anybody else... why you should kick I do not know." Sing Lee remained in the area, buying furs, trading, and seeking gold until his death in 1906. Well known on the coast, a frequent traveller on the coastal steamers, his death received a lengthy mention in the Victoria newspapers—at the time, an unusual tribute for a Chinese person.

Descriptions of social life among settlers in the early years rarely surface, but on occasion Filip Jacobsen welcomed groups for celebratory events. *The Colonist* describes how thirty people gathered at Clayoquot for a New Year's Day dance and celebration in January 1896, in the "new building erected by the Clayoquot Fishing & Trading Co, which had been most tastefully decorated for a magnificent banquet provided by Mr Jacobson, the manager." This event could very well have taken place up Tofino Inlet at the recently constructed Clayoquot cannery.

Following many "loyal and patriotic toasts," the assembled crowd, including a good number of Norwegians, drank to the health of the Queen. John Grice then spoke at length of the connections between the British empire and the Norse people; Father Van Nevel, the Catholic priest living at Opitsat, waxed eloquent about the help settlers provided in his missionary work, and another Catholic father recited a short poem in Chinook, complimenting the Clayoquot chief. John Chesterman rounded off the evening with his "humorous versatility" and his impersonation of Santa Claus.

Several months later, Filip Jacobsen organized another remarkable event. To celebrate Queen Victoria's birthday in May 1896, a sports day took place at Clayoquot, with aboriginals "in gala attire." Among the judges of the competitions: Constable Spain; Father Van Nevel; Harry Guillod, the Indian agent at Ucluelet; and Chief Joseph of Opitsat. Canoe races, sack races, every type of race imaginable offered prizes ranging from hats to shoes to silk neckties—even a new bonnet for one of the ladies' events. Jacobsen did not know at the time, but he had set a precedent for what later became known as "Clayoquot Days." For decades, local people consistently gathered at Clayoquot on the May long weekend for community picnics and for sporting events. Sometimes such events also took place at Clayoquot on Dominion Day, now called Canada Day—the first of July.

After Harlan Brewster took over as manager and postmaster at Clayoquot in 1899, Filip Jacobsen briefly took up mining, but eventually he returned to the Bella Coola area. He remained there until his death in 1935. Brewster remained in charge of the Clayoquot store for just over two years, during which time Thomas Earle ran into severe financial difficulties. Back in 1891, Earle had entered federal politics, and his business ventures began to suffer. He also had invested heavily in an American railway that drained his resources to the point he declared bankruptcy in December 1901, much to the shock of the business community in Victoria. Earle never recovered his losses and died financially broken in Victoria in 1910.

Rumours of Earle's impending bankruptcy reached the ears of Walter Dawley and Thomas Stockham early in 1901. They acted quickly to

In 1902, Thomas Stockham and Walter Dawley abandoned Stockham Island and took over Thomas Earle's larger store and hotel at Clayoquot on Stubbs Island, just across the harbour. The coastal steamers regularly called at the long dock, and the community had a resident policeman, mining recorder's office, post office and telegraph. A substantial townsite seemed poised to develop here. *Image A08865 courtesy of Royal BC Museum, BC Archives*

acquire his business interests at Clayoquot, and in February 1902 they bought out Earle's entire holdings on Stubbs Island: land, store, hotel, and dock. Turning their backs on Stockham Island, they moved across the harbour. With their two satellite stores up the coast at Ahousat and Yuquot, with their business interests flourishing, and with all the facilities of Clayoquot at their disposal, Stockham and Dawley became the most influential businessmen on the west coast north of Victoria. Dawley became the new Clayoquot postmaster, a position he held until 1937. The Methodist medical missionary Dr. McKinley, who succeeded Dr. Rolston, shortly afterward took over their original establishment on Stockham Island. The Methodists eventually purchased the property from Stockham and Dawley for $1,500 and transformed the former hotel into a small hospital.

The summer of 1902 saw much agitated lobbying about the telegraph line being extended from Alberni toward Clayoquot. John Chesterman and other settlers wanted the line to terminate on the peninsula, where they firmly believed a new townsite would emerge. Dawley and Stockham wanted it to extend to Stubbs Island by underwater cable. They had their way, and in December 1902 the telegraph instruments were installed at their store, and the telegraph connection to the outside world came alive, radically changing the nature of communication on the coast.

Without doubt, Stockham and Dawley helped set in motion a new and dynamic era in the history of Clayoquot Sound—although perhaps not in the manner they originally wished. Given the burgeoning activity locally, it became evident that a permanent community would emerge. However, apart from a few stubborn settlers like John Chesterman and John Grice, no one at first believed that a community would spring up on the Esowista Peninsula, nor that it could ever eclipse Clayoquot on Stubbs Island. Walter Dawley dismissed the entire notion. He had established himself at Clayoquot confident that all future settlement and commercial activity would take place right there on Stubbs Island. He was wrong.

Chapter 9:

"ALIVE WITH FISH"

WHEN THE FIRST EUROPEANS ARRIVED on Vancouver Island's west coast, the sheer wealth and variety of marine resources amazed them. "The Coast is alive with fish," coastal trader Hugh McKay told the *British Colonist* in June 1859. "Herrings, large and fat, can be taken in shiploads, and so can salmon and dogfish. Along Clayoquot Sound, codfish can be taken in large quantities." Yet despite the evident potential, several decades passed before any serious attempts at commercial fishing began in Clayoquot Sound. This changed when Thomas Earle came on the scene in the spring of 1893. Within a short time of his arrival, Earle determined to open a salmon cannery in the Sound. He knew the business well, for in 1888 he had become a partner in the Alert Bay Canning Company on Vancouver Island's east coast.

Initially, Earle seized the opportunity to exploit the annual salmon runs by opening a saltery at Clayoquot, salting down fish in barrels. On September 25, 1892, the *Colonist* reported: "Steamer *Mystery*, Captain Brown, returned to Victoria last evening from a long and wearisome trip down the West Coast, she brought back as passengers a number of salmon fishermen who early in the season had been supplied with a large number of empty barrels along with several tons of salt to go down to Clayoquot Sound and there catch and pack salmon." *Mystery* returned to Clayoquot in early December 1892 "with four Norwegian fishermen, a quantity of lumber and a large amount of supplies, for the fishing station located there. The Norwegians are men who came out from their native country about 7 weeks ago with the object of leaving on their present expedition. In their own land these men were regarded as experts at their business." Several months later, *Mystery* again delivered salt to the station, and in May 1893 she headed to Stubbs Island with Thomas Earle and Alfred Magnesen on board. Even after Earle opened his cannery at Kennfalls in 1895, the saltery at Clayoquot continued packing fish in barrels for years to come. The *Colonist* reported six years later, on October 1, 1901, that "Talbot and Jacobsen of Clayoquot, and Feker of Kyuquot, have put up from 80 to 100 barrels of salted salmon." A barrel usually held ninety kilograms of salmon.

By 1893, Earle had entered a partnership with Magnesen, his book-keeper and accountant. Magnesen had arrived in Victoria six years earlier from Stavanger, Norway, and he had strong connections within the Norwegian immigrant community in British Columbia. Following two seasons of salting salmon in barrels, on December 22, 1893, Earle and Magnesen formed the Clayoquot Fishing and Trading Company. The *Colonist* announced: "The Clayoquot Fishing & Trading Co Ltd liability, publish their memorandum of association, Alfred Magnesen, Cecil Fletcher and Robert A Cunningham, all of Victoria, as the trustees. The settled object is to engage in the business of fishing, sealing and trading generally, the capital stock to be $15,000, in 100 shares." Typically, Earle's name does not appear at the forefront of the new company. Because of his involvement in so many business ventures, he generally stayed in the background, allowing his managers to assume control of the day-to-day affairs. He also may have been trying to avoid any perception of a conflict of interest associated with his position as a Member of Parliament.

By the summer of 1895, Earle and Magnesen had employed a number of settlers to help build a one-line cannery some twenty kilometres east of Clayoquot, at the mouth of the Kennedy River, where the fish congregated before swimming up to their spawning grounds in Kennedy Lake. By August, according to the *Colonist*, "The cannery at Clayoquot, established somewhat as an experiment, has already 3,000 cases of salmon ready for the market with another 1,000 to follow this week. The supply of fish greatly exceeds the capacity of the cannery." At that time, the industry standard for a case of salmon consisted of forty-eight one-pound cans, most exported to Britain, where it was not uncommon for a working man to eat a can of salmon, at half the cost of beef, for lunch. By 1897, British Columbia canneries shipped $3 million worth of salmon to Britain.

John Eik's well-known seiner *Annie H.* tied up at the Clayoquot cannery. The cannery operated at Kennfalls between 1895 and 1932, providing employment for aboriginal, Chinese and Caucasian workers alike. Note the water barrels on the roof as fire protection. *Monks collection, courtesy of Lois Warner*

The establishment at Kennfalls, typical of canneries at that time, came to resemble a small village. The main cannery building sat on pilings surrounded by a series of docks, and within stood rows of washing and cutting tables where Chinese workers cleaned, washed, and cut the fish into pieces. Aboriginal women packed the pieces into the cans. The Chinese soldered lids onto the tops, leaving a small vent hole, and the cans went into the steam retort for cooking. Afterward, with the vent holes soldered shut, workers lacquered the cans to prevent rust, tested them, labelled them, and packed them into cases for shipment. The cannery boiler needed a mountain of firewood to keep it running during the canning season. Accumulating that firewood gave many Clayoquot Sound settlers paid work during the winter.

Right beside the main cannery stood the can loft and tin shop, which opened for business well before the fishing began, with workers preparing cans for the season. A cavernous net loft stood in another separate building. Here seine nets, made of linen and cotton, hung to dry or to be repaired. The floor of these lofts had to be very smooth so as not to snag the nets, and it served a double purpose as a perfect dance floor on occasion. "The old cotton nets tore easily and needed a great deal of skill to repair them," recalled Ian MacLeod, who used these nets fishing out of Tofino as a young man.

Although considered small by industry standards, the Clayoquot cannery still needed a substantial and steady supply of fish during the season. Alfred Magnesen sought out Norwegians already fishing for Fraser River canneries, enticing them to come to Clayoquot Sound with their small sailing vessels to catch salmon for the cannery. He also employed aboriginal fishermen, who fished from their canoes, often using their wives for additional paddle power. None of the fishermen had to go far afield, for the salmon schooled around the mouth of the Kennedy River, right in front of the cannery.

Sid Elkington, who worked at Kennfalls from 1923 until 1929, described in his unpublished memoirs how the fishery worked: "The sockeye fishing was concentrated at the head of Tofino Inlet near the mouth of the river, close to the cannery. When the later runs of salmon, Chum Cohoe—with scattered Pinks and Spring, entered the Sound, they scattered to various streams in various inlets to spawn, so fall fishing was carried out over a wide area, and additional boats, owned and crewed by Indians from Opitsat and Ahousat reservations joined in the fishing. The total salmon runs of Clayoquot Sound were just sufficient to amply supply a small cannery such as Kennfalls, all taken by purse seines in inside waters." In the early years, fishermen pulled their purse seine nets aboard by hand—power-driven rollers and winches, invented in the 1920s, eventually relieved them of this back-breaking task. Sometimes, to avoid hand-hauling the net, fishermen towed the net to shore and there dispatched the fish into skiffs.

From the skiffs, the catch went into a nine-metre-long scow and then was towed to the cannery. Fishermen worked from dawn till dusk in their open boats, their pay based on the numbers of fish caught, ranging from a few cents to ten cents a fish, depending on demand. Sometimes the catches proved so large the cannery could not keep pace; with no refrigeration, the company had to impose fishing closures,

Crew of seiner *Newcastle #4*, skippered by Jack Lokholm, mid-1920s. Before the days of powered drums and blocks—and for trollers the powered "gurdies"—fishermen had the back-breaking job of hand-hauling heavy, wet nets onto their boats. *Monks collection, courtesy of Lois Warner*

never popular with the fishermen. The *Colonist* described one such closure on August 16, 1895, in the first season of operation: "For a week or more the operations at the Clayoquot Sound cannery had been all but at a standstill, though a 2nd run of salmon started the rush again. There was trouble with the fishermen, too, for a few days the men wanted pay for their idle as well as busy spells, and refused to work until their demands were accorded to. An amicable settlement was arrived at with the canners, however, and the trouble terminated suddenly." As time passed, gasoline engines, reliable "one-lungers" built by Easthope Brothers in Vancouver, made fishing easier, although the motorized boats increased the catch, forcing yet more closures.

Hired as storekeeper and bookkeeper, Sid Elkington also tallied the number of fish, kept an eye on temperature and pressure in the steam retorts, ran supply vessels up and down the inlet to Clayoquot, and even stoked the boiler when the engineer had a break. He also would tow the "gut scow" full of fish offal out into the inlet, and one of the Chinese workers would shovel all the fish waste directly into the water.

Although the cannery offered a variety of accommodations, the aboriginal workers mostly lived in their nearby summer village, Okeamin, at the mouth of the Kennedy River. In the 1920s, some six or eight families from Opitsat would live there and work at the cannery, arriving every spring to prepare the nets, and staying on to work the season. Other workers stayed in separate, segregated quarters. The Chinese had their "China House," where they slept, cooked, played mah-jong and fan-tan, and sometimes smoked opium, legal in Canada until 1908. They also grew large vegetable gardens, took care of their chickens, and tended the pigs they brought in to fatten up and eat. As a young boy, Bob Wingen was intrigued by those pigs; he had never seen a pig before. In the early years of the cannery, the Chinese also did some prospecting, sluicing for gold in their spare time. According to the *Colonist* in 1897: "The Chinamen employed about the cannery devote their evenings and early mornings to the search for the hidden wealth, and although reporting no very important discoveries they are quite as enthusiastic as the rest and can produce at any call quite as many specimens." The cannery manager lived in a grand house, well distanced from the noise and smell of the workplace. "At our cottage near the cannery there was a big wrap-a-round porch, and sleeping space for fourteen," recalled Nan Beere. The youngest daughter of Harlan Brewster, who eventually managed and owned the Kennfalls operation, Nan spent her childhood summers at the manager's house after the turn of the century. "There was a marvelous beach at Kennfalls and I swam there often." She clearly remembered the dignified presence of Tla-o-qui-aht Chief Joseph, who cut firewood for the Brewsters, and his wife, Queen Mary, who did their laundry.

Alfred Magnesen added another ship to Earle's fleet in 1896 when he commissioned the *Clayoquot* to be built, an 24.5-metre coal-fired steamer capable of carrying large freight loads. The *Clayoquot* set off down Tofino Inlet to Clayoquot every ten days or so to meet coastal steamers—initially the *Maude* and *Willapa*; later the *Queen City*, *Tees*, and *Princess Maquinna*—when they made their regular stops there.

Clayoquot Cannery, probably around 1916. *Courtesy of the late Nan Beere*

The *Clayoquot* loaded up all the food and supplies for the cannery and often took cases of salmon to Clayoquot for shipment to Victoria. The vessel even made occasional trips to the capital city to deliver cases of salmon and to pick up supplies. In 1903 she was replaced by the *Edna Grace*, which was in turn replaced in 1912 by the gasoline-powered *Isku* as the cannery's tender.

Encouraged by the success of the Clayoquot cannery, other fish-processing enterprises began to appear along the west coast. In 1896,

Thomas Hooper, the architect from Victoria who designed Thomas Earle's warehouse and office building, opened a cannery at Nootka. The first season proved a bust for this new facility; few salmon showed up, and it packed only fifty cases. Although it shut down after operating for only two years, another cannery opened at Nootka in 1917 and ran successfully for three decades. In 1897, Messrs. Hackett and McDougall began a small smoked-cod operation at Ahousat, helping to diversify the area's fishing industry and providing work for local fishermen ahead of the summer salmon runs. That year they shipped forty to fifty barrels in a two-week period. In 1903 the Alberni Packing Company opened the Uchucklesit cannery on the Alberni Canal, a very successful venture that sold out in 1906 to Wallace Bros. Packing and became the Kildonan cannery. In 1911 another cannery opened farther up the coast at Quatsino.

Ambitious fish-processing schemes have surfaced from time to time in Clayoquot Sound. In 1918, George Brown, principal shareholder in the Union Fish and Cold Storage Company based in Vancouver, proposed building a cold storage plant at Clayoquot on Stubbs Island. The Canadian Pacific Railway's Mr. H. Brodie, on an inspection trip along the coastal steamer route, reported the plant would have the capacity to "handle as many as a million salmon." Company documents in the British Columbia archives reveal that Union Fish and Cold Storage bought an 18.5-square-metre parcel of land from Clarence Dawley for $8,000 on March 16, 1918. This small slice of land stood adjacent to the dock at Clayoquot. Construction began on a cold storage plant in 1918, but the following year the Union Fish and Cold Storage Company ceased to exist, leaving at Clayoquot a large and distinctive red building with vents on the roof. Three years later, on November 18, 1922, the *Daily Colonist* reported that Harry West, a resident of Clayoquot, in partnership with Walter and Clarence Dawley, had applied for a foreshore lease alongside the dock on Stubbs Island, including a building described as "Fish House." The West Mildcure Salmon Company variously operated a cold storage, smoke house, saltery, and mild cure fish plant in that building in the 1920s, and in later years the building continued to be used as a saltery. In the 1940s, it briefly housed a small crab cannery.

In November 1898, New Brunswick-born Harlan Brewster began working as a purser on the coastal steamer *Willapa*. Earlier in the decade Brewster had worked with his brother at the Carlisle cannery on the Skeena River, and he had developed an interest in the cannery business. Thomas Earle met Brewster on one of his many trips up the coast and quickly recognized his talents; in August 1899, Brewster became the new manager of the Clayoquot cannery. Like Earle, Brewster took a lively interest in politics; in 1907 he became a member of the provincial legislature for Alberni and the West Coast, and in 1916 became premier of British Columbia.

The Clayoquot cannery averaged 4,000 cases per season until 1900, when it produced 7,500 cases. In 1901 it put up 7,000 cases and added Japan to its markets. Yet despite the positive outlook for his cannery, Thomas Earle's fortunes dramatically collapsed. Forced into bankruptcy in December 1901, two months later he sold the Clayoquot store to Walter Dawley and Thomas Stockham, with Harlan Brewster purchasing the cannery in partnership with J.L. Beckwith and A.G. McGregor. They renamed it the Clayoquot Sound Canning Company, and Brewster continued in charge until his death in 1918. Over the years he made a number of changes in the cannery's operation, including installing the first commercial fish trap on the west coast in 1906 at Ginnard Point on Meares Island. A heavy tide washed it away that winter, but another, built farther up the inlet, worked more successfully. His most notable contribution to the canning industry remains his introduction of an enhanced sanitary canning system, which saw cans crimped shut and soldered entirely by machinery.

In 1910 the Department of Fisheries built a sockeye salmon hatchery at what became known as Hatchery Beach, on Clayoquot Arm of Kennedy Lake. To construct and to supply the hatchery, all materials and stores had to travel along Tofino Inlet to the Kennedy River rapids, up a trail alongside the rapids, then some twenty kilometres by launch to the hatchery site. This hatchery operated from 1910 until 1935, providing a number of jobs and increasing traffic up and down Tofino Inlet and past the cannery.

Local residents enjoyed occasional visits to the hatchery, where the manager warmly welcomed them. Mike Hamilton, who lived in the area from 1914 to the mid-1920s, first working on the telegraph line and later as a machine shop operator in Tofino, chose to spend his honeymoon at the hatchery, staying in the manager's house. Mike assured his dubious fiancée that it was "a wonderful place, where there have been several honeymoons already." Another well-known local couple, Ted and Dorothy Abraham, spent two weeks there in the mid-1920s, enjoying the scenery and the excellent cooking at the manager's home. The energetic Dorothy investigated the hatchery thoroughly, and asked the manager, William Forsythe, to describe the most exciting event during his time there. His reply came swiftly: "When it rained 11.2 inches [28.5 centimetres] in twenty-four hours!" The overall success of the rain-drenched hatchery remains questionable. Lifelong Tofino resident Ken Gibson said, "It produced a lot of fish but when they put the fingerlings into Kennedy Lake the cutthroat trout ate most of them."

When the telegraph line arrived at Clayoquot in 1902, the cannery patched into it on a branch line. From the cannery, sixteen kilometres of line extended along the shoreline of the inlet, reaching across to Long Beach, where it hooked into the main west coast line. Maintaining the fragile telegraph line and its various branches provided regular employment over many years to different linemen along the coast, each one responsible for a lengthy stretch. They were often obliged to walk the line in terrible weather in search of breaks, which occurred all too frequently due to storms and fallen trees. After 1914, the line extended beyond Clayoquot all the way to Nootka, looping crazily from tree to tree and over bays and inlets along many shorelines, connecting remote homesteads and enterprises and the ever-increasing number of mining camps.

By the 1920s, pilchards began appearing on the west coast for the first time in living memory. Edgar Arnet first noticed them in Tofino

This Clayoquot Sound Canning Company label dates back to the pilchard bonanza on the West Coast in the 1920s. Canning these small, fatty fish proved unsuccessful because the fish were too oily. Pilchard plants up and down the west coast reduced tons of pilchards for oil and fish meal. At the height of the pilchard fishery twenty-six reduction plants existed on the west coast of Vancouver Island. *Courtesy of Roly Arnet*

Inlet in 1917; after talking to aboriginal people he learned that these fish had long been used for cooking, heating, and lamp fuel during the intermittent periods when they showed up on the coast. No one quite knew where they came from, or why, but these extremely oily fish, about the size of a sardine, began turning up in such staggering numbers that the shoals extended for kilometres. "There were literally millions of tons of them," recalled Mike Hamilton. "The Sound teemed with them. They made a sight to be remembered when after dark one could stand in the bow of a power boat and watch the phosphorescent millions hastening out of the way." Eleanor Hancock, in *Salt Chuck Stories from Vancouver Island's West Coast*, described them as "bubbling silvery carpets in the inlets." Their arrival in such numbers ushered in a period of intense commercial activity on the coast. Some canneries, including the Clayoquot cannery, attempted to can pilchards. In 1917, Nootka Cannery put up 10,000 cans of herring and pilchards, along with 45,000 cans of salmon. Mr. H. Brodie of the CPR, who visited Nootka Cannery in 1918, reported that during the one night he stayed there, twenty-five tons of pilchards came in, at least some of which would be canned. "When cooked at a pressure of fifteen pounds for eighty minutes," wrote Mike Hamilton, "this reduced the many bones they possessed out of existence and made them very pleasant eating." Not everyone agreed, and canning pilchards proved unprofitable.

The real value of the pilchards lay in reducing the fish for oil, then drying the remains for fish meal. By the mid-1920s, no fewer than twenty-six pilchard reduction plants had sprung up on the coast, scattered along the inlets between Barkley Sound and Quatsino Sound. Through the 1920s, while the pilchards remained abundant, these plants thrived, many becoming regular stops along the coastal steamer route up the west coast. The Clayoquot Sound Canning Company opened a reduction plant at Shelter Inlet, one of six such plants within the Sound. The Gibson brothers, based at Ahousat, used their piledrivers to set the foundations of many of these plants, and in 1926 they built their own reduction plant at Matilda Creek near Ahousat. In the 1928 season, fishermen harvested 80,000 tons of the little fish, sometimes hauling in 200 to 300 tons of them in a single set. Yet even during the boom years the pilchard runs could be unpredictable, and the reduction plants opened and closed accordingly. In his diary, Father Charles Moser, then the Roman Catholic missionary at Opitsat, noted a temporary shutdown in September 1926, when all the reduction plants on the coast closed because the pilchards had stopped running. Even so, no one dreamed that the pilchards would stop completely. They did. Just as mysteriously as they had arrived, the pilchards began to recede. "They just kept farther and farther out to sea until they disappeared altogether," recalled Mike Hamilton.

In his book *Bull of the Woods*, Gordon Gibson described the final season:

> In May 1932 we started to get ready for the fishing season, which started about the first week of July. We had spent at least $20,000 to get ready: nets were prepared and hung, boats chartered and crews brought in. July passed, then August, and no fish came. There were a couple of hundred boats and 1,000 or more crew aboard as well as 400 men at...reduction plants scattered along the coast from Barkley Sound to Quatsino Sound.

The government sent out its fishing patrol boat, the *Givenchy* with six skippers including myself, to locate the pilchards. We ranged as far south as the Columbia River, zigzagging back and forth making about a 1,000 mile [1,600-kilometre] run searching for the fish. We didn't find them and the pilchards never came back to the West Coast in quantities that are economical to harvest. According to aboriginal sources, the *tsepin*—the Siwash name for pilchards—disappear for long periods, and are one of the continuing mysteries of the sea. There is no explanation for the summer of 1932.

The famous sealing schooner *Favorite* returned to Clayoquot Sound just as the pilchard era began. After the fur seal trade ended in 1911, she had been used as a workshop in Victoria, but in 1916 former sealing captain George Heater took her out of mothballs, rebuilt her interior, and towed her to Sydney Inlet at the north end of Clayoquot Sound. Dismasted, she provided accommodation for some twenty young women Heater brought out from Aberdeen, Scotland, to work at his saltery and fish bait plant. The women set to work salting herring and later pilchard, though that fish had too much oil for the salting process to be entirely successful. The girls' presence attracted immediate attention from the bachelors in the area, as Mike Hamilton noted. As the telegraph lineman for the area, Hamilton frequently stayed at a cabin in Riley's Cove, not far from Heater's enterprise. "A company of girls," he wrote, "...incurred considerable excitement and fun in that far flung outpost." The girls likely inspired the name given to the site of Heater's saltery near the head of Holmes Inlet: Pretty Girl Cove. In 1920, left unattended, the *Favorite* sprang a leak in a fierce winter storm, which also destroyed the large floathouse, various rafts, and the saltery shed. The remains of the once famous schooner still lie at the bottom of Pretty Girl Cove, her final resting place on the coast she had served so long and so well.

During the dying years of the fur seal hunt, another West Coast industry began to make its presence felt in Clayoquot Sound. In 1909, the *Directory of Vancouver Island* described the area around Clayoquot in detail, ending with: "This is...a supply centre for whaling and sealing schooners." By 1909, commercial whaling on the coast had begun in earnest, although in its earliest form it dated back to the 1830s. Then, whaling ships from the eastern seaboard of the United States sailed round the Horn to hunt sperm whales in the Pacific Northwest. By 1834, enough whaling ships were hunting off the West Coast that the Hudson's Bay Company governor, George Simpson, briefly considered making plans to provision them.

In 1869, Captain James Dawson joined forces with Captain Abel Douglas to form the Dawson and Douglas Whaling Company, setting up whaling stations at Whaletown on Cortez Island and at Whaling Station Bay on Hornby Island in the Strait of Georgia. The company hunted humpback whales for their oil, which it sold to the logging industry. Within three years, Dawson and Douglas fell into insolvency because of a scarcity of whales in the confined strait. In 1904, Captains Sprott Balcom and William Grant formed the Pacific Whaling Company to hunt whales off the west coast of Vancouver Island, establishing a whaling station at Sechart in Barkley Sound in 1905, and a second station at Cachalot in Kyuquot Sound in 1907. Their third station, at Page's Lagoon near Nanaimo, halted operations in 1908 because of a lack of whales.

Initially, the company hired experienced whalers from Norway and Newfoundland, a fact noted by Father Charles Moser, who visited the Sechart whaling station in June 1906, where he met "nine Catholic men from Newfoundland [who] are employed and engaged to instruct westerners [in] the whaling business." The company also hired former sealing captains, including Captains Bill and George Heater, to take command of the new steam-driven, harpoon-firing whale catchers. Within two years, and with profits growing, Balcom and Grant formed the Queen Charlotte Whaling Company and opened two more stations at Rose and Naden Harbours in Haida Gwaii. That year, their four whaling stations processed a total of 1,624 whales.

Each plant hired scores of workers, many of them Chinese, Japanese, and aboriginal, to flense and render the carcasses. The sheer volume of whale products emerging from these whaling stations beggars description. Shipments of up to 1,100 barrels of oil at a time from Cachalot and Sechart would arrive in Victoria aboard the steamer *Tees*, along with vast quantities of fertilizer, mostly destined for international markets in Glasgow, San Francisco, and Japan. According to the *Colonist*, on September 14, 1905, during Sechart's first season, the steamer *Queen City* expected to carry "100 tons of guano [fertilizer] and 300 tons of whale oil" on her next trip down the coast.

The plant at Cachalot employed up to 200 men, half of them Kyuquots who lived with their families in small houses supplied by the company. In later years, Cachalot began processing and canning the whale meat, dubbed "sea beef," for domestic and Japanese markets. At times of full production, up to 2,000 cases of meat emerged from the plant each day. Father Charles Moser's diary mentions receiving one of the first cases of canned whale meat from Kyuquot in July 1918; subsequently, the school received canned whale meat on several occasions.

The whaling industry on the coast slowed down around 1909, and the following year Balcom and Grant, whose fortunes remained tied to the dying fur seal trade, sold out to railway magnates Mackenzie and Mann for $1 million. The industry rebounded, only to suffer another setback in 1913, given the glut of whale products on the international market. Two years later, with World War I underway, and aware that whale oil could be used to make explosives, William Schupp bought the company in 1915, renaming it the Victoria Whaling Company. Within a short time, Schupp showed profits of over $1 million annually. Whalers and processors raked in bonuses throughout the war, but the following two decades proved leaner, as the number of whales diminished. Sechart ceased operations in 1917, and the Cachalot plant at Kyuquot closed in 1925.

Between 1908 and 1923, these two west coast whaling stations processed over 5,700 whales. Bizarrely, during their years of operation the whaling stations became a significant tourist attraction on the coastal steamer route. Passengers and crew would disembark for a quick tour, keen to view the great piles of bones and baleen and eager to be photographed alongside the immense carcasses awaiting flensing. Mr. H. Brodie, the CPR inspector touring the coast in 1918, could not comprehend this, appalled as he was by "the most indescribable stench [that] prevails at the whaling station...and makes a large number of people very ill."

The Rose Harbour and Naden stations in the Queen Charlottes continued operating until 1942 when, due to wartime restrictions on travel and the loss of the Japanese market for whale meat, the industry became less viable. In 1948 the Western Whaling Corporation, owned by the Gibson Brothers, established a whaling plant at the old Royal Canadian Air Force station at Coal Harbour, at the northern end of Vancouver Island. Later acquired by BC Packers and a Japanese company, the plant largely processed oil and fertilizer, as well as whale meat for the Japanese market. It remained in operation until 1967, when processors hauled the last whale taken in BC waters up its slipway. By then, Russian and Japanese whaling fleets, equipped with large factory ships to process the whales, were operating offshore and continued to do so until 1975. British Columbia's whaling industry could not begin to compete. With its antiquated ships in need of replacement, with prices falling, and with the whale population diminishing, commercial whaling came to an end on the West Coast.

By the late twentieth century, few if any observers on the west coast of Vancouver Island shared coastal trader Hugh McKay's mid-nineteenth-century optimism about the potential of the coastal fishery. As McKay indicated in 1859, fish of many types could be "taken in shiploads" from the waters so "alive with fish." No longer. Since McKay's time, fishing fleets had harvested enormous, unsustainable quantities, leaving the fishery in dire straits. Fish stocks declined so precipitously that between 1995 and 1997 the Mifflin Plan, put in place by the federal government's Department of Fisheries and Oceans, bought back half the commercial fishing licences on the West Coast in an attempt

Two seine boats, *Aliema* on the left and *Annie H.* on the right, set off for a day's fishing, mid-1920s. These seiners represent a way of life that had entirely vanished by the 1990s. *Monks Collection, courtesy of Lois Warner*

to remedy the situation. This plan reduced the fishing fleet by half and made commercial licences so expensive that only the owners of very large fishing vessels, capable of catching huge numbers of fish, could afford them. The plan did not, however, significantly reduce the number of fish being taken. Stocks continued to decline. Fewer and fewer commercial seine boats plied the waters around Clayoquot Sound.

Thrown out of work, some of the former fishermen opened sport fishing enterprises, or became fishing guides. In Tofino, as in other locations once dependent on commercial fishing, sport fishing gradually evolved during the 1990s to become an integral part the economy—by the 2010s it involved dozens of local outfits and guides. On February 11, 2013, the *Vancouver Sun* reported that "British Columbia's recreational fishery is worth as much to the provincial economy as commercial fishing, aquaculture and fish processing combined."

By 2009 the fleet of BC-based trollers, that had numbered 1,800 in the mid-1990s, dwindled to some 160 trollers fishing the mid-West Coast, following the reductions of the Mifflin plan. That same year, the ten-year Pacific Salmon Treaty signed between Canada and the United States saw numbers decline even more. That treaty saw Canada receive $30 million compensation when it agreed to a 30 percent decrease in the number of chinook (spring) salmon caught by Canadian trollers, in an attempt to protect the fish stocks returning to Washington and Oregon rivers. These catch limits led to the *Victoria Times Colonist* (December 17, 2009) reporting that "this coming fishing year [will] provide enough fish to support 15 to 30 troll boats in the 160-license fleet." The newspaper was quoting Kathy Scarfo, president of the West Coast Salmon Trollers Association, who later commented to the *Globe and Mail* (March 13, 2009), "The days of looking at a harbour and seeing it full of salmon trollers are over."

The future of West Coast fishing remains highly uncertain. Climate change and shifts in water temperature affect the migration paths of salmon, while sea lice and diseases spread from salmon farms further diminish wild salmon stocks. Meanwhile, conscientious groups valiantly continue to repair spawning streams damaged by logging and other industries, hoping for better days ahead. In 2014, the First Nations in Clayoquot Sound won a landmark Supreme Court decision giving them the right to catch and sell fish commercially, and as treaty talks continue, First Nations look set to play a far bigger role in the future of the Sound's salmon, the fish that has sustained them for millennia.

Chapter 10:

"TEEMING WITH RICHES"

THE TANTALIZING POSSIBILITY OF FINDING rich mineral deposits gripped the imagination of many early settlers on Vancouver Island. "The West Coast lands teem with riches in the shape of gold, copper, coal, iron and other metals," declared Dr. J.S. Helmcken of Victoria in a letter to the *British Colonist* in May 1899. While hopes ran high for discovering all these valuable resources along the coast, nothing ever equalled the feverish dream of finding gold.

When the Cariboo gold rush ebbed in the mid-1860s, many of the miners who had come to seek their fortune stayed on in the new colonies of Vancouver Island and British Columbia. Some ventured up the west coast, encouraged by early rumours of gold and other minerals. In 1861, prospectors found small quantities of gold in San Juan Creek near what is now Port Renfrew, and others found copper in Barkley Sound. Four years later, John Buttle unwittingly launched the first rush of gold seekers into Clayoquot Sound.

Formerly a botanist at London's Kew Gardens, Buttle took part in the Vancouver Island Exploring Expedition of 1864, led by Robert Brown and commissioned by Victoria business leaders to explore Vancouver Island and to search for viable mineral deposits. The following year, Buttle led another expedition at the request of the colonial government, then headed by the third and last governor of Vancouver Island, Arthur Edward Kennedy, after whom Kennedy Lake and River are named. As part of his mandate to explore and survey the west coast of the Island, Buttle was responsible for assessing the area in and around Clayoquot Sound. He left Victoria with a six-man party on the HMS *Forward*, and for the next two months they explored every inlet, bay, and river of the Sound. Buttle sent intermittent reports to his superiors in Victoria, which the *Colonist* eagerly reprinted or quoted. In April 1865, he reported that members of his party had found payable quantities of gold in the Bear (Bedwell) River at the eastern end of Bedwell Sound. Buttle then carried on with his explorations elsewhere in Clayoquot Sound and up at Nootka Sound, unaware that his newspaper report had set off a minor gold rush to the area. In August 1865, a group of some 200 avid prospectors set out to Bear River aboard the steamer *Otter*, angrily turning away Chinese gold seekers because, according to the *Colonist*, "feelings of antipathy to the Chinaman setting foot on white men's diggings is too general." But once the prospectors began panning in the Bear River, they discovered very little gold. They remained in the area only a week before returning to Victoria in disgust. The disillusioned men complained bitterly of being duped, accusing Buttle of being irresponsible, and the once enthusiastic reports in the *Colonist* now condemned Buttle as "not fit to command a cook's galley, much less a party of exploration." Soured by this experience, Buttle sailed to California, putting British Columbia behind him. Buttle Lake, in Strathcona Provincial Park, the oldest park in the province, bears his name.

Twenty years later, another burst of activity took place at Bear River. In September 1886 the *British Colonist* reported: "We learn that about a month ago 5 Chinese miners who came from a creek in Alberni Sound made a prospect on Clayoquot Sound, and found on Bear River, which empties into the sound, splendid prospects. The find is good enough to justify the Chinese to break camp at Alberni and 25 Chinese have also gone there." The numbers quickly increased, and in December 1886 the *Colonist* reported that some eighty Chinese had built huts along the Bear River and intended to stay for the winter: "A boss Chinaman brought about $600 in gold dust from Bear River, and he also speaks encouragingly regarding future prospects." Later the newspaper reported: "It is understood that a steamer has been chartered to take in another cargo of Chinese and supplies. It is regrettable, if the diggings are as rich as it is now supposed they are, that they should be exclusively controlled by the Chinese. Some of our white mining population should at once take a trip to the new field and make an effort to open it up." Nonetheless, few Europeans ventured into the area, and mining experts who did go remained dubious about the prospects there.

In July 1887, the provincial minister of mines, John Robson, sent Captain Napoleon Fitzstubbs to Bear River to make an assessment of the situation. Fitzstubbs reported back: "From all I saw on Bear River...I am of the opinion that no remunerative discoveries of gold have been made there hitherto, and...there will not be hereafter." That December all the Chinese, possibly driven away by the sudden death of one of their number, returned to Victoria, "bringing with them the most gloomy reports of their mining operations during the year, and say there is very little gold on the river, at least it does not pay to look for it."

A decade later, hope ran high yet again in the Bear River area. Prospectors returned in numbers to try once more, staking new mining claims and working them more aggressively, now tunnelling and blasting the bedrock to get at the ore rather than sluicing for placer gold flakes in the sands of the riverbed. Promising findings of copper and silver and veins of gold-bearing quartz kept the excitement alive, with hundreds of men coming and going at Bear River in the late 1890s. This surge of activity saw a hastily constructed community called Port Hughes scramble into existence near the mouth of the Bear River. On August 22, 1899, the *British Colonist* described this little settlement as having "assumed very considerable proportions. It is to have a good wharf shortly, and is already the headquarters of 60 or more located mines, a score or more of which are being actively developed." For a short while, Port Hughes became a regular stop on the coastal steamer route, and the place seemed so promising that former Victoria alderman Moses McGregor financed the construction of a fourteen-room hotel "which would not be out of place in any city." This hotel would accommodate not only Bear River prospectors and miners, but others investigating their mining claims in the general area.

The enthusiasm for mining and prospecting throughout Clayoquot Sound and all along the west coast spread like wildfire in the late 1890s. Prospectors flocked onto the coastal steamers, heading north to try their luck. The *Colonist* described the scene aboard the *Tees* on April 21, 1897, the steamer en route from Clayoquot to Ahousat and other stops: "With very few exceptions, every passenger was a prospector, with a formidable looking pack at hand's reach." Any whisper of a positive showing strengthened the determination of the miners and prospectors as they laboured on their claims, chipping and blasting into the rock. They fanned out all around Clayoquot Sound and along the coast, following rumours of good prospects and high-priced sales of properties. The *Colonist* never missed a transaction: "A good deal of interest is being taken in the West Coast mines, as witness the bonding not long ago of 2 groups of claims on Bear River owned by Chris Frank and Mr. Jacobson for $40,000 and $25,000 respectively. The lead on the Black Cap, which shipped 1 ton of ore by *Tees* on her last trip, is 3' wide and assays $67 a ton."

With returns like these, small wonder nearly everyone in the vicinity became involved. Even the Presbyterian missionary at Ahousat and the priests at the Roman Catholic missions began staking claims, hoping to strike it rich. On June 10, 1897, the *Colonist* observed that "Indians, klootchmen [aboriginal women], Chinamen, white men and in general every resident of Clayoquot is a prospector and a firm believer that a great future for that section as a mining country is not very far distant." Filip Jacobsen, then Thomas Earle's manager at Clayoquot, eventually held interests in about thirty claims, while Walter Dawley and Thomas Stockham also held a great many mining interests. From July 1898 onward, as the first official Mining Recorder for the area, Dawley knew every lump of ore and every ounce of gold removed from anywhere in Clayoquot Sound. By the end of that year he had recorded 114 mining claims, four of them placer claims. With such traffic through his store, he heard all the gossip and did a brisk trade with the miners. For a number of years around the turn of the century the store's letterhead declared "MINERS' SUPPLIES A SPECIALTY: A Full Line Constantly Kept in Stock."

Although the Bear River/Port Hughes excitement did not last long, at its peak dozens of men toiled long and hard at their claims. At first they carried their ore out in haversacks, later by packhorse, along the rough fourteen-kilometre trail and over the seven rudimentary bridges they had constructed, extending from the claims high up in the mountains at the head of the Bear River, down to the mouth of the river.

From there, the ore travelled to Victoria aboard the coastal steamers *Tees* or *Queen City*, and on to smelters at Ladysmith or Crofton on the east side of Vancouver Island, or to Tacoma in Washington. Americans took a keen interest in this mining boom, buying up a number of promising claims. On March 8, 1898, the *Colonist* reported: "One sale is that of the Crow group which Messrs. Jacobsen, Drinkwater and Peterson have disposed of to Spokane and Tacoma people for $20,000 cash. Another deal just made is the transfer of the BeShaklin claim owned by Stockham and Dawley, Clayoquot, for $10,000. This claim is situated on Sidney Inlet adjoining the Jones and Kincaid property." The following year the newspaper declared that "the coast is overrun with American mining speculators looking for 'good things.'"

Canadian speculators also rushed to invest, evidenced by the flood of reports in the Victoria newspapers. In December 1897: "Leslie Jones, who has just returned from spending 8 months in that mineral belt of the Island, states that all the way from Sidney Arm to Hesquoit, a distance of 6 miles [10 kilometres], is staked out. Mr. Jones is associated with Messrs Morris and C. E. Cooper, of this city, in the ownership of a number of claims on Bear River, besides 6 at Hesquoit and 3 more, which are a continuation of the Jones and Kincard [Kincaid] group on Sidney Arm." The same Leslie Jones wrote to Stockham and Dawley from one of his claims in mid-1897, requesting that they send a case of rye whiskey on the next boat. Such orders arrived often from men marooned at their isolated claims, requesting booze, blasting caps, dynamite, tobacco, "prospecting shoes," and food.

The mining claims in Sydney Inlet turned out to be the most promising and active in all of Clayoquot Sound, championed in the late 1890s by the irrepressible prospector James Jones, known as "Black Jones." His cheerful letters to Walter Dawley brim with optimism and good humour. "Excuse this writing," he announced in one letter from Sydney Inlet in July 1898, "my only table is a gold pan." By then, Jones and his partner, James Kincaid, had been keenly working their claims on Peacock Mountain, alongside Stewardson Inlet on the west side of Sydney Inlet, for nearly a year. With a team of a dozen or so men they had erected cabins and a blacksmith shop and driven at least one tunnel eighty metres into the rock. Their sacks of ore travelled out to the smelters on the coastal steamers, sometimes picked up from Fred Thornberg's trading post at Ahousat. Thornberg grumbled in his letters about having to load what he called "Jones oar" from freight scows and canoes to the steamer, a task he loathed almost as much as loading barrels of dogfish oil. Delighted with his initial findings, Jones became known as one of the best prospectors in the district, praised by the newspaper in 1897 for finding "the prettiest peacock copper seen in Victoria in recent months."

Such reports kept optimism alive among the miners and prospectors as they laboriously made trails to their claims and chipped their way into the rock. They ardently followed rumours of good prospects and stories of high-priced sales of properties. They christened their claims with evocative names like Iron Duke and American Wonder on Tranquil Creek; Indian Chief in Sydney Inlet; Iron Cap and Kalappa on Lemmens Inlet; Brown Jug at Hesquiat Lake; Jumbo on Deer Creek; Good Hope on the Trout (Cypre) River. The Bear River gold rush inspired names like New York, Seattle, Corona, Castle, Belvedere, King Richard, and Galena. In 1898, Clayoquot Sound boasted thirty-two prospects enjoying varying degrees of activity, with only a very few, including the Rose Marie on Elk River above Kennedy Lake, showing much promise for future gold production.

While these small-scale endeavours continued in Clayoquot Sound, the massive gold frenzies of the Klondike and Alaska captured the world's imagination with dramatic tales of fortunes won and lost. Any mention of gold, anywhere, stirred up eager interest. In June 1899, word reached Victoria that Carl "Cap" Binns, the man who carried the mail from Ucluelet to Clayoquot, had discovered gold flakes in the black sands of Wreck Bay (Florencia Bay), just south of Long Beach. Binns discovered the gold accompanied by Klih-wi-tu-a, or "Tyee Jack," who may have been first to spot the gold. A new rush of mining claims ensued along the three-mile beach of Wreck Bay: the Presbyterian missionary in Ucluelet, Melvin Swartout; the officers of the steamer *Willapa*; and the skippers of several sealing schooners visiting Clayoquot all staked claims, and the *Colonist* declared that if the reports of gold

Carl "Cap" Binns re-enacts his discovery of gold on the beach of Wreck (Florencia) Bay as James Sutton looks on. A short-lived placer mining frenzy gripped the area at the turn of the nineteenth century, but wind and waves made panning difficult and a flume built by Sutton to facilitate extraction of the fine gold washed away in winter storms, ending this west coast gold rush. *Image PN02704 courtesy of Alberni Valley Museum*

proved true, it existed "in quantity sufficient to bring 10,000 miners to the field in half a year."

Prospectors found the flaky, floury, very fine gold of Wreck Bay difficult to extract from the sand; while some boasted exceptional hauls of $4.50 a pan, others came up entirely empty owing to the patchy distribution of the gold on the beach. Nevertheless, miners worked all that summer using rockers and pans, and enticing reports kept surfacing of how much gold travelled out on the coastal steamers, at times over a thousand dollars' worth in one shipment. Winter storms brought that first season to an end.

James Sutton of Ucluelet had staked claims at Wreck Bay immediately after the initial discovery. He and his brother William owned Sutton Lumber and Trading Company in Ucluelet, and both became involved in the excitement at Wreck Bay. James formed the Ucluelet

Placer Company in partnership with a "San Francisco mining man," Mr. T. Graham, and in the spring of 1900 he hired twenty-five men to construct a water flume in twelve weeks. According to the *Colonist* of July 1, 1900, this two-kilometre-long flume cost $10,000 and used 80,000 board feet of lumber, extending from a dam on Lost Shoe Creek to the beach, bringing the fresh water essential for sluicing the placer gold from the sand. Salt water could not be used because it held sand and because wave action made it difficult to obtain. Meanwhile, other methods of gold extraction came into play, with several ingenious machines at work on the beach. On September 30, 1900, the *Colonist* reported that the steamer *Willapa* had "brought $1700 in dust from Wreck Bay. This was taken from the Sutton properties on a 10 days run of a small gold-saving machine. Two larger machines are being installed, and when these are put to work the output will be greatly increased." By early October the Sutton and Graham flume sluiced its first gold, but by the end of that month high tides and storms washed out whole sections of the flume, forcing operations to shut down for the winter. The Sutton syndicate claimed to have recovered $12,000 in gold from the year's production, prompting some prospectors to begin looking at the sands of Long Beach for similar returns, but lack of promising "colour" there discouraged them.

In April of 1901, with the flume repaired, Sutton and Graham's hydraulic machines recovered an average of $450 worth of gold flakes a day, but foul spring weather and high tides forced constant closures. By the following year, due to the perpetual interruptions caused by tides and storms, claim owners were looking to offload their properties. John Eik, G.R. Talbot, and Filip Jacobsen sold their Wreck Bay Mining Company to a Seattle real estate agent, Mr. Starbuck, for a reported $60,000. Sutton and Graham sold theirs to two San Franciscans, Mr. Riffenburg and Dr. Gunn. By 1903, with most miners having given up on Wreck Bay, Tofino store owner Sing Lee leased the claims and hired a few of his fellow Chinese to rework the tailings to recover what gold they could. In the three years of the Wreck Bay gold rush, an estimated 35 to 40 thousand dollars' worth of gold emerged from the black sands of the beach. How much Sing Lee and his Chinese workers gleaned remains a mystery, but they persevered. According to the *Colonist* in August 1903: "The purser [of the *Willapa*] brought 53 ounces of dust which was shipped to Victoria by Sing Lee."

Within Clayoquot Sound, the Sydney Inlet claims eventually developed into the most successful mine in the area, the Indian Chief Mine, on the property originally worked by James Jones and James Kincaid. After their initial efforts, unable to finance further development, Jones and Kincaid sold out in 1899 to Edgar Dewdney, BC's first Lieutenant Governor, and his Dewdney Canadian Syndicate based in England. The new owners added five nearby claims to their holdings and carried out development work until 1904. The mine then fell idle until 1907, when the Vancouver Island Copper Company reopened it and built an aerial tramway extending from the mine entrance, high on the steep side of the inlet, down to a wharf they constructed on the foreshore. From there, ore could easily be loaded onto ships for transport to the Tacoma smelter. In November 1907, Father Charles Moser noted in his diary: "My first Mass at Sidney Inlet, a copper mining camp, where quite a few Indians are employed." In 1908 the Tyee Copper Company purchased the property and began to develop it, initially hiring some twenty-five men to work the mine and to operate the small sawmill providing pit props and shoring. By 1909, thirty-seven men worked at the site.

James Jones followed all these developments in Sydney Inlet with keen interest, even writing to inquire about his former mining claims from South Africa after he volunteered to serve in the Boer War. Throughout subsequent misfortune and ill health, Jones's heart remained fixed at his old mining claim. He returned to Sydney Inlet a couple of times, but his health failed and in June 1911, James Jones took his own life, shooting himself in Beacon Hill Park in Victoria. He never saw the enduring success of his copper mine. The man who discovered "the prettiest peacock copper" on the west coast lies buried in an unmarked grave in Ross Bay Cemetery in Victoria.

The copper mine in Sydney Inlet became the most successful in Clayoquot Sound, operating on and off from 1899 until 1939, extracting what an early prospector called "the prettiest peacock copper" he had ever seen. The coastal steamer *Princess Maquinna* called here regularly to load tons of ore during the mine's heyday. *Mike Hamilton photo*

After a hiatus of several years, activity had increased at Sydney Inlet by 1916 as copper prices soared during World War I. The mine came back into action under the name Tidewater Copper, managed locally by Silas P. Silverman. A 100-ton-per-day concentrator helped improve production, and despite a short-lived strike at the mine in 1918, by 1920 it was producing 300 tons a day. Father Charles often mentioned the mine in his diary during those years, mostly because the coastal steamer so often faced lengthy delays there, loading copper concentrate and unloading large amounts of cargo. With declining copper prices, the mine closed down in 1923, putting sixty miners out of work and leaving many unpaid bills.

In the mid-1930s, Japanese investors purchased the mine and production resumed. With the onset of World War II, suspicions circulated locally that the Japanese in Sydney Inlet were using the mine as a front to build a submarine base and other facilities. The mine closed again in 1939. BC's Ministry of Mines and Energy reports that between 1904 and 1939 the overall production of the mine came to 722 ounces of gold, nearly 54,900 ounces of silver, and 2.43 million pounds of copper.

During the early years of World War II, members of the Fishermen's Reserve ripped up rail tracks that had been part of the mine and took them to the air base being constructed at Ucluelet, where they were re-laid and used to haul Canso planes out of the water on a dolly. A Fishermen's Reserve veteran later recalled being ordered to go to Sydney Inlet and blow up the mine. "I remember the mine was way up on the hillside...There was a big powder magazine with big vents in it. So somebody said, well, there isn't any use blowing us all up, so we plugged the vents with rocks and when she blew, the ship was about half a mile down the inlet on anchor, and these rocks went out like cannonballs...big plumes of water all around the boat as these rocks crashed."

Although the Indian Chief mine at Sydney Inlet became the most productive mine in Clayoquot Sound, interest in the Bear River area persisted over a longer stretch of time—as gradually the name "Bedwell" replaced "Bear." The area fell silent following the excitement at the turn of the century, marking time until 1912. That year, a group of English investors purchased the mining properties known as Big Interior and Ptarmigan, located on the summit far up Bedwell River, and established Ptarmigan Mines Ltd. to work the rich copper ores of the properties. The company set up a camp at the mouth of the river, and for a couple of months in the summer of 1914, work began in earnest: developing and extending a wagon road along the steep terrain by the river, building a large new bridge, and starting work on at least six tunnels. Materials, including great spools of steel cable, arrived for a planned aerial tramway at the head of the inlet. It was never built. With the outbreak of war in August 1914, the men left to enlist, the management returned to England, and everything was abandoned. The same fate befell the Rose Marie mine, and the Kalappa mine in Lemmens Inlet. Owned by John Chesterman and others, this mine had shipped out 1,500 tons of ore in 1913; the war brought all activity to an abrupt end.

When a Ptarmigan Mines engineer came to investigate the possibility of reopening the mine in 1919, he found much had been damaged or stolen, and the hard-won wagon road was in serious disrepair. The company attempted some work in the late 1920s, but it did not amount to much. In his book *Jack's Shack*, Jack Crosson described the mine area following his visit to Bear River in 1931 as a member of the Hydrographic Survey:

> We...found most of the heavy equipment still there. Sheds and barns had all fallen down and lay rotting on the ground and there was enough wire on reels to build a two mile [three-kilometre] aerial tramway. We also hiked up the trail; some of it was blasted out of solid rock and was a single road width; other parts remained as a foot trail.
>
> About three miles [five kilometres] up the road we came to a well-built shake building...We found it was full of all kinds of hardware and small mining tools. Stores, such as many new small barrels of horse shoes and other barrels of horse shoe nails, were in good condition.

Small flurries of mining activity continued in the vicinity of Bear River. Bill Bond came to Tofino in 1922 to work on the You Creek Mine, a set of four mining claims near the Ptarmigan Mine, owned by J.B. Woodworth of Vancouver. Bond took freight to the head of Bedwell Inlet by boat, then trekked twenty kilometres along the trail up the river to the mine, with packhorses carrying the freight. The return journey sometimes saw the horses' rawhide packs laden with gold concentrates extracted by a small cyanide mill at the mine. In the end, this mine, like so many others, failed to become viable, partly because of the onerous challenges of transport. By 1933 it lay abandoned.

In 1933, Alfred Bird and his associates staked their claims on a rich vein of gold at Spud Creek, near Zeballos Inlet on the west coast of Vancouver Island, eighty kilometres northwest of Tofino. Another rush for gold ensued, centred on the hastily created boom town of Zeballos. During its first hectic decade, the Zeballos gold rush saw over $13 million worth of gold, at $35 an ounce, extracted from a number of mines in that area. Such rich findings led to a renewed surge of interest in the potential for gold at the Bedwell River mining properties. In 1938 the Pioneer and Bralorne mining companies opened mines there, the Musketeer and Buccaneer. They worked for three years just prior to and in the early years of World War II. The original wagon road and trail leading upriver underwent considerable improvements, and hopeful miners once more headed to the mines.

Walter Guppy described the scene at Bedwell River in his book *Wet Coast Ventures:* "There was a grocery store and a flophouse where lodgings, meals and bootleg booze could be obtained at the beach, and a truck and taxi service to the mines. The madam from Zeballos even paid a visit with a view to establishing a branch facility." Miners flew in and out from Vancouver on float planes that landed near the Tofino dock, overnighting in town before heading to the mines. In his unpublished memoirs, Sid Elkington, who owned a store in Tofino and acted as agent for Canadian Airways, recalled: "Pilot Tom Laurie would call on the radio; advise me that he was over Kennedy Lake and descending... and advise me to bring a funnel out to the float, so he could pour off his passengers. This would indicate to me that he was bringing back a load of miners, who had been in Vancouver to celebrate, blow their wages and were returning, badly hung-over, and quite unsteady on their feet, or worse than that." But as with the earlier Bedwell

(Bear) River gold rushes, this one also ended in war. "It was said locally that Bear River...was jinxed," wrote Walter Guppy. "Every time a boom started a war broke out to end it; first the Boer War, then the First and Second World Wars."

The industry destined to bring the greatest riches, the most activity, and the most notoriety to the west coast began in an unspectacular manner when Captain Edward Stamp, financed by British investors, established a steam-powered sawmill at Alberni in 1860–61. He received a 6,070-hectare timber grant from Governor James Douglas and reportedly "purchased" the logging rights to Barkley Sound from the Tseshaht people for "twenty pounds sterling, fifty blankets, a musket, molasses, food and trinkets."

By August 1861, William Banfield, agent to the Colonial Secretary, informed Douglas of 14,000 board feet of lumber being cut at Alberni Settlement every day; when better machinery arrived he believed the daily production should rise to 50,000 board feet. Head logger Jeremiah Rogers supervised operations there for four years as his crew fed logs to the mill; his name lives on at Jericho Beach in Vancouver where he later worked at what became known as "Jerry's Cove." Increasing costs and growing competition from mills in Washington and Oregon saw the Alberni sawmill close in 1864, after exporting 35 million board feet of lumber to markets in Britain. Some of the lumber cut at the Alberni mill found its way to the 1862 World's Fair in London; the *Colonist* announced this as a sign of "what Vancouver Island can do in the tree-growing department."

By the 1880s, other smaller mills began operating in Barkley Sound and in scattered locations up and down the coast, cutting and milling for specific local markets. Early settlers highly valued milled wood, which often proved difficult to obtain. Sometimes shipwrecks obligingly cast up loads of lumber on the coast, free for the taking, but hardly a reliable source.

In October 1894, Bernt Auseth, originally from Trondheim, Norway, pre-empted 56.6 hectares at Mud Bay (Grice Bay). A month later, fellow Norwegian Thomas Wingen pre-empted the adjacent property. Highly inventive men, Auseth and Wingen together built a small waterwheel-driven sawmill at the mouth of Kootowis Creek on Auseth's property. They laboriously ditched and dammed a slough, using lumber to make the dam, constructing it so that the force of the water pushed the joints together to make it tighter and stronger. Then they made a waterwheel, nine metres in diameter, using yew wood for the cogs and crabapple for the pinions. Next followed the axle, created with squared fir, tapered at the ends and strapped together with scrap iron. For bearings they scoured the beach for big round stones, which they hollowed out, fitting the axle into them, and the whole apparatus ran smoothly with generous lubrications of dogfish oil. The sawmill could handle logs up to 1.25 metres in diameter on the hand-cranked carriage that fed the saw. When Wingen and Auseth finished an order of lumber, they bound it into a raft, set a 3.6-metre-long sailboat on top, and sailed with the tide down the inlet for delivery. Many of the earliest homes of settlers in the area used lumber from this unique mill. After a number of years of running the mill, Auseth left the area. Tom Wingen acquired Auseth's land and continued operating the mill until he moved to the emerging settlement at Tofino.

In 1883, James and William Sutton came to the west coast. Already involved in mining and sawmilling at Lake Cowichan and Deep Bay, the brothers established themselves at Spring Cove, near Ucluelet, and built a sawmill. Ten years later, with capital of $100,000, they incorporated as Sutton Lumber and Trading Company, and as they became more established and successful they began acquiring a vast number of timber leases in the Kennedy Lake area, and later on Meares Island and elsewhere in Clayoquot Sound. In 1903 they sold shares in their company to the Seattle Cedar Lumber Manufacturing Company, then expanding into Canada. With the American company financing the project, the Suttons began constructing what would become the biggest cedar mill on the west coast, at Mosquito Harbour on Meares Island. The site provided ample fresh water to create the necessary steam to run the mill, and its protected bay was deep enough to

The large Mosquito Harbour cedar sawmill, owned by the Sutton brothers and the Seattle Cedar Manufacturing Company, operated on Meares Island between 1905 and 1907. Forced to close when teredos (shipworms) honeycombed the dock pilings and destroyed twelve million board feet of boomed logs, the mill never reopened. For many years, Jacob Arnet of Tofino worked as watchman there; his boat *Mosquito* can be seen tied up to the dock. *Tofino Municipality collection*

accommodate large ships that would carry away the finished products. By 1905, 150 workers laboured to complete the ambitious mill, with a wharf and small townsite at Mosquito Harbour. The total cost of this immense project reached $460,000. "Preparations are in active progress to commence construction of logging roads, mills, wharves, etc., plans for machinery are in preparation, and this promises to become one of the largest and most successful lumber enterprises in BC," trumpeted the *Colonist* in November 1905. "The company has a capital of many millions, a disposition to spend wisely but freely, and abundant successful experience in the lumber position. The fact that they will cut, carry and dispose of the lumber in a market which they already control makes their position an exceptionally strong one." In June 1906 the newspaper claimed the mill would employ "400 or 500 white men," that it would ship two or three loads of wood each week to international markets, and that this mill would be "the very largest in the manufacture of cedar in the Dominion."

Loggers began felling immense red cedars in nearby Warn Bay to be milled into shingles and lumber for markets in New York and New England. These "handloggers," as they were called, chose trees growing near the water's edge so the logs would fall or skid into the water, where they would be boomed and later towed to the mill site. Once the loggers selected a tree, they cut smaller trees to fall crossways and downslope from the bigger tree, ensuring that it would have a cushion to fall on and a surface to skid along down to the saltchuck. When they began work on the bigger tree, the loggers cut notches into the trunk, facing in the direction they wanted it to fall, and inserted springboards into the notches. Standing on the boards, they cut another deep notch, or undercut, after which they inserted additional springboards on the opposite side of the trunk. Then they went to work with the two-man, 3.3-metre crosscut saw. It could take two men a full day to cut one tree. Accuracy was vital; if the tree missed the pre-cut skid trees, it would hang up before reaching the water's edge. If this happened, loggers could spend countless hours using peavey poles and Gilchrist jacks to force the tree into the water. Once the tree had fallen, the loggers then faced the chore of limbing it and cutting it into manageable lengths. When enough logs had been cut and boomed, a tug towed the boom to the mill site.

The Mosquito Harbour mill began operations in November 1906, producing "500,000 shingles and a large quantity of lumber a day," according to the *Colonist*. Workers lived in the townsite near the mill in houses provided by the company, and they even had their own Mosquito Harbour post office to serve them. By May 1907 the mill had over four million board feet of lumber ready for shipment. The future seemed rosy—but then catastrophe struck. Saltwater teredos (*Teredinibacter turnerae*), or shipworms, had infested the entire inventory

Though short-lived, the townsite at the Mosquito Harbour mill had a post office from 1906–8, and the company had its envelopes embossed with stamps. The Mosquito Harbour postmark is rarely seen and highly valued by postal enthusiasts.
Courtesy of Tim Woodland

of logs—12 million board feet—in the booms near the mill. Ranging in length from 7.6 to 90 centimetres, these teredos had bored into the logs, feasting on the cellulose and honeycombing each log with tiny passages, degrading its strength and rendering it useless for milling. The company laid off all the loggers, but the mill continued processing logs untouched by the pests. By July, teredos had infested the wharf pilings so badly that the wharf collapsed, throwing "two to three million board feet of lumber and shingles into the water," according to the *Colonist* of July 12, 1907. Workers scooped up the bundles of shingles and the lumber and loaded them onto the freighter *Earl of Douglas,* which had arrived to carry whatever it could of the salvageable lumber and shingles to the eastern United States. The vessel carried four million board feet of lumber around Cape Horn to New York, arriving in November 1907, only to find that a financial collapse had caused a dramatic slump in the lumber market. This broke the Mosquito Harbour mill, and it closed. Hopeful that a profitable market for cedar products might arise in the future, the company continued to maintain the mill, going so far as to replace its pilings with concrete foundations in 1924, and for many years hiring Jacob Arnet as caretaker to look after the site.

In 1931, twenty-four years after it closed, Jack Crosson visited the mill. "We discovered Mosquito Harbour and what was left of a large wharf and shingle mill. The only indication of the wharf was at low tide when long rows of piling could still be seen. They were eaten in half by teredoes...The upper part and decking were long gone, but the lower third of the piles stood in lines in the mud, showing their pointed ends skyward. The remaining part was just a shell as the inside was honeycombed by the teredoes." Crosson and his companions went into the engine room, finding everything in good condition, and they examined the six shingle-making machines, all seemingly in perfect order. The main building had no leaks, and all the windows remained intact. "The Americans had built a row of nice homes for their workers. We went into one after fighting our way through the young alder saplings, ferns, small trees, and other bushes. The house was well built and there was no leaky roof. All the windows were in and none broken. You could scarcely see the house next door through the West Coast jungle, although it was not that far, about twenty-five feet [7.5 metres]. I don't know what has happened to the sawmill and cottages since then."

Ten years later, in 1942, the Gibson brothers from Ahousat received a federal contract to dismantle the machinery at Mosquito Harbour mill and dispose of it for war use. The Gibsons definitely knew their way

Chinese workers hunt through the debris, salvaging useable material, following the collapse of the docks at Mosquito Harbour mill in 1907. *Tofino Municipality collection*

around sawmills, having been involved in logging and mills for many years. Their father, William F. Gibson, had been active on the coast since before World War I, coming and going seasonally, harvesting wood for various markets, and encouraging settlers in the region. Gordon Gibson joined his father in Clayoquot Sound in the summer of 1916, helping to fell and skin logs for telephone poles, and the following summer found them at Trout (Cypre) River, working on a contract to harvest "ships' knees"—the large knee-shaped roots used for right-angle joints in wooden sailing ships. That work continued the following year, at the head of Herbert Inlet. All four of Gibson's sons, John, Clarke, Earson, and Gordon, became involved in the family enterprises, turning their hands to any job that would make money. They fished; drove piles for docks, wharves, and booming grounds; transported goods; built docks and canneries; and towed log booms. By 1918 the Gibsons were cutting massive spruce trees as fast as they could under the terms of the new Aeroplane Spruce-Cutting Act, which issued special permits to cut spruce on public or private lands for aircraft construction. When the war ended, the Gibsons found themselves with a lot of spruce on their hands. They moved their operation to Ahousat and built a small sawmill on the west side on Matilda Creek, initially to mill their left-over spruce into oar stock. A bunkhouse for their staff followed, and a home for themselves. In 1920, William Gibson, in partnership with Tommy Atkins, established his Gibson Lumber and Shingle Company, beginning a powerful family dynasty. Renowned for their risk taking and roustabout living, the Gibsons' reputation grew, year by year.

Before William Gibson established his mill at Matilda Creek, John Darville had arrived on the west coast and set up his own small saw-mill. Hailing from Seattle, where he worked as a pattern maker in a foundry, he built a water-powered mill at Calm Creek (Quait Bay) on the mainland behind Meares Island, about thirty-two kilometres from Ahousat. With his sons Roy and Fred and one other helper, Darville produced lumber to order, establishing himself as a trustworthy and respected figure on the coast, able to turn his hand to anything. The Darvilles also built fish boats, and Fred developed the technique of inserting refurbished car engines into boats. John leased his mill to Fred Knott in the late 1930s and moved to Tofino, where he continued building boats. When his beloved mill burned down in 1939, he returned to Calm Creek and tried single-handedly to rebuild it, without success.

In 1926, following the success of the Whalen brothers' pulp mill at Port Alice, Sutton Lumber came up with the idea of building a pulp mill, in conjunction with Crown Zellerbach, at the mouth of the Kennedy River. The plan included damming the river to raise the level of Kennedy Lake by fifteen metres to produce enough power to run the operation. This grandiose proposal came forward at the same time as, and possibly in conjunction with, an equally ambitious scheme for a west coast rail link. A proposed branch line linking Alberni to the coast would service the future pulp mill and allow the company to log the area by rail, particularly the flat land along the peninsula between

Ucluelet and Tofino. Survey crews arrived to assess the feasibility of the pulp mill, but nothing came of this scheme—in part due to the financial collapse of 1929. Similarly, plans for a proposed hemlock sawmill at Mud Bay came to nothing. The plans for a railway never extended beyond the drawing board.

The west coast of Vancouver Island consistently attracted industries, ambitious projects, and people with grand dreams. Over many decades, schemes for mills, for mines, even for settlements, often in highly unlikely locations, have flourished and faded. The harsh realities and challenges of living and working on the coast have defeated many enterprises and undertakings, sometimes after years of persistent, back-breaking effort. Countless quiet inlets, bays, and mountainsides bear traces of broken dreams and abandoned ventures. Yet whatever the odds of making good, the coast has consistently drawn optimistic people willing to work hard, convinced they will succeed. In the late nineteenth and early twentieth centuries, the settlers arriving on the coast came with high hopes, encouraged by the abundance of the sea and all the apparently empty land, so readily available to them. They looked to make a fresh start and they were determined to remain.

Chapter 11:

THE HOPEFUL COAST

THE SUMMER OF 1895 found Victoria-based surveyor Mr. T.S. Gore slogging his way through the bush on the Esowista Peninsula, survey gear and notebook at the ready. As he and his crew beat their way through thickets of salal and salmonberry, trudged through swamps, navigated gullies and deadfalls, and endured clouds of mosquitoes, they took sightings and measurements and blazed perimeter marks onto trees. By the autumn, when Gore had finished, almost all the land from the northern tip of the Esowista Peninsula right down to Ucluelet had been officially surveyed and given lot numbers. The numbers Gore gave the parcels of land he surveyed in 1895 are still used today.

Gore's field books describe in precise detail every feature of the land, the shores, and the waterways, including the size, type, and density of timber on the land. The few existing structures on the peninsula also appear on his intricate maps, including the new cannery on land pre-empted in 1894 by the Clayoquot Fishing and Trading Co. at the mouth of the Kennedy River, the new sawmill belonging to Thomas Wingen and Bernt Auseth in Mud Bay (now Grice Bay; called Mill Bay by Gore), and the dike under construction at Jens Jensen's place, in Jensen Bay. Out at Long Bay (Long Beach), Gore's map of Lot 162 even includes "Dawley's potatoe patch," planted on land Walter Dawley pre-empted the previous year.

Following Gore's survey, the lands on the Esowista Peninsula officially stood open to settlement and development. All this took place with scant, if any, reference to the local First Nations. In the mid-1880s, the government had established the extremely limited reserve lands for aboriginals living in Clayoquot Sound (the establishment of Indian reserves is covered in Chapter 12). By assigning these reserves, the government had, in its own estimation, "given" sufficient lands to the indigenous inhabitants; the rest of the land now could be inhabited by newcomers or earmarked for resource exploitation. As the late nineteenth century gave way to the twentieth, aboriginal chiefs and leaders watched with growing concern and perplexity as more and more settlers arrived in their traditional territories, intending to stay. Speaking in 1914, nearly a generation after the earliest wave of settlement, Chief Jimmy Jim of Ahousat stated: "Some white men have 200 acres [81 hectares] or more, and some have 80 acres [32.4 hectares]. And why have we such a small place here? We were born here, and white settlers have a bigger place."

The parcels of land surveyed by Gore ranged in size from sixteen to eighty hectares. These could be "taken up" as pre-emptions, timber licences, or mining properties, or they could be purchased outright. To obtain a Crown grant for their land, pre-emptors had to satisfy the authorities and "improve" the land, by building a dwelling, adding fencing, and attempting some form of agriculture—hence "Dawley's potatoe patch." While they were expected to live on the land they had pre-empted, many pre-emptors did not do so. They had little interest in agriculture, making half-hearted efforts while pursuing other interests such as handlogging, prospecting, or establishing businesses. Many pre-emptors, throughout the province, did not bother even with token gestures of "improvement," and their lands reverted to the Crown.

A number of highly significant parcels of land in the Tofino/Ucluelet area had been pre-empted, purchased, or acquired as timber licences before Gore's survey. William Sutton, of Sutton Lumber in Ucluelet, took up immense tracts of land around Kennedy Lake, Toquart Bay, and Ucluelet Arm in the early 1890s, a prelude to further land acquisitions by Sutton in Clayoquot Sound in the early 1900s. Many decades later, the fate of much of that land, including the original Sutton timber licences on Meares Island, would ignite intense controversy about logging practices. Nearer to Long Beach, the earliest pre-emption occurred in 1890 when James Goldstraw staked forty-eight hectares of land in Schooner Cove. The following year, George Maltby and William Kershaw took up parcels of land adjacent to Goldstraw's. In 1894, Jacob Arnet, Bernt Auseth, and Thomas Wingen pre-empted land in Mud (Grice) Bay, along with Jens Jensen, in Jensen Bay. Also in 1894,

Thomas Stockham took on the island bearing his name in Tofino Harbour, and Walter Dawley pre-empted land at Schooner Cove.

In the Tofino area, settler John Grice registered his strategic pre-emption on May 1, 1893: Lot 114, described in land records as "Low Pen, Hd of" (the Esowista Peninsula appears as "Low Peninsula" on early maps, a name used off and on until the early 1920s), encompassed the northwestern tip of the peninsula, an area of eighty-three hectares. Abutting his pre-emption to the east and south, the adjacent Lot 115 appears on Gore's survey map as "Low's Pre-emption." Little is known of Mr. Low. He did not hold the land long, nor is his pre-emption properly registered, and Gore's reference to his pre-emption is one of the few solid pieces of evidence about him. In 1896, John Eik and fellow Norwegian Svert Huseby took over Low's property, eventually receiving a Crown grant for it in 1908. These two parcels of land, Lots 114 and 115, account for the present-day town centre of Tofino.

When John Grice acquired Lot 114 with its commanding view of Tofino Harbour, he sensed right away he had a superb property with future prospects. Only seven years later, in 1900, he had this land surveyed and subdivided into lots for a future townsite. At the time, this scheme for a town on the Esowista Peninsula seemed wildly optimistic, given the few settlers, the isolated setting, and the existing settlement just across the water at Clayoquot on Stubbs Island. Yet this type of optimism fuelled the schemes and dreams of countless settlers in British Columbia as they travelled hopefully to distant places, doggedly determined to establish themselves and to make good.

The survey map for Grice's Lot 114 identifies the proposed settlement as "the town of Clayoquot." His choice of name added to a confusion of "Clayoquots" that persisted for a number of years, with the name variously used for the community on Stubbs Island, for Stubbs Island itself, for the emerging townsite on the peninsula, sometimes for the village of Opitsat, often for the Tla-o-qui-aht First Nation, and more generally for the whole of the Sound. In 1904, Father Charles Moser, the Roman Catholic missionary at Opitsat, first used the name "Tofino" in his diary, referring to the peninsula townsite. This is one of the earliest known uses of the name.

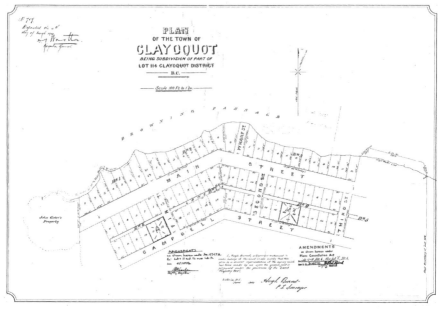

Several years before Tofino became an established settlement, John Grice foresaw a town emerging on this site. He had these plans drawn up on a section of his original pre-emption, Lot 114. Initially he called this "Clayoquot" as if challenging the older "Clayoquot" on Stubbs Island, but by 1904 the name "Tofino" began to be used.
Alberni-Clayoquot Regional District

Like all other settlers, John Grice set out to make his mark in this new territory. He quickly learned to communicate in the Chinook trading jargon and began to act as an intermediary between the local hunters and the sealing schooner captains in their hiring negotiations. As a literate Englishman, later described by Dorothy Abraham in her book *Lone Cone* as "a very learned man, a great lover of Shakespeare and all the classics, also something of an astronomer," Grice possessed a decided advantage when it came to acquiring local government jobs that provided stipends. By 1895 he had been appointed shipping master and Justice of the Peace for Clayoquot. Later years would find him filling other official positions, including customs officer, tide and rain gauge supervisor, and fisheries officer.

For most of his first two decades on the west coast, Grice lived as a single man. In 1912 his wife, Jane, joined him, setting sail from England aboard the *Empress of Ireland* with their daughter, Jennie, by

John Grice from Newcastle-upon-Tyne first came to Clayoquot Sound in 1891. Two years later, he shrewdly acquired land on the tip of the Esowista Peninsula where the village of Tofino later emerged. His wife, Jane, did not join him in Canada for many years, but became a beloved resident of Tofino in her later years. The couple died within three days of each other, in 1934. *Ken Gibson photo*

then in her late twenties. The couple's long separation still perplexes their descendants, some believing that John Grice may have fallen into disfavour for fathering a child or children out of wedlock in England. The birth certificate of his young son, Arthur, who accompanied Grice to Canada, names one Mary Nesbit as Arthur's mother, not Jane Grice. Dorothy Abraham wrote glowingly of the Grices in their later years. "He was rather like a rosy apple to look at," she declared, describing a punctilious early riser who drank gallons of cold water, and whose frail, sweet-natured little wife dressed in old-fashioned silk frocks and beribboned bonnets. They both lived out their days in Tofino; Grice died of cardiac failure in 1934 at the age of eighty-four. His wife, also eighty-four, died three days afterward of chronic bronchitis.

Looking at Grice's earliest plan for the townsite that became Tofino, his own personal property stands out. He retained the very tip of the peninsula, now called Grice Point, for himself and built a house there.

From 1901, the Chinese trader Sing Lee operated his store on the shoreline nearby, possibly on the same site briefly used as a trading post by Hugh McKay in the 1860s, and later by David Evans in the 1880s. Much to Walter Dawley's chagrin, Sing Lee enjoyed a brisk trade in furs and attracted some of Dawley's regular customers to buy provisions in his store, including Elizabeth Chesterman, who, when her husband could not take her by boat over to Clayoquot, found it easier to trade at the "China store."

No one lobbied more energetically on behalf of the new settlement than John Chesterman. He felt sure the early settlers would succeed in creating a lasting community, with a dock, post office, school, stores, and many other amenities. Chesterman had been in the area since taking up his first seventy hectares of land in 1895, adding the adjacent sixty-seven hectares in 1900, which gave him ocean frontage encompassing all of what are now called North and South Chesterman Beaches. He cleared land and built a house on the sheltered inlet side of the property, and settled there with his young wife, Elizabeth, following their marriage in 1901. Their first child, John Filip Reginald, was born later that year. Chesterman kept his finger on the pulse of every potential development in the area, informing himself about local politics, remaining close to Harlan Brewster of the cannery and to A.W. Neill, the west coast Indian agent, later elected Member of Parliament for Comox–Alberni. When word came in 1901 that the Dominion Government Telegraph Service intended to extend the telegraph line from Alberni to Clayoquot, Chesterman pushed to have the terminus at "the settlement" on the peninsula rather than extending it underwater to the community on Stubbs Island. Although the telegraph, completed in 1902, officially terminated at "the settlement," an underwater line did reach over to Stockham and Dawley's establishment, possibly because they lobbied even more energetically than Chesterman and likely resorted to bribery to make this happen. At least initially, most of the telegraph business went through the telegraph operator at Stockham and Dawley's.

Chesterman found lucrative employment for an eighteen-month period as foreman of the local telegraph crew during the installation

John Chesterman stoops over a cookstove, cooking for his crew who were building trails on Vargas Island in anticipation of many settlers living there. Virgil Evans stands at the right of the picture, circa 1911. *W.A. Drader photo, Tofino Municipality collection*

of this line. He obtained many jobs over the years: building roads to Ucluelet and to Bamfield, on the telegraph line, at the cannery, and on the construction of Estevan lighthouse in 1908. Many of his letters to Walter Dawley survive, placing orders from his various workplaces for everything from "jap rice" to dynamite, all written in a meticulous script and often including wry jests.

In the spring of 1901, settler George Maltby landed the job of enumerator for the census in Clayoquot district. Over nearly three months, travelling mostly by rowboat, he listed the settlers in the Tofino area, on Stubbs Island, and at Opitsat, Ahousat, and Hesquiat; he even included the staff of the recently established Christie Indian Residential School at Kakawis on Meares Island, and the Chinese workers at the cannery and the hotel. No aboriginals appear; records of their population relied on the efforts of government agents and missionaries, and later on band lists assembled by Indian agents.

Most of the seventy-two men enumerated by Maltby in 1901 described themselves as farmers or miners, with a handful of carpenters and prospectors. Seventeen had wives living with them, and eleven of the wives had children. The Guinard (or Ginnard) family, living at the southwestern corner of Meares Island, then had five children; the Arnets three; the Wingens one. With the pace of settlement gradually increasing and the birth rate rising, a school was needed. To qualify as an "assisted" school, with the provincial government covering a teacher's salary, at least seven children had to attend regularly. According to Catherine (Katie) Monks's brief history of Tofino, in the booklet *Cedar Bark and Sea*, "Two French-Canadian families had pre-empted up the Inlet...between them they had over twenty children." The 1901 census does not reflect these numbers, but Katie Monks could have been referring to the Guinard family and possibly the families of Paul and Nelson Fayette, who pre-empted land up the inlet in the mid-1890s but did not remain long in the area.

A newspaper clipping in a scrapbook created years ago by Daphne Gibson mentions a receipt dated April 23, 1899, made out to Auseth and Wingen for materials for the "Clayoquot Schoolhouse." This shows that the schoolhouse had purchased some 8,000 board feet of lumber from these local sawmill owners, who forgave part of the $57.60 owing, donating $17.50 to the "Clayoquot School Fund." Not much evidence survives of this early Clayoquot school, but its location is recognized in a commonly used place name: Schoolhouse Point, up Browning Passage, at the entrance to South Bay. Provincial school records indicate the school opened in 1898, with twelve children enrolled the first year; the teacher, Miss A. Doran, received fifty dollars per month. The following year, three different teachers worked at the school, a high turnover perhaps explained by the drop in salary to forty dollars per month. In 1900–1901, still with twelve children in attendance, the doctor at Clayoquot, Dr. P.W. Rolston, served as teacher. The school operated only forty-four days that year, and it likely closed the following year. Hints of moving this original schoolhouse to "Clayoquot" emerge in Walter Dawley's correspondence, not indicating if that meant to Stubbs Island or to the emerging Tofino townsite, nor if the building

Jacob Arnet, his wife Johanna, and their seven children, Alma, Edgar, Harold, Karl, Bjarne, Trygve, and Walter pose outside their house in Tofino, around 1910. Note the massive stumps looming in the background. *Courtesy of Roly Arnet*

was ever moved. In 1903, James Redford, an Alberni merchant active in provincial politics, wrote to Dawley saying, "The schoolhouse will remain where it is and the townsite also."

Young Alma Arnet attended school at Schoolhouse Point only briefly before it closed, her father Jacob taking her there by rowboat or sailboat. When interviewed later in life, Alma remembered her family moving to Ucluelet for a year and a half, where she attended school with several other youngsters in the front room of their teacher's home. Jacob found work with the Sutton sawmill in Ucluelet during this period, all the while continuing his seasonal work at the Clayoquot cannery and keeping an eye on his homestead and livestock at Mud Bay. Every summer, with Jacob working at the cannery, the Arnet family moved onto a floathouse anchored near the cannery, much to the delight of the children.

In 1906 the Arnets returned from Ucluelet to find a small school operating in Tofino. Accounts of this school vary, but it likely started in a private home, shortly afterward replaced by a one-room schoolhouse built by volunteers on land cleared by George Maltby at the corner of what is now Third Street and Campbell. To be near the school, Jacob Arnet built a home on the waterfront in Tofino, and the family moved from their homestead into "town." Several other families who initially lived farther away from the townsite also moved into town, including John Chesterman and Tom Wingen. In addition to the Arnet family, Chesterman and his wife, Elizabeth, contributed to the required head count for the new school, as did Francis Garrard and his wife, Annie, whose children bravely came to school in Tofino by rowboat, a perilous journey from their isolated home on the new Lennard Island light, constructed in 1904. Formerly employed in the construction of the telegraph line between Alberni and Clayoquot, Garrard had come to Lennard Island to assist in building the new light station. He stayed on as lightkeeper until 1908, when he moved his family to Vargas Island and later into Tofino. He and Annie had eight children in all, several of whom attended school in Tofino.

The first Tofino school and its teacher received an approving nod from the *British Colonist* in June 1906: "The school started on Clayoquot townsite, so ably presided over by Miss May Clark of Victoria, has been very successful so far, the daily attendance averaging 12 scholars." In fact, some twenty-eight students appear on the official enrolment for the school that first year—absenteeism clearly ran high—but nonetheless the school at Tofino, called Clayoquot School until 1924, never looked back. In 1909, W.A. (Bert) Drader came to teach there; thanks to him, many early photographs of the area now survive.

The coastal steamers sometimes called at Tofino now, on their twice-monthly trips up the coast, even though the place did not as yet have a dock, and all supplies had to be offloaded onto scows and small boats. With ambitious new developments underway, like the Mosquito Harbour sawmill, newcomers continued to arrive at the townsite, a few at a time, some just passing through, some coming to stay. Among the long-term players was the quick-witted trader James Sloman.

Sensing a golden opportunity at the emerging townsite, Sloman abandoned his storekeeping job with Walter Dawley to become his direct competitor across the water at Tofino. Dawley was not amused. He had already been double-crossed by Thomas Stockham, who walked out on their partnership in 1904 in a bitterly acrimonious dispute. Stockham then purchased two sealing schooners and carried on trading seal skins and furs in defiance of Dawley, using Sing Lee, the Chinese storekeeper in Tofino, as a middleman. Stockham even provisioned his boats through Sing Lee, the very man he and Dawley had tried so hard to put out of business. With Sing Lee's sudden death in 1906, Stockham and James Sloman acted together to seize the moment. Sloman formed a partnership with Stockham's brother-in-law John McKenna, and together they purchased the "China store," almost certainly with help from Stockham, knowing full well that Dawley had also been trying to acquire this store.

A wily operator, James Sloman learned all the tricks of the trade from Dawley, having worked for him at the Nootka store for five years, and briefly at Clayoquot. He well knew the importance of acquiring additional services to create a thriving enterprise, and within three years a post office found a welcoming corner in Sloman's store, bringing with it increasing traffic and trade. With the arrival of its own post office, the name "Tofino" became formally accepted in the community: the names "Lone Cone" (for the mountain) and "Riley" (for Reece Riley, an early settler) had been considered, but "Tofino" triumphed, taking its name from Tofino Inlet. The inlet had been named in 1792 by Spanish captains Galiano and Valdés, honouring Spain's chief hydrographer, the renowned astronomer and mathematician Vicente Tofiño de San Miguel.

E.B. (Burdett) Garrard, Francis Garrard's brother, became the first Tofino postmaster in 1909, by then having already served two years as the Tofino telegraph operator. Burdett built his home around the telegraph office and later expanded operations when he moved the post office to the same location. This communication hub remained in the Garrard family for years to come. In 1911, when Burdett and his family moved to Alberni, Francis Garrard became Tofino's next postmaster and telegraph agent He held both positions, with the assistance of his wife and daughters, until 1924.

While it became increasingly evident that this new Tofino townsite had come to stay, the strong arm of the law remained firmly based at the established settlement of Clayoquot on Stubbs Island. Following the departure of Constable Spain in 1902, Constable Daniel McDougall took over at Clayoquot, remaining there for over five years before Ewen MacLeod took over from him. MacLeod had first seen the area early in 1905 when working as a seaman on the sealing schooner *Charlotta G. Cox*. According to his niece Mary Hardy (née MacLeod), "When he viewed Lone Cone and the mountains surrounding the harbour, it reminded him so much of the island he came from (Raasay, on the northwest coast of Scotland) he determined to return." In 1906, Ewen joined his older brother Murdo, who had arrived on the coast the previous year and was working on the road at Bamfield. Ewen heard of the opening at Clayoquot for a police constable and applied. Both brothers came to Tofino, Murdo finding work at the Mosquito Harbour sawmill—for which he received $1.10 per day—and in various construction jobs. Murdo and Ewen were the first of several MacLeods to come to the area—another brother, Alex, followed in 1911, accompanied by his cousin John (Jack) MacLeod and an unrelated John MacLeod, whose sister Julia later married Murdo MacLeod.

Ewen MacLeod felt entirely at home in the damp, grey, island-strewn landscape, and far better suited to this life than to his earlier police work in Glasgow. He enjoyed the hunting and fishing, and like Constable Spain before him he travelled far and wide around Clayoquot Sound in his rowboat, ranging farther afield, to Nootka and to Kyuquot, by steamer when necessary. Having been brought up in a crofter's cottage, both Ewen and Murdo MacLeod well understood hardship and poverty, and they felt an affinity for the growing plight of the aboriginal people as their access to traditional lands and resources diminished.

When he began working at Clayoquot in 1907, Constable MacLeod's pay stood at seventy-five dollars per month, five dollars of which went toward renting a cottage from Walter Dawley. Attached to this cottage stood the rudimentary jail, built in 1906, complete with ringbolts embedded in the walls. Over the years, this jail occasionally housed prisoners for short periods—sometimes those awaiting transport to face charges in Victoria, sometimes seal hunters who jumped ship, breaking their agreements with the captains. In March 1907, when Father Charles Moser's motor launch *Ave Maria* suffered mechanical problems, he turned to the Clayoquot jail for assistance from the "2 Nootka Indians in jail [who] had deserted their sealing schooner. At my pleading and promise they would return to jail these 2 Indians towed my launch to Opitsat with their canoe and after a good meal returned to jail." In later years, rebellious runaways from residential school were sometimes tracked down by police and truant officers and held in this jail before being returned to school. More often than not, though, the jail simply served as a drunk tank. With many sealing schooners still visiting Clayoquot Sound to pick up hunters and replenish supplies, the bar at the hotel on Stubbs Island, the only one on the west coast north of Victoria, did a booming business. Veteran sealing captains like Alex MacLean and George Heater would stop by, needing to boost their morale as their livelihoods slowly vanished, and the bar regularly welcomed workers from Mosquito Harbour, along with the usual traffic of prospectors. This kept Constable MacLeod busy, for often the "uncivilizin' influence of Clayoquot liquor" led to barroom brawls, forcing him to intervene.

Prior to his marriage in 1911, Ewen MacLeod often took his meals at the Clayoquot Hotel, paying twenty-five cents for breakfast, fifty cents for dinner. His precise account book shows that for $2.50 per month he had a standing order for milk from the one cow at Clayoquot, and that he bought salt cod from the fish saltery on Stubbs Island for twenty-five cents per fish. For seventy cents he could purchase over a kilogram of smoked salmon from the Natives, and tins of salmon from the Clayoquot cannery cost twenty-five cents each. He made no mention of buying a drink at the Clayoquot Hotel, but clearly various MacLeods enjoyed good times there. In later years, Ewen wrote to Walter Dawley, saying: "I trust you will keep the MacLeod boys in order...don't let them drink too much boose."

In 1910, on a trip to the sawmill at Mosquito Harbour, Ewen MacLeod met Mabel Reeves of Seattle, holidaying with the summer caretakers. Evidence of his attraction surfaces in his account book: one box of chocolates, $1.00. They married the following year, and Mabel gamely settled into life as the local policeman's wife. One of the perks, when the first baby arrived, was the extra space in the jail next to the house: an excellent place to dry diapers on a rainy day. The MacLeods left Clayoquot in 1914, first moving to Hope, and later to Lytton. They had purchased their cottage at Clayoquot from Dawley, and it remained in the MacLeod family until the 1960s.

The year 1908 saw significant changes at Tofino. The much-desired government dock went in that year, at the location occupied today by the First Street dock. This large structure, extending sixty metres offshore, finally established Tofino as a regular stop for the coastal steamers. Prior to this, the coastal steamer *Tees* would not stop at Tofino unless at least three tons of freight had to be unloaded, which meant the *Tees* holding her position offshore, arduously shuffling freight from her cargo deck onto a scow, and landing goods on the beach. With a decent dock, Tofino could now rely on mail and supplies arriving three or four times each month. The 1909 schedule for the British Columbia Coast Steamship Service of the CPR still insisted on calling the community "Clayoquot townsite," but by 1910 the name "Tofino" appeared as a fixed stop on the schedule.

Another proud new institution began in 1908 with the establishment of the Clayoquot lifeboat, an essential service that over subsequent years employed scores of local men. As coxswain, John Chesterman had charge of maintaining the vessel and managing a crew. Bernt Auseth constructed the boathouse for the new lifeboat on a waterfront lot in Tofino that had been purchased for fifty dollars by the Department of Marine and Fisheries. Powered by oar and sail, the lifeboat required ten men to row any distance, leaving little space on board for shipwrecked victims; at most three or four passengers could be safely taken aboard at one time. Originally manned by volunteers, before long the lifeboat crews received hourly pay when on duty, and the coxswain enjoyed an annual salary. Apart from being on call for emergencies and regular drills, the crew also cleared land, built fences, and maintained the property around the boathouse. One crew member kept watch

The Clayoquot lifeboat service, established in 1908 in Tofino, played a pivotal role in the community. First powered by oar, this "surf boat" was replaced in 1913 by a motorized vessel. *Image F03431 courtesy of Royal BC Museum, BC Archives*

at night, and the single men on duty slept at the boathouse in the uncomfortable loft. Married men, if they lived nearby, slept at home. In the early days, the lifeboat sometimes even served as a means of transport for taking new settlers to their homes. By 1913, because the original "surf boat" faced increasing criticism for its evident limitations, the inspector from Victoria recommended that the boat be replaced by a motorized vessel.

As time passed, the lifeboat station took on an increasing roster of duties: provisioning and delivering mail to Lennard Island light; monitoring the official gauges for tide and rainfall; maintaining the increasing number of whistle buoys, markers, and lights in the harbour. The lifeboat crew could be called on to assist at any local emergency, including fires and medical calls, ranging all over Clayoquot Sound and down the coast along Long Beach to Ucluelet. The lifeboat also served to transport coffins for burial in the town cemetery on Morpheus Island. It became a fixed point of reference in town; a reliable source of employment for many men, and a source of considerable local pride.

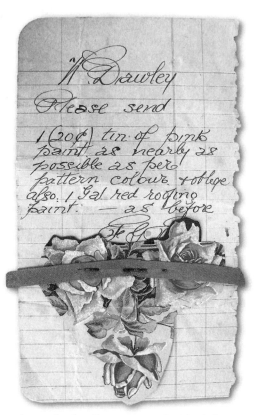

A sample of wallpaper covered with pink roses, sent by Fred Tibbs to Walter Dawley in 1909. Writing from his home at Long Bay (Long Beach), Tibbs requested Dawley obtain matching pink paint.

Image MS1076 courtesy of Royal BC Museum, BC Archives, Walter Dawley Papers

Frederick Gerald Tibbs, pictured here with his cousin Vera Marshall, stands out as one of Tofino's best-known eccentrics. He settled at Long Beach in 1908, later moving to his "Dream Isle" off Tofino, clear-cutting the island and erecting a castle-like home. *Image F03427 courtesy of Royal BC Museum, BC Archives*

The year 1908 also marked the arrival on the west coast of a self-effacing young man, Frederick Gerald Tibbs, destined to become one of Tofino's best-known characters. At first glance not a prepossessing character, Tibbs appeared stocky and rather shy, painfully self-conscious about a facial disfigurement dating back to a childhood injury in England and made worse by various surgeries. Benignly good-natured and cheerfully eccentric, Tibbs first settled on land he pre-empted at Long Bay (Long Beach), a considerable distance from Tofino and from other settlers, the area now occupied by Green Point Campground. Strangely keen on physical exercise, Tibbs caused locals to shake their heads when they heard he took a plunge in the breakers at Long Bay every morning, followed by an energetic run round and round a huge tree stump on the beach. Tibbs wrote voluble, friendly letters to Walter Dawley, including fussy and precise shopping lists. He ordered such items as "limewater glycerine" for his hair, lemons, mousetraps, nails, thimbles, a blue sweater, and on one occasion a can of bright pink paint, enclosing a sample of rose-covered wallpaper providing the hue to be matched. After passing on good wishes to everyone in the "liquid dominion of Clayoquot," as Tibbs called Dawley's establishment, he signed his name in a flourish of calligraphic curlicues. While living at Long Bay, Tibbs gave his return address as "Tidal Wave Ranch." He did no ranching there, but filled his days clearing land and establishing himself in a rough little cabin "built out of driftwood and gas cans and made quite ornamental," according to Mike Hamilton's memoirs, and featuring—if the paint did arrive as ordered—a rosy pink interior.

Early in 1910, Tibbs left Tidal Wave Ranch and took a job on remote Triangle Island off the northern tip of Vancouver Island, which he described as "this mountain top, surrounded by ocean." Tibbs assisted there with the construction of a new lighthouse, sending to Dawley for tennis shoes and a "good deep-toned mouth harp," to be shipped up on the supply vessel *Leebro*. He saved enough money for a trip to England, but by November 1911 he was back at his "ranch," in his spare time busying himself as president of the Clayoquot Conservative Association. The following year Tibbs took a job at the Kennedy Lake salmon hatchery and found himself increasingly drawn to Tofino. A small 1.2-hectare island in the harbour caught his fancy, so he sold his property at Long Bay and bought the island, which he christened Dream Isle, painting the name in huge white letters on the rocks. Here, Tibbs began to pursue his dreams, with the village of Tofino watching in complete astonishment.

In the first of many unexpected moves, Tibbs set about clear-cutting the entire island, blasting out stumps whenever he could. He had a

fondness for using large amounts of dynamite; loud explosions from Dream Isle became commonplace. Ignoring Jacob Arnet's kindly suggestion that he leave at least some trees for wind protection, Tibbs left only one tree in the centre of the island, an enormous spruce that he topped at thirty metres. Over time, he removed every limb, leaving a tall standing spar. Up this he built a sturdy ladder, almost a small scaffolding, mounting all the way, step by step, to the top, where he constructed a narrow platform. According to local legend, he would climb to the platform every morning with his cornet and serenade Tofino with lively tunes, in particular "Come to the Cookhouse Door, Boys." Having first lived in a tent on the island, Tibbs gradually built his dream home, a wooden castle, three storeys high, complete with a crenellated tower and battlements. Painted red, white, and blue, held to the rocks with steel guy-wires, the castle eventually housed a piano and a phonograph, with a garden alongside featuring trellised roses, a loveseat, and a sunken well. Inside, the walls were "beautifully ornamented by artistic designs in plaster work," according to George Nicholson, who managed Dawley's hotel at Clayoquot during the 1920s. Tibbs lived on the ground floor; the upper levels remained unfinished and

Fred Tibbs's "tree rig" on Dream Isle. He left one tall spruce standing on the island, limbed it, built a ladder, and ascended every day to the top, where he played his cornet. *Image F03431 courtesy of Royal BC Museum, BC Archives* accessible only by ladder. In the years leading up to World War I, Tibbs had just begun all this work; he continued doggedly on, year after year, with each new development establishing him ever more firmly as one of Tofino's leading eccentrics.

Although few could compete with Tibbs's highly visible idiosyncrasies, from the earliest days of settlement the west coast consistently attracted its fair share of oddballs: independent, stubborn individuals determined to go their own way, brooking no interference. Solitary, a little—sometimes very—peculiar, these men (and they were always single men) tended to disappear up the inlets or into the bush, finding remote places to live undisturbed, coming to town only when it suited them. Dorothy Abraham described how one of them, "tucked away in the most remote part of Kennedy Lake...lived year in and year out in the solitary wilderness," and how another, "the dirtiest specimen of humanity you could ever imagine," built a house on a cliff on a distant outside beach, lived on "coon meat and candied peel from kelp," and astounded everyone near the piano at the Clayoquot Hotel on one occasion with his exquisite rendition of Beethoven's *Moonlight Sonata*.

In his memoirs, Mike Hamilton also noted the presence all over Clayoquot Sound of "weird individuals, bearded and long-haired who somehow lived hidden away in some remote location," particularly recalling the American known as Fitz. Formerly a cowboy in Montana, Edward Fitzpatrick arrived on Flores Island in 1915, having pre-empted land sight unseen on the northwest coast of the island. He arrived aboard the *Tees* with a bull, two cows, two horses, some chickens—and even a plough, according to Hamilton. With no dock at Ahousat, the large animals had to swim for shore, while the missionary John Ross helped Fitz land the rest of his gear and the chickens by canoe. Fitz insisted he would farm his remote tract of land, even though, in John Ross's words, it consisted only of "muskeg and moss...[with] hard pan not far below." Laboriously, Fitz transported everything to his property by canoe, driving the larger animals along the shore and through the forest. He led an entirely solitary life in the cabin he built, emerging every month or so to purchase supplies, "a gaunt, unshaven figure, barefooted and clad only in overalls." In October 1915, Fitz came to the Ahousat store to purchase flour and coal oil, and headed out the next day in his skiff, planning to row the long distance home. Several people saw him off, including Mike Hamilton. Over two weeks later, a group of local boys, combing the shoreline for debris from the Chilean barque *Carelmapu*, recently wrecked off Schooner Cove, discovered Fitz's homestead deserted, the chickens dead, and no sign of life. Fitz had never made it home. Some Ahousahts finally spotted him marooned on an exposed rocky islet in a terrible state of emaciation and distress. He had survived the swamping of his boat and struggled to shore, salvaging the sack of flour, a can of kerosene, and a few other items, including five precious matches, stashed in his hair to keep dry. He sheltered in the roots of a tree, lit a small fire, and somehow survived for nineteen days. Father Charles Moser received word of Fitz's rescue from Pascal, one of the men who saved him. Fitz had written a note to the priest, explaining what happened: "Mr Pascal he got me of Iona Isl in sea where I was wrecked and I froze and starved 19 days. Will pay him well...God will be praised and glorified." Mike Hamilton wrote of Fitz with awe, in part because of his spectacular body odour and the caked black mud that had to be scraped off him by John Ross in an enforced bath at the Ahousat mission. Fitz returned to the United States in 1920.

A German man named Edmund Proestler also attracted considerable attention from time to time on his property at Long Beach. Strikingly bowlegged and very shy, he generally avoided people, working hard on his property where he could be, as Mike Hamilton recalled, "a one-man nudist colony. He worked so much with nothing on that he was almost as brown as an Indian." Occasionally, surprised visitors would come upon Proestler working naked, and he would flee into the bushes. He rarely came into Tofino, especially after World War I began. He so feared being arrested and interned he would only visit the village after dark to buy food.

Another storied local character, Bill Spittal, hailed from Glenshiel, Scotland. For many years he lived on the north side of Tofino Inlet in a leaky one-room shack, its walls streaked with tobacco juice, his sole companion a disreputable old dog named Joe Beef. Everyone had tales to tell of Bill Spittal, and he spun many a yarn himself about his prospecting experiences in the interior of British Columbia—how his nose had nearly frozen off, and the number of toes he had lost to frostbite when he had been given up for lost by his companions. "You know, he never washed his teacup," Ian MacLeod claimed. "It was just as if it had been varnished inside." Ian and his six siblings grew up in Tofino, where their father, Alex, was in charge of the lifeboat for many years. Bill Spittal and his dog made a lasting impression on local youngsters, perhaps because big, shaggy Joe Beef had such a fearsome reputation. "He was vicious," declared Ian. "The dog was deaf and dumb and he couldn't bark or nothing but he went around showing his teeth all the time." Bill and Joe Beef were inseparable, even sharing the same, unvarying diet of clams and ducks and fish. "You'd hear [Bill] passing down to Clayoquot to get drunk," Winnie Dixson recalled. The daughter of Tofino's first resident doctor, Winnie arrived as a young woman in 1912. "I've seen him singing for dear life and rowing. The tide was so strong he was going backwards when he thought he was going forwards." Brisk, matter-of-fact Winnie declared in an interview with Bob Bossin in 1981 that she never had much interest in men, nor time for them; she had milking to do, and people she checked on and people who needed to be fed. Nonetheless, she had a soft spot for Bill Spittal. They became unlikely partners in several of his mining interests, and when he died he left everything he had to Winnie. After his death, another reclusive Scot, Bill MacKay, lived in Spittal's cabin.

The BC Directory for 1910 contains an entry for Clayoquot that includes the Tofino townsite, giving the population of the overall area as "300 whites and 250 Indians." The directory provides names and employment of the male settlers, most of them described as carpenters or farmers, some as prospectors and miners, only two or three as fishermen. The directory lists several local amenities, the Methodist hospital on Stockham Island, the lifeboat station, and telegraph and post office among them. The newly constructed community hall, built by volunteer effort, and measuring 19 by 12.5 metres, receives no mention, but no fewer than four local stores can be counted: one at Clayoquot cannery, Dawley's store on Stubbs Island, Sloman's store, and that of William Stone and his son Stuart in Tofino.

A few years earlier the Stones had set up a little store on the island still bearing their name in Tofino Harbour—likely just a small operation in their own home. They had lived on the island since 1904, and the highly capable Christina Stone did her best to create a productive garden there, even bringing over a number of cows and setting up a small dairy. Later they moved into Tofino from the island and briefly ran their small store there, assisted by Wallace Rhodes. For many years Stone had been the Methodist missionary at Clo-oose, and his store-keeping efforts so close to Clayoquot annoyed Walter Dawley. Just as he did with Sing Lee and James Sloman, Dawley tried to prejudice his suppliers against Stone, even though Stone posed no threat. Writing to Dawley in May 1908, he apologetically stated "that our little venture in the store business was not against you but simply a means to a living."

Actively involved in local politics, Stone further infuriated Dawley by becoming leader of the newly formed Liberal Association, in response to the election of the Conservative Richard McBride as provincial premier in 1903. Following this election, the first in British Columbia involving party politics, Conservative and Liberal factions squared off locally, Dawley staunchly behind the Conservatives, Chesterman favouring the Liberals, in company with Stone. While Stone and his family lived in Tofino, his sons Chester and Stuart took over the machine shop started by Jens Jensen. After moving to Alberni in 1915, the family started a commercial transportation business that eventually boasted two well-known vessels, *Tofino* and *Roche Point*, frequently seen on the coast for years to come, delivering cargo and passengers.

Also in the 1910 directory listing for Clayoquot, an entry appears describing Dr. Melbourne Raynor, the Methodist doctor and missionary, as president of the Clayoquot Development League. This ambitious little organization, to which many prominent settlers belonged, emerged from the larger Vancouver Island Development League. Formed in 1909, the parent league brought together delegates "from...Quatsino; from Nootka, where marble quarries promise wealth...; from Clayoquot, from St. Josef and Holberg, from Banfield." They gathered to discuss the needs of their communities, radiating boundless optimism about the future and a shared passion to acquire roads. All league members, in every location, campaigned vigorously for roads. At meetings of the Vancouver Island League, roads to Quatsino, to Nootka Sound, to Tofino and Ucluelet, to Port Renfrew all came under discussion. Mountain ranges, budgets, and all other obstacles seemed not to matter. "Modern engineering laughs at the obstacles presented by mountain heights," declared a 1910 report on the development league's work. Such minor details must be overcome, for "the pressure of an immense Dominion, rapidly being peopled with incoming settlers from every part of the world, is behind the west coast of British Columbia, and before it lies the unlimited and only partially explored markets of the far East."

Writing of the development league in October 1910, the *Colonist* noted the recommendations made by Mr. J.J. Shallcross and other delegates who met with the premier and cabinet. "He recommended that the government be prepared to plant orchards to replace the Douglas Fir once the forest was logged." The delegates also suggested "reducing the pre-emption acreage—say from 160 acres to 80 acres [65 hectares to 32.5 hectares]—as a means to encouraging closer settlement...to remove or minimize the isolation so keenly felt by the majority of pioneer settlers." Harlan Brewster attended this meeting, announcing that "Alberni would be a railway terminal point in the very near future." Here he proved correct: the Esquimalt and Nanaimo Railway did indeed come to Alberni in 1911. Less accurately, Brewster also said that "considerable progress had been made last summer on the Alberni-Clayoquot road," a statement more hopeful than true. Perhaps because of this type of overstatement, the *Colonist* noted MLA John Jardine's dry comment: "With respect to the settlers who were finding their way to Vancouver Island, he regretted to learn that they not infrequently found things not as they had been led to believe...He thought the Vancouver Island Development League might with advantage be more careful in its advertising campaign."

In the years leading up to World War I, several development schemes on the west coast of Vancouver Island proposed wildly ambitious plans for settlement. Planners dreamed of remote Quatsino becoming a major railway terminus, a gateway to trans-Pacific trade. Land developers from Chicago created the short-lived Hesquiaht Land Company, noted in Father Charles Moser's diary when some unknown Americans came to investigate their holdings. Walter Dawley fielded letters from many hopeful speculators, including a Mr. A.R. Love in Liverpool, England, who claimed he could invest untold millions in land, any land. At Clo-oose, the most difficult boat landing on the coast, the West Coast Development Company put forward the wildest of all schemes, promising unwary investors the next Atlantic City, a major seaside resort complete with an amusement pier, tennis courts, and golf links. Dozens of people bought land sight unseen on the exposed coast at Clo-oose, expecting a bustling settlement, only to be greeted with nothing whatever on their arrival.

Nothing so grandiose occurred near Tofino, but the same sense of immense possibility fired the imagination of some settlers, along with a tendency to minimize practical problems. By 1912, with Francis Garrard as president, the Clayoquot Development League published a pamphlet explaining that although a good deal of land in the area was already taken up, lots remained available for pre-emption or purchase, costing from five to ten dollars per acre. While extolling the mild climate and the fertile soil, and providing detailed prices for agricultural produce—"butter brings 35 cents to 45 cents per pound, chickens, dressed, from 75 cents to $1.25"—the pamphlet conveniently failed to mention problems of transport or access to outside markets.

The most ambitious land development scheme near Tofino occurred on Vargas Island. Following the tragic death of their infant son, Edward, who died on Lennard Island in 1908 after accidentally eating a piece of lye, Francis and Annie Garrard decided to leave the light station. Pierre Hovelaque invited Garrard to join him in "taking up land and...holding it for sale making some profitable transactions," as Garrard wrote in his memoirs. On Vargas Island they obtained as much land as they could by pre-emption, lease, and purchase, "making in all 1280 acres [518 hectares] we would have control of, for our purpose." The two men started energetically, as Garrard's memoirs attest, each building a cabin and then clearing a "fair sized track" of land and seeding it in grass for future ranching. They even attracted the attention of "an American stock owner who looked over the land with a view of running stock on it," but the idea fell through. Having expanded their cabin, planted some fruit trees, and started a small garden, the Garrards split their time between Vargas and a home they had in Tofino. By carrying out various "improvements" to the land on Vargas, including land surveys and some clearing, fencing, and building, as well as bringing goats and a cow or two to the island, Garrard felt sure its value had increased. "We could feel we were rapidly becoming wealthy, on paper...we hoped by the disposal of the land as planned to make ourselves into a solvent concern."

Pierre Hovelaque made a trip to England shortly after he and Garrard acquired land on Vargas, and while there he likely advertised the land as being available for settlement, or he may simply have circulated the information among friends and acquaintances. Word spread, and Vargas Island succeeded in drawing a good number of British settlers, most without the faintest idea of what faced them. Young, single men arrived first, including Arthur and Ted Abraham, Donald Forsythe, Frederick Sydney Price, Freeman and Frank Hopkins, and their distant cousin Harold Monks. Several of them regularly ordered supplies from Dawley's store at Clayoquot, including Harry Hilton, who wrote for advice in March 1912: "Two or three weeks ago a party of four of us...secured a pre-emption each. We intend going into Residence in the near future & would like to know if it would be advisable to take up a stump puller." Expecting to be able to farm, they grappled with acidic and boggy soil, isolation, and major logistical challenges on an island well removed even from the marginal settlements nearby. Before long most of the young men sought additional employment, and after building their cabins on Vargas, several of them, including Harold Monks, found work at Clayoquot cannery.

Some of the men attracted to Vargas later brought their wives and extended families to the island. A small group settled at the north end, naming their cluster of homesteads Port Gillam, after the well-known steamer captain Edward Gillam; some surviving letters also refer to it as Port Vargas. They optimistically constructed a wharf there in the winter of 1914; it did not last one season before being destroyed in winter storms. The coastal steamer called regularly at Port Gillam for several years, even after the wharf disappeared. Away from this community, other settlers could be found in scattered homesteads around the island, several in the southeastern section, and one couple, the Clelands, in Open Bay (Ahous Bay) at the western side of the island. Famously, Cleland and his wife took horse and buggy rides, just for the fun of it, along the vast stretch of sand in the bay. Just how the horse and buggy came to be at this remote location beggars the imagination; no road but a rough corduroy trail stretched across the island, often floating in mud across boggy sections. Building and maintaining this trail was an arduous and thankless undertaking requiring the assistance of oxen. Traces of the trail can still be seen on the island.

Helen Malon stands out as one of the more unlikely settlers on the island. In July 1912, freshly arrived from England and en route to Vargas, she wrote in her diary: "Arrived Clayoquot about 3PM. Had to stay there the night as our beds had only arrived the same boat as us. Very primitive little place, hotel, one store, P. Office, Police station... there are other small settlements and Indian villages on the mainland and islands round. Hotel queer and primitive, but clean. John Chinaman cook, housemaid etc. We were introduced to various [settlers] all more or less queer, mostly more."

Helen came to this "queer" place at the urging of her two sons from her first marriage, Ted and Arthur Abraham, and her brother Arthur George Anderson. All three had taken up land on Vargas Island in 1911, a combined total of 203 hectares. Perhaps dazzled by this amount of land, Helen, widowed by her second husband, emigrated with her grown daughters, Violet and Eileen Abraham, and her two younger children, Pierre and Yvonne Malon. They planned to build a comfortable house, establish a farm, and start anew.

Vargas Island proved a far cry from the comfortable middle-class life the family had led on the Isle of Wight, in their large home with servants. "It was quite a shock to our feelings to find no house, only a shack," Helen wrote after her first nerve-wracking trip over to Vargas, with the family's goods loaded into a canoe and towed to the south-facing beach. "We have gone to a primitive life and no mistake, but I think we shall like it all right," she bravely asserted a month later. With significant gaps, her diary covers the years from 1912 until 1919, providing a terse commentary on the difficulties faced by a settler who found herself isolated, facing hard physical work, and in many ways entirely ill-suited to the life. She longed to be able to attend church regularly; she brought both a piano and, on one occasion, a piano tuner over to the island; she loved doing fancy needlework; and she suffered persistent ill health.

According to Francis Garrard, Helen Malon purchased less than a hectare of the land he and Hovelaque had owned, in the bay just east of Garrard's own Vargas home, looking over toward Stubbs Island. Garrard had quickly lost interest in the Vargas Island land scheme; by the time the Malons arrived, he and his family had moved into Tofino, and his partnership with Hovelaque had dissolved. Hovelaque remained on Vargas, and in 1920 he married Violet Abraham. They stayed on the island longer than any others and were still there in 1926, leading, as Garrard stated, "a very secluded life."

Helen Malon hired Hovelaque, along with other Vargas settlers, to build her new house in the bay she called "Suffolk Bay," from where she could see the boat traffic heading in and out of Tofino Harbour. Her sons Ted and Arthur settled into cabins on the more remote western side of the island, facing Wickaninnish Island. Years later, after World War I ended, her daughter-in-law Dorothy Abraham, married to Ted, decisively concurred with Helen's choice about where to settle on Vargas. "It seemed so difficult to believe that literally there were no roads of any sort, only blazed and partly cut out trails leading through the dense bush, through swamps, sometimes on floating corduroy on which we slipped and slithered, often more or less under water or mud. No fields! No grass! No people! No anything!" After the briefest experience of Ted's remote cabin, Dorothy declared, "My heart sank...then and there I told him I could not endure such loneliness...we decided right away to build on the other side of the island, next door to my in-laws."

Despite its brevity, Helen Malon's diary provides clear insights into the life of a European woman in Clayoquot Sound. No comparable document has survived. In particular, her diary shows the relentless amount of work required to establish and maintain a garden, and the urgent need to produce all the vegetables and fruit possible. Helen coaxed a profusion of black and red currants, strawberries, gooseberries, asparagus, peas, marrows, celery, cabbages, potatoes, beans, and other vegetables from the soil, not to mention the roses and geraniums she so loved. She fertilized with starfish, herring roe, sacks of herring, chicken manure, seaweed, and she never ceased trenching, digging, expanding. Once into her new house, she planted fruit trees of all descriptions. Jam-making filled a great deal of her time at harvest season; even in the dark of winter she did not stop, making nine kilograms of apricot jam one November from dried apricots, similarly peach jam from dried fruit, and always vast quantities of marmalade—13.6 kilograms in one go early in 1916—using marmalade oranges from the store at Clayoquot.

Unlike many settlers, Helen Malon evidently had at least some disposable income. She hired other settlers to build her home; she frequently employed aboriginals—named in her diary as Skookum Charlie, Big William, and Mr. Tom—to help clear land and cut wood; a woman named Jessie came to do the laundry. The new house had plenty of space and some elegant touches, including decorative panels of stained glass and carved corbels. Insofar as she could, Helen maintained the habits of a gentlewoman, passing days writing letters, devoting considerable time to making lace, confessing to being "too slack to do much but read all day." Her diary describes many occasions when she spent entire days in bed feeling unwell. Subject to fits of malaise, which she described vaguely as "felt rather seedy," "tired and stupid," "felt rather a wreck," Helen went through many bad spells and took to her bed.

Some diary entries revel in the natural beauties surrounding her. She took time to marvel at the "lovely great waves dashing in to the bay," "the sea magnificent, lovely bright dark green." She wrote of feeling "breezy and free" walking over the sands, and delighted in moonlit nights and the "phosphorous" in the sea. Settlers rarely indulged in

Vargas Island Picnic, circa 1913. Many of the men here would not survive World War I. Filled with zeal for "King and Country" (note the Union Jack) most of them enlisted and went overseas. After the war, the short-lived settlement on Vargas Island disappeared. *Ken Gibson Collection*

such comments in their practical, matter-of-fact diaries or letters. In nearly thirty years of diary writing, Father Charles Moser expressed almost no interest or pleasure in the surrounding scenery; nor did Francis Garrard in his memoirs. Yet in the few years she kept this diary, Helen Malon frequently did so.

Repeated themes in the diary show unceasing anxiety about boats and weather, near-desperate anticipation of mail, and continual worries about the children's health and about bad teeth, which plagued everyone. Oddly, Helen Malon received dental care on one occasion from "Young Brewster," who came to Vargas and removed two of her teeth—apparently Raymond Brewster, the eldest son of cannery owner Harlan Brewster. Another day she went up the inlet to the cannery with a family member "to have teeth seen to." Her diary gives vivid snapshots of unusual events: the entire lifeboat crew arriving on Vargas unannounced and having to be fed; the astonishment of an aboriginal woman seeing Violet Abraham wearing only a "bathing dress" as she worked in the chicken coop; the eager anticipation of a visit from the Chestermans, with a special cake baked, and sharp disappointment when they did not come. Detail after detail unfolds: bartering for fish with local people, purchasing woven baskets, awaiting news of a delayed steamer, and whenever possible getting off the island and going over to Tofino, in whatever vessel proved seaworthy—and many did not—to attend church.

Churchgoing initially meant going to services in the Tofino community hall; occasionally services even took place on the beach at Vargas, if a clergyman would come over. In July 1913, however, a team of volunteers, including Francis Garrard, Jacob Arnet, and John Chesterman, started to build a church in Tofino. On October 13, the first church service triumphantly took place in the new St. Columba Anglican Church. The idea for a church first arose in 1910, "during a picnic...on Vargas Island, at which were most of the inhabitants of Tofino and Stubbs Island," according to Garrard's memoirs. They held a meeting and decided to approach the Anglican diocese about establishing a parish. Fundraising soon began, staunchly supported by many locals and assisted by an endowment from the British philanthropist Baroness Angela Burdett-Coutts. The church also benefited from a bequest to the diocese by the family of Francis Beresford Wright in England, who wanted to contribute to build a church in a place of beautiful natural scenery. Over a century later, this church still stands in the town centre, lovingly maintained by a dedicated handful of people.

No substantial information appears in Helen Malon's diary about how the Vargas settlers interacted with aboriginal people living nearby, but evidently conflicts and tensions did arise. The Vargas people had placed themselves in traditional territory of the Kelsemaht people, now amalgamated with the Ahousaht, and the presence and attitudes of the newcomers caused much consternation. In May 1914, speaking of the Vargas settlers in his testimony to the McKenna–McBride Royal Commission on Indian Affairs, Chief Billy of the Ahousaht stated, "We are having trouble all the time." Chief Charlie Johnny of the Kelsemaht also testified to the commission about Vargas: "We had houses there, and we used to live there all the time—It was not Reserve but we used to live there all the time...I wrote to Mr. Neil about it, he was then the Indian Agent. I got an answer in which he said that white people had come on that place, and we would have to take our houses down, and said if we didn't Abraham would burn all the houses down."

Accustomed to coming and going freely on Vargas Island, the Kelsemaht and Ahousaht people simply could not comprehend white people settling there. Several aboriginal houses, most occupied seasonally, stood on lands taken up by settlers. According to George Sye's testimony to the McKenna–McBride Commission, one of the Abraham brothers felled a tree right through his house. "I said to him you had better not take down that tree until I have moved my house. But that same day he felled the tree, smashing my house all to pieces." At least two other settlers, Frank Perrotta and one of the Hopkins brothers, took possession of aboriginal houses and lived in them for a while. "The House was there before Hopkins came along," Chief Billy protested. "It was built a year before he came, and I want to know if it is right for a whiteman to come along and live in the place where the Indians have been living long years ago. Is it right—I would like to know—I don't want whitemen to come along and take the places where the Indian houses are."

To provide background to this dispute, Indian agent Gus Cox explained to the commission that one or both of the Abraham brothers had taken up land on an old Kelsemaht village site. "Mr. Abraham" had offered to provide 1.2 hectares of land elsewhere on the island in return for the village site, and an agreement had been drawn up to that effect. This arrangement quickly proved unworkable, because in the shuffle of lands the local people lost their excellent landing beach on the southeast corner of Vargas. Their objections led them to apply for extra reserve land on the land bordering this beach, at the old village site. The application proved successful, with the granting of a new eleven-hectare reserve there in 1916.

Before World War I, opportunity and optimism abounded for the settlers in and near Tofino. With a good dock, regular steamer service, a community hall, church, customs office, post office, school, and even a short-lived hotel/boarding house called the White Wing Hotel, the place seemed set to thrive. Lots in the Tofino townsite sold for about a hundred dollars, and eager campaigning for a road to Ucluelet continued. Energized by service organizations like the Women's Auxiliary of the church, the Settlers' Association, the Clayoquot Development League, and the Overseas Club, the town now had far more people than Clayoquot on Stubbs Island. Nonetheless, Garrard's memoirs darkly hint at more than one political plot in the pre-war years to "cause the spoiling of Tofino." Such plots threatened to close the Tofino telegraph and post offices, shifting them over to Stubbs Island, and abandoning all maintenance of the Tofino wharf.

Walter Dawley involved himself closely in such machinations, pitting the Conservative and Liberal factions of the area against each other. Never one to give up his schemes easily, Dawley clung for many years to his belief that a bustling community would grow up around him on Stubbs Island. In the early 1900s, this notion seemed entirely feasible to him, and his political allies bolstered the idea. In 1903 the like-minded James Redford, reassured him, "Not in our lifetime will there be sufficient business to establish a larger centre of population then you can acomadate [*sic*] on the island."

Holding to the dream, in 1906 Dawley arranged for a survey of Stubbs Island, laying out a future townsite on the northeastern section of the island, in the area behind the store and hotel. The plan for this imagined community, officially registered, outlines several blocks, each with ten lots, intersected by a proposed grid of streets named Manson, King, Queen, and Cordova Streets. None of this ever became a reality. In 1916, Dawley submitted a scheme for a further subdivision, on a larger tract of land, covering the northwestern section of the island. These subdivisions attracted no settlers, no investors, no development. At some point Dawley must have realized the futility of such schemes, but nothing indicates that he gave up easily.

By the time World War I began, the Clayoquot cannery provided steady employment; the Ptarmigan mine, with its new roads and tramways at Bear River, buzzed with activity; and the copper mine at Sydney Inlet and the Kalappa and Rose Marie mines seemed full of promise. Even more exciting, a spanking new west coast steamer, the *Princess Maquinna*, made her first voyage up the coast in July 1913, promising a vastly improved service.

The war changed everything. The mines closed down or went into liquidation, Walter Dawley found his suppliers could not fill all his orders, being obliged to attend to military orders first, and the international market for furs collapsed. One by one, younger men in town enlisted and went off to fight: Charlie Dixson, the doctor's son; Murdo MacLeod; Joe Grice; Arthur Grice; Arvo Haikala of the cannery; the schoolteacher Bert Drader; Burdett Garrard Jr.; Harold Sloman; Frederick Tibbs; the new police constable Robert Beavan. Lillian Garrard, having been encouraged by Dr. Raynor of the Methodist hospital on Stockham Island to study nursing, set off to England as part of the Canadian Army Medical Corps to nurse wounded soldiers. Jack Ross of Ahousat, the son of the Presbyterian missionary, enlisted, as did Harlan Brewster's son Raymond. Over the course of the war all four of Fred Thornberg's sons signed up: William Thornberg returned so badly wounded he died in Victoria in 1916; John joined the 28th Battalion and was seriously wounded.

On Vargas Island, Helen Malon wrote very little about the war in her diary, although it engulfed her life. When the guns of August 1914 sounded, the Malon and Abraham families had been on Vargas less than two years. Both Ted and Arthur Abraham enlisted immediately; September 1914 found them both at training camp in Valcartier, Quebec. Fletcher Cleland also enlisted at once; his attestation papers give his occupation as "rancher" and his address as "Westward Ho, Vargas Island"—the name he and his wife gave to their "ranch" on Ahous Bay. As the war progressed, other Vargas settlers signed up: Harold Monks, Frederick Sydney Price, Gerald Lane, George Anderson, the brothers Donald and William Forsythe and their uncle William, Harry Harris, the Hopkins brothers, Allan Carolan.

Freeman Hopkins and his brother Frank both enlisted in May 1916, leaving their young wives, Esther and Lillian, at Port Gillam on Vargas Island. When he left, Freeman instructed Esther to do business only with Walter Dawley. This led to a pathetic exchange of letters, with

Esther valiantly explaining to Dawley how she could not hire a motor launch to come to Clayoquot to make her purchases. "I trust you will pardon me," one letter ends. Unmoved, Dawley wrote to Freeman Hopkins at training camp in England, demanding he change his wife's shopping habits. In the subsequent exchange of letters, Hopkins promised that his wife would comply, suggesting she may have been "induced by others in this respect." In all likelihood, Esther Hopkins merely wished to purchase basic necessities on the island from local settler Helen Carolan, who briefly attempted to run a small store at Port Gillam. She gave it up a year or so after her young son Allan enlisted, aged only seventeen. "I understand young Carolan is going to Victoria this boat," wrote Dawley's assistant, Mr. Johnson, in a note to his boss on February 4, 1916. "His mother has at last consented to his joining up." Perhaps to console herself, Helen Carolan started up a small school for ten children on Vargas Island in 1916. She received seventy dollars per month in salary; the two school trustees were Esther Hopkins and Harry Hilton. The school lasted less than two years. Dorothy Abraham later wrote that, "like the wharf which was swept away at the first big storm, [the school], in turn, was swept away by the first school inspector who paid a visit to the island."

Francis Garrard noted in his memoirs how, "at the beginning of the war, there seemed to be a considerable amount of distrust between the Norwegians & the British element at Tofino, but later on after hearing of the sinking of many Norwegian vessels by the Germans, the former seemed to view matters more from the Canadian point of view." The tensions in the town spilled over in an angry letter from James Sloman, published in the *Colonist* on November 19, 1915, defending Tofino against accusations of being "pro-German." While admitting that in the early days of the war a few locals "who lacked...both brains and patriotism" made pro-German statements, he pointed out how "in Oct 1914, under the auspices of local Overseas Club, we called a patriotic meeting and raised $315 towards the patriotic fund; and since that time we have on different occasions raised toward the tobacco fund the following sums: $57, $45, $30, through the same agency, the Overseas Club." Sloman stated that out of a population of seventy-five men over the age of eighteen, ten had already enlisted as volunteers. "It is unfair, un-British," he fumed, "to rope, throw and brand a whole community for the actions and utterances of a few."

On November 7, 1917, Helen Malon wrote in her diary: "Mrs G. [Garrard] came over in the morning to tell us about my darling Arthur. God Keep Him." Arthur Abraham had died overseas. One letter survives from him to his mother, dated October 5, no year given, likely written from northern Europe. "It's about time for another letter I think especially as I have not gone into the trenches this time... So far as I have discovered at present my duties when the battalion is in the trenches consist of (I touch wood) looking after the requirements of one horse." With her two younger children and daughters Violet and Eileen, Helen Malon remained on Vargas for nearly two years following Arthur's death, never again mentioning him in her diary. By 1919, the family spent more time in Victoria than on Vargas, and by 1921, according to Helen's granddaughter Joan (Malon) Nicholson, the Malon house on Vargas stood deserted. Most other homes on Vargas met a similar fate.

Only a small handful of wartime letters from the local men who enlisted have survived. Some appear in Walter Dawley's correspondence. "Jerry Lane and Harry Harris are now over in France in the thick of it," Freeman Hopkins wrote in September 1916. That same month, Murdo MacLeod wrote: "I hope to live to see you & have a yarn about some of my experience since I left...That is if I don't get knocked out before that. It's the easiest thing in the world to get knocked to Kindom [Kingdom] come here...Writing under difficulties." In a letter to his two younger sisters in 1918, Raymond Brewster wrote: "Well dears I expect to be away to France before very long...I'll try to catch a nice little Kaiser for you." In one of his letters, Freeman Hopkins asked, "When is this war going to finish, as I am ready for home-sweet-home," a sentiment echoed by Murdo MacLeod: "Well we will be all glad when it's all over & back to God's Country again."

When the war ended, the list of dead from Tofino and Clayoquot Sound included Arthur Abraham, Raymond Brewster, Donald Forsythe, Burdett Garrard, Joseph Grice, Arvo Haikala, John MacLeod, Frederick

Sydney Price, Jack Ross, Frederick William Thornberg. The injured who returned included Murdo MacLeod, Wallace Rhodes, Jack Mitchell, Fletcher Cleland and John Thornberg. MacLeod had received serious facial injuries in 1916 at Courcelette and returned to the front, only to be seriously injured once again in 1917. Recuperating at Keighley War Hospital in Yorkshire, his astonishment only matched hers when he met Nurse Lillian Garrard from Tofino working on his ward.

Only two of the Vargas men who enlisted returned to live on the island following the war. Harold Monks returned and also Ted Abraham, bringing with him his energetic wife Dorothy. The Abrahams built a house near the Hovelaques, and Dorothy tried to come to grips with the isolation. In her book *Lone Cone*, she lamented how, with only her in-laws, the aboriginals, and one male settler nearby, she had "no-one to see all my nice English trousseau." Dismayed by the ugly masses of stumps on cleared land, yearning to play tennis on a groomed court, and hating to travel to Tofino over that "horrid piece of water," she tried to imagine life on the island before the war, with some thirty hopeful settlers in residence. Their places now lay abandoned and "it was very pathetic to come across little clearings and houses with desolate gardens, which had been laid out with such care and hard labour."

An era had ended on Vargas Island. In Tofino, the community regrouped and carried on.

Chapter 12:

DISCONNECTION

"MR GUILLOD [the Indian agent] used to say to the Indians that there would not be any white people here," Chief Jimmy Jim of Ahousat stated in May 1914. "They will not come here; it is too wild, he said, and white people would not use this land. That is what Mr. Guillod told my father." The chief was appealing to the officials of the McKenna–McBride Commission, trying to make them understand the Ahousahts' need for access to their traditional lands, and expressing his peoples' baffled disbelief at the changes being forced upon them. The commission, a group of government appointees, travelled the province for several years, visiting Indian reserves, hearing testimony from local leaders, considering requests for additional lands, and conferring with Indian agents, with the declared aim of settling once and for all the boundaries of Indian reserves.

Jimmy Jim's testimony to the commission reflects similar statements from many other aboriginal leaders in Clayoquot Sound and throughout the province. "Now the Indians are beginning to know...," he said. "Today they know they have so small a piece for my people. Some white men have 200 acres [81 hectares] or more, and some have 80 acres [32 hectares]. And why have we such a small place here. We were born here, and white settlers have a bigger place. Why don't we have bigger lands?"

The McKenna–McBride Commission hearings took place when "the life of the Nuu-Chah-Nulth people was uprooted, causing many different cultural 'breaks,'" as Ahousaht chief Earl Maquinna George stated in *Living on the Edge*. The population had dramatically decreased, and almost every bond in traditional aboriginal society had suffered some form of "cultural break": certain customs, such as the potlatch, had been banned; the people had lost traditional forms of barter and exchange for a cash economy; children were facing removal to residential schools; nations were gradually losing their languages; and perhaps most confusing and alarming of all, they were losing traditional territory and fishing grounds. The Nuu-chah-nulth's access to their traditional lands became radically restricted as settlement expanded, and the patches of land set aside as Indian reserves bore little relationship to the long-established understanding of traditional territories.

Most of the limited reserve lands set aside for Nuu-chah-nulth peoples of the west coast date back to the 1880s. Between 1882 and 1889, over the course of several trips to the area, Indian Reserve Commissioner Peter O'Reilly allotted reserves to all the different tribes on the coast, based on the assumption that people who relied on fishing did not need much land. When in the field, he worked fast, rarely spending more than a few days setting out reserve lands for any given tribe, carefully scheduling and planning his visits, attempting to see local authorities and chiefs, and briskly assigning the reserve lands as he saw fit.

In 1882, O'Reilly visited Barkley Sound and the Alberni area, and in the space of a week designated thirty-six reserves, almost all linked to sites of traditional fisheries. If Europeans happened to be living in a potential reserve area already, their claim to the land took precedence. Even so, O'Reilly assured one of the local chiefs that "the Government were anxious to secure to them all their fishing grounds." In 1886, O'Reilly arrived in Hesquiat Harbour, where he allotted five reserves. Three years later, in 1889, he spent most of June and early July in and around Clayoquot Sound, determining the reserve lands for the Tla-o-qui-aht and Ahousaht peoples.

For the Ahousaht, including the Manhousaht and Kelsemaht bands, he designated nineteen reserves; on the map these appear as a scatter-shot of small dots, mostly situated at traditional village sites and fishing grounds. The largest of the Ahousaht reserves, the traditional winter village site of Maaqtusiis in Matilda Inlet on Flores Island, measured 105 hectares, the next in size being 57 hectares at Wahous, located at the mouth of the Cypre River. Most of the Ahousaht reserves measured between 9 and 20 hectares; the three smallest measured 5, 4.5, and 2.5 hectares. O'Reilly allotted ten reserves for the Tla-o-qui-aht people, the two largest being 73 hectares at Opitsat and 44.5 hectares at Clayoqua

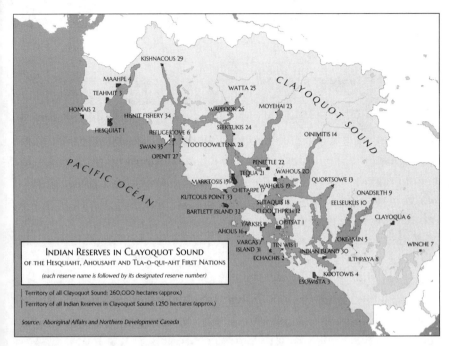

Established in the 1880s, Indian Reserves represent less than 0.5 percent of the total territory of Clayoquot Sound.

at the mouth of the Clayoquot River. The smallest Tla-o-qui-aht reserve, Ithpaya, measured 1.4 hectares and was on the "northerly shore of Kennedy Lake at the rapids," according to the Schedule of Indian Reserves. The Okeamin reserve, a traditional fishing village on the eastern bank of the Kennedy River near Tofino Inlet, measured 9.7 hectares and had fourteen houses. As Douglas Harris pointed out in his book *Landing Native Fisheries*, this last reserve included for the Tla-o-qui-aht the right to fish in the river from the boundary of the reserve downstream for about a kilometre and a half to the tidal waters of the Tofino Inlet. Yet only a few years after these reserves were established, the Clayoquot cannery began operating in that fishing area, having acquired 64.7 hectares of land nearby, specifically to access this same fishery. So the fishing rights granted to the Tla-o-qui-aht people on the Kennedy River, where they had always fished, proved far from exclusive. O'Reilly later denied he had allocated an exclusive fishery.

By the time his term as Indian Reserve Commissioner came to an end in 1898, Peter O'Reilly had established 654 Indian reserves throughout British Columbia, bringing the total number to just over 1,000. With these reserves set aside on the West Coast and elsewhere in the province, government authorities and incoming settlers perceived all the rest of the land to be entirely unoccupied, thus available for settlement and for industrial exploitation. As Cole Harris wrote in *Making Native Space,* "Opening land for others to own is what Indian reserves were intended to do." With the diminishing population of native people officially corralled within their small, assigned spaces, others now took over the vast remaining spaces of British Columbia.

Few colonists ever questioned this; one notable exception was Gilbert Sproat. In 1860, Sproat overruled the objections of the Sechart people in the Alberni area when he arrived with two armed vessels and some fifty men to take possession of land at the head of Alberni Inlet, enabling Captain Edward Stamp to establish a sawmill and a settlement. Governor James Douglas contributed the gunboat *Grappler* to add to this show of force, and to ensure the takeover of the land. "We often talked about our right as strangers to take possession of the district," Sproat later wrote. While he believed that strangers did have the right to purchase the land, he recognized that at Alberni "it was evident that we had taken forcible possession of the district." His book *Scenes and Studies of Savage Life,* published in London in 1868, reveals how, as time passed, he felt increasing concern about the "injuries and discouragements [that] come upon the aborigines, through the occupation of their country by the settlers. Their hunting and fishing places are intruded upon, their social customs disregarded, and their freedom curtailed, by the unwelcome presence and often unmannerly bearing, of those who are stronger than themselves." In 1876, Sproat became one of the first three Indian Reserve Commissioners, appointed as a team, before Peter O'Reilly took over. Sproat's increasing sympathy for the aboriginal point of view, and his assumption that aboriginal people would control the fisheries on their reserve lands, made him unpopular with government authorities. The three-person team disbanded in 1878, and Sproat continued as the sole commissioner. Considered too generous with his land settlements, he was forced to resign in 1880.

Peter O'Reilly initially appeared to share Sproat's assumption about aboriginals controlling their fisheries, but later he backed away from this position. In the 1880s the federal government began the process that ended in its taking over legal control of all fisheries, relegating aboriginals to a subsistence food fishery. The result, according to Cole Harris, is that "many Native people today live in settlements that once depended on fisheries, and on reserves that were allocated to be fishing stations, but, because of one licensing scheme or another, have access to only a small share of the fisheries at their doorsteps."

In May 1914, the evidence given by Nuu-chah-nulth leaders at the McKenna–Mc-Bride Commission's hearings at Opitsat, Ahousat, Hesquiat, and Nootka consistently focused on a few main points. They all wanted more lands made available to them; they wanted to be free to harvest cedar trees for canoes and bark; above all, they expressed confusion, dismay, and sometimes anger about the restrictions on hunting and fishing, particularly fishing. Chief Napoleon of Nootka spoke for all First Nations on the coast when he told the commission "I don't want any white men to...[take away] any of our land or fishing places or hunting places, because God made us this way and put us in the places where we live." A young man at the time of the McKenna–McBride hearings, Chief Napoleon had been educated at Christie Indian Residential School at Kakawis on Meares Island. In 1908 he married Josephine, who also had attended Christie School, in a lavish Christian ceremony at Friendly Cove, the first such ceremony

Mowachaht chief Napoleon Maquinna with his bride Josephine on their wedding day in 1908. They both attended Christie School in its earliest years, and were married in the Roman Catholic church at Yuquot, with the Christie School band in attendance. Chief Napoleon gave testimony in 1914 at the McKenna–McBride Royal Commission hearings, speaking eloquently about his people's need for more land.
Mount Angel Abbey Library

The McKenna–McBride Royal Commission held its hearings in various locations in Clayoquot Sound in the spring of 1914, hearing testimony from aboriginal leaders as they argued for more land for their people. This scene shows the hearings on May 18, 1914, at Maaqtusiis. "My people are not going away from the places where they used to live," declared Chief Billy, during his long and powerful testimony. *Image H07174 courtesy of Royal BC Museum, BC Archives*

for a native leader on the west coast. Like the older Nuu-chah-nulth leaders, Chief Napoleon pointed out very basic problems concerning his people's access to resources, including how they could no longer even gather logs from the beach freely. "The white people that are around here," Chief Napoleon explained, "...stop us taking the logs and timber along the beaches. [They] don't want us to take any of that lumber or any of the wood."

The testimony of Chief Billy of Ahousat fills several pages in the published record from the McKenna–McBride Commission. He repeatedly stated his fear that white men would destroy the houses of Native people, giving examples from Vargas Island of aboriginal houses that had been either used or destroyed by settlers. He also told of other aboriginal houses on non-reserve lands that had been there for many years for seasonal use when the people fished there; he feared their removal. He commented on the increasing scarcity of fish; he described many traditional fishing sites and their various uses; he solemnly stated, "My people are not going away from the places where they used to live." He also specifically asked the commission about beach wood on Vargas

Island, and whether his people could take wood from the beaches in front of the new settlers' homesteads: "One time we went on to the beach and picked up a piece of 2 X 4 lumber and he ["Mr. Abraham"] said to us you can't take that—that lumber belongs to me. And don't you come on this beach any more, because that is my beach. Therefore I want to know when he buys the land does he get the beach?" The chairman of the commission replied, "If a man buys a piece of land the beach on which it fronts belongs to him. And it is the same with the Indian on his reserve."

In his testimony, Jimmy Jim of Ahousat spoke of access to good timber: "The white settlers can take up timber limits on the lands, stay here in Clayoquot a few years, and after they have cleared up a little place of farm land, they sell it for a good many hundred dollars and sometimes thousands of dollars and then get away...we know that us poor Indians here have nothing. We cannot sell any timber land or we can't down the timber on our own reserves. It is just like holding us as blind men." He elaborated: "There are a few cedar trees around the shore from the bark of which we made baskets. We cannot do that anymore. We cannot cut down the cedar trees so that we can make canoes or can get the bark. What are we going to do for a living?" He spoke of the restrictions imposed on his peoples' use of their traditional summer camp area on Kennedy Lake; they were no longer permitted to fish or even trap there. The land around Kennedy Lake, and all of its rich resources, had always been central to Tla-o-qui-aht life; here stood their heartland, their major source of sustenance. Their increasingly curtailed access to the lake and its resources, and to many other traditional sites, baffled and angered them. "We wish to have a place to make canoes and some other things...We want to ask you to be allowed to do the same as the white men are doing here with their lands and timber limits."

The Nuu-chah-nulth leaders all faced questions from the commission about how they used their various reserve lands, and why they required the additional lands they were requesting. All of their answers related to long-established patterns of fishing or sealing or some form of harvesting from the sea or land: they explained their connection to these lands in terms of access to different salmon runs or to clams, berries, seal, halibut, cedar trees. They described how and where they harvested and processed these and other resources, season by season. Every village site or summer fishing camp or stream had a story behind it of long-standing, usually seasonal, occupation and specific usage. When asked to explain why the Ahousahts had so many different traditional places for fishing in one area, Chief Keitlah gave the obvious reply: "So that we could go from one place to another. That is how we got the fish." With some twenty-four fishing streams and rivers in their territory, the Ahousahts simply followed the salmon, travelling anywhere from eight to thirty-two kilometres from the main village of Maaqtusiis. The name of the village reflects these movements; it means "moving from one place to another."

Chief Joseph of Opitsat expressed his perplexity at no longer being allowed to fish from the 44.5-hectare Clayoqua reserve. "They put us in jail for it," he stated. The restrictions on fishing at Kennedy Lake dated back to October 1905, when John Grice, as fisheries officer, and fisheries inspector Edward Taylor first informed the local people they could not continue to fish there. Father Charles Moser attended the meeting with the fisheries inspector on October 30, 1905. His diary reports that Taylor forbade the Tla-o-qui-aht to fish in the lake and also banned "the use of nets (they still could use spears) in the river coming from Kennedy Lake. The Indians were wild and used insulting language to the Inspector." Taylor also banned traditional fish traps in the river. In subsequent letters to Taylor, John Grice commented that the ban on fishing in Kennedy Lake seemed a "desperate remedy" and that "I came in for my share of abuse."

Nine years later, at the time of the McKenna–McBride Commission hearings in the area, fishing in Kennedy Lake remained contentious. Tensions increased following the establishment of the hatchery on the lake in 1910. Limitations on fishing in the Kennedy River had become even stricter, the Clayoquot cannery effectively having taken control of that fishery. Kelsomaht Charlie testified to this before the commission, saying, "I want to tell you that Mr. Grice does not like to see the traps in the creek so we took them down, and Mr. Grice used to go down to [Harlan] Brewster and tell him to get the fish right in the creek, with a seine...There used to be lots of fish in the creek, but since the cannery has come on that creek there is no fish there at all." Jasper Turner of Opitsat also gave evidence: "The canneries get all the fish and we have nothing for the winter. Of course we cannot live on the white people's food, we have to live on our own."

The McKenna–McBride Commission also scrutinized the monetary value of reserve lands, and the value of the extra lands being requested by the various tribes. At the Tla-o-qui-aht hearings, John Grice gave evidence about this, generally valuing reserve land for the tribe at twenty to forty dollars per acre (less than half a hectare), with the exception of Esowista, the seven-hectare (seventeen-acre) reserve out at Long Beach. "That is the most valuable, for this reason," Grice explained. "There is a lot of talk about the CPR building a hotel on Long Beach which practically adjoins this particular reserve. A section was sold, consisting of about 70 acres, for $5,000 not very long ago. And I should think the value of this 17 acres would be $4000." The short-lived rumour about a CPR hotel at Long Beach quickly died away, along with rumours about a railway line extending to Long Beach. Without such speculative value, Grice estimated the Esowista reserve to be worth only thirty dollars per acre.

The Nuu-chah-nulth leaders who gave testimony to the McKenna–McBride Commission requested that specific areas of land, clearly identified, be granted to them. Like his fellow chiefs, Chief Joseph of Opitsat spoke with straightforward eloquence. "I am the Chief here. I am going to tell you what I have in my mind...I have 221 Indians and this place is too small for that number of people. I am very anxious to get more land for my people." His requests for land on behalf of the Tla-o-qui-ahts included all of Wickaninnish Island, all of Indian Island in Tofino Inlet, and four small fishing stations out at Long Beach. The Ahousaht, Kelsemaht, and Manhousaht requests included both Blunden and Bartlett Islands, Kut-cous Point, various lands on Vargas Island, and some land in Mosquito Harbour, "all covered with timber limits [licences]," according to Indian Agent Gus Cox.

If the requested lands had already been assigned as timber licences, the aboriginal people stood little to no chance of acquiring them for additional reserves. An immense amount of land had already passed beyond their reach in this way. Between 1905 and 1909 a rush of timber speculation occurred in British Columbia, with the government granting thousands upon thousands of timber licences. These encompassed vast tracts of land around Kennedy Lake, on Meares and Flores Islands, and throughout Clayoquot Sound, much of it going to Sutton Lumber, anticipating construction of the Mosquito Harbour mill. With this timber-licence land off limits, the Tla-o-qui-aht request for all of Indian Island seemed doomed to fail, as one of William Sutton's many timber licences covered most of the island. The Tla-o-qui-aht did eventually acquire a small new reserve on Indian Island: "that portion of the island exempt from the Sutton timber license." Although logging in Clayoquot Sound had scarcely begun at the time of the McKenna–McBride Commission, this system of granting renewable timber licences set the standard for future logging practices, effectively alienating huge swathes of heavily timbered land. The fate of this land became the flashpoint of an international storm of controversy in the late twentieth century.

Land pre-empted, Crown-granted, or purchased by settlers also stood beyond the reach of Nuu-chah-nulth requests. By 1914, such land accounted for almost all of the Esowista Peninsula and the land bordering on Tofino Inlet, large tracts around Kennedy Lake, most of Vargas Island, and numerous islands and scattered parcels of land throughout Clayoquot Sound. Settlers or land speculators holding land had nothing to fear from aboriginal requests for additional reserves; they knew their claim to the land would be considered superior and upheld. So when Chief Joseph requested all of Wickaninnish Island for the Tla-o-qui-aht people, Walter Dawley had absolutely no cause for concern. Dawley had applied to purchase the entire island in March 1912, declaring he would use the land "for agricultural purposes." He paid a total of $2,145 for the 156-hectare island. The Crown grant (Number 6654) ceding the island to him was registered in Victoria on May 13, 1914, only two days before the McKenna–McBride Commission met with Tla-o-qui-aht leaders and heard Chief Joseph's request for the island. The commission denied the chief's request.

Some of the local chiefs indicated, in their testimony to the commission, that they realized their requests for particular parcels of land would prove hopeless. When Chief Billy of Ahousat recalled some land at Bear River that former Indian agent Harry Guillod had promised to Chief Billy's father, he commented: "A white man came along, and he is living there now, and I don't know that I'm going to get that place, because a white is living there now...I don't think I am going to get that land any more." He was right.

As west coast Indian agent at the time of the commission hearings, Gus Cox tried his best to help with various requests for land in his testimony to the commission. He supported several, including the Ahousaht applications for both Blunden and Bartlett Islands. He endorsed many statements the Nuu-chah-nulth leaders made to the commission, and he encouraged every action possible to preserve their right to fish, saying, "I think they ought to have the privilege of catching fish at any time of the year for their own use." He firmly asserted that the responsibility for depletion in fish stocks in Clayoquot Sound lay with the cannery owners, that it had nothing to do with the native fishery, which never harmed fish stocks. He stressed the futility of officials insisting that aboriginals on the coast should clear the land and grow vegetables, saying the land did not lend itself to this. He also stated, "I think it is absurd that the Indians should not be allowed to cut down the timber on their reserves," explaining that "the Department won't allow them to cut down any timber on their reserves without first getting a permit from the Agent and then that permit only covers two or three trees...I think the Indians ought to be allowed as much as they want."

The hearings of the commission did not last long, just a few hours in each location. The officials stuck to a strict schedule, always needing to move on to the next reserve and the next tribe a day or so later. Questions posed by the commissioners consistently focused on the same matters: they asked about numbers of people, canoes, and gasoline boats on each reserve; they asked about agriculture, about cows, about fish stocks and clam beaches, about hunting and trapping, about firewood supplies, about summer fishing camp sites. They always asked for named beaches and tracts of land to be identified on maps, a process entirely unfamiliar to the chiefs giving testimony; they knew their territories intimately, but not on printed maps.

The dauntingly formal hearings proceeded with sworn testimony heard before government authorities seated behind a table. The chiefs giving testimony faced close questioning, and most had to speak through an interpreter. Discouraged by such an alien process, many potential participants decided not to attend. Some, like Police George of Opit-sat, submitted a letter instead. At Hesquiat, the day after the Ahousat hearing, Father Charles Moser noted in his diary the arrival of the commission on board the *Tees*. "Only few Indians being here word was sent to Home-is for men to come and make suggestions and put in claims in regard to Indian claims for lands. But these did not arrive before 8 PM, which time was too late for a meeting." Pleased to have officials visiting, Father Charles boarded the *Tees* and enjoyed a slap-up dinner courtesy of the visitors. "When I left them in the evening Chief Steward Richards gave me a box along with apples, oranges, bananas, grapefruit, nuts, cucumbers and a bottle of cognac." Of the meeting with Hesquiaht leaders the following day, Father Charles wrote only "it was short." Mike Hamilton happened to be at Hesquiat, working to install the new telegraph line, at the same time as the McKenna–McBride Commission hearings. He noted the presence of the visiting officials in his memoirs: "I have no knowledge of who they were and just what they accomplished; not very much by all evidence. Poor Indians!"

The commission's work in Clayoquot Sound produced few changes, granting only a few new reserves in 1916, not nearly as much land as requested. The Tla-o-qui-aht acquired only 36.5 hectares on Indi-an Island. The Ahousaht gained Bartlett Island and Kut-cous Point at the south end of Flores Island, and the Kelsemaht acquired an 11-hectare patch on the southeast corner of Vargas Island, an old village site adjacent to the property owned by the Abraham family. Although Indian Agent Cox stated that "it has always been my policy to try and keep the whites and the Indians as far apart as possible, for the sake of both," at this one corner of Vargas Island they were in close proximity, for a while at least. Elsewhere in Clayoquot Sound, at the time of the commission, most reserves stood some distance from settlers. Nonetheless, aboriginals felt hemmed in and surrounded, if not directly by settlers, certainly by the alienating force of fisheries restrictions in waters they had once freely used, and by timber licences on land they thought of as theirs. As Chief Joseph put it: "[The land] is all taken up by white settlers who surround the reserve all round, and pretty soon there will be no room." Possibly more than any other Nuu-chah-nulth leader in Clayoquot Sound, Chief Joseph had reason to hope his requests for extra land might be heeded. For many years he had been held in high regard by settlers, by various employers, by the storekeepers, by the missionaries. And as George Nicholson pointed out in the *Daily Colonist*, Chief Joseph's "counsel was of inestimable value to both the department of Indian affairs and provincial police." But none of this helped when he asked for more land for his people.

As the McKenna–McBride Commission concluded its hearings, the Nuu-chah-nulth people struggled to adjust to a social and economic framework that had changed incalculably in only a few decades. Outsiders had assumed control of their lands and waters. The fur seal industry brought them into the cash economy but that source of income dwindled away, and the people now sought seasonal work in canneries and on hop farms, often far from home. The traditional seasonal rhythms of fishing and food gathering were faltering, and many people, particularly the elderly or the sick, now depended on the Indian agent to provide handouts of flour, sugar, and tea for their very survival. On top of all this, the potlatch ban, in effect since 1884, began to be enforced in an entirely new manner, so this traditional means of wealth redistribution, this institutionalized, engrained generosity among the people, no longer worked as it had in the past.

For many years the potlatch ban had little impact, and on the West Coast these traditional giveaway ceremonies and gatherings continued more or less as before. Potlatches had expanded in the late nineteenth century, becoming increasingly lavish as more money and trade goods became available. In British Columbia, the most elaborate potlatches occurred among the Kwakwaka'wakw (Kwakiutl) people in and around what is now Alert Bay. Host families sometimes gave away canoes, motor launches, money, jewellery, furniture, sewing machines, and

253

musical instruments as well as the more traditional potlatch fare—flour, rice, clothing, basins, plates, blankets, and apples. On the west coast of Vancouver Island, potlatches never reached the proportions of Kwak-waka'wakw potlatches, being smaller and less lavish, yet they served many needs in the changing coastal communities, for all concerned. As Chief Maquinna cleverly pointed out to Indian agent Harry Guil-lod back in 1886, potlatches acted as "an incentive to industry, a great help to the white trade in Victoria." Local traders like Walter Dawley consistently benefited from them, carrying items for what he noted in his ledgers as "Ind. Trade," often cheaper goods of lesser quality for potlatching. "Ind. shawls," as Dawley called them, sold for twenty-five cents in 1899, destined for potlatches; better-quality shawls then fetched one dollar. Crates of soup plates, washbasins, apples; stacks of blankets; and countless bolts of print fabric passed through Dawley's hands, at a profit, for potlatches.

Stories of wife swapping, prostitution, and drinking tainted reports of some potlatches, as well as tales of European men taking advantage of these events by providing alcohol, abusing women, and spreading venereal disease. Yet despite occasional outbursts from government authorities about the perceived evils of potlatching, and about the dangers of spreading contagious illnesses like tuberculosis or measles at such crowded gatherings, little concerted effort went into enforcing the ban. "The priests and ministers of all denominations condemn the feast," wrote Father Augustin Brabant, a comment that seems little more than a nod to the authorities. "As for me, I cannot see any harm in it, although I would rather have it abolished," he added, with evident disinterest. His successor at the Hesquiat mission, Father Charles Moser, largely shared this indifference. In his diary spanning the first three decades of the twentieth century, containing thundering denunciations of many other aboriginal customs, Father Charles never once condemned the potlatch, though he mentioned it frequently. "Four painted up and feathered Indians invite me to a potlatch to be held on the 10th," he wrote on February 6, 1906. Being too busy offloading freight from the schooner *Allie Alger*, he could not attend, "but a dollar was given to me anyhow."

The generally laissez-faire attitude toward potlatching came to an abrupt end under the stern eye of Duncan Campbell Scott, deputy superintendent of the Department of Indian Affairs from 1913 to 1932. Dismissing the "senseless drumming and dancing" of potlatches, as well as the sun dances and thirst dances of the Prairie First Nations, Scott determined to enforce the federal law against all these practices. He questioned how anyone could sympathize with such traditions, maintaining that "the original spirit has departed, and...they are largely the opportunities for debauchery by low white men." Repelled by the "prolonged idleness and waste of time, by ill-advised and wanton giving away of property and by immorality," Scott demanded that Indian agents and police take action against potlatching.

Renowned for his poetry as well as his career as a bureaucrat, Scott often wrote of aboriginal people in highly romantic terms. In his verse, they appear as a noble and doomed people, famously summarized as "a weird and waning race" in his poem "The Onondaga Maiden." Waning indeed. When Scott ruled the Department of Indian Affairs in Ottawa, the aboriginal population had been diminishing for decades as the twin scourges of tuberculosis and alcohol did their worst. Some schoolchildren growing up in BC during the 1920s and 1930s heard in the classroom that aboriginal people would likely not exist in the future; they were all dying out.

In their book *An Iron Hand upon the People*, Douglas Cole and Ira Chaikin describe how enforcement of the potlatch ban in Scott's era led to arrests and even to imprisonment, particularly for the Kwakwaka'wakw people, during the 1920s. The potlatch took a beating, more so in some areas than others, but the tradition survived. Hosts chose hidden locations, and they and their guests became expert at evading the authorities or putting up organized resistance and argument. Among the Nuu-chah-nulth, according to Cole and Chaikin, the practice survived, particularly in out-of-the-way places unfrequented by law enforcement officers. Gordon Gibson attended a number of potlatches at Ahousat in the 1920s, during the height of the enforcement period, and witnessed the generous and practical gifts—everything from smoked salmon to a dugout canoe—being lavished on guests from as far away as Nootka.

In the twelve- by twenty-four-metre longhouse, with walls made of 3.6-metre cedar splits, some ten or twenty families would gather for a few days. "The dirt floor was raked smooth, and a little light came through holes made in the roof for the smoke...Three separate cooking fires were often needed for a big potlatch...Some guests would be sleeping while others were dancing, singing or swapping tales."

Government opposition to the potlatch gradually fizzled out, and by the end of World War II had all but disappeared. More pressing issues of social justice, education, housing, and resource management came to dominate the agenda for First Nations. The law against the potlatch dropped from the statutes in 1951. As the cultural revival of First Nations became increasingly strong through the ensuing decades, potlatch traditions have been revitalized up and down the coast.

As Tofino grew and began to flourish in the early decades of the twentieth century, as more settlers arrived, as more small enterprises took root, as more newcomers plied the waters of Clayoquot Sound, the connections among the various new arrivals slowly strengthened, and a sense of community grew. During these same decades, local First Nations reached their lowest ebb as tuberculosis and other diseases, including measles, whooping cough, venereal disease, and alcoholism, ran rampant. The people became increasingly disconnected from their former way of life.

In the villages on the west coast, missionaries were eager to exert ever more control in their zeal to Christianize and control the people they called pagans. Increasingly, the attention of the missionaries turned to influencing the children. Schools for aboriginal children arrived gradually in Clayoquot Sound: first a handful of sectarian day schools opened and closed sporadically; then, from the turn of the century onward, residential schools appeared. Of all the disconnections faced by the aboriginal people of the area, this would be the worst of all: the growing disconnection from their own children as one generation after another passed through these schools.

Chapter 13:

SEPARATION

BY 1914, THE PROVINCE OF BRITISH COLUMBIA operated sixteen church-run and government-funded residential schools for aboriginal children. Three of these stood on the west coast of Vancouver Island: the Presbyterian school at Alberni, which opened in 1891, and the two residential schools in Clayoquot Sound. A mere 14.5 kilometres separated the Roman Catholic Christie School at Kakawis on Meares Island from the Presbyterian residential school near the village of Maaqtusiis on Flores Island. These schools dominated their surroundings. The Nuu-chah-nulth Tribal Council's book *Indian Residential Schools* explains: "In the past, the largest building...was the house belonging to the head Chief of that community. The comparatively huge residential school buildings implied an importance above and beyond that of any local traditional authority...Residential schools had an overwhelming physical-cum-political presence in Nuu-chah-nulth territory."

In the many decades of their existence in Clayoquot Sound, the residential schools at Kakawis and Ahousat housed thousands of children from up and down the coast. During the 1920s and 1930s, attendance at Christie School hovered between 60 and 75 students. The Ahousat school always had fewer students, averaging in those years 35 to 50, though enrolment peaked at 75 in 1939. That same year, following expansion, student numbers at Christie School increased to 101, giving a joint enrolment at the two schools of 176 children. The Ahousat residential school closed in 1940, leaving Christie School as the only residential school in Clayoquot Sound from then on. Following World War II, Christie School consistently housed well over 100 students each year, some years more than 120. When Christie School closed in 1971, the school still had over 100 students.

One of the earliest group photographs of Christie School students, taken in the early 1900s in the school chapel. *Mount Angel Abbey Library*

Christie School at Kakawis first opened in 1900 with thirteen children, increasing to twenty-eight within weeks. A group of priests, brothers, and nuns, all members of the Benedictine Order based at Mount Angel, Oregon, formed the original staff at the school, arriving only twelve days before the first students. Many of these Benedictines came from Belgium and Switzerland; they arrived in North America believing they would be working among the aboriginals of Oregon, near Mount Angel Abbey, never dreaming of ending up on the West Coast of Canada. But Bishop Alexander Christie of Victoria arranged with their superiors to have them come to Christie School and so, with English as their second language, absolutely no experience of boats or the sea, and after years of living in supportive religious communities, they arrived. Among them was the school's first principal, Father Maurus Snyder; also Father Charles Moser, determined to record events in his diary:

"In the year of our Lord 1900 on May 16th," he wrote, "there arrived at Clayoquot on the West Coast of Vancouver Island, BC, Canada the following: Rev P. Maurus, Rev Chas. Moser, The Ven Bros. Leonard and Gabriel, also the Benedictine Sisters Sr M. Placide, Sr M. Frances, and Sr M. Clotilde. We were to take charge of the recently built Christie School." The school awaited them, freshly painted, still smelling of sawdust, standing high on a south-facing bank overlooking a curving sand beach. Large, imposing, gleaming white, this structure became far larger over the years with various additions and changes. It would stand at the base of Lone Cone for most of the next century.

Father Augustin Brabant had vigorously campaigned for this school since 1895, when he approached Bishop Jean Lemmens in Victoria with the idea. Without a school, Brabant feared his bitter adversaries, the Protestants, would prevail. "Their efforts to invade the coast are very pronounced," he wrote anxiously. Protestants had been making their presence felt on the coast since the early 1890s, mostly in Barkley Sound and at Nitinat, but by the mid-decade Brabant knew they had infiltrated "his" part of the coast, intending "to give us trouble and pervert our Indian children." Bishop Lemmens died in 1897, and in 1899 his successor, Bishop Alexander Christie, approved the construction of the Catholic residential school on Meares Island. Brabant selected the site and considered it ideal, because it distanced the children from their own villages and from settlers. The school received a per capita government grant for the education of fifty children. "If we do not accept the grant," wrote Christie, "it will be given to one of the sects; your children will be perverted and you will lose the fruit of all your labours."

Father Maurus Snyder (left) and Father Charles Moser, both Benedictines from Mount Angel Abbey in Oregon, arrived in Clayoquot Sound in May 1900. Father Maurus served as principal at Christie School until 1911. Father Charles became missionary at Opitsat for ten years, later replacing Father Brabant as missionary at Hesquiat, and then working at Christie School in the 1920s. His diary spans thirty years, a valuable source of west coast information. *Mount Angel Abbey Library*

Although the residential school at Ahousat opened five years after Christie School, it had been a gleam in the eye of the Presbyterians ever since 1896, when missionary John Russell first arrived there and opened a day school in the village. In 1901 he applied to the Department of Indian Affairs for the bigger prize. He wanted a residential school because only then, in his estimation, could he exert the control he desired. By removing the children from the influences of their home life, he could more readily convert them to Christianity, turn them from their "pagan" ways, and ensure they spoke only English. Russell argued that although over sixty children "received instruction" at the Ahousat day school in 1901–2, the average attendance had been only twelve per day, a number that had dropped from previous years. He attributed this "to the wandering of the parents for fishing and hunting purposes. As the sealing industry decreases they go in larger numbers to the Fraser River Salmon fisheries and to the hop fields in Washington and can take more of their children with them...This can only be avoided by the erection of a Boarding School." Faced with the Roman Catholics operating their government-funded residential school at nearby Kakawis, Russell believed the Presbyterians deserved an equal opportunity. Indian agent Harry Guillod supported this notion, pointing out in a letter to his superiors in Victoria in 1902 that Ahousat had fifty-five school-age children, with forty-one enrolled in the day school. According to Guillod, this provided inadequate exposure to English, for "the rest of the day they are speaking their own language and conforming to the Indian irregular and improvident mode of life."

The presence of these Presbyterians at Ahousat enraged Father Brabant. In his early days, Brabant counted Ahousaht territory as Roman Catholic, having baptized 135 children there on one day during his first visit to the coast in April 1874. Yet over the years Ahousat presented many challenges to the Catholics, no priest ever lived there for an extended period as they did at the Hesquiat and Opitsat missions. Brabant built a small Catholic church at Maaqtusiis in 1881, and in 1885 Fred Thornberg helped construct a priest's residence for Father Jean Lemmens, who remained only two years before becoming bishop of Victoria. Father Heynen succeeded Lemmens there, and like his predecessor he briefly attempted to run a Catholic day school at Ahousat, reporting to the Indian agent in 1889, probably with some exaggeration, that he had twenty-seven pupils. Statistics for all day school enrolments tend to be sketchy and unreliable, frequently exceeding the estimated number of children living nearby, and often failing to report actual attendance. Father Heynen's school petered out after a couple of years, like most other sectarian day schools on the west coast. Heynen's name appears on the 1891 census for Ahousat, but by then he likely lived there only part time—Father Brabant, who definitely did not live at Ahousat, also appears as a resident in that census. Father Van Nevel served there on and off in the 1890s, but according to Brabant, Van Nevel neglected Ahousat in favour of Opitsat. In 1896 the Presbyterians seized their chance and moved in, setting up both a mission and a day school at Ahousat. By 1900, when Father Maurus Snyder tried to recruit children from Ahousat for the newly opened Christie School, he noted that "a burly fellow wanted to shoot me for going on the Ahousat reserve for children."

Such territorial disputes occurred repeatedly between Catholics and Protestants in many locations on the west coast. At Nootka, around the turn of the century, Father Brabant waged a vigorous battle against the "preachers," who in turn, according to Nootka storekeeper William Netherby, seemed ready to "fight the priests...and make it hot for the Catholics." At Clayoquot, the Methodist medical missionary Dr. P.W. Rolston arrived to work among the Tla-o-qui-aht in 1898, followed by Dr. Charles Service until 1902, then by William Stone, Dr. McKinley, and later by Dr. Melbourne Raynor, who established a small hospital on Stockham Island, which the Methodists had purchased from Stockham and Dawley for this purpose after the storekeepers left the island in 1902.

From his established mission at Opitsat, Father Charles Moser grimly observed these Methodists making incursions into the village he considered his own. In 1901 a Methodist day school opened at Opitsat in direct competition to the Catholic one; in 1905 the Methodists purchased property near the village and began conducting church services in a house there. The tension continued for years. On November 8, 1909,

Father Charles resorted to bribery. "From the beginning of October until today I had empty school days. Nobody would come, they all went to the Methodist school. On All Saints day I offered an Indian 25 cents each day whenever three of his five very near relatives would come to my school. In spite of this offer I had none of them till today and then only one of the five." A month later, Dr. Raynor staged a pot-latch to attract local people to his church. "His church bell rang three times for the meeting," wrote Father Charles. "About 20 men attended. They were treated with coffee, bread, crackers, pies and fresh pears which latter were furnished by John Grice of Tofino who...exhorted the Indians to join the Doctor in school and church and for so doing were promised free medicine when sick and the best kind of medicine." Providing medical care, often with government-supplied medicines, played a central role in the work of all missionaries on the coast.

At Ahousat, where both Catholics and Protestants had set up shop, the local community had no hesitation playing one against the other. In June 1904, as soon as the Presbyterians established a residential school there, a group of Ahousaht leaders protested the actions of the newly arrived Presbyterian teachers in a petition sent to Ottawa. Addressed to Clifford Sifton, Superintendent General of Indian Affairs, and signed by "Chief Billy, Chief Moquiney, Chief Benson, Chief Atlin and Chief Nokhamas [Nokamis]," it stated: "A number of the Indians were frightened and compelled to sign a paper and give up these children to this new [Presbyterian] teachers, and for them to have control of the children until they are 16 years of age." The letter also pointed out that "the church-house belonging to our old teacher the Priest was standing here on our land, and they could see it alright, so why did they come here to make trouble." Along with several other petitions from the local community during the early years of the Ahousat resi-dential school, this document clearly states that parents did not wish their children to attend the school. It also seems to favour the Catholics over the Protestants, declaring of the Catholics that "it was all right with them we had respect for them. They made us better people. We kept from work and trade of a Sunday. There was less whisky and gambling." In the same letter, the chiefs also wrote: "We know how

2 of the [Presbyterian teachers] assaulted an old white man here and took his children by force from him and why because their mother [an] Ahouset Indian was a Catholic and so was the children. We don't want such trouble here, we did not ask for these new people to come here."

This "old white man" was Fred Thornberg, formerly the trader at Clayoquot. Often in the thick of village disputes, Thornberg suspected everyone around him of ill-will and conspiracy; he even believed his water barrels and door handles had been tainted with tubercular blood by the people he called the "Divels of Ahouset Indians." Although he had married an Ahousaht woman, Thornberg managed to be at odds with almost everyone in the village. He wrote voluminous and angry letters to the priests, to government agencies, even to the Victoria newspaper, complaining about countless perceived wrongs in Ahousat. A number of his letters detail his fury with the Presbyterian missionaries, accusing them of turning his daughter Hilda against him, and forcing her and his younger son to attend their school. In the long run, little Freddy Thornberg attended the Roman Catholic Christie School like his older brothers. Daughter Hilda, after many dramatic arguments and a volley of letter writing from her father, endured a brief period at the Ahousat school and then refused to go to school at all.

Despite his contrarian ways, or perhaps because of them, Thornberg fit in fairly well at Ahousat. The village seemed to thrive on confrontation, and disputes continually flared up, for the Ahousahts never hesitated to challenge anyone trying to impose authority upon them. Back in the late 1880s, Father Jean Lemmens remarked on how his Ahousaht converts would argue hotly during Mass, disputing the homily "with all the noise they could make." Indian agents, missionaries, storekeepers, and sealing captains had known for many years to expect challenges at Ahousat. A.W. Neill, the Indian agent who succeeded Harry Guillod, described the Ahousahts as "the most impudent and aggressive on the coast."

In the heyday of sealing, Captain Sieward wrote to Walter Dawley expressing concern about doing business at Ahousat. "Billy is here and wants me but I am afraid that...there will be a hot time in Ahousat." The "Billy" in question was most likely Billy August. One of the most vocal leaders of his time, Billy August figured in many Ahousaht disputes, never afraid to stand up for himself and his people. In the teeth of shrill protests from Fred Thornberg, Billy August set up a small store on the Ahousat reserve in 1899. Thornberg jealously reported to Dawley that Billy was selling overalls (ninety cents a pair), neckties (twenty-five cents each), and sacks of onions. "I askt him how much he had clearet on his trade he said $20.00 August can read & write and I supose he has lerned from Mr Russell how to write & order goods." Billy August had his own store letterhead printed and ran his store for a number of years, despite Walter Dawley repeatedly badgering wholesale suppliers in Victoria to stop selling him goods. "Sales to Billy August will cease," declared Johnson Brothers Dry Goods in 1909, and the Hudson's Bay Company also agreed to stop trading with Billy August. Yet his little store kept going.

Being literate, August retaliated by sending his complaints about Dawley's store at Ahousat directly to Ottawa, going over the head of the local Indian agent. "Dear Sir," he wrote to Clifford Sifton in June 1904. "We have found out that you are boss of all the Indians, so we ask you for justice." His complaint focused on Dawley owing rent to the Ahousahts for having his store on their land. "Please have the whiteman's store removed," he wrote. The controversy about stores at Ahousat, and who had the right to be there, provoked agitated streams of correspondence for several years. Meanwhile, both stores stayed put, and Billy August continued to lodge his protests about a number of other issues. In 1911 he complained to Indian Agent Neill that a survey party, hired by the Gibson family, had damaged Indian houses on Ahousaht land at Moyeha, and he asked for reparation. Later, in 1914, he appealed to the Department of Indian Affairs in Ottawa when four Ahousaht people, including his wife, "Mrs Bill August," were threatened with jail and then fined seven dollars each for potlatching. The Ahousat missionary, John Ross, who had by then taken over from Russell, made the arrests and brought the charges. "Mr Ross is not good teaching for the children," wrote Billy August angrily. "He is Policeman all over the west coast Indians they know that he is Policeman...Mr Ross always make a lots of trouble."

The Superintendent of Indian Affairs in Victoria, A.W. Vowell, clearly believing Billy August to be the troublemaker, once described him as "an agitator and a mischievous man."

On occasion, the authorities took the grievances of Ahousaht leaders very seriously, never more so than in 1900, when William Netherby, who had taken over as the Ahousat storekeeper, found himself facing death threats. The Ahousahts accused him of grave robbing. Constable Spain from Clayoquot and Indian Agent Guillod became embroiled in the fray, understanding, as Spain explained in a letter to the Attorney General, that grave robbing was "about the greatest crime in the eyes of the Indians." Spain evidently believed Netherby to be guilty, yet when Netherby appeared before the magistrates at Clayoquot, they dismissed the case. The enraged Ahousaht leaders did not have a chance to air their case in court because, delayed by bad weather, they did not arrive at Clayoquot until after Netherby's hearing. Head Chief Nokamis of Ahousat protested in a letter to the Attorney General, demanding Netherby's removal from Ahousaht land and enclosing a petition from the Ahousaht people. Highly anxious about the situation, Constable Spain lent all the support he could to the Ahousaht complaints. Netherby departed Ahousat, never to return.

Despite such successes in protesting to government authorities, when it came to the Presbyterian residential school at Ahousat, local opposition and petitions to Ottawa proved futile. Confident his application would be approved, missionary John Russell began taking day school children into his own home, starting a *de facto* residential school in advance of government approval. By 1903 he had twenty-six boarders living with him, and he soon received the go-ahead to build a school for up to fifty children. His wife's health broke down under the strain of all the work, and he resigned before the school had been completed, succeeded by John Ross.

Russell's bid to set up this school did meet at least some opposition in official circles. Martin Benson, clerk of the Schools Branch of the Department of Indian Affairs in Ottawa, spoke against the idea. Benson had protested before within the department about another residential school matter. In 1897 he noted the spread of tuberculosis in residential schools across Canada: "It is scarcely any wonder," he wrote, "that our Indian pupils who have an hereditary tendency to phthisis [tuberculosis] should develop alarming symptoms of this disease after a short residence in some of our schools, brought on by exposure to draughts in school rooms and sleeping in overcrowded...dormitories." Years would pass before others publicly protested the fatal flaws in the hygienic arrangements at residential schools.

In a letter to the head of the department dated November 29, 1901, Benson outlined his objections to a residential school at Ahousat. He explained that such a school appeared unnecessary, listing all the Indian schools on the west coast of Vancouver Island at the time: boarding schools at Alberni and Clayoquot (Kakawis), and day schools at Ahousat, Ucluelet, Opitsat, Kyuquot, Nitinat, Ohiat, and Dodger Cove; two of these Roman Catholic, four Presbyterian, and one Methodist. According to Benson, the west coast had no need of another residential school. "While a boarding school would ensure constant attendance and quicker progress," he wrote, "it is a question whether what they can acquire at the day school will not be sufficient for their future needs." In his view, the children would likely grow up and live as their parents had lived; therefore, he stated, "it seems to me that they will be better fitted to follow these pursuits...when they are young, than after several years residence in a boarding school." Benson had often seen religious denominations facing off in the mission field, and he knew all too well the "disputes between opposite religious denominations in their endeavours to obtain Government support for their schools." He wearily pointed out that "whatever concessions are made to the one will be demanded by the other." In short, he felt the application for an Ahousat residential school had more to do with local religious factions jostling for position than it had to do with the children's needs.

His advice went unheeded. John Ross oversaw the building of the Ahousat school on a 56.6-hectare tract of land near the Maaqtusiis Reserve. It opened in 1904, with twenty-five students and the first principal, Rev. J.C. Butchart. Within a year of opening, forty children lived at this school, twenty-three boys and seventeen girls. The first school inspection report in November 1905 describes the children as

In 1905, two wings were added to the original Christie School to accommodate increasing enrolment, making this building the largest anywhere in Clayoquot Sound. Students used the sandy beach in front of the school as their playground; the sisters sometimes took girls to the beach to do physical exercises, believing that could help prevent tuberculosis. *Mount Angel Abbey Library*

being bright and well, despite an outbreak of whooping cough and an inadequate water supply. Arithmetic and singing receive praise in the report, but the lack of order in the classroom came in for censure.

Christie School responded to the arrival of the Ahousat school by expanding. Two substantial dormitory wings, added to the original box-like structure in 1904, could now accommodate up to seventy-five students. With staff, support workers, and visitors, this meant the community frequently numbered well over a hundred people. Parents wishing to visit their children could see them in the specially constructed "Indian House" under a strictly controlled timetable allowing no more than a couple of hours on specified Saturdays; parents did not have access to the school or to the dormitories. Visiting parents sometimes came by canoe from Kyuquot, Nootka, or Hesquiat, as well as from nearby Opitsat—all the Catholic missions on the coast aggressively recruited schoolchildren from these nominally Catholic villages.

From the outset, Father Brabant warned that "it is terribly hard for the parents to part with their children," describing a bereft mother to Father Maurus in a letter: "You have no idea of the distress the mother of Mamie is in since the little girl left. I am sure she would do anything to have her back. But it will wear off." Father Charles's diary contains several descriptions of distraught parents and crying children being forcibly removed at the time of saying goodbye. One account outlines a miserable scene at Echachis in 1905, when Sister Placida forced little Emma Peter into a canoe bound for the school: "The child don't want to go and hides under blankets. The parents of course side with the daughter. Sister grabs the child and carries it in spite of howling and kicking like a wild animal down the beach and deposits it in the boat." Emma Peter's mother took the unusual and brave step of seeking help from the police constable at Clayoquot to get her child back, to no avail. "The Policeman rightly informed," wrote Father Charles, "turned against the Indians and sent them home minus Emma who is to stay in school." Most families did not openly resist in this way; fearing repercussions if they refused, they allowed the children to be taken away to school with stoic acceptance. Nonetheless, the undercurrent of resistance and unhappiness ran very deep, and a familiar pattern emerged: grief-stricken partings, children sometimes hiding or being hidden, police involvement when trouble arose, children forced back to school. Time and again, in subsequent years, police acted as truant officers, seeking out children who had run away from school or whose parents attempted to hide them.

Because of the seasonal work undertaken by most of the parents, often at distant canneries and hop farms, children at the schools could find few people to turn to in their home villages. The villages lay semi-deserted for months at a time during fishing season, when the canneries operated, and when the hop harvests occurred; only old people remained. So if the schoolchildren ran away, their families might not be there. To make matters more difficult, from the earliest days of the schools, many students came from families fractured by disease and death. When recruiting children for Christie School, Father Brabant sought out those he called the "semi-orphans" of tubercular parents, knowing these children, less well-protected by family, would be easier to recruit. All of the children, though, whatever their circumstances, found themselves marooned at the schools, cut off from their own communities, wearing strange clothes, eating strange food, and following stern rules that forbade girls and boys to speak to or play with each other, even their own siblings and cousins. Worst of all, they could not speak their own language, even to each other, and they faced punishment if they did so.

Just over a year after the Ahousat School opened, serious trouble arose following the death of Will Maquinna, son of hereditary Chief Billy of Ahousat. Only eight years old, Will was the last of Chief Billy's children. The others had already died. Will died at the school in November 1906, apparently of food poisoning, following a visit to his grandparents. The school, then with the Rev. J. Millar as principal, insisted he had eaten tainted food while visiting his grandparents and this had caused his death on returning to school. Chief Billy's outrage and grief could not be appeased. He had been in Victoria when the boy died, and by the time he returned to Ahousat the body had been buried.

Determined that his complaints be heard, Chief Billy sent a petition to Ottawa, signed by a number of community members, demanding that all the teachers at the school be removed, threatening that no more children from the village would ever attend, and saying parents were removing their children from the school. He met with Indian Agent Neill, who angrily reported to his superiors that Chief Billy had "publicly done his best to injure the school," dismissing him as "one of the worst Indians on the Coast." Neill warned the distraught father "in fairly strong terms...he had better take care of how he sets himself to undermine [the school]." Further, Neill insisted that Chief Billy had no right to the title of "Chief," explaining he had "removed him from being Chief" and instructing others not to use this title in any correspondence with Chief Billy.

Nothing came of Chief Billy's angry complaints. The Ahousat school carried on as before, although it learned a lesson from the little boy's death. Several years earlier, Christie School had learned the same lesson when a boy named Mike, son of the Kyuquot chief Hackla, died at school of pneumonia within months of the school's opening. Given the outcry that followed these deaths, and the volleys of blame hurled at the school authorities, both schools knew they must try to avoid having children die in their charge. Put simply, if a child became dangerously ill at either school, the administrators preferred to send the child home to die.

On numerous occasions in subsequent decades, sick children were discharged and sent home, encouraging the spread of tuberculosis to the villages. Examples of this abound in surviving records of both Christie and Ahousat schools. In 1911, John Ross reported from Ahousat that in a list of sixteen former students, six had died of tuberculosis. In 1912 he wrote that "in the early part of the year two girls were discharged on account of symptoms of decline," adding that both girls died of consumption at home shortly afterward. From 1904 to 1916, one or two students at the Ahousat school died each year, the average enrolment being thirty-five. In 1913, three students of Christie School died, "one through tuberculous glands and two through consumption," according to a letter from Father Frowin Epper to the Department of Indian Affairs. Father Charles Moser frequently described in his diary his travels up and down the coast to attend the deathbeds of former students at home in their villages; he would arrive determined to administer the last rites, remaining by the bedside, whether or not the family wanted him there, until the person died.

A number of letters written by Christie School students to Father Maurus Snyder in 1911 describe their own illness and the illness of other students. "I am sorry to tell you that I am sick yet. Please pray for me," wrote Maggie Stevens, later sent home. Cosmos Damian William wrote, "I am sorry to say that I am spitting blood for three days." From Emily Jacob: "I have a sore on my neck both sides." From Cosmos in another letter: "I am sorry to say that Didac is dead...he lived only four days after he left here." The sisters also often wrote to Father Maurus, the health of the children dominating their letters. "We lost dear little Barnabas," reported Sister Mary Clara. "Alice is improving, Maggie...has also bad consumptive cough."

Treatment of the evidently serious illnesses at Christie School and

Ahousat relied on a limited array of medicines provided by the Indian agent. A surviving "Requisition for Drugs for use of Indians," dated July 1910, indicates the diseases being treated by the missionary John Ross both at the school and in the village: "Scrofula, Consumption, Rheumatism, Syphilis, Sore eyes etc." The "drugs" include sulphur and zinc ointment, turpentine, castor oil, Listerine, boracic acid, mustard, iron pills, and carbolated Vaseline. Children who were sick at school appear routinely to have been treated with laxatives and enemas, and in later years with half an aspirin tablet. Each of the schools had an infirmary where children with infectious diseases would be kept, but all too often ailments like influenza or measles proved fatal, in many cases because the children's health was compromised by underlying tuberculosis or congenital syphilis. The most commonly cited cause of death, whether for children who died at the school or for those who had returned to their villages, was "tubercular meningitis."

From about 1905 onward, the first wave of children who attended residential school in Clayoquot Sound began returning to their villages to embark on their adult lives. "In 1908 my school days came to an end," wrote August Murphy, one of the earliest students at Christie School. "I had learned to read and write and speak the English language...Every morning we learned our catechism. Now I went out and started work." His first job took him to the short-lived marble quarry near Yuquot. "I was the first Indian to work with the *mamuthlne* [white people] at this work. Later I went with the whaling ships." In his brief, unpublished memoir, August Murphy noted the many challenges of transition from school. He wrote of how people at home "began using the clothing and food of the white people. Not knowing how to use them the health of the people suffered...The children, it is true, learned the proper preparation of these foods and the way to look after wet clothing, but when we got back to the reserve we didn't care to force our knowledge on the others. It was the turning point of our civilization." His memoirs reiterate the appalling death toll of tuberculosis. "One family lost nineteen of twenty children. Another family has only one living of seventeen. Another lost all of eighteen children." He continued: "Then we learned to make home brew...[and since] the opening of a beer parlour not far from here, many of our boats have been lost and many lives with them." August Murphy remained a devout Catholic for the rest of his life. His letters to Father Maurus Snyder, along with his brief memoir, are at Mount Angel Abbey. "Remember us in your prayers," one letter ends.

Apart from their different religious persuasions, the schools at Ahousat and Kakawis had far more in common than they may have cared to admit. Classes usually took place in the mornings, conducted strictly in English. Religious instruction, chapel, or Bible reading took up part of every day. After 1921, when schooling became compulsory, the schools shared the same basic curriculum for reading, writing, and arithmetic. At one point, the reading included a primer for Grade One entitled *Two Little Indians*, while the Grade 7s tackled *Treasure Island* and *The Lady of the Lake*. Afternoons at the schools meant doing chores: for the girls, housework and cooking and laundry and needlework; for the boys, an unceasing round of chopping firewood, clearing land, maintaining buildings, and gardening. At Christie School the sisters did much of the classroom teaching, and the brothers and priests took charge of practical tasks and taught skills like carpentry and shoemaking. Each school, at different times, taught the boys boatbuilding skills, and each attempted to keep various types of livestock, with immense effort and marginal success.

Some teachers at Ahousat longed to enter the foreign mission field, arriving at the school for their introduction to missionary work. Usually in their early twenties, with little if any teaching experience, they aspired to go to China or India once they had served time in Clayoquot Sound. Staff turnover was very high. The teachers at Christie School, all Benedictine sisters and fathers and brothers, tended to stay for longer periods, yet they too had been sent to their remote school with little if any idea of what lay before them. From the very beginning

Wearing their best clothes and straw hats, this group of Christie School students stare solemnly at the camera in the early 1900s on an excursion in a large canoe. The sisters found such canoe trips challenging; their cumbersome habits made it difficult for them to get in and out of canoes. *Mount Angel Abbey Library*

they faced shock after shock at Kakawis. On their arrival in May 1900, Chief Joseph of Opitsat kindly provided a great number of clams for a feast—the horrified sisters had never seen a clam and had no idea how to cook them. The sisters also had trouble getting in and out of canoes, thanks to their heavy woollen habits, and faced serious difficulty in mounting a rope ladder from a canoe to board the coastal steamer. But at least the sisters did not suffer the kind of scrutiny endured by the younger female teachers at Ahousat. The appearance of any young single woman in the early 1900s always occasioned comment on the coast, with its shifting population of prospectors, surveyors, fishermen, and adventurers. The Ahousat storekeeper William Netherby once wrote to Thomas Stockham, telling him to come immediately to survey the newly arrived teacher, with a view to matrimony. He assured Stockham that marrying her would cure his rheumatism.

In practical terms, both Christie and Ahousat schools faced similar challenges; access and transport for each was a logistical nightmare. "Here again is a residential school awkwardly situated for transfer of freight," wearily commented one of the school inspectors following a visit to Ahousat. Transporting goods and people gave rise to endless small dramas. Cargoes offloaded from the coastal steamers into freight scows and canoes risked being dumped into the ocean on rough days. To land construction materials, school provisions, and large furnishings required careful timing, reasonable tides, and a good deal of assistance. Landing flour was particularly tricky, for once wetted it could not be used—and huge amounts of flour arrived regularly. A single batch of bread at the Ahousat school required at least forty kilograms, while Christie School, with its higher enrolment, needed far more. By the late 1950s an estimated 30,000 loaves of bread were baked per year at Christie School; one breakfast disposed of forty-four loaves. Deliveries of up to two tons of flour at a time could arrive at Christie School, requiring every able person to swing into action. Not all of the flour reached shore safely, as Father Charles glumly attested on February 3, 1920 (one of many such comments): "One ton spuds, ½ ton flour... besides a few hundred lbs groceries were received. On landing on the beach our freight boat got swamped in the surf."

By 1912, nineteen boys and sixteen girls attended the Ahousat school. That same year Christie School had sixty-six students. Nothing indicates that the two schools ever interacted or visited; they functioned as if the other did not exist. Students at Christie School faced far greater isolation than those at Ahousat, for Christie lay seven and a half kilometres from the village of Opitsat, connected only by a rough trail, and many students at the school came from distant villages up the coast. At the Ahousat school, most children came from the adjacent village of Maaqtusiis, only a short walk away. Although they saw little of their families, some Ahousaht students were allowed home on Saturdays, but not to stay overnight. On Sundays they all attended church in the village, marching single file along the slippery raised boardwalk; a teacher led the boys first, then the matron followed with the girls, and the rest of the staff trooped along behind. When they reached the village, in order to prevent children slipping off to visit their homes, they walked two by two, closely watched by the staff. In the church, the girls and women of the village sat on one side, boys and men on the other. The schoolchildren occupied the front pews, their family members behind, with mothers and fathers and grandparents craning to glimpse their own children.

Both the Indian agent and the school inspectors made regular visits to all residential schools. The annual reports of the west coast Indian agents follow the activities of Christie School and the Ahousat school closely in their early years, describing the numbers of children and their health, education, and surroundings. Detailed accounts survive of land being cleared, of the boys learning trades and the girls becoming good housekeepers, learning to sew and cook and excel at "fancy work." Displays of the fancy needlework from Christie School appeared at the St. Louis World's Fair of 1904, along with prizewinning samples of the handwriting of the students, who all learned the Palmer method, an immaculate copperplate hand that many students practised for the rest of their lives.

Almost every official report on each school also commented on fire precautions, repeatedly urging improvements, assessing the exits from dormitories, the available ladders, the firefighting water supply and pumps, the students' training in fire drills. The large wooden buildings, badly heated by inadequate wood and later coal stoves, posed serious fire hazards. At the Ahousat school, the practice of locking the children into the dormitories at night, presumably to prevent their running away, put them even more at risk from fire. In response to a query from Ottawa in 1913 about how the children could exit locked dormitories in the event of fire, John Ross explained that inside each dormitory "a duplicate key is kept in a...box with a glass cover." If the need arose, the glass could be broken and the key used. As for the bars on the dormitory windows, Ross reported that "an iron bar is left in each dormitory to break off wooden bars on windows in order to escape...The bars are not iron but wood, 3/4" x 2" [1.9 x 5 centimetres]." He added that each dormitory had a rope fire escape; this consisted of a single rope extending along the roof.

On May 5, 1917, the Ahousat residential school burned to the ground, along with several outbuildings. No one suffered injury. Up at Hesquiat, Father Charles heard the news over the telephone: "I could hear through my phone the roaring of the fire and the crackling of wood." One month later, Father Charles wrote in his diary of "two more Indian schools having burnt down, the one in Alberni and the other at Sechelt near Vancouver." In all cases, students set the fires in what John Ross described as an "epidemic of arson."

Christie School escaped, but only just. In early June, students repeatedly tried to set fires, managing only to damage the roof slightly in one case, but making several attempts, hiding matches and stashing kindling under their beds. "So many times the boys tried to burn the school, but no success," exclaimed Father Charles in a letter. "The finger of God! *Deus etiam providebit.*" Far more successful as arsonists, the Ahousat students destroyed their school, but two of them were caught. John Ross reported two girls confessing that they set the fire "by soaking bundles of rags with coal-oil up in the attic and putting a match to them. They hurried down and sat by the kitchen stove busy at their knitting." Along with six boys who had set the unsuccessful fires at Christie School, these two girls spent time in the Clayoquot lockup on Stubbs Island before appearing in front of local magistrates. Later they faced further legal proceedings in Victoria. Two of the boys served two years each in reform school in Vancouver; one of the girls spent two years in a penitentiary.

The stormy, confrontational atmosphere prevailing at Christie School before and after the fires of 1917 emerges vividly in Father Charles Moser's diary and in surviving letters from Father Joseph Schindler, principal at Christie School from 1916 until 1919. They each noted the "rebellious spirit" of the students and "a kind of revolution" breaking out in April 1917, when Father Joseph called the police from Tofino to help control the boys. Threats of prison and reform school did not stop the persistent attempts to run away from the school, the stealing of food and Mass wine, the frequently violent clashes between staff and students. Common punishments, especially for the boys, included clipping their hair and confining them for many days in the photographic darkroom or in a bathroom, with only bread and water. Persistent offenders were confined for up to two weeks in the school jail, a newly created facility housed in the old blacksmith shop near the school.

Father Brabant would have been outraged by this. The older priest had died in 1912, forced by ill health to leave Hesquiat and to spend his final years in Victoria. Trapped there by his age and infirmities, he fretted helplessly about his missions on the coast and about the school he founded, always yearning to return, fearing everything would fall apart without him. Brabant's powerful influence lingered for many years in the lives of priests who succeeded him, particularly Father Charles Moser and Father Maurus Snyder. During his years as principal of Christie School from 1900 to 1911, Father Maurus frequently sought advice from Brabant. It arrived in lengthy, often irascible, letters in which Brabant shared in great detail his experience on the west coast, his familiarity with aboriginal families and customs, and his determined ideas about how the school should operate and how the priests should behave. He even warned Father Maurus against fasting too much, and chastised him severely for a risky canoe trip that had endangered the lives of students. Brabant also issued an unequivocal warning about physical punishment. "Be sure to abstain from bodily punishment," Brabant wrote in a letter dated February 13, 1901. "Indians never resort to it and do not tollerate [sic] it on their children."

Under Father Maurus, the school seems to have developed much as Brabant would have wished, and children rarely faced corporal punishment. But in 1911, Father Maurus left Kakawis and returned to Mount Angel Abbey. Under his successor, Father Frowin Epper, and the following principal, Father Joseph Schindler, the atmosphere in the school changed. In 1917, Father Charles Moser, happily ensconced at the mission at Hesquiat, reluctantly obeyed a command from his abbot to leave and go to Kakawis. "It will be a sacrifice on my part to move there," he wrote to Father Maurus, "as Kakawis as it is at present has no attraction for me." Once there, he soon discovered physical confrontations with students to be commonplace. Between 1919 and 1922, he unwillingly served as principal, finding the position impossible. "[The boys] shake their fists in my face and try to fight me," he explained to

Christie School boys with Father Maurus Snyder, around 1910. Some boys here could be as young as five years old. Father Maurus left the school in 1911 to return to Mount Angel Abbey in Oregon. That year, many boys and some of the sisters wrote anxiously to Father Maurus about his successor, Father Frowin Epper, who was very severe. *Mount Angel Abbey Library*

the Indian agent. At the trial of four boys charged with theft, Father Charles confessed his inability to handle them: "I cannot fight with my light weight and height against several of the boys." The judge responded that Father Charles had lost control of the students and should be replaced, concluding, "You are not severe enough in your punishments." The next principal of Christie School, Father Ildephonse Calmus, described by the bishop in Victoria as a strict disciplinarian, had no fear of the older boys, nor of inflicting severe punishments. In 1922 he faced assault charges for severely beating one of the boys; the incident came to the attention of Dr. Dixson in Tofino, who examined the boy's injuries, and the case against Father Ildephonse was heard by Ted Abraham, then a Justice of the Peace in Tofino. It settled out of court.

The nature of punishments meted out at these residential schools depended on the nature of the principal and staff in charge at any given time, and could vary considerably in severity from one period to another. In 1934, with the Rev. Joseph Jones in charge and sixty-three children enrolled, the Ahousat school received a glowing report from school inspector Gerald Barry. "The whole atmosphere in this school is in advance of our other BC Indian schools." He continued, "This is one of the best administered Indian Residential Schools in British Columbia. The children are very happy, a condition I do not find prevailing in all our schools, and they are in the best of health. There is little if any corporal punishment." Five years later, with the school now under principal A.E. Caldwell, the same school inspector, Gerald Barry, reported that "every member of staff carried a strap" and "children have never learned to work without punishment." Elsie Robinson, who attended the school in the late 1930s, recalled other forms of punishment: "They were always holding a big stick, ready to hit you if you didn't obey," she stated in an interview for the *United Church Observer* in 2010. She also remembered being struck for speaking her native language, a common cause for punishment at residential schools across the country. Other punishments involved humiliation or hard work or both: "Some supervisors made us use a toothbrush to wash the floors. We were forced to do it...Just to be cruel, I guess."

One of the students at the Ahousat residential school in the 1920s, McPherson George, became "a very strong believer in the Christian faith that he received through the teachings of the Ahousaht Residential School," according to his son Chief Earl Maquinna George. Descended from Chief Billy, Macpherson George acquired his name at the school courtesy of the Presbyterians, who could not pronounce his Native name; many children received new names from residential schools. McPherson George and his future wife, Mabel, both attended the Ahousat residential school, and in the 1930s their son Earl, born in 1926, went to the same school. His mother died when he was two, and in the summers, with his father away working at canneries, in fish plants, and on seine boats, he and his younger brother, Wilfred, were cared for by the school staff.

"Back in Ahousaht, the summer months became very lonely," he wrote, "because all that was left in the village site of Maaqtusiis were the elders, who were unable to work in the fish canneries. There were very few of us left; I was one of those when I was young because I didn't have any place to go at times. There were times that I stayed right at the residential school for the summer months." From 1938, when he was twelve years old, Earl Maquinna George joined his father, the older children, and other adults and commuted every summer to work in the canneries on Rivers Inlet. McPherson George by then had a nine-metre-long combination gillnet–troller named *Native Lass*, powered by a single-cylinder Fairbanks "one-lunger" engine. This boat would transport large groups of Ahousaht people up to Rivers Inlet for the summer of fishing or working at the cannery, taking three days to travel up the coast past Kyuquot, rounding Cape Scott on the northern tip of Vancouver Island, and ending up at Good Hope Cannery. In his book *Living on the Edge*, Earl George recalled some 300 to 400 boats being there when they arrived, all preparing to go fishing when the gun went off, announcing the start of the salmon season. Earl found work in the cannery, overseen by the Chinese boss, for fifteen cents an hour. During his first summer, he netted thirteen dollars.

By the 1930s, both Christie and Ahousat schools made sporadic attempts to encourage at least some traditional skills, often taught by earlier graduates from the schools. In this way lessons in carving, beadwork, and basket weaving occurred at the schools from time to time. Gerald Barry, in his report of 1939, approved of the "mat-weaving and basket making" at Ahousat, praising one of the beadwork belts as the highest quality he had ever seen anywhere in British Columbia. It was later exhibited at the Canadian National Exhibition in Toronto. At Ahousat, Nellie Jacobsen, who had attended the school as a child, taught beadwork, weaving, and other crafts. By way of contrast, Elsie Robinson and the other senior girls also attended an evening class called "Charm," in which, she said, teachers from the Ladies' Missionary Society "taught [us] how to dress and how to act. We had table etiquette and sex education." Ahousaht elder Peter Webster also attended the Ahousat school around this time. In his book *As Far as I Know*, he wrote: "My memories of attending the school are not pleasant ones. I entered knowing no English. I found that every time I used my native tongue I was punished...we had to listen, morning and night, to readings from the Bible. We did not understand any of it."

Following the fire at the Ahousat residential school in 1917, Presbyterian authorities had not wanted to rebuild, but the Women's Missionary Society provided the funds to construct a new school. Like so many residential schools across Canada, the building went up hurriedly, relying on second-rate work, shoddily and cheaply done, leading to many problems later on. Within little more than a decade, the place was a mess. In 1929, the newly appointed principal, William R. Wood, wrote to Duncan Campbell Scott of the Department of Indian Affairs, describing how the children had suffered in recent years because of the lack of heating, good water, and acceptable toilet facilities. "Looking back over the record of the School during the past two or three years I find that there have been an unusual number of deaths among pupils and ex-pupils, and unusual number of discharges from the School on account of ill health, and that at the present time the number of pupils, especially of girls, who are normally healthy is startlingly low. I am convinced that they suffer constantly from the lack of elementary conditions of human comfort." In another letter to A.W. Neill, now sitting as a Member of Parliament in Ottawa, Wood stated, "There is scarcely a machine or a utensil about the place that is not worn out and in need of replacement," pointing out that students "sleep in dormitories from which the chill of the BC winter is never removed by artificial heat...the water they drink is never ordinarily drinkable...the toilet system exhibits none of the features of ordinary decency, much less comfort." Wood's warnings went unheeded. He remained at the school a little over a year, perhaps leaving in despair. Few principals of residential schools dared to raise their voices in this manner; if they did, they risked being removed from their positions and posted to other residential schools, even more isolated and deprived.

In 1936, when nurse Bessie Jean Banfill came to work at Ahousat, she and the newly arrived younger schoolteachers shared their anxieties about the conditions at the school. Among themselves they discussed "how the government allowed six-year old children to be locked in the dormitory of a School, which had been condemned for years as a fire hazard; how the government officials apparently considered cod-liver oil a cheaper way of maintaining the health of the children than to provide them with decent living conditions." The mandatory requirement that each child receive a dose of cod liver oil twice a day from November to April appalled the nurse; she thought it "awful stuff." The children seemed resigned to it. After meals, "each child tipped back his head and opened his mouth...I dropped the allotted, compulsory dose...into those gaping mouths." When a new arrival at the school, a little boy only four years old, refused to open his mouth, an older boy warned him "You'll catch it!" but the nurse "did not have the heart to hold him, force it down, or to report to [the principal] who no doubt would have strapped him."

Nurse Banfill's book *With the Indians of the Pacific* presents a thinly fictionalized account of her time at Ahousat, changing some names of places and people. Inspired to come here by glowing reports of the wonderful work done at far-flung missions among aboriginal people, she arrived full of hope, only to be quickly dismayed. When she and one of the teachers challenged the principal about conditions at the school, he replied, "If I could do what I think right for the Indians I would change the whole set-up here!" He explained defensively that his exaggerated official reports about the success of the school ensured its existence, and his position as principal. "Do you mean to say," one of them asked, "that if you wrote the truth officials would ask for your resignation, because you disagreed with them?" "Wouldn't they!" the principal replied, adding, "High-up government officials and church congregations want glowing reports to extract generous contributions. They do not want to hear, or let the public hear, about the other side of the picture."

Every child had to pass a medical examination to be admitted to residential school. The nurse checked all children for infections, impetigo, venereal sores, colds or coughs, and signs of tuberculosis and other infectious ailments. From the outset, she realized that some very young children at the school showed signs of congenital syphilis, a diagnosis confirmed by the doctor in Tofino, who indicated to her that "practically all the five and six year olds had been venereally infected before they were admitted to the School, and that every home had, or had had, tuberculosis." The principal of the Ahousat school made it clear to the new nurse that he did not "adhere strictly to government regulations," and that he could admit students at his own discretion, regardless of their medical condition. Less than impressed by the medical attention the children had been receiving, Nurse Banfill also discovered a boy in the school suffering from diabetes, one of the symptoms being chronic bedwetting. He had been "whipped, starved, threatened, and given... pills" because of this bedwetting, and the principal had concluded "He is too lazy to get up at night." When the doctor saw the boy, he again confirmed the nurse's diagnosis, saying, "An interesting case, because I have never seen an Indian with diabetes. I doubt if he will live to be twenty." Even though the nurse offered to provide injections of insulin, the doctor decided not to treat the disease, for no one in the boy's family could give hypodermics when he went home.

Nurse Banfill stayed less than a year at Ahousat. The place and the work overwhelmed her. She had not expected to be put in charge of health care for the entire village as well as the schoolchildren. She discovered on her arrival that her duties included making daily visits to most houses; during one such visit, a young Ahousaht woman further explained her duties to her: "You know we have to keep our houses clean for daily inspection, and you have to report any signs of whisky or drunkenness on the reservation." The nurse commented, "I wondered if I was supposed to be a policeman as well as a nurse, and why I had not been informed about this unpleasant task." She grew increasingly uncomfortable with her role, and angered by the visits of the "white bootlegger," whose boat often stood offshore, attracting local customers.

In 1939, school inspector Gerald Barry wrote to his superiors in Ottawa that the Indian agent was not satisfied with the Ahousat school, and it would soon close. Several letters reiterate this theme, with Barry also mentioning that the principal, A.E. Caldwell, carried out his duties with the help of a barbiturate called Luminol. Barry continued to repeat his fears about fire safety in the school, a concern of every inspector since the school had been rebuilt in 1917.

In 1940, before the school could be closed, it once again burned down. It was not rebuilt. From this time on, a series of different day schools served Ahousat, catering largely to elementary students. Some students from Ahousat went to the Alberni Residential School, particularly in their high school years. When he visited Ahousat in 1945, marine biologist Ed Ricketts saw no evidence of a school nor of any missionary activity, commenting only that the place seemed "one of the sad and dirty Indian Villages," but he missed a good deal on that brief visit. The United Church did continue to operate a day school for Ahousaht children, and in 1955 a new mission-funded day school was built there. In 1962 the provincial government assumed responsibility for the Ahousat school.

Few indications suggest the settler communities at Clayoquot, Tofino, or Ahousat ever had much awareness of day-to-day realities at either of the residential schools in Clayoquot Sound. The two schools existed in separate spheres, not far away yet maintaining a clear distance from the growing settlements. At Ahousat, the emerging white community clustered around the sawmill, store, post office, and steamer landing, just across the inlet from the aboriginal village of Maaqtusiis. The Ahousat school kept itself as isolated as possible, both from Maaqtusiis and the newer settlement. Christie School remained largely invisible to people living at Clayoquot and Tofino, although once in a while the brass band from Kakawis would perform at special events. Very occasionally both schools would be invited to attend public events, but apart from that, little mingling occurred. Few outsiders saw much of the schools and the students, apart from the doctor, various government visitors, and the police who went in search of truant children and brought them back to school.

In the 1920s, Dorothy Abraham visited Christie School several times, accompanying her husband when he went there in his role as magistrate "to straighten out their difficulties," as she put it. And the Abrahams sometimes took their visitors to the school after visiting the "Indian ranch" (reserve) at Opitsat, as part of the local tourist attractions.

Christie School brass band, around 1908. Formed shortly after the school opened in 1900, for many years the band played at major events like Clayoquot Days, and for special church events and social gatherings. Only boys played in the band. *Mount Angel Abbey Library*

"Like all children the Indians were unruly at times," she wrote, "and would make off into the bush with sides of bacon and a dozen or so loaves of bread, and be missing for days at a time...I remember the boys drank all the alcohol out of the specimen bottles (snakes, toads etc) and became very drunk. They were up to every prank." Tirelessly enthusiastic about everything she saw, Dorothy wrote of "the very good Presbyterian Mission" at Ahousat, and of Christie School being "splendidly run and up to date with all the latest devices, where Indian boys and girls are trained and educated to a very high standard."

Mike Hamilton also visited Christie School on his travels up and down the coast. He had become friendly with Father Charles Moser, who helped to rescue him from a serious boating accident in Hesquiat Harbour in 1917. Years later, the priest again rescued Mike when he fell off the dock in Tofino. Unable to swim and weighed down by his oilskins, Mike found himself hauled out of the water by Father Charles. "Born to be hung, not drowned," he commented. Always prepared to help out if the school needed him, in the early 1920s Mike would

285

go there to do mechanical repairs and to service the movie projector, allowing the children to enjoy an occasional Charlie Chaplin movie as a special treat. He told visitors to Clayoquot Sound that a visit to the school would be "extremely interesting and educational," and that the staff would "spare no pains to welcome and entertain any visitors who call." How often such visits occurred is unclear, as is the nature of the tour visitors received.

Christie Indian Residential School outlived the Ahousat residential school by more than three decades, continuing to operate at Kakawis until it closed in 1971. By then, residential schools were closing all over Canada, as the emphasis on integrated public education grew. As the years passed following these closures, former students began speaking out publicly about their experiences. Gradually, and then more frequently, accounts of mistreatment, humiliation, and physical and sexual abuse were heard across the country, implicating school after school. Inevitably, people on the west coast began to wonder what really went on at the residential schools that had operated right there, in Clayoquot Sound, for so many decades.

Chapter 14:

COMMUNITY

Late 1920s, looking east toward the government dock, with Sid Elkington's store at the end. The dock in the foreground led to Towler and Mitchell's store, visible on the far right. On the left, the Tofino Trollers' co-operative fish-buying camp. The clear-cut "Dream Isle," now Arnet Island, is in the background. *Image B04222 courtesy of the Royal BC Museum, BC Archives*

"IT WAS LIKE THERE WERE THREE or four different villages," observed Mabel Arnet, recalling Tofino in the 1920s and '30s. "You knew you were in the Scandinavian group. Or if you were in the Scotch group, you knew you were in that group. Then there was the Indian village, which was hands off, and the Japanese people. You spoke with them but you didn't associate with them socially."

Several different worlds of people came together in Tofino. The Norwegians hailed from hard-working fishing and farming stock, stoic, unpretentious, and clannish, described by Dorothy Abraham as "tall, handsome women...and taller handsomer men"; the Scots and English groups included Gaelic-speaking Orkneymen, stubborn north country folk, and a handful of educated expatriates clinging to the notion of the British empire. The First Nations occupied separate spheres around

Wheelbarrow race at Clayoquot Days on Stubbs Island, early 1930s. People travelled from all over Clayoquot Sound to participate in this May 24 event, the largest, most important gathering of the year. Sporting events of all kinds, boat races, and a community picnic drew hundreds of people: aboriginals, Japanese, and European settlers alike. The growing town of Tofino can be seen in the background, also Bill Bond's pile driver. *Monks collection, courtesy of Lois Warner*

Clayoquot Sound: on reserves, in villages, in schools, and in social groupings largely unknown, and unfathomable, to most outsiders. The numerous Japanese settlers who arrived in the area in the early 1920s, all of them fisher-folk, clustered in settlements known locally as "Jap towns" in Tofino, at Clayoquot, and at Ucluelet

Despite their clear divides, everyone in the area knew each other, or knew *of* each other, at least by sight and by racial type. They knew each other's boats; they met on the docks; they glimpsed each other at the stores, at church, at dances, and at special events, when they met in large numbers. Perhaps most importantly, they met for Clayoquot Days. From the first such event organized by Filip Jacobsen in 1896, sports and picnic days occurred at Clayoquot, initially on the May 24 weekend to celebrate Queen Victoria's birthday; later on Dominion Day on July 1. Over the years this all-inclusive gala event became the best-loved and largest gathering in the area. "The morning of the 24th would be a time of great excitement," Ronald MacLeod recalled in his memoirs. "Women packed picnic fare with families sharing the catering. New running shoes and light summer clothing for the children. Local fish boats swarming to the government wharf to pick up people to ferry them across to Clayoquot. Indians in flotillas of gas boats and canoes making their way to *the* event of the year."

Recalling the Clayoquot Days of the 1920s and '30s, Ian MacLeod described crowds of "twelve or fourteen hundred people from Tofino, Ucluelet, the reduction plants, the sawmills, the hatcheries, from Hot Springs Cove, Ahousat, Nootka. There would be dozens and dozens of fishboats." Students from Christie and Ahousat residential schools also attended Clayoquot Days and the brass band from Christie School would play. The local Japanese community participated enthusiastically at Clayoquot Days, the children joining the races and enjoying "Canadian" ice cream cones, as the Christie School band entertained everyone with tunes like "Bicycle Built for Two."

The races and sports competitions welcomed everyone. "Foot races for all, from the very young to the aged," Ronald MacLeod recalled, "three-legged races, sack races, high jump, broad jump, hop-step-and-jump, pole vault, relay races, hurdles, tug-of-war, canoe races, upset-canoe races, skiff races, rowboat races, fish boat races—we had it all, even a greasy pole hung off the wharf and out over the water." Epic feats of strength took place, the star event being the tug-of-war. Onlookers sang out encouragement to their teams—aboriginal chants, Norwegian Viking tunes, songs in Gaelic. By the late 1930s, according to Walter Guppy, during the short-lived mining boom, the tug-of-war pitted local fishermen against miners. The fishermen, accustomed to pulling heavy ropes, always won. In the sporting events, Ian MacLeod, age seventeen, excelled at the broad jump, making a twenty-one-foot (6.5-metre) jump. "But Isaac Charlie...he could make over twenty-four feet, twenty-five maybe. According to...the judges in those days, he broke the world record, but it was unofficial."

"I won all the skip races," Arline Craig recalled, with a laugh. "And there were softball games out on the sandspit—Ahousat against Opitsat, and a Ucluelet team too." Because Arline so often rowed from her family's home on Bond (Neilson) Island to Tofino, she also won the rowing races. She enjoyed seeing Mamie Dawley, Clarence Dawley's wife, enjoying herself at Clayoquot Days, wearing a sun hat wreathed with flowers, greeting everyone, telling funny stories, and playing the piano at the hotel, where a good number of men could be found in the beer parlour, having come in "for a quick one when the throat got too dry from cheering and hollering," according to Ronald MacLeod.

"All the Indians turned out in their war paint," Dorothy Abraham reminisced, claiming that she too won a good many of the rowing races. To her delight, tennis arrived in Clayoquot by the late 1920s, becoming a regular feature of Clayoquot Days. When George Nicholson took over management of the Clayoquot Hotel in the mid-1920s, he convinced Walter Dawley to establish tennis courts on a "nearly level enough" patch of grass, fenced to keep the local bull away. Thirty-eight people signed up to join the tennis club, paying a dollar each, and according to Dorothy Abraham, membership soon swelled to seventy. The club bought "racquets and balls and shoes of every size, which were housed in the hotel so that anyone coming in off a survey or fishing boat would find everything provided." During Clayoquot Days, tennis also took place on the curving sandspit.

"The beach was so much bigger then," Lorraine (Arnet) Murdoch recalled, "Everything took place over on the beach, all the games, but in later years most of that beach just disappeared. It's never been the same." Barry Campbell, formerly of Parks Canada, and an authority on invasive species on the west coast, knows why. He holds Walter Dawley responsible. Determined to firm up the sandy shoreline, at some point during his years on Stubbs Island, Dawley planted a European species of beach grass, *Ammophila arenaria*. Instead of protecting the sandy beach, this grass rapidly spread, drastically reconfiguring the beach by directing most of the windblown sand out toward the northerly sandspit, at the cost of the crescent-shaped beach in front of the hotel and store. Aerial photographs of Stubbs Island from the early 1930s onward reveal immense changes in the shape of the beach and the length of the spit. By the 1940s this erosion had become so serious that the area in front of the store threatened to drop into the sea. Ruth White lived at Clayoquot during the 1940s, and in later years she observed how "the

Vancouver photographer Frank Leonard took this photograph in the 1920s. The saltery stands at the end of the dock, and Walter Dawley's store, with its square white front, on the far right. The Clayoquot Hotel, rebuilt after the fire of 1922, is the dark building to the left of the store. The European beach grass in the foreground, brought in by Dawley to firm up the sandy beach, proved to be invasive and damaging, spreading to other beaches in the area. *Image 16677, Vancouver Public Library*

sea had gradually taken the buildings away." Despite valiant efforts to shore up the area with hefty log cribs, the erosion continued, slowly undermining the old store completely. Eventually loads of rock were barged over to the island to protect the shoreline.

The same beach grass that caused this erosion subsequently spread down to the Wickaninnish Beach area, where the delicate ecosystem of the sand dunes behind the beach has been seriously harmed by this and another non-native beach grass, *Ammophila breviligulata*. These firmly rooted, fast-growing beach grasses trap vast quantities of sand on a rising fore-dune crest that now stands two metres higher than the dunes in earlier years. This crest rises in front of the natural dunes, depriving them of windblown beach sand they need to survive, and without which the native plants on the dunes die. Barry Campbell, who since his retirement has led heroic efforts to combat invasive species, initially went to war against Scotch broom and English ivy before tackling the invasive beach grasses. Volunteers and Parks Canada employees now follow his lead, patrolling the sand dunes and pulling up dense clumps of the destructive grasses, allowing the native beach grass (*Leymus mollis*) to return, along with endangered plants like the pink sand verbena.

Back in the 1920s and 1930s, the annual Clayoquot Days offered the largest local get-together, but residents enjoyed other comparable events from time to time. Sports days took place regularly at various First Nations villages and at the residential schools, baseball being particularly popular, and invitations often extended to all living nearby. Community picnics occurred: on Vargas Island, at Long Beach, at Echachis, and especially at MacKenzie Beach, organized by the Legion, the Japanese community, or the church. "A monster picnic was held at Mackenzie's Beach recently, King's Jubilee Day," reported the *Daily Colonist* in May 1935, one of many such notices. Royal landmarks often inspired special events; the coronation of George VI in 1937 called for a day of "celebration sports" at Clayoquot, with prizes of "Coronation mugs, plates, cups and saucers and knives" donated by Robert Guppy, likely also responsible for handing out 100 coronation teaspoons to local schoolchildren.

A staunch royalist, formerly with the British civil service in India, Guppy came to Tofino with his wife and family in the early 1920s. Initially they settled on John Chesterman's original property some distance from town, where the family endured their first winter in a leaky shack, tacking a leopard skin to the wall to keep out drafts, and placing a tiger skin on the bare floor. They then moved into Tofino, to a newly built house the family called "Clay Bank." Robert Guppy returned to India for two years, leaving his wife, Winifred, in charge. Accustomed to having servants in India, she did not even know how to make porridge when she first arrived in Tofino, but she quickly adapted. On her husband's return, he did not live with the family, preferring to live across the harbour on Stone Island, which he had purchased from William Stone. Guppy had a liking for islands: he also bought Strawberry and Beck Islands, renaming the latter Garden Island and establishing a hobby farm with cows and sheep and goats. He rowed into town almost every day with milk and produce for the family; his grandson Ken Gibson recalled watching the sun shining on his grandfather's long, spooned oars as he feathered his way across the harbour, sculling in the manner he learned as a rowing blue for Pembroke College, Oxford. He would climb out of the boat and walk barefoot up the beach over the barnacles, in Ken's memory always wearing the same outfit: short pants and a pith helmet.

Guppy's attraction to the islands in Tofino Harbour has been shared by many over the years. From the earliest days of settlement, these islands have been repeatedly bought and sold. Thomas Stockham became the first island pre-emptor in 1898, promptly giving Stockham Island his name. Filip Jacobsen followed suit in 1899, pre-empting an island listed in the land records as "Clayquot Snd, small island," at first simply called "Jacobsen's," and later Stone Island. In 1907, when James Beck and Thomas Gardhouse acquired an unnamed "Island nr Jacobsen's I.," it became Beck Island, and two years later Aksel Nilson pre-empted the island now called Neilson Island. Not all of these early island-seekers lived on their islands, though some did. In 1898, Mrs. Rolston recorded that "on all or most of these lonely scattered islands a family or bachelor is struggling to clear the dense bush and have a patch ready for vegetables or garden." Notwithstanding the tidal rips, the winds and storms, the difficulties of moorage, and the lack of fresh water, the romance and charm of these islands have won the hearts of many over the years. Others considered island life and quickly abandoned the idea, among them Mike Hamilton, who briefly owned Strawberry Island in the 1920s. His fiancée, Mabel, liked the notion of living there, but Mike hastily sold the island, pointing out the practical difficulties of such a residence in a letter. "I was jolly glad even to see 150 bucks as the island would have been a white elephant," he wrote, assuring Mabel that "we can get lots more islands bigger and better ones and close to hand." They never did. Strawberry Island has been owned for many years now by well-known diver and whale researcher Rod Palm.

Of all island dwellers in the harbour, none ever matched the impact made by Fred Tibbs during his years on his Dream Isle—also called Castle Island and Arnet Island. Before Tibbs headed off to serve in the Canadian Forestry Corps in World War I, he sounded one final blast on his cornet from his treetop platform, saying goodbye to his island domain. He told no one he was going, simply boarded up the windows of his wooden castle and left. On one window, up in the tower, he painted a picture of a beautiful princess; some say she looked like Olive Garrard. No one knew at the time, but Tibbs harboured secret romantic attachments, not only to Olive but also to Alma Arnet. Some thought he also fancied Winnie Dixson. "Oh he tried all of us, all the different girls," Winnie later commented. "I didn't have much interest...I had about 300 chickens."

Neither Alma nor Olive had any idea what lay ahead. Tibbs had made his will before setting off to war, leaving the island "and everything thereon, excepting the house and ten feet of land on either side of the house site," to Alma Arnet, "because she's the nicest girl I know." He left the house and contents, except for his gramophone, to Olive Garrard, "because it was built for her." If Olive married, the house should go to Alma "if she is still single." Returning intact from the war in 1919, Tibbs resettled on his island and resumed his land-clearing, his gardening, and his risky experiments with explosives. On New Year's Eve in 1919, he tried to explode dynamite from his tree platform thirty metres up in the air, to "blow the old year to the four winds," but the explosion did not go off with the bang he had hoped, the dynamite being frozen. In his wooden castle, Tibbs entertained visitors who came to listen to his gramophone and drink cocoa, and he often went to Tofino to collect mail and to "have some music, as there are two or three damsels here who play very nicely." He attended community events and dances—though he never danced—and he also took up a new job. Rowing his skiff around the harbour, he tended the navigation lights, coal-oil lanterns mounted on tripods on wooden floats. Every second day when the lanterns required refilling, Tibbs would tie up to the floats and clamber on to fuel the lights.

In early July 1921, Francis Garrard noted that Tibbs had been blasting rock on his island; "he had got badly powdered and had been quite ill from the effects." Immediately after this, on July 4, the Clayoquot Hotel went up in flames. Along with every other available man, Tibbs rushed over to Stubbs Island to assist in fighting the fire. The following day he went out to tend the lights, but after landing on one of the floats, his skiff drifted away. He dived in to swim after the boat. Not realizing what had occurred, a Tla-o-qui-aht man who saw the empty skiff towed the boat to Opitsat. Tibbs turned and made for the nearest land, on Stubbs Island. Perhaps overexertion, combined with the effects of the dynamite powder, had weakened him, for although he was usually a powerful swimmer, the effort proved too much. "He made the spit alright," Bill Sharp recalled. "He crawled up on the sand and lay there." A Japanese fisherman alerted the authorities; the telegram sent from the Clayoquot police to their superiors in Victoria read "Frederick Gerald Tibbs found exhausted on beach at Clayoquot by Jap fisherman early this morning." Tibbs could not be revived. "When the Doctor arrived...," wrote Francis Garrard, "Tibbs was already dead... it was a very sad affair." The gravestone for Frederick Gerald Tibbs stands in the old Tofino cemetery, on Morpheus Island.

Following Tibbs's death, the Garrard and Arnet families reached an agreement about his unusual will. Olive Garrard relinquished her share of the inheritance, his castle home, to the Arnets, and Dream Isle became Arnet Island. A group of men went over to the island shortly after Tibbs's death to cut down the thirty-metre-high "tree rig," deeming it unsafe, and as time passed the clear-cut island slowly greened over. A few others attempted to live on the island, renting out Tibbs's castle, but the place became associated with bad luck and sudden death. According to Anthony Guppy, after several unfortunate fatalities and mishaps there, the "strange little castle remained unoccupied for a long time...People began to believe it was haunted. It became a sort of game for young people to go over there, get inside, and make the most hair-raising ghostly noises." The stories of Tibbs lingered and grew; by the late 1920s, "Fred Tibbs had already acquired the gloss of a legendary figure," according to Guppy. The year after Tibbs died, Alma Arnet married Harold Sloman; Olive Garrard also married in 1923. Had Tibbs lived a bit longer, perhaps he would have reconsidered his will. He certainly would have enjoyed the livelier social scene that began to emerge in Tofino in the ensuing years.

In the winter, with picnics and sports days off the agenda, lively gatherings in Tofino were few and far between. For those seeking excitement, dances occasionally took place over at the Clayoquot Hotel, and the beer parlour there always welcomed thirsty men. Following the fire in July 1922, determined to lose no drinking time, Walter Dawley promptly rebuilt both the hotel and beer parlour, just as he had following an earlier fire in 1908; the second time around, having learned from experience, he had the place insured. Yet despite the busy scene in the beer parlour, and the comings and goings in the hotel, on the whole Dawley's establishment held limited appeal for townsfolk, especially families and young people. In the dark rains of winter, they remained grounded in Tofino, hemmed in by thick bush, their scattered homes joined up by muddy tracks and dimly lit by kerosene lamps. A "mug up" of coffee with the neighbours, getting together to listen to one of the few radios in town, arranging meetings to voice community concerns, and attending church services provided the limited distractions. "Do you know, they had never had a bazaar, or even such a thing as a whist drive!" wrote Dorothy Abraham in amazement after she and her husband left Vargas Island and moved into town in the early 1920s.

Social life in Tofino took on a fresh dimension in 1923 with the construction of a new community hall. The original hall in town had been built before the war by a group of settlers, all of them shareholders in the undertaking. Following the war, the Great War Veterans' Association of Tofino purchased this hall for its clubhouse, calling it the Clayoquot Sound Great War Memorial Hall. Because some townspeople felt the Legion Hall, as it became known, functioned more as a club for its members than as a community hall, a group formed to build another hall. The Tofino Community Hall Association raised funds for a larger structure by selling shares, with a minimum of five and a maximum of 100 shares per person. Volunteers built the new hall in a series of work bees, within months producing a simple and solid building: wooden floored, red roofed, painted cream, with one large hall, a smaller anteroom, and a covered porch. The hall officially opened in mid-July 1923, with its first whist drive and dance. Over the years this hall hosted countless badminton tournaments, strawberry teas, box socials, whist drives, even early movie shows, including Felix the Cat and Charlie Chaplin, magically brought to life courtesy of Mike Hamilton's hand-cranked projector. The hall became famed for hosting elaborate New Year's masquerades and wedding receptions—yet in its glory days, nothing the Tofino Community Hall offered could eclipse the Saturday night dances.

Saturday after Saturday, decade after decade, the dances continued, the social heartbeat of the town. In the afternoon before a dance, the big wood stove would be lit, and willing young men fetched the piano from a nearby home. This instrument could not be left in the hall because the damp spoiled the tuning. An accordion and a violin often joined the piano, and in a pinch, a gramophone played. The musicians tuned up and never faltered. "Three waltzes, three fox-trots, three polkas, a sequence that repeated over the course of the evening," Jan Brubacher wrote in an article for *The Sound*. "With a whooshing of dresses and a tap, tap, tap on the hardwood floors, Norwegian traditions of dancing passed down through the community with dances like the Hambo and the Schottische." And Dorothy Abraham enthused, "The Norwegians were the most wonderful dancers."

Men lined one side of the hall on the big benches, ladies on the other, while at the back, tables groaned with the food laid out for the dancers. Alcohol not being permitted in the hall, those who wished to drink stashed their liquor in the bushes, and men would pop outside from time to time to their designated spots; no one would ever touch another's bottle. "If you were a lady," Vi Hansen observed, "you did not step outside." Everyone came to the dances: children and old people; loggers and fishermen passing through; people off visiting boats; miners and prospectors who hiked down from the mines for the weekend; all the girls in town, dressed in their finest; and sometimes, depending on the state of the road and the season, even people coming up from Ucluelet.

Special occasions called for extra dances; Walter Guppy recalled a "cougar dance" in the mid-1930s, held after a group of men tracked and shot a trapped cougar that had dragged itself up a creek, trap and all. No single man could claim the bounty, so they shared it, rented the hall, invited everyone, and danced away the proceeds. The prospector Sam Craig trekked into town from Bear River one weekend, expecting a dance. Finding none planned, he started asking friends if they planned to come to the dance that night. "Dance? There's a dance?" Word spread, and within hours the event became a certainty, a piano had been moved to the hall, food and alcohol mysteriously appeared, and the dancing began. The following Sunday mornings could be tough, especially for the men who had to move the piano back to its home and then make the return trek to their mines, or go out on their fish boats, heads throbbing.

The promise of entertainment could entice party-going locals a good distance out of town. At Calm Creek, the Darville family liked to have parties, despite being some twenty-three kilometres from town. On December 22, 1925, the *Colonist* reported: "An enjoyable party and dance was given at John Darvil's mill at Calm Bay and, although...a furious southeaster prevailed at the time, the young folks braved it with true Canadian determination." Three years later, in April 1928, the Darvilles hosted a masquerade ball at the Tofino Community Hall. "About 150 guests were present. Costumes worn by Miss Ethel Darville, Tyomi Onami, Miss Audrey Coton, the Misses Nicholson and Wallis, Andy Gump, Mrs McKenzie, 'Mickey' Nicholson, Mrs E W [Dorothy] Abraham, the Darville brothers, Mrs Norman Thomas, Miss Winnie Dixson, Daphne Guppy, Mrs Trygve Arnet."

In 1929 the Tofino Community Hall Association and the Great War Veterans' Association of Tofino reached a compromise. Rival events had sometimes occurred on the same night at their halls, so the two groups agreed to hold dances on alternate Saturdays, an arrangement that lasted for a number of years. The Legion Hall also hosted the occasional vaudeville show, and it acquired the added attraction of a poolroom and a barber shop, both operated by the one-legged "Peg" White. From time to time, Legion members raised the question of whether they should obtain a beer licence, but the red tape proved too daunting, and they settled for temporary liquor permits at special functions.

Weightier political matters preoccupied Legion members much of the time. Made up of returned veterans from World War I, the Clayoquot

Legion included Murdo MacLeod, who had been seriously wounded in action twice, as the first president. Other members included Harold Monks, Fred Tibbs, Harold Sloman, Rowland Brinckman, Jack Mitchell, Wallace Rhodes, Alex MacLeod—to name only a few. In 1921, this group accepted Lillian Garrard, who had been a nursing sister overseas, as an honorary member, though she no longer lived locally. The Legion took its responsibilities seriously, using its lobbying power to ensure returned veterans received jobs on the fisheries patrol, at the lifeboat station, or in other government-funded positions. Legion meetings addressed many matters of concern to the community, helping to defend the Tofino post office in 1921 when it faced the threat of closure, and initiating discussions about how to obtain better medical care in town. Legion members also participated energetically in the perennial campaign for a road.

For decades, west coasters had hankered for a road. The notion of linking to Alberni via a permanent route across the mountains had persisted since the earliest days of settlement. Back in 1896, Clayoquot storekeeper Filip Jacobsen petitioned for funds to improve the trail leading out of Ucluelet toward Long Beach. The provincial government allocated $500 in funds, keeping eighteen men and a foreman busy working that winter on a section of the path "a distance of 3 miles [4.8 kilometres]...building four bridges...and making a trail...passable for either horse or cattle." In 1898 another $500 kept the project moving slowly forward.

Ten years later the *Colonist* expounded on the importance of a proper connection between Ucluelet and Tofino, stressing the potential tourist benefit. The newspaper declared that the imminent arrival of a railway in Alberni would draw visitors down the Alberni Canal to Ucluelet, and then up to Long Beach—if a road existed. Later that year, the village of Ucluelet acquired more funds to improve the connection to Tofino and, "using wheelbarrows, picks, shovels and crosscut saws, the only equipment affordable from the paltry government grants," kept a crew of men busy, achieving little more than allowing surveyors to mark where the road eventually would run.

Despite such spurts of activity, prior to World War I the "road"

The corduroy road under construction outside Tofino, heading toward Ucluelet, circa 1920. *Monks collection, courtesy of Lois Warner*

linking Ucluelet to Long Beach consisted only of straggling stretches of overgrown trail through the bush, with occasional lengths of corduroy logs laid over boggy sections. Yet the dream of this and future roads persisted, fuelled by news of the forthcoming "Canadian Highway." On May 4, 1912, near Alberni, road crews began "surveying the new road from Sproat Lake to Long Beach...The Long Beach road will connect up at Alberni with the Canadian highway, so that in the very near future this highway from Victoria will find a true seaboard terminal on that ocean, at one of the finest beaches in all North America"—or so declared the *Colonist* on May 9, 1912.

300

Given such optimistic forecasts, in the pre-war years settlers and land speculators began snapping up every available section of land between Ucluelet and Tofino. In 1910, over 200 land transactions took place in the Ucluelet/Tofino area, many at Long Beach: pre-emptions, purchases, Crown grants, and a handful of mining claims and timber licences. By 1912, over 300 transactions occurred. Many parcels of land changed hands several times within a few years, and a significant number of people acquired multiple adjacent tracts of land; short-term land speculation was rife. By contrast, a handful of earnest settlers tried valiantly to settle on their newly acquired lands, working every daylight hour to clear land, packing supplies on their backs over rough trails if they were not on the waterfront, and labouring against considerable odds to keep their families fed and their livestock safe. The coming of the war put an end to many of these early homesteads, and the land rush petered out. In 1918, only eight land transactions took place in the entire Clayoquot District, extending from Hesquiat to Ucluelet.

While the pre-war fervour persisted, the *Colonist* breezily reported in 1914 that construction continued on the Ucluelet/Tofino road. Because motor cars had by then arrived in BC, the paper noted that "Long Beach, which will be connected with Tofino before long by the road, is the finest stretch of hard sandy beach...and will someday be the scene of automobile racing such as is practiced on the Florida beaches." Given that no one in Tofino or Ucluelet owned a car until the early 1920s, such a notion must have seemed foolish nonsense to most locals.

Postwar road-building efforts saw little progress and increasing local irritation. Leading the charge against ineptitude and wastefulness, the Great War Veterans' Association of Tofino convened a public meeting in July 1920. "It appears the road foreman is frittering away the money by making trails to land which is neither in occupation or cultivation," snapped the *Daily Colonist*. Even so, postwar road work did provide sporadic employment for locals. When Harold Monks returned from the war, he initially worked at the Tofino lifeboat station for $105 a month, but in May 1920, when the lifeboat service cut its winter crew for the summer months, he took a job with the Tofino road-building crew, receiving $76.43 for eighteen-and-a-half days' work.

In 1921, to press for more action on the road, James Sloman, Francis Garrard, and others from Tofino joined forces with a group from Ucluelet and travelled to Victoria to lay their case before the Good Roads League, an organization created by cyclists in Rhode Island in 1892 to lobby for improved roads. A Tofino branch of the BC Good Roads League formed in 1922, with Captain John W. Thompson as secretary. Known as "Cap" Thompson, and considerably older than most war veterans, he became one of Tofino's most beloved citizens. Thompson claimed to have been the oldest person serving in the Canadian army during the war; he had lied about his age, knocking off a couple of decades, and joining up in 1918 at the real age of sixty-eight. Renowned in Tofino for greeting every coastal steamer at the dock, Thompson's flower garden boasted dahlias as big as dinner plates and prize gladioli. Local children vied to help out in the garden for a nickel a time.

The short-lived Tofino Good Roads League put out a publicity leaflet mincing no words. After a spot of purple prose extolling the town and its location—the "verdure-clad fairy islands" of the harbour, and the "sunlit summer seas that lie embosomed among the everlasting hills"—a blunt subheading came straight to the point: "What the West Coast Needs: Good Roads. More Settlers. Much Advertising." Then another headline, "What we want You to Do," and the command "Boost For a Road—Yell For a Road." While the Good Roads campaigners set their sights on a connection to Alberni, the first step still remained completing the laggardly connection between Tofino and Ucluelet. Yet despite the local campaigners winning a meaningless "Good Roads Pennant" in 1923, the road extended only three kilometres outside Tofino at the end of that year.

By 1925 the road from Tofino stretched nearly to Long Beach, and local optimists hoped that Tofino residents wanting to picnic there would no longer have to rely on the tides to make the journey. Until this time, excursions to Long Beach had to coincide with high tide so people and supplies could be unloaded from their boats in Grice Bay before walking the trail across the peninsula to the beach. The return trip had to meet the next high tide in the evening; missing the tide meant a very messy trek through the mud flats of Grice Bay out

The early road between Tofino and Ucluelet, late 1920s. Completed in 1928 after decades of effort, for many years part of the journey required vehicles to drive a considerable distance on Long Beach, rejoining the road at the other end of the beach. *Image NA05425 courtesy of Royal BC Museum, BC Archives*

to deeper water. Helen Malon reported in her diary how she was "a little late in coming back and had to walk three or six hundred yards [275 to 550 metres] in the mud, barefoot, not at all a pleasant experience."

Anthony Guppy recalled the Tofino road of his childhood days as "nothing more than a rough gravel trail that began at the government dock in the village and wound its way through the village into the woods. This trail...continued on for some three more miles [five kilometres]...then turned into a sort of rough road bed that led through the forest to Long Beach." Overgrown with flourishing vegetation, this "so-called road remained an almost unusable trail, winding up and down steep little hills and through marshy land." In winter, any car foolish enough to venture out of town "would sink to its axles in the soft brown quagmire" before reaching Chesterman Beach.

Slogging through thick mud is an apt metaphor for the road. The Tofino–Long Beach section became infamous for its washouts, axle-deep mud, and waist-deep sinkholes. After that came the easy part—driving many kilometres on the sands of Long Beach before joining up with the better, but still very rough, road to Ucluelet.

Rough or not, vehicles began to make the journey. In early June 1928, the *Daily Colonist* noted that "H.T. Fredrickson brought the 1st tourist car over the road from Ucluelet to Long Beach," and two months later Peter Hillier of Ucluelet seized the opportunity and established an occasional bus service to carry sightseers from Ucluelet to Long Beach in the summer months. Tom Scales and J.R. Tindall of Vancouver drove a motorcycle at 145 kilometres per hour across the sands of Long Beach in August 1930, proclaiming it "the finest speedway ever seen." The following month, Arthur Lovekin, who had bought 244.5 hectares of land fronting on Long Beach a few years earlier, had a car shipped to Ucluelet. After driving it up to Long Beach, he took a spin along the sand accompanied by his wife and daughter, driving at speeds up to 112 kilometres per hour. The Lovekins had built a large house and extensive gardens on their property, and used the place as a summer residence for thirty-five years; Lovekin confidently expected development would follow them to Long Beach, once declaring it to be "the playground of the Western World."

Travelling by road in and out of Tofino remained a nightmare for many years. Ronald MacLeod remembered that "by the late 1930s, if the summer was dry, a truck could make its way to Ucluelet with great difficulty but only if the driver had an axe to cut poles and branches to lay across the sinkholes." Yet residents stubbornly clung to the road dream. After all, ever since 1926 a sign had stood near the government dock proclaiming the location to be the "Pacific Terminus of the Trans-Canada Highway." Surely one day this would come true. Meanwhile, the sign became a favourite rubbing post for the local cows roaming the town. On one occasion it disappeared and emerged mysteriously in Ucluelet, and for many years it provided photo ops for tourists disembarking from the *Princess Maquinna*. Tom Gibson, later the mayor of Tofino, repainted the sign year after year, keeping the dream alive. With the formation of the Tofino Board of Trade in 1929, yet another lobby group took up the cudgels in the fight for a road link out to Alberni. This road campaign still had thirty long years to run; it needed all the fresh energy it could muster.

When I first saw Tofino in the nineteen twenties,
I felt the inaccessibility of my abode.
But people said, "Don't worry; all the money being spent is
A guarantee that soon we'll have a Lovely Road."

Kilkenny-born Rowland Brinck-man arrived in Vancouver in 1914, and served in World War I for the Canadian Expeditionary Force. On his return to Canada, he spent several years at Ahousat and came to Tofino in the late 1920s. A skilled artist and writer, he staged many light-hearted dramatic productions, writing the material himself and bringing the community together in a new manner.

Tofino Municipality collection

Rowland Brinckman dashed off these lines about the road with his usual insouciance. One of Tofino's most popular residents, Brinckman neatly captured the spirit of the town in his tongue-in-cheek writing and quirky paintings. An energetic organizer, he established a dramatic society and put on many light-hearted skits, plays, and concerts in the town, writing the material himself and uniting the community in a new manner. He designed and painted elaborate backdrops for these events, wild, colourful flats of scenery featuring imaginary monsters. The children loved him. On summer evenings they would wait till "Brinky" went on his night watchman shift at the lifeboat station, and they would visit him there, begging for stories. He introduced the little crowd of MacLeod boys to a hitherto unknown world, reading them the recently published *Winnie the Pooh*, among other books. "He gave us a sense that there was a world beyond our cocoon called To-fino," Ronald MacLeod wrote, marvelling at "the rich flow of wonders that sprang forth from his brain."

A gifted artist, musician, and writer, Brinckman's charm and keen humour won the hearts of everyone he met during his time in Tofino. Even the most phlegmatic Scot had to admit he was not bad—for an Englishman. His puckish wit emerges in his illustrated map of Clayoquot Sound, still hanging in the Tofino municipal offices. The map lists the languages spoken in town—including Gaelic, Norwegian, and Japanese—and its intricate cartoon sketches and captions poke fun at "fierce fishermen" and the "Presbyterian Mission (very holy)" at Ahousat. Off Lennard Island, in exposed waters, Brinckman wrote: "Here ye sick transit spoileth ye gloria Monday," punning on the Latin *sic transit gloria mundi*.

Born in Kilkenny to a privileged Anglo-Irish family and raised in England, Brinckman came to Canada in 1914, perhaps to free himself from the pressures of his background. His father, a career military man who served in many colonial campaigns, received the Order of the British Empire for his services during World War I. His Irish grandfather, John Elliot Cairnes, an economics professor at both Queens University in Belfast and Trinity in Dublin, gained renown for his writings on economics and the slave trade. Brinckman arrived in Vancouver and found work as a farmhand. A year later he signed up to join the Canadian Expeditionary Force, giving his occupation as "Architect." He spent the rest of the war overseas, serving in the Machine Gun Corps, and taking part in the battle of Vimy Ridge in 1917. On his return to Canada in 1919, he worked for a while as a clerk in Vancouver before heading to the west coast with some friends, seeking adventure.

According to Gordon Gibson, Brinckman and his friends arrived on the coast in 1923 in their small six-horsepower boat. They settled initially at White Pine Cove, on the southern shore of Herbert Inlet, near where dozens of marines and sailors began their infamous land attack on the Ahousahts following the *Kingfisher* incident in 1864. Before long, these inexperienced Englishmen were cutting shingle bolts, enthusiastically and ineptly, for the Gibson Lumber and Shingle Company at Ahousat. The hard labour of felling trees, then bucking and splitting them, proved too much for Brinckman's friends, who retreated to Vancouver, but he stayed on for a number of years, settling on land he pre-empted at the head of Matilda Inlet on Flores Island, and spending a great deal of time with the Gibsons in Ahousat, where he worked in the sawmill and in the cookhouse.

The tough-talking, hard-drinking Gibson boys, four brothers famed for their risky and ambitious ventures, had never seen the like of Rowland Brinckman. "[He] brought an entirely new dimension to our lives," wrote Gordon Gibson. "He was a music buff and a fantastic cartoonist...an avid reader and had a standing order with a bookstore in Vancouver to send him novels as soon as they were available." Thanks to Brinckman, the Gibson house rang to the music of Gilbert and Sullivan, and the works of P.G. Wodehouse and Arnold Bennett entered the home. Evenings around the piano, rousing singsongs, and hours listening to the gramophone became part of their lives. "He was such a gracious man that all of us were grateful for the warmth and new interests he brought into our lives." Possibly Brinckman encouraged Gordon Gibson's unexpected passion for poetry. A colleague once described Gibson as "such a complex character...a person who could talk like a muleskinner...and in the next breath recite verse after verse of the most complex poetry without missing a word."

Brinckman no doubt encouraged the impromptu dances that often occurred at the Gibson household on Saturdays, when the teachers and staff from the Ahousat mission came over, or whenever the *Princess Maquinna* called. "In the early days the *Maquinna* tied up overnight at Ahouset," Alder Bloom of Tofino recorded in his memoirs, "and the Gibson boys would escort the passengers across the island, on plank walks that they had built over the wet ground, to the local hot springs for a refreshing dip, then they would return to their home where they danced in their living room to the wee hours of the morning." If young single ladies were aboard, "lady tourists" as they were known, taking the round trip up the coast and back, the dancing became even merrier. "Up the coast we were good dancers," Gordon Gibson wrote. "We would dance all night when there was a fiddle and enough light." But all too soon the *Princess Maquinna* would be on her way, with a shriek of her whistle, manoeuvring slowly away from the dock at Matilda Creek—

no small feat in the dark or the fog, because the ship had to back down the narrow inlet for about a kilometre before she had enough room to turn around and head off.

When little Mary McKinnon was growing up in Ahousat in the 1920s, she would walk over to see Rowland Brinckman, and he showed her the children's books he was writing and illustrating. Her mother, Gladys (Izard) McKinnon, formerly a concert pianist in England, bitterly resented being transplanted to Ahousat, where her husband worked for the Gibsons after losing his family fortune, but she took comfort from finding in Brinckman someone she could talk to about books and poetry and music. Fearing tuberculosis, Gladys did not allow Mary to play with Ahousaht children; the solitary little girl could hear their laughter and see them playing, but she had to make her own entertainment. She collected shells and learned to row all by herself in a little skiff in the harbour, but her best moments came when she could visit the *Princess Maquinna*, for Captain Edward Gillam always allowed her to come aboard and have a meal at his table. Other than this, her great delight lay in visiting Brinckman and hearing his stories.

After moving into Tofino, Brinckman lived in a cottage opposite the present-day Maquinna Hotel. He soon befriended the entire town, including the sometimes testy George Nicholson, who had moved to Tofino in 1930 after managing Walter Dawley's hotel and beer parlour for several years. Nicholson took over the Tofino Hotel, formerly owned by Hans Hansen. Not renowned for a sense of humour, Nicholson suspected Brinckman was in cahoots with the local teenagers who, on occasion, enjoyed playing pranks. One Halloween proved particularly lively: pranksters tied Nicholson's doors shut from the outside, and boys throwing firecrackers managed to damage a small totem pole Nicholson had erected outside the hotel. The figure had a prominent penis, which strangely vanished. The enraged Nicholson took up his shotgun and let loose a volley, and some of the shot peppered the backside of one of the boys. A local feud led to charges of assault being brought against Nicholson. The Ahousat magistrate came to town to hear the case, but dismissed the charges.

Despite any differences, Brinckman and Nicholson, as Great War

In May 1931, Rowland Brinckman and George Nicholson organized a re-enactment in Tofino of Captain Cook's 1778 landing in Nootka Sound. Several Tla-o-qui-ahts, including Queen Mary and Chief Joseph, played the parts of Mowachaht people, and a few blonde Norwegian girls also took on aboriginal roles. This "Nootka tribe" greeted "Captain Cook," played by George Nicholson, welcoming him and his men ashore. *Courtesy of Leona Taylor*

veterans, addressed each other as "comrade" at the local Legion gatherings, and they collaborated successfully on several dramatic productions. The most ambitious occurred in May 1931 when, backed by the Legion and the BC Historical Association, they mounted an elaborate re-enactment of Captain Cook's landing at Friendly Cove in 1778. Described in the *West Coast Advocate* as "by far the most elaborate performance ever attempted locally," the pageant aimed to be a "performance identical in every detail of the actual occurrence." This extravaganza took place on a Tofino beach, likely Tonquin Beach, and according to the *Daily Colonist* practically everyone in the district attended, including "hundreds of Indians from nearby reservations." Featuring accurate period costumes for Cook and his men and for the aboriginal characters, and with "exact detail paid to the Indian language of the time," the pageant included a boat landing, scenes on board ship and in war canoes, and song, dance, and dialogue. Large flats painted by Brinckman depicted the scenery of Friendly Cove, and the two producers had obtained elaborate props: "a priceless collection of old totems, masks, cedar bark blankets, monster mounted eagles that moved their wings and heads, and many other old valuable Indian articles." Many of these items were loaned by people from Opitsat; others came from George Nicholson's private collection.

The cast numbered twenty-two, including five elders from Opitsat, named by the *Colonist* as "Chief Joseph, Queen Mary, Paul Avery, Iskum Jack and Chief E. Joe." Chief Joseph and Queen Mary carried great authority locally, being the best-known Tla-o-qui-aht elders; their participation in the pageant added considerably to its status. Nicholson described them "both arrayed in their war paints...and clothed in bearskin rugs." Queen Mary nearly stole the show, holding everyone spellbound "for as long as she continued her friendly gestures in both song and dance." Not having a sufficient number of aboriginal participants to represent the Nootka people, "a band of young ladies from Tofino [acted] the part of the Nootka tribe." This explains the distinctly Norwegian appearance of some of the "Nootka" girls in surviving photographs. George Nicholson took the role of Captain Cook, and the part of Chief Maquinna, according to Nicholson's account of the event, fell to Chief Joseph. The *Colonist* reported that Brinckman played Maquinna, but he more likely acted as Maquinna's interpreter during the long speeches made by Chief Joseph in that role.

The pageant opened with Chief Maquinna and his men discussing rumours of a big "devil man" coming to threaten their way of life. A white sail then appeared out at sea, and the "Nootka tribe" danced defiantly, interrupted by gunfire. After an encounter at sea, a sailors' hornpipe, more Indian dances, and an elaborate exchange of gifts, the boat sailed into "Friendly Cove," peaceful accord was established, and Cook and his men came ashore to a welcoming ceremony. A concert in the Legion Hall followed the pageant, and according to Nicholson, "Chief Joseph and Queen Mary put on a song and dance act that certainly brought the house down, and called for several encores."

The historical importance of Captain Cook had been commemorated on the west coast well before the famous pageant. August 12, 1924, saw the unveiling of a cairn at Friendly Cove to honour Cook's "discovery" of Nootka Sound. Several dignitaries from Victoria participated, including Lieutenant Governor Walter Nichol, Dr. C.F. Newcombe of the Provincial Museum, and the influential historian F.W. Howay of the Historic Sites and Monuments Board of Canada.

The group travelled to Friendly Cove by steamer, its numbers swelling en route as local participants in the event came aboard, including a group of schoolboys from Kakawis. "I joined the *Princess Maquinna* at Tofino, there was quite a party aboard," Dorothy Abraham enthused, delighted when her newly formed Brownie troupe received a Union Jack from the dignitaries on board. When the crowd of visitors arrived at Friendly Cove for the unveiling of the eleven-foot-high (3.3-metre) cairn, Father Charles Moser acted as interpreter between the Lieutenant Governor and Chief Napoleon of Yuquot. This cairn joined another commemorative cairn already in place nearby. The earlier one, known as the Meany monument, had been erected by the Washington State University Historical Society in 1903, through the efforts of history professor Edmond Meany.

Following the 1931 Captain Cook pageant, the area witnessed yet another attempt to make the road between Tofino and Long Beach passable in winter. With thousands of unemployed men left idle by the Great Depression, the Canadian government set up relief camps in remote locations to keep them busy on public works projects—and also to keep them out of the cities, fearing the spread of communist agitation. Camp 101 went up near Chesterman Beach, alongside the road, to house 100 men, mostly fishermen from Tofino, Ucluelet, and Ahousat. Another section of the relief camp went up at Long Beach. The young Guppy boys often went out to the Chesterman camp and chatted with the men, who "would tell us tales about wild animals around the camp...hungry mosquitoes, atrocious food and damp beds in damp tents...the place was driving them crazy." The men laboured at ditching, grading, and gravelling the Tofino–Ucluelet road, doing all the work by hand with pick and shovel, the only machine available being an old Ford truck. They earned twenty cents a day plus room and board. The Guppy boys also visited the Long Beach camp once, meeting the camp foreman, who whiled away his time building a highly finished Welsh dresser from wood collected on the beach. "I doubt the crew there did much work," wrote Anthony Guppy. "I think they likely spent their time walking the sands and discussing ways to reform the capitalist system when and if they ever got back to civilization."

Following the first winter, local people began to reach out to the unemployed men in the camps, offering support and entertainment. This followed a letter to the *Colonist* asking "if anyone would donate a battery radio for use at Long Beach Unemployment Camp; there are now over 100 men there, and they have very little contact with the outside world. Mail delivered twice a week, and no form of entertainment." The men received a radio, and Captain Neroutsos of the Canadian Pacific Coast Steamship Service sent three bundles of magazines. Later, "a football game between the Camp and Opitsat Indians was played, ending in a win for the road camp by 4 goals to one," reported the *Colonist* on March 29, 1932. "In the evening the men were entertained to the Legion show and dance." A month after that, some local entertainers took their show out to the camp; performers included Rowland Brinckman, Rev. John Leighton, George Nicholson, and Eileen Garrard. Such diversions must have been more than welcome at the dismal work camp, although other excitements did occasionally present themselves. On August 24, 1932, a Boeing five-passenger flying boat crash-landed on Long Beach. Pilot Gordon McKenzie had taken off from Nootka for Vancouver but flew into fog, forcing him to make an emergency landing. Swells caught the plane and carried it out into the surf, rolling it over and over, as men from the relief camp rushed to the rescue, fixing ropes to the plane, and the Tofino lifeboat hurried to the scene. The pilot escaped serious injury.

For many years, a silent undercurrent of activity all along the west coast involved selling booze. Since 1854, the sale of alcoholic drinks to aboriginals had been against the law, a prohibition based entirely on race that gave rise to decades of bootlegging, along with persistent, unavailing efforts to stop this activity. During the sealing era, schooner captains frequently provided alcohol to bribe hunters to sign on; in later years, bootleggers sold whiskey or moonshine from their motor launches, anchoring off the villages and waiting for customers to come out in their canoes. At the Clayoquot beer parlour, some customers regularly bought beer for aboriginal people, who would wait outdoors for the surreptitious handover.

During the years of prohibition in British Columbia, from 1917 to 1921, alcohol could not legally be bought or sold at all, inspiring highly inventive ways of obtaining liquor. After 1920, with the introduction of prohibition in America, many Canadians entered the lucrative rum-running trade, a cross-border traffic that thrived until US prohibition ended in 1933. Tall tales of illicit booze sales in and around Tofino have been told for decades, mostly unsubstantiated, always colourful, and generally leaving more questions than answers: about bottles of booze hidden in the piano at Clayoquot; about a large stash of liquor in a disused fishing scow on the waterfront; about scowloads of rum leaving Tofino for offshore vessels; about one of the prettiest houses in Tofino having bottles hidden in a little-used cellar. Impossible to verify and improving with age, such stories live on. When America ran dry, various local citizens probably did have extra liquor on hand, perhaps a fair amount, to sell to visiting American boats, either at the local docks or offshore. As Douglas Hamilton commented in his book *Sobering Dilemma*, "The illicit booze trade was a small entrepreneur's dream."

In 1932, Tofino officially incorporated as a village, a coming-of-age process enabling the community to govern itself. A board of three commissioners became the first town council; Jacob Arnet acted as chairman of the commission, working alongside John Cooper and Robert Guppy. Wilfred Armitage served as town clerk. In the ensuing years, most prominent local citizens served as commissioners at various times. At first, meetings took place monthly in the home of one or other of the commissioners, the minutes recorded by hand in imposing ledgers. The commissioners gravely discussed all matters of local concern, large and small. The safety of pedestrians came up at one of their meetings during Tofino's first winter as a fully fledged village. The commissioners agreed to ban vehicles from Main Street because of its deteriorating condition, and to allow people to walk safely. An overly cautious decision, considering the town had, at most, half a dozen vehicles.

The question of health care in Tofino frequently surfaced as a matter of concern for village leaders. Medical care in the area had never been adequate, and a series of different physicians came and went at Clayoquot in the early years of the century, followed by the establishment of the short-lived Methodist hospital on Stockham Island. After only a few years of operation, that hospital closed around 1912. Father Charles Moser noted its demise in his diary: "The Mission was given up by the Methodists. The Hospital used to be a Hotel was bought by Chief Joseph for something like $20.00 for the lumber that was in it."

No doctor lived in Tofino until 1912, when Dr. Douglas Dixson arrived; he remained the only doctor permanently based in Clayoquot Sound for nearly twenty years. Appointed to provide medical care for aboriginals on the coast, Dixson faced an impossible job. He ranged from Tofino to Kyuquot, travelling continually up and down the coast by rowboat, fishing vessel, and coastal steamer, attending to the residential schools and the villages. Whenever he could, Dixson hired the *Agnes*, a vessel owned by the Grant family and regularly used to transport mail and workers up Tofino Inlet to Grice Bay and the Clayoquot cannery. Every month Dixson received his "Indian cheque" for around forty dollars, and filed his "Indian report" and "Schools report." His duties included checking children for contagious ailments and deciding if they were fit for admission to residential school. Dixson also cared for the Tofino townspeople and for scattered settlers requiring his help on a fee-for-service basis.

Dixson's surviving diary from 1916 lists all his patients by name or nickname: Topsail George, Big William, Bachelor Tom, Bill Spittal, Reece Riley, Lockie Grant, and many others, along with their various ailments. Phthisis appears often—a term used for tuberculosis—along with measles, mumps, whooping cough, syphilis, pneumonia, rheumatism, teeth extractions. In his travels, Dixson visited the workers at the copper mine in Sydney Inlet, settlers on Vargas Island, the storekeeper at Nootka—and he made regular runs to the hotel at Clayoquot to see patients, followed by a meal at the hotel and a few shots of rum or whiskey. The diary indicates that he sometimes received urgent summons to visit isolated homesteads, like that of the Rae-Arthur family in Hesquiat Harbour, and on one occasion to visit a serious burn victim at Ahousat. Bad weather could easily prevent him making such emergency calls; far too frequently his boat had to turn back.

Dixson also checked the Tofino schoolchildren for signs of tuberculosis. The schoolteacher, Katie Hacking, who later married Harold Monks, recalled the doctor's much-dreaded visits to the school. At first she failed to understand the children's unhappiness when they knew he was coming. Eventually she learned they did not like how Dixson used the same tongue depressor on all of them. She suggested they bring an implement from home, perhaps a teaspoon or butter knife, to serve as a personal tongue depressor. On the day of the health checks, Dixson expressed amazement at all the cutlery the children produced. When Katie explained, he expostulated, "But I do nothing of the kind! I use one end of the depressor for the girls, and the other end for the boys!" Described by Dorothy Abraham as "a funny old boy," easily overexcited and unable to suture a badly cut hand, Dixson did not inspire confidence as he grew older. He remained in Tofino until just before his death in 1932, succeeded by Dr. A. Swartzman.

It became increasingly clear that one doctor could not adequately serve the area, and that sending seriously ill people out by boat to hospital in Alberni often imperilled lives. The lifeboat, fisheries patrol vessels, lighthouse tender, and coastal steamer all dealt with medical emergencies, but they could not always respond quickly enough, nor could they provide proper care to patients en route. Dr. John Robertson, who took over from Swartzman in the autumn of 1934, set about making changes. On contract to the Department of Indian Affairs, he was primarily responsible for serving the aboriginals, but inevitably he served everyone who needed him. He recalled his early experiences in an article for *Canadian Hospital* in June 1937. "When I first came here... I found it necessary to do emergency appendectomies in the homes with no running water and no means for safe sterilization."

According to George Nicholson, who often ferried the doctor to visit patients in remote areas during his five-year tenure in Tofino, Dr. Robertson performed a total of three appendectomies in the Tofino Hotel, one in a floating logging camp, two in private homes, and four at the mission schools. "Many a mulligan pot had to improvise as a sterilizer," wrote Nicholson. Robertson's young wife, Marguerite, assisted at one of these appendectomies, carried out by gaslight on a table in the Tofino Hotel. With no sterile linen available, Marguerite turned to her trousseau because her tea towels "were quite new." She put them in a disinfectant solution, donned rubber gloves, and laid out surgical instruments—including bent forks in place of retractable forceps. The surgery proceeded, and the patient recovered. Robertson conducted another of these emergency appendectomies on the kitchen table in the home of Murdo MacLeod, who stoically held the gas lamp for the doctor during the operation on his young son Ronald.

From the moment of her arrival in Tofino, Marguerite Robertson learned to expect the unexpected. She arrived after her husband, disembarking on Christmas Eve 1934 from the same boat carrying the much-anticipated order of Christmas liquor, eagerly awaited by revellers at the dock. Her introduction to Tofino came the following morning in church, when even the minister, Rev. John Leighton, felt the effects of too much Christmas cheer. He left the service halfway through to be quietly sick in the churchyard and returned with a smiling apology. Dearly loved in the community, "Padre" Leighton could do no wrong in the eyes of his parishioners. Another memorable event occurred when Queen Mary and Chief Joseph of Opitsat came to visit Marguerite. As a sign of her status and wealth, Queen Mary arrived wearing three hats. Marguerite presented tea and cookies to her visitors; when she offered a refill, Queen Mary declined, "but I would have if you'd had coffee." Queen Mary came to know Dr. Robertson well; he gave her the empty hypodermic glass vials from his surgery, and she made them into a treasured necklace. She wore it on special occasions, including the day in August 1936 when she and Chief Joseph greeted the visiting BC premier, Duff Pattullo, on the dock at Tofino.

Mid-1930s, Chief Joseph and Queen Mary at Opitsat with unidentified Roman Catholic sisters and priest. *Mount Angel Abbey Library*

At first, Dr. Robertson saw patients in a tiny damp shed on the waterfront. He had to coat instruments with Vaseline to stop them from rusting, he fetched water in a pail, and he kept the wood stove going in a space too small for an examining table. A frail partition that did not reach the ceiling divided the examining area from the cramped waiting room; sometimes the doctor asked patients to wait in Towler and Mitchell's store next door, to afford privacy for others. This store, formerly Sloman and McKenna's, had changed hands twice during the 1920s, before being purchased in 1928 by two former employees of Walter Dawley, Fred Towler and Jack Mitchell. Although on the site of the original store in Tofino, Towler and Mitchell's was no longer the only store. Shortly after Duncan and Maude Grant arrived in Tofino in 1916, they built a store on pilings at the end of the government wharf, just a short distance away. Grant's store operated until 1930, when former cannery employee Sid Elkington took it over, changing the name to Elkington's.

The doctor's "office" perched on the boardwalk known as Grice Road, near the homes of several early settlers. First John Grice built his house on Grice Point, later the MacLeods, Larkins, Rileys, and others built their homes along the waterfront here. In 1927, John Cooper, originally at Long Beach, built his new Tofino home just above the road, and shortly after, Cooper opened the Imperial Oil marine station on the waterfront below. Harold Monks later bought Cooper's home and business. With the oil station, two stores, post office, mining recorder's office, several homes, doctor's office, and government wharf all in close proximity, this became the commercial centre of Tofino. And as daily gathering places in town, nothing beat the conviviality of the stores. Often a good number of townsfolk could be found hanging around the potbellied stoves, talking politics and local gossip with whoever came by. First Nations families also whiled away their time in the stores, including Chips George and his wife, who sometimes spent entire days at Towler and Mitchell's. Comparing prices between the stores provided a special pleasure; if tinned corn, print fabric, lamp wick, hair ribbon, or flour varied by as much as a cent, word would spread at once. Being asked to wait in the store, watching all this activity, never seemed a hardship for Dr. Robertson's patients.

The doctor, though, knew he needed a facility offering patients better care and a guarantee of privacy. This became particularly clear to him when treating venereal disease. Both gonorrhea and syphilis were rife on the coast, cutting across all populations of fishermen, settlers, and aboriginals. Syphilis also affected children, who could be born with the condition. Records survive of one little girl at the Ahousat residential school who received eight treatments for congenital syphilis before dying of tuberculosis at the age of only eight. Her case was not unique. For adults affected by venereal disease, particularly rampant during fishing season, the doctor had to put aside a good deal of time for the required treatments. Robertson had so many cases of syphilis coming his way that at certain times of year he dedicated every Friday to treating the condition, privately dubbing the day "Dirty Friday" as a steady stream of patients attended his clinic for IV treatments of the pre-antibiotic drug known as Salvarsan, compound 606, or arsphenamine.

Knowing that local women could act as nurses to their own families, Robertson believed that, with ingenuity and volunteer help, Tofino could support a small hospital. It would mostly serve emergency cases, using relatives to nurse the patients, and the doctor would rent a section of the building for his offices. Robertson discussed the idea with community leaders and found eager local support. The idea quickly took hold, leading to one of the most extraordinary volunteer efforts the town ever witnessed. From the outset, everyone understood that this hospital would be a labour of love, relying on local generosity and volunteers. It would serve a wide area and a wide range of people, from Ucluelet to Estevan Point, a population of about 900 settlers and 1,400 aboriginals.

Formed under the Friendly Society Act of British Columbia, the Tofino Hospital Society took on the challenge of fundraising. Government funds would cover 40 percent of the cost; the rest had to be raised by the society. Local merchants came forward to donate goods, services, and money, and many businesses and individuals from outside the area also contributed. Rowland Brinckman, a good friend of the Robertsons, donated the land for the hospital building. Well before construction began, the redoubtable Ladies' Hospital Aid group sprang into action, numbering from twelve to twenty-five members at different times. They first met in February 1935 and decided to purchase fabric and start sewing all the bed linens, pillowcases, gowns, and curtains. Their subsequent fundraising efforts included raffles, bake sales, fashion shows, bazaars, and dances. For decades to come the Ladies' Aid remained a local force like no other, tirelessly raising money for specific hospital expenses. "It was amazing," Marguerite Robertson recalled, "how everyone pulled together. Whites, natives, Japanese—everyone." By the spring of 1935, work had begun, described in the *Daily Colonist* on May 2: "Community spirit working overtime, all the men-folk of Tofino district turned out each day to help clear the site for the proposed hospital...a very few days had the property transformed ready for building."

To contribute to the fundraising, Rowland Brinckman organized a "monster vaudeville show." The curtain rose at the Legion Hall on May 18, 1935, for the first of two packed-house performances, admission twenty-five cents. The audience included aboriginals and Japanese, visiting fishermen, lighthouse personnel, dozens of people from Ahousat and Ucluelet, plus, on the first night, officers, crew, and passengers from the *Princess Maquinna*. The steamer changed her schedule, staying in port overnight for the spectacle. Following the second night's performance, a huge dance took place in the community hall. Over 200 people attended, the Ladies' Aid served supper, and musicians from the lighthouse tender Estevan provided the music. The vaudeville show included an "Indian war dance in full costume," led by Chief Joseph of Opitsat and performed by eight dancers. The talent also featured an accordion concert, and a trapeze act by the doctor, who hit a rafter and broke a rib in the excitement. The centrepiece, a play written by Brinckman, poked fun at what he defined as the main interests of Tofino inhabitants: gas engines, fishing, rum, and *sake*, the powerful rice wine made by local Japanese.

Everyone in Tofino knew about, and many happily shared, the abundant homemade *sake* around town, thanks to the Japanese residents. Yoshio (Johnny) Madokoro recalled the local "part-time law-man" who would drop by to drink *sake* with his parents. "A few times when someone came in from 'outside' he would drop a warning and all signs of the illegal *sake*-making would magically disappear." In a memoir written for his church newsletter in Toronto, Tatsuo Sakauye recalled proudly that his mother made "the best booze on the West Coast." Mrs. Sakauye brewed her *sake* twice a year in her home at Eik Bay, each batch requiring two forty-five-kilogram sacks of rice. No one ever sold *sake*; it featured as a gift on special occasions. Padre Leighton had a great fondness for it, consuming impressive amounts without ill effect. Bill Spittal, the old prospector who lived on Tofino Inlet, became friendly with the Kami family, and their *sake* very likely inspired him when the family asked him to name their newborn baby. Spittal named him Napoleon Bonaparte Kami.

Fundraising efforts for the hospital continued unchecked. According to George Nicholson, the Vancouver radio announcer Earle Kelly raised many donations. Known as "Mr. Good Evening," and sometimes hailed as Canada's first personality broadcaster, Kelly regularly mentioned the *Princess Maquinna*'s progress up and down the coast during the 1930s. His comments about the vessel he dubbed "The Good Ship *Maquinna*" won him many friends on the coast. From 1929 onward, west coasters tuned in to catch his nightly broadcasts on radio news service CKCD from

Vancouver, straining to listen through the scratchy reception. As Kelly wound up his show, he bid goodbye to all his listeners "on the land, on the water, in the air, in the woods, in the mines, in lighthouses," often adding "and especially to everyone on the Good Ship *Maquinna*. Good night." Marguerite Robertson recalled these broadcasts vividly: how everyone would tune in at 6 p.m. on the days the *Maquinna* was due; how "Mr. Good-Eve-en-ing" spoke so slowly and formally; how he spoke always of Clay-oh-kwot—never "Klakwot"—and To-fee-no. In Tofino, if the boat was delayed unloading freight at You-cloo-let or at Clay-oh-kwot, hearts would sink: "'Oh dear, canned sausages for dinner again,' we'd say."

By October 1935, the Tofino Hospital Society agreed that to keep costs down, the hospital would have no furnace but would be heated by wood stoves and a coal-fired kitchen range; it would not be wired for electricity, but would instead use Coleman lamps; and the upper floor would be finished at a later date. Construction began in 1936, all done by volunteers. Every day, groups of women prepared large noonday meals for the workers. Within a few months the building became a reality.

In the early years, patients came to hospital with their own "nurse," usually a relative, and paid one dollar a day to be there. The Ladies' Aid did the mending and some of the cooking and cleaning, and continued to raise funds for whatever need arose. Marguerite Robertson assisted at surgeries in the new hospital, lighted by battery-powered headlamps and performed on an operating table built by the doctor. She would cautiously administer ether or chloroform, with her husband intoning "Drip, drip, drip," but before long, trained nurses came to help. One travelled over from Clayoquot, where her husband ran a mink farm, and the nurse from the residential school at Ahousat also came when needed. Bessie Jean Banfill wrote of one occasion when she received a telegram at Ahousat to come at once. The lifeboat from Tofino came to fetch her, her severe seasickness en route to the hospital eased by the "cheerful spirit of the huge, big-hearted, life-saving crew, as they vied with each other to serve me." She assisted at the surgery, and the local telegraph operator, who had never before witnessed an operation, also helped. Within a few hours, the nurse found herself back in the lifeboat, heading to Ahousat, while the patient recovered in hospital, attended by "a local Norwegian girl and a relative."

Rowland Brinckman never saw the hospital completed. He had accepted a job in Ottawa, working for the National Theatre. Excited at the prospect of new horizons, he sold his possessions and came to stay with the Robertsons in April 1936, just prior to his departure. To the dismay of all his friends, the severe cold he had been nursing worsened into pneumonia. Despite the efforts of the doctor, assisted by Hilmar Wingen, who provided oxygen from his machine shop, Brinckman's condition deteriorated. "We couldn't save him," Marguerite Robertson recalled sadly. He died in their home. "And bitter tears we children wept," wrote Ronald MacLeod.

Unable to attend the funeral, Marguerite stayed home with her new baby. The rain lashed down in torrents, water poured off the handmade casket in the Tofino lifeboat, and the solemn cortege of boats heading to the cemetery on Morpheus Island looked so dismal that she made her husband promise if anything happened to her he would "never take [her] body to that dreadful place." Not everyone shared her dread of the Morpheus Island cemetery, and the place still exerts a strong hold on local imagination. Twenty-two people are buried there, including John and Jane Grice, Jacob and Johanna Arnet, John and Annie Eik, Fred Tibbs, Harold Kimoto, and several members of the Garrard family. The island ceased to be used as a cemetery in the late 1940s, with the opening of a cemetery outside Tofino, near the airport.

With the building of the hospital and with a growing local economy, Tofino came into its own as a hub for the west coast. The population in town stood at around 250 by the late 1930s, nearly one third of the people in town being of Japanese descent. Well-established and well-respected, the Japanese had become an integral part of the local scene in Tofino. Given their growing families and increasing involvement in the community, their future here looked bright.

Chapter 15:

THE JAPANESE

"BOY, THEY WERE GOOD," Trygve Arnet declared in his 1981 interview with Bob Bossin. "They made all their own spoons [fishing lures]. They'd get these big pieces of brass and cut them and polish them up and bend them the way they wanted them. Then they'd try them in the water, pulling them along to see they worked right. I fished right along with them. They were really good."

Ian MacLeod, like Arnet a salmon troller, recalled that when his family arrived in Tofino, all but two of the local trollers were Japanese. He described them as "the greatest people on earth when it came to fishermen. They co-operated so well. There were no radio telephones, but there were methods of communicating. If a man was in trouble, he raised one pole...If the weather looked bad, everybody would stay out until a certain point and then they'd all go in together. They wouldn't leave one guy by himself...it was bred in them to have respect for the ocean and everything pertaining to it."

Not everyone shared this admiration for the Japanese. From their earliest days in the province, their success as fishermen sparked bitter resentment within the fishing community throughout British Columbia. Japanese immigrants had been in British Columbia from the late 1880s, although initially in very small numbers. Like the early Chinese immigrants, single working men made up the bulk of these Japanese, and most intended to return to Japan after making their fortune. Many ended up staying, outfacing as best they could the antagonism they attracted from the fishing community and, more broadly, from Canadian society at large.

For over two decades, from the early 1920s until 1942, scores of Japanese lived in or near Tofino. By the time they faced evacuation as "enemy aliens" during World War II, they numbered nearly 100 in the Tofino area and over 200 Japanese lived in Ucluelet. At the time of their arrival on the west coast, most of these Japanese spoke marginal English and "fisherman's Japanese." Many came from Steveston, at the mouth of the Fraser River, where they had been fishing and working in the canneries. They shared a determination to make good on the west coast, to raise their families and educate their children there, participating as best they could in community affairs. But above all, they came to fish—a trade at which they excelled beyond measure.

Their arrival introduced a new type of fishing on the west coast of Vancouver Island. Rather than fishing only in the summer months to support the canneries, the Japanese adapted the small gillnet boats they used on the Fraser River to handle west coast conditions, and they began salmon trolling throughout most of the year. Interviewed for *Westcoast Fisherman* in June 1995, Johnny Madokoro recalled the first commercial troller to fish out of Tofino, Yasumatsu Isozaki, who "claimed to be able to catch a spring salmon with a table spoon." The prowess of the Japanese fishermen entirely changed the pattern of local fishing. Alma (Arnet) Sloman recalled how "the men who lived in Tofino [followed] in the footsteps of the Steveston people...taking up fishing on a serious basis."

Although a small Japanese community existed in Victoria throughout the 1890s, far larger Japanese communities sprang up around the sawmills, docks, and canneries along the Fraser River, in Steveston, and in Vancouver. The fishing skill of the Japanese, and their growing dominance in the industry, sparked resentment and anger from white and First Nations fishermen alike, which sometimes erupted into confrontations and violence. In 1893 the Fishermen's Benevolent and Protective Association in New Westminster lobbied to curtail the right of Japanese and Chinese to obtain fishing licences, and demanded a reduction in the number of licences granted to them. In various guises, such campaigns continued on and off for decades. Even so, according to Ken Adachi in his book *The Enemy That Never Was*, by 1901 Japanese fishermen held 1,958 of a total of 4,700 licences issued in the province, and by 1919 they held 3,267 fishing licences, nearly half the number issued that year.

The earliest Japanese in Clayoquot Sound appeared in the late nineteenth century, during a surge in emigration from Japan that brought thousands of Japanese into British Columbia. The majority of these new arrivals headed south to the United States, but a significant number remained; by 1901, some 4,600 Japanese lived in British Columbia. A handful of these showed up on the west coast as itinerant workers before the turn of the century, evidenced by a note to Walter Dawley in 1899 from Mr. J. Tanaka in Alberni, asking Dawley to provide for Japanese workers hired to cut cordwood at the Rose Marie mine. The *Colonist* also noted the presence of a handful of Japanese fishing off Port Renfrew as early as 1901.

Due to long-standing Japanese involvement in the fur seal hunt in offshore international waters and in the North Pacific, Japanese vessels and Japanese faces became familiar in Victoria and along the outer coast of Vancouver Island during the heyday of sealing. Sometimes Japanese sealing schooners showed up in Canadian waters seeking safe harbour or to take on water and provisions, and in the later years of the fur seal hunt, some Japanese sealers offered employment to experienced Canadian seal hunters and captains who set sail under the Japanese flag. In April 1909 the schooner *Matsu Maru* carried several seal hunters from Victoria to help man the nine "hunting boats" on board, and the vessel put in at Hesquiat en route north. Two Japanese crew members jumped ship there. According to the *Colonist*, "The Japanese had watched their opportunity and swam ashore, taking to the bush beyond the spit at Hesquoit...They took to the woods and hid until nightfall when they found a small canoe belonging to an Indian and made their way 10 miles [16 kilometres] down the coast to Sydney Inlet. They landed there and met an Indian, by name Hesquiot Frank, with whom they arranged for the trip to Clayoquot." Whether or not he intended to, "Hesquiot Frank" delivered the men straight into the hands of the acting police constable at Clayoquot, who detained them and sent word to their captain. The *Matsu Maru* picked them up off Lennard Island, from "a gasoline launch belonging to Mr. Jensen," their bid for freedom foiled.

The following year, in 1910, the *Colonist* commented on the movements on the west coast of the Japanese sealing schooner *Shinano Maru*, under the command of the well-known Captain Voss of Victoria. Father Charles Moser observed this schooner with interest, commenting in his diary that it "anchored near Opitsat to get a supply of water. Sailors in gumboots rowed their sealing boats into the creek behind the village filled them with water and rowed them back to sch. In this fashion many trips had to be made." Having provisioned at Clayoquot, the vessel then headed for Quatsino Sound, where once again two Japanese sailors jumped ship. Captain Voss, "aware of troubles in store for his vessel if the men were left on Vancouver Island, urged the Indians to join in a search for them." Two days later, attracted by the smell of cooking, the "hungry deserters came out of the bush glad to escape from the timber and hunger among the trees."

The whaling stations on the BC coast attracted a considerable number of Japanese workers. At Rose Harbour on Haida Gwaii, where whaling began in 1910, the station relied almost exclusively on Japanese to do the skilled and difficult job of flensing, while Chinese labourers rendered the carcasses. Although exact records are no longer available, the whaling stations on Vancouver Island's west coast, established several years before Rose Harbour, also employed many Japanese workers. In February 1913, Captain Gillam, on board the *Tees*, heard the case of two Japanese workers from the Kyuquot whaling station who had been arrested by Constable Ewen MacLeod for selling liquor illegally. As Justice of the Peace, Gillam found both men guilty, charging each a fine of $200 or six months in jail. They paid the fines.

In 1907, following a period of nearly seven years when Japanese immigration to Canada declined to a trickle, over 8,000 Japanese arrived in British Columbia, largely single men. Even though nearly half of these subsequently went on to the United States, their presence ignited vitriolic protest in BC, inspired by fearsome propaganda about the "yellow peril" posed by Japanese and Chinese alike. Fearing for their jobs in the face of competition from these hard-working immigrants, anti-Asian elements ran amok. The scene in Vancouver turned particularly ugly, fuelled by labour union rhetoric, by some politicians, and by editorials like that of September 9, 1907, in the Vancouver *Daily Province*: "We are all of the opinion that this province must be a white man's country...We do not wish to look forward to a day when our descendants will be dominated by Japanese, or Chinese, or any colour but their own." The newly formed Asiatic Exclusion League staged a protest and parade in Vancouver in September 1907, which ended with a mob of several thousand people rampaging through Chinatown and through the area around Powell Street known as "Little Tokyo." Singing "Rule Britannia" and shouting anti-Asian tirades, the crowd broke windows, damaged property, and rioted for several hours.

Despite escalating anti-Japanese sentiments in BC, and another sharp reduction in immigration, the Japanese communities in the province continued to grow slowly, in part because Japanese women, exempt from the immigration restrictions, began to arrive in numbers. Married men sent for their wives and families to join them, and single men sought out "picture brides," who courageously set sail from Japan to wed men they did not know. As the families grew, the Japanese communities gained stability and grudging acceptance from the surrounding population. By 1921, the number of Japanese Canadians in British Columbia had risen to 15,000; a decade later it reached 22,000. According to historian Jean Barman, given the complete halt of all Chinese immigration in 1923, "racism was increasingly concentrated on the Japanese," not only because of their numbers but also because they "were becoming increasingly economically competitive."

Continued pressure from both white and aboriginal fishermen led to tighter licensing restrictions for the Japanese on the Fraser River during the 1920s, and a significant reduction in Japanese fishing licences there. According to Geoff Meggs in his book *Salmon*, "between 1922 and 1925 more than 1,000 [Japanese] men would be driven from the industry." For those determined to continue fishing, the reduction in Fraser River licences, combined with poor sockeye runs there, led them to fish elsewhere.

Japanese fishermen had long been aware of the potential on the west coast, and they also knew the tricky politics involved in fishing there. As early as 1904, Mr. J. Tanaka revealed his knowledge of the situation in a letter to Walter Dawley, asking about the dog salmon run at Clayoquot. He asked if "the Indians make trouble if some another men will do catch it by net." Having heard from other Japanese of the abundance of dog salmon, Tanaka wanted to send "many fisher," but he was unsure of the timing. "I shall be glad if you will kindly let me know about the season and complaint of Indians."

From 1917, Japanese fishermen made their presence more widely felt on the west coast of Vancouver Island, by then appearing often around Ucluelet and Tofino. One of the first to fish near Tofino, Yasumatsu Isozaki, reportedly returned to Steveston saying the salmon seemed so plentiful and easy to catch they virtually jumped into the rowboat. As troubles within the Fraser River fishery grew, the number of Japanese fishermen heading toward the west coast increased. According to Mr. W.G. Ellison of Port Renfrew, quoted in the *Colonist* on April 16, 1919, "An average of 15 Japanese small fishing craft were in the harbour each night on their way up the West Coast...Three years ago a Japanese would not have been seen around Renfrew during the fishing season." That same spring, Father Charles Moser remarked in his diary the presence of Japanese boats fishing off Hesquiat for spring salmon, alongside the local aboriginals.

In the spring of 1921, over a hundred Japanese fishermen came to the Ucluelet area to troll for salmon, sparking angry protests from local fishermen about the number of trolling licences allotted to the Japanese. The presence of these and many other Japanese fishing on the west coast emerges clearly in the census of 1921. In early June, when the census enumerator for Ucluelet, Wilfred Thornton, made up his lists, he noted over 120 Japanese fishing vessels in the immediate area. His enumeration also reveals several Japanese families already living at Ucluelet. Up at Clayoquot, enumerator George Anderson of Vargas Island also diligently listed all the Japanese vessels that happened to be in the Tofino area during the first week of June when he was counting heads. His records reveal over eighty "gasboats" with Japanese crew anchored at Clayoquot or Tofino; no Japanese households or families yet appear at either location. The census names every boat owner and crew member, though most boats had only one person aboard. These Japanese vessels far outnumbered the boats owned by local people in 1921, and they must have presented an extraordinary sight at the time, lying at anchor en masse in Ucluelet harbour and at Clayoquot and Tofino. The Japanese fishermen listed in the 1921 census include many who subsequently took up residence on the west coast. In November 1921, the *Colonist* described one Toyojiro Nakamoto as "Japanese fish broker of Tofino." Nakamoto evidently stationed himself there as a fish buyer for the sizeable Japanese fleet; some records indicate the presence of a Japanese fish buyer in Tofino as early as 1917. By April 1922, the *Colonist* sternly noted that "Fishery patrol vessels...have gone to the West Coast to keep an especially sharp eye on Japanese trollers."

In response to this growing presence, both Caucasian and aboriginal fishermen on the west coast demanded the Department of Fisheries enact a local residency requirement for salmon trollers. On March 1, 1923, the residency requirement came into effect. By the end of that year, some ninety Japanese fishermen and their families had settled on the west coast: fifty in Ucluelet, ten in Bamfield, twenty-five in Tofino, and six at Clayoquot on Stubbs Island. Most of these people hailed from the Wakayama prefecture in Japan, and according to Masako Fukawa in her book *Spirit of the Nikkei Fleet*, two-thirds came from one village called Mio.

Prior to the residency requirement, the Madokoro family had already settled near Tofino. In 1922, nine-year-old Johnny Madokoro travelled from Steveston up to Tofino aboard his father's 9.75-metre boat *KM*, a gillnetter powered by a seven-horsepower Vulcan engine. They made the trip in tandem with Johnny's uncle Denjiro, in his boat the *DE*. When they rounded Grice Point, the tide was running, sweeping them rapidly toward Tofino. Johnny, who was used to the bigger town of Steveston, felt disappointed by the place: "'How rinky-dinky!' I was not impressed...'Yikes!'" Two years earlier, Dorothy Abraham's first impressions of Tofino when she arrived as a war bride from England were much the same: a "little village of a few straggling houses, a life-boat station and a road, if it could be called a road...[that] did not reach anywhere." The Madokoros chugged up Tofino Inlet to the property on the arm of South Bay known as Maltby Slough, where his uncle had already settled, along with some six other families, about eight kilometres from Tofino.

This earliest Japanese settlement at South Bay became established in an area near a number of older settler homesteads, some of them still occupied in the early 1920s. Most settlers who pre-empted land in the vicinity of South Bay, like the early settlers in Grice Bay, had either moved into Tofino or given up and gone elsewhere. When the Japanese arrived, Haray Quisenberry and his wife still maintained their homestead on Maltby Slough, where they had lived since before the turn of the century in their little home with its wide verandahs, described by Dorothy Abraham as "scrupulously clean and a haven of happiness." Their garden boasted a small orchard, and they became famed locally for their strawberry wine. In the late 1920s, forced by ill health to leave their beloved home, the couple sold what they could and rowed for one last time down the inlet, both wearing their best clothes in which they had been married some forty years earlier. "They were a picture..." wrote Dorothy Abraham. "She in her voluminous garments, the long skirt and the hat with plumes looking so out of place in a row-boat, rowing for all she was worth." The Quisenberrys' orchard provided fruit to chance visitors for years to come; even in the late 1960s, young hippies exploring the area found apple trees still bearing fruit.

George Maltby also lived nearby, sturdily maintaining his large vegetable garden at the head of the tidal slough that bears his name in local parlance, known on the maps as English Cove. Maltby rowed regularly down the inlet on the ebb tide to visit Tofino on Boat Days, and to sell his vegetables. Arline Craig recalled Maltby stopping by her family's home on Bond Island; her mother relied on his produce and would save all her cotton bags for him, every sugar sack and flour sack she could spare.

John Grice had taken up two large tracts of land on South Bay, and according to Walter Guppy in *Clayoquot Soundings*, the first Japanese who came to the area rented their land from Grice. Johnny Madokoro believed that his uncle Denjiro had purchased the land he occupied in South Bay, but he likely rented the land from Grice, for legal documents show it to be in Grice's name at the time of his death in 1934. Only sketchy accounts survive of this Japanese settlement in South

Bay, but evidently the place proved unsuitable for the newcomers. The fishing grounds were far away, the anchorage difficult, and navigating the channel through the mud flats presented too many risks. The little settlement, with its cluster of houses and makeshift wharf, did not last long, and the Japanese there moved nearer to Tofino. Traces of their first settlement lingered well into the 1930s, recalled by Anthony Guppy in his book *Tofino Kid.* "I can remember when I was still quite a small boy going up the inlet...and seeing the old village where the Japanese community had once lived...The Japanese houses, precariously built on slender tree trunks driven into the muddy bottom of the slough, had mostly all tumbled down by then, but I was greatly intrigued by the sight of an entire village devoid of its inhabitants."

Kamejiro and Tama Kimoto, with their seven children, and two other families chose a different location to settle when they first arrived in 1922. They moved into the old abandoned hotel on Stockham Island. The Kimotos travelled from Steveston in the family's gillnetter, the 9.75-metre *KK*, and tried to make the most of their uncomfortable new home. "The hotel used to leak. We'd put pots and pans all over the place," Tommy Kimoto recalled. "It was pretty wrecked and it was haunted." Fearing the spirit of an aboriginal woman said to haunt the hotel, Kamejiro Kimoto reportedly refused to sleep there, preferring his boat. At Christmas the children decorated a tree to cheer the place up: "We had no money for fancy store-bought decorations, so we used the most colourful things that we had," Mary Kimoto recounted, "bright orange, shiny red and light yellow fishing plugs and flashers. We also stuck some oranges in the branches, but they were special and expensive."

Within eighteen months, the Kimotos moved over to Stubbs Island, which the Japanese called *Nakanoshima.* Along with half a dozen other Japanese families, they leased land from Walter Dawley and built their houses toward the southeastern end of the island, above a small rocky beach. The Kimotos eventually had a home with four bedrooms, an attic, and a porch with the *ofuru*, the heated Japanese bath. Everything was carefully crafted by hand; even the sink was made from local wood. "I guess you could say the place on Clayoquot was more or less a shack," recalled Tommy Kimoto, "but it was nice there." Like the other families, the Kimotos grew vegetables, and they shared a well with the Seguro family next door, the water "so clear and sweet that the hotel folks [from Clayoquot Hotel] would come to draw water for their guests." Other families on Stubbs Island included the Igarachis, Seguros, Karatsus, Katsuros, Yoshiharas and Okadas. The children all enjoyed exploring the island, some of the boys particularly intrigued by the old disused jail. Tommy Kimoto's mother would try to scare them with mock threats, saying badly behaved children would be locked away there.

In 1923, Umetaro Morishita went to live in Storm Bay on Tofino Inlet, just past Grant's Point, becoming the first Japanese resident to build a house in the area the Japanese called *Nishikage*. Others followed suit, including the Madokoros, who built their home in Storm Bay with lumber from the Darville sawmill, rafted down from Calm Creek. In the end, some six adjoining tracts of land in Storm Bay, about half a hectare apiece, became home to Japanese families. This land had been part of John Eik's original Crown-granted pre-emption, Lot 115; due to various land deals among the early pioneers, it had been subdivided in 1928. The subdivision, containing the sections where the Japanese lived, belonged jointly to Eik, Jacob Arnet, and John Grice.

Several clusters of Japanese settlement, locally called "Jap Towns," emerged in and around Tofino. The one at Clayoquot, home to at least six families, stood on land rented from Walter Dawley. The one at Storm Bay comprised six narrow strips of land stretching from the water, crossing the main road leading into town, and extending up the opposite bank. Near the Storm Bay properties at least one other Japanese family, the Kondos, built a house. Another Japanese settlement, the one nearest town, stood on land leased from John Eik, at the site of his former chicken ranch, on the waterfront below the now famous Eik Tree. Five families initially built their houses and lived here, each household paying Eik two dollars rent per month. Later, a few more families also settled there. Other Japanese lived near the current location of the Marina West Resort, and in various houses they rented around the town. In the 1930s, the Mori family rented a house belonging to the much-loved local character "Cap" Thompson, regularly providing him with meals.

A sketch by the late Edward Arnet, detailing the layout of the Japanese community on John Eik's property in Tofino. Note the now famous Eik Tree in the left background. *Courtesy of Dorothy Arnet*

Of the Japanese families living at Clayoquot on Stubbs Island, Naoichi and Sen Karatsu had the largest family, raising nine children there. One of the six Karatsu children born at Clayoquot, Ruby (Karatsu) Middeldorp came into the world with the assistance of their neighbour, Mrs. Okada. "My dad gave us all Japanese as well as English names," Ruby explained. "I don't know how he dreamed up our names, but my brother Rennie was named after the name on the packages of Rennie Seeds, and my sister Norah after the *Princess Norah*." Their father had served as a medical orderly in the Russo-Japanese war, and his skills came in handy locally. He provided medical aid to the Tla-o-qui-ahts when requested and became a regular visitor to Opitsat. He helped to vaccinate children in that village against smallpox, as well as inoculating the children on Stubbs Island. In *Spirit of the Nikkei Fleet*, Masako Fukawa described how, "on one occasion a local tribe repaid [Karatsu] with a canoe full of *kazunoko* (herring roe)." Another Japanese resident of Clayoquot also provided medical care for the surrounding community. From her years growing up on Bond Island in Tofino Harbour, Arline Craig vividly recalled Mrs. Igarachi, a trained Japanese nurse: "She was really nice. We saw her whenever we needed help." According to Mickey Nicholson, who lived at Clayoquot, where his father George managed the hotel and beer parlour from 1925 onward, "[Mrs. Igarachi] was almost the same as a doctor. Everybody depended on her."

In Tofino, the Japanese children attended public school, followed by three hours of Japanese school. The public school in Tofino expanded in 1927 to accommodate them, becoming a two-room structure with two teachers, one for the "Little School" and one for the "Big School." From only sixteen children in 1923, enrolment grew to forty-three in 1926, and by 1935, fifty-eight students attended school in Tofino. For the children over at Clayoquot, a government-funded school operated from 1924 onward, initially with an enrolment of eighteen children, though it generally stood at fourteen or fifteen. In July 1927, the Clayoquot teacher, Stanley Flitcroft, "gave all his senior pupils a very enjoyable outing with a launch ride to Lennard Island," according to an article in the *Colonist*. "Flitcroft states that some of his pupils are of far above normal intelligence, the names on his honor roll are: Tommy, Bobbie, Jackie & Mary Kimoto, Yoshize Yoshihara and William Okada." An earlier teacher at the Clayoquot school, Miss M.E. Thompson, taught the children a rousing school song that Mary Kimoto never forgot. Every day, to the tune of "O Christmas Tree," the children belted out "Our school is by the seashore, O Clayoquot, O Clayoquot."

Ruby Karatsu attended this "little red schoolhouse" at Clayoquot for her first years of school in the late 1930s, with Mrs. M.G. Barr as her teacher. The Barr family, with their six children, lived on Stubbs Island in a house next door to the school during the 1930s, providing a needed boost to the enrolment. But by 1938, with only half a dozen or so children attending, the school no longer met the provincial quota and had to close. The closure may have been hastened by the school's location; erosion of the sandy beach on Stubbs Island caused more than one building to collapse onto the beach over time, and the school stood near the edge. Children from Clayoquot then went to Tofino to school, rowing two kilometres back and forth every day. Along with the other Japanese children in town, Ruby Karatsu attended Japanese school after her regular classes, and rather than row back and forth every day to the island, she often stayed in town with her older sister Alice, who had married and was living there. After one year, the Clayoquot School reopened, again with Mrs. Barr as the teacher. It closed permanently halfway through 1942, following the expulsion

Clayoquot School on Stubbs Island, around 1930. Built in 1924 for the Japanese community there, the school closed in 1942, when all Japanese were evacuated from the West Coast. The younger children in this picture were likely born on Stubbs Island, where some eight to ten families lived, including the Igarachis. Mrs. Igarachi acted as nurse, doctor, and midwife for many people in the Tofino area. *Image 2001.5.76 courtesy of the Japanese Canadian Cultural Centre, Toronto*

of the Japanese from the coast.

In his book *Tofino Kid*, Anthony Guppy recalled the rough little Tofino school building he attended in the late 1920s and early 1930s, "surrounded by a jumble of logs, stumps and salal thickets in the cedar and hemlock rainforest," with a plank walkway leading over swampy ground to the front steps. He never forgot how various teachers enforced discipline. "Peter Grant employed a long, polished wood pointer; Miss Apts used a highly flexible fly-swatter. Miss Coaton [Coton] acquired a piece of belting from the machine shop, while Bob Gale used a regulation school board supplied leather strap, and not always fairly. I remember Murdo MacLeod spending hours beating the palms of his hands on a rock to toughen them up." With no lighting other than an oil lamp, the classroom often became too dark to read or see the blackboard, and in heavy storms the teacher's voice would be drowned out by the hammering rain on the roof. Parents and other volunteers cleared a patch of land for a playground, and the boys could play soccer, although "since the field was dirt, not grass, we played a local version of the game called mud sharks."

During the 1920s and 1930s, strong childhood connections developed between the Tofino and Japanese schoolchildren. Ronald MacLeod vividly recalled his best friend, Ikua Nakai, and another boy, "a truly spoiled child," whom some Japanese thought to be a reincarnation of the Buddha. Over at Clayoquot, Joan (Malon) Nicholson, granddaughter of Walter Dawley, became inseparable best friends with Gloria Karatsu. The two little girls happily played together on the beach and in the sand dunes, scampering back and forth along the boardwalk linking

the Clayoquot Hotel to the Japanese section of the island. Ruby, Gloria's older sister, walked the same boardwalk every day several times: back and forth to the school, and also every afternoon at the behest of her mother, when she went to stand on the hotel porch, looking to see if her father's boat had yet come into sight, returning from his day's fishing. Sometimes the children would play at the old fish saltery on the island, running noisily up and down the outside wooden stairs.

Gloria Karatsu and Joan Malon (Nicholson) at Clayoquot, late 1930s. These two best friends were inseparable as little girls growing up on Stubbs Island. Joan's grandfather, Walter Dawley, ran the store and hotel. The Karatsu family had nine children, and like other families on the island, rented their land from Dawley, at the Japanese settlement on the southeastern section of the island.
Courtesy of Joan Nicholson

At the Clayoquot Hotel, managed by George Nicholson, his son Mickey recalled, "We saw a lot of the Japanese. They were good customers. The Japanese liked beer. They made a point of trying to get along with the white people and they did." Ruth White, who lived on Stubbs Island from 1941 onward with her husband Bill, remembered two Japanese girls named Celia and Ivy who would ride a horse bareback up the beach. "They were both

March 3, 1928, Japanese girls at Clayoquot celebrating the annual *Hina Matsuru*, or Doll Festival, also called Girls' Day. All are in traditional kimonos, holding their valued dolls, with Lone Cone in the background. *Image 1994.84.4 courtesy of the Nikkei National Museum and Cultural Centre, Dr. David Gray Collection*

very Canadian," she said. Father Charles Moser approvingly noted in his diary the numerous occasions when Japanese fishermen offered him free boat rides to Kakawis: "Charges nil. White man would not do that." Once Father Charles travelled down from Kyuquot on a Japanese fish packer, the owner insisting that he take the only berth aboard. Like other boat owners, Japanese fishermen could also be drawn into the unhappy business of helping police take runaway children back to the residential school at Ahousat or to Christie School at Kakawis on Meares Island. On one occasion in 1926, Father Charles noted that Constable Bradner arrived at Kakawis on board a "Jap boat" with "two truant girls from the cannery."

The Japanese of the Tofino area became actively involved in community events, often organizing large, inclusive gatherings. Mike Hamilton, who worked with Hilmar Wingen in the Tofino Machine Shop in the

1920s, recalled: "It was customary for the Japanese community after the fishing season to put on a sort of party and banquet to which all the village was invited...No expense was spared in providing a feast to gladden the heart of any gourmet." Japanese-hosted picnics in the summertime also became regular events. On Dominion Day in 1927, they hosted a community picnic on Echachis Island, making a special trip over to Kakawis to invite the entire school. Father Charles wrote: "A spokesman of the Japanese colony here spoke to me inviting the Christie school to their picknick tomorrow at Echachislet, they would furnish the boats." The *Colonist* covered this same "picknick" in detail: "Field sports were staged under Tyomi Onami, secretary of the Japanese Fishermen's Assn. Foot race: Rev Mr Walter, Mr Morishita, Mrs Hamanaka, Mrs Jennie McLeod, Mrs Kami, Mrs V Evans. In the evening a grand entertainment and ball was staged at the Clayoquot Hotel, at which Harry Hay and Jimmy Williams, assisted by Mrs Grant, amused the audience with skits and monologues, and humorous recitations by Sgt Major Bailey, of Little Qualicum. Music by the dungaree band, Andrew Emerson and Japanese songs were sung and interpreted by Tyomi Onami, followed by Mrs Jim Anderson on piano."

More such events followed. "A children's party was given by the resident Japanese at the Clayoquot Hotel," reported the *Daily Colonist* on March 10, 1929, "in celebration of the opening of the fishing season, to which all white residents and their children were invited. The Japanese were splendid hosts, and spared neither pains or expense. There was music, dancing, games and supper." A few months later, another special event for Dominion Day: "The Japanese residents gave a grand picnic at Kelsomat Beach, to which all residents were invited, and entertained royally, being conveyed there by a small fleet of launches...Mr Morishita and Mr Onami spoke on behalf of the Japanese colony." Later that year, just before Christmas, the *Daily Colonist* noted a "pre-Xmas entertainment given by the Japanese residents at the Tofino Community Hall, at which over 100 local residents partook."

The Japanese in Tofino always took pains to participate in significant community events. In late August 1927, scandal rocked Tofino when well-known resident Edward Leach was murdered. Dorothy Abraham discovered his body in his boat on Clayoquot Spit, together with the body of his beloved dog. A war veteran and fisheries patrol officer, Leach had lived for a time in Fred Tibbs's castle on Dream Island, and later on Strawberry Island. His murder sent shock waves throughout the area. Father Charles Moser recorded in his diary: "Sept 1 Arrived at Clayoquot wharf by outside passage 5:30 AM. Got a Japanese fisherman to bring me to Kakawis for $1.00. He told me that 3 Indians from Opitsat are suspected of having murdered Mr. Leech." The whole of Tofino turned out for Leach's funeral in a long cortege, including all the local Japanese. Leach's coffin was placed in the lifeboat and escorted to the town cemetery on Morpheus Island by a mass of boats: seiners, Japanese trollers, launches, rowboats, and canoes. Three men from Opitsat were arrested and charged with Leach's murder. The trial took place in Nanaimo, with many witnesses from Tofino called to give evidence. "When the time came, twenty-four witnesses left Tofino on the *Princess Maquinna* for the trial," Dorothy Abraham wrote. "It was quite a holiday for everyone, at the Government's expense...The morning we left Tofino, one of the witnesses committed suicide, which rather complicated matters." The witness in question, Henry Hansen, may have visited Leach on his boat the evening he died. Speculation and rumour abounded in the town, and Hansen's death only deepened the mystery. The jury acquitted the three accused men, and Leach's murder has never been solved.

As a child growing up at Clayoquot, Mary Kimoto met "a tall English minister...[who] came calling on Clayoquot Island. He wanted all the Japanese kids to come to his church...We were all baptized...If you were wondering how my [Buddhist] parents felt about this Anglican Church thing, I think they wanted us to become part of the larger Tofino community." The minister, Rev. Philip Frank Ardagh-Walter, welcomed all Japanese families in Tofino to St. Columba Church. During his tenure in the parish from 1927 to 1930, he performed fifty-two baptisms, including thirty-five Japanese children. Many of them attended Sunday School regularly, bearing their weekly offering of one penny for the collection plate. "Being baptized and going to church meant they were becoming Canadian," according to historian

Masako Fukawa. By contrast, the MacLeod children did not attend the Anglican church. Determined to maintain the traditions of the Free Presbyterian church, Alex MacLeod conducted a strict Gaelic Sunday School for his children and their cousins. "We couldn't play on the Sabbath," Ronald MacLeod wrote. "Couldn't go outside our yard except to go to Sunday school; no music except...singing the Psalms of David. No work except for works of mercy."

The Japanese boys had a lot more fun on Sundays. "We would meet the boys from Storm Bay at church and each of us had a can of worms and a fishing line," Tatsuo Sakauye reminisced in a letter to Dorothy Arnet. The boys hid the worms and line underneath the wharf at Wingen's machine shop, and then ran back after church to go fishing for perch off the wharf. Unlike the Anglican minister, the Roman Catholic priests in the area made no attempt to attract Japanese converts, focused as they were on the First Nations, although Father Charles did note on one occasion in 1923 that "a Jap boy" showed up at Mass at Opitsat.

For Tatsuo Sakauye, born in Tofino, his most vivid memories of growing up involved fishing and gathering seafood: "fishing for coho in the inlets, crabs, four kinds of clams, abalone, shrimps, snappers, perch and all that fresh *nori* [an edible seaweed]." The Sakauye brothers—six in all—would go every February to Chesterman Beach to gather *nori*. "We would come home with 20 100 lb [45 kilogram] bags of *nori*. After washing and rinsing the nori it would be spread to dry all over the neighbourhood."

Along with most other children in Tofino in the 1930s, Tatsuo loved seeing seaplanes land in the harbour. Although planes had been appearing sporadically along the coast since the early 1920s—first noted by Father Charles Moser in his diary in September 1921, when "a large flying machine passed over our school"—seeing them right in Tofino Harbour gave a special thrill. "We would drop everything we were doing and run along the beach to watch the plane land on the sea," Tatsuo recalled. Lorraine (Arnet) Murdoch did not share this delight. She recalled seeing a plane land in Tofino Harbour, a "wooden flying boat," when she was four or five years old in the early 1930s. It arrived to pick up her grandfather, George Nicholson, and a passenger on board asked Lorraine if she wanted to go for a ride. She refused, terrified by this unusual offer. In quiet Tofino, such excitements came around rarely; even a car ride provided significant bragging rights for the little boys. Tatsuo remembered only one car when he was growing up. The Wingens owned it, and one memorable day Harvey Wingen offered the Sakauye boys a ride through town to the government wharf. "It was a Model T Ford and had to be cranked at the front to start the engine... on the way back we had to jump out of the car and push the car up the [government wharf] hill...That was our first car ride."

Wanting the sons of the family to have a better Japanese education, the Kimoto family of Clayoquot sent their eldest son, Harold, to Cumberland, where a sizeable Japanese community had grown up around the coal mine. Johnny Madokoro also attended school in Cumberland. Other Japanese families sent their older children off to Victoria or to Vancouver for school if they could do without their help on the fish boats or around the house. For a year, Mary Kimoto attended high school in Victoria, boarding with Walter Dawley's family and helping with housework. Walter's wife, Rose, and their children had lived in Victoria for many years by this time, with Walter coming and going from Clayoquot. Mary, who had attended dances at the Tofino Community Hall, found herself teaching fourteen-year-old Clarence Dawley to dance "so that he could be ready for the Victoria socials...Clarence had to be 'proper' in his entrance into the local high society."

The dances in the Tofino Community Hall in the 1920s and 1930s saw many Japanese of all ages joining in. "The dance music was from a piano and I think Mrs. Nicholson played the cello," Mary Kimoto recalled. "That was our big night out. The *hakujin* [Caucasian] ladies made sandwiches and cakes, which were a treat for us." Johnny Madokoro, quoted in *Settling Clayoquot*, remembered, "We would go to all the dances. Even the first generation used to dance. I remember... one particular small man, he just learned to dance a little bit...and here was a tall, tall, white woman and they were dancing together. That was Mr. Nakagawa and Mrs. Abraham. We laughed our heads off."

Johnny Madokoro returned abruptly to Tofino from school in

Cumberland when his father died in 1928. Overnight, he became head of the family, and his uncle Rinshiro helped him to take charge of his father's fish boat, the *KM*. "Man, I was one worried fourteen-year-old," he recalled. "I would follow [Uncle] out each morning...and he would guide me around the fishing grounds." Within a short time, Johnny single-handedly took charge, managing his boat and his catch of salmon just like the other men. With the other Japanese fishermen, he would be out on the trolling grounds by 4:30 a.m., often fishing off Round Island, which the Japanese called *Maruyama*. The Japanese trollers, by now mostly using two-cylinder, twenty-horsepower Palmer engines, took an hour or more to get out to the trolling grounds. Once there they generally set out eight lines with separate leads at four-fathom intervals. According to Johnny Madokoro, in their early years the Japanese set lines with four or five "Japanese-style lures," until Umetaro Morishita developed the lure he called the "shiny wobbler." "He saw a native Indian throwing something shiny from the shore one day. This fellow was catching salmon right from the shore...he saw it was a shiny piece of tin with a hook attached. That day he went home and made his own version of a 'wobbler.'" After many attempts, Umetaro came up with one that moved like a fish. His catch improved dramatically, and he shared the "shiny wobbler" with Johnny Madokoro's father and a few others. "The rest is fishing history," Johnny commented.

Settled into his routine as a fisherman, some days the teenaged Johnny Madokoro would haul in 226 kilograms of salmon by hand: "The best was the spring salmon, they could go to forty or fifty pounds [18 or 22 kilograms]. Usually they were smaller, perhaps twenty-five or thirty pounds [11 to 13.5 kilograms]. Coho were our bread and butter fish, they ran about six to ten pounds [2.75 to 4.5 kilograms]." Johnny's sisters and brothers now deferred to him as the head of the household: he had the first servings of food, and he could no longer roughhouse with his brothers. Nonetheless, he had to wait until he turned eighteen before he could join the men drinking *sake* and eating *gochiso* (special treats) during the New Year's Day celebrations. At New Year's the Japanese often put on a children's concert, with an open invitation for everyone in town to attend. A dinner afterward provided copious amounts of *sake*. According to Ronald MacLeod, "Only the ultra-strong made it home without some help."

When Kamejiro Kimoto drowned in a fishing accident off Wicka-ninnish Island in 1933, his children Mary and Tommy, both at school in Victoria, returned to Clayoquot. His eldest son, Harold, took charge of their father's fish boat, the *KK*, and the family all pulled together to help. Mary found work in Tofino helping the doctor's wife, Marguerite Robertson, around the house. Mary recalled Marguerite's concern that she might overhear improper songs when "Doc" and his friends were drinking, but Mary politely reassured her she heard nothing. "Later," she admitted, "when I was hanging out the wash, I absentmindedly started singing 'The bells of hell go ting-a-ling.' I looked up to see Mrs. Robertson shaking her head as she walked away."

Over on Stubbs Island, Mrs. Okada established a *kamaboko* (cod fish-cake) factory in 1935. Her husband constructed the factory in a shed near their house on the island, and devised machinery to assist the production. In an article about Mrs. Okada's enterprise, Larry Maekawa described the ingeniously fitted-out shed where she processed ling cod into *surumi*, or fish paste, by means of a small engine that powered a series of belts and crankshafts wielding a large wooden mallet. This pounded cod fillets to the right consistency in the large concrete *usu*, or bowl, standing ready under the mallet. The *surumi*, once seasoned and cut into pieces, was deep-fried in a large vat. Cooked to a golden brown, the patties of *kamaboko* went into one-pound cans, vacuum-sealed by Mrs. Okada in a complex two-step process. She lined up the cans on her small conveyor belt, tightly hand-crimped each top, and pasted labels on the cans before packing them in wooden crates, forty-eight to a box. This *kamaboko* travelled on the *Princess Maquinna* to Victoria, and on to markets in Vancouver and also Kelowna, to satisfy the enthusiastic demand of the Japanese communities there. Mrs. Okada could barely keep up with their orders; her business generated as much income as her husband made fishing.

In Tofino, at her home on the Eik property, Mrs. Nishimura also made *kamaboko* in a small shed. In the summer of 1940, a local mechanic, Ralph Telvik, helped her rig up the machinery, using a car engine to turn a belt that drove the wooden hammer, pounding the fish into paste in the concrete *usu*. Decades later, Edward Arnet told historian Midge Akukawa, that the Nishimuras hoped to export their *kamaboko*, but war intervened. When they were evacuated from the coast in 1942, the family left behind some twenty cases of *kamaboko*, each containing forty-eight cans. "In 1946 when [Ed] and his father checked the cans," wrote Midge Akukawa, "the ends were bulging, and the contents were a pale yellow. They opened the cans, poked holes, and dumped them off-shore."

At the age of eighteen, in September 1938, Mary Kimoto married Johnny Madokoro in Tofino at St. Columba's Church, a big event for the whole community. One of the little Arnet boys enlivened the proceedings by "dancing around trailing toilet paper from his head saying, 'I'm Mary Kimoto, I'm Mary Kimoto.'" "Mary looked so beautiful, but she did not look up, she did not want to appear bold," recalled Marguerite Robertson. Everyone attended a reception afterward in the community hall, vividly remembered by Sid Elkington because he had to leave abruptly, in high spirits thanks to the *sake*. As one of the local storekeepers, he had to respond when salesmen came knocking, which they did at any hour, depending when their boats arrived. The Mackay, Smith and Blair Drygoods man came to find Elkington at the wedding reception, taking him away to the company's boat to view samples and place an order. Elkington's festive eye lit upon some "rather striking ladies' panties and bras with bright coloured flower patterns," which he decided would be just the thing for Tofino. "When the order arrived, in the cold sober light of a working day, they did look rather bright." His wife, unamused, told him they would never sell, but "to my great relief, they went like wildfire, catching Mrs. and Miss Indian's eyes—the order was too small."

Johnny Madokoro became actively involved in the Tofino Trollers' Co-operative Association. Formed in 1924 and continuing until 1941, the Trollers' Co-op became a central feature on the Tofino waterfront. The fish-buying vessel *Rose N* often appeared there, along with the co-op-owned *Western Chief*, both packing salmon to the Seattle market. According to Ronald MacLeod: "The Japanese were much more accommodating than the non-Japanese. They bought fish from whites and Indians and took non-Japanese in as members...It cost a dollar a year to be a member, at least in the early 1930s." As president of the Trollers' Co-op for many years, Mitsuzo Nakagawa developed good working relations with the Tla-o-qui-aht fishermen. According to Masako Fukawa, he was the "only non-Indian to be permitted on the Indian Reserve in Tofino [Opitsat] at that time."

During the years the Japanese lived in and near Tofino, they became an integral part of the community, garnering respect from all quarters as fishermen, as residents, as generous hosts. Describing his business at the Tofino Machine Shop in the 1920s, Mike Hamilton wrote to his fiancée, Mabel, that he had scant use for some of his customers. He dismissed First Nations clients because "they have inferior boats and engines and anyhow they don't look after them," and he had equal disdain for "the white people with boats [who] are few and are also poor customers, what few there are usually broke." Then he described his Japanese customers: "Our best customer in every way...They usually have splendid boats & engines they keep them in good condition...They are good payers, always cheerful and ready to lend a hand let it be financial or otherwise. They will subscribe to any good cause to their last cent. In short they are ideal citizens notwithstanding all that has been said against them."

"Ideal citizens" or not, the period of Japanese Canadians living in Tofino as productive members of the community would soon come to an abrupt end. When World War II began in 1939, their days on the coast were numbered. Drastic change lay ahead.

Chapter 16:

BOAT DAYS

Princess Maquinna in Tofino Harbour, mid-1920s, taken from Grice Point.
Mike Hamilton photo

NO SUCH VESSEL HAD EVER BEEN BUILT in British Columbia. Anticipation of her imminent arrival on the west coast route gripped everyone's imagination. The largest ship ever built in the province, launched on Christmas Eve 1912 at Yarrow's Shipyard in Esquimalt, the SS *Princess Maquinna* would surely transform travel along the coast. Proud descriptions fill the annals of the CPR, with detailed litanies of her technical merits: "3 cylinder Triple Expansion. Single Screw. 1500 Horse Power, 2 Scotch Marine Single Ended boilers. Speed in knots 12.5. Working pressure 180 lbs. [81.5 kilograms] 6 Furnaces, Fuel Capacity 1,705 barrels...Overall length 244' [74.3 metres] Length between perpendiculars 232' [70.7 metres] Breadth 38' [11.5 metres] Gross tonnage 1,777, 50 rooms, 100 beds or berths, 70 crew members." Translated, this meant a ship bigger, better, stronger, faster, and far more reliable than any the coast had seen before.

The *Daily Colonist* revelled in describing the interior, "all panelled in mahogany, with cornices and pilaster finishing," and the bevy of "furnishers, decorators and others" feverishly preparing the ship for her maiden voyage up the west coast of Vancouver Island in July 1913. "A fine boat," concluded the laconic Father Charles Moser, who travelled on this first voyage. His confrere, Father Joseph Schindler, commented a few months later: "The *Tees* looks like a wash tub along side of [*Maquinna*] and small." Everyone compared the splendid new ship to her unfortunate predecessor, SS *Tees*.

Even though she had been built specifically for the west coast route, with her double hull and ease of manoeuvring in narrow inlets, the *Maquinna* did not serve full time on the route until 1917. Initially, the wharves along the coast, many of them flimsy, worm-eaten structures, could not cope with her size; some needed to be doubled in length to allow her to dock, and much rebuilding had to take place to accommodate her. So during her earliest years, other routes often claimed the *Maquinna*, and west coasters felt cheated; they had been promised this gem of a vessel, yet most of the time they still had to make do with the much-derided old-timer *Tees*.

The *Tees* had served the west coast on and off since her inaugural trip from Victoria to Alberni in 1896. Initially praised for her elegant finish, "all done in birds' eye maple" with the ladies' cabin "a wonderful dark red plush," she even garnered approval from the captain who piloted her to Victoria from her home port of Stockton-on-Tees in England. "She rides the water like a duck," he declared fondly. No one concurred when *Tees* embarked on the coastal route. "That blinking old tub could roll and take a nose dive at the same time so that hardened sailors got seasick on her," Mike Hamilton declared bitterly. She became known as the "Holy Roller" as she pitched and rolled her way through rough seas, year after year. Slow, with her best speed nine knots, and known as a "wet ship"—mostly underwater in bad weather—she measured 50.2 metres in length. During her years of service on the coast she carried untold thousands of passengers—her record load being 147—and countless cargos of whale and dogfish oil, fish meal, cans of salmon, building supplies. Still, no one grieved when this "blunt-nosed ugly duckling" finally left the west coast, giving way finally and permanently to the *Princess Maquinna* in 1917. Yet the *Tees*, along with earlier steamers serving the west coast, particularly *Queen City*, *Willapa*, and *Maude*, truly set the stage for the *Princess Maquinna*. These ships established the pattern of regular steamer traffic: for many years their arrivals were awaited with almost painful anticipation, and they served the coast long and honourably. In subsequent years, though, *Princess Maquinna* took all the laurels; she set a new gold standard and became perhaps more beloved than any vessel in the CPR's *Princess* fleet. "If ever a ship took on body and soul and personality...loved by all who sailed in her, it was the *Princess Maquinna*," wrote Dorothy Abraham. No one ever disagreed.

From 1913 to 1929, Captain Edward Gillam had charge of the *Princess Maquinna*. Universally liked and respected, Gillam seemed as much part of the boat as the green leather seats in the saloon or the ungainly funnel with its cracked-tone whistle. He knew the coast from Victoria up to Port Alice as well as any man alive, and he also knew most of the people who lived along it. At one time or another most people on the west coast became his passengers: their stories and dramas were paced out on the deck, recounted in the saloon, discussed in the dining room, witnessed at close quarters. Captain Gillam knew that he provided not just *a* link between people and places on the west coast; he provided *the* link, the only consistent, regular, long-standing means of travel and communication on the coast. A large, companionable man, kindly and firm, Gillam became renowned on the coast for his outstanding seamanship, his ability to navigate in thick fog through the trickiest of channels. He knew every rock and reef, every echo when he sounded the ship's whistle, and how the echoes varied from location to location. He knew the very dogs barking in the dark nights as

Captain Edward Gillam, long-time officer on several coastal steamers. Renowned for his exceptional skills as a navigator and for his friendliness to all passengers, Gillam was captain of *Princess Maquinna* from 1913 until 1929, the year of his death.
Image PN04450 courtesy of Alberni Valley Museum

he approached different settlements, he knew how to manoeuvre his large ship into position on any given dock by calculating the tricks of wind, tide, and current. Originally from Newfoundland, Gillam came to Victoria in the latter days of the sealing industry, eventually joining the Canadian Pacific Navigation Company as a deckhand. Later, with the company renamed the British Columbia Coast Steamship Service, he served as an officer aboard *Willapa* and *Queen City*, and became captain on both *Queen City* and *Tees* before taking command of *Princess Maquinna*.

Early in his years aboard *Princess Maquinna*, Captain Gillam gained widespread renown for his valiant attempt to save the foundering Chilean barque *Carelmapu*. In November 1915, this three-masted ship came to grief off Gowlland Rocks, just up the coast from Schooner Cove at the north end of Long Beach. Driven off-course by extremely high seas and winds, with her sails shredded, the ship had been drifting helplessly for two days, ever closer to the rocky shore of Vancouver Island. Travelling southbound on the *Maquinna*, Captain Gillam tried his utmost to come to the rescue of the vessel, approaching as close as he dared in the towering breakers, close enough to make himself heard through a megaphone. Positioning *Maquinna*'s stern toward land, he dropped both anchors and ordered half-speed from the engines to maintain position. Two attempts to shoot a line to the doomed ship failed. The captain of the *Carelmapu*, Fernando Desolmes, lashed himself to the ship's railings and ordered the two lifeboats to be lowered, hoping they could reach the *Maquinna*, knowing the chances to be slim. The first boat did not even hit the water before spilling all passengers into the heaving sea. Gillam ordered fuel to be spilled over the water to break the crests of the waves, but when the second lifeboat tried to steer toward *Maquinna*, a huge wave flipped it over. No one in the lifeboats survived. Meanwhile, the danger for *Princess Maquinna* became too extreme; her straining cable winch seemed about to heave the deck apart. "The terrific strain injured the winch," according to Mike Hamilton's account, "to such an extent that the anchor could not be hauled in. The first mate, Captain Kinney, was obliged to crawl forward with a hack saw and saw through the link, letting chain and anchor go." Captain Gillam had to leave the *Carelmapu* to her fate. Desolmes waved a despairing farewell as *Princess*

Maquinna headed out to sea, her fifty passengers looking back in horror as the mizzen mast of the shipwrecked vessel ripped off, tossing two of the remaining men on board into the sea. Desolmes released himself from the railing, genuflected, and dropped into the ocean. Against all odds, he made it to shore. Four others also survived. Nineteen perished.

At Long Beach, settler John Cooper buried eleven of the bodies that eventually washed up on the shore; he later wrote "nobody knows where they are but myself." Captain Desolmes and one of the survivors, Rodrigo Dias, stayed at Long Beach with Cooper; the other three went to the hotel at Clayoquot, in care of the Tofino lifeboat crew. "All were in very bad shape," according to Cooper. The captain's Great Dane dog, named Nogi, somehow made it to shore, and Cooper kept him—he wore a brass collar with the name of the ship on it. Two years later someone shot Nogi and stole his collar. Cooper, who lived at Long Beach for eleven years before moving into Tofino, had bad luck with his pets. He had "quite a herd of cattle, a team of Arabian horses, pigs, chickens, ducks and a tame deer known as 'Jackie of Long Beach.'" Jackie also was shot by a hunter, and the sea lion Cooper befriended, "a tame one, quite a pet, that used to come up to the house," was happily snoozing on the sand near Cooper's home when a hostile logger attacked and killed it.

The *Maquinna* era on Vancouver Island's west coast has acquired the glow of legend over the years. From the heroic attempt to rescue the *Carelmapu* to simple stories of gathering around the ship's warm funnel, nothing in the collective consciousness of west coast residents can match the shining memories of the *Maquinna*. Every ten days for nearly four decades this faithful ship ran up and down the coast of the Island, leaving Victoria at 11 p.m. on the 1st, 11th, and 21st of every month, arriving Tofino northbound on the 3rd, 13th, and 23rd. On those northbound trips, when *Princess Maquinna* steamed into sight in Tofino Harbour, the town and the whole harbour came alive. This was "Boat Day"; the very words evoked an inner tremor of anticipation. "People came from all the outlying parts," Dorothy Abraham wrote, "in launches and craft of all kinds: also the Indians, gay with colour, in their canoes." "It was during 'boat-day' that one could expect every one, queer, odd and otherwise to make their appearance," wrote Mike Hamilton, "to get their groceries, mail and...mysterious crates, jars and packages...They would converge upon [the wharf] in canoes, skiffs and rowboats, from all directions."

Maquinna's strangulated whistle sounded as she passed by Lennard Island and entered Tofino Harbour. Everyone in the village knew that sound, and hearing the whistle, children rushed down to the government wharf, along with anyone meeting the ship to collect goods or visitors or mail—and pretty much everyone else in town came too, just for the fun of it. "All of us kids wanted to catch the rat line," Ken Gibson recalled. "We'd hear that whistle out in the harbour and just run like heck down to the dock to be there when the *Maquinna* came in." Catching the monkey's paw, that heavy ball of spliced rope connected to the thin rat line, in turn connected to the heavier line, the hawser, "meant we were bringing the boat in!" Local children would stampede onto the ship and run straight for the commissary with their nickels and dimes to buy Cracker Jack popcorn, Superman and Flash Gordon comics, chocolate bars. Even during the days of World War II rationing, the *Maquinna* still sold chocolate and candy, adding to her aura of magic for local children.

On board, the "ear-splitting and nerve-shattering" noise of her steam whistle, heard up close, would send Mike Hamilton's young children screaming to their mother, hands clapped to their ears. "That whistle was History all in itself," Mike Hamilton wrote in his unpublished memoirs, describing how it "would begin with a sort of squeal of a one-or-two second duration before the shattering blast commenced which...gave you time to steel yourself against the shock." Joan (Malon) Nicholson has happier memories of that sound; to her great delight, as a young child coming home to Tofino, she had the privilege of going up onto the bridge and, on a signal from the captain, pulling the whistle cord. "I think I was the only kid in Tofino who did that."

"The sound of the *Princess Maquinna*'s steam whistle meant more... than Santa Claus himself," wrote Alder Bloom, and the bustle at the dock, as recalled by Ronald MacLeod, provided non-stop entertainment with "freight and mail unloading; salesmen coming off with their large sample cases and rushing to cover the two general stores in the limited time before the ship sailed on; a host of tourists in summer, travellers to upcoast communities enjoying a brief visit on the dock with friends... Up and down the wharf would trundle handcarts carrying newly arrived freight to the two stores. A hive of activity!" People waited anxiously, wondering if their mail orders had arrived or their liquor orders, mysteriously wrapped in brown paper, having been paid for and requested ten days earlier by filling out a special form.

As for the sheer fun of seeing strangers—nothing could match that. "What oddball tourists in their strange getups will we see today?" Ronald MacLeod always wondered. In the summertime, those tourists would stroll along the dock, where they met aboriginal people selling their crafts: baskets, mats, and covered bottles the most popular items. The visitors would roam around the village, pause for snapshots, and drift along Grice Road on the waterfront to see all the activity at Towler and Mitchell's store.

Lorraine (Arnet) Murdoch particularly liked Towler and Mitchell's store on Boat Day. Her parents did most of their trade here, running a tab, like everyone else, to be paid off after fishing season—she never saw them pay cash. She was fascinated by the carcasses and sides of meat being unloaded and carried along the dock. People would line up and wait for their fresh meat while Jack Mitchell did the cutting—preparing the roast or stewing beef or the special cuts he would put aside for special customers. Dr. Robertson and his wife, Marguerite, often found that Mitchell had put aside a choice cut for them, although the real highlight of Boat Day for Marguerite depended on the ship's stewards. Because Dr. Robertson had worked on the Alaska steamship run as a young man, he knew many of the crew, and they often presented Marguerite with a treat of fresh fruit from the ship's stores: oranges, grapes, or, even more wonderful, a banana.

In their local shopping, the doctor and his wife took care to trade at both stores, showing no favouritism. Sid Elkington's store, at the head of the government wharf, also buzzed with excitement on Boat Day. Aboriginal customers favoured this store, possibly because Sid had spent many years trading in northern British Columbia, he spoke the Chinook trading jargon, and he had worked with many Tla-o-qui-aht at the cannery. Operated by Elkington and his wife, Kit, from 1930 onward, Elkington's store, like Towler and Mitchell's, never really closed; the storekeepers could be called out of bed at any hour by demanding customers. In his memoirs, Sid Elkington even recalled a customer hammering on the store door on Christmas Day.

The length of time the *Princess Maquinna* spent at the dock on Boat Days varied. It could be less than twenty minutes on days with light freight; on August 18, 1918, the precise CPR inspector, Mr. H. Brodie, noted that the *Maquinna* arrived at Tofino 11:16 a.m. and left at 11:34. A record copied from the *Maquinna*'s logbook on May 26, 1925, indicates the ship arrived at 2:29 and departed at 2:55. On other occasions, when a lot of freight had to be unloaded, or if the ship had time to spare, she could spend several hours at the dock. Little boys would watch the unloading with spellbound fascination, especially if something heavy or unwieldy—a large engine, an unhappy cow, a load of furniture, a large order of hay—had to be winched up in a sling and swung onto the dock. Ronald MacLeod recalled the rare excitement of a day in April 1931 when a Ford Model A truck arrived for Borden Grant. According to the *Colonist*, on that day the *Princess Maquinna* outdid herself, for she offloaded not only the truck but also another vehicle "over her side with derrick and sling [depositing them] on the wharf as easily as a few cases of salmon. One was a passenger car and the other a two-ton truck." Local traffic was picking up; several cars now jolted their way through town from time to time. Mike Hamilton had brought the very first car, a 1916 Model T Ford, to Tofino several years earlier, thrilling the children, many of whom had never seen a car, by giving them rides. This car did not survive long on the so-called road in town. "In a very short time," wrote Dorothy Abraham, "it was lying on the side of the road a total wreck."

No one in Tofino ever received an unusual delivery off the boat without everyone knowing. In 1924 the newlywed Mabel Hamilton attracted more comment than she wished when her bedroom furniture arrived; the two single beds surprised everyone. Similarly, Winifred Guppy's shopping habits, according to her son Anthony, caused "some people to think we were better off than we actually were...and we were resented for our perceived affluence," in part because his mother bought in bulk, mail-ordering goods from Woodward's in Vancouver rather than shopping locally: "fifty-pound [22.6 kilogram] sacks of flour and sugar, fourteen-pound [6.3 kilogram] boxes of butter, five-pound [2.2 kilogram] pails of shortening, large tins of Rogers' Syrup, a case of two dozen cans of Pacific milk, and so on. It was much cheaper to buy our groceries in bulk." Clothing, too, arrived by mail order; sometimes mothers hastily bundled their children into new clothes right there at the dock, checking to see if they fit. If not, they could immediately be returned.

Dorothy Abraham and her husband lived about 1.5 kilometres from the dock, and they usually met the *Princess Maquinna* with their old wheelbarrow, which they bumped along the road, often in torrential rain, coming to and from the boat to fetch their supplies. "It was quite a chore, to wheel a barrow over such a road as we had. Not a road at all...stumps, holes, mud and rocks...we got to know every inch of it, and every hole and stump...we would have to wait for the mail to be sorted... and many a time we trudged home with the old barrow at midnight or in the early hours of the morning...My job was to hold the lantern and pick the way."

Waiting for the mail to be sorted and the parcels handed around meant many people crammed into the small post office attached to Towler and Mitchell's, especially around Christmastime. Francis Garrard retired as postmaster in 1924, followed for brief periods by Mabel Hamilton and two other short-term postmasters until 1928, when Fred Towler took on the job. He held the position for eighteen years, assisted by Wilfred Armitage, and the good-natured mayhem at Christmas always kept them both busy. "I occasionally added to the problem as a paid helper," Ronald MacLeod recalled, although his ten cents hardly seemed proper pay. "I emptied the mail sacks on the floor, stacked the empties in a corner and tried to keep the floor cleared of waste paper. Outside the Post Office there would be a long line of people, fretting and anxious to know whether their Christmas mail orders had arrived."

By the time the mail was sorted, the *Maquinna* had departed. Five minutes before leaving, the ship's whistle screeched, warning visitors on board to disembark. The steam winches clanged and clattered, seagulls took off in whirling cacophony from the dock and nearby boats, little children would cry at all the noise, and after a flurry of farewells the excitement faded. The boat pulled away. Silence resumed. "Skiffs, canoes and rowboats fanned out in their homeward direction," Mike Hamilton wrote. "A period of semi-desolation would descend upon the scene until the next steamer arrived, and so it went on year in and year out." The freight manifest of the ship, posted inside the large freight shed at the dock, revealed exactly what the ship had carried and enabled anyone who had not collected their freight to check if it had arrived. Anyone so inclined could also see who had received a liquor order and plan social visits accordingly. Mike Hamilton remembered two locals in particular who always took nocturnal rambles down to the freight shed after the boat had left: one unnamed gentleman, known to be constantly thirsty, and Sophus Arnet's cow, looking for leftover hay. This cow famously roamed the town, raiding gardens, opening gates with her tongue, visiting the dock, rubbing against fences and signs. Oblivious to shouts and blows, she draped herself with laundry left on clotheslines, positioned her cowpats in busy areas, obstructed access to buildings, and generally received the blame for anything that went missing. "One man went so far as to suggest facetiously to his neighbor Hamanaka...whose precious woodpile had unaccountably diminished overnight, that perhaps the cow had been in the locality...and so the fun went on."

Steaming out of Tofino, the *Maquinna* travelled only a short distance to her next stop at Clayoquot, pulling up at the end of the long curving dock with its railcar that took freight up to the store and hotel. From Clayoquot, the next stop was Kakawis, with freight for Christie School unloaded into scows that came alongside the steamer, and nervous passengers encouraged down the rope ladder into waiting canoes. Then came Ahousat. On the trip made by Inspector Brodie in August 1918, many cannery workers disembarked there, following their summer's labour away from home: "It is very interesting disembarking them, as they are all handled in dugouts. These come along side of the ship, which anchors in the bay. The Indians pile into the dugouts, baggage, men, women, children, dogs, pots, pans...Among other things there were small cook stoves, stove pipe, hats, strips of oil cloth and all sorts of paraphernalia. It took about an hour to disembark all the Indians." In later years, the *Maquinna* could dock at Ahousat, navigating up Matilda Inlet to the wharf that had been built in front of the Gibson sawmill.

From Ahousat, the *Maquinna* continued through Clayoquot Sound and up the coast, over the years her scheduled stops shifting, changing, and increasing to include any and all short-lived settlements and enterprises: Port Gillam, Bear River, Herbert Inlet, Sydney Inlet—at various times all of these appeared on the steamer's schedule, along with the various canneries, pilchard reduction plants, mining developments, whaling stations, and logging camps that sprang into being. By 1931, the *Princess Maquinna's* schedule listed forty-five locations between Victoria and Port Alice where the steamer could call—half of them scheduled stops, the others serviced on request.

In distant inlets she might be greeted by one person in a canoe, looking for mail or cargo, for even in the most remote locations everyone knew they could count on the *Maquinna*. "She would often pull into a small float camp or a booming ground and unload the loggers' cargo out the side hatches," wrote Bill Moore in *B.C. Lumberman* in 1977. "She had two large iron doors on her sides down near the water's edge, and when these were opened freight could be passed out to waiting hands. It may be the middle of the night in a snow storm or it may be in a strong tidal inlet...the captain of the *Maquinna* would hold her in position while the logger or fisherman took his freight off." People waiting up these lonely inlets could sense the thrum of the ship's big engines long before hearing the whistle tooting her arrival; they knew every sound of that ship approaching and leaving, especially the grating sounds of winches and chains. Once on board, everyone revelled in the familiar, welcoming smells: blasts of dark smoke from the funnel, warm gusts from the engine room, the rich aroma of steamy cooking in the ship's galley.

When the boat stopped for any length of time, local residents could come aboard and treat themselves to a meal. The dining saloon, panelled with "dark expensive wood," according to Alder Bloom, seemed a place of great elegance, a far cry from everyday life on the coast "Several heavy mahogany tables [were] placed about the room," Bloom recalled, "covered with fine linen cloths, heavy silverware and fine dishes. All done in true CPR style with a ship's officer at the head of each table. An immaculate waiter took my order." Children travelling on the boat were simply awe-struck by the impressive surroundings. Bob Wingen recalled, "When we sat down at the dinner table on the boat there was this beautiful dinner service laid out with all this cutlery. We were dumbfounded and the stewards would have to teach us how to handle it all. We couldn't afford all those knives and forks." Mary (MacLeod) Hardy has never forgotten the details of dining aboard: the polished banister leading into the dining room, the welcoming smells, the amazement of reading the menu with "new words such as à la mode' or à la carte' and the finger bowls, it was a whole new world to us." The ship's officers always took their place at tables with the passengers; well-behaved children might even find themselves invited to sit with the captain. In the early 1920s, breakfast or lunch aboard ship cost seventy-five cents; dinner one dollar. By the late 1940s, the price of lunch had increased to a dollar and ten cents. Gene Aitkens described a lunch she and her son enjoyed aboard the *Maquinna* in 1948: "We had soup, turkey, potatoes, and cauliflower, mixed salad and pudding, tea for me, milk for Art and then a banana. Art also had an apple." Such workaday fare, though, could not compare to the more exciting midnight suppers, with buffet tables lining the starboard side of the dining lounge and offering cold salmon, roast beef, and turkey; fruit salad, chocolate cake, crème caramel, and raisin pie for dessert—to name only a few items.

On special occasions, the food served aboard the *Maquinna* could be amazingly elaborate. Take Christmas Day of 1924. The handwritten menu, decorated with sketches of holly, excitedly capitalized every item of the many courses: Salted Almonds and Ripe Olives for starters, fol-lowed by a choice of soups: Consommé à la Reine and Cream of Oyster. Then the fish course: Boiled Halibut with Shrimp Sauce and Lobster Salad with Celery, also Boiled Ham with Champagne Sauce. Orange Fritters and Chicken Patties also make an appearance. Then the choices for the main course, including Roast Ribs of Beef with Yorkshire Pudding, Roast Turkey with Cranberry Sauce, and Roast Goose with Apple Sauce, all served with Mashed Potatoes and Green Peas. Dessert next: Plum Pudding with Rum Sauce, Deep Apple Pie, Mince Tartlets, Cream Puffs. To round off the meal: Maraschino Jelly Creams, Nuts, Raisins, Figs, and Dates.

Weddings in all communities along the route often took place to coincide with the arrival of the *Maquinna*—and sometimes even took place aboard. Ivan Clarke, a Victoria-born tugboat master, arrived at Hot Springs Cove in 1933 on the *Maquinna*, pitched his tent and decided to stay. With $500 worth of provisions, he built a house and store with lumber salvaged from nearby Sydney Inlet Mine and began catering to fish boats and fishing camps in the area. Thirteen months later his fiancée, Mabel Stephens, arrived at Ahousat on the *Maquinna*. The Presbyterian minister, Rev. J. Jones, came aboard and married Ivan and Mabel, with Captain William Thompson serving as best man. Also in 1934, Daphne Guppy and Tom Gibson, who had recently arrived in Tofino to work on gold prospects up the Kennedy River, were married by the ship's captain on board the *Princess Maquinna*. Weddings in Tofino often were timed to allow newlyweds to go straight from their wedding reception onto the southbound boat, heading off on their honeymoon. This explains why Tofino wedding anniversaries, for decades, fell on the 6th, 16th, and 26th of the month. On those dates the coastal steamer appeared in town late at night on its return voyage down the coast, heading south to Victoria. The Community Hall buzzed with festivity on wedding days, and according to Ronald MacLeod, "practically everyone in the village would be invited to these events...By midnight, the *Maquinna* would arrive and the newlyweds would board the vessel under a shower of rice and hearty good wishes for a joyous honeymoon."

Once aboard ship, stewards would usher passengers into their staterooms. For ten dollars and fifty cents, in the 1930s, Tofinoites could go to Victoria, with a stateroom and all meals included, including afternoon tea and a midnight supper. "She could take 400 passengers," Alder Bloom recalled, "but the fifty staterooms with their large upper and lower berths could not accommodate everyone. Many people spent the night in the lounges." Those in the staterooms found the lower berth had its own electric reading light, and the cabins offered two folding seats, a wardrobe, a washstand with a pitcher and basin, and a chamber pot tucked discreetly away. Over time, the *Maquinna* acquired hot and cold running water in her staterooms.

In the morning, chimes awakened the passengers, as the steward walked up and down, sounding the bell and announcing, "First call to breakfast, first call to breakfast." Mealtimes had three sittings, with each passenger assigned a time. People could while away some of the hours of travel out on deck, weather permitting, sometimes clustered around the warm funnel of the ship. In good weather, the ship's crew would be out there chatting to passengers, even playing deck games. The cargo hatches on the ship were forward, and the cabins, smoking lounge, social hall, and dining room aft of the hatches. Cecil Maiden, who travelled often on the *Maquinna*, recalled the facilities on board with deep affection, despite his assertion that she never proved herself a comfortable vessel. "Those who travelled in her will never forget her," he wrote, "the strange zig-zag passageways, the unpretentious homey lounge, the tiny smoking room, the cozy dining saloon with its atmosphere of a kindly home." Everyone eventually spent time in the *Maquinna*'s central saloon because, as one of her crew commented, "There wasn't anywhere else to go. Everyone had to be friendly." Although parts of the deck could be piled high with building supplies and cargo, some stout-hearted passengers regularly chose to travel outside, in sheltered positions on deck, weather permitting. According to Cecil Maiden, some did so even in stormy weather: "they gathered around the warm funnel, as the ship rolled and plunged, the salt sea spray in their faces...the boards groaning and creaking."

Regular travellers on the route always knew the location of the *Maquinna* when she stopped, even in the dark and the rain, by the sounds and the smells of each port. According to Anthony Guppy, the reduction plants had "a particularly rancid oily smell," and a salmon cannery had a "fresh fish smell." Passengers could also tell without looking if the ship had stopped for a boat landing or at a dock. A boat landing meant that people and goods transferred to smaller vessels that came alongside the *Maquinna* for loading and unloading; the loud clanging of the big steel cargo doors opening signalled a boat landing. If passengers chose to look out, "down below on a cold misty sea there would be people struggling to unload perhaps a stove, building materials, or boxes of food into a pitching skiff or canoe." As Captain H.G. Halkett wrote in *The Islander* in 1980, recalling the *Maquinna*, "Unfamiliar passengers who may have expected nights of quiet sleep aboard would soon be disillusioned as the chatter and blather of three sets of steam cargo winches created an unholy row in all cabins." At scheduled stops along the route, passengers soon knew to expect the shuddering of the ship, the sounding bells and whistle, the rattling chains, the hurried footsteps along passageways and decks, and the noisy shifting of freight from within the cargo deck.

For aboriginal passengers, the coastal steamers provided frequent and reliable transport, especially for those travelling to and from seasonal employment at the canneries. Since the early days of the Canadian Pacific Navigation Company, seasonal workers travelled to the canneries in large groups, taking with them the household goods they would need for several months away from home. These travellers did not experience convivial times in the dining saloon, and comfortable berths to sleep in. They travelled "deck class," sitting out on deck, making little shelters where and how they could, sometimes travelling in the cargo hold in bad weather. When the ship stopped for any length of time, they would take their big iron cooking pots and prepare a meal on the beach nearby, sometimes catching fish right then and there to eat. More privileged passengers often noted the large numbers of cannery workers on board: "a hundred or more Indians, men, women and children...sleeping on deck for two or three nights...On arrival at the cannery...they disembarked with all their weird paraphernalia slung over their shoulders...each carrying their little load."

Exceptionally, at a time of segregated steamer travel, Father Charles Moser's diary provides accounts of obtaining staterooms for Christie School students when travelling to and from the school. June 4, 1924, found him at Kyuquot, shepherding a large group aboard the *Maquinna*: "I had 29 children to take care of after leaving the Whaling Station and at 9 P.M. at Nootka got four more. The 33 spent the night divided in eleven staterooms. For fares and rooms I paid the Purser $146.90."

Three years later, on April 24, 1927, he wrote of children heading back to the villages from Christie School: "Said Mass at 4 AM. When we heard steamer whistle got baggage and children ready...I got staterooms for the girls and placed the boys in the steerage."

Despite this evidence from Father Charles of aboriginal children occupying staterooms aboard the *Princess Maquinna*, most often the schoolchildren travelled "steerage" in the cargo area or, if the weather permitted, out on deck. In 1936, Nurse Banfill of Ahousat accompanied three schoolchildren to Alberni, recounting the trip in her book *With the Indians of the Pacific:* "As Indians are not allowed to eat or sleep in the quarters used by white people, I found a place below the hatch for the boys to sleep and eat their lunches. Mary, with the features of a white girl, was more or less smuggled into my cabin; sleeping on a leather couch and eating her school lunch." The boys paid little heed to the restrictions and wandered all over the boat anyhow, to the disapproval of other passengers. "Whenever I took [Mary] out on deck," Nurse Banfield wrote, "I noticed two wealthy tourists, lounging in chairs...peering down their noses at my little brood and me." Former students who attended Christie School in the late 1930s and early 1940s still recall how they had to stay below decks. Violet George first travelled to Christie School when she was six years old, with her two older sisters. Her father paid their fares from Nootka Cannery, and the girls went aboard and went down to the hold, where they stayed for many hours before reaching the school. With no benches provided, they sat on their suitcases; a bucket served as a toilet.

Although treated as second-class passengers aboard the coastal steamers, aboriginals provided a major tourist attraction along the west coast route. On Boat Days at many stops between Victoria and Kyuquot, aboriginal artisans sold their baskets and carvings to passengers from the early years of the twentieth century onward. In September 1910, the *Colonist* noted a group of Natives gathered in Victoria, waiting for the steamer *Tees,* "some of the women engaged in weaving hats and baskets, some of the men busily carving small totems and other wares for the tourist trade. Many Kodak fiends were engaged 'snap-shotting' the picturesque groups."

According to Douglas Cole in *Captured Heritage*, around the time of World War I, aboriginal art began to gain prestige in British Columbia, adding a certain cachet to up-market settings. Totem poles and reproductions of aboriginal motifs were featured in murals or as decoration in places like the Empress Hotel and the Lieutenant Governor's ballroom in Victoria. From 1911 onward, largely thanks to the energies of Dr. C.F. Newcombe, the province made concerted efforts to acquire aboriginal cultural material for the provincial museum—decades after major museums in America and Europe had led the way in pillaging every artifact they could obtain from villages up and down the northwest coast. Local museum interest developed in step with popular interest in aboriginal art and design, in turn feeding the growing touristic interest in "Indian curios."

Tourist traffic along the west coast of British Columbia had developed well behind that of Alaska. Boatloads of Alaska-bound tourists travelled by steamer from the continental United States from the early 1880s onward. In 1889 the Alaska tourist traffic had increased to the point that one steamship company alone carried over 5,000 passengers that summer. Tourists swarmed ashore at every small port, keen to see the indigenous people and to buy their handicrafts. Eventually the CPR woke up to the fact that the same potential existed along the west coast of Vancouver Island and began to capitalize on it ruthlessly.

Once the pulp mill at Port Alice opened in 1917, this town became the turnaround point for "round-trippers," those curiosity-seeking tourists who boarded the steamer just to see the coast. When the CPR began to promote the west coast route to tourists, its popularity grew rapidly. A publicity leaflet of 1922 notes that "only recently has the route been featured as a tourist route," and it admits the already serious problem of seasonal overbooking—a problem noted in Father Charles Moser's diary, with his dour comments about the growing numbers of tourists and the difficulty of reserving bunks. Mike Hamilton had even more to say: "It was a continual nuisance to the coastal residents to find every single cabin and bunk booked up...the company never held sleeping quarters for [coastal residents] which wasn't fair as they were the mainstay for the service when there were no tourists."

By the 1930s, publicity about the west coast route made much of the presence of aboriginal people along the way. "The coast is rich in Indian colour," an undated press release effused, "and the aborigines do much to brighten the way." A brochure from 1934 promised that "the Indians of this district are still noted for their skill in basket weaving and offer their wares for sale to tourists at various wharfs." Growing up in Tofino, Ronald MacLeod remembered seeing "how Indian women would take up stations on the wharf and sell woven basketwork, carvings and other artifacts." Well-circulated publicity images showed totem poles, canoes, and local women busily weaving their baskets. They featured in posters and leaflets and on the front of brochures advertising the "Sunset Cruises" up the coast aboard either the *Princess Maquinna* or, after her introduction to the coast in 1929, the *Princess Norah*. Explanatory notes about aboriginal culture told tourists of the locals they could meet. The 1936 brochure stated: "Although the influence of civilization has had much to do with changing the mode of living of these aborigines, much remains to show that in earlier days they were a highly cultured race, enjoying a normal and happy existence." And later in the brochure: "On the whole a jovial and carefree people, these Indians offer interesting studies. Many opportunities for meeting these people are afforded to travellers during this leisurely and picturesque cruise along the Pacific Coast."

Before long the CPR advertised the west coast as an alternative to the Alaskan cruises, and people sometimes booked their travel a whole year in advance. Weather permitting, these summer tourists found no lack of entertainment aboard. Shuffleboard on deck became a special attraction, along with dancing and card games in the saloon. Seasickness affected only a "small minority," according to the CPR's mendacious publicity; furthermore, those affected "look upon it as an experience to be talked about on their return home."

Although Inspector Brodie conceded in his 1918 report that the west coast route did have some tourist attractions—his favourites being the cemetery at Nootka and the village of Yuquot, with little good to say about Tofino and Clayoquot Sound—he presented only lukewarm ideas of how to improve the *Maquinna* for tourists. "A few deck chairs are required," he wrote, "a phonograph for dancing, and an awning over the after deck. A bath room or two would require to be provided." Brodie entirely failed to see how popular this route would become. Ten years after his inspection trip, a splendid new steamer was built for the west coast route, specifically to accommodate all the tourists. The much-trumpeted arrival of the *Princess Norah* on the west coast ushered in a whole new era of tourism on the coast.

Larger and more elaborate than the *Princess Maquinna, Princess Norah* measured 76 metres long and 14.6 metres wide, offering much more cargo space as well as greatly improved amenities for the travellers. She could carry up to 700 passengers at a time. Of her sixty-one staterooms, four deluxe suites offered private baths, fourteen of the cabins had showers, and all had hot and cold running water. Her berths accommodated 165 people, and up to a hundred at a time could eat in the dining saloon. She had a dance lounge, and on busy runs a band travelled on board to provide music. "She was a sleek and gracious beauty of a ship, a real Princess, with something new—a bow rudder, to help her navigate the narrow passages and inlets of the rugged West Coast," wrote James Nesbitt.

As a junior reporter for the *Daily Colonist*, Nesbitt nabbed the assignment of covering the *Norah*'s highly publicized inaugural run up the coast in April 1929. In later years he recalled

Promotional leaflets from the 1930s for the growing tourist traffic on the CPR steamships' west coast route. They stress the attractions provided en route by aboriginal people, who sold their carvings and baskets at stops along the way. The coast was advertised as "rich in Indian colour," with Native people who "do much to brighten the way." At this time, aboriginal people continued to die in large numbers from tuberculosis, and when travelling on the coastal steamers, they had to remain on deck or travel in the cargo hold. *Private collection*

Passengers play shuffleboard on deck aboard the *Princess Norah* on a calm day.
Image D021718 courtesy of the Royal BC Museum, BC Archives

the experience: "The very special guests were the Governor General of Canada and the Countess of Willingdon, the latter a peppy lady who missed nothing and had a sharp tongue." Also on board: Lieutenant Governor Robert Randolph Bruce of British Columbia; the Governor General's aide-de-camp Major Selden Humphreys; and the mayor of Victoria, Herbert Anscomb. Captain Cyril D. Neroutsos, the "stern, autocratic, every-inch-a-sailor...manager of the CPR's BC Coast service," also came along. During these glory days of the CPR ships, James Nesbitt reported, an employee who failed to call Captain Neroutsos "Sir" was fired forthwith, and when inspecting his ships, Neroutsos wore a white glove to enable him to detect the least speck of dust.

When the Governor General's toplofty aide-de-camp came to Nesbitt's stateroom to bid him and another reporter to have dinner at the vice-regal table, Nesbitt shook with nerves. He struggled into his first black tie for the occasion and braved a formal dinner. The other reporter, irritated by the tone of the invitation, which began "Their

A stateroom aboard the *Princess Norah*. Note the satin-covered eiderdowns. *Image D02717 courtesy of the Royal BC Museum, BC Archives*

Excellencies command you...," refused to attend the dinner, suggesting to Nesbitt they both hide in the engine room rather than put up with such condescension. The resulting empty space at the table annoyed Captain Neroutsos and led to the unnamed reporter being suspended from his paper for being rude to the "representatives of the Crown." Lady Willingdon credited Nesbitt with more journalistic strategy than he possessed when she congratulated him "for having kept [his] rival out of the way."

"Boatloads of Indians, in native attire, swarmed around the *Norah* as she came in," wrote Nesbitt, describing the steamer's arrival in Ucluelet. Similar welcomes awaited her all along the route, with elaborate presentations from local leaders, community groups, First Nations, and always with crowds of local people flocking to the docks to participate in gala receptions. Ucluelet children had a day off school, and youngsters of all races, Japanese, aboriginal, and others, scrambled aboard the *Norah*, wildly excited to see the grand new boat with its distinguished guests. Also at Ucluelet, the enthusiastic Lord Willingdon expressed such interest in seal skins that he clambered right into a bin of skins at Edwin Lee's store to examine them. At Lennard Island, approaching Tofino, a flotilla of Japanese fishing boats and every other vessel imaginable converged to escort the *Norah* into harbour. George Nicholson's *Miowera*, with Ronald MacLeod and many others on board, joined the "fishing boats, tenders, pleasure boats, whaling canoes, small canoes, skiffs, rowboats and whatever else that would float…bedecked in colourful flags and banners."

Winnie Dixson recalled the lavish ceremony awaiting the visiting dignitaries on the dock in Tofino: "The wharf was lined with these painted backdrops and spruce boughs. Then the Indians did their dances with all the masks. And all the school kids were down there singing the national anthem…Oh, it was a real reception!" Hundreds of people attended, and the Tla-o-qui-ahts invested Lord Willingdon with the honorary rank of chief. Japanese girls danced wearing traditional attire, and Mitsuzo Nakagawa, president of Tofino Area Fishing Co-op, presented the Governor General with a huge sturgeon as a mark of esteem. Dorothy Abraham's Girl Guides and Brownies stood for inspection and then "danced around the regal party on the wharf, which had been transformed by the veterans into a bower of loveliness." The Tofino Board of Trade hosted a reception for the illustrious guests; among those honoured, Chief Joseph and Queen Mary of Opitsat.

The most repeated tale of the viceregal couple's visit to Tofino on the *Princess Norah* involves their encounter with the old Scottish prospector Bill Spittal and his famously ugly dog, Joe Beef. The Governor General and his wife agreed to walk up the trail from the dock to look around the village of Tofino. John Cooper, formerly of Long Beach and now a leading citizen of Tofino and Legion president, escorted them—although the escort could have been George Nicholson; accounts vary. After the couple politely admired Cap Thompson's large dahlia garden and meandered down the road into the village, "who comes limping down the path with his dog but old Bill Spittal…he used to lead [Joe Beef] around on a piece of anchor chain," Walter Guppy recalled. Bill Spittal, with his tobacco-stained beard, floppy hat down to his eyebrows, old coat dragging on the ground, could not have been less impressed by the august company facing him. Politely, Cooper introduced Bill as one of Tofino's original prospectors and pioneers. "'Mr. Spittle [*sic*], I want you to meet Lord and Lady Willingdon, and I'm their escort,'" Ian MacLeod recounted in one version of the story. "Bill Spittle let out a great big spit of snoose and he said, 'Howya doing? I'm Bill Spittle from Glenshee, Scotland, and this is my escort, Joe Beef.'"

The *Princess Norah* continued her triumphal progress up the coast, met with great enthusiasm everywhere. At Port Alice, Father Charles Moser joined the celebrity crowd on board and travelled back down the coast, enjoying the good cheer just as he had on the inaugural run of *Princess Maquinna* back in 1913. On that trip, as on this, Captain Edward Gillam had charge of the vessel. Gillam had been appointed captain of the *Norah*, relinquishing command of the *Maquinna*, and he foresaw finishing his career aboard this newer, larger boat. He did so, but not as foreseen. Three weeks later, Father Charles noted in his diary: "The sad news was told us that our good Captain Gillam had passed into eternity...RIP. He was a good friend of mine." On board the *Norah* on her second trip along the west coast, Gillam fell down a short flight of steps and died, likely of a heart attack. In Tofino, Dr. Dixson examined the body, and John Grice, as coroner, signed the death certificate. According to Dixson, Gillam's face was tranquil.

For the rest of her first season, Father Charles boarded the *Princess Norah* regularly on his mission trips along the coast—Nootka to Hesquiat, Hesquiat to Kyuquot, Port Alice to Kakawis, Opitsat to Hesquiat, his usual

Princess Norah steams south, leaving Tofino Harbour, with Grice Point on the left and Felice Island in the background. Note the oil tanks on the shore, where Katie and Harold Monks ran the Imperial Oil marine fuel depot. The seiner *Kenn Falls* is at the oil dock, and the Tofino Trollers' Co-operative fish-buying camp lies offshore. *Courtesy of Leona Taylor*

peripatetic summer—frequently commenting on the new ship and the numbers of tourists on board. "June 4, 1929: *SS Pr Norah* at Hesquiat at 4 AM...About 20 tourists aboard making the round trip." In July, Father Charles commented on a special stop the *Norah* made, anchoring "alongside the survey steamer *Lillooet*. Chief Surveyor Parizeau came aboard our boat for the sake of dancing until daylight." Later in the month the priest counted ninety-two tourists on board. He began to find travelling on the *Norah* a bit too lively for his taste: "July 23, 1929: Left 9 P.M. per *SS Norah*. Big freight for Kakawis, lumber for fire escapes. Tough salesmen and others on board, dangerous company, not suitable for a priest. Age and experience became me well on this trip. Steamer full of tourists; had a berth in a room with 2 others."

Despite her more lavish facilities and touristic gaiety, *Princess Norah* never won the hearts of west coasters as the *Princess Maquinna* did. She served the coast in tourist season throughout her early years, but increasingly she was deployed on other runs, particularly to Alaska, and also on the Gulf Island run and up to Prince Rupert. *Princess Maquinna*, despite occasional assignments on other runs, stuck firmly to the west coast of Vancouver Island, becoming known over the years as "Old Faithful." Following Gillam's death, several other popular captains served on the *Maquinna*: Captain Robert "Red" Thompson, then Captain William "Black" Thompson, followed by Captains Peter Leslie, Martin MacKinnon, Leonard McDonald, and R.W. Carthew. Two of the ship's captains spoke Gaelic fluently, often enjoying a chat with Murdo MacLeod in Tofino; on Boat Days near Christmas they would visit the MacLeod home for a dram of whisky, and *Princess Maquinna* would leave a bit later than scheduled.

Significant as the coastal steamers were, arriving every ten days at stops all along the coast, the routine movement of smaller boats coming and going in Tofino Harbour, around the Sound, and up the inlets made every day a boat-filled day. Without these boats and all their activity, nothing could happen. Fishing, transport, provisions, communication, recreation—everything relied on boats. Recognizable at a glance to local people, all these fish boats, workboats, scows, skiffs, canoes, rowboats, government vessels, mission boats meant the world to their owners, each one carrying its own cargo of stories. Knowing these boats, their background, their activities, meant knowing what was going on in town and along the coast. Small wonder their comings and goings attracted such interest.

During the many years when Clayoquot cannery operated, from 1895 to 1932, cannery vessels frequently appeared, the two tiny steam-powered tugs *Bulldog* and *Bison* or the early fishing boats *Iskum, Beth, Eastpoint,* and *Bertha L.*, some of the fleet overseen by John Eik, head skipper of all cannery-owned boats. As the years passed, with the arrival of Japanese fishermen, the increase in salmon trolling, and, later, the bonanza years of the pilchard fishery, the numbers of boats coming and going in Tofino Harbour mounted dramatically. Early in the morning, dozens of boats would head out fishing, presenting a calm, silent rush hour of fish boats, outlined against the lightening sky. Dorothy Abraham recalled the scene: "It was a fascinating sight if ever one was up early enough to see them go out in formation, a steady stream, and it was always interesting to see who would be 'high boat' for the day." High boat meant the highest catch of the day—everyone wanted that honour, most often captured by Harold Kimoto and other Japanese fishermen. Among the vessels heading out before dawn, the small, sturdy Japanese salmon trollers usually bore only the initials of their owners as names, including the *KK, DE, KM,* followed by their fishing licence numbers. The Japanese vessels all fished for the Tofino Trollers' Co-operative Association. The fish packers awaiting them at the fish-buying station in Tofino Harbour in the 1930s included the chartered *Rose N*, which packed salmon for the Seattle market, and the *Western Chief*, owned by the fishing co-op.

The *West Coast Advocate* periodically reported fishboat activity as if the vessels were alive, setting off on their travels as sentient creatures quite independent of their owners. "Seiner *Ginger Boy* has gone to Barclay Sound to fish dog salmon...*Yankee Boy* has arrived to spend a week-end in Tofino." "The seine boats *Kenn Falls* and *Aliema* returned from the [bait] herring fishing at Kyuquot for Christmas." During the July–August sockeye season, *Kenn Falls* and other Tofino-based seiners, *Aliema, Calm Creek, Annie H., Yankee Boy, Ginger Boy, Silver Horde, Anna B.,* would head up the inlet for sockeye, joined by numerous seiners from elsewhere on the coast. John Eik and his crew of five sometimes invited local boys aboard *Kenn Falls* for a week or so as a special treat during the season, giving the boys bragging rights among their friends. Other boats did the same: "I begged to get a couple of weeks on first Roy Darville's boat *Calm Creek*, and then on Karl Arnet's boat, the *Aliema*," wrote Anthony Guppy. "They took me on without pay...and knew I just wanted to see how things were done on a seiner."

Aboriginal fishermen operated several of the fishing vessels often seen in Tofino Harbour in the late 1920s and 1930s—*Axmaxis, Margaret C.,* and *Skill* among them—as well as a Nootka Packing Company seiner skippered for many years by the highly respected Kelsemaht fisherman George Sye. Other local trollers and seiners included Oscar Hansen's *June W* and Louis Fransen's *Pete*, and many fish boats from other home ports came and went: the *Cape May* and *Ohiat* from Bamfield, the *Bramada* from Alberni, the *B.C. Kidd* from Steveston, the *Newcastle #4* from Vancouver, the *Skill* from Port Alberni. The United Church mission boat *Melvin Swartout* became a frequent visitor, and American trollers would anchor in Tofino harbour when weather dictated. Edgar Arnet's well-known *Cape Beale* appeared in the spring and fall when he needed to store or pick up gear, which he stored in his father Jacob's shed. George Hillier's Ucluelet-based boats also regularly showed up. A successful fishermen on the coast, Hillier started his career hand-trolling from an Indian canoe and subsequently owned *Ucluelet Kid, Doolad,* and *Cupid* before acquiring the large *Manhattan I,* from which he seined salmon and anchovies and long-lined halibut.

A good number of the boats based in and around Tofino had been built there by their owners, John Hansen's salmon seiner *Ginger Boy* among them, and many smaller vessels like Anthony Guppy's *Tofino Kid*. Many of the best known boats in the area originated at Wingen's shipyard, including Joe MacLeod's salmon troller *Loch Monar*, the Catholic mission's *Ave Maria II*, the gillnetter *June W*, and trollers *Sharlene, Bear*

Island, and *Cumtux*. John Eik had his seiner *Kenn Falls* rebuilt by the Wingens in 1935, and the Gibson brothers of Ahousat commissioned two tugs: *Gibson Girl* in 1938 and *Tahsis No. 1* in 1943. Although most boats built by Tom Wingen and later by his son Hilmar did not remain in Tofino, ranging far and wide in their careers as motor launches, tugs, or fish boats, the launch of any Wingen boat always gave rise to local celebration. Boat launches, especially of larger vessels like George Hillier's 18-metre seiner *Manhattan II* in 1941, often turned into gala events involving almost everyone in Tofino, and ending in a dance at the Community Hall. Bob Wingen, Hilmar's son, remembered how he and his brother Harvey discovered the champagne hidden safely away for boat launches. "We figured that spilling all that good booze at the launch was a great waste. So we got the bottle and worked the wire loose and took the cork out, drank the champagne and refilled the bottle back up with ginger ale and re-sealed it. So a lot of the boats in my time were christened using ginger ale and not champagne."

T.H. Wingen's Shipyard had opened for business on the Tofino waterfront in 1929, initiated by Tom Wingen, and later expanded, adapted, and carried on by son Hilmar and grandson Bob. The shipyard grew out of Wingen's earlier enterprises, the Tofino Boat Yard, which he established with Mike Hogan after moving into Tofino from the family's original homestead out at Grice Bay, and the Tofino Machine Shop, which Hilmar Wingen opened in partnership with Mike Hamilton in 1917. The earliest Wingen-built boats predate the official opening of the shipyard, the *Tofino*, built in 1918 for the Stone family, being the first.

At one point the third-largest small-boat shipyard in British Columbia, Wingen's employed forty-five men by 1944. These included labourers, machinists, cabinet makers, and six Norwegian shipwrights, all able to "lay down a board, mark it out and cut it to shape with a broad-axe, and the damn thing fit!" as Bob Wingen explained. The war years kept the shipyard humming. Renowned for his exceptional craftsmanship, Hilmar Wingen, like his pioneering father, became famed for his ingenuity. Determined to use local materials as much as possible, he devised a method of laminating yellow cedar and yew wood to make ships' ribs, bypassing the need to import cants of white oak, the tough, springy wood traditionally employed. The Wingens salvaged Douglas fir for boat keels from trees that came down in slides from the mountains above Kennedy Lake, and they used red and yellow cedar for planking. When it came to engines, "by the late 1930s the Wingens were pouring their own bearings and rebuilding engines from the block up," according to Andrew Struthers, who lived aboard the *Loch Ryan*, a vessel rebuilt by the Wingens. They created "pistons, heads, rods—right out of raw metal." Hilmar even built a two-stroke gas engine from scratch.

In the late 1920s and 1930s, when a strong westerly or southeaster blew the offshore pilchard purse seine fleet into Tofino harbour for a "tie-up" day, these boats could be found six abreast at the wharf and on floats. Company-owned boats dominated the scene, each one painted in company colours and flying company pennants—over the years the companies included Nootka Packing Company, Nelson Brothers, BC Packers, Anglo-British Columbia, Francis Millerd and Company, and the Canadian Fishing Company. Local boys loved visiting the pilchard vessels, peppering the fishermen with questions and "learning neat things like net mending and fancy rope splicing," according to Ronald MacLeod.

The movements of the Tofino lifeboat provided another constant source of interest, even though most trips tended to be routine or practice runs. Still, even the most mundane trip on the lifeboat could be exciting for a young boy, and because his uncle Alex MacLeod worked as coxswain on the lifeboat for twenty-six years, Ronald MacLeod sometimes enjoyed short trips to fill the lamps in the harbour navigational system. He remembered the lifeboat as a "double-ender about 38 or 40 feet [11.5 or 12 metres] in length. It had buoyancy tanks which were supposed to ensure that the vessel would right itself if it ever tipped over... fortunately, an assumption never tested. A canvas canopy from the bow section to mid-ships provided the only cover for the crew." Occasionally he and his cousins went out on the lifeboat with a delivery run of mail and supplies to the light at Lennard Island. Seas could be huge, and seasickness almost inevitable, but the boys thrilled to watch the large workboat offloading cargo for the light, and crew members battling to hold it in place in a surging sea as a large canvas sling descended from an overhead cable to carry the goods ashore.

Looking out from the town, no one could mistake the larger, official boats that sometimes showed up in the harbour. These included the lighthouse tender *Estevan* and one of the offshore fisheries patrol vessels, the coal-burning *Givenchy*, whose Captain Redford spent nearly twenty years (1919–38) enforcing the five-kilometre offshore limit along the West Coast, inside which no foreign vessel could fish. Canada's other Pacific offshore fisheries patrol vessel, the *Malaspina*, with Captain Henderson in charge, also appeared from time to time. In the 1930s the hydrographic survey vessel *Lillooet* became a familiar sight for several years as she worked along the coast. The fifteen-metre police motor launch *PML7* also showed up periodically on patrol duty, carrying out the usual jobs of collecting taxes from canneries and from fishermen, monitoring events in First Nations villages, providing assistance to destitute trappers and prospectors out in the bush, or tracking down stolen boats. This boat meant business; handcuffs hung from the wall of the cabin, and she carried a Thompson submachine gun on board. Also appearing from time to time was the *Otter*, for thirty-five years a passenger vessel all around the coast until purchased by the Gibson brothers in the early 1930s and refitted as a fish packer. She made regular visits until she went up in flames in 1937. The Department of Indian Affairs' launch *Duncan Scott*, skippered by Indian agent Noel Garrard, showed up in the harbour fairly often, as did the Catholic mission boat *Drummond*, succeeded by the *Brabant*. During the 1930s, the well-known mission boat *Messenger II*, operated by the Shantymen's Christian Association, also became a frequent visitor.

The famous *Malahat* loomed into sight occasionally, now stripped down and glumly functional, working as a log barge for the Gibson brothers at Ahousat. Built in Victoria in 1917, during the years of American prohibition this 74.5-metre five-masted schooner had served as the most famous of all rum-running vessels out of Vancouver. With immense loads of liquor, she sailed south and loitered in the danger-ous offshore waters of "Rum Row," off the Californian and Mexican coasts. Captained by Stuart Stone for several years during that period of risk-taking and high seas adventure, the *Malahat* acted as a floating warehouse, remaining largely in international waters and provisioning smaller vessels that ran for shore with their loads of booze packed into gunny sacks. Stone had been involved in rum-running from 1920 onward, starting in a small way on the family's Alberni-based launch *Roche Point*, then as master of several important rum-running ships, including *Federalship* and *L'Aquila*. Jailed briefly in California in 1927 for his activities, Stone carried on undaunted, in 1929 taking command of the mothership, *Malahat*. Two years later he married his second wife, Emmie May Binns, daughter of Carl Binns of Ucluelet, aboard the *Malahat*. Many years his junior, Emmie May lived aboard the *Malahat* with Stuart for eighteen months, revelling in the adventure and romance. Their time together was cut short by his sudden death in 1933, after he fell ill aboard the *Malahat*. Built "in the grand old style with a coal burning fireplace in the owner's quarters and two full size bathtubs," according to Gordon Gibson, no ship could compare to the *Malahat*. In her altered state, she served the Gibsons as a self-powered, self-loading and self-unloading log barge until 1937, carrying upward of $15,000 worth of logs at a time. In her last few years, with her engines removed, she served as a lowly barge before foundering in Barkley Sound in 1944, the famous vessel "pounded to pieces by Pacific waves and BC logs," according to the *Vancouver Sun*.

By the mid-1930s, Murdo MacLeod's 11.5-metre *Mary Ellen Smith*, an inshore fisheries patrol vessel, provided another familiar sight, heading out to monitor salmon streams along a 100-kilometre stretch of coastline, from Wreck Bay to Estevan Point. In earlier years, MacLeod had hired George Nicholson's 12-metre *Miowera*, well-known locally for her role in fisheries patrol, freight and passenger charters, and also rumoured to have been a rum-runner. Since obtaining the *Mary Ellen Smith*, "kindly in a sea and comfortable to live on," MacLeod could stay out longer and travel farther. His strong voice, singing in Gaelic, could sometimes be heard from shore as he headed out on his patrols.

On calm days, voices and scraps of song often carried clearly over the water; Anthony Guppy's abiding childhood memory of George Maltby recalled the old pioneer in his big red rowboat, returning back up the inlet to his home, tired at the end of a day in town, and talking to his boat: "Come on, old boat, come on, take me home quickly now."

For boys growing up in Tofino and elsewhere along the coast, their first boats were rowboats or canoes. "When you were a kid in Tofino in those days, because there were no roads, you didn't want a bicycle like other kids—you wanted a dugout canoe," Bob Wingen stated. "The Natives would carve them for fifty cents a foot, so an eight footer [2 metres], which was the most popular, cost four dollars." Looking back to his early days of canoe building in the 1920s and '30s, Peter Webster of Ahousat also commented on the prices: "It seems strange now, but in those days a twenty-one foot long canoe [6.5 metres] would sell for about thirty-five dollars."

The Tofino boys would take their prized canoes to the beach and surf them ashore, two or three boys to a canoe. On occasion, Father Victor at Christie School would call the telegraph station in Tofino, spreading the word that the "surf was up" near the school. "Half a dozen of us would row our dugouts up there and join the native kids from the school and then surf our canoes," Bob Wingen recalled. "After we'd surfed for a while Father Victor would ring a big bell and we'd all go ashore and go into the gymnasium. The nuns would have us strip off our wet clothes and, after giving us kimonos to wear, served us hot cocoa while our wet clothes dried in a big drying machine they had somewhere. After that we put our dry clothes back on and rowed for an hour back to Tofino. That was a big day for us." Up at Ahousat, the young Gordon Gibson also delighted in his first canoe, a gift from his father when he was fourteen years old: "I had more pride in that boat than any we have owned since. It was so tender that if I put up my sail about 2 feet down from the first bow thwart, I could tack close into the wind and shoot back and forth across the Inlet regardless of the wind's direction."

As the boys became older, they wanted bigger and more powerful boats. About to turn fifteen, Anthony Guppy told his parents he "had to have a bigger boat if [he] was going to earn any real money." He purchased an old, unpopular vessel, the *Ivy H*, used earlier as a fisheries patrol boat and mocked locally as the "Piss Pot." He put the *Ivy H* to work, taking customers back and forth to the Clayoquot Hotel; they would pay anything from fifty cents to two dollars depending on their level of sobriety, and he found himself "always helping some inebriated person down the dock from the hotel and then onboard the boat."

None of the Tofino boys in those years ever could forget the early summer mornings in the harbour with the commercial fishermen long gone, already out at their fishing grounds off Portland Point or Cleland (Bare) Island. The lads then took to their skiffs, rowboats, and canoes, also going fishing. "Mostly in pairs, one rowing and the other tending the lines, a fleet of boys would troll near the kelp beds...along the shores of the several channels that led from the wide-open Pacific Ocean to the sheltered inside waters," recalled Ronald MacLeod. In the evening, some of these small boats would be out again, hand-trolling for coho along the sandbars and channels among the islands in Tofino Harbour.

At the end of the day, well before dark fell, families in Tofino would be watching, anticipating the return of the various boats, the sounds from the dock. Whatever the season, whatever the reason, someone on shore always waited, someone watched and listened, for the bustle of fish offloading to the fish camps, the sounds of gear being stowed, the careful adjusting of tie-up lines, the progress from floats and docks up to the rough trails and roads leading home, the small boats being dragged ashore. The day would slowly fade and the lights on the harbour markers, initially those kerosene lamps on wooden tripods, guided latecomers in through the channels and sandbars of Tofino Harbour. Another day of boats ended.

Chapter 17:

WARTIME

WHEN HIKERS WALK TWO KILOMETRES along the Bomber Trail, south of Tofino and just beyond the Radar Hill turnoff, they arrive at the wreckage of Canso aircraft #11007. This Royal Canadian Air Force (RCAF) plane crashed here on the night of February 10, 1945. "The Bomber," as it is locally known—although it was not a bomber but a multi-use transport plane—is a reminder of the time when large air bases in Tofino and Ucluelet served as the first line of defence for western Canada during World War II. Along with other isolated bases along the British Columbia coast, they faced the Pacific Ocean, constantly on the alert for signs of Japanese hostilities.

Given Japanese aggression in Manchuria and China in the early 1930s, Canada's Ministry of Defence concluded by 1935 that Japan and the United States might well become involved in a war, and that Canada could be drawn in. Three years before World War II began, military planners started constructing an RCAF base at Ucluelet, anticipating war in the Pacific, and in 1938 Western Air Command came into being to coordinate West Coast defences. The war officially began in Europe on September 3, 1939, and Canada declared war on Germany a week later; at that stage, Canadian defensive efforts focused on protecting the East Coast and safeguarding ships and convoys in the Atlantic Ocean.

Early in 1939, Western Air Command ordered RCAF No. 4 General Reconnaissance Squadron, based at Jericho Beach in Vancouver, to send a detachment of obsolete, amphibious Stranraer flying boats to Kennedy Lake near Tofino. Called the Barkley Detachment, the aircraft and crews carried out reconnaissance flights when weather permitted, with crews and mechanics camped in tents awaiting favourable flying weather the rest of the time. The planes continued their patrols from Kennedy Lake until June 1940, when the Western Air Command, anxious to activate its coastal defences, deemed the Ucluelet base ready for occupancy. When RCAF personnel arrived at the base in July 1940, they found nothing complete: the hangars, barrack blocks, storm sewers, wireless masts and workshops all needed a great deal of work. Stumps littered the area, and slash fires spread a haze of smoke over the base. Many personnel camped in tents, and those allocated to the unfinished barracks crammed into every available corner. The water reservoir had dried up that summer, and at high tide it filled with salt water.

The mechanics managed to keep the two ancient Shark seaplanes and the two four-man Stranraer flying boats ready for crews to make what patrols they could. They flew out over the Pacific, often in appalling conditions, on the lookout for submarines and Japanese vessels. Soon after the squadron arrived at the Ucluelet base, the air force equipped the planes with bombs, and the squadron's name changed to No. 4 Bomber Reconnaissance. The Canadian Army sent a detachment of the Canadian Scottish Regiment to guard the Ucluelet base; shortly after, members of the Veterans Guard of Canada replaced them. By late 1941, some 400 servicemen were stationed there, as conditions at the base slowly improved thanks to the many construction workers also based there.

In 1938, keen to increase surveillance on the coast even before the outbreak of war, the Royal Canadian Navy created the Fishermen's Reserve (FR), its motto: "Ships of Wood, Men of Steel." Unofficially called the Gumboot Navy, this outfit consisted of fishermen and towboat men using their own or fishing company boats. When the men joined up, they took their boats down to the Esquimalt naval base to undergo basic training—at times a bit too basic for these experienced men. "In the early days they even had a course to teach us how to row, for God's sake!" remembered one Fishermen's Reserve captain. Each boat had huge identification letters and numbers painted on the hull near the bow. Kitted out with .303 Lewis machine guns, as well as wireless/telegraph sets, and depth charges or minesweeping gear, the small craft became even more cramped than usual. Due to a shortage of radios, some FR boats took along carrier pigeons to keep in touch with headquarters in Esquimalt.

Typical of boats in the Fishermen's Reserve, the HMCS *Margaret*, shown here, patrolled the west coast during World War II. Equipped with light armament, depth charges, and sometimes minesweeping gear, none ever actually engaged the enemy. A number of men from Tofino served in this "Gumboot Navy," as it was called.
Image E004665419 courtesy of Library and Archives Canada

On the payroll of, and commanded by, the Royal Canadian Navy, members of the Fishermen's Reserve patrolled the coast on the lookout for suspicious activity, assisting police whenever needed and keeping in close contact with naval authorities. Called upon to investigate a reported sighting of a submarine, one member of the force commented wryly, "Our total armament was a half dozen depth charges, a few rifles, and some stripped Lewis guns. Don't know what the hell we would have done if we had bumped into it." The 975 volunteers of the Gumboot Navy never fired a shot and spent most of the war investigating all the inlets along the coast and dealing with wild West Coast weather.

A total of eight Fishermen's Reserve units operated along the west coast, ranging from Port Renfrew to Kyuquot. From Tofino, members included Andy Johnson; Roy Erickson; Hubert Eik; Oscar and Alfred Hansen; Ian, Joe, Donald, and Ron MacLeod; Wallace Grant; and Bjarne, Douglas, Edgar, Norman, Trygve, and Waldemar Arnet. Arthur Park headed up the unit at Nootka, and George Rae-Arthur had charge of the Ahousat unit. Although no Tofino-based boats participated in the Gumboot Navy, Edgar Arnet skippered his *Cape Beale*, registered out of Vancouver, as part of the fleet. In the five years of its existence, the Fishermen's Reserve lost only one of its boats, the *Midnight Sun*, which sank off Cape St. James with a loss of all hands.

The Pacific Coast Military Rangers, also known as the BC Rangers, provided further surveillance along the coast during the war years, bringing a number of volunteers into action. The Rangers recruited loggers, trappers, prospectors, and aboriginals living in remote locations to be on the alert for suspicious activities. Each volunteer carried his own rifle and received a pair of binoculars from the government, along with training in how to identify fifty-five types of enemy aircraft and all classes of Japanese submarines. Teenage boys and men too old to join the regular forces took part in this outfit; later, many of the younger ones joined the Canadian forces. According to Walter Guppy, various Rangers units received Sten guns: "Tofino had one and the Ahousat Indian Band four."

On December 7, 1941, when Japanese planes attacked the US naval base at Pearl Harbor in Hawaii, the worst fears of Canadian military planners became a reality. America entered the war, heightening the possibility of a Japanese attack on the Pacific coast. Immediately, Canadian military activity increased along the coast. Plans already existed for a series of air bases along the outer BC coast, and with the Ucluelet base now open, construction crews moved north to Coal Harbour, at the tip of Vancouver Island, to begin building a base for amphibious aircraft there. At the same time, the Sea Island base in Richmond (now Vancouver International Airport) and the Jericho Beach base near Point Grey in Vancouver, underwent expansion. Construction also began on an airport at Boundary Bay in Delta, another at Patricia Bay near Victoria, one at Bella Bella on the central coast, and a fourth on Digby Island off Prince Rupert. Most significantly for the west coast of Vancouver Island, development of a proposed airfield and RCAF base

The Tofino Air Base under construction in late 1942, with the waves of Long Beach and the Tofino-Ucluelet road visible in the lower section of the photo. The aircraft hangars had yet to be built but most administrative buildings appear to be completed, including the 128-bed hospital, a recreation hall, a canteen, a thirteen-bay garage, barracks, a diesel power plant, and mess halls. Over 2,000 air force servicemen and eighty members of the Women's Division served at the Ucluelet and Tofino bases during World War II. *Courtesy of Fran Aitkens*

at Long Beach suddenly became high priority. Within weeks of Pearl Harbor, the area near Long Beach buzzed with activity as throngs of construction workers and road builders arrived.

The site the RCAF chose for the Tofino air base occupied what locals called the "Burnt Lands," an area once swept by fire, extending from Long Beach over to the mud flats on Grice Bay, adjacent to property owned by the Lovekin family. Poorly drained and difficult to access, the site posed immense logistical challenges. Coast Construction Company, hired to prepare the site and build the air base, found its machines repeatedly bogged down in mud, while the military focused its initial efforts on completing an all-weather gravel road between Ucluelet and

Long Beach, also pushing side roads through to Chesterman Beach and Cox Bay. While crews punched the roads through, Coast Construction struggled to clear land at the base site. The company realized the job was beyond its capacity and subcontracted Gordon Gibson of Ahousat to prepare the site. "When we took the contract," Gibson wrote, "we changed the whole procedure. We divided the area into 200 sections, each 400 feet square [37.16 square metres]. Between the sections, we put in the roads, and set up spar trees, so that the donkeys [steam engines] could yard out the logs. The stumps were gathered into piles every 800 feet [244 metres] and burned...We built a wharf for unloading our barges [in Grice Bay] and brought in thousands of yards of gravel. Then, after our contract came to an end, Coast Construction leveled the ground and built the airport."

In his book *Eighty Years in Tofino*, Walter Guppy recalled the frenetic activity in the spring of 1942. Lines of barges filled with gravel from Cypre River headed along Tofino Inlet into Grice Bay. A bustling work

Fran Aitkens atop a piling on Long Beach in the late 1940s. Placed there in long lines to deter landing craft and airplanes in case of Japanese invasion during World War II, some pilings can still be seen at low tide on the beaches. *Courtesy of Fran Aitkens*

site emerged at August Arnet's long-abandoned property in Grice Bay, with workers hacking a couple of old buildings free from the salmonberry and salal to be used as a bunkhouse and cookhouse. The gravel barges offloaded into trucks that headed out through a sea of mud along the newly created mile-long road to the airport site. There, crews struggled to build the ambitious airport with three 1,500-metre runways and all the structures required for the expected influx of military personnel. Gordon Gibson and his crew built anti-aircraft bunkers and gun emplacements at the airport site. To prevent enemy airplanes, landing craft, and tanks coming ashore, the RCAF also commissioned Gibson to drive pilings every 300 metres, from high water to low water, into the sands of Long Beach and adjacent beaches, stringing wire and cables between the pilings. "We also assisted the army in building machine gun redoubts along the beach, which we made using huge drift logs bulldozed over with sand as cover. Demolition experts laid charges across the runway in trenches every 500 feet [152 metres] so that it could be blown up in the event of a Japanese attack," wrote Gibson. As the rush of construction work continued at Long Beach, hundreds more workers arrived, camping out in a primitive collection of shacks thrown up amid the mud. The number of construction workers employed at the Ucluelet and Tofino bases peaked at 1,500 in late 1942. The RCAF Tofino base was still far from completed, and month by month the fear of Japanese aggression in the Pacific Northwest mounted.

Even before Japan's attack on Pearl Harbor, nine Japanese submarines had been positioned along the west coast of America. In the weeks following that attack in December 1942, observers reported some 147 submarine sightings between Alaska and California. The I-series B-class submarines measured 105 metres long and had a range of 25,000 kilometres, enabling them to stay at sea for ninety days. On December 20, 1941, Japanese submarine I-17 attacked the oil tanker SS *Emidio* off California's Battery Point Lighthouse, killing five crew members. On February 23, 1942, the same submarine fired twenty-five shells at an oil tank complex near Santa Barbara, California; following that attack, the submarine sank two ships on its way back to Japan. An imminent invasion along the west coast of North America seemed all too possible. To aggravate matters, Japanese submarines launched dummy periscopes made of buoyed bamboo poles with a weight at one end to hold the mock periscope upright. This ruse kept anti-submarine patrols busy on useless missions long after the I-boats had returned to Japan following their initial sorties along the West Coast.

On December 7, 1941, the same day as Pearl Harbor, Japanese forces launched attacks on the Philippines and set off with electrifying speed down the coast of Southeast Asia. They soon occupied much of Eastern

China, including Hong Kong, Thailand, the Dutch East Indies, and Malaya, and within five weeks had reached the Burma/India border. Japanese planes, flying from occupied Port Moresby in New Guinea, bombed Darwin, Australia, and in April 1942 Japanese bombers sank Britain's newest battleship, the *Prince of Wales*, as well as the battle cruiser *Repulse* near Singapore, killing 840 seamen in total. The speed of Japanese advances threw the west coast of North America into an even greater state of alarm, putting the Ucluelet base on active war alert. Patrol flights out of Ucluelet increased, personnel on the base began carrying gas masks and steel helmets at all times, blackout curtains and shades blanketed all windows, and before long Western Air Command had over 200 men guarding the base. Additional Veterans Guard members arrived to set up four gun emplacements around the base.

After war broke out in Europe, the ladies of the Red Cross in Tofino busied themselves knitting for victims of the Blitz in England. The *West Coast Advocate* reported on November 12, 1941, that the Red Cross in Tofino had provided "Forty attractive sweaters for the refugees," to be sent to England. In addition, "twenty nightgowns were handed in by the Japanese ladies, to help out with the local war effort." Shortly after, Japan attacked Pearl Harbor. According to Mary Kimoto, recently wed at St. Columba's Church and raised in Tofino, "the world we knew disappeared forever."

Right after the attack on Pearl Harbor, Johnny Madokoro encountered Jack MacLeod, who told him what had happened. Madokoro called Mr. Nakagawa, president of the Tofino fishing co-op. "'Gee whiz,' I said, 'What are we gonna do?' It never entered my head that it would be real trouble for us, because we were all naturalized Canadians. But I guess there was anti-Japanese feelings building up right from the day the first immigrants came. It was building up, building up and bang!" Some Japanese cut their firewood for the winter as they listened anxiously to the radio, filled with disbelief but hoping life would continue as normal even as "the news got worse and worse."

On a Christmas visit home in 1941, Ronald MacLeod became keenly aware of the increasing tensions in Tofino. His father, Murdo MacLeod, as the local fisheries inspector, "had the unhappy chore of escorting RCMP around when they came in their patrol boat late at night to check Japanese papers." Every fisherman in the area knew Murdo MacLeod; the local Japanese addressed him as "Sensei," a sign of respect. MacLeod did his best to quell the fears of the Japanese, and on one occasion he reprimanded an officer who acted harshly toward them. "He [gave] the officer a dressing down and made the point that even though there was a war, there was no excuse for uncivil behavior. My father made a point of emphasizing what fine community-minded people the Japanese were and that they deserved better treatment. He could get away with this because he was a veteran of WWI...and he was the local Fishery Inspector on whom the officer depended for information."

During his visit, Ronald MacLeod walked down the hill toward the government dock. "Standing there with his hands behind his back stood Mr. Mori. He was staring at a sign that read 'Western Terminus of the Trans-Canada Highway'. This sign had been put there at a time when locals were pushing for a road link to Port Alberni and points east. As I approached Mr. Mori, I could see tears streaming down his cheeks. It was obvious even to an insensitive lad like me that he was very much moved...I can only assume that Mr. Mori had expected to be in Tofino for all the days of his natural life."

Rumours about political plots and treachery spread in the town: of local Japanese boys receiving military training; of Japanese newcomers to the area who had trained in Japan as spies; of naval officers in the pay of Japan infiltrating the fishing co-op; of Morse code messages being transmitted to the Japanese military on secret radio equipment. "There was a feeling that, if Japan invaded the coast, a lot of local Japanese would help them," Walter Guppy later wrote. "Whether this was right or not, I don't know. How can you tell?"

"We heard all the stories," Tommy Kimoto commented. "Like we had gas ready for the Japanese navy to come and load up. I mean, maybe they were using diesel fuel, how would we know?" He tried arguing

In 1942 the Canadian government seized all fishing vessels owned by people of Japanese descent on the west coast of Canada and impounded them at Annieville on the Fraser River. The Royal Canadian Navy and the Fishermen's Reserve seized 1,200 boats in total, many of them shown here. *Image C07293 courtesy of Royal BC Museum, BC Archives*

with local fishermen: "They said there were two or three ex-Japanese naval officers fishing, but I never heard of any. They were all ignorant fishermen, every one. All guys like me."

"How quickly attitudes in Tofino changed," Ronald MacLeod wrote. "Suddenly our friends and neighbours were enemies...We are all guilty to some extent—those who preached hate and those of us who remained silent...My father was an exception. He remained sympathetic and supportive of the Japanese residents of Tofino until he died." Interviewed for *Settling Clayoquot*, Johnny Madokoro described how Murdo MacLeod kept the fishermen informed as tensions and uncertainties rapidly mounted. Then the government ordered the Canadian Navy to seize all 1,200 fishing boats owned and operated by the Japanese in BC coastal waters. In mid-December 1941, all Japanese boats in Tofino had to be rounded up on the waterfront. "I was sort of the spokesman," Johnny Madokoro said, "so when the Coast Guard came in, I had to talk to the commander. He said we would have to take our boats to New Westminster. I said, 'But when do we get them back?'"

"Boy, there was all hell broke loose around here then," commented Trygve Arnet. Most West Coast Japanese fishermen took their own boats over to the mainland, under escort and at their own expense, Johnny Madokoro among them aboard his troller *Crown*. His brother Hiroshi also took part in the sixty-strong flotilla of boats from Tofino and Ucluelet, heading to New Westminster under guard of the navy vessel *Givenchy*. The boats left Tofino Harbour in a long string. Each fish boat had a soldier aboard; the one aboard *Crown*, a prairie boy, was terribly seasick. Foul weather forced the boats to seek shelter for three days at Bamfield; the trip took five gruelling days instead of the usual day and a half. Once at New Westminster, according to Harold Kimoto, "a whole gang came aboard and they took everything that was left on the boat. Some of the men were beaten up. They took batteries, everything. I didn't care because we were leaving the boat anyway, but gee whiz." Tommy Kimoto blamed the "navy guys" for most of the stealing, adding, "They even stole anchor chains."

"We were detailed to the Fraser River," recalled Trygve Arnet, then working with the Fishermen's Reserve out of Victoria. "Our job was to round up all the Japanese owned boats and put them away...It was heartbreaking. I remember seeing Japanese there and, you know, they were crying. There were men in their old World War One uniforms, wearing Scottish tams and the jackets with the brass buttons buttoned up. It was pretty tough. Those who were Canadian-born were the same as you or I, they'd never seen Japan...The Government sold all the boats. There were some good buys there...Oh yes, the Japanese got a pretty dirty end of the stick on that deal."

On January 14, 1942, the Canadian government declared all Japanese in Canada to be enemy aliens, decreeing that all persons of Japanese descent be moved inland at least 160 kilometres from the coast. Although rumours of evacuation had been circulating, Canadian-born Japanese citizens could not believe they would also be included. "Then the lifeboat crew came and took away our telephones," Johnny Madokoro recalled. "But I never heard anybody say we should be in a concentration camp or prison or anything like that. Those guys were old friends. They all said, gosh, it's too bad."

When the evacuation order came, it came fast. "One day, bang, came this Mountie and told us they were going to move everybody," Madokoro recalled. The officer arrived by float plane in Storm Bay. "Mr. Nakagawa and I walked down to the plane. He said 'We have to move you guys tomorrow morning. The *Maquinna* is coming down.' I said, 'We can't do anything in that short time. We have to get rid of our belongings. At least give us 24 hours.'" Within a day, all Japanese residents had packed up their allowance of one bag each, making frantic last-minute plans for keeping their homes and possessions safe in their absence. Complete confusion reigned. Isabel Kimoto lived in Tofino at the time, newly married, nineteen years old, and with a small baby. "I remember police just pushed the door open and took the radio," she says. Tatsuo Sakauye's mother hoped to save her remaining twenty bottles of *sake* until they returned. "She told me to go to the beach away from the tide and bury them," he related in a letter to Dorothy Arnet. "The *sake* will be gone but I am sure the empty bottles are still there." At least two Japanese residents of Tofino had only recently acquired new homes: Harold Kimoto had purchased Ole Jacobsen's home early in 1941, and the Nakagawa family had built a house in Storm Bay that same year.

The day of the evacuation is etched in the memories of those who witnessed it. March 15, 1942. Damp and chilly. All local Japanese assembled at the government wharf in the morning: twenty-seven people from Clayoquot, sixty-eight from Tofino. The *Princess Maquinna* kept them waiting for hours, not arriving till late in the day. Looking out from her window over the crowded wharf, Katie Monks worried about the long wait the Japanese were enduring. "I said 'Harold…there isn't even a public toilet over there and the women and all those kids—could I go over and get some of them and bring them over here and at least give them a cup of tea?' He thought about it quite a while because it was bothering us. He finally said, 'Well, I don't think you should. Just look at it this way: they're leaving but we have to stay.'"

"I sure was heart-broken," Ken Barr, a teenager at the time, recalled. "I remember old Japanese ladies sitting there with the few belongings they could take with them…I remember crying, seeing them go."

"I didn't go down to see them off," said Marguerite Robertson. "There was no way I was going to see people herded aboard a boat like that."

As a schoolgirl, Islay MacLeod watched the confusion in disbelief:

"There were my friends, Emiko and her sister, Sachiko...and there was the Japanese boy who had won a place in my heart forever by helping me with my arithmetic. And there were all the others, milling about on the Government wharf...I had never seen so many Japanese adults and children together at one time. It seemed to my young eyes that half the population of Tofino was leaving. And there we were, the other half...watching, watching watching...These friends who had almost overnight become our enemy...there was no communication between 'us' and our friends." The *Maquinna* arrived, looking "drab and ominous in her wartime grey," and the Japanese embarked with their suitcases and bundles. "Not one of them looked back and not one of them waved goodbye...I never heard their departure discussed—ever—by children in my age group, or by the adults."

Over on Stubbs Island, Joan (Malon) Nicholson, aged eight, pestered her mother with the same question, over and over again. "Why did they take Gloria away?" Joan and Gloria Karatsu, also eight, had been best friends since they could remember. Madeline Malon, Joan's mother, had no answer. Eventually Joan stopped asking, but she never stopped wondering about Gloria. Decades later she tried to track down her long-lost best friend. She managed to contact Ruby (Karatsu) Middeldorp, Gloria's older sister, only to learn Gloria had died several years earlier.

The Canadian government interned a total of 22,000 Japanese during World War II, including a number of veterans from the previous war. During the 1914–18 war, 222 Japanese Canadians had fought for Canada; fifty-four had died, eleven won the Military Medal for bravery.

Older people in Tofino still recall the sharp realities of the war, and the genuine fear of a Japanese attack. "You had to have buckets of sand upstairs in the attic in case of incendiary bombs," Ken Gibson commented when interviewed for *Settling Clayoquot*. "You really knew there was a war going on." Ken still owns a copy of the "Air Raid Drill Precautions" handwritten by his teacher, explaining that the school bell would ring in "three short, sharp soundings" for an air raid drill.

On hearing this, the children were to head into the playground and "seek shelter without delay in the stumps and bushes...each should seek shelter separately; avoid grouping together." At Christie School on Meares Island, the children also carried out air raid and fire drills, and by 1943, according to Indian agent P.B. Ashbridge, all the children there had gas masks. "The threat of attack was so real," wrote Gordon Gibson in *Bull of the Woods*, "that the military authorities insisted a box of groceries be kept in every home in case it became necessary to evacuate the women and children. I carried a gun in my car at all times as did many others." Blackouts became part of everyday life on the coast following Pearl Harbor, with people putting tarpaper over their windows. Enforcing the blackout regulations was the task of the local Home Guard, which sometimes put the men in awkward situations, as Arthur Guppy discovered when he had to row over to Beck Island to tell his curmudgeonly father to douse his lights. Guppy Senior angrily refused, outraged by his son's impudence and by this affront on his liberty.

On June 3, 1942, Japanese planes launched the first of two attacks on the American military installations at Dutch Harbor, Alaska, in the Aleutian Islands, killing 100 servicemen and civilians. This prompted American authorities to send a contingent of fifteen radio-detection specialists to Ucluelet to provide early detection of future attacks with their equipment, a forerunner of modern radar. In June 1942, within a month of the attack on Dutch Harbor, Japanese forces captured and occupied Kiska and Attu, the two most westerly of the US Aleutian Islands.

Japanese submarines returned to the west coast in June 1942. On June 7, 1942, submarine I-26 torpedoed the SS *Coast Trader* sixty-four kilometres off Port Renfrew, and on June 20, I-25 torpedoed the British freighter *Fort Camosun* in Juan de Fuca Strait, only eighty kilometres from Victoria. Then came the attack that electrified the west coast of Vancouver Island and sent shock waves across Canada. On the night of June 20, 1942, submarine I-26 shelled Estevan Point lighthouse at the entrance to Hesquiat Harbour—the first attack on Canadian soil since the war of 1812. Twenty-two people then lived at Estevan Point, one of the biggest installations of its kind on the coast, with its lighthouse, telegraph office, weather centre, and powerful radio that coordinated shipping throughout the North Pacific. As salvoes of enemy fire erupted at Estevan Point, the residents reacted in stunned disbelief.

Robert Lally, the lightkeeper, immediately doused the light. He later claimed to have seen more than one hostile warship offshore, as well as the submarine, and a strange white light emanating from one of the vessels. Radio operator Edward Redford stated that "the submarine surfaced about two miles [three kilometres] offshore and was plainly visible. Shelling commenced at approximately 9.40 p.m. and continued for about forty minutes. The first shells landed on the beach about one hundred yards [90 metres] in front of the lighthouse...The submarine pulled out on the surface and everyone could see her and hear her diesel engines quite clearly." Some twenty-five shells were fired, the noise terrifying as they exploded near the light or whistled overhead toward Hesquiat village.

The telegraph operators stayed at their post, contacting Pacific Command, while everyone else evacuated the light station. According to Redford, "except for a few buildings hit by shell fragments, no damage was caused either to the lighthouse or radio station." Meanwhile, over at Hesquiat village, panic-stricken people ran from their houses and headed to sea in canoes and motorboats to be out of range of the shells flying overhead. The lighthouse tender *Estevan* had anchored off Hesquiat earlier in the evening, unloading supplies that later would be taken along the eight-kilometre wooden road to Estevan Point. Working as fireman on the vessel, Tommy Rae Arthur recalled the intense excitement. When the *Estevan*'s skipper heard that a submarine had been sighted, Tommy reported, "He told me and all of the ship's whole crew that he was going to go full steam ahead, getting to hell out of Hesquiat."

Everyone in the vicinity related slightly different versions of the events of that night. Ada Annie Rae-Arthur (Cougar Annie) came up with one of the more colourful: she claimed to have seen the submarine surface right inside Hesquiat Harbour. "My great old mother [saw] a real submarine out in Hesquiat Harbour," wrote Tommy Rae-Arthur proudly. "So she...made a very special phone call on the old land line phone to Estevan Point to let them know." Later, Cougar Annie said a shell had hit the beach near her place at Boat Basin; this would have been eighteen kilometres off target, given that the submarine was aiming at the lighthouse.

Commodore W.J.R. Beech coolly dismissed some of the more excitable eyewitness accounts of the shelling. His official report to Ottawa stated that "the excitement during the bombardment may have caused those present to see and hear things which did not actually occur." Calmer than most witnesses, Edward Redford commented: "While naturally there was some nervousness, everyone, including the women and children, took the whole incident in their stride, then spent the following day souvenir hunting." Searching for Japanese shell casings provided entertainment for years to come. Shortly after the attack, coastal missionary Harold Peters found one measuring 16 inches long [40 centimetres]; the last shell to be discovered turned up in 1973.

Bjarne Arnet served as a skipper in the Fishermen's Reserve at the time of the Estevan Point shelling. He received orders to take his boat out and intercept the submarine. His weaponry on board at the time amounted to three old Enfields from World War I and a stripped-down Lewis gun. Arnet had been born and raised in Tofino and knew every shoal, rock, and sandbar on the coast, but he decided to take no chances on this mission. "The next thing you know," recalled a fellow Fishermen's Reserve member, "Esquimalt got a message from Bjarne that they were 'aground on a sandbar!' No way was he going after a sub equipped like that!"

The attack on Estevan Point has sparked much debate over the years. Some historians maintain a complex conspiracy lay behind the event, and that ships of the US Navy, not a Japanese submarine, fired on the lighthouse. Writer Douglas Hamilton supports this argument, suggesting the attack was meant to "scare the bejesus out of Canadians and wake up those reluctant Quebecois and other 'lukewarm patriots' to the very real dangers of the deepening war." The attack came at a time when conscription had become a hot topic in Canada; shortly afterward, the pro-conscription lobby prevailed. Also following the attack, according to Frank Rae-Arthur, "War bonds went on sale the next week, and sold out!"

Not even the testimony of the submarine captain, Yokota Minoru, convinced everyone about the nature of the attack. Many years after the war, in 1973, the captain stated: "It was evening when I shelled the area with about 17 shots. Because of the dark, our gun crew had difficulty in making the shots effective. At first the shells were way too short—not reaching the shore. I remember vividly my yelling at them, Raise the gun! Raise the gun! to shoot at a higher angle. Then the shells went too far over the little community toward the hilly area...the people were very quick to put out lights in the buildings but the lighthouse was slow to respond—the last light to turn off."

Only a day after the Estevan Point attack, Japanese submarine I-25 launched a similar attack, firing seventeen shells at the US Army's Fort Stevens near Seaside, Oregon. Most of the shells hit the beach, and residents of nearby Astoria watched the gun flashes far out to sea as the submarine fired its rounds. Within hours, Radio Tokyo boasted that the attacks on both countries had left citizens from Mexico to Alaska "panic stricken," and that Canada was now suffering "attacks by Axis navies from the East as well as the West."

Although submarines continued patrolling West Coast waters, no further shelling or sinking of Allied ships occurred on the coast for the rest of the war. Japan turned its attention to other means of attack. The I-series submarines, though they possessed no radar, each carried a small float plane that could be assembled and dismantled in under an hour. A compressed-air catapult launched the plane from the deck of the submarine, and when it returned a crane lifted it aboard where it could be disassembled and folded up for storage. Powered by a 340-horsepower radial engine capable of doing 150 knots, the little aircraft could remain in the air for five hours and could carry two seventy-six-kilogram bombs. At dawn on September 9, 1942, submarine I-25 launched its small float plane off the coast of Oregon, and the plane dropped two bombs in the forest near Brookings. A forest ranger spotted the resulting fire and managed to douse the flames. Three weeks later, a similar attack occurred, but with no ill effects. Given such incidents, people along the west coast of North America remained edgy.

On October 14, 1942, Coast Construction declared the new Tofino airfield ready for use, and the first military aircraft touched down on the east-west runway. The pilot of this Lysander, a British high-wing airplane primarily used for artillery spotting and army reconnaissance, ignominiously lost control and ran off the end of the runway. The plane had to be trucked to Ucluelet and shipped by barge to Vancouver for repairs. After this inauspicious beginning, the Kittyhawk fighter planes of No. 132 Fighter Squadron landed at Tofino the following day. The air crews found their new home in an appalling state.

Personnel bunked down in the construction camp and looked around in complete dismay. Nothing seemed remotely ready. Only the east-west runway could accept flights; the other two runways were still covered with trees and stumps. When the barracks opened a few days later, they offered little more than a roof, walls, and a floor. "No partitions, no electricity, no water, no toilets, washing facilities or showers. Lavatories were of the outdoor multi-holed variety reached by a trek through mud and construction debris," recalled Leslie Hempsall. "A few wood-burning stoves provided heat, their chimney pipes stuck through the nearest window...At times food was so short that rationing began. To add to the confusion, knives and forks were in short supply and not everyone could eat together at one time." No hangars had been completed, so maintenance personnel and ground crews had to stand by, huddled in tents at the end of the runway during October storms. Tarpaulins over the noses of the fighter aircraft provided minimal protection during maintenance work. In a desperate move to speed up completion of the base, the RCAF assigned airmen to construction duties, never bothering to ask if they knew a hammer from a chisel, nor checking with the unionized construction workers, who promptly threatened to strike.

Adding to the overcrowding and confusion, No. 147 Squadron and its Bolingbroke bombers then landed at Tofino. By the end of 1942, the Tofino base had eight Kittyhawk fighter planes, three single-engine Harvard trainers, two Cessna twin-engine trainers, and three Boling-broke bombers. These Bolingbrokes required a crew of four, carried four 115-kilogram bombs or depth charges, and flew at 290 kilometres per hour. On patrol, the planes undertook twelve-hour flights extending 800 kilometres out into the Pacific, looking for submarines and monitoring shipping activity. Among the pilots of No. 147 Squadron were a number

Aircrew of No. 147 Bomber Reconnaissance Squadron pose in front of one of their Bolingbroke Bombers at the Tofino RCAF Station in 1944. *Image PA162822 courtesy of Library and Archives Canada*

of New Zealanders, who must have wondered how they ended up on this dismally uncomfortable west coast base. One week after arriving, the Kiwis, with their great love of rugby, organized rugby training sessions on the sand of Long Beach in preparation for a forthcoming game against a Navy team.

Thirty officers and 357 non-commissioned officers and men ushered in 1943 at Tofino air base. The place by then boasted six toilets, some electric lights, and running water—if the pipes had not frozen. More army personnel soon arrived to protect the new airfield and the newly installed fuel tanks at Grice Bay, and four army encampments sprang up between Tofino and Ucluelet. To keep the soldiers active and to hone their skills, the army set up a rifle range and survival school on the Long Beach sand dunes, and conducted a rigorous obstacle course. The planes from the Tofino base also used the sand dunes for strafing and to bomb mock targets; as recently as February 2012, police were forced to cordon off a section of the sand dunes while demolition experts dismantled yet another unexploded bomb, one of several discovered over the years.

The Ucluelet-based Sharps and Stranraers continued making their lonely patrols out over the Pacific, rarely spotting anything, but every now and then the station would be on high alert. In early December 1942, Western Air Command warned that an enemy strike force might be off the coast, intent on an attack to mark the anniversary of Pearl Harbor. All aircraft from both Ucluelet and Tofino headed out to sea on patrol; finding nothing, the general state of boredom resumed. One veteran recalled how "there was so little to do, and so many to do it." To boost morale the Tofino station printed its own newspaper, the *Western Flight*, and hosted movie nights. They also welcomed the Kitsilano Boys Band, and Barney Potts and his dance band, who made their way over from Vancouver. Sports and clubs of every description also kept the men occupied during their non-working hours. By the end of 1943, nine Canso and two Catalina aircraft had replaced the obsolete Sharks and Stranraers at Ucluelet.

With no liquor outlet in Tofino during the war, the beer parlour at Clayoquot became a popular destination for military personnel and construction workers keen to escape the monotony and discomfort of life at the base. Walter Dawley did not witness these wartime boom years; he had left the area around 1937, having stubbornly remained at Clayoquot as long as he possibly could, and he died in Victoria in 1944. He passed his business on to his daughter Madeline and her husband, Pierre Malon. At some point following their marriage in 1933, he gave all of Stubbs Island to them for the sum of one dollar, and they moved there to help run the place. Madeline Malon never much liked living at Clayoquot, constantly waiting on others, emptying the "thunder mugs" (chamber pots) in the hotel bedrooms, and dealing with the demands of the bar at the hotel. In 1942, following the Japanese evacuation, the Malons sold the entire island to Betty Farmer and her brother Bill White.

Born in England and raised in Victoria, Betty Farmer came to the west coast in 1941 following the death of her husband, at the suggestion of her brother Bill, then living at Clayoquot and working for Pierre

Malon. Betty began cooking for the Clayoquot Hotel, and she fell in love with the whole setup on the island, then comprising five cottages, beer parlour, hotel, and store—not to mention the school and the jail, still standing. Along with Bill and his wife, Ruth, Betty ran the place. Petite, strong-minded, and extremely capable, she became the heart and soul of Clayoquot for the following twenty-two years.

Entirely undaunted by the challenges of running the beer parlour, during the war years Betty Farmer became famous for her ability to control the large numbers of men who came to drink, sometimes too much, at Clayoquot. If an unruly customer refused to leave when asked, she would simply stop serving that table, or even the entire room, until the other customers had removed the troublemaker. "Throw that man out, or make him sit on the porch, or no drinks for anyone." According to American biologist Ed Ricketts, who first visited Clayoquot in 1945, "many were sent to sober up under the rhododendrons before being allowed back in."

Dr. Howard McDiarmid came to know Bill White well in later years, and his memoirs recount Bill's story of one particularly memorable weekend during the war at the Clayoquot Hotel. "One Labour Day weekend when the miners were busy, the loggers were cutting spruce for Mosquito bombers, and there was a huge crew building...[what became] the Tofino airport. The workers had all downed tools for the long weekend and headed for Clayoquot, quickly overwhelming the tiny beer parlour. The party flowed out to the adjacent lawns, beach and dock, continuing through Saturday, Sunday and into Monday, at which point the RCMP patrol boat arrived at the dock. Bill came down to meet [the boat] and the corporal told him, 'All right, Bill, shut her down.' To which Bill replied, 'No, you shut her down. You've got the gun!'"

A number of the wives and families of air force and army personnel came to visit for varying periods of time, offering a welcome break for the men posted to the grim, muddy isolation of RCAF Tofino. With no married quarters on site, the cabins at Singing Sands and Camp Maquinna on Long Beach often hosted visiting families, charging around fifteen dollars per month. Others used the collection of cabins earlier occupied by construction crews, some of which had been moved to Schooner Cove. Officially dubbed Pacific Heights, this scrappy hamlet, with no electricity or running water, became known as "Dogpatch," after the hillbilly town in the comic strip *L'il Abner*. Some wives and families staying for longer periods rented rooms in the town.

When Catharine Whyte's husband, Peter, was posted to Tofino air base as a photo technician, he found two rooms for them to rent in Mrs. Ragnhild Ericksen's home. Catharine wrote to her mother every day about her life in Tofino. She vividly described walking in the pouring rain to meet the *Princess Norah*, battling with the oil stove, chasing cows out of the yard, and her daily treks with the "WC bucket" to dump it in the sea. The Ericksen home consisted of "six rooms and two bathrooms and four families...and yet we are so comfortable and cozy." The other renters in the house included air force families and a schoolteacher. Peter Whyte travelled back and forth to the base every day, with Sundays off and "a 48 once a month." Both Catharine and Peter Whyte had close associations with the art world and painted throughout their lives. They founded the Whyte Museum of the Canadian Rockies in Banff, Alberta, where they made their home after the war.

The presence of the RCAF base at Long Beach had an immediate impact on Tofino. Even though an "arm's length" policy officially prevailed between the town and the base, the presence of hundreds of young men in the area, and their planes flying overhead continually, brought a huge amount of excitement to the town. The people of Tofino went out of their way to make the military men feel welcome when they came to town, hosting dinners in their homes, holding Red Cross fundraising dances and whist drives at the Legion Hall, and playing various sports with members of the forces. Local girls enjoyed the frequent dances at the air base, on the strict understanding that no local women could spend a night there.

"It was a great time for the ladies," Ken Gibson commented, recalling how the pilots went out of their way to court local girls. "Marg Sloman was about eighteen or nineteen at the time and she lived next door to the school. The Kittyhawk pilots would fly over her house and do 'chimney sweeps' which involved screaming down from a great height and pulling out at roof level. When the pilots started this air show, the teacher couldn't get a word in edgeways and we would all be at the windows watching the show. The squadron leader who organized the air show would tell Marg at the next dance at the base how he had led his squadron in serenading her."

With his store now powered by a diesel generator, "thus doing away with Coleman gasoline lighting or Aladdin kerosene lamps," and with a modern refrigeration unit, Sid Elkington felt well-equipped to meet the demands of the young air force men and their wives. He did run into unforeseen challenges, though. "With so many young marrieds," he wrote in his memoirs, "we got requests in the store for such pre- viously unheard of things as condoms. I had then to delicately advise local young girls working for us what they were, so that they might not be embarrassed." Sid also noted the occasional presence of attractive, well-dressed women who arrived on the steamer and passed through his store; he learned from the local constable that these were ladies "of ill repute...planning to reap a bonanza...with so many unattached young men there." Several of the air force wives found part-time work at Elkington's store on the weekends, "when we were tremendously and excitingly busy."

Wartime on the West Coast inevitably gave rise to mishaps and snafus. In July 1943, a fighter aircraft flying over the islands in Tofino Harbour experienced engine trouble; after spluttering and banging, the motor quit entirely. The pilot bailed out by parachute, landing in a tree near Lemmens Inlet, and the plane crashed on the far side of Meares Island. When two Opitsat men found the pilot swinging from the branches, with the help of the lifeboat crew they climbed up and lowered him to the ground with ropes, returning up the tree to re- trieve the parachute. Long-time coxswain Alex MacLeod arranged for a "medical plane" to come to the scene, and reported that the rescue had taken four hours. Grateful for the help of his Tla-o-qui-aht rescuers, the pilot gave them his gun and flare gun. A few weeks later, when his superiors learned that he had given away air force equipment, they made him go back to retrieve his gifts.

Six months later, on December 18, 1943, personnel at the top-secret installation at Ferrer Point, a radio-detection station near Nootka, radioed headquarters that they were under attack, with shells exploding nearby. Coal Harbour and Tofino RCAF stations immediately launched aircraft; they located two small fishing boats in the vicinity but found no sign of an invasion fleet. Intelligence later revealed that the *Princess Maquinna*, on one of her usual runs up the coast and entirely unaware of the installation at Ferrer Point, had chosen to do some gunnery practice, firing off a number of 5.5-kilogram shells from the lone gun mounted on her foredeck.

On another occasion, Ruth White and Betty Farmer paddled from Clayoquot over to Vargas Island for a picnic. As they sat contentedly picnicking on an isolated beach, a fighter aircraft suddenly zoomed in low over the trees and began machine-gunning the beach. "We dove for cover under a huge log. We couldn't tell where the plane was from—it all took place in seconds—then we heard it again, machine gunning in the distance. From then on we stayed close to the bush, just in case the plane should come back, which thank goodness it didn't." The attacker was probably a bored pilot having a bit of gunnery practice on what he thought was a deserted beach.

In May 1943, US forces advanced on the Alaskan island of Attu and reclaimed it from the Japanese, who had taken it in June 1942. After fierce fighting the Japanese forces surrendered: the US suffered 3,929 casualties, with 549 killed. Three months later, after bombing the island relentlessly, a combined Canadian and American force of 35,000 succeeded in recapturing the island of Kiska, with a loss of twenty-five Americans and three Canadians. Securing these islands dramatically reduced the Japanese threat to North America, but forces along the West Coast continued to remain vigilant.

One further Japanese threat materialized along the coast early in 1945, when Japan launched its "Windship Weapon." Knowing that the prevailing winds (later termed the jet stream) flow eastward across the Pacific Ocean from Japan to North America, the Japanese built large balloons to carry incendiary devices to the West Coast, hoping to ignite massive forest fires. Ten metres in diameter and twenty metres in height, each hydrogen-filled balloon carried four incendiary bombs weighing a total of ninety kilograms. The balloons could climb up to 10,000 metres and took three days to reach North America, their altitude maintained by an altimeter-driven control system. At the end of the calculated period of travel, the bombs aboard dropped one at a time.

Only about 1,000 fire balloons of the 9,300 launched reached North America, travelling as far east as Detroit, Michigan; as far south as the California/Mexican border; and as far north as Alaska. Few forest fires resulted, but a woman and five children on a church picnic near Bly, Oregon, died when they discovered one of the devices, and the bomb exploded. Most of the balloons landed in remote areas, and three were shot down by the RCAF. In May 1945, American bombers destroyed two of Japan's balloon factories, forcing an end to this scheme. To this day, loggers and hikers continue to find remnants of these balloons.

In order to relieve crews in remote locations who had been on active service for extended periods, the RCAF made a practice of rotating squadrons through its various stations. Those on remote bases went to more populated settings, which perhaps saved the sanity of many serving at the Tofino airbase, unaffectionately known as "Mudville." In January 1943, No. 4 Bomber Reconnaissance Squadron at Ucluelet switched with No. 120 from Coal Harbour. On October 31, 1944, No. 4 Squadron moved to Tofino; less than a month later, on November 25, 1944, it was disbanded as the Japanese threat to the coast receded. On July 1, 1943, No. 132 Fighter Squadron flew its Kittyhawks to Boundary Bay, and No. 133 Fighter Squadron flew its Hurricanes to Tofino. Nine months later, the two squadrons switched places again. On March 12, 1944, No. 115 Bomber Reconnaissance Squadron from Patricia Bay flew its fifteen Venturas to Tofino, replacing No. 147 Squadron, which officially ceased to exist on August 23, 1944. Over 2,000 air force servicemen and eighty member of the Women's Division served at the Ucluelet and Tofino bases during World War II. In addition, some 8,000 army personnel served at the two air bases during the war, as well as many hundreds of construction workers. In their thousands of hours in the air, the aircrews and aircraft based at Ucluelet and Tofino never fired a shot in anger, or sank any enemy submarines. On September 1, 1944, both RCAF Ucluelet and RCAF Tofino became inactive. Left with no aircraft and a complement of only 186 personnel, the Tofino base became a signals unit, used by planes from other bases for practice landings and takeoffs and for flight training

With the war virtually over, on the afternoon of February 10, 1945, RCAF Canso #11007 landed at Tofino. Pilot Ronnie Scholes wanted to do some landings and takeoffs to test repairs on the aircraft's port engine. Crew members went to Ucluelet to pick up some parts, and after they spent time in the mess at the Tofino base, the Canso took off to return to Coal Harbour at about 11 p.m. with twelve people, four 115-kilogram depth charges, and a full load of fuel on board.

Shortly after takeoff, the port engine died and Scholes tried to turn back to the Tofino airfield. With the plane quickly losing altitude, he put it into a full stall to slow down, then "pancaked" it into the tops of the trees on the southern slope of Radar Hill. Miraculously, all twelve aboard survived. Scholes suffered a fractured forehead and broken nose; others had only minor bumps and bruises. No sooner had the plane hit the ground than a broken fuel line in the port engine began spewing fuel, which caught fire. One of the survivors doused the flames as the others scrambled to get away from the crash. The survivors made themselves as comfortable as possible and waited. When the plane failed to arrive at Coal Harbour, a search plane took off from Tofino and soon spotted the wreckage, and ground parties rescued the survivors. Later RCAF personnel from Tofino returned to the crash site, retrieved the radios and machine guns and exploded the depth charges near the downed plane.

At the end of the war, along with the two runways and the nearby wreckage of the Canso, some fifty-odd buildings remained at the Tofino air base as visible reminders of the military presence there, including two hangars, a 128-bed hospital, a two-chair dental clinic, a recreation hall, a canteen, a thirteen-bay garage, barracks, a diesel power plant, and mess halls. The military also left nine enormous 113,650-litre fuel tanks at the head of Grice Bay. Too big to remove, authorities fenced them off and all but forgot about them until 1993, when remediation crews took two weeks to safely remove what was left of the very old fuel.

Over the years, local people found many uses for various buildings at the air base, moving some to new locations; dismantling others and integrating them, or their lumber, into different structures. The firehall, the Schooner Restaurant, and the Maquinna Hotel in Tofino all made use of military buildings, as did the original St. Francis of Assisi church. The local curling club created an ice surface in one of the disused hangers and used it well into the 1960s. Today only four or five of the original buildings still stand at Tofino Airport.

Commercial flights began using the airport following the war, sporadically at first, increasing over time. The year 2010 saw the construction of a new terminal building with a twenty-five-seat waiting room to handle daily scheduled flights to and from Vancouver and Seattle. Yet however much traffic or excitement or improvement Tofino Airport may see in the future, it seems unlikely anything will ever rival the events here during World War II, or will match the heightened atmosphere that affected the whole area at that time.

Main Street in Tofino with an array of vehicles, the Community Hall on the right. This photo was taken at the time of a boat launch at Wingen's shipyard in the late 1940s, hence the crowded street. The shipyard is to the left and the Model A Ford truck with one headlight belonged to Bob Wingen. *Anthony Guppy photo, courtesy of Carol and Robert Windley*

Chapter 18:

Peacetime

DISEMBARKING FROM THE *PRINCESS MAQUINNA* at Clayoquot in June 1945, Ed Ricketts looked around at "a lovely place of green gold hummingbirds, I never saw so many in my life before, and thrushes always singing, and rhododendrons in bloom until you can't see over them, and white seagulls flying by the black mountains. I can't think of a prettier or better place to work and rest." Following "the unpleasantness of wartime travel" up the coast from California, on ships still painted battleship grey, Ricketts based himself at Clayoquot for the following five weeks. A pioneer ecologist and marine biologist, Ricketts came from Monterey, California, where he ran Pacific Biological Laboratories on the street later known as Cannery Row, made famous by his close friend, novelist John Steinbeck, who also lived in Monterey. Ricketts had a profound influence on Steinbeck, encouraging in him a deeper understanding of the human factors causing ecological crises of the time, including the dust bowl of the 1930s, powerfully described in Steinbeck's *Grapes of Wrath*, and the overfishing of sardines off California, a subject central to Steinbeck's *Cannery Row*.

Ricketts came to Clayoquot to study marine life, collecting specimens and attempting to map what he termed a "biological picture" in and around Clayoquot Sound. He planned to include his findings in a second edition of his well-known book *Between Pacific Tides*, a study of Pacific Coast marine life. During the time he and his common-law wife, Toni, spent at Clayoquot, Ricketts recorded his keen observations in his diary, writing of the exciting varieties of marine life, and also providing vivid details of the social life he encountered. The "peppy and drunken country dances at Tofino" came in for comment, as did the fluency of Father Mulvihill, then principal of Christie School, when he spoke the Nuu-chah-nulth language to schoolchildren there, and the unspoken racial protocols. Ricketts noted that "visiting of unauthorized whites at these Indian villages isn't customary and I believe it's actually prohibited."

Ricketts stayed at Clayoquot as a guest of Betty Farmer for most of his time on the west coast, living with Toni in the apartment above the old store. Betty, along with her brother and sister-in-law, Bill and Ruth White, remained happily in charge of the Clayoquot Hotel, store, and post office; the place now had cows, chickens, guinea fowl, and a pig to clear the land. Betty was establishing a remarkable garden, and the hotel had a reputation for serving excellent meals. Bill White served as Clayoquot's postmaster until he and Ruth moved into Tofino in 1947, when Betty took over as postmistress, holding the position until 1964. In her early years, mail still went out on the *Princess Maquinna*. When the coastal steamships no longer called, she did three mail runs a week to Tofino in her boat. From there letters went to Ucluelet by car and then by boat to Alberni. During her many years on the island, Betty commanded both respect and admiration, described in an article by Mildred Jeffrey as a "wonderful little character...strong as a man [she] runs boats, a tractor, acts as fisherman-hunter guide... day or night she is on hand ready to serve her hotel guests, visiting fishermen, hunters." In 1949, Betty's widowed sister Jo Brydges joined her at Clayoquot, and they operated the place together, both sharing a passion for gardening. Freddy Thornberg of Ahousat, youngest son of pioneer trader Fred Thornberg, became their faithful jack of all trades, working closely alongside them for many years.

In the decade after Ed Ricketts visited the area, Clayoquot's beer parlour began to face competition. For a number of years the Tofino Legion arranged a temporary liquor licence once a month to host "The Smoker," an evening when alcohol was served, but in 1954 a licensed bar finally opened there. In 1955 the Tofino Chamber of Commerce (formerly the Board of Trade) wrote to the provincial Liquor Control Board about the "clear necessity" of a provincial liquor store in Tofino. The wait proved long, for the liquor store did not open in Tofino until the mid-1970s. A beer parlour started up in Ucluelet in the 1950s, and by 1959 the new Maquinna Hotel in Tofino opened, with its own beer parlour and a cocktail lounge. Yet despite this competition, the Clay-oquot establishment continued to thrive; in 1954 the hotel expanded, with a room for dancing added, and the beer parlour enlarged.

Famous for her sharp tongue and generous spirit, Betty Farmer kept the tradition of Clayoquot Days alive during her years on Stubbs Island, and she also established an enduring legacy there and elsewhere through her love of gardening. She planted many species of trees, shrubs, and flowers at Clayoquot, but above all, as Ed Ricketts immediately noticed, she planted rhododendrons. In 1963, Mildred Jeffrey reported some 130 varieties of rhododendrons growing on Stubbs Island, the damp and mild climate being ideal for this plant. Many of Betty's rhodos still bloom around the Tofino area, for she shared plants liberally. Because of her encouragement, Ken Gibson took up growing rhododendrons in Tofino in the 1960s; since then his expansive garden has become widely famed and now features nearly 1,000 varieties and some 2,500 shrubs. Responsible for officially naming a dark red rhododendron "Clayoquot Warrior," Ken named another "Brianna," and all over Vancouver Island a species form *(R. praestans)* is known as "Dot Gibson," for his late wife. Renowned among rhododendron growers in western North America, particularly for promoting tender *maddenii* and broad leaf species, Ken Gibson is one of only a handful of Canadians to receive a silver medal from the American Rhododendron Society. Every year he welcomes hundreds of visitors to his "rhodo heaven," ablaze with colour, near downtown Tofino.

Long before this, outstanding rhododendrons were growing on the west coast in the garden of the genial Scottish pioneer George Fraser, in Ucluelet. An experienced horticulturalist, Fraser settled there in 1894, gradually establishing his extensive nursery garden that would eventually supply the Empress Hotel in Victoria with plants and flowers. Fraser had worked in many well-known parks and gardens, including the newly created Beacon Hill Park in Victoria, before settling at Ucluelet. Renowned as a botanical hybridizer, his garden became a favourite destination for the fledgling tourist traffic on the west coast. Captain Gillam of the *Princess Maquinna* often delayed the steamer's departure from Ucluelet to allow tourists time to visit Fraser's garden, and on the *Princess Norah*'s inaugural run in 1929, Governor-General Willingdon and his wife also visited the garden. No one returned to the steamer without flowers, particularly rhododendrons. By the time he died in 1944, Fraser had gained international recognition for his work. He sent pollen of his rhodos to Kew Gardens and to growers in England, America, and New Zealand. Fraser's hybrids, including the one named after him, *R. fraserii*, flourish in many countries, and plants from his garden appear in a number of places on the west coast, including Cougar Annie's garden in Hesquiat Harbour. Over at Clayoquot, "bright with hummingbirds" in the early summer, many rhododendrons share this coastal lineage.

To the eye of outsider Ed Ricketts in June 1945, despite the brilliance of flowers and birds and the generous welcome he received, Clayoquot at first seemed a bit ramshackle. He noted "lots of tumbledown buildings by the wharf, the remains of a blacksmith shop...signs of the Japanese fishing village still in place," and he heard how the *Princess Maquinna* no longer always stopped at Clayoquot; in bad weather, especially in the winter, she sometimes bypassed this former coastal hub completely. But the place surprised Ricketts, the comfortable apartment complete with generator-powered electricity and running water, the delicious meals, the lively life of the hotel bar. He had a keen eye for the unexpected, noting the collection of Burmese art at the hotel, including a giant Buddha, acquired by Betty Farmer's late husband, who had been a magistrate in Burma; the "fantastic library" with titles on communism, labour unions, socialism, and Russian literature; a young aboriginal girl doing chores, effortlessly singing the Gregorian *Kyrie* from the *Missa de Angelis* as she worked around the hotel, then paddling home to Opitsat in her canoe.

Besides collecting samples of marine life from the beaches on Stubbs Island, Ricketts also explored Round Island and Deadman's Island, as well as visiting Vargas on Dominion Day 1945. "Walked 3 miles along the trail. I should say through the trail since sometimes we were literally tunneling under the underbrush, and we had to crawl on our bellies." Built by the long-departed Vargas settlers, the sturdy plank trail across the island, with its footbridge over the marshy interior, had been all but obliterated. Later that evening, Ricketts and Toni enjoyed "a swinging dance, complete with brass band, at the Royal Canadian Airforce base." Four days later they hitched a ride in a jeep heading down Long Beach, collecting specimens en route to Ucluelet, where they joined an impromptu Independence Day celebration at the seaplane base. "I don't know where the army gets all its liquor under rationing," mused Ricketts. Fond of a drink, he often made his own concoctions in his lab on Cannery Row, and he found the west coast decidedly odd concerning alcohol. "On the whole west coast of Vancouver Island a shore line of at least a thousand miles [1,600 kilometres], there are only two liquor stores and three pubs. At the pubs you can only get beer." At the Clayoquot beer parlour he noted how "on Saturday nights people come in from 30-40 mile [48- to 64-kilometre] boat trips," and how wartime restrictions allowed patrons to buy only one case of beer to go. But despite these apparent shortages, no one wanting a drink went thirsty. Plenty of homebrew could be found in town, and as Jacqui Hansen realized when she arrived in Tofino in the early 1950s, "there were always bootleggers, someone would get a case in and sell bottles to friends."

At evening gatherings over a few drinks, Ricketts regaled the Whites, Betty Farmer, and others with stories of Monterey and of John Steinbeck, whose *Cannery Row* had just been published, to great acclaim. In that novel, Steinbeck based his leading character, "Doc," on Ed Ricketts, and even 2,400 kilometres away at Clayoquot, the fame of this character dogged Ricketts. Yet later on, recalling his time with them, Ruth White remembered Ricketts not as the larger-than-life "Doc" but as an astute and dedicated collector, able to discern imperceptible creatures in seemingly empty tidal pools. "He would see things in tide pools where I would see nothing," she stated. "One time he found these little transparent fish and all you could see were two little black dots for the eyes." Ricketts and Toni collected hundreds of marine specimens during their time at Clayoquot, carefully preserving them in their makeshift lab above the old store. Five weeks after they arrived, after a final party, Ricketts and Toni departed on the *Maquinna*. Bill White recalled in a letter: "After the Ricketts departure, we all got gloriously drunk...Betty went to milk the cow and passed out, hanging onto its tail."

A year later, Ricketts and Toni, accompanied by his son Ed Jr., returned to Clayoquot aboard the *Princess Norah*, as the *Maquinna* was having her wartime grey painted over. They stayed for a month, roaming the intertidal zones as before, collecting specimens, constantly amazed by the immense variety of species. Describing a reef off Wickaninnish Island, spangled with thousands of starfish of every imaginable colour, Ricketts wrote: "There are more species here, and incomparably more individuals too, than anywhere else in the world." They headed north to continue collecting in Haida Gwaii and in Alaska, and on their return they saw the destruction caused by the June 23, 1946, earthquake. Measuring 7.3 on the Richter scale, this had been "one of the most severe which has been recorded in Canada within historic times," according to the Seismological Division of the Dominion Observatory in Ottawa. On Stubbs Island, many chimneys had been knocked down, windows smashed, and most of Betty Farmer's dishes broken. Ricketts's sample bottles, with their specimens preserved in alcohol, mostly remained intact.

True to form, Ricketts threw another farewell party when they left on July 20, 1946, this time aboard the *Princess Maquinna*, attended not only by his Stubbs Island friends but also by Captain MacKinnon, who kept the ship tied up in Tofino for an extra half hour while he continued partying. "Everyone including Capt. MacKinnon got quite swacko," wrote Ricketts. When the ship finally got underway, the officer on duty, "so young and gold braid and trim and disapproving," disputed with the captain exactly where they were in the fog that enshrouded the ship once they left Tofino, and about when and where to change course. "And of course it worked as you'd suppose. The drunken Capt., by this time cold sober, was right, and the precise and sober younger office was minutes and a half a mile off. The Capt. was on the nose."

Ricketts planned a return trip to Clayoquot in the summer of 1948, accompanied by Steinbeck, so the two of them could work on a new book, *The Outer Shore*. A week before departing, Ricketts's car collided with a train at a railway crossing in Monterey. Ricketts died a few days later. Bill and Ruth White heard the news on the radio, shocked by the death of the charismatic man they had expected to see within days, who once said his "idea of heaven was to be out on the reef near [Lennard Island] on the west coast at low tide when the sun was rising and marine life was just teeming."

The teeming life of Clayoquot Sound has attracted countless scientists and researchers both before and since Ricketts's day. Initially they came as collectors, trying to gather, preserve, mount, and catalogue every specimen they could find, marine life, insects, birds, and mammals, working to establish an inventory of the amazingly rich biodiversity of Clayoquot Sound. Professor George Spencer of the University of BC spent a summer at Tofino in the mid-1920s, boarding with Dorothy Abraham and her husband. He set up a laboratory in a shed where he dissected and bottled his specimens, much to the fascination of his landlady, who greatly enjoyed the "wonderful collection of crabs and every kind of marine life, every bug and beetle that crept upon the earth at Tofino: we all became biologists that summer!" In 1931, as a very young man, Ian McTaggart-Cowan arrived for his first visit to the area, ranging far and wide as he collected small mammals and birds. This work involved shooting and trapping them, then skinning, cleaning, drying, and stuffing the creatures at makeshift field camps. McTaggart-Cowan went on to a distinguished career as a professor at UBC, gaining international recognition for his work as a wildlife biologist and conservationist, and later awarded both the Order of Canada and the Order of BC. He worked with a wide range of environmental organizations over the years, inspiring many scientists and naturalists who followed in his wake, including Charles Guiguet. For two summers in the early 1960s, Guiguet came to Clayoquot working as a field biologist for the National Museum of Canada. A specialist in birds and small mammals, he focused on collecting varieties of mice, becoming known locally as the "mouse man." His wife, Muriel, and his children accompanied him, camping on Stubbs Island. "We had 5 tents: the boys' tent, our tent, the girls' tent, and then a skinning tent," Muriel recalled in an interview with Briony Penn. "Charles would make up the birds, and skulls had to be dried. So there was a little packet of skulls hanging above the stove." Like his mentor Ian McTaggart-Cowan, Guiguet visited Cleland Island, enthralled by the many varieties of marine life, birds, and small mammals there. On his recommendation, and with the active involvement in later years of Bristol Foster of the BC Provincial Museum, Cleland Island became the first ecological reserve in BC in 1971.

In postwar Tofino, dances took place every month at the Legion, and twice a month at the Community Hall, with live music provided by Walter Arnet and Sam Craig on violin and piano, and other musicians and dancers often coming up from Ucluelet to join the lively whirl. "We danced polka, schottische, foxtrot, waltzes," remembered Jacqui Hansen. "Everyone went." And thanks to Les Busswood, ex-RCAF, now living in Tofino with his wife, "we have a permanent movie in town!" Islay MacLeod wrote excitedly for the *West Coast Advocate* in January 1946. Delighted that the Busswoods had chosen Tofino as "a home for their movie projector," she described the first show in the Community Hall, attracting "swarms of 'first-nighters'" to a Bob Hope movie. Les Busswood's van, emblazoned with *L.D. Busswood, Mobile Movies, Tofino - Ucluelet*, travelled the region showing films in community halls, First Nations villages, and logging camps.

The immediate postwar years found Sid Elkington and other store-keepers in Tofino regretting the departure of RCAF personnel from the area. Trade decreased considerably following the bustling days of the war, with so many people coming and going from the air base. Yet though business slowed, Tofino's population increased slightly, for a number of discharged air force personnel and workers decided to settle there, some building homes right in the town. Many practical improvements also resulted. "Tofino benefited by being connected to the large airport electric power generating plant, with the capacity of supplying power and light for the whole district," wrote Elkington in his memoirs, relieved he no longer had to maintain and produce his own power from a generator. Two street lights appeared in the town in

1947, provided by Hilmar Wingen; not long afterward, lights appeared on the government wharf, and a long-awaited water system for the village seemed about to become a reality, having been approved by the village council. "Also, the old telegraph service was replaced," Elkington reported, "with an adequate telephone service, connected to the cities."

In April 1947, after seventeen years in Tofino, Sid Elkington sold his store to the Kyuquot Trollers' Co-operative Association. Some Tofino fishermen already belonged to this co-op, for it had a fish-buying camp in town. Now the co-op wanted to add Elkington's store to its chain of fish camps and stores stretching along the coast from Barkley Sound to Quatsino Sound. Elkington left Tofino and started working for the co-op as purchasing agent and stores manager in Victoria. The Kyuquot Trollers' Co-operative continued under that name for a few years before becoming the Tofino Consumers Co-op. It remained at its original site at the head of the government dock until 1964, when it moved to a new building up the hill on First Street, now the site of the Co-op Hardware Store. Towler and Mitchell's store also changed hands after the war, becoming Sinclair and Boyd's, and later the Tofino Fishing and Trading Co. Even the Tofino Hotel changed hands, in July 1949 becoming the Tofino Lodge under its new owner, Bud Fillies, who installed a soda fountain and a freezer unit, making his café the first on the coast to serve ice cream sodas. "He also plans to cater private parties and banquets with meals served by candle light," announced the *West Coast Advocate*. "His wife will operate a beauty parlor in the same building."

Having expanded the T.H. Wingen Shipyard considerably during the war, Hilmar Wingen continued to build and launch boats. An enthusiastic crowd attended the 1946 launch of the twelve-metre troller *Cash-in*, built for Mickey Cashin of Bamfield. In April 1948, *Hillier Queen* skidded down the ways and entered the water, built for George Hillier of Ucluelet in just three months. She was "48 ft [14.6 metres] long, 13 and a half [4 metres] beam, 30 tons. 6 cylinder Murphy Diesel, 135 horsepower. With automatic controls, 75 watt radio telephone, and a 'Bendix Sounding Unit' for all types of fishing, first trip being for halibut." Two tugs and one other troller emerged from the shipyard in

1948–49. In 1950 Wingen built the crab boat *Jo-Anne* for Pierre Malon and Bill White, along with two other vessels, and 1952 saw the launch of the fourteen-metre tug *Dog Star,* with its "360 hp Cummings Diesel, first of its kind to be used on a marine installation." In 1950, "another new progress for Tofino was the opening of the Standard Oil station, operated by H. Wingen. The station is situated near the Tofino Marine Service with a float and wharf for the convenience of all boats." The whistle marking the beginning and end of the workday at Wingen's, at 9 a.m. and 5 p.m., continued to sound until 1955, when boat building ceased and the business diversified. The shipbuilding records of the company, dating back to 1918, reveal twenty-seven new vessels built there, including six tugs (two for the Gibson brothers), six boats rebuilt from the waterline up, and six other substantial rebuilds. The Wingens' various operations over the years had immense influence in Tofino, creating steady employment and serving as a cornerstone of the local economy well into the 1970s.

A new enterprise started up in Tofino shortly after the war, when Pierre Malon and William Lornie built a crab cannery at Armitage Point, where the Malons had bought property. Lornie originally tried to start this cannery at Clayoquot, where he worked for some years, but the idea proved unworkable there. At Armitage Point, Pierre Malon and Bill Bond built the cannery, and within its first year the Tofino Packing Company employed three workers from Opitsat to pick and can the crab. Bill White moved from Clayoquot into Tofino in 1947 and became Pierre Malon's partner in the crabbing business. By this time the Malons had moved into their new home near the cannery; Joan (Malon) Nicholson remembered the excitement of seeing her family's future home, consisting of two sections of the former RCAF hospital, floating down the inlet on a scow toward their property.

A *Daily Colonist* article by George Nicholson in February 1956 described the cannery, which then operated two boats and offered year-round employment for a dozen men, and part-time work "for the same number of local housewives...and...several salmon fishermen during the off-season." The business by this stage had expanded, occasionally canning salmon and clams as well as crab; the salmon came from

Ben Hellesen's fish-buying plant in Tofino when he had surplus fish. In the following few years the cannery took on more employees and built larger facilities, as well as extending the dock, still known locally as the "crab dock." A larger boat, the 11.5-metre *Stubbs Island*, built in Nova Scotia and designed along the lines of lobster-fishing vessels, arrived on the scene to boost production. Over its years of operation, many employees at the cannery came from Opitsat, although plenty of Tofino people also found employment there, including many women. The cannery closed in 1964 when Pierre Malon decided to sell the property and move away. Betty Farmer, by that time ready to leave Stubbs Island, bought his property and moved to Armitage Point with her sister, Jo Brydges. With Freddy Thornberg helping, they brought with them many plants from Stubbs Island, digging up a number of their special rhododendrons, some 3.5 metres high. Freddy paddled the plants from Clayoquot to Tofino in his canoe, their foliage trailing through the water. They rinsed them off with a garden hose, and every rhododendron survived.

The aftermath of war saw heated political arguments in many coastal locations in British Columbia about whether the thousands of interned Japanese residents should return to their former lives on the coast. Ed Ricketts wryly noted "a fine political fight going on" in the 1945 federal election: "one candidacy was announced on the bald platform 'We don't want the Japs in here—ever.' In the Comox–Alberni constituency encompassing Tofino and Ucluelet, A.W. Neill had served as MP for six consecutive terms, voicing his virulent opposition to Japanese immigration and to the presence of Japanese fishermen in British Columbia since 1921. In 1945, Jack Gibson succeeded Neill as MP, promoting the policy of repatriating all displaced Japanese back to Japan. Many leading citizens of Tofino favoured this policy, clearly stating they did not want any Japanese returning to the village. The first indication of this appears in the minutes of the Tofino Board of Trade in September 1942. At a meeting attended by A.W. Neill,

"C.A. Elkington called Attention to the Japanese Question and strongly urged the repatriation of all of Japanese origin." Three years later, as the war drew to a close, the Tofino Board of Trade sent a telegram to Ottawa, dated December 13, 1945. Signed simply "Tofino Board of Trade," and addressed to J.L. Gibson MP, House of Commons, Ottawa, it reads: "We wish to again vigorously protest the expected return of persons of Japanese origin to the West Coast and feel we should warn of likely trouble from unanimously determined Canadians against such policy." A year later, on December 12, 1946, the Board of Trade's minutes state: "A discussion was held on the Japanese question and it was moved by T.H. Wingen and seconded by H. Sloman that we wire and vigorously protest the return of persons of Japanese origin to the West Coast and feel that a warning of possible danger should be voiced as people in these parts are determined on this matter."

Early in 1947, the Tofino commissioners, the municipal council of the day, weighed in on the Japanese question. A number of these local officials also belonged to the Tofino Board of Trade, and they expressed in council the sentiments repeatedly voiced by the board. The minutes of January 24, 1947, record a resolution passed by council: "The Commissioners of the Corporation of the Village of Tofino hereby resolve that, at the request of the residents of the Village of Tofino, all orientals be excluded completely from the Municipality, and shall be prevented from owning property and carrying on business directly or indirectly within the Municipality. " The handwritten minutes add the following information: "Copies of this resolution to be sent to Mowat (MLA) Gibson (MP), Legion and Board of Trade."

No official motion supporting this resolution appears in the minutes, and no subsequent reference to this subject appears in the ensuing months and years of council minutes. No law or bylaw excluding "Orientals" ever officially passed, nor was any such law or bylaw proposed. Nonetheless, this resolution proved highly effective. No Japanese returned to Tofino after the war. Furthermore, a widely held assumption spread, and continues to be repeated, that a law had indeed been passed banning Japanese from owning property or living and working in the town. The extent of local resistance to their return effectively made any such law unnecessary. It had been passed in spirit, if not in fact. The leaders of Tofino made their point.

Tofino's attitude toward the returning Japanese reflected similar positions held by communities in Ontario and in the Fraser Valley, where other local councils also attempted to exclude "Orientals." "Municipal councils actually didn't have the authority to impose any exclusion of Canadian citizens," wrote Ken Adachi in *The Enemy That Never Was*, "but the Department of Labour generally operated on the principle that it would not permit Japanese to reside anywhere in Canada where there was an official protest."

In 1949, all talk of repatriation to Japan had faded and Japanese Canadians again had the right to vote—a right taken away from them in 1895 and never restored, except to the 222 Japanese Canadian veterans of World War I. Also in 1949, wartime restrictions on the movements of the Japanese ended and they could return to live within the 160-kilometre protected area along the coast. Those who did so risked hostility. In the Skeena district, the Native Brotherhood declared, "We flatly do not want the Japs back in our coastal region," and many farmers in the Fraser Valley openly resisted Japanese attempts to return. In Ucluelet, some twelve Japanese families did return to live, but not to their former land and homes, which had been absorbed into the adjacent Indian Reserve land. No Japanese returned to Tofino.

Even if he had been welcome in Tofino, Naoichi Karatsu, a Canadian citizen, would not have returned. Like many other families, the Karatsus had left their home intact, believing they would be back, and leaving behind many of their valued possessions, including two precious dolls in glass domes, beloved by the Karatsu girls. The notion of returning withered away in the bitter years of internment. After the war, Naoichi Karatsu took his family to Toronto and started a new life; he never talked about the war years to his children, other than to say he would never return to the coast. Their home in the "Japtown" on Stubbs Island disappeared into the bush like all the others; its contents mysteriously vanishing over time. In August 1948, an article in *Island Events* by E.M. Watson described a stay on Stubbs Island, and a tour of the island with Betty Farmer. They visited "the now deserted Jap-town" and its "once lovely gardens...completely overgrown." They peered into one "poor little lost house, now almost completely swallowed up in a jungle of vegetation. The door stood—or rather, leaned—permanently ajar; there were holes in the roof; the windows were gone." Nothing of any value remained.

During the war years the elderly and respected John Eik faced an impossible task. Surviving correspondence from Mr. H.F. Green, the "Custodian of Enemy Property" in the Secretary of State's office in Vancouver, indicates that at the request of the custodian, Eik did what he could to safeguard the property left behind in the houses of his Japanese tenants. He made inventories and sold various bits of Japanese fishing gear, stacks of firewood, and other items, submitting monies received to the government agency in charge, to be passed on to the owners. Monitoring the Japanese homes proved very difficult, as the custodian acknowledged in a letter dated November 13, 1944. Alluding to the "general conditions at your end" and the "difficulties you have met with," Green wrote: "We appreciate that you have done what you can and we would not expect you to be responsible for any losses after the precautions you have taken." The Japanese homes and possessions fell prey to looting; the houses quietly rotted away or passed into other hands. "People in Tofino had a heyday as soon as the Japanese people left," Ellen Kimoto commented in an interview in 2012. "They were in there taking absolutely everything." But this was wartime; no one commented, no one raised awkward questions. A veil of silence fell over the whole subject of Japanese possessions. "I never sold my house in Tofino, but somebody got it," Johnny Madokoro said, years later. "We never put up a squawk. We thought 'Oh, the heck with that place, it's not worth anything.'"

Curious to see where she grew up on Stubbs Island, Ruby (Karatsu) Middeldorp revisited the site of the old Japanese village on several occasions. Members of the Karatsu family from later generations have made the same pilgrimage, noting the bits of broken Japanese pottery and the domestic artifacts marking the area. In the 1980s Rennie Karatsu, Ruby's older brother, unexpectedly found himself hailed on the street during a visit to Tofino. "Hey, I know you," said an aboriginal man, who recalled fishing alongside the Karatsu boys. The Karatsus' eldest daughter, Alice, who had married Tohachiro "Toki" Kondo in 1937, settled in Toronto following the war, where Toki took a series of different jobs, "but his heart remained on the west coast," according to his granddaughter Christine Kondo. In 1950, Toki began making annual trips out to the coast, fishing every season out of Ucluelet. Because of a recruitment drive by BC Packers, seeking experienced fishermen on the coast, some ten former west coast Japanese fishermen returned to their fishing careers in 1950. Some resettled on the coast, including Mary and Johnny Madokoro and their three boys, who had been living in Toronto. They relocated to Alberni in 1951, and Johnny resumed fishing on his new boat, *Challenger II*. Mary's brother Tommy Kimoto and his family settled on a property in Spring Cove at Ucluelet, and Tommy took the helm of the well-known troller *La Perouse*.

The Tofino municipality's 1947 resolution to exclude "Orientals" hovered uneasily in the back of many minds for many years. It resurfaced in 1981 when cited by Bob Bossin in *Settling Clayoquot*, and later came under scrutiny in 1997 when the Tofino council addressed the subject. Councillor Roly Arnet moved to search the records to ensure the resolution was not in effect, and he raised the challenge of issuing an apology to the Japanese. The motion passed, but no apology ensued. The subject has again come up for discussion among local leaders recently, but to date no apology has been issued by the council. In 1988 the federal government apologized to all Japanese Canadians who had been interned, and each surviving internee received $21,000 reparation. In 2012 the BC provincial government issued its own apology to the Japanese.

During the postwar years, protracted debates arose in Tofino and Ucluelet about how best to make use of the infrastructure left behind at the air base. One of the earliest suggestions aroused strong local opposition. In 1945, the west coast Indian agent, P.B. Ashbridge, suggested closing the aging Christie School at Kakawis and using the former air force hospital as a new residential school. The school's principal, Father Mulvihill, petitioned to have the school relocated, and the summer of 1946 saw an intense flurry of letter-writing to authorities in Ottawa. Most writers expressed strong objections to the idea. Jack Gibson, MP, stated that an Indian residential school near Long Beach "would prejudice the value of the adjoining property for summer resort purposes." The Alberni District Board of Trade concurred, declaring such a school would "seriously affect Long Beach as a Summer Resort." Protests also came from Arthur Lovekin and his lawyer. Lovekin, whose property at Long Beach abutted the hospital site, had donated the four hectares of land for the hospital to the RCAF during the war "as a patriotic gesture." His lawyer stressed that Lovekin had given the land for this specific purpose, and if a residential school were located there his home property and the house, on which "he expended...in excess of $10,000.00," would suffer "tremendous depreciation." The lawyer added that other nearby property owners also opposed the school, intimating that if the idea persisted, Lovekin would take legal action to prevent it. Meanwhile, Andrew Paull weighed in from Vancouver. As president of the North American Indian Brotherhood, he stated that Christie School had a legitimate claim to be relocated on government property, that the old school was a fire trap and must be replaced, and that the government should "exert every effort to defeat the rapacious hand of the exploiter." By the end of August the idea had been quashed, and Father Mulvihill withdrew his application. The Tofino Board of Trade then made another proposal: that the hospital be used as a home for war veterans. Nothing came of that, either, and the land in question reverted to the Lovekins. Fleetingly, the RCAF seaplane base at Ucluelet came under scrutiny as a potential site for relocation of Christie School, but to no avail. The school remained where it was, and the "old fire trap" continued as a school until 1971, later becoming a family treatment centre. In 1983, as long predicted, it finally went up in flames. The RCAF hospital buildings eventually found other quarters; one section still stands at the corner of Campbell and Third Street in Tofino, a long, rectangular structure that once served as a church run by the Shantymen's Christian Association, and later as Tofino's maritime museum.

At Kakawis, on Meares Island, the Oblates of Mary Immaculate had been in charge of Christie School since before the war. The founding order, the Benedictines of Mount Angel Abbey, Oregon, had withdrawn from the school in 1938 following many years of internal debate. The responsibility for Christie School had always been an uneasy burden for the Abbey, requiring more administrative effort and support than the abbot in charge felt able to provide. The Benedictine fathers and brothers all returned to Mount Angel, while the Benedictine sisters of Mount Angel remained at the school to assist the Oblates. Under the Oblates, enrolment at Christie School remained consistently around 110 to 120 students. Ever more staff came to work at the school, including, as time passed, a handful of former students who worked as assistant cooks or mechanics, in maintenance jobs, and assisting with sports activities. In the early 1940s, former student Barney Williams agreed to work as the school's boat builder; with the boys at the school he built a school freight boat in 1941, a new *Ave Maria* mission launch in 1945, and a motor launch for the Nootka mission in 1947, among other vessels.

In a booklet produced for the Golden Jubilee of the school in 1950, messages of commendation for Christie School appear from many sources. Noel Garrard, then superintendent of the Indian Agency, congratulated all of the staff for how "Christie School has taken a rightful place in the history and progress of the West Coast." Photographs of the children reveal a total of 122 children attending Grades 1 to 8 that year. Only four appear in the Grade 8 photograph, all of them girls; Grade 1 had a total of forty boys and girls. Photographs of the staff also appear in the booklet, with captions providing their names and positions. These include a brother identified as "Brother Samson OMI, Disciplinarian." "Disciplinarian" had become a job description. To this day, former students remember Brother Samson as a cruel and unjust man. Many years would pass before the nature of the discipline at this school, and at other residential schools, came under public scrutiny. In the 1950s, few people thought to ask searching questions.

The mid-1950s saw three new Roman Catholic churches under construction in Clayoquot Sound. The large new St. Lawrence's Church at

Ahousat opened in the summer of 1956, with a 6.7-metre-high steeple. Mr. J. Bonn of Mount Angel did all the interior carpentry, constructing the altar and pews at Kakawis and barging them to Ahousat. Tofino's Roman Catholic church, St. Francis of Assisi, opened in 1958, with much of the construction material salvaged from airport buildings. Work also began around that time on the Church of the Immaculate Conception at Hot Springs Cove. Delayed in its construction, the church finally opened in 1963, its opening procession led by Chief Benedict Andrews. At Opitsat, St. Anselm's Catholic church had been completely destroyed by a massive fire in June 1925, when flames raced through the village, engulfing twenty-three homes and leaving the church in smoking ruins. Father Charles Moser heard the news up at Nootka, sadly observing, "It was a very hot day with a SE gale." According to Dorothy Abraham, "the wailing and lamentation could be heard for miles." Rebuilt by Father Charles in 1927, the church continued to exert considerable influence in the village. At a first communion in May 1958, in a packed church, the *West Coast Advocate* reported, "All girls wore sheer white nylon dresses, silk veils and orange blossoms, carrying white rosaries...Following mass, a banquet-like breakfast was enjoyed by about seventy-five persons...Harry Charlie of the Opitsats made an interesting speech in his native tongue...there was a procession of the sacrament through the village with the children's choir singing and reciting."

Determined to promote the west coast to tourists and visitors, the Tofino Board of Trade decided in 1947 to invite the editor of the Victoria magazine *Island Events* to Tofino. Board members provided ideas and photographs, and several glowing articles ensued, promising wonderful west coast experiences to visitors. Breathless with hyperbole, most of these articles described raking crabs from tidal pools, fishing in the surf on Long Beach, enjoying nightly beach parties where everyone could "pop corn, steam clams and crabs, roast wieners and tell stories," with "rousing sing-songs" as part of the fun. Advertisements from many local businesses appeared alongside the articles, offering accommodation at the Tofino Hotel and Café, with "Rates Reasonable. Home Cooking." The Clayoquot Hotel declared it had a "Homey Atmosphere" and could provide "Fishing. Boating. Hunting," while the Singing Sands Camp on Long Beach offered daily or long-term accommodation in its cabins: the monthly rate, forty dollars. Situated on Fred Tibbs's former property at Green Point in the middle of Long Beach, Singing Sands had been offering cabins to rent since 1937. Established by Peg and Dick Whittington, it became an annual retreat for many families;

Peg Whittington, who ran Singing Sands Resort on Long Beach from 1936 onward, with an array of glass fishing floats. Used by Japanese fishermen to float their nets, the glass balls often detached and followed the currents across the Pacific. *Courtesy of Fran Aitkens*

in the postwar years, Gene Aitkens and her two children, Fran and Art, came every year. Gene had first come to Singing Sands during the war to visit her husband, Chas, then posted at the air base, and she became a close friend of Peg Whittington. Fran and her brother delighted in playing on the beach and finding many sizes of glass balls, those translucent fishnet floats from Japan that slipped their nets and floated across the Pacific Ocean to bump gently ashore, sometimes in great numbers, at Long Beach. They also enjoyed seeing guests arrive at Singing Sands. The local bus dropped them some distance away on the beach, and Peg would harness her pony, Duchess, to the resort's wagon, and drive along the sand to meet them. The children played around the pilings on the beach with Peg's beloved dog, Posh, and swam fearlessly in the surf. "Art would swim out to get logs, he loved surfing in on them," Fran recalled.

Peg Whittington remained at Singing Sands for over thirty years, operating her small resort and becoming one of the most respected residents of the area. Her husband died in 1946, a victim of the aftermath of war. A large unexploded mine floated onto the beach near their home, and after the Whittingtons reported it, a naval demolition crew came ashore in a skiff to detonate the mine. Returning to the ship, the small boat flipped in the churning surf. Dick Whittington and the local policeman from Ucluelet courageously tried to save the men in the water, at great danger to themselves. Both Dick and one of the naval men drowned.

As time passed, more accommodation became available at Long Beach. In the late 1930s, only the Whittingtons' Singing Sands and Hazel and Jim Donahue's Camp Maquinna had small cabins to rent, but following the war, Nellie and Joe Webb opened the Wickaninnish Lodge at the south end of Long Beach. They moved a section of the RCAF hospital building to the site and transformed it into the main lodge, offering a room with all meals for forty-five dollars per week. Before long they also rented cabins. In the early 1950s, Edgar and Evelyn Buckle arrived in the area with their sons, Neil and Dennis; they built Combers Resort at Long Beach. Shortly after, Jack and Norah Morae built their Long Beach Bungalows, near the Wickaninnish Lodge. Most of these places attracted regular customers who returned year after year: one of the most famous, painter Arthur Lismer of the Group of Seven, came to Wickaninnish Lodge every year from 1951 until 1968, painting daily from his chosen spot, which became known as Lismer's Beach.

As well as these early resorts, several dozen people built summer cottages, and some thirty permanent homes appeared; by the late 1950s, over sixty residents lived at Long Beach full time. In those years, the now hard-to-find glass fishing floats from Japan floated ashore continually, "a dime a dozen," according to Neil Buckle. One day in 1956, an unusually large number came in at once; the Buckles collected 236 balls that day in a 2.5-kilometre stretch of beach. Everyone collected the glass balls, competing for the most and the best. Nellie Webb made regular forays along the beach with her Clydesdale horse, Punch, hitched to a wagon, loading up with the balls whenever they drifted in.

A fresh influx of military personnel arrived at the RCAF station at Long Beach in the 1950s, bringing considerable excitement to the area

The radar station on what is now called Radar Hill, under construction in 1952. Fearing communist aggression in the early 1950s, Canada and the United States built the Pinetree Line radar network across the continent to warn of pending attacks. The Radar Hill installation closed in 1958, rendered obsolete by the Distant Early Warning (DEW) Line in the Arctic. *Image PA067592 courtesy of Library and Archives Canada*

for a few years. At the outbreak of the Korean War in 1950, Canada contributed 26,000 men and women to a United Nations force attempting to prevent the communist takeover of Korea. This war intensified the tensions of the Cold War; fears of communism became ever more heightened, along with a growing dread that the Soviet Union might attack North America with long-range bombers and intercontinental ballistic missiles (ICBMs). In response, the US and Canadian governments joined forces in the early 1950s to build thirty-nine radar stations, known as the Pinetree Line, along the 50th parallel stretching from Newfoundland to Tofino. Construction on the Tofino station, named C-36 and located on what is now called Radar Hill, began in 1952. Although only a hundred people served at the radar station, the RCAF base at Long Beach reopened to house these personnel, including a number of families. To serve these families and other local children, in 1954 the Tofino Airport School opened in an RCAF building near Schooner Cove, enrolling twenty-six elementary students the first year. High school students took the bus to attend school in Ucluelet, along with their counterparts from Tofino, who had started to make that daily bus trek to high school in 1952.

Although an armistice ended the Korean War in 1953, dividing the Korean peninsula at the 38th parallel into North and South Korea, fear of communist aggression remained intense. The buzz of activity around Radar Hill carried on with the installation of complex radar and communications equipment, and in 1954 the radar station opened, becoming fully operational the following year. At the air base, the presence of military personnel, support staff, and their families created a busy social hub, and it became the scene of frequent dances and other events that often included the townsfolk. Everything from square dancing to bingo and children's parties took place at the base, and the RCAF baseball team played against teams from local logging camps or the community of Opitsat. Considerable effort went into these social and sporting events; the 1954 diary of the commanding officer, J.R. Ashworth, states: "More thought being given to future station entertainment—facilities that are most necessary in winter."

During the height of the Cold War, local boys experienced some of the greatest excitement of their lives when Long Beach became a shooting gallery. Early every morning for about six weeks in 1953, combat exercises and target practice took place there as military aircraft strafed the beach with rockets and machine guns. With the beach closed off to locals, fighter planes roared in, guns blazing. Neil Buckle remembered the screams of the shells flying, heavy thuds of rockets landing, and metre-deep holes left in the beach: "They set up targets on the beach and had a target on Florencia Island in Wreck Bay and Mitchell bombers dropped 500-pound [226-kilogram] bombs on it for weeks on end. They set up cheesecloth targets, about ten feet by ten feet [three by three metres] with a big bulls eye, in front of the sand dunes...The Mustang fighters would start about six in the morning and start strafing the beach...They had so much ammunition that toward the end, they were firing all six rockets at once. As kids we used to collect the .50-caliber brass shell casings."

In January 1958, Pinetree Station C-36 at Radar Hill closed, made redundant by newer technology and by the building of the Distant Early Warning (DEW) Line in the Arctic, which could provide more lead time in the event of a Soviet attack. The personnel stationed at the RCAF's Long Beach base departed. Once again, a period of intense military involvement in the area ended, leaving large facilities deserted. Traces of the radar station remain visible on Radar Hill, and near them stands the Kap'yong Memorial honouring Canada's contribution to the Korean War, in particular noting the battle fought by the 2nd Battalion of the Princess Patricia's Light Infantry on April 22–26, 1951, a battle that helped stem a major breakthrough by enemy forces. On January 10, 1997, the Pacific Rim National Park Reserve, now encompassing Radar Hill, twinned with the Hallyo Haesang Sea National Park in Korea. Veterans and their families continue to hold a memorial service at the Kap'yong Memorial each Remembrance Day.

The Tofino Airport School continued operating under that name until 1964, when it became the Long Beach School. It carried on serving the growing community in the Long Beach area until its closure in 1970, at which time it had thirty-eight students. During its years of operation, enrolment in this school fluctuated; at its peak in 1956 it had forty-one students, but in other years as few as seven children attended. Meanwhile, in Tofino, enrolment in the village school stood at around forty students per year, remaining at that level through the 1950s.

In this postwar period, Long Beach and Tofino were gradually emerging as two distinct communities, closely linked, but different. Tofino clustered around its fishing industry, commercial activities, and community events, with the Board of Trade and the village council voicing matters of local and regional concern. Long Beach enjoyed a more fluid population made up of visitors, scattered residents, a few resorts, and summer people; also, by the 1950s, a few Tla-o-qui-aht families lived permanently at the traditional Esowista village site. Thanks to the military presence in the area, the road between Ucluelet and Tofino had greatly improved, although its washboard surface and potholes still gave rise to many complaints.

Transportation on the west coast underwent many changes in these years, with ever more small aircraft flying up and down the coast. Commercial air traffic had begun arriving in Tofino in the mid-1930s, with Ginger Coote Airways serving the gold-rush community up the coast at Zeballos in single-engined Fokkers and Fairchilds. These

In the 1940s, the Tofino Hotel was the only hotel in town. Still standing today, the building now houses Tofino Sea Kayaking and Wildside Booksellers. In the mid-1930s Dr. John Robertson performed a total of three appendectomies on a table in the hotel before the town had a hospital. *Image I26227 courtesy of Royal BC Museum, BC Archives*

airplanes often stopped in Tofino, becoming famed for their mercy flights, rescuing injured or sick people in remote areas. The Gibson brothers at Ahousat often flew with the red-haired Ginger Coote in the 1930s, never worrying about safety. As Gordon Gibson put it, "Ginger never flew very high so there was more chance of flying into a fishboat mast or a lighthouse than into a mountain." But in May 1938 a Ginger Coote Airways flight crashed near the Alberni Canal, killing everyone on board, including George Nicholson's wife Mary; the wreckage was not located for ten months. At the time, the Nicholsons' daughter, Bonnie Arnet, worked as the agent for Ginger Coote Airways in Tofino. In 1941, Ginger Coote sold his company, which was soon absorbed into Canadian Airways.

Sid Elkington in Tofino became the local agent for Canadian Airways, and in the early 1940s local air traffic picked up considerably with two gold mines, the Pioneer and Bralorne, in production on the Bear (Bedwell) River. For a brief time, Elkington operated a branch store up the Bear to cater to all the miners, and he also took over the Tofino Hotel to accommodate their comings and goings. Mrs. Harold Arnet, known as Benny, managed it for him, proving highly adept at handling miners who had been "poured off the plane" from Vancouver after spending their days in the big city drinking away their paycheques. Knowing the state the miners could be in, Canadian Airways provided Elkington with "effective medication in pill form to calm heavy hangovers up to *Delirium Tremens*." During the war years, Queen Charlotte Airlines (QCA) also began flying into Tofino; all planes landed out in the harbour, and passengers and freight came ashore in small boats operated by the agents. Later, Canadian Airways installed a small float near the government wharf, and de Haviland twin-engined Rapides, Noorduyn Norsemen, and Barkley-Grows began to arrive in the harbour, carrying more passengers. By the late 1940s, QCA dominated the west coast scene, even negotiating a franchise to land planes at the Tofino air base from 1948 onward. By 1952 it flew daily from Vancouver to Tofino, charging twenty-one dollars for the forty-five-minute flight. Pacific Western Airlines bought out QCA in 1955.

The small float planes operated by these various airlines served the larger coastal communities of Ucluelet, Tofino, and Zeballos, but would also put in at lonely outposts and inlets, speedily whisking people and supplies in and out. "Isolation was a thing of the past," wrote Tofino resident Alder Bloom in his unpublished memoir. "A small float plane could land on the water at any camp and take a passenger to Vancouver in an hour." Despite the convenience, he mourned previous times. "The glamour days were gone forever," he stated wistfully, "when the loggers, fishermen, cannery workers, tourists and business men all dressed up in their best clothes for two days of elegance and fine meals, a touch of class that the *Maquinna* brought to a group of people whose lives were far from glamorous." Yet even those who dearly loved the *Princess Maquinna* could see that the ship was showing her age.

For seven years following the war, the *Maquinna* soldiered on. In 1951, the journalist Cecil Maiden wrote of her: "She has stolen the hearts of the people, for she is not just a part of their history, she has made it." He described how she "has taken the sons and husbands of the west to fight in two world wars. At times when no fish boat could fight through the wild seas...always around the headland or behind the driving rain, has been the *Maquinna—The Maquinna* has just gone on going on." But she could not go on forever. Month by month, the Good Ship's problems multiplied. "Passengers will never forget the cockroaches which infested *Princess Maquinna* in her last years, and the co-operative stewards who improvised traps to catch them—a tumbler, with a little water, greased on the inside with butter. The cockroaches climbed into the glasses, drawn by the butter, but couldn't climb out again." Passengers arose repeatedly in the night to empty the water tumbler and its victims out the porthole. Much more seriously, repeated mechanical difficulties, particularly involving her old boilers, afflicted the *Maquinna*. Even worse from the CPR's viewpoint, the passenger and freight traffic had steadily declined on the west coast route. Nearly 11,000 people travelled on the route in 1939; by 1951 this dwindled to 7,215. Internal memoranda of the CPR and its subsidiary British Columbia Coast Steamships reveal equally woeful data about cargo. Most of the canneries on the west coast of Vancouver Island had closed by 1951 as companies centralized operations in Steveston, at the mouth of the Fraser River. The remaining plants on the coast processed fewer fish than in earlier years, and by 1952 only a few herring-reduction plants operated consistently. From 1942 onward, the west coast route ran at a considerable loss, each year becoming more of a financial liability. In 1945, Ed Ricketts airily commented of the CPR steamers: "I think they got done years back with the idea of making money...They seem to make an attempt to serve the region." Yet making money did matter, and losing it mattered even more.

By 1952 *Princess Maquinna*'s boilers could not raise enough steam, and her speed reduced from fourteen knots to nine. The end came even sooner than expected. CPR authorities had planned to withdraw the ship from service following a final sailing on September 18, 1952, but she did not make that trip. "She was already loaded, passengers and mail aboard, and about ready to sail...Captain Carthew...assembled his passengers in the saloon and informed them that she had made her last trip and would sail no more. They would be permitted to stay on board—many had already retired for the night—and be provided with breakfast, but must find their way up coast as best they could."

Reaction to the news of the *Maquinna*'s demise came swiftly. "Coast up in Arms at Loss of Service," declared one newspaper headline. "The whole economy of the West Coast is at stake," said R. Barr, member of the Tofino Board of Trade. "We are facing an intolerable situation. We must have steamship or highway connections in order to survive." The CPR had anticipated such reaction, but its memos and reports also reveal keen anticipation that the long-awaited west coast road would soon connect Alberni to Tofino and Ucluelet. As a result, any planning for a post-*Maquinna* steamship service amounted to stopgap measures designed to continue just until the road came through. The resulting service, provided by the small and ugly *Princess of Alberni*, followed by the *Northland Prince* and the *Tahsis Prince*, did just that. For a number of years these vessels served the coast, carrying ever fewer passengers, never inspiring much enthusiasm in the hearts of west coasters. Increasingly, passengers chose to travel out to Alberni on the *Uchuck*, which left three times a week from Ucluelet.

When Padre John Leighton heard that the *Maquinna* faced her end, he wrote to the superintendent of the British Columbia Coast Steamships. "As Vicar of the West Coast for some years I developed a very warm spot in my heart for the dear old *Princess Maquinna*. I am sorry to see how gravely ill the poor old lady seems to be, but naturally old age is getting her down." He requested that the bell of the *Maquinna* go to the Vancouver Mission to Seamen, where Leighton served as chaplain. In April 1953, after the *Maquinna* had been broken down to become an ore-carrying barge, Captain Carthew presented her bell to the mission. It accompanied Padre Leighton to Tofino when he retired there, and now hangs in Tofino's Legion Hall. Ivan Clarke of Hot Springs Cove insisted on witnessing the breaking up of the *Maquinna*, attending as self-appointed chief mourner; he bought her stateroom keys as souvenirs. Stripped down to a shell and renamed *Taku*, the former *Princess Maquinna* stoically served as an ore barge for several years before being scrapped for metal.

By 1952, the Tofino hospital, so proudly built by local volunteers, had been serving the area for fifteen years. Now a fifteen-bed, two-storey institution, it employed three nurses and a doctor, providing service for patients from Amphitrite Point to Estevan Point. Patients living farther north went to Port Alice or to the little mission hospital at Esperanza, near Ceepeecee, which had opened in 1937 and was run by the Shantymen's Christian Association. Having successfully raised funds for a nurses' residence, the ever-busy Ladies' Hospital Aid in Tofino continued organizing a seemingly endless procession of "linen showers," "superfluity sales," and "silver teas" to fund specific projects and to purchase equipment. By May 12, 1952, the Tofino hospital had admitted a total of 438 patients so far that year. Then disaster struck.

"It happened on a Sunday while many of the Tofino people were at church," according to an article in a Ladies' Aid cookbook from 1983. "The fire horn blew and Maidie Hansen went to the church and quietly entered. She walked over to Katie Monks and whispered, 'The hospital is on fire.'" Katie Monks yelled out loud, ending the service abruptly. "The parson jumped up on the rails, tripped and fell flat on his face. He got up and went to pull the church bell (also used as a fire alarm), but the rope broke." Everyone raced for the hospital and joined in fighting the fire, including a group of twenty Freemasons visiting from Alberni. The Ucluelet fire brigade careened wildly up the road to assist; some reports say they covered the forty kilometres to Tofino in thirty-five minutes flat. All patients were safely evacuated, and no one was injured. Rescuers managed to save most of the valuable medical equipment and hospital records, and the nurse's residence escaped harm, but the hospital building did not stand a chance. Grim-faced Tofino residents looked on despairingly as it went up in flames, reduced in under two hours to charred ruins.

With temporary hospital facilities set up in the nurses' residence and an RCAF hut, moved into Tofino from Long Beach, controversy erupted about whether Tofino or Ucluelet should be the site for a new hospital. According to Walter Guppy, "considerable animosity was displayed" over the ensuing months in a protracted series of meetings and debates about what to do next. Given Ucluelet's population of around 700 to Tofino's mere 300, the larger community felt it had a superior claim. However, factoring in the 1,400 aboriginals in Clayoquot Sound, and the fact that few of them had cars to drive to hospital in Ucluelet, Tofino won the day, but not before the battle between the two communities caused much ill will.

The hospital board sold the old hospital site, had volunteers clear the wreckage, and agreed to a new site on land donated by the Garrard and Monks families. Hospital fundraising once again began in earnest, with the local hospital board required to raise nearly one third of the hospital's projected cost of over $200,000. Everyone chipped in: some 100 loggers and fishermen each donated $100, and local businesses contributed generously, as did the Advance Logging Company, Mac-Millan Bloedel, and BC Forest Products. The Ahousaht band donated $2,500 from the sale of timber rights; normally such revenue would have been shared among all members of the band, but the Ahousahts unanimously agreed to donate the funds to the hospital. In Ucluelet, a "rather risqué fashion show" also contributed its profits to the cause, and a dance at the RCAF station raised funds for a hospital incubator. Everything appeared to be going well, when a last-minute crisis arose. With costs escalating, another $23,000 was needed before construction could start, and the organizers had only thirty days to raise it. The hospital board invited the bank manager from Alberni to explain the situation to local residents. At that meeting, the bank manager accepted promissory notes totalling more than the required amount, with many local people putting up their homes, and in some cases their fish boats, as collateral. Construction on the hospital began in April 1953, relying heavily on volunteer assistance. The official opening took place in August 1954, at a ceremony attended by BC Minister of Health Eric Martin; Paul Sam, the first elected chief councillor of Ahousat, also took his place among the dignitaries. Dr. Howard McDiarmid arrived to start his new job in the hospital less than six months later. The hospital had "17 beds, four bassinettes and a pediatric ward of ten cribs...a surgical operating room and an obstetrical delivery room... and an x-ray machine," he recalled.

Fundraising continued long after the hospital had been rebuilt. The Tofino nurses put on a large dance at the air base in the summer of 1955 to raise funds; the "Loggers' Party" of May 1955, sponsored by Knott Brothers Logging, passed the hat and raised eighty-nine dollars. A performance of the "Jerry Gosley Smile Show," a popular Victoria-based song-and-dance revue, at the airport on September 23, 1955, produced forty-four dollars for the hospital, with Mr. Gosley planning to repeat the show in Tofino and Ucluelet. "Our hospital means so very much to us all," the *West Coast Advocate* stated on May 10, 1956. "In addition to serving the villages of Tofino and Ucluelet, RCAF air base and radar stations, Long Beach, Port Albion, Kennedy Lake Logging Company, Knott Bros Logging, C&B Logging and several other logging camps, many Indian villages and staff and pupils of Christie's Residential School, officers and members have all worked hard to ensure its success."

Dr. McDiarmid found he had to cover a lot of ground in his new job; his schedule demanded he be in Tofino on Mondays, Wednesdays, and Fridays, and in Ucluelet Tuesdays and Thursdays. McDiarmid became actively involved in local events, helping to establish the Long Beach Curling Club, which set up a two-sheet curling rink at one of the old airport hangars. "The curling club went a long way to heal the bitterness that existed after the two towns' long fight over the location of the hospital," he wrote. "It drew residents of Tofino and Ucluelet together." For several years during the mid- to late 1950s, in order to raise funds to operate the curling rink, the club became involved with the Aero Club of BC, helping to organize large scale "fly-ins" to Long Beach and Tofino Airport on the July 1 weekend. This event attracted small planes from flying clubs all over British Columbia and the United States, some from as far away as Texas. In 1958, 110 private aircraft and a chartered DC-6 passenger plane carried more than 500 people to the shindig. The following year, according to the Vancouver *Province* of June 22, 1959, a total of 138 planes landed, all of them at the airport—"for the first time they were not allowed to land on the beach." The Toronto *Star Weekly* hailed this annual fly-in as "one of the gayest events in the Pacific Northwest." The Long Beach Curling club catered a massive crab feast for the hundreds of people attending; in 1959, volunteers cooked up 1,800 crabs for the crowd, in huge pots over propane stoves on the beach. "We also sponsored a hangar dance, for which we hired a good outside band," McDiarmid wrote. "The dance featured the longest bar in Canada, stretching the whole length of the hangar. It was staffed by ten bartenders, all volunteer curlers."

Because the Ministry of Defence had transferred control of the Tofino Airport to the Department of Transport in 1958, commercial and recreational planes now regularly used the runways. Yet with all the improvements in air traffic, the west coast still had no road link to the rest of the island. Following the war, the Tofino and Ucluelet Chambers of Commerce formed a joint committee to advocate energetically for a road connection to Alberni. In July 1949, to publicize how much the two isolated communities wanted a road, a delegation of the committee—Doug Busswood, Robbie McKeand, and Walter Guppy—undertook a three-day hike over the mountains to Alberni. They then proceeded on to Nanaimo by car to attend the Associated Chambers of Commerce of Vancouver Island convention, which passed a resolution urging the provincial government to build a road to the west coast. At that time, though, other coastal communities were also demanding roads, and to make matters more difficult, the provincial government changed the official terminus of the Trans-Canada Highway to Victoria, rather than Tofino, in an attempt to attract federal funds for the Malahat Drive between Nanaimo and Victoria. All of this put the west coast road on the political back burner. Yet again, the campaign for the road stalled.

Even without a road to the rest of the island, optimistic Tofino residents purchased vehicles "really hot off the market," according to the *West Coast Advocate*. "Tofino will soon be classed as the city of cars," the paper enthused in September 1950, going on to list a few: Dr. Monteith owned "a dashing 1949 Chev," Borden Grant "a striking 1949 Plymouth," Bert Knott a "streamlined 1950 Chev," and the Wingens "a 1950 Mercury."

In 1952, the Social Credit party headed by W.A.C. Bennett took office in Victoria, heralding a twenty-year era of growth in the province, particularly in the resource industries. Forestry companies had long eyed the riches of the west coast of Vancouver Island, and in 1955, in return for logging concessions, BC Forest Products signed an agreement with the government to build the most difficult, westerly section of the west coast road, which involved a good deal of drilling and blasting of a sheer rock face near Kennedy Lake. MacMillan Bloedel would build the eastern section of the road around Sproat Lake, incorporating and connecting already existing logging roads. This included a notorious set of switchbacks, with unimpeded 300-metre drops into the lake below, at either end of a high, narrow, logging road. The Department of Highways, under the leadership of Phil Gaglardi, would build the twenty-kilometre middle section of the road to the coast.

Now that the road seemed a certainty, nervous reaction to the coming change mounted. After all, not everyone favoured the idea. Through all the decades of clamouring for a road, voices of dissent had been raised: "I can only hope that the road never gets through to Long Beach," wrote a visitor to George Jackson's Long Beach home back in 1929, "otherwise the place will be cluttered with a lot of millionaires, hot-dog stands and chocolate bar papers." At a community meeting held at the Legion Hall around 1949 to discuss the matter, half the audience talked about the economic advantages the road would foster while those opposed argued that the town would become a tourist trap. The "pro" side won the debate by a margin of one vote. "Not that the vote counted for anything, but it did reflect the attitudinal changes introduced by 'in-comers,' as the returning veterans were called," commented Ronald MacLeod in his memoirs.

Long-time resident Mary Evans definitely favoured a road to Alberni. "It took a war and the building of an air base to eventually get a halfway decent road [between Tofino and Ucluelet]," she wrote in her unpublished memoir. "Let us hope that we do not have to resort to the same measures in order to get our Tofino–Alberni road." But others, including Jacqui Hansen, felt anxious. "The Chamber of Commerce really pushed for the road, but we knew what was coming, we knew the tourists were coming and we were real worried." Many years later, when the road had become a reality and its full impact dawned, Walter Guppy looked back almost sadly on the many years of intense yearning for the road. "We thought of the advantages of being able to drive out without going to the expense of making a three or four day trip of it. We thought of how our property values would increase and of the employment opportunities that would result. We also thought of sharing the natural attractions of the area with others from the 'outside.' But we had little inkling of the extent of the development that would take place once the road was actually built." All that lay ahead.

Chapter 19:

LOVELY ROAD

ON AUGUST 22, 1959, every roadworthy vehicle in Tofino and Uclue-let—all seventy-four of them—assembled to form an excited cavalcade and set off to make history. Carrying a total of 300 passengers, the cars gathered at the junction of the road leading to Alberni. Travelling in a convoy, they departed at 6 a.m. to inaugurate the new road, with each vehicle displaying a ticket—purchased for five dollars—for the privilege of participating. It had taken five years for the logging companies and the Department of Highways to patch the various sections of the road into a more or less navigable thoroughfare. Some work trucks had already gone along the road, but this cavalcade of local vehicles truly marked the opening of the road.

Each driver signed a waiver absolving the road builders of any lia-bility for damage or injury and agreed to adhere to four rules: to stay in line; not to stop except at the four designated stopping points; not to throw matches or cigarettes from their cars, and not to smoke at the stopping points; and to drive as near as possible to the car in front. Some creeks still had no bridges, and the vehicles had to ford them, one by one, led by a pilot truck. Everyone made it through safely, arriving in Alberni three hours later, covered with dust, car horns sounding triumphantly. Many continued to Nanaimo, where they posed for a photograph in Beban Park, and some did not want to stop, carrying on to Victoria. "The experience of driving over paved roads with traffic lines...was new for most of these people," commented George Nicholson in the *Colonist*. He drove in the lead car with Tom Gibson, president of the Tofino Chamber of Commerce. The oldest person making the trek out, Anton Hansen, aged eighty-five, had waited for this road for fifty-five years; next in age, Fritz Bonetti, seventy-five, had lived at Long Beach since 1912.

Bob MacKenzie leans on his car door at one of the rest stops during the drive to Port Alberni over the newly opened road on August 22, 1959. His daughter Kathy is in the car. Note the Tofino, BC pennant on the side window. *Courtesy Bob and Doris MacKenzie*

Not long after, on Labour Day, forty cars travelled westward from Sproat Lake to Long Beach. By the end of that weekend, an estimated 3,000 people and some 700 cars had travelled over the road in one direction or the other, according to George Nicholson. Many unwary drivers hit the sands of Long Beach, delightedly revving their engines and racing across the open stretches with absolutely no understanding of what could happen or what areas to avoid. That weekend, local resident Paul Norton pulled fifty-four cars off the beach with his jeep, saving them from sinking into areas of soft sand. He charged ten dollars per car. A new local business had been born.

When Rowland Brinckman wrote his poem in the 1930s, expressing hope for a "lovely road," he may not have had quite this road in mind. Most people who drove over it more than once soon had a section or sections they feared, dreaded, or hated: the switchbacks, the washouts, the dizzying heights, the drop-offs, the spectacular slippages, the stretches that seemed to zigzag crazily for no good reason. Alex Masso of Opitsat believed he knew the explanation for one particularly scary and winding section of the road; it was obvious, he said. The surveyor was on a drunk at the time.

Following the much-publicized opening, the road, officially named Highway 4, remained closed to the public during daytime hours, with locked gates at both ends, to allow the loggers to get on with their work. The gates stayed in place until 1964. For years after the opening, the road remained extremely challenging for drivers, and the journey fraught with peril. Noel Hamlin of Alberni inaugurated a bus service, valiantly navigating his thirty-three-seat vehicle over the new road three times a week. In December 1960, with eleven people on board, he had to drive through a massive washout in the dark, with water up to his headlights, pushing floating logs out of his way. "Water gurgled under the bus door" a local newspaper reported. A year later, Hamlin made the news by commandeering a Department of Highways grader one night, and grading a particularly bad five-kilometre stretch. Accused of stealing and damaging the grader, he faced a hefty bill from the department, and a fine. "I'm damned if I'll cough up," he told a reporter. "I'd rather go to jail than pay a cent."

Driving Highway 4 was not for the faint of heart: extremely narrow in places and devoid of barriers along its edges, its steep switchbacks, climbing to 580 metres above Sproat Lake and back down to lake level, reduced some drivers to tears. "Many of the people who had come to Tofino by road refused to return over it, opting either to fly out or go by boat," commented Dr. Howard McDiarmid. He recalled the time he and his family drove his powder blue Chevrolet Bel Aire over the road in the early 1960s, suffering not one, but two, flat tires. They spent the night in the car waiting for a truck to come along the next morning. The truck took McDiarmid and the tire rims to town to be re-shod while the family awaited his return.

The doctor saw the impact of the road on his patients. "I had more than a few requests for tranquilizers from people who were heading out on the road...Most locals who had to use the road carried two spare tires, extra oil, food and, in winter, sleeping bags. Everyone had their favourite horror story...mine involved a night during the winter when it was snowing heavily. We had chains, so we made it up the west end of the switchbacks fairly easily, but going downhill on the east end, even with chains, was like going down a ski jump with curves." The district highways manager sent out a sanding truck in response to McDiarmid's call, "but it was so slippery the truck flipped over. They closed the road." As journalist Jack Scott dryly commented, the road was "not yet suitable for a gay party in an open convertible."

Despite all these difficulties, the new highway brought immediate changes. Fish and freight companies began shipping their goods to market over the road. This change in transport saw several ice plants pop up along the Tofino and Ucluelet waterfronts, allowing fish caught at daybreak to be iced down and trucked out to Victoria and Vancouver within twelve hours. This meant more fish could be caught and shipped, so ever more fish boats began working on the outer coast. At one stage in 1964 during a particularly good salmon run, over 400 fish boats tied up in Tofino. At night, the lights of seemingly countless boats could be seen lined up at anchor on the inside of Wickaninnish Island, waiting to go out at dawn. Bob Wingen, now the third generation of Wingens working in Tofino, became the first in Tofino to acquire a fish-packing vessel, the *Harriet E.* This boat would load up with ice and head out to buy fish from camps up the coast as far as Winter Harbour, returning to Tofino to be met by trucks ready to load the iced fish and drive out of town. This system continued into the 1970s, fading out when larger fish boats carrying their own ice came on stream, making the large fish packers redundant.

For a few years in the early 1970s, Bob Wingen attempted to speed up fish transport by adding the element of air travel. He acquired two Norseman seaplanes for his Sea-Air-Pac Company, employing local pilots Doug Banks and Gary Richards to collect fish from the fish camps along the coast, then return to Tofino to load the fish onto trucks for transport to Vancouver or Victoria. Wingen's long-term dream was to fly fish into Tofino from isolated fish camps, and fly it out again from the airport in big cargo planes. This never happened; even the short-haul flights of Sea-Air-Pac did not last long, running into too many technical problems.

The 1960s boom in salmon fishing could not be sustained. Salmon runs, by their nature, fluctuate from year to year, and the 1965 sockeye run proved a huge disappointment, even as improvements in fishing equipment and larger boats allowed greater catches. In an attempt to rectify these imbalances and to maintain sustainable yields without impairing the survival of the salmon stock, in the late 1960s and early 1970s the Department of Fisheries implemented a number of measures. It limited the number of fishing licences, it regulated the size of the harvest, and it introduced a salmon enhancement program by building new hatcheries. The limitations in the salmon fishery led some Tofino fishermen to branch out and harvest halibut, shrimp, crab, and anchovies. For a while the Japanese market demanded sea urchins, harvested by divers, packed on ice in small wooden boxes, and shipped to Japan by air. Divers also harvested abalone, a practice banned by the mid-1970s, as well as geoducks and sea cucumbers.

Once the locked gates on the road to Alberni disappeared and daytime restrictions ended in 1964, visitors began travelling out to the west coast in ever greater numbers to camp and party on Long Beach. More and more vehicles appeared on the beaches, with some people overnighting in campers and vans, and others in tents amid the driftwood above high-tide level. Often tents pitched by the unwary flooded when the tide rose. In short order, residents living on or near the beach, including Peg Whittington and the Lovekins, "found themselves dealing with uninvited visitors knocking at the door looking for water, a toilet, a phone, or help to rescue a vehicle stuck in the sand," according to Adrienne Mason in *Long Beach Wild*. The Lovekins ended up erecting a barbed-wire fence along the front of their property to keep people away.

Among the many who wanted to see just how fast they could drive their cars along the beach was *Vancouver Sun* columnist Allan Fotheringham. On June 30, 1961, he wrote: "I drove the length of the beach, most of it at 70 mph [112 kilometres per hour]...When the tide is out and the hard-packed sand stretches a half-mile, you can hit 100 [160 kilometres per hour]." Navigating around the World War II pilings, which still studded the beaches since being installed to prevent enemy craft landing, made the wild drive even more exciting. These pilings remained on Long Beach and Chesterman Beach, and in Cox Bay, long after the war, although many disappeared with the action of surf and tide. Eventually Tom Gibson and his sons accepted a contract to blast the remaining ones away at five dollars apiece. They missed a few, and to this day traces of these wartime defences still emerge at the lowest tides.

The notion of driving on Long Beach had seemed such a grand idea in earlier years, when newspaper articles anticipated the thrill of driving along the beach, several cars abreast. But now, "residents watched, both amused and appalled as tourists tore up and down the beach and through the surf," wrote Adrienne Mason, "often becoming swamped at the mouth of Sandhill Creek or mired in the wet sand. Many cars were so hopelessly stuck...that the owners just left them. To this day, every once in a while, especially in winter when storms and high tides have scoured the beach, a corroded chassis emerges from the sand." Jim Hudnall counted himself lucky; unlike many, his vehicle survived its submersion in sea and sand. "We had the VW van on the beach and it began to sink in the soft sand as the tide came in, so we took out the battery, plugged the carburetor with rags and removed everything. The tide covered it and we waited until low tide the next morning, got it towed to higher dry land, hosed it off in fresh water from a nearby stream, and lo and behold, it started right away, and we drove it back to Seattle."

"I towed over 200 cars off the beach," Neil Buckle recalled of his years living at Combers' Beach. "One time, these guys had soaked the ignition and...they finally came up and said they needed a pull to get started...I pulled and pulled them with my old Ford car and in the end we did get it going. They asked what they owed me and I said 'Oh this will be twenty dollars,' or something like that. 'Well, we don't have any money but we have a set of Snap-On Tools. Can we leave them with you until we come back and pay you tomorrow?'...I was *really* hoping that he wouldn't come back and pay me, but he did, unfortunately." According to Buckle, "People drove on Chesterman's Beach, too, but it was pretty hard to get stuck on Chesterman's because it was so hard-packed. The old chassis at Chesterman's that appears in the sand now and then is from a 'car-be-que.'" So-called car-be-ques occurred when revellers decided to set fire to old cars.

Unquestionably, all the newcomers and visitors to the beach had an immediate influence on the economy of the area and the services offered. From 1965 onward, Abbott's Store, located just behind Long Beach, also housed the Long Beach post office, with Archibald Henry

Abbott as postmaster. This was the first post office at Long Beach since Hazel Donahue briefly acted as Long Beach postmistress from her home at Camp Maquinna in 1946–47. Abbott's also operated a gas station. Another, the Long Beach Service Station, opened in 1958 just south of Green Point, with Surfway Market opening across the road. The Kimola Motel stood near the road now leading to the golf course, and in 1962 the provincial campground opened at Green Point, offering eighty-nine campsites for visitors. The Long Beach School near Schooner Cove welcomed over eighty students during the early 1960s; numbers later fell to around forty before the school closed in 1970.

With the road open, and with a growing number of visitors looking for places to stay, Robin Fells and Jeff Crawford sensed an opportunity. The Vancouver businessmen partnered with Joe Webb, who owned the Wickaninnish Lodge, and together they secured financing and began building the impressive new twenty-two-room Wickaninnish Inn, on the site of Webb's lodge. The hotel stood on a rocky outcrop, offering stunning views of the beach and the ocean. People flocked here from far and wide to sit in front of the fire, enjoying the relaxed atmosphere and upscale service, including world-class cuisine. A 1964 newspaper article, appearing just after the new inn opened in July of that year, described the Wickaninnish Inn as "an improbable first-class hotel." Few expected to find such top-notch accommodation in such a remote location, particularly in a hotel that took pride in offering no radio, television, newspapers, or telephone. Many guests flew in to Tofino Airport rather than face the not-so-lovely road from Alberni.

Beachfront accommodation in the area also included the MacKenzie Beach campsite, nearer to Tofino. The MacKenzie family had owned property there since Donald MacKenzie, a veteran of Vimy Ridge, came to work as the Lennard Island lightkeeper in the mid-1920s. In 1929, for $250, he purchased 400 metres of shoreline on sixteen hectares of land at the beach now bearing his name, previously known as Garrard Beach. Francis Garrard had pre-empted two large tracts of land there in 1906 while working as Lennard Island's first lightkeeper. Because Lennard Island had an unreliable water supply, the Garrards often came over to the beach to do laundry, washing their clothes in the stream. In the 1930s, Donald MacKenzie and his wife Mina built a home on the beach from lumber milled by the Darvilles at Calm Creek and towed around to their site. They had nine children in all, the four younger boys born in Tofino. Bob MacKenzie recalled walking into school in Tofino at the age of seven, four reluctant kilometres there and back each day, along the rough trail to and from what Rowland Brinckman dubbed "MacKenzieville."

By the late 1950s the MacKenzies had sold their sixteen-hectare beach property and moved away, but the family maintained a foothold on the beach. In 1956, Bob MacKenzie purchased a parcel of land adjacent to his family's original property, and in 1965 he and his wife Doris moved from Tofino to their MacKenzie Beach home and opened a campsite and mobile home park there. By 1968 they offered thirty campsites and started developing plans to offer further accommodation.

The new road provided ready access to the swells of Long Beach and the other beaches for a small number of surfing enthusiasts who had already begun surfing farther down the coast at Pachena Bay and Jordan River. This band of surfing pioneers launched an industry that fifty years later has become one of the main economic engines of the Tofino area. Though surfing as a board sport originated in Hawaii, the Nuu-chah-nulth people had long practised surfing their canoes onto beaches. In 1912, John Ross, principal of the Ahousat residential school, mentioned in a report to the Department of Indian Affairs that "canoe racing and surf riding are common amusement during the summer months." Two years later, Mr. H.N. Clague, in his report to the Department of Lands, wrote of the beaches on the west side of Vargas Island: "No more enjoyable sport can be imagined than surf-riding at any one of these delightful stretches of clean sand." Bruce Lucas grew up canoe surfing at the surf break at Hesquiat Point, always trying for bigger and bigger waves. Despite his mother's anxiety, he and his friends loved braving the big seas in their small canoes, "paddling as fast as we could [to] catch the wave when it started breaking."

"Boarding," as some early settlers called it, appears to have been practised in the 1920s. In the *Colonist* of December 1, 1929, Gertrude Jackson mentioned the attraction of surfing: "Long Beach...could become a most popular Summer resort with golf, horseback riding, motor racing, as well as hunting, hiking, boating and surfboard riding, the latter providing a thrill that is hard to excel." Two years later, in an article dated March 19, 1931, the *Colonist* commented: "The first bathers of the season plunged into the Long Beach breakers. There was quite a ground swell caused from the last gale, thus making it very interesting riding the surfboard."

The modern surfing era began in the mid-1960s with Jim Sadler, Ralph DeVries, and Bruce Atkey, among others, setting the pace. They braved the six degree Celsius water, wearing wetsuits and using home-made surfboards. "The thick, heavy, diving suits weren't very supple and to add warmth they coated themselves with Vaseline to ward off the cold," Ruth, Sadler's wife, remembered. They ordered surfboards from California, and as Ruth recalled, "They held their breath hoping [the boards] would arrive in one piece." Later, as demand grew, Atkey drove to California from time to time, buying surfboards for under fifty dollars, loading them into his VW van, and bringing them back to Vancouver Island for resale.

Ralph DeVries, who worked as a carpenter building the Wickaninnish Inn in 1963–64, stayed on as a cook and learned the rudiments of surfing from some Californians visiting Long Beach. He went to Victoria and purchased a surfboard from a pawnshop. When the inn's manager, Robin Fells, saw DeVries enjoying himself so much on his board, Fells purchased a few boards so that he and his guests could also try surfing. Instead his staff co-opted most of the boards. "We had a hell of a lot of fun," remembered DeVries. "I'd cook in the morning and surf in the afternoon."

By then Jim Sadler and his family, who had been surfing at Pachena Bay, had arrived in Tofino. Having come temporarily to help local businessman Jack Walters build his grocery store in the town, Sadler fell in love with Tofino and the surfing and stayed, becoming a leader in the Tofino Bible Fellowship as well as a legendary surfer. Often these surfing pioneers had the "long beaches"—Wreck Bay, Long Beach, Chesterman Beach, Cox Bay—entirely to themselves.

By 1966, enough enthusiasts surfed on the west coast to inspire the

A P44 Volvo with surfers and surfboards on Long Beach, part of the early surfing scene in the 1960s. *Courtesy of Ruth Sadler*

Jordan River surf club to sponsor Canada's first surfing competition, the Long Beach International Surf Contest, at Wickaninnish Beach on the May 24 weekend. The two-day event drew forty contestants, each paying an entry fee, and some 2,000 spectators. With contestants from the Americas, New Zealand, Vancouver Island, and the Lower Mainland, as well as local surfers, the event proved a huge success. New Zealander Paul Griffin won the men's division, with local Jim Sadler, riding his own homemade board, placing second. New Zealander Ginty Bigwood came third, with local Paul DeVries fourth. Victoria's Joan Oliver won the women's trophy with Lynn Bissel, also from Victoria, placing second. Terry Ismay won the junior men's award. This event received mainstream—if incredulous—publicity. "Surfing in Canada? Aw, go on!" declared an article in the *Vancouver Sun* on June 10, 1966, following with an admiring description of the success of this first ever event.

The surfing competition continued for another two years, but by 1968 so many rowdies turned up to party rather than watch the surfing that the organizers cancelled further events. The termination clearly showed how the uncontrolled party atmosphere at Long Beach on summer week-

The winners of the first surf competition held at Wickaninnish Beach in May 1966. New Zealander Paul Griffin (third from left in the back row) won the men's division, with local Jim Sadler (head bowed at the front) placing second with his homemade board. *Courtesy of Ruth Sadler*

ends was beginning to wreak havoc. On holiday weekends, thousands of people—up to 7,000 at a time—descended on Long Beach to camp. Cars careened around on the beach, towing riders balanced on drift logs or old car hoods; this "sand sledding" developed into "pallet surfing," with riders perched on wooden pallets tied to back bumpers of cars. In 1966 an eighteen-year-old from Vancouver died when struck by a car on Long Beach. Visitors raided the beach, digging indiscriminate quantities of razor clams—some collecting hundreds of kilos at a time—and hauling them off the beach in garbage cans. People also collected large numbers of sea stars as souvenirs, all too often leaving the creatures to rot in plastic bags. Heaps of garbage remained on the beach after the crowds departed, and with no public toilet facilities, as Peg Whittington bluntly stated, "the beach stunk."

In his essay "The Beaches of Clayoquot," Brian Brett described the scene: "Windsurfers on wheels whistled down the beach, and cars dodged families and children and hippies...The police were chasing a drug dealer and they...sank into a sand pool. The car could have been rescued. No-one helped them, they were too busy cheering as the tide came in, pounding the car out of sight. There was dog shit everywhere. Garbage and plastic bags and tarps littered the driftwood line, and toilet paper hung in the trees. Endless parties. Stoned-out hippies. It was a carnival on sand."

By the late 1960s, a different scene appeared south of Long Beach at Wreck (Florencia) Bay, where members of the "Tune in, Turn on, and Drop out" generation chose to make their stay more permanent. They turned that beach into a mecca for the counterculture of the time. Hippies, dropouts, and flower children, Vietnam draft dodgers, Vietnam vets, and other itinerant young people began trickling onto Wreck Bay in 1968–69, selecting it for its isolation, away from the more mainstream visitors on Long Beach. They erected semi-permanent dwellings high on the beach, where they "[lived] off youth and a dream in plastic and driftwood shacks," as Adrienne Mason wrote in *Long Beach Wild*. Ridding themselves of inhibitions, many went naked, smoked marijuana, dropped acid, and lived a laidback lifestyle as far away as possible from the restrictions of a society they felt had gone badly awry. Many of the beach dwellers drifted back to urban settings during the winter, but a few chose to remain at the beach year-round. The loosely knit community also attracted those who dropped by for a few days or weeks, just to see what was going on. One summer the young Margaret Sinclair spent time there; a few years later she married Prime Minister Pierre Trudeau, and their son Justin now leads the federal Liberal Party in Canada.

Not all of the beach dwellers lived right at Wreck Bay; some lived on the outer islands, a number in shelters at Schooner Cove, and in the winter months some stayed at cabins at Peg Whittington's place on Long Beach. Members of this group valued Peg's encouragement of their artistic pursuits. A few went on to become well known in the Canadian art scene, including the musician Valdy; writers Susan Musgrave, George Ryga, and Sean Virgo; and actress Frances Hyland, as well as environmentalist Vicky Husband.

At Wreck Bay, the flock of newcomers dispersed all along the five-kilometre beach, some even along the cliffs, in their shelters and tents. According to Adrienne Mason, "They played drums and flutes, carved sculptures from driftwood, cast candles of the Wreck Bay cliffs. A joint, a jug of cheap wine, or a tab of acid was rarely far out of reach." At the height of their tenure, as many as 500 people occupied the Wreck Bay beach during the summer months. Among them, Bruce Atkey, who split cedar shakes from driftwood and sold them or used them to build various structures along the beach. "We were hippie shakers," Atkey remarked. He continued living around Tofino for years, well known for building beautiful and inventive structures from beach wood and split cedar. Many others at Wreck Bay produced highly creative arts and crafts, some of which sold through local shops. Acclaimed sculptor and wood carver Godfrey Stephens became a familiar presence on the beach during those halcyon days, working on his carvings and revelling in what he termed the "panorama of Florencia...raining in light." On July 20, 1969, he joined the "wild people listening to short wave radio at the exit of Lost Shoe Creek, full moon above. Listening to... one step for mankind," as astronaut Neil Armstrong descended from Apollo 11 to walk on the moon.

In 1971, Ucluelet resident Pat Hutchinson worked as an enumerator for the Canadian census, a task that included counting heads at Wreck Bay. "I interviewed as many as I could," she wrote. "To try to count them with their daily comings and goings was a quite impossible chore. Many were non-Canadians, some refused to be interviewed, some refused to give surnames or addresses, others said they were just passing through. For some three miles [five kilometres] one could see a continuous stretch of great piles of logs...arranged and re-arranged to make so many styles of dwellings that one could only say that they were indescribable...along the top of the cliffs, for at least two miles, in every nook and cranny and in every small clearing other, more comfortable shelters had been erected." Along the beach she saw "great imagination coupled with ingenuity to utilize driftwood boards and beachcombed chains and old pieces of iron gratings...to improvise dwellings that were comfortable and extremely picturesque. There were kettles strung from chains, old pots strung from log frames, stone fire boxes, benches, tabletops, and hollowed out holes in the sand for sheltered sleeping quarters. Although a few had paid slight heed to such niceties, most had also set privy holes well back from the main beach."

For the most part local residents tolerated the offbeat newcomers, picking up the hitchhikers and sometimes helping them sell their arts and crafts. Their way of living may have shocked some, but it fascinated almost everyone, and few could resist going to have a look. One summer day, Charles McDiarmid, aged about twelve, went to visit Wreck Bay with his mother, who maintained this was a sight not to miss: "I remember the beach being absolutely packed, with lots of little shelters along the shore in the driftwood, and half the people were naked." A young man wearing ragged, multicoloured bellbottoms walked toward them. Naked to the waist, deeply tanned, and completely oblivious to others, he played his silver flute, seemingly in a trance. With his flute flashing in the sun, the music faded as he passed; for Charles McDiarmid, this seemed the essence of Wreck Bay.

Some local residents complained that the hippies discouraged public use of the various beaches by their appearance and behaviour. "They are not helping us to attract legitimate tourists," declared Mike McGeein, chairman of the Ucluelet Chamber of Commerce, in a *Vancouver Sun* article. "We have discussed ways to get rid of these undesirables, but there is nothing we can do. We have checked with everyone and they are free to come and go as they please." Certain locals even talked of forming vigilante committees to take unilateral action against people with long hair and beards who, they felt, having taken over various areas such as Wreck Bay and Schooner Cove, regarded these beaches as their own. "Some of the working people of Tofino resented the idleness of the hippies," commented Ruth Sadler.

A significant number of the young people who landed in the Tofino area in the late 1960s and the 1970s relied on welfare cheques to get by. The welfare office in Port Alberni sent an official to Tofino once a week to distribute cheques from the municipal offices. Jacqui Hansen, then the town clerk, recalled: "I remember the smell when they came into the office to get their cheques—it was that oil they all wore, patchouli oil. The place just reeked after they left, we always had to air it out."

Jim Hudnall felt differently about that odour. He enjoyed picking up hitchhikers in his VW van and the "combined smell of wood smoke and human scent, and the lovely patchouli oil smell."

Jim Hudnall and his wife, Carolyn, made their first trip out to the coast in August 1967. "When we got to Port Alberni there was a bad forest fire burning and the road was closed during the day for firefighting but they allowed cars through at night," Jim said. "So we drove into unknown territory with the fire burning on both sides of the road and all around Sproat Lake, and we arrived at Green Point campground in the dark. We woke up next day and saw the view for the first time. I thought I'd died and gone to heaven." That first summer they stayed on Frank Island off Chesterman Beach, parking their VW van on the island above the high tide mark. In subsequent summers they camped at various locations before finding a cabin at Schooner Cove, built by Bruce Atkey. "*The Whole Earth Catalog* was our Bible. It was full of ideas about how to build, about septic and water supply systems etc. We were pretty isolated and cut off so we had to fend for ourselves."

Whatever isolation newcomers and beach dwellers on the coast may have experienced, it could not compare to that of earlier years. After the rough, narrow ribbon of a road punched its way over the mountains to the coast in 1959, the isolation of Tofino and Ucluelet effectively ended as commercial and recreational traffic grew, and as outside influences arrived, affecting everyone in the area. The Tla-o-qui-aht people bore the impact of this change more than the other First Nations of Clayoquot Sound because large areas of their traditional territory became accessible by road for the first time in history; their traditional village of Esowista lay directly alongside the road. Only a handful of people lived there permanently before the 1960s, but in subsequent years the village expanded considerably in size; its population now exceeds that of Opitsat, the principal Tla-o-qui-aht village. Yet even Opitsat, across the water from Tofino, soon felt the effects of the road, as goods and services became more easily available. In 1964, Opitsat became electrified when BC Hydro laid 2,500 metres of submarine cable across the harbour from Tofino. All homes in the village quickly wired up, and local merchants did a brisk trade as Opitsat residents rushed to buy televisions, fridges, washers, and dryers.

Because of its more remote location, the Ahousaht village of Maaqtusiis did not experience such abrupt changes. By the 1960s it had fallen on hard times, out of sight and all too often out of mind of government authorities. "Man comes in a boat, usually every month," commented Mark Atleo, a band councillor at the time, describing the Indian agent's visits. "All the time he's got one foot on the dock and the other foot on the boat." Following a visit in April 1965, journalist Terry Hammond wrote a damning article in the *Daily Colonist*. "Ahousaht village is a collection of weathered, grey, rot-infested shacks...inhabited by 400 human beings. Of these a dozen have jobs, the rest exist on the scanty pickings of welfare and unemployment insurance." The fleet of fish boats at Ahousat had numbered fifty in the mid-1950s; now only about twenty did any fishing. Hammond described the village as a living ghost town, the homes ravaged with decay, broken windows boarded up or stuffed with rags, and up to sixteen people crammed into each tiny fire-trap home. One family with eleven children lived off $136 per month. A four-room schoolhouse had some eighty children enrolled, but "many parents prefer to send their youngsters to a residential school in Port Alberni where, they claim, a better education is offered." The two churches, Roman Catholic and United, stood in stark contrast to the rest of the village, with their "sparkling paint and solid construction."

Hammond interviewed Paul Sam, the first elected chief councillor of the Ahousahts, and also the "hereditary speaker for the hereditary Ahousaht chiefs." Sam spoke of the losses his people had experienced: "This was a fishing village, but the salmon are going because the white man has not cared for the spawning beds and the cod have been over-fished by the trawlers. The clams have died from the waste of the herring reduction plants. The sea otter is gone and we can no longer shoot the seal. Now we can't even cut down a tree to make a dugout... Now Ahousahts can't live like Indians, but white man has no jobs for us. Maybe by and by there be no Ahousaht village."

Shawn Atleo (A-in-chut), former chief of the Assembly of First Nations, and a hereditary Ahousaht chief, remembered hearing as a child about Ahousat's grim prospects. "When I was five or six, we were living in Bella Bella in the Central West Coast," he told a reporter for the *Vancouver Island University News.* "There was a superintendent at that time who was advising a teacher who was considering going to Ahousaht. He said, 'Don't bother going to Ahousaht'—in essence he was saying it's a dying community. Nobody will be there in 20 years." Shawn Atleo's father, E. Richard Atleo, responded to this by taking his family to Maaqtusiis where he became school principal in the early 1970s, helping revitalize the community.

In 1973 Ahousat had a brief brush with fame when chosen as the location for the movie *I Heard the Owl Call My Name.* Featuring actor Tom Courtenay in the leading role, as well as Alberni's George Clutesi and Ahousat's Margaret Atleo, the filming took several weeks in September of that year, with local residents and others enjoying walk-on roles. The cast and crew filled every available room in the Tofino area during the shoot, and the movie premiered at the Tofino Legion, to hoots of recognition as familiar faces appeared onscreen.

The idea of creating a national park around Long Beach dates back to 1929, when the Canadian National Parks Association first put the idea forward. Following a visit to the coast with two government surveyors in 1931, J.M. Wardle, chief engineer of the federal Parks Department, praised the beauty of the area but did not support the idea of establishing a park here, seeing far too many drawbacks, including the cold water temperature and the fog. Despite strong local support for a park, the initiative faded into the background for many years. The provincial government acted first, setting aside land at Green Point in 1948, which later became Wickaninnish Provincial Park. Lobbying continued for a national park at Long Beach, backed by Tofino's mayor Tom Gibson and other local businessmen, but no real action occurred until after the completion of Highway 4. Through the 1960s, the mounting summertime chaos on the beach could not be ignored; as Adrienne Mason wrote, "the need to protect the land *from* the public [gained] serious attention."

By 1966, discussions had advanced to the point that the provincial government offered Wickaninnish Provincial Park as part of a larger national park. Dr. Howard McDiarmid took up the cause, championing the idea of a national park during his successful 1966 provincial election campaign. Like all other local people he saw conditions rapidly deteriorating on Long Beach year by year, and in February 1968 he gave a famous speech outlining the situation to the provincial legislature: "Are you aware, Mr. Speaker, that on July 1 of last year there were 7,000 campers tenting on Long Beach provincial park, crammed in cheek by jowl, defecating, micturating [urinating] and copulating—not separated by so much as a blade of grass, Mr. Speaker? In fact, barely a grain of sand. Motorcycles racing up and down the beach, airplanes landing and taking off, no water and two toilets for 7,000 people?" An irritated editorial in the *Vancouver Sun* on March 1, 1968, pointed out that west coast visitors were still putting up with "slum conditions" on their major beach, while politicians endlessly talked.

In 1968, Jean Chrétien became minister of Indian Affairs and Northern Development, the department responsible for national parks. Ken Kiernan, BC's minister of recreation, invited Chrétien to tour the area by helicopter, followed by lunch at the Wickaninnish Inn. Impressed by what he saw, Chrétien agreed to work with the province to establish a park that would encompass not only Long Beach and an area extending over the peninsula to Grice Bay, but also the more than 100 islands and islets of the Broken Group in Barkley Sound, and the area from Cape Beale to Port Renfrew, including the seventy-five-kilometre West Coast Lifesaving Trail, giving a total park area of 511 square kilometres. In 1969 the two levels of government agreed to split the cost of acquiring land, and the BC government set in place a plan to create the park in three units, one by one: first Long Beach, then Barkley Sound, then the West Coast Trail section. The two levels of government finalized the deal in April 1970.

On June 16, 1970, in a much publicized visit, Prime Minister Pierre

In 1970 Prime Minister Pierre Trudeau visited Long Beach where he tried surfing. Here he is on the right coming out of the water with Robin Fells, centre, then owner of the Wickaninnish Inn. Vancouver Sun *photo*

Trudeau helicoptered in to Long Beach to survey the area of the new park and to try his hand at surfing. Robin Fells of the Wickaninnish Inn provided Trudeau with a wetsuit and a surfboard, and along with two other surfers they braved the frigid water. The prime minister managed to stand on his board on his first attempt, and they enjoyed over half an hour in the waves. According to the *Daily Colonist*, Trudeau returned to shore with "legs pink as Tofino crabs from the slap of icy waves, yellow towel draped rakishly around his ears," to greet a small crowd. During his visit, a bearded youth with long hair asked him "When are you going to legalize marijuana?" and Trudeau quipped, "You mean you need grass to get high on in this magnificent area?"

On May 4, 1971, Princess Anne, accompanied by Jean Chrétien, cut a ribbon at Long Beach, officially opening Pacific Rim National Park. By then, the full impact of establishing the park had become devastatingly clear to residents and business owners within its boundaries. In the years leading up to the creation of the park, people in the Long Beach area generally favoured the idea, keen to protect the area from the hordes of out-of-control incomers. They assumed their homes and businesses would be grandfathered in, co-existing with the park and adjusting to its rules and infrastructure; after all, similar arrangements had been reached in other national parks. But in keeping with Ottawa's policy of establishing new national parks as wilderness areas, entirely free of development, residences, or commercial enterprises, all those living and operating businesses within the park received notice they must leave. All privately held properties would be acquired for the park through purchase, exchange, or expropriation.

"This news just came out of the blue," said Neil Buckle, forced to face the reality of giving up Combers Resort on Long Beach, operated by his family since the 1950s. For long-time residents like Peg Whittington, the Lovekin family, the Buckle family, the Moraes, and many others, the news came as an overwhelming shock. Subsequent negotiations, disputes, and appeals left many landowners frustrated, angry, and bitterly hurt by what seemed like an autocratic takeover. Between 1970 and 1975, all homes, buildings, and businesses within the park boundaries were either moved or razed, leaving little more than a detailed inventory in the archives of Parks Canada, with photographs of every structure in the park prior to its removal or destruction. The Lovekins' large home, Peg Whittington's Singing Sands, Long Beach Bungalows, Combers Resort, Abbott's Store, Surfway Market—all went, along with dozens of homes and summer cabins. A few structures, including the Kimola Motel, remained intact for use as park offices or staff accommodation.

At the Wickaninnish Inn, Robin Fells fought back, mustering substantial support from horrified former guests across Canada who petitioned for the inn to be allowed to continue operating. After huge effort, he gained a five-year extension. The inn carried on under different management, but its former glory faded away. It closed in 1977, and the building became an interpretive centre for Parks Canada.

Right after the park officially opened in May 1971, and with land expropriations and negotiations in the Long Beach area underway, the Wreck Bay community, nestled in makeshift homes along the beach, received notices of eviction. Protests proved futile, and so, in

Godfrey Stephens's words, "Wreck Bay became wrecked for people like us." Everyone had to leave by the end of September 1971; if the owners destroyed their structures and cleaned up, they would receive compensation of up to fifty dollars. Beach dwellers at Schooner Cove received the same offer. In the autumn of 1971, when most of the summer folk had left for the winter, Parks staff, along with demolition crews, dismantled and burned the remaining structures. Ken Gibson and his crew were contracted to do this work and found a few people still living at Wreck Bay, refusing to move. "I remember one gal, standing naked in front of her shack in November, trying to stop us getting it," he said. The crew stood back while a policeman from Ucluelet and a Parks representative did the talking. In another cabin, Ken found an angry sign left for him and his men: "May you burn in hell." "Some of the cabins were real nice," he remembered "very inventive in their use of space, the squatters had done their best with what they had. Most were down low on the beach, a few were treehouses." In an attempt to avoid conflict, Ken and Parks staff established a policy of dismantling only one habitation from any one area in a day. Around the same time, Parks staff asked Ken to collect old abandoned cars on and near Wreck Bay, paying twenty dollars per car. He collected scores of derelicts, some barely more than scrap metal.

The traditional Esowista village site, on Indian Reserve land belonging to the Tla-o-qui-aht people, fell within the new park's boundaries. Lengthy discussions took place about how the park should deal with this reserve land, and whether it too should be expropriated. Asked if they would be willing to do a land swap and shift the reserve out of the park to other locations, Tla-o-qui-aht leaders refused. In the end the park adjusted its boundaries to exclude Indian Reserve land. In subsequent years, more and more Tla-o-qui-aht people chose to live permanently at Esowista village, and overcrowding became a problem. Complex negotiations began, with the Tla-o-qui-ahts wishing to expand the reserve into park land to accommodate more people. In 2006 the park ceded eighty-four hectares of land to the Tla-o-qui-aht, allowing the construction of a new village site, called Ty-Histanis, adjacent to Esowista.

The coming of Pacific Rim National Park did not bring an end to problems on Long Beach. Far from it. The park attracted even more people to the coast, and early Parks staff faced stiff challenges as they tried to impose a degree of order on the seasonal chaos. Word of the attractions of the area began to spread far and wide. In "Coast of Unsung Grandeur," an article in the June 1971 edition of *Westways*, the magazine of the Automobile Club of Southern California, journalist Dolly Connelly waxed lyrical about the glories of the scenery, describing the two-day-long July Fly-In at Long Beach as a non-stop beach party, now accessible by car, despite the "tooth-shattering misery" of the "roller-coaster gravel road." She also provided details of the daily Orient Line bus service, the regular commercial flights to Vancouver, and the twice-daily flights from Port Alberni, while lavishing praise on the Wickaninnish Inn and the "venerable lodge" at Clayoquot.

In the autumn of 1972, the Department of Highways improved the road to Port Alberni, eliminating the dangerous switchbacks around Sproat Lake in favour of a lower level alternative, and paving the entire route. With travel made so much easier and quicker, Easter weekend of 1973 saw 1,700 groups camping at Long Beach, Wreck Beach, and Schooner Cove, probably amounting to over 6,000 people. On the May 24 holiday weekend that same spring, the situation became even worse. An estimated 10,000 people arrived on the coast, including two motorcycle gangs. The *Daily Colonist* reported the number to be even higher, stating 15,000 people had been on the beaches, and mourning how "few of these people know, or care, that a vital element of Long Beach has gone forever, driven away by their presence." One unruly group set fire to a car (some reports say two cars) and rolled it—or them—down the beach, prompting the RCMP to read the Riot Act and arrest eleven people. This convinced Parks officials to set in motion a plan they knew would be unpopular, but which they believed to be essential: camping and driving on the beaches would be completely banned.

When the Department of Highways paved the road to the west coast in 1972, hordes of people arrived to camp on the beaches. The numbers escalated out of control. On the May 24 weekend in 1973, an estimated 10,000 people camped on Long Beach.
Photo courtesy of Pacific Rim National Park Reserve

Achieving this took time and met with angry opposition, but in 1975, at the end of the summer, the beaches within the park officially closed to camping and to cars. Local business owners feared that the ban would discourage tourism; instead it changed the nature of tourism, expanding its scope and leading to a rush to provide tourist facilities and housing outside the park boundaries. This rush took on proportions no one ever imagined possible.

Tofino from the air in 1965, the Maquinna Hotel standing out as the town's most prominent structure. *Tofino Municipality Collection*

Chapter 20:

ADJUSTMENT

THE SPIKE IN DEMAND for herring roe took Tofino by storm in 1971. Highly valued in Japan for *kazunoko*, a traditional dish symbolizing fertility and family prosperity, roe became the most valuable commodity on the west coast following the depletion of herring stocks in both Japanese and Russian waters, driving a fishing extravaganza even wilder than the pilchard boom in the 1920s and '30s. Hundreds of seiners, gillnetters, and herring skiffs arrived in Clayoquot Sound that spring, looking to scoop up as many herring *(Clupea pallasii)* as their boats could hold, while fish buyers vied for their catches with suitcases full of cash. "It was like the Wild West on water," commented a witness.

When herring spawn in coastal waters in late February and early March, the female herring, each carrying 20,000 to 40,000 eggs, swim into bays and inlets at high tide and deposit their roe on the kelp and eelgrass near the shore. The male herring turn the water milky white as they deposit their milt on the roe. Seabirds fly about in a feeding frenzy, sea lions and seals gorge themselves on herring until they can eat no more. Every season is different, every spawn is different, but in the 1970s the herring consistently flocked in, demand soared, and the roe industry boomed.

Fishermen have only a matter of hours to capture the female herring before they deposit their roe. Because timing is so critical and the window of opportunity so small, boats would stand by in great numbers, awaiting permission from the Department of Fisheries to begin netting the fish. In the rush for herring roe, this led to chaotic fishing in very tight quarters that sometimes saw boats ramming each other while jockeying for the best locations to set their nets. Fish companies chartered float planes to scout for herring from the air. Doug Banks became the first pilot to install a sounder on his plane, so if he landed amid a school of herring, he could report the extent and number of fish.

"We radioed our reports in code, so other planes and the fish boats wouldn't understand. Soon everyone was doing the same. It was cut-throat competition," Doug recalled. Occasional fist fights broke out, and fishermen threatened each other with guns, for fortunes could be lost if a boat and its crew failed to catch as many fish as possible in the allotted time. Those lucky enough filled their holds and even their decks to overflowing; in 1975, ten overloaded boats went down on the west coast in the unpredictable March weather.

Fish packers cruised the fleet in the boom years of the 1970s, offering astronomical amounts of money to fishermen. "Japanese fish buyers skulked around town in business suits, carrying briefcases full of fifties," wrote Andrew Struthers. "'Just a gift,' they would say. 'Please remember us when you catch some herring.'" One fisherman recalled a fish buyer paying him with 341 thousand-dollar bills from a briefcase that held $1.25 million in cash. Asked to carry a paper bag from a float plane to a boat, a local woman obliged, unaware until later that she had held over $300,000 in cash. One boat made $1.6 million in one set, according to Walter Guppy, and fisherman Frank Rae-Arthur maintained that with so much cash circulating on the coast, no hundred-dollar bills could be found east of Winnipeg. Ladies of the evening arrived from Vancouver and set out for the fishing grounds in the *Marabel* and other yachts; some women reportedly accepted payment in herring roe if the men had no bills small enough.

While the United States allowed frozen whole herring to be shipped to Japan for processing, Canadian law demanded that the herring roe be processed in Canada. In 1972 this led Bob Wingen into partnership with Andrew Tulloch and Ned Easton, to expand his involvement in the fishing industry. Wingen had taken over the family business in 1955, renaming it Tofino Marine Services. The Wingens' days of boatbuilding had come to an end, and Bob's interests diversified to include fish packing for various companies, harvesting and processing oysters, and managing fish-buying camps on the west coast of Vancouver Island. With the herring boom in full swing, and confidently expecting a $1.7-million grant from the federal government as part of an initiative to employ aboriginal workers, Wingen and his partners borrowed money in 1972 to develop new facilities. The first stage of the new operation, now called Tofino Fisheries Ltd., started up in 1973, processing herring, groundfish, oysters, and shrimp. By 1974 the second phase had been completed, replacing the machine shop and boat shed with a reduction plant, freezer, and cold storage. By then the operation stood out as the largest enterprise in town, employing 240 workers, including 125 aboriginals. However, changes in the federal government radically affected the financing of the operation, with the result that the company received only $319,000, instead of the expected $1.7 million, forcing it into receivership. Canadian Fishing Company took over Tofino Fisheries that year, selling it to BC Packers in 1980.

During the herring boom, the plant hired hundreds of workers to handle the catch, process the herring roe, and render the herring into fishmeal. "The plant hummed around the clock and there was overtime galore," according to local writer Frank Harper, who worked there, wearing two of the mandatory hairnets (one on his beard). In *The Sound* magazine, Harper described the all-important fish line, where only women worked, popping the "jewelled roe" out of the swollen bellies of the female herring. "Squeeze, pop, squeeze, for 10, 12 hours a shift, the ladies sometimes singing songs in time with the great grating machinery to break the monotony...as many as 80 women crowded in at the long table, elbow-to-elbow, popping, singing." The roe, stored in airtight containers, was airlifted to Japan; the rest of the herring rendered down and shipped out of town.

According to Harper, Tofino's population tripled in springtime during the years of the roe fishery. "Fishermen and migrants swarmed here in all sorts of weird vehicles: rickety homemade houses on wheels with stovepipes poking through the roofs, and in hippie busses painted psychedelic, trucks pulling skiffs stacked three high." Tofino's St. Francis of Assisi Roman Catholic church on Main Street opened its doors to a group of Ahousaht women who worked in the fish plant, allowing them to sleep and stay in the church so they would not have to travel back and forth.

"The whole town reeked of money and herring," as Jacqui Hansen put it. "Everyone complained about the fishy smell, but to me it was the smell of money because my kids were working in the fish plant making fifteen dollars an hour, huge money at the time. We had herring scales over everything; they stuck to the skin; they stuck to the shower, they got inside the washing machine and attached to clothes. They were everywhere." Janis McDougall's essay in *Writing the West Coast* describes how she recognized fish plant workers "by the flash of silver scales on their clothes and by the invisible cloud of odour that remained in the bank long after paycheques had been cashed."

With so much money floating around, the bars in Tofino did a booming trade as groups of people gathered to spend some of their cash and wait for the next herring opening. "We lived in herring then...," Frank Harper wrote. "It was a rush, a chore, a thrill, a drag, a bonanza." Even the bears were happy. On one occasion a truck carrying a load of herring meal tipped over on its way out of town, spilling its load. The bears feasted royally.

The herring roe fishing frenzy lasted only a few years, with prices rising from $60 a ton to $5,000 a ton before Japanese consumers balked at paying $26 per pound in their stores. By 1980 the bottom fell out of the market, leaving prices at $9 per pound. Some Japanese companies, having stockpiled tons of US frozen herring, went broke, and on the west coast many BC fishermen rued the downturn. One fisherman summed the whole herring episode up: "It was very intense. It could be very, very dangerous but, boy, it was super exciting. I don't think you'll ever see another fishery like that again."

The herring boom gave the village of Tofino a small taste of what it meant for the town to be overtaken by a new industry and assailed by an influx of new people. The town had been facing constant adjustments since the creation of the road; by the mid-1970s, the days of living in tranquil obscurity as an isolated fishing village seemed like a distant dream. The park had come to stay, the long beaches were becoming widely known, the youth culture of the beaches continued to influence the town, and the numbers of visitors kept increasing.

In Tofino village the first wave of small motels and resorts appeared from the mid-1960s to the early 1970s: Duffin Cove Cabins, Lone Cone Motel, Esowista Place Motel, the Mini Motel, and the Apoloma Motel (later the Pacific Breeze). Available tourist accommodation in the village faced a temporary reduction in the summer of 1973 when fire destroyed part of the Maquinna Hotel. Originally owned by Reuben Parker, Frank Bull, and Dennis Singleton, the Maquinna had opened on July 1, 1959, built with material salvaged from the Tofino air base. Initially, the hotel housed a grocery store on its lower floor facing Main Street, with the beer parlour on the main floor. By the time of the fire, the hotel had a dining room, lounge, and cabaret; the beer parlour, with its separate entrances for "Men" and "Ladies and Escorts," then occupied the ground floor. The fire destroyed the cabaret and caused considerable water damage. All forty-five guests had to be evacuated, but the main part of the building remained intact thanks to Tofino's volunteer firefighters. For a short while the hotel closed, but the beer continued to flow.

Out at MacKenzie Beach, the MacKenzie family expanded their campsite, by 1972 offering twelve cabins and a mobile home park to visitors, plus several cottages to rent. Farther along MacKenzie Beach, Ben Hellesen, who had earlier operated a fish plant in Tofino, opened Ocean Village Resort in 1976, with its distinctive beehive-style cabins. Hector Bodchen opened Crystal Cove Resort as a small campground in 1979, later building a number of log cabins for guests. At Cox Bay, the Pettinger family acquired their resort in 1973. Having spotted an advertisement in the *Edmonton Journal*, they bought 16.5 hectares of oceanfront in Cox Bay where the Pacific Paradise Motel stood, a lodge built several years earlier with recycled materials from the airport. The Pettingers renamed their venture the Pacific Sands Beach Resort; now much expanded, it remains the longest-running resort in the area.

While all these new facilities provided more accommodation in the area, other local amenities remained scant. Maureen Fraser arrived on the west coast in 1975, after driving across Canada and visiting both Banff and Jasper National Parks en route. She had enjoyed the amenities the towns of Banff and Jasper offered to park visitors, and she arrived at Pacific Rim National Park expecting at least some services for visitors. Out near the park, she found nothing. All services at Long Beach had disappeared by then: the little stores and the gas stations had gone, along with the Fiddle-In Drive-In that had once boasted "The Finest in Fish 'n' Fountain," serving "Hamburgers, Abalone Burgers, Oyster burgers, Prawn burgers." Maureen went to Tofino in search of a cinnamon bun: "I couldn't find one because there was no bakery in Tofino. Nothing. I looked around and thought, 'This town doesn't know what's hit it.' Pacific Rim National Park has just been created right next to it, and it had this amazing Sound, and it had almost no services. No bakery. No bookstore. No place to rent canoes and kayaks." Maureen continued on her planned road trip down to South America, noting how tourist centres catered to their visitors, and developing ideas of what she would do. A year later she returned to Tofino to start a business that has become arguably the town's most notable gathering place, the Common Loaf Bakery and Café, famed for its bread and cinnamon buns, and for its freewheeling community notice board.

In the mid-1970s, deciding where to go out in the evening in Tofino was not difficult. The Maquinna Hotel restaurant served dinner, or customers could go there for a drink in the Tiki Cocktail Bar or in the beer parlour. The only other choices were the small Kakawin Café (later the Loft Restaurant) or the Schooner Restaurant. The Schooner occupied the site of Vic's Coffee Bar, which had first opened in 1949 in a section of a disused RCAF hospital building, moved into town that year by Tofino's Masonic Lodge. The Masons occupied the top floor, renting out ground floor units to local businesses. In the postwar years, this building stood on the outer edge of the village, backing onto the forest; the Masonic landlords promised their early tenants that one day this would be the centre of Tofino. Vic's Coffee Bar morphed into the Lone Cone Café before being transformed into the Schooner Restaurant by Jerry Gautier in the early 1960s. In 1968, Gloria Bruce took over the restaurant, making the place famous for its burgers and fish and chips. Still run by the Bruce family, still in its original location, the Schooner carries on a thriving business to this day, now right in the centre of town.

In 1974, the municipal council turned over the town's Community Hall to a collective of young people as a coffee shop, gathering place, and arts centre. The old hall had been used less and less frequently during the 1960s, for social life in Tofino changed noticeably with the coming of television, which arrived around the same time as the road. Even with only one channel offering fuzzy black-and-white images, the new medium—and *Hockey Night in Canada*—proved mesmerizing. The Saturday dances no longer exerted their old appeal, and people stayed home more. Re-created as the Gust o' Wind Arts Centre, the hall took on new life and became the heart and soul of Tofino for many young people who drifted into town and stayed there. Here they gathered to drink coffee, read, pursue their crafts, dance, and listen to live music. Artists and craftspeople leased spaces for around twenty dollars per month where they could create and sell their work from small studios and workshops, and the centre offered classes in different disciplines: music, dance, pottery, carving, yoga, and breadmaking. Well-known carver and photographer Adrian Dorst had a space here; Michael Mullin, now owner of Tofino's Mermaid Tales Bookstore, shared his collection of books here; Maureen Fraser started her Common Loaf bakery as the Gust o' Wind Bakeshop. And here, over many cups of coffee, concerned discussions arose about environmental issues, many of them focusing on Meares Island, due to be logged by MacMillan Bloedel. From such discussions, the Save Meares Island group took shape, later evolving into the Friends of Clayoquot Sound. Membership included many of the Gust o' Wind regulars. While the place attracted mostly young and like-minded people, townsfolk also came in occasionally, some out of curiosity, some to purchase crafts. Dorothy Arnet became a regular customer: "I came for that wonderful bread!"

Not everyone in Tofino approved, many expressed great unease about providing a drop-in centre for a seemingly irresponsible young crowd. The loud music, late-night celebrations, dances, and drumming, along with the wafting scent of marijuana, led to repeated complaints to the town council. In September 1980, council heeded the complaints and closed the centre with a disapproving thud of the gavel, following what the local paper termed "a long and unpleasant feud." At that time, council could not have foreseen that the 2014 Arts and Culture Master Plan for Tofino would acknowledge the Gust o' Wind as the town's first arts society, going on to praise the "free and communicative flair [that] came out of those times that can still be seen within the works of local artists today."

The closure of the Gust o' Wind marked the end of an era in Tofino. "Perhaps they thought that if we close the building all these people will go away," commented Maureen Fraser. Some did leave, but many remained. A new breed of Tofinoite emerged from the counterculture, settling in and near the town to raise families, some buying property; some establishing themselves as small business owners, entrepreneurs, and artists; many becoming actively involved in community affairs and the growing environmental movement. The Community Hall, emptied of its noisy and creative crowd, housed Tofino's library for a number of years before being demolished in 1997.

The paving of the road, the thriving herring fishery, and the increasing logging activity attracted many new residents to Tofino during the 1970s and '80s. The town's population stood at 461 in 1971; by 1991 it increased to 1,103. So many Americans took up residence that an area of town on Olsen Road became known as "Little Seattle." "Increasingly there were different layers of people in Tofino, and not as much mingling as there had been before," Leona Taylor noted. In 1972, a twenty-eight-lot subdivision was created on the new Cypre Crescent, largely to house MacMillan Bloedel employees, with lots selling for $2,200. Some of the newcomers became actively involved in local groups, the men coaching local sports teams and running organizations like the Boy Scouts. A few of the women joined the long-established Ladies' Hospital Aid. Although initially dubious of new members with newfangled ideas—"But we've never held a dance at the Legion on Valentine's Day!"—the older Ladies' Aid members soon recognized the success of these energetic new fundraisers.

In 1969, Jim Hudnall and his wife, Carolyn, having camped out for three summers in the area, decided to buy property in Tofino. They chose a lot on Tofino Inlet, costing $5,000. "We could have bought land at Chesterman Beach for way less, but no one wanted to live there," Jim related. "It was too swampy and there was no place for a boat." At that time, any land for sale at Chesterman Beach belonged to Dr. Howard McDiarmid. In the mid-1960s, he had purchased 490 metres of waterfront property at Chesterman Beach, with an option to buy another 550 metres. Eventually he owned land all along North and South Chesterman Beach, over 120 hectares extending across the Pacific Rim Highway to the inlet. Bit by bit he subdivided sections of this land, initially offering lots for sale for $2,000 each. At first only one sold. Leona Taylor shared the incredulity of most Tofino residents. "Who would buy property way out there? We thought anyone who bought out there was crazy. It was below water level in places and it was way too expensive."

Slowly, in the late 1960s and early '70s, lots at Chesterman Beach did begin to sell. Prices crept up. A brochure from late 1971/early 1972 offered lots at Chesterman Beach with 30.5 metres of shoreline for $12,500, and semi-waterfront lots for $4,000. Mary Bewick, among the earliest purchasers, has lived there ever since, walking the beach every day. Mary Oliver purchased her land for a dollar down and a promise to pay later, as did Neil and Marilyn Buckle, displaced by Pacific Rim Park from their lodge at Combers' Beach. The Buckles became the first to build on North Chesterman Beach in 1970, having acquired their waterfront lot for a mere $10,000. According to Charles McDiarmid, "My father gave [Neil] a discount if he would build a house within a year of purchase [because] there were rumours that homes... would sink into the sand at high tide...Neil did build his house and with a basement to boot, to prove that all would be fine...the house he built still stands today."

By the mid-1980s, some twenty homes, many of them small cabins, dotted the shore along both North and South Chesterman Beach, with a similar number of homes set back from the water along Lynn Road. Neil Buckle milled a good deal of the wood used in these homes at his mill on Vargas Island; he would bring wood over and sell it from his home at Chesterman Beach, operating on an honour system. If no one was at his place to sell the wood, customers simply took what they required and recorded their purchase on slips of paper provided.

Some of the early Chesterman beach dwellers in the 1970s brought with them alternative lifestyles reminiscent of those from Wreck Bay, no doubt surprising the "townies," who until then had regarded the beach as a local hangout for drag racing up and down the sand. According to Adrienne Mason: "There was 'Laser Dave,' who on clear, starry nights, would set out rows of lit candles to show the alignment of the planets (or some say it was a landing strip for aliens). There was the naked carver, Henry. His end of the beach was the nude end. There were the early surfers...There were houses shaped like pyramids and octagons, and those built of salvaged wood by weekend work parties fuelled by beer and clams."

Increasingly, Chesterman Beach began to attract like-minded families raising young children. A tightly knit community took shape, some of the children home-schooled, many of them taking to the waves on their Boogie Boards and becoming the "beach babies" of Chesterman. The people of Chesterman even initiated their own tsunami warning system, setting up a "phone tree" among themselves. In the mid-1980s, the beach residents formed an association and launched a valiant, although unsuccessful, effort to purchase Frank Island for public use. The island, just offshore and accessible at low tide from Chesterman Beach, would then have cost $48,000. By 2006 the asking price for the island stood at $2.9 million.

At the north end of Chesterman Beach, carver Henry Nolla became an institution on the beach, in the early years walking around nude in the summer, wearing nothing but a bandana and a knife slung around his hips. With quiet, Zen-like concentration, he carved totem poles, bowls, and all manner of other objects in his workshop at the end of the beach known as "Henry's End." From time to time he carried out commissioned work, as when the municipality asked him to carve a "Welcome" sign to be placed on the roadside at the entrance to the town. Having grown up in Europe with a Swedish mother and a Spanish father, English served as his third language, and spelling could be problematic. When unveiled, the sign read "Wellcome" and had to be redone.

Described by Andrew Struthers as resembling "Father Time in a

Blake engraving," the much-loved Nolla garnered great respect for his work, acting as a mentor to many other wood carvers. He died in 2004, having lived some thirty years on Chesterman Beach. His work can still be seen all around Tofino: at the Common Loaf Bakery, on the Village Green, and, most prominently, in the distinctive facade of Roy Henry Vickers's Eagle Aerie Gallery. "I wouldn't be here if it wasn't for Henry," Vickers once said. Nolla's large carving shed, adjacent to the Wickaninnish Inn, remains open to visitors and carvers.

If Henry Nolla had walked down to South Chesterman Beach in the late 1980s and early 1990s, he would have noticed the next generation of west coast surfers taking to the sport like ducklings to water. Vern and Gisele Bruhwiler's children, Raph, Sepp, Francis, and Catherine, and Ralph and Alice DeVries's son Peter all lived right on Chesterman Beach, as did Kathy Long, Jack and Brian Greig, Amy Henderson and her three siblings, Mike and Ben Campbell, and the Buckle boys, among others. Along with other young enthusiasts, including Jenny and Sarah Hudnall, Sarah Kalkan, Ryan Erickson, Asia Dryden, Seth Amhein, they formed the first generation of homegrown Tofino surfers. They graduated from Boogie Boards to surfboards, and once out there catching the wave, certain members of this group never looked back; they would take west coast surfing to the next level. Because they lived on or near the beach, they could surf before and after school, or in some cases during school hours. "We used to have to go to school by bus," Sepp Bruhwiler recalled. "Some days Frank and I would purposely miss the bus, sneak back home, grab our gear, go surfing and hang out on the beach all day. Other days if the surf was up mom would allow us to stay home and surf."

The alternative, slightly offbeat sport of the 1960s and '70s had changed its image by the time these young surfers were growing up. While still very cool, surfing had become more mainstream, attracting a far more diverse crowd. The popularity of skateboarding and snowboarding, and improvements in wetsuit design, helped, while the California-inspired trendiness of surf clothing and accessories further boosted the sport's appeal. By the early 1980s, enough surfers had begun haunting the beaches to encourage Liz Zed to start up the first surf shop in the Tofino area; Live to Surf opened in 1984 in an addition she built onto her house at Chesterman Beach. The young surfing crowd vied for the fun summer jobs there.

In 1977, Howard McDiarmid bought the land at the northwest end of Chesterman Beach, including the rocky headland, the area fronting on Shell Beach, and around onto MacKenzie Beach. He built himself a house at the very tip of the headland, employing Don McGinnis—who shortly afterward became Tofino's mayor—to build the house, with Henry Nolla assisting. Nolla became McDiarmid's caretaker, living in a cabin nearby. McDiarmid had eyed this property at the headland for many years, dreaming one day he would own it. Having played a leading role in the creation of Pacific Rim National Park, he realized early on the development and tourism potential of the west coast of Vancouver Island, and had long imagined building a resort on this site.

After the original Wickaninnish Inn on Long Beach closed for good in 1977, McDiarmid bought the rights to the Wickaninnish name the day the previous ownership lapsed. His ambition of opening a second Wickaninnish Inn then waited in the wings for many years. By the time the current resort opened in August 1996, Chesterman Beach had been transformed. In the late 1990s, properties hit the million-dollar mark when a Vancouver businessman offered Jim Schwartz a million dollars for his recently completed house on the beach. The new owner later flipped the house for $1.9 million; in 2014 it sold for $2.55 million. The little cabins that once dotted the beachfront fell to sledgehammers or to flames to make way for ever larger, more ambitious homes. Singer Sarah McLachlan bought and built there, also Sunkist CEO Ralph Bodine. No one now can purchase a property on Chesterman Beach for under $1.5 million, and newcomers take for granted services that the early residents never imagined possible. Many hard-won changes in Tofino's infrastructure had to occur over the years to enable such development; none more important than the establishment of water and sewer connections to Chesterman Beach in the early 1980s.

From the early days, Tofino residents had generally looked after their own needs in terms of water and garbage disposal. Garbage could be buried but often went straight into the sea, sometimes right off the government wharf, even into the 1960s. For water, people dug wells, tapped into creeks, or simply collected rainwater in barrels. Such water systems could be problematic, as Catharine Whyte mentioned in a letter to her mother in 1943: "The pump water is nice and brown and not very tasty, so we boil it before drinking it." In 1949, the village voted to create a communal water supply by damming the small creek running into Duffin Cove near Grice Point behind the hospital. The map of Clayoquot Sound made by John Meares in 1778 notes this creek as a "watering place"; Meares and other mariners evidently used it to replenish their ships' fresh water supplies.

To provide Tofino with water, workers built a forty-five-cubic-metre wooden reservoir near the creek. It fed into a network of water mains painstakingly hand-dug or blasted into the underlying rock throughout the village. Initially, Tofino's new community water system required someone to make a daily journey to the creek to start the gas-powered generator that pumped water from the creek to the reservoir. When BC Hydro electrical power arrived in the village in 1961, this job became redundant.

Although plagued by a series of misfortunes in subsequent years, for its first few years this water system worked fairly well. Nursed along by Tom Gibson, chairman of the hospital board, later mayor of Tofino, and owner of Gibson Contracting, the water kept flowing. "Tom knew where every pipe in Tofino's primitive water system was located, and he was always right there to repair the numerous leaks," Howard McDiarmid wrote. Because Tofino had no sewer system at the time, faulty septic tanks also kept Gibson and his sons busy with ceaseless repair jobs. Sewer connections did not arrive in Tofino until the early 1980s.

Tofino's water system faced its first crisis in 1958 during a severe summer drought. The lowest rainfall ever recorded in Tofino's history, only 185 millimetres of rain from May until August, meant most of the rivers in the area dried up, leaving the village with no water. After surviving this ordeal, and with the wooden reservoir by then leaking badly, in 1960 the village built a new forty-five-cubic-metre wooden tank on Meares Island, collecting water from Close Creek. A three-kilometre-long PVC pipe carried the water under Browning Passage to Tofino. Disaster struck in 1964 when the earthquake in Anchorage, Alaska, sent a tsunami surging into Browning Passage. It ripped apart the plastic submarine pipe, depositing pieces of it in crab traps and all over the sea floor. To maintain the needed water supply, a temporary pipe carried water to the village while the original pipe was being repaired and upgraded. Once reinstalled, calamity again intervened. In 1968, unseasonably cold temperatures caused the pipe on Meares Island to freeze and burst, even though water was constantly flowing through it. After repairing the pipe, village officials recognized that the system needed further upgrading because the altitude of the tank at Close Creek provided very limited water pressure; Tofino residents at higher altitudes needed water pumps to ensure they had service. And the submarine pipe continued to pose problems. With new ice and fish plants being constructed on the waterfront, demanding more and more water at a higher pressure, something had to be done.

In 1970, just when Tofino proposed upgrading its water system, Noranda Mines, which had worked the recently closed Brynnor iron ore mine at Maggie Lake south of Tofino, wanted to dispose of a 455-cubic-metre steel tank, free of charge. Seizing the opportunity, the village had the tank cut in half, loaded it onto a flatbed truck, and transported it to Barr Mountain, just behind Tofino village. With the tank welded back together, and with a new and larger submarine pipeline extending from Meares Island to feed the tank, the village's water pressure shot up from 35 to 126 pounds per square inch.

More adversity hit the water system in November 1975. This time heavy rains sent a mudslide down the side of Mount Colnett on Meares Island, completely washing out the Close Creek dam, the settling tank, and 457 metres of pipe. In April 1976 the *Westcoaster* described how the town "haywired a workable system together" while lobbying desperately for financial assistance from the province. Finally, with the aid of a $50,000 provincial grant, the village built a dam on Sharp Creek, north of Close Creek, and laid a new pipeline, 4.7 kilometres long, to the village. Just as the forms for the dam had been built and stood ready for the concrete to be poured, a sudden very heavy rainstorm completely wiped out the structure. Workers had to begin the whole building process anew.

With the growing number of residents and visitors, the water requirements of the area increased. The new resorts south of the village, and the expanding community at Chesterman Beach, wanted to be connected to Tofino's water system. The village council lobbied the federal government for an $11.3-million grant to build an entirely new water system and sewer infrastructure between 1983 and 1986. To expedite the application process and to qualify for the grant, in 1982 the village of Tofino became the District of Tofino, expanding its boundaries to include all the land south on the Esowista Peninsula as far as the northern border of Pacific Rim National Park.

The federal money allowed the District of Tofino to build a water system served by Ginnard Creek, south of Close Creek on Meares Island, and to run a supply line to two large concrete reservoirs, one just south of the village (on District Lot 117), and the other on Lovekin Hill, between Chesterman Beach and Cox Bay. The grant also covered the cost of an infiltration gallery and water settling tank at Close Creek. In 1988, calamity again hit Tofino's water system. Only three years after it had been constructed, the DL117 concrete reservoir began leaking from the bottom, washing away its sand base. The tank collapsed and was removed from service. To compensate for its loss, in 1992 the District linked #1 Creek on Meares Island into the system. In 1995 a new reinforced concrete base allowed the DL117 reservoir to be put back in service, and Tofino's water system finally appeared ready to handle the District's water needs for decades to come.

No matter where one lived in Clayoquot Sound, by 1978 improved medical aid could handle emergencies far more effectively than before.

The Tofino Ambulance Service began serving residents of the Sound that year, using an ambulance, planes, and the Tofino lifeboat. The paid employees of the Ambulance Service included about a dozen Tofino townsfolk, including loggers, hippies, fisheries officers, and Co-op workers, headquartered in the old ambulance station behind the hospital. Two remained on call all the time, and the service fielded an average of 200 calls a year. At the hospital, Dr. Harvey Henderson arrived to replace Howard McDiarmid, who left Tofino in 1972. Henderson initiated regular visits to Hot Springs Cove and Ahousat, flying in to hold local clinics. The nurses' residence in Tofino had expanded over the years to house half a dozen nurses. The matron, Australian-born Dilys Bruce, ruled her domain with a strict hand. Actively involved in the community, she also co-owned the Mini Motel with Mary Mac-Leod, and both Dilys and Mary staunchly supported the environmental movement in later years. One of the nurses who served many years at the Tofino hospital, Midori (Sakai) Matley, had survived the bombing of Hiroshima. She and her husband, Peter, became long-time Tofino residents. For years, she was the only Japanese person in town.

A handmade poster advertising one of the earliest wildlife tours in Clayoquot Sound in the early 1970s. Jim Hudnall and his wife Carolyn ran tours from Long Beach taking tourists out to see whales and sea lions, charging four dollars for an hour and a half.
Courtesy of Jim Hudnall

As Tofino worked to improve its infrastructure and services, many in town explored ways of tapping into the economic potential created by visitors. Among the earliest to sense that tourists would pay to see wildlife, Jim and Carolyn Hudnall bought an old survey boat in 1970 and started their Clayoquot Cruise and Charter business. As Carolyn explained, "This was the beginning of the environmental era and we were part of that consciousness, and had become acquainted with some of the scientists who were working to preserve the wild." Leaving from the crab dock, they gave "sunset cruises" as well as wildlife tours around the islands in Tofino Harbour and up the inlet, viewing birds on the mud flats, eagles, raccoons, and seals. No one thought, at that point, of whale or bear watching. Sea lions, though, already had proved an attraction. In the late 1960s, Ernie Bach, who ran the gas station and VW repair shop on the Tofino waterfront, started taking groups of visitors on "Sea Lion Cruises." They left from Tofino in his large cabin cruiser and went to Sea Lion Rocks off Long Beach. "We were appalled at how he blew his horns and disturbed the sea lions," Carolyn said. These original sea lion tours stopped in 1970. Jim and Carolyn then approached the director of the newly formed Pacific Rim National Park "to describe our vision of an 'environmentally conscious' Marine Mammal Interpretive Cruise," requesting permission to run such tours from the park amphitheatre at the north end of Long Beach. They proposed going directly from there out to Sea Lion Rocks with a park naturalist on board to talk about the wildlife.

Every summer from 1971 to 1976, these cruises ran from Long Beach. "At first we advertised them just as sea lion tours," Jim Hudnall recalled, "but we soon realized we could always count on seeing grey whales so we began advertising as whale tours—the first in the area." Jim strung a rope from the beach to an anchored buoy out beyond the surf and pulled his Boston Whaler to and from shore. "People sometimes got wet." Once he had loaded a maximum of twelve passengers, he would haul the boat out to sea until the water was deep enough to lower and start the engine. A trip to Sea Lion Rocks cost four dollars and took ninety minutes; Jim ran four trips daily in the summer. Carolyn took care of the bookings and publicity, posting cheerful hand-coloured signs around Tofino. As the operation grew, Doug Palfrey and Jim Darling joined the ranks of employees, along with Marta Fiddy, who worked as office manager from a disused home on the beach.

Others soon realized the potential of adventure travel and ecotourism and began offering wildlife and whale-watching trips around Meares Island and to other areas of Clayoquot Sound. Jamie's Whaling Station began operations in 1982; Shari Bondy started up the first whale-watching business using Zodiacs in 1985; Remote Passages Whale Watching and Sea Kayaking opened in 1986, as did Ospray Fishing Charters. Dorothy Baert of Tofino Sea Kayaking first offered kayaks to rent in 1988. In 1987, Tofino hosted its first annual Whale Festival. From these beginnings, the town's fame as a centre for whale watching and wilderness adventure grew and spread.

In 1983, sport fisherman Dick Close began building the Weigh West Marine Resort on the Tofino waterfront. One of the first tourism entrepreneurs, Close offered fishing charters, rental boats, and "all in" packages to visitors. "The whole thing kind of evolved over the next decade or so," Close commented. "First we built some rooms, then added a pub, then more rooms, then a restaurant, then more rooms."

Some of the adventure tours of Clayoquot Sound began taking visitors to Hot Springs Cove on the Openit Peninsula, about thirty kilometres northwest of Tofino, at the entrance to Sydney Inlet. Al Pineo offered visitors the first day-long return trips to Hot Springs Cove in 1982, aboard his boat *Barkley Pacific*. He went up "the inside" through the passages and inlets of Clayoquot Sound, returning on "the outside" along the open coast, viewing basking sharks, birds, orcas, and grey whales en route, with a relaxing soak in the hot springs as the highlight of the trip. Long known to the Nuu-chah-nulth as *Mok-seh-kla-chuck*, meaning "smoking waters," the hot springs average 50 degrees Celsius. Visitors walk for some twenty minutes along a boardwalk to reach the springs, where geothermal water bubbles out of the ground at 455 litres a minute, cascading down a series of pools and small waterfalls to the open ocean. Most of the early tourists happily joined in the tradition of entering the springs naked. "People who wouldn't have taken their socks off in public would strip off buck naked there," Al Pineo remembered.

For years, mariners referred to this location as Refuge Cove, noting the safe anchorage it afforded from the open Pacific Ocean. Local storekeeper Ivan Clarke served as postmaster there from 1936 onward; first known as Sydney Inlet Post Office, the name changed in 1948 to Hot Springs Cove Post Office. The following year the Hydrological Survey of Canada officially changed the community's name from Refuge Cove to Hot Springs Cove, to distinguish it from Refuge Cove

Hot Springs Cove filled with fish boats. From the mid-1930s, Ivan Clarke ran a store, gas dock, ice plant and fish packing business here for many years. A small school, originally called "Sydney Inlet School," was built there for his eight children and other locals. Note the airplane tied to the wharf at the right. *Courtesy of Leona Taylor*

on Redonda Island in Desolation Sound. When the Clarke children, eight of them, needed to go to school, local fishermen helped Ivan build a one-room schoolhouse. This Sydney Inlet School opened in 1946, with thirteen children attending—mostly Clarkes, plus a few of the younger Rae-Arthur children from Boat Basin in Hesquiat Harbour. The school ran until 1960, with the name officially changed to Hot Springs Cove School in its final year. For many years without a school, in 2008 the Hesquiaht First Nation Place of Learning opened at Hot Springs Cove, a large, beautifully designed building combining community centre and elementary school, overseen by a totem pole donated by Chief Dominic Andrews.

Back in the 1930s, Ivan Clarke began selling fuel as Standard Oil's agent at Hot Springs Cove, and he established a busy fish-buying station there. For years, he and his family packed, iced, and shipped fish out to Victoria. Art Clarke remembered working there even at the age of eight: "We iced fish all night, as much as 30,000 pounds [13,600 kilograms]. Once we iced 75,000 pounds [34,000 kilograms]." Upward of 200 trollers made Hot Springs Cove their base during the eight-month-long fishing season. When not out in their boats, the fishermen often soaked in the springs, using the hot water to wash their clothes.

Bruce Lucas grew up in Hot Springs village in the 1950s and knew every fish boat in the cove: "Some of the boats I remember were the *Coho King,* the *Boulder Point, Eileen C, Swan, Restless,* SS *Hesquiaht Flyer, Lenny Boy, Tidewater, Audrey S* and of course the mighty *Seven Oaks.* These boats fished just about all year round, fishing for spring salmon in April and progressing into coho, sockeye and pinks in the summer. During the winter months, these boats would troll and jig for ling cod and other ground fish. Our fishermen did not rely on employment insurance benefits or welfare; they were very hard-working men."

Hot Springs Cove became home to many Hesquiaht people by the 1950s. It had long been a place they used as a safe refuge and a fishing station, and in 1874 Father Brabant noticed, on his first visit to the cove, that "here quite a number of Hesquiaht Indians were living." The traditional winter village site of the Hesquiahts, on the outer shore of Hesquiat Harbour, became less viable as the twentieth century advanced, given the increasing number of motor boats. Although an ideal location for launching dugout canoes, the village could not provide safe moorage. Father Charles Moser's diary documents many instances of motor launches being damaged at Hesquiat during storms, and Father Charles mentioned discussions about moving the village site as early as 1915. The move happened slowly—in 1931, when visiting Hot Springs Cove with the hydrological survey, Jack Crosson noted "no buildings of any kind, not even an Indian shack." But gradually, most Hesquiahts did move away, many to Hot Springs Cove, abandoning the old village. By 1950, when Father Maurus Snyder visited the west coast after many years' absence, he described Hesquiat village as "nearly depopulated." In the late 1950s, Father Fred Miller twice visited Hesquiat to report on conditions there to his superiors. "Poor old Hesquiaht," he wrote. "It was a little the worse for wear." He found houses that had "given in to the inevitable and laid down in the sallal brush." The once dominant church of St. Antonin stood vacant and unused, silently rotting away, its windows broken, its roof leaking, the buckling floor strewn with mildewed books and vestments. The era of the ambitious mission had ended, and the "great herd of cattle [Father Brabant] started now roams wild through the woods."

Following the Alaska earthquake in March 1964, a tsunami surged into Hot Springs Cove sweeping houses away, some igniting when coal oil lamps and stoves overturned. No one died but many residents of the village left the vicinity. Some years later, the community was rebuilt on higher ground. *Courtesy of Dr. John Clague*

On the night of March 28, 1964, an earthquake near Anchorage, Alaska, measuring 9.2 on the Richter scale, sent a tsunami surging down the west coast. It wiped out the Hesquiaht village at the head of Hot Springs Cove, carrying away sixteen of the eighteen houses. Some of them burst into flames as coal oil lamps upset, igniting the buildings. Luckily everyone survived the experience, save one cat. "It was the second wave that pulled about four or five houses out into the bay," reported Sue Charleson, who lived through the horror. "They were drifting on top of the water with people inside. A couple of the houses were in flames...In the meanwhile, the fuel lines must have broken at the [Clarke's] store near the government dock. It was lucky that those burning houses did sink before they reached the spilled fuel." After the event, most residents left the cove and it was more or less deserted for a few years. During the late 1960s, "Refuge Cove IR 6" became a Hesquiaht Indian Reserve, and eventually Hesquiaht people returned there, re-establishing themselves on this new village site, on higher ground northwest of the original village site.

In 1955, Ivan Clarke donated fourteen hectares of his original 48.5-hectare pre-emption to the provincial government for a park, leading to the creation of Maquinna Marine Provincial Park. Forty years later, in 1995, the Clayoquot Sound Land Use Decision saw the province add an additional 2,665 hectares to the park, incorporating many kilometres of coastline in Clayoquot Sound. The park then encompassed Hesquiat Peninsula, the coastline around Hesquiat Harbour and down to Hot Springs Cove, the outer coasts of both Flores and Vargas Islands, as well as other sections of coastline. In 1968, Ivan Clarke sold the rest of his land and retired, having lived over thirty years at Hot Springs Cove.

On Meares Island, Christie Indian Residential School at Kakawis closed for good at the end of June 1971, condemned as a fire hazard. During the school's final two years, at the insistence of the fire inspectors, the dormitories all moved downstairs, with the upper floors used only for recreation and for sewing classes. In the decade before it closed, the school had undergone many changes. The Benedictine sisters withdrew in 1961, handing over to the Immaculate Heart sisters from California. From then on, the school offered full days of classes, rather than only a few hours of instruction. During the 1960s, pupils no longer had to attend daily mass in the chapel, and boys and girls—formerly so strictly segregated—could now socialize, sharing sports activities and holding occasional dances, with rock 'n' roll music coming from the record player. Volleyball and basketball remained the favourite sports; one team called themselves the "Mush Eaters." Everyone hated the school's oatmeal.

Faced with the old school's closure, the Christie School Board reached a landmark decision. The board, made up largely of First Nations representatives, decided to build a residence for 100 Christie students in Tofino. After much deliberation, they decided that aboriginal students from around Clayoquot Sound, at least those in elementary school, would live in this purpose-built residence and attend an integrated

public school in Tofino. School integration had already begun in Tofino, for when the Opitsat elementary school closed in the mid-1960s,
students from Opitsat entered the public school in Tofino, commuting
back and forth to their village. In the latter years of Christie School
on Meares Island, only a few students attended from Opitsat or from
Ahousat; most came from villages farther up the coast—Hot Springs
Cove, Hesquiat, Yuquot, and Kyuquot. Ahousaht students attended the
publicly funded elementary school in their own village, the Presbyterian
school having closed. Most Ahousaht students attending high school
went to residential schools at Alberni, Mission, or Kamloops. Those
same residential schools also absorbed the high school students who
had attended the old Christie School on Meares Island; the move into
Tofino to attend school did not include high school students.

The plan to bring all the Christie School elementary students into
Tofino led to the federal government agreeing to fund construction of
a large new school in Tofino as well as a residence for the aboriginal
students, at the location now known as Tin Wis on MacKenzie Beach.
By September 1971 the residence had been completed, and 100 students
moved to their new accommodation. Administered by the same staff
who had worked at Christie School, most of whom lived on site, this
new residence provided recreational facilities and far more space. "Each
boarder will have his own room," declared the *Colonist*, "a far cry from
Christie School's crowded dormitories." The new Wickaninnish School
in Tofino would not be ready for another year, so during the 1971–72
school year, Tofino students from Grades 5 to 7 took a bus to the "New
Christie" residence, as it became known, and attended class with students from the former Christie School there. Children in Grades 1 to
4 living at the New Christie residence bused into Tofino each day to
attend classes at Tofino Elementary School. After that initial year, no
classes took place at New Christie; students there all travelled by bus
to the Wickaninnish School in Tofino. Following the closure of New
Christie residence in 1984, the building became offices for the Tla-o-
qui-aht administration, then a guest house, before being incorporated
into the Tla-o-qui-aht-owned Best Western Tin Wis Resort.

The eleven-room Wickaninnish School opened in Tofino with

grand ceremony in April 1972, declared "the most modern [school] in BC" by the *Tofino-Ucluelet Press* of April 20, 1972. Participants at the opening included Len Marchand, then the only aboriginal member of Parliament; Donald Brothers, minister of Education; and well-known aboriginal writer George Clutesi. "Mr Clutesi declared," according to the local newspaper, "that today's Chief Wickaninnish, George Frank of Opitsat, gave his most cherished possession, his name, to the new school." Alma (Arnet) Sloman, "the oldest graduate of Tofino's original one-room school," also took part in the ceremony, unveiling a commemorative plaque.

Across the water from the ever-busier Tofino scene, the old hotel at Clayoquot on Stubbs Island soldiered on. After Betty Farmer sold the place in 1964, mining developer Andy Robertson of R&P Metals took it on, hiring caretakers who managed the property for him for a number of years. Robertson did not live there but came and went, pursuing various mining interests in the area. In 1964 he also purchased a half interest in Tofino's Maquinna Hotel, in partnership with one of the original owners, Dennis Singleton. Robertson anticipated lively comings and goings of mining men and their families in his two hotels if his mining interests flourished. In the end, this failed to happen, yet the hotel at Clayoquot carried on, serving dinners and drinks and attracting visitors to stay at the eight-room hotel. Under the management of Paul and Freda Brown, the place became well known for its excellent food, and the island still welcomed locals for memorable get-togethers. In a reminiscence written for *The Sound*, Frank Harper described the Clayoquot Day festivities in 1974, with over a thousand people on the island, featuring baseball, mass drumming, picnics and barbecues, boats going in all directions, the bay alive with activity. He wrote of the eccentric chef at Clayoquot: "a genius cook and intellectual from Belgium named Yves who wore bright-striped robes and yellow wooden shoes and smoked a pipe and cursed you if you put salt or pepper on the food he'd prepared."

In 1977, Lucas Stiefvater purchased Stubbs Island, essentially working in partnership with Andy Robertson, who held a mortgage on $450,000 of the $500,000 sale price. Stiefvater ran the hotel and restaurant at Clayoquot, acting as chef, boat operator, and gardener. During his time there, the old store still stood, teetering on the edge of ruin on the eroding beach, its floor and roof slowly collapsing, used mostly as a storage shed. Stiefvater and his staff recognized the historic value of Walter Dawley's boxes of dusty old papers, which had lain around for decades, first in the old store, then in the hotel. They contacted the provincial archives in Victoria, an initiative that led to the archives acquiring the papers. Dawley's incoming correspondence of more than thirty years now fills 8.3 metres of shelf space, a treasure trove of historical information about the coast.

In 1978, rooms at the Clayoquot Hotel, meals included, cost forty dollars per day, and dinner commanded a set price of fifteen dollars, including transport to and from the island, according to a *Vancouver Sun* article of June 23, 1978. "The ancient beer parlour is long gone," lamented the writer, not mentioning that the liquor licence for the entire establishment had quietly lapsed years earlier. No one dreamed of asking awkward questions when the hotel restaurant continued serving alcohol.

By 1980, ownership of the island had become highly convoluted, and would remain so for the next decade. Stiefvater and Robertson attempted to sell the place to Frank Neufeld, who brought a complex and dubious property scheme into play. Sun and Sea Development set out to attract shareholders who invested believing they would receive a small plot of land on the island and a time share in the hotel.

Publicity for Sun and Sea Development announced that the Clayoquot Hotel and restaurant would close following the summer of 1980, and from then on the island would "accommodate less than 120 individual owners with their own private island retreat," sharing a central park, the lodge, and the dock. Neufeld advertised plots of land for sale at $15,000 each, with $3,000 down, selling the lots from a hand-drawn map never officially registered as a subdivision with the Alberni–Clayoquot Regional District. The planning department at the regional district first heard of this scheme in the advertisements and repeatedly refused to sanction such a subdivision. Nonetheless, many people stubbornly believed the subdivision would eventually obtain planning permission, and over 100 people invested in the scheme. All lost their money. A *Vancouver Sun* article of June 23, 1984, headlined "Investor dreams sour in $1 million loss," described how "a fantasy island...turned into a million dollar financial nightmare," following a BC Supreme Court decision stating that the would-be investors had no claim on the island. Any agreement they had signed proved non-binding, being conditional on the approval of the regional district. In a personal memoir, former Clayoquot Hotel manager Al Pineo wrote, "I find it hard to believe how many people bought a piece of Stubbs Island with nothing to show for their investment but a hand crafted map with a lot number on it that was never going to result in actual ownership."

In 1982, with the property development scheme going nowhere fast, Al and Dorothy Pineo took over as caretakers and managers on the island, and they set out to revive the hotel and restaurant. Determined to bring new energy to the place, and realizing that accommodation was increasingly difficult to find in Tofino, they announced that the eight-room hotel was once again ready for guests. They offered to cater banquets and special events, and before long the old place had come back to life. "I think people were dying to have Clayoquot back," Al Pineo explained. During their three years on the island, the hotel ran at capacity during the season, and the forty-seat restaurant booked solid with two sittings each night, customers reserving tables up to two weeks in advance

In 1985, the Pineos left. Following foreclosure, the island changed hands and local businesswoman Olivia Mae took it over. Under the business name Boardwalk Developments Ltd., Mae approached the regional district about selling lots on Stubbs Island based on Walter Dawley's early subdivisions. She and her partner, Annaliese Larsen, prepared publicity information, offering ten beach lots for sale and stating in their publicity that "arrangements are in place to pipe water from nearby Tofino." Tofino council knew nothing of this and "strongly recommended" that Olivia Mae stop these advertisements, according to an article entitled "Fingers Rapped," in the *Westerly News* of January 23, 1985. Sporadic marketing efforts continued while local rumours whirled about further development schemes, including time shares, a golf course, foreign investment, and another subdivision. The *Westerly News* of February 26, 1986, reported a major expansion planned for Clayoquot Lodge to transform it into "a world-class destination," but the owners "won't yet make public their plans for the resort," other than saying trips to the island would be available for afternoon tea. As time passed, the island welcomed fewer and fewer visitors, the hotel and restaurant closed, and locals looked on, nonplussed. By the end of the decade, the old hotel had suffered a fire, and the house where Ruth and Bill White had lived in the 1940s burned to the ground in 1985. Busy, bustling Clayoquot, once the major hub of all commercial activity in Clayoquot Sound, ceased to exist.

In 1990, Susan Bloom bought the island, once again in foreclosure, and all talk of development and subdivision ceased. Determined to tidy up what remained there, to restore the gardens, and to preserve the island and its forest intact for future generations, Susan Bloom brought in caretakers Sharon Whalen and Chris Taylor, who have worked tirelessly ever since. With the help of local contractors, they first had to dismantle the old crumbling buildings, rid the place of disused machines and debris, and rebuild the dock. With much care and hard work, Stubbs Island's gardens gradually expanded and found new life, and extensive boardwalk trails on the island have been built and maintained. This renaissance at Clayoquot does not include a hotel or restaurant; those days have ended. Yet every year on the May 24 long weekend, the tradition of welcoming people at Clayoquot continues, for then the gardens open to local people who visit the island in great numbers, ferried back and forth in boats provided by the owner. Since 2007 the forest on the island, covering some 75 percent of its area, has been protected with a conservation covenant, registered through The Land Conservancy of British Columbia.

Farther offshore, Wickaninnish Island has remained even less affected by all the recent change in the area. Difficult to access and with no safe moorage, the island fell into private hands before World War I, when Walter Dawley pre-empted and later purchased the entire island. It has never been subdivided, remaining intact as one large parcel of land as it passed through the hands of several owners over the years. No one logged it or built any substantial structures there, and in the early 1970s the island again came up for sale. Vicky Husband and Suzanne Hare, two former beach dwellers from Schooner Cove, reached an agreement to purchase it, with a view to maintaining the island as a place where a small group of like-minded people could create a co-operative land use and living agreement. Under the terms of a re-zoned "land use contract," the island was designated for "co-operative seasonal development under strict environmental controls." Several leaders in the environmental movement became involved: Greenpeace pioneer Lyle Thurston, early Greenpeace supporters Myron Macdonald and David Gibbons, and Vicky Husband, who became conservation chair of BC's Sierra Club. Now some sixteen people share ownership of the island. Most come and go seasonally; only Suzanne Hare and her husband, Steve Lawson, live there year-round.

Through the 1980s and '90s, the Tofino community became increasingly polarized around environmental and land use issues; years of strife and division ensued, leading to intensely bitter local disputes and enmities. Yet at the same time a keen entrepreneurial spirit kicked in locally, and irrespective of the socio-political divides, people of all stripes sensed they could profit from the growing tourist trade, realizing it had come to stay. The early ecotourism enterprises involved everyone from former hippies to developers, as did the service industries in town, and everyone catering to tourists knew that visitors did not want to see clear-cuts. Around Ucluelet, and in many other locations on the coast, vast areas had been laid waste by clear-cutting, mudslides, and slash-burning; such landscapes silenced and appalled visitors. No one in Tofino with a finger in the pie of the growing tourist trade wanted to see that in their own backyard.

A group of the new entrepreneurs in town seized the chance to make their voices heard early in 1987. Maureen Fraser of the Common Loaf bakery; Joan Dublanko, who opened the first bed and breakfast in Tofino at Chesterman Beach in 1986, and who also ran the Three Crabs Deli along with Cristina Delano-Stephens; Al and Dorothy Pineo, who in 1986 took over management of the Loft Restaurant; Shari Bondy, who ran whale-watching tours; and Dorothy Baert, about to open her kayak rental business, decided to attend a Chamber of Commerce meeting. None were members, but they joined then and there as local businesspeople. They outnumbered the old guard and basically took over the local branch, voting each other in as officers, passing all their own resolutions, and starting to actively promote Tofino as a tourist destination, putting forward the idea that clear-cut logging must stop if the town wanted tourists. In the late 1980s, the Tofino Chamber of Commerce sent a telegram to the provincial government asking for a halt to logging in Clayoquot Sound—an unprecedented action for a Chamber of Commerce.

Wholesale promotion of tourism troubled some long-time residents. "At first people resented the tourists as an infringement on their privacy," Mayor Penny Barr admitted to the *Seattle Times* in July 1983. "But we're right next door to a national park that has about half a million visitors a year. So we don't have a choice of having tourists or not... More visitors are coming every year—people always want to see the end of the road." She stressed the need for good long-term planning, acknowledged the growing pressure for development, and concluded, "We have to get our act together." These concerns would prove very real for Tofino, for the visitors just kept coming. An article in the *Victoria Times Colonist* dated May 12, 1985, estimated the town's population at 350 in the winter and over 3,000 in the summer.

A perfect storm of events led to the introduction of aquaculture in Clayoquot Sound in the mid-1980s. With both the herring and salmon fisheries in decline, with opposition to logging growing, with BC suffering through a recession, and with the Social Credit government looking to stimulate foreign investment in the province's resource industries, the government opted to allow fish farms on the west coast. This occurred just as Brian Mulroney's federal government passed a bill rescinding the requirement that Canadians hold majority ownership in Canadian-registered companies. At the same time, Norwegian fish farm companies were looking to move to Canada and other countries because the Norwegian government had placed limits on the size of fish farms there. Fish farming promised to provide jobs, to help feed the world, and to reduce pressure on salmon stock; it seemed, on the face of it, a perfect solution to several problems.

In 1985, Ian Bruce, a fisheries biologist, became a partner in the first fish farm in Clayoquot Sound, Sea 1 Aquafarms Ltd., located in Irving Cove in Tofino Inlet, where its nets hung below floating cedar logs. Other farms opened shortly after at Mussel Rock and Saranac Island, both northwest of Meares Island. These early farms began by raising native chinook and coho salmon, but by 1993 most salmon farms were producing Atlantic salmon because of their faster growth rate. As more and more fish farms began raising Atlantic salmon at various locations on the BC coast, environmentalists began voicing their concerns about these alien fish escaping and breeding with wild Pacific salmon. In April 1995, in response to these concerns, and also because of a decline in wild fish stocks and the death of 100,000 fish at a farm on the Sunshine Coast, the provincial NDP government placed a moratorium on new fish farms. In 2002, the newly elected Liberal government of Gordon Campbell lifted that ban.

In 2000, when salmon prices fell drastically, the aquaculture industry underwent consolidation. With the lifting of the seven-year moratorium, a few multinational corporations secured even more control of fish farming in BC. They built new, larger, more automated fish farms in order to cut costs, at the expense of small, family-owned operations. By 2007, Norwegian-based corporations controlled 89 percent of all fish farming in British Columbia—Marine Harvest had 56 percent, Cermaq (Mainstream Canada) 23 percent, and Greig 9 percent.

When fish farming arrived in the Sound in 1985 it created much-needed local employment. As wild salmon runs declined, the Tofino Fish Plant, owned by B.C. Packers since 1980, began to founder. It closed in 1982, throwing people out of work. The Meares Island logging standoff in 1984 (described in Chapter 21) also caused Tofino to suffer economically. "Thankfully the fish farming industry began and that kept the town going," said former mayor Whitey Bernard. Yet over time, opposition to fish farms increased steadily as environmental groups highlighted a growing litany of problems related to the industry. These included an increase in sea lice in the ideal incubation conditions provided by net pens; escaped Atlantic salmon infiltrating wild Pacific salmon stocks and habitat; the use of antibiotics, pesticides, and steroids to control disease in caged salmon stocks; and the further decline in wild salmon stocks since fish farming began. Farming fish is inefficient; as Peter Robson noted in his book *Salmon Farming: The Whole Story*, 2.45 kilograms of oil and fish meal from herring, mackerel, anchovies and sardines are required to produce one kilogram of farmed salmon. Opponents of fish farming also point out that the feces, the uneaten food, the pesticides, and the colouring agents (to make the flesh pink) end up deposited in the bays and inlets below the fish pens, smothering the seabed and depriving shellfish and other bottom-dwelling sea creatures of oxygen. "They're like floating pig farms," said Daniel Pauly, professor of fisheries at the University of British Columbia in an interview with the *Los Angeles Times*. "They consume a tremendous amount of highly concentrated protein pellets and they make a terrific mess." Jeff Mikus, a commercial prawn and shrimp fisherman from Tofino, reported to the BC Aquaculture Review in 2005–6: "As time has gone on (about the last five years) we started catching fewer prawns, shrimp and other sea life in our traps around fish farms...Sea lice are a huge problem in fish farms. They use a chemical called Slice to kill sea lice infestations in the net pens...[it] kills crustaceans, like sea lice, but it also kills prawns, shrimp and crabs...The problem here is that there are so many farms in such a high density in such a small area that there are very few places to go to get away from them."

In 2002, 200 tonnes, or 80,000 fish, died at Cermaq's Bedwell Sound farm from a suspected outbreak of infectious hematopoietic necrosis (IHN); in 2003 another spate of IHN hit five of Cermaq's farms, forcing them to cull their stocks and to close for a year. Nine years later Cermaq had to destroy another 570,000 fish at its Dixon Island fish farm, and when the IHN virus hit Mainstream's farm at Millar Channel, the firm lost an estimated $10 million when it was forced to cull all of its stock and disinfect the site.

When Cermaq gained approval to build a new fifty-five-hectare fish farm in Clayoquot Sound in 2012, a dispute erupted between the Tla-o-qui-aht and the Ahousaht. The farm would be located at Plover Point on Meares Island, an area traditionally shared by the Ahousaht and Tla-o-qui-aht First Nations. Sixty Ahousahts worked with Cermaq, and the Ahousaht First Nation favoured the fish farm being located at Plover Point. The Tla-o-qui-aht opposed the farm and threatened a lawsuit to prevent its establishment. "Fish disease outbreaks and pollution could devastate our already stressed salmon runs and shellfish sites near Plover Point," said Tla-o-qui-aht councillor Terry Dorward, interviewed by the *Times Colonist* in October 2012. In the end, despite petitions and much opposition, Premier Christy Clark allowed the project to go ahead.

Despite its many problems and consistent opposition from environmentalists, fish farming in British Columbia appears to be here to stay, with aquaculture producing 30 percent of all the seafood consumed in the world. As Peter Robson argued in *Salmon Farming*, "To supply the fish people want, there is no option but to continue to develop aquaculture, and BC waters are well suited to raising cold-water species such as salmon." In 2012, the fish farming industry provided 6,000 direct or indirect jobs and $800 million to BC's economy. Interestingly, the state of Alaska, to the north, has resisted the temptation to allow fish farms into its waters.

Some progress is slowly being made to rectify some of the problems associated with fish farms, including efforts to establish closed-containment, land-based fish farms. In 2013 the 'Namgis First Nation, known as "People of the Salmon," established BC's first such plant near Port McNeill. However, until closed containment becomes more widespread, opponents of fish farms are calling for the industry to regularly leave existing farms fallow to allow the bays and inlets where they are located to recover. Also, in order to reduce the risk of disease, they recommend having 20 to 30 percent fewer fish in each pen. Some opponents want to rid the British Columbia coast entirely of all fish farms, proposing that BC live up to its "Super Natural" slogan and create a niche market for fresh wild salmon as a superior product fetching higher prices from those willing to pay more for good natural food. British Columbia is hard pressed to compete in the farmed fish market with nations like Norway and Chile; because of their economies of scale, those nations produce farmed salmon far less expensively. Meanwhile, with twenty-one fish farms operating in Clayoquot Sound in 2013 (Marine Harvest holds two licences in the Sound, raising Atlantic salmon; Cermaq has thirteen licences and also raises Atlantic salmon; Creative Salmon operates six farms, raising Pacific chinook salmon), restaurants in Tofino offer nothing but wild salmon on their menus. Many Tofinoites rely on the fish farming industry for their employment, but not a single restaurant in Tofino serves the product to customers.

Environmentalists and marine scientists generally endorse the farming of oysters, clams, and mussels, as these bivalves filter and clean the water they live in. With this in mind, Roly Arnet retired from both school teaching and salmon fishing in the 1980s. The grandson of Jacob Arnet, who held Tofino's first salmon fishing licence in 1898, saw the writing on the wall: "I could see that the salmon industry was declining. It was being over-exploited and there was no commitment by the government to protect salmon habitat." In 1985, Roly borrowed $50,000 from Ecotrust and established an oyster lease on the west side of Lemmens Inlet. After a run of successful harvests, he increased the size of his lease to ten hectares in 2000 and involved his nephew Derek in the project. A fourth-generation Arnet now operates this eco-friendly commercial enterprise in Clayoquot Sound. "It's one of our goals to create a quality brand locally and internationally." About 3.2 million oysters a year are currently harvested in Clayoquot Sound; Lemmens Inlet supports most of the commercial oyster farms, with some half-dozen leases there. Since 1997, Tofino has hosted a two-day Oyster Festival in November, with eager participants downing over 10,000 oysters.

Just as new local enterprises came on stream during the 1980s, the forestry industry faced its west coast Waterloo. A logging blockade on Meares Island in 1984 saw the opening salvo fired in a gradually mounting storm of protest, confrontation, and publicity, pitting logging interests against environmental activists and aboriginal leaders in Clayoquot Sound. A titanic confrontation lay ahead, one that would eventually attract worldwide notice. International attention had last focused on the west coast of Vancouver Island almost two centuries earlier in 1790, when the Nootka crisis nearly led to a war between Great Britain and Spain. This time the "war" would be confined to Clayoquot Sound, but news of the battle would, once again, reverberate around the world.

Chapter 21:

The War in the Woods

IN THE EARLY 1930S, TOFINO'S Rowland Brinckman composed a few lines of verse to protest plans to log Cathedral Grove, the stand of old-growth forest alongside the highway east of Port Alberni, near Cameron Lake. Part of the poem reads:

What's all this talk of Cathedral Grove?
Why shouldn't we cut it down?
What right have people who beauty love
To shake their heads and frown?

Why shouldn't we spoil the countryside?
Why shouldn't we chop and slash?
Who in mere landscape would take a pride
If it can be turned into cash?

"Pardon me," he wrote in a postscript, "if I utter a small squawk in defense of one of the loveliest spots I've ever been lucky enough to see."

Appeals in defence of Cathedral Grove date back to 1911, when James Anderson, secretary of the newly formed British Columbia Natural History Society, put forward a proposal to protect the area, supported by the Vancouver Island Development League. A renewed campaign arose in 1929, led by the Associated Boards of Trade of Vancouver Island. Finally, in 1947, the provincial government established the 136-hectare MacMillan Provincial Park to preserve this area of old-growth forest.

The preservation of Cathedral Grove was highly unusual. Through-out the twentieth century, the prevailing attitudes in British Columbia broadly aligned with the stance of provincial politician Phil Gaglardi, who once declared: "Those trees weren't put [there] by God to be praised, they were put there to be chopped down!" And so most of the old-growth forests and great trees of eastern Vancouver Island fell to axe and saw, and the advent of the chainsaw, which could cut down as many trees in a day as six handloggers, accelerated the pace of logging enormously. The easily accessible valley-bottom timber fell first, with railways carrying logs to the water's edge, where they could be boomed and towed to sawmills. By the late 1950s, logging trucks had replaced steam locomotives, leaving many mountainsides on Vancouver Island zigzagged with steep gravel roads, as trucks retrieved timber ever higher on mountain slopes. These roads became so steep that some logging trucks carried 1,350-litre tanks of water to cool their brakes as they negotiated the switchbacks on their way down carrying log loads of over 100 tonnes. Exports of wood products and an increased number of pulp and paper mills within the province led to an ever greater demand for new sources of trees.

In 1959, when the road to the west coast opened, forestry giants MacMillan Bloedel (MacBlo) and BC Forest Products thrilled at the prospect of logging huge stretches of untouched old-growth forest. Long before the road, logging had been done in Clayoquot Sound, but only as a relatively minor industry, feeding logs to early sawmills such as those run by Tom Wingen in Grice Bay, John Darville at Calm Bay, the Gibson Brothers at Ahousat, and the Suttons in Ucluelet. Most of this early logging could not be seen from Tofino, although since the mid-1950s one highly visible logging scar had stared Tofino residents in the face. Fred Knott and his brother John then owned a logging outfit based in Tofino, Knott Brothers Logging; with the agreement of the Tla-o-qui-aht, this company logged the southern face of Lone Cone, directly opposite Tofino, in 1954–55. "It was a terrible scar, they just shaved the side of that mountain, you could see it from everywhere," Jacqui Hansen recalled. "But it's all grown over now." From out at sea, a few more clear-cuts could be spotted, including a large area on Catface Mountain. Ron Dalziel spent the summer of 1964 fishing offshore, and in his memoirs he wrote of the view looking toward land from his boat: "Except for the odd scar, from a fire or a clearcut—such as Catface Mountain that you could pick up from twenty miles out—untouched timber spread out on the hillsides all the way from Kyuquot right down to Tofino."

When MacBlo and BC Forest Products (BCFP) began logging in earnest on the west coast, they focused on cutting trees in the vicinity of Kennedy Lake and around Ucluelet. Through the agreement they struck with the provincial government in the 1950s to help build the Ucluelet-Tofino road, the two companies had acquired the rights to log a vast amount of land, including all the timber licences once held by the Sutton Lumber and Trading Company, located around Kennedy Lake, Toquart Bay, and Ucluelet, on Meares Island, and in various other locations in Clayoquot Sound. Additionally, in 1955, BCFP was granted a vast area encompassing 101,214 hectares between Port Renfrew and Estevan Point along the west coast of Vancouver Island. The political shenanigans behind the BCFP grant led to one of the biggest scandals in BC's political history. The provincial minister of Forests, Robert Sommers, earned the distinction of being the first government minister in the British Commonwealth to be jailed; he went to prison for twenty-eight months after his conviction for accepting a bribe to facilitate the awarding of timber licences to BCFP.

For a while, Clayoquot Sound remained comparatively unscathed, even as clear-cuts began to spread far and wide around Ucluelet. By the early 1970s, several small "gyppo" logging outfits operated within the Sound. One logged at Windy Bay on Meares Island, out of sight of Tofino in Fortune Channel; others set up camps in Shelter Inlet and on Flores Island. Hamilton Logging took over from Knott Brothers and operated a camp from Hecate Bay near the mouth of the Cypre River, under contract to MacMillan Bloedel; in 1972, owner Tom Hamilton died in a plane accident when taking off from that operation. Greenwood Logging also operated under licence to MacBlo in Herbert Inlet, Hot Springs Cove, and later Stewardson Inlet, its operations stretching across the peninsula past Cougar Annie's garden in Hesquiat Harbour. Even smaller gyppo logging outfits, like Sam Craig and Dave Bond Logging (C&B Logging), operated in the Kennedy Lake area and Stewardson Inlet. Meanwhile, Lowry Logging was cutting on Catface Mountain, and Ray Grumbach had a small operation first at Hot Springs Cove and later in the Bedwell River area. These independent logging operations, including Pacific Logging and Coulson Prescott among others, peaked around 1976, when

MacBlo and BCFP began bringing in their own crews, changing the general mood of logging in the Sound. MacBlo built the Cypre Crescent subdivision in Tofino to house some loggers and their families, and the Maquinna Hotel expanded to serve the influx of new workers. While he accommodated certain MacBlo housing developments, Mayor Don McGinnis worked hard to keep Tofino from becoming a company town.

The agreement the forest companies signed with the provincial government when they agreed to help build the road to the coast required them to harvest on a sustainable yield basis, to replant new trees, to replace the ones cut, and to take precautions against fire. However, the agreement did not stipulate how the companies would harvest the trees, and clear-cutting proved the most efficient and economical method. It also proved to be the most visible. As logging roads extended farther and farther and the clear-cuts grew in number, the cutting methods of the forest companies came under increased public scrutiny. Truck logging gave loggers greater access to wilderness areas, but the roads they built also allowed more and more members of the public to view their logging practices. As an increasing number of British Columbians took to the wilderness along logging roads to camp, hike, fish, and recreate, they were appalled by the landscapes of utter devastation left by clear-cuts. Entire mountainsides had been stripped. Trees had been cut to the edge of lakes, leaving shorelines choked with debris. Rivers and streams ran brown with silt and rocks, rendering them unusable for the fish that had once spawned in them. Soil that would have sustained new growth had been washed away, leaving only bare rock, and erosion caused by logging roads had led to landslides that gouged massive scars on hillsides, visible for kilometres.

This was not the wilderness visitors expected to see, and people began to speak out against clear-cut logging. At the same time, the environmental movement gained ever greater momentum following its protests against nuclear testing in the late 1960s and early 1970s. Groups such as US-based Sierra Club, founded in 1892, and Vancouver-based Greenpeace, founded in 1972, eventually joined forces with Friends of Clayoquot Sound and the Western Canada Wilderness Committee to protest the practices of the BC logging industry. Clayoquot Sound's two leading industries, logging and tourism, soon reached a crossroads and a bitter collision pitting economic prosperity against the preservation of wilderness.

The first major, widely publicized confrontation in Clayoquot Sound between environmentalists and the forest companies occurred in 1984 on Meares Island, directly across the harbour from Tofino. In November 1983 the provincial government gave MacMillan Bloedel permission to log 90 percent of Meares Island, deferring for twenty years the remaining 10 percent. Rumours had been circulating around Tofino for years of MacBlo's intentions to log the island. Young people gathering at the Gust o' Wind Arts Centre in the late 1970s anxiously discussed what could be done to stop this, and those discussions led to the creation of Friends of Clayoquot Sound (FOCS). Everyone in town had seen the results of clear-cut logging around Ucluelet, and even if they supported logging elsewhere in Clayoquot Sound, they did not want that kind of devastation happening within sight of Tofino.

At the request of Tofino municipal council, the provincial government established the Meares Island Planning Committee in 1980. Consultations began among concerned citizens, local environmentalists, First Nations, forestry union representatives, the provincial government, and MacBlo to see what could be done to prevent a repetition of the ugly mess left around Ucluelet. "We didn't want to look out our windows and see a clear-cut on the south side of Meares Island," commented Whitey Bernard, who served as Tofino's representative on the committee. "We even flew Premier Bill Bennett and some of his cabinet ministers up from Victoria in a Beaver to let them see Tofino's 'viewshed,' as they called it, and told them how concerned we were." Over the next three years, the committee tried to reach consensus, suggesting a number of options to preserve Meares Island. One proposal was to log only half the timber; another to log half now and the rest after twenty-five years. "There were a lot of balls in the air at the time," said Bernard. "Tourism was beginning to take hold, and many people in the community made their living from logging, but I think MacBlo was beginning to realize that if they were going to log Meares Island they were going to have to do it in a totally different way."

Frustrated at the slow pace of these negotiations, MacBlo walked out of the Meares Island Planning Committee, calling all the options unfeasible and suggesting that it be allowed to log 53 percent of Meares Island over the next thirty-five years, most of it on the north side of the island, out of sight of Tofino. Around the same time, Tofino resident Harry Tieleman decided to take action. A member of FOCS, and owner of the Esso gas station and Happy Harry's Restaurant in Tofino, Tieleman purchased a hundred shares in MacMillan Bloedel, which allowed him to attend the 1984 annual shareholders' meeting at the Hyatt Regency Hotel in Vancouver. At that meeting he put forward a motion that MacBlo cease all plans to log Meares Island. Though his motion ended in defeat, Tieleman gained widespread publicity, prompting MacBlo chairman Adam Zimmerman to blurt in frustration in front of a CBC camera: "Who needs tourists? Tourists are a goddamn plague! Tourists are the most polluting thing you can introduce into the environment!" Zimmerman also asserted that logging Meares Island would look like only a minor dose of acne. "Every time he opened his mouth, we gained another 10,000 supporters," commented Michael Mullin, one of the leading anti-logging activists in Tofino and a founding member of FOCS. A veteran of the riots in Chicago in 1968, and having, as he put it, "cut [his] political teeth in Chile during the Allende period," Mullin had a keen sense of how protest movements worked. Along with others in FOCS, he knew the vital importance of attracting publicity and media coverage.

To raise awareness of the proposed logging of Meares Island and to emphasize their total opposition to any logging there, FOCS held the Meares Island Easter Festival at the Wickaninnish school gymnasium in Tofino on April 21, 1984, bringing some 600 people together from around the province. The short-lived *Tofino Echo* reported that "the media was here in full force." Regional and international musicians and other entertainers performed in front of the tall carving called *Weeping Cedar Woman*, created for the event by Godfrey Stephens. Representing the guardian spirit of the area, Cedar Woman became a powerful symbol for conservation. At that Easter Festival, Tla-o-qui-aht chief councillor Moses Martin declared Meares Island to be a Tribal Park, a term he coined to assert Tla-o-qui-aht territorial rights over the island.

Fired up by this declaration, FOCS worked with the Tla-o-qui-aht to make a trail on Meares Island from Heelboom (C'is-a-quis) Bay to some of the oldest and biggest trees on the West Coast, one of which measures over nineteen metres in diameter. The "Big Tree" trail let visitors and journalists see close-up the giant trees that would be lost if logging took place. Local residents also set up camp on the site where logging would start, and Tla-o-qui-aht carvers Joe and Carl Martin began carving dugout canoes on the shore of C'is-a-quis Bay, where they also built a cabin. Anti-logging protesters organized a large Meares Island protest rally in Victoria on October 21, 1984, attracting 1,200 people to the Legislative Buildings. At the protest, the Tla-o-qui-aht raised the 8.5-metre-tall welcome figure *Haa-hoo-ilth-quin*, a carving by Joe David that stands today outside the Museum of Anthropology at the University of British Columbia.

During this period of intense campaigning and publicity seeking, some of the more militant, self-proclaimed eco-warriors began driving spikes into trees on Meares Island, a practice that would destroy chain-saws, cause injury, and impede logging when and if it began. Neither FOCS nor the First Nations condoned tree spiking.

On the morning of November 21, 1984, the MacBlo crew boat *Kennedy Queen* arrived at Heelboom Bay, with loggers aboard prepared to start operations. A flotilla of boats awaited them, filled with people who had been waiting to be called to the scene when the loggers were en route, to prevent their landing. The organizers radioed the code message "Coffee's On," and the boats converged on the bay. Media helicopters flew overhead, and other reporters, who had been alerted to this event well in advance, followed the action from other boats. On the foreshore, sixty or more protestors stood waiting and watching, and a standoff ensued. The RCMP spent several hours trying to negotiate a compromise, and finally, at 1 p.m., the loggers landed. Chief Councillor Moses Martin, waiting on shore, stepped forward to greet them. Taking a paper from his pocket, he began reading the terms of the original timber licence issued to Sutton Lumber and Trading Co. in 1905, the same licence MacMillan Bloedel had acquired in order to log Meares

MacMillan Bloedel's crew boat, *Kennedy Queen*, navigated through a flotilla of boats in Heelboom (C'is-a-quis) Bay on the morning of November 21, 1984. Anti-logging protesters filled the boats and lined the shoreline of Meares Island in this historic faceoff, to prevent loggers going ashore with chainsaws. *Adrian Dorst photo*

Tla-o-qui-aht chief Moses Martin on Meares Island on November 21, 1984, defying MacMillan Bloedel loggers. Several months earlier he had declared Meares Island to be a Tribal Park, setting in motion years of protest against logging in Clayoquot Sound. *Adrian Dorst photo*

Island. Martin pointed out that the Land Act, in defining the terms of the timber licence, stated: "You will respect all Indian grounds, plots, gardens, Crown and other reserves." He then said that the land was a Tribal Park and declared, "This land is our garden. If you put down your chainsaws you are welcome ashore, but not one tree will be cut." Speaking of this historic faceoff in later years, Moses Martin told of an RCMP officer confronting the Nuu-chah-nulth Tribal Council leader George Watts, who stood beside Martin. "He said, 'I've got room to put a thousand Indians in my jail,'...George said, 'You go ahead. We'll bring a thousand more.'"

Two days later, MacBlo sought a court injunction against anyone who obstructed their work. The Tla-o-qui-aht and Ahousaht First Nations filed for their own injunction to prevent MacBlo logging their territorial land, occupied by indigenous people for 4,200 years. They documented the many sites showing aboriginal land use on Meares Island and launched their court case based on aboriginal title. In subsequent years, significant and far-reaching research has documented the history of aboriginal land use throughout Clayoquot Sound, stretching back thousands of years.

In January 1985 the BC Supreme Court ruled MacBlo could go ahead with its logging on Meares Island, a ruling immediately appealed by the Tla-o-qui-aht and Ahousaht. The BC Court of Appeal overthrew the Supreme Court ruling, and on March 27, 1985, the court granted an injunction freezing all plans to log Meares Island until First Nations claims could be resolved. The immediate threat of logging Meares Island had ended. Complex legal proceedings then dragged on for years. Supporters set up the Meares Island Legal Fund, and major fundraising efforts took place, with funds coming from all quarters: high-end art auctions, raffles, dances, and humble bake sales. The Martin brothers of Opitsat donated two specially carved dugout canoes to be raffled for the fund. As late as 1991, MacBlo continued its efforts to overturn the injunction; the company's lawyer, John Hunter, told *The Sound* magazine that summer that the chances of lifting the injunction were good. He was wrong; the injunction held firm.

"The Meares Island confrontation was the first time the whites and natives have gotten together on anything that was worthwhile," Joe Martin, then a Tla-o-qui-aht band council member, stated in an interview in the *New York Times*. Reflecting back on events ten years later, local writer Frank Harper agreed, pointing out that "the folks who lived in Clayoquot Sound had probably never before or since been so united around a political issue" as they were on Meares Island. However, Leona Taylor did not sense such a degree of unity in the town: "You had to be pro-logging or anti-logging, there was no room for discussion," she commented. "It split the town into two factions." The battle was difficult and sometimes bitter, but Meares Island became a template for future environmental actions and First Nations land claims in British Columbia. It also proved a watershed moment for the people of Tofino.

"The town of Tofino paid dearly for...the Meares Island process," recalled former mayor Whitey Bernard. "The industry and government weren't particularly happy that a town had stood up and said 'We have some very, very serious concerns about logging this particular piece of land.'" According to Steve Lawson in the documentary film *Tofino: The Road Stops Here*, "MacBlo moved its office to Ucluelet. The Bank of Commerce, some of whose directors also served on the Board of Mac-Millan Bloedel, became a branch office of the bank in Ucluelet. The Forestry office relocated, the Fisheries and Wildlife Officer left town and the government even threatened to shut down the liquor store."

"House prices dropped twenty percent and it took a long time for the town to recover," Bernard noted. "All of this, a direct result of the community standing up to the forestry companies. Thankfully the fish farming industry began and that kept the town going." Others pointed out that during the years after the Meares Island confrontation, tourism in Tofino began to fill the economic breach, growing slowly but steadily, and attracting many new enterprises to the area.

Following their efforts to help the Tla-o-qui-aht prevent logging on Meares Island, environmentalists kept a watchful eye on logging practices elsewhere in Clayoquot Sound. In June 1988, wildlife photographer Adrian Dorst raised the alarm when he spotted workers blasting a logging road in Sulphur Passage on the east side of Obstruction Island, south of Shelter Inlet. This proved to be the work of Fletcher Challenge, the New Zealand-based company that had bought out BC Forest Products in 1987. A small number of protesters descended on the area, first blockading the road builders' boats, then lying along the route of the proposed road. By law, blasting could not occur with people in close proximity, so the protesters aimed to maintain a presence in the area. Some even suspended themselves in makeshift hammocks from the cliff edges and from trees within the blast safety zone. In one incident during the Sulphur Passage protests, loggers cut down a tree in which a protestor was suspended in his hammock.

Fletcher Challenge responded by applying for a court injunction to prevent the protests. Undeterred, the protesters defied the injunctions and remained in the area, forcing the RCMP to arrest thirty-

In 1988 during the campaign to stop Fletcher Challenge from building a logging road in Sulphur Passage, protesters strung hammocks and suspended themselves above areas where road builders planned to blast.

Mark Hobson photo, courtesy of Clayoquot Action

five of them, among them Ahousaht hereditary chief Earl Maquinna George. Twenty of those arrested received sentences ranging from three to forty-five days. Suzanne Hare was flown to Vancouver in handcuffs, along with local fisherman Pat McLorie, also arrested at Sulphur Passage, to appear before a judge. Their plea of "not guilty" did them little good; some time later Hare again boarded a plane, this time en route to jail with five other women arrested at the protest: Shari Bondy, Valerie Langer, Julie Draper, Bonny Glambeck, and Shelley Milne. Along with five of the men arrested, they chose jail time over paying a fine.

On April 27, 1989, a headline in the *Victoria Times Colonist*, accompanying a photograph of Suzanne kissing her three children goodbye, read "Mum kisses her children, takes jail for forest fight." The women had hoped to serve their eight days at a halfway house in Victoria, but instead they went to Oakalla, a maximum-security prison in Burnaby. According to Suzanne, the judge decreed, "If they are going to do time, they are going to do hard time." On arrival at Oakalla, she recalled how they "were put into a cramped little cell for hours, Shari Bondy was pregnant at the time, and there wasn't even room to lay down. We were then stripped down, given prison clothes and doused with a chemical delousing poison...until we were finally settled into our cell area."

These arrests at Sulphur Passage, and the jail sentences meted

Protestors on the steps of the Nanaimo Court during the Sulphur Passage campaign in 1988. *Mark Hobson photo, courtesy of Clayoquot Action*

out, gave a taste of what lay ahead. For Valerie Langer of Friends of Clayoquot Sound, three more arrests would follow in various logging confrontations over the next decade. "After you've been arrested once, the other times don't really matter," she later commented. "You already have a criminal record from the first time."

The environmentalists attempted to acquire their own injunction against the road building in Sulphur Passage and requested a six-month moratorium on logging. Chief Earl Maquinna George also sought injunctions to stop the logging on his tribe's traditional lands. "This was traditional Ahousaht territory and I, as chief, decided to protest the logging," he wrote in *Living on the Edge*. In his traditional role as streamkeeper for Shark Creek, a salmon stream in Ahousaht territory draining into the northwest side of Millar Channel near Sulphur

Passage, he saw he had a clear duty: "I am the person who watches and sees that no damage is done to Shark Creek." None of the court actions succeeded in stopping Fletcher Challenge, but the growing publicity created by the activists, using the age-old war slogan "No Pasarán" (they shall not pass), attracted a great deal of media attention. After five months of protests, Fletcher Challenge shelved the Sulphur Passage project and built a road farther back in the mountains, less visible from the water, where it clear-cut the slopes of Shelter Inlet. After the protest, Bob Bossin wrote his song "Sulphur Passage," which became a rallying cry for protests that followed.

> No pasarán, Megin River,
> No pasarán, Clayoquot River,
> No pasarán, Sulphur Passage.

In the early hours of December 23, 1988, the towboat *Ocean Services* lost its tow, the tanker barge *Nestucca*, off Grays Harbor, Washington. Attempting to set another line, the boat rammed its barge, causing 5,500 barrels of heavy, thick, bunker oil to spill. Tides and currents soon caused the oil slick to drift northward onto the west coast of Vancouver Island. The residents of Tofino and Clayoquot Sound forgot their differences in responding to this emergency, which threatened local beaches and wildlife. Over Christmas and New Year, groups of volunteers spent every waking hour dressed in white plastic protective suits, patrolling the beaches at each high tide and collecting bag after bag of seaweed clumps, covered in thick tarlike oil. "The oil was several inches deep in huge raised lumps that came in sections up to the size of dining tables," according to Barry Campbell, then with Parks Canada. "Staff had to remove thousands of dead birds immediately so that predators wouldn't try to eat them and die themselves." Local businesses and individuals donated food for a soup kitchen to feed the volunteers; others attempted to save as many birds as they could. An estimated 56,000 birds died. Crab and shellfish beds, as well as herring spawning grounds, suffered from oil contamination. Tofino people focused on the task at hand and kept at it until, finally, the provincial government stepped in to help. Eventually some 5,500 volunteers showed up, some arriving from Vancouver and Victoria to take up the cause and relieve the locals. This incident focused further attention on the fragility of the west coast ecosystem and also demonstrated the unity that still existed in Tofino.

In an attempt to understand more about the environmentalists and to come up with a new approach to "the whole nightmare," as a company spokesman termed the continuing protests, MacMillan Bloedel hired consultant Rosy Siney in 1989 to assess matters. Her internal report, "The Land Use Controversy: How did we get into this mess?" was to be shared with front-line foresters. In this report, Siney attempted to explain to MacBlo executives how significantly times had changed. Rather than supporting patriarchal/masculine values that saw men conquering the wilderness and felling giant trees as an honourable means of earning a living, society now placed increasing value on matriarchal/feminist ideals relating to "sustainability, conservation, nurturing, caring, slow or no-growth, emphasis on equal opportunity, consensus, [and] choice." The author pointed out that "the preserva-tionists are attacking not our numbers, but our values." Stuck in its business-as-usual mentality, MacBlo's management and, indeed, its individual employees had great difficulty accepting this new reality.

The Sulphur Passage confrontation led to yet more government-appointed committees. These included the Clayoquot Sound Sustain-able Development Task Force Steering Committee (CSSDTF), formed in 1989, and its subcommittee, the Clayoquot Sound Sustainable Development Steering Committee (CSSDSC), which grew out of the CSSDTF in 1991, both formed to decide which areas of Clayoquot Sound should be logged and which should be protected. Unsurprisingly, this committee-heavy approach gave rise to frustration. Environmental-ists called it the "talk-and-log" period: "While we talked, they logged," Valerie Langer told Tim Palmer, author of *Pacific High: Adventures in the*

Rufus Charleson stands in front of the massive clear-cut on Mount Seghers, part of Hesquiaht territory, in the early 1980s. Such logging practices ignited international protests. *Adrian Dorst photo*

Coast Range from Baja to Alaska. "For fourteen years we tried to protect what was left uncut, and for fourteen years the rate of cutting increased." Despite the efforts of environmentalists who staged small-scale protests, set up blockades, and sometimes faced arrest, vast clear-cuts continued to spread in Clayoquot Sound and up the coast, many on slopes and watersheds in remote areas unfrequented by tourists and the media, and difficult for protesters to access. Around Hesquiat Harbour, the sides of Mount Seghers and others stood stark naked; the infamously scalped Escalante watershed north of Hesquiat could be seen from outer space; and the clear-cuts on the mountainsides above Shelter Inlet, Cypress Bay, and other inlets "look[ed] like they've been napalmed," in the words of protester Betty Krawczyk.

Outraged by the continuing devastation, some activists took matters into their own hands. In April 1991, protesters set fire to the Kennedy River Bridge, putting it out of commission, preventing access to an active MacBlo logging area, and throwing 210 loggers out of work. When MacBlo tried to barge eleven vehicles and their crew up Tofino Inlet to access the area from another direction, the barge sank in Tofino harbour, costing MacBlo huge embarrassment and its insurance company $250,000. "Tofino was a town bewildered this week," wrote Frank Harper in *The Sound*, describing "a half-mad, bizarre dance that can only go on at westcoast levels." In rapid succession the bridge burned, the barge sank, the beloved Legion Hall went up in flames, and the Tla-o-qui-ahts began to boycott Tofino businesses in response to Tofino council's refusal to support the First Nation's bid to have land at Tin Wis set aside as an Indian Reserve. Any one of these events would have had the town on edge, but the burning of the bridge particularly shocked everyone. Following a telephone threat that his art gallery would be burned down in retaliation for the bridge destruction, Roy Henry Vickers of the Eagle Aerie Gallery, who had been supportive of the environmental movement, issued a public statement in *The Sound*. He reiterated his environmental concerns but condemned the burning of the bridge as a criminal act. The town became ever more divided against itself, and the protests continued. Later that year, in September, when the government allowed limited logging in the Bulson Creek watershed, activists blocked the logging road, leading MacBlo once again to seek injunctions, which led to further arrests. Protests and arrests at Bulson Creek continued off and on for years.

A British Columbia-based logging company, International Forest Products or Interfor, entered this tense environment in October 1991. The company had purchased Fletcher Challenge's tree farm licences when that multinational wound down its operations in the province. Vowing to operate in a different manner, Interfor established an office in Tofino, with Dean Wanless in charge. "Our Chief Forester told me to think 'outside the box' and mandated me to practise sustainable forest management; to practise innovative harvesting techniques and to still make a profit," Wanless said. "It was a tall order and to accomplish it we set out to make ourselves part of the community, to work with the First Nations, and to work to preserve habitat by using helicopters and smaller logging equipment so as to make a smaller imprint on the environment." By attempting this, Interfor generally managed to avoid the high-profile bad publicity and disruptions to its operations that MacBlo was experiencing, although its local offices periodically attracted groups of protestors holding signs with slogans like "Interfor—Clear-cut Destruction." Interfor continued harvesting in Clayoquot Sound, although in smaller cutblocks than MacBlo and Fletcher Challenge. Its largest clear-cut of 1994 measured 31 hectares, but as Frank Harper pointed out in *The Sound* in January 1994, "31 hectares is about the size of greater Tofino."

Around the time Interfor appeared on the scene in 1991, BC's Ministry of Forests released a discussion paper as it prepared to develop its Forest Practices Code, which would eventually become law in 1995. After years of rapacious logging practices, signs of change were beginning to appear in British Columbia's forest industry, but these changes were not happening nearly fast enough for some.

International publicity decrying logging practices in British Columbia mounted steadily in 1991, largely due to the efforts of Greenpeace Canada through its connections with environmental groups abroad. Several European countries began discussing the possibility of banning Canadian wood products from old-growth forests. In March 1991 a German television program, *A Paradise Despoiled*, came up with the phrase "Brazil of the North" to describe the effects of clear-cutting, and in December 1991 the British newspaper *The Observer* published a four-page feature accusing the BC forestry industry of a "chainsaw massacre." More such coverage would follow.

In January 1992, NDP premier Mike Harcourt's new provincial government announced the formation of an independent and impartial Commission on Resources and the Environment (CORE), which would create a land use plan for every region of BC. Headed by Stephen Owen, CORE possessed a mandate to consult local interest groups, including environmental organizations and First Nations, about land use, forest practices, and stewardship, encouraging consensus on these issues. Clayoquot Sound was not included in the CORE process because of the ongoing deliberations of CSSDTF and CSSDSC, then trying to reach agreement on how best to deal with short-term logging in the Sound. Nonetheless, Owen's final report would undoubtedly have ramifications for the Sound.

Early in 1993, Greenpeace, the Sierra Club, and a coalition of other environmental groups began their international campaign in earnest. Drawing on their wide membership, and using their proven ability to attract media attention, they spread the news of Clayoquot Sound's clear-cuts around the world. In January, the *New York Times* ran a full-page advertisement headlined "Will Canada do nothing to save Clayoquot Sound, one of the last great temperate rainforests in the world?" The ad named many Hollywood stars who lent their support to the protests, including Tom Cruise, Nicole Kidman, Robert Redford, Tim Robbins, Martin Sheen, and Oliver Stone. Activists placed prepared articles in leading European, American, Asian, and Latin American newspapers, using the term "Brazil of the North" for Clayoquot Sound, and publishing graphic pictures of clear-cuts. Protests organized by different environmental groups took place in front of Canadian embassies in a number of countries, and talk of boycotting Canadian wood products continued.

All the while, the provincial government had been planning its own form of action. On April 13, 1993, Premier Mike Harcourt descended from a helicopter at Radar Hill and announced his government's Clayoquot Sound Land Use Decision. Billed as a "compromise solution," the decision allowed the forest companies to log 62 percent of the Sound, while placing 17 percent of the old growth in the Sound under "special management." The decision also promised to end clear-cutting, to set higher standards for logging road construction, and to monitor more closely the logging practices of forest companies. Those companies generally welcomed the decision, although not all were happy. "That decision reduced Interfor's allowable cut from 171,000 cubic metres to 66,000 cubic metres—a reduction of over 60 percent," said Dean Wanless of Interfor. "Which made it ever more difficult to run a profitable forestry operation." In addition, as part of the land use decision, the government promised to work to establish a UNESCO Biosphere Reserve in Clayoquot Sound.

The details came as a complete shock to most environmentalists.

Viewing the Clayoquot Sound Land Use Decision as a call to arms, the Western Canada Wilderness Committee, Friends of Clayoquot Sound, the Temperate Rainforest Alliance, and the Valhalla Wilderness Society all immediately resigned from the ongoing CORE deliberations, unwilling to put any further trust in government-led environmental initiatives. Many also saw the Clayoquot decision as a conflict of interest, as the BC government had purchased $50-million worth of shares in MacBlo in February 1993, making the government one of the company's largest shareholders. Without doubt, the badly handled and badly timed decision provided the spark that ignited the largest protest in Canadian history, leading to the largest mass arrests in the country, and drawing national and international media attention. *The San Francisco Chronicle* published a lengthy front-page story about the decision, again repeating the "Brazil of the North" slogan.

Shortly after the Harcourt government announced its decision, another bridge came under siege in Clayoquot Sound. In May, Michael Mullin and two others attempted to set fire to the Clayoquot Arm Bridge in an effort to cut access to most of MacBlo's logging sites in the Sound. They were arrested, given short jail sentences, and ordered to do community service. Mullin did his for FOCS; he had been a director of the organization but resigned when he was arrested.

As the summer of 1993 approached, FOCS prepared to take action. At one of the early strategy meetings, the six people present boldly proposed they try to draw a large number of people to Clayoquot Sound, maybe as many as 200, for a mass protest. In hoping for 200 people they were "dreaming big," according to Tzeporah Berman. Building on a base of support from other organizations, they sent out invitations for participants to attend training sessions on civil disobedience and non-violent protest, and to learn about the rainforest and media skills. The first training camp took place at Clayoquot on Stubbs Island in early June 1993. The headline in the *Westerly News* declared "Learning Disobedience in Tofino," and the accompanying article described people attending from as far away as California and Germany. The organizers had expected a hundred or so people; 250 showed up. Another highly visible training camp took place in Stanley Park in Vancouver, attracting several hundred people, with news reporters in attendance. Central to the training were principles of non-violence and civility, and all participants had to agree to FOCS's code of conduct: "We will not run, we will not shout and will carry ourselves in a calm and dignified manner; we will respect all other beings; we will carry no weapons and we will not be under the influence of drugs or alcohol when at a function in public."

FOCS began to realize its movement might grow into something far bigger than anticipated; the group hired eight people to coordinate events for the summer, and other environmental groups mustered resources, support, and strength to face a summer of protest. Faxed notices sent to the media said only "Clayoquot Blockades will start July 1," providing no details in the hope of exciting curiosity about what lay ahead. By the end of June, a small group began to set up tents and a makeshift kitchen for what would become the Clayoquot Peace Camp.

Hundreds of people from across Canada and from the United States, Mexico, Australia, and Europe began converging on the Sound. Galvanized into action by all the publicity about clear-cut logging, they gathered at the Peace Camp. It opened on Canada Day, July 1, 1993, in an old clear-cut commonly called the "Black Hole," which had been burned to allow for natural regeneration. One of the ugliest examples of logging practices, the Black Hole lay right beside the Tofino–Alberni Highway a few kilometres east of the Ucluelet–Tofino junction. Mountainsides defaced by washed-out logging roads and mudslides, and huge piles of logging slash, provided a backdrop for the camp, vividly illustrating what the environmentalists were protesting and offering a dramatic background for media pictures and interviews.

The organizers hired Tzeporah Berman, a twenty-four-year-old graduate student from the University of Toronto, to coordinate and run the camp—an extraordinary challenge given the magnitude of what followed. Some 10,000 to 12,000 people passed through the Peace Camp by the time it finally closed on October 9, 1993, and throughout that time it exemplified the non-violent principles of civil disobedience observed by Mahatma Ghandi in India against British rule, and by Martin Luther King in the American Civil Rights movement. "I was very concerned about making sure that the protest would be peaceful," said Berman. "We organized mandatory training sessions in non-violence every day. We developed talking circles as a way of decision-making, and we gave people a sense of ownership in the process." Over that summer, women comprised an estimated 80 percent of those staying in the camp, many inspired by the eco-feminist successes of the Women's Pentagon Action in the United States, and the Greenham Common Women's Peace Camp in Britain. Jean McLaren, one of the earliest of the "Raging Granny" protesters in British Columbia, brought her experience of the Civil Rights movement and Greenham Common to the Peace Camp. Having been arrested in 1992 at another logging protest, and banned from going within 200 metres of any logging road in the province, she stayed put in the camp for four months, giving daily training sessions in non-violent communication and peacekeeping skills.

While previous protests and logging blockades on Meares Island, at Sulphur Passage, and at Bulson Creek had taken place in relatively inaccessible locations, the Peace Camp could not be missed; anyone travelling toward Tofino and Ucluelet had to see it. Similarly, all of the logging blockades and protests during the summer of 1993 took place at the readily accessible Kennedy River Bridge, giving the media un-precedented access to all the action. "One of the reasons the Clayoquot protest grew so big so fast," said Vicky Husband, of the Sierra Club, "was that people could easily drive to the area and see for themselves the horror show of what was going on with the logging." The protests gained momentum far faster than anyone expected. In early August, FOCS campaign organizer Valerie Langer commented in a CBC News interview, "When we started this five weeks ago we were told it would fizzle in a week. Look at this! If this is a fizzle let's keep fizzling."

Each morning at 4 a.m., activists formed a motorcade at the Peace Camp and drove up the West Main logging road leading off the highway opposite the camp. They travelled about ten kilometres, to the Kennedy River Bridge, where the protestors, often carrying signs with slogans like "No Trees, No Fish, No Jobs" and "No Fish, No Forests, No Future," took their positions, waiting for the trucks. Some people sang, some drummed, many linked arms. Some stood beside the road; others sat or stood directly on the logging road, forming a human barrier in front of the bridge as a cavalcade of logging trucks, crummy wagons, and RCMP vehicles arrived. "All of the laughing and the talking and the drumming and whatever was happening would just end," said Berman. "There'd be complete silence as all of the people of different ages and different backgrounds stood in front of the trucks." An RCMP officer would then inform the protestors that they were breaking the law—both MacBlo and Interfor had taken out court injunctions preventing protests. When the protestors refused to move, officers began making arrests, often carrying those arrested to a nearby bus, which then transported them to the athletic centre in Ucluelet to be processed. Those who stood by the side of the road and chose not to be arrested that day would return to the Peace Camp for one of the meals, cooked three times each day in the camp kitchen, that fed 200 people at a time with donated food.

The well-organized, peaceful blockades aimed to attract the broadest possible support and to encourage more and more ordinary citizens to join the protest. The daily ritual continued all summer long. By September, 932 people had been arrested, the single largest mass arrest occurring on August 9, when it took RCMP officers seven hours to arrest 309 protestors. The protests and arrests garnered increasing worldwide media attention as the environmental movement kept up, and won, the publicity battle. Marches and demonstrations in support of Clayoquot protesters took place in Vancouver, Munich, Bonn, London, and Sydney, Australia.

"We wanted to run a campaign that raised a profile beyond Vancouver Island," said Valerie Langer. "We wanted to run it in a media-savvy style, one that your grandma would feel comfortable joining." The protesters sustained a clear, well-planned media campaign, every day presenting news outlets with ready-made copy. As well, by continually offering reasoned solutions to the problems at hand, the movement garnered more credibility, while the logging companies and the government looked and sounded completely unnerved. The events of the summer provided rich fodder for the crowds of reporters, given the almost daily scenes of police dragging off peaceful, non-violent protesters from all walks of life, the highly photogenic surroundings, the scenes of devastation on the surrounding hills.

Nonetheless, journalists had their work cut out for them in that pre-digital age, as CBC television reporter Eve Savory vividly recalled.

> I made eighteen trips there that summer, usually with cameraman Rob Douglas. We would catch a late ferry after I filed, drive to Tofino...We'd be up at 2 a.m. and be at the barricade at Kennedy Lake by 4 a.m. where the activists were waiting. We would shoot the confrontations as the buses and trucks and cops arrived, the loggers shouting out the windows, angry, anxious, upset. Baffled, really. The cops would tell the protesters to move. They didn't, they sat down, they were picked up, dragged off, taken away...We always tried to interview a logger at the site but they were so angry they would either refuse or harass us so my cameraman and I would head to Ucluelet where most of them lived. I got seriously hassled because they saw us every day at the barricades and figured we were tree-huggers too. Very frustrating, as I wanted to give them a voice...Oh, they were mad at all of us, no matter how we tried. And then, the race to the dock where the float plane had arrived to take me and the tapes back to Vancouver, and the cameraman would make the long drive back. Crazy time.

Robert F. Kennedy Jr., an environmental lawyer in Washington D.C., made an appearance in support of the protestors, as did Tom Hayden and the Greenpeace-sponsored enviro-rock band Midnight Oil. The band flew from Australia to play a concert in front of an estimated 5,000 people at the Black Hole in mid-July 1993. The band's towering, six foot six, arm-swinging, bald-headed lead vocalist, Peter Garrett, encouraged the crowd to continue its protest, declaring he was "bugged by a government who bought shares in the forest industry prior to making a pro-logging land use decision like Clayoquot," and he found it "scandalous, immoral and improper." Renowned environmentalist David Suzuki sat in the front row near the stage, which was constructed of burned wood from the Black Hole site. The international press turned out in force for the event.

Matt Ronald-Jones, who worked at the newly opened Middle Beach Lodge, where the band stayed, recalled cars parked on both sides of the road for kilometres leading to the concert site, and noted that a cloud hung over the clearing from all the marijuana being smoked. "After the concert we were heading back to my car, when I saw a brand new Pontiac Trans-Am sports car loading passengers by the side of the road. The door sat open. Just then a crummy wagon full of loggers came up the road moving pretty fast. Seeing the open door of the Trans-Am the crummy driver didn't slow down one bit...and the big van ripped the door clean off that Trans-Am and kept right on going. It was something to behold!"

"The loggers were angry and frustrated," reporter Eve Savory commented. "Most of the protesters were young females who spoke softly and sang. What's an angry man to do? Yes, there were many angry words, but my impression was they felt baffled, out of their depth, deeply frustrated, and probably, deeply anxious. With good reason." Some of the loggers had spent decades of their lives in the forest; they took pride in their work, and they could not begin to comprehend this mass opposition to everything they had ever done, much of it coming from people who did not know the area at all. Small wonder anger erupted. Tzeporah Berman received so many death threats on her voice mail that a colleague began filtering them so she would not hear any more; she also received anti-Semitic hate mail. Opponents often targeted the Peace Camp, leaning on horns in the middle of the night, throwing stones at tents, and harassing people from the gates. Tensions rose in Ucluelet and Tofino, with families becoming estranged, car and truck tires being slashed, boats being sunk. Warring bumper stickers could not begin to reveal the depth of feeling in the area; "Logging Feeds My Family" and "Hug a Logger, You'll Never Go Back To Trees!" only hinted at how threatened the logging community felt.

In mid-August 1993, the logging-industry-sponsored pressure group

Share BC organized a two-day rally in Ucluelet to express support for the government's Clayoquot Sound Land Use Decision, and to bring loggers together in a show of solidarity. Some 5,000 loggers and their supporters from all over BC came to Rendezvous '93, billed as a "protest against the protesters" in the *Westerly News*. Many participants sported yellow ribbons and T-shirts, and "along with the yellow were countless yells, yells everywhere of support for the embattled loggers of the West Coast...The yellow army rallied in support of the government and encouraged it time after time to stand its ground on the decision." Rousing speakers urged the local loggers not to lose their backbone, with Jack Munro of IWA-Canada saying, "Maybe you feel by yourselves in the morning some days, but we're sure as hell there with you, we appreciate you keeping your cool." Gerry Stoney of the IWA stated, "This will be a moment of truth that will put an end to the distortion and plain unadulterated BS that the preservationists are feeding to the people of BC and the world. I want to say to anyone watching on TV or listening on the radio, folks you're being swindled, you're being conned, you're being lied to by the so called leading lights of the environmental movement."

As the summer of 1993 wore on, the RCMP continued their arrests, which came to include women from the Raging Grannies, one of them eighty-one years old. One day four grandmothers linked arms with MP Svend Robinson and several others, "and all launched themselves and Clayoquot into the international sphere with the simple words, 'No, I will not move,'" as Valerie Langer wrote later. A great-grandfather of eighty was arrested, children as young as eleven and twelve, Anglican priests, professors, lawyers, teachers, doctors, high school students, politicians, aboriginals, and even some loggers. "Theme days" saw only people from specific groups blockading: on one day, those from the Gulf Islands; on another, artists, including nature painter Robert Bateman; and on it went, with people of faith, business and professional people, tourists, foresters, and even deaf people taking their turns to be arrested.

In his autobiography, Premier Mike Harcourt wrote: "But despite the protest, the arrest of almost eight hundred protestors and the Greenpeace-inspired boycotts, I was not about to give in to the protestors.

I was not about to give in to the clear-cutters either. I was not about to give in to the forest industry. I was not about to give in to aboriginal demands. I would most certainly not give in to the likes of [Robert] Kennedy's grandstanding. He said he was outraged over our decision. I wrote of him and his 'outrage' that 'he was asking loggers and forestry workers to live off their inheritance—just like he does.'"

In August 1993, the first of a series of eight trials began before Justice John Bouck in the theatre of the Royal BC Museum in Victoria, the number of defendants so great that the provincial courthouse proved too small. In order not to clog the courts, protestors were tried en masse, leading to complaints of Canada's Charter of Rights and Freedoms being violated and basic legal rights denied. The first trial of forty-four protestors continued for five weeks; the rest followed in 1994. Most of those arrested faced criminal contempt charges for defying MacBlo's court injunctions rather than the charge of civil contempt, which carried a less severe penalty. Even though the court documents stated that the case pitted MacMillan Bloedel against John and Jane Doe, no MacBlo lawyers appeared in court, as they would have done had the protesters faced civil contempt charges. Instead Crown counsel from the Attorney General's office prosecuted the case, which made it look like the province of British Columbia had quietly taken over the prosecution of the cases for MacBlo. As lawyer Jim Miller stated, this left the impression "that the Attorney General is joined at the hip with MacMillan Bloedel." By taking over the prosecution, the Attorney General's office saved MacBlo thousands of dollars in lawyers' fees, passing those expenses on to the province's taxpayers.

Most of the accused appeared in court for the first time in their lives. Most appeared without lawyers to represent them and could not opt for trial by jury or call witnesses to appear in their defence. The court denied them the opportunity to explain why they had stood on the road at the Kennedy River Bridge. Each defendant was asked: "Were you there? Did you hear the injunction read?" In most cases, videotaped evidence provided by MacBlo proved the defendant had been there, and then the defendant was found guilty because, as the judges stated over and over, "If you were on the road and knowingly disobeyed the injunction, then you are guilty. That is the law." The judges imposed widely inconsistent sentences: fines ranging from $350 to $3,000; sentences ranging from suspended sentences to six months in jail, and sometimes probation. MP Svend Robinson received a fourteen-day sentence. Local doctor Ron Aspinall was slapped with sixty days in jail and a $3,000 fine. When two of the arrested grandmothers—Judith Robinson, aged seventy-two, and Betty Krawczyk, sixty-five—refused to sign undertakings that they would stop protesting, they each served eighty-five days in prison. At one point during their sentence they were transferred by air, with another older woman, from Nanaimo to Victoria, a trip made "unbelievably complicated by the leg shackles and handcuffs we were forced to wear," wrote Betty. "Three grandmothers in leg irons for protesting the demolition of one of the world's last old growth rainforests! Lord have mercy on us." The severity of some of the sentences came as a terrible shock; many of those participating in the blockades had expected to do community service, not to be taken from the courtroom in handcuffs by a sheriff.

Tzeporah Berman had always made sure she was not on the road among those willing to be arrested. Nonetheless, one day the RCMP arrested her from the side of the road and charged her with aiding and abetting the commission of 857 criminal acts. The charge, which potentially carried a six-year prison sentence, outraged prominent criminal lawyers Clayton Ruby of Ontario and BC's David Martin. They stepped up and defended Berman pro bono. "A Macmillan Bloedel representative [admitted] during the trial that the firm had lobbied for months to have the charismatic woman arrested," reported Kim Westad in the *Victoria Times Colonist*. In rendering his decision after Berman's four-day trial, Justice Richard Low opened with harsh words for the Crown, then dismissed the case. In 2013 the "whacked-out nature worshipper," as one TV reporter dubbed Berman, received an honorary degree from the University of British Columbia, and today she appears on a list at the Royal BC Museum of 150 people who have "changed the face of British Columbia."

Following their sentencing, each defendant reserved the right to speak to sentencing, giving rise to eloquent and moving statements.

Peter Holmes stated, "I believe that these trials themselves are doing at least as much to bring the administration of justice and the courts themselves into disrepute as, and probably quite a bit more than the original actions of the arrestees that triggered these trials." Margaret Ormond said, "I went to Kennedy Bridge, not as an environmentalist... but as a private citizen, out of concern for the world my children and grandchildren will inherit." Carol MacIsaac said, "We are at a point in history where direct and urgent action is needed. If it does not come from government then it must come from people of conscience." Kim Blank went on record saying, "The idea that the democracy of Canada has been threatened by the Clayoquot protestors is overstated. If our wonderful country is truly threatened by the action of a few protesters sitting quietly on a dirt road in the middle of the night, then it is time to hang up the old hockey stick and move to a different planet." George Harris, a logger arrested with his two sons Adam, twelve, and Tyson, eleven, concluded his submission: "I was thinking what the parents of the eleven and twelve-year-old children said in Nazi Germany in the 1940s when their Jewish neighbors were taken away to be exterminated. This was done legally, this was done with everyone's knowledge. What did parents say? What will I say when my children grow up and look at the destruction of this province? I will say that I stood with my friends on the line at Clayoquot Sound. Thank you, Your Honor."

The arrests, the trials, and the convictions did nothing to stop the protests. Instead, environmental groups broadened their horizons, organizing a "markets campaign." Careful research into which companies used paper products manufactured from logs harvested in Clayoquot Sound led the protesters to large American companies like Scott Paper and Pacific Bell Telephone. Faced with demonstrations in front of their offices and factories, and with activists offering to place stickers on their products bearing slogans like "I destroy rainforests" and "Let your fingers do the chopping," the companies, fearing negative publicity, cancelled their orders. "Things didn't turn around until we worked with international markets for wood products," said Valerie Langer. The activists expanded their campaign to Europe and organized boycotts of MacBlo products in England, Australia, Germany, and Austria. According to author Lorna Stefanick, "In Britain activists were arrested for chaining themselves to the doors of Canada House; in Germany, Sweden, Australia, Italy, Japan and India groups protested the logging of Clayoquot Sound outside Canadian embassies and consulates." The environmentalists brought with them a 3,600-kilogram red cedar stump, two metres in diameter, that was reckoned to be a young 390 years old—given that some cedars live to 1,500 years. Named "Baby Stumpy," it toured North America before Greenpeace transported it to Europe, where it fascinated thousands and became a powerful symbol for the anti-logging campaign. European corporations began cancelling contracts with MacBlo. "They canceled over five million dollars in contracts in England and at least that much in Germany," said Langer. "We were called 'traitors' by company executives and provincial officials." She said that the publicity campaign in Europe and the United States "linked with the campaign for alternative paper fibers, recycling and reduced paper consumption. It was the most outrageously reasonable campaign. There is no question that ancient forests should not be used for telephone directories and newspapers."

In October 1993 the Harcourt government launched a two-pronged strategy to defuse the situation. It first established a nineteen-member Scientific Panel for Sustainable Forest Practices in Clayoquot Sound, headed by Dr. Fred Bunnell, with Nuu-chah-nulth hereditary chief E. Richard Atleo as co-chair. The panel set out to find the most scientifically rigorous standards for environmentally sustainable logging. In March 1994, the BC government signed an Interim Measures Agreement with the Nuu-chah-nulth. This put land use decisions for Clayoquot Sound into the hands of a ten-member board made up of First Nations and provincial representatives, giving the First Nations a veto over all decisions, pending the completion of treaty negotiations. The Interim Measures Agreement also gave First Nations in Clayoquot Sound $4.5 million over two years for economic development. This agreement drove a wedge between First Nations and the environmental movement,

In the meantime, in February 1994, Stephen Owen released his CORE report recommendations. Although Clayoquot Sound had been excluded from his deliberations, among his recommendations he proposed preserving 13 percent of the rest of Vancouver Island as wilderness. He recommended that the government create new logging practices and standards, and impose heavy penalties for non-compliance; provide funds to oversee resource and environmental management in Clayoquot Sound; create a biosphere reserve in the Sound; and receive and respect policy advice on land use allocations reached by consensus at regional tables. Owen also asked that the Conflict of Interest Commissioner investigate the provincial government's purchase of shares in MacBlo.

The CORE recommendations riled loggers all over BC, many of whom united behind the Share BC movement. They viewed the CORE recommendations as an assault on their livelihood that would eliminate 3,500 forestry jobs, cost $42 million in wages, and devastate their industry. On March 21, 1994, Share BC staged a massive event at the Legislative Buildings in Victoria, drawing a crowd estimated at between 14,000 and 20,000 loggers and their supporters, many wearing yellow ribbons. They came from all over Vancouver Island and elsewhere in BC, travelling by bus and in cavalcades of cars and logging trucks to hold the largest demonstration ever seen at the legislature. This rally, targeted not only the government and Owen's CORE recommendations, but also, as Jack Munro of the IWA put it, "the cappuccino-sucking, concrete-condo-dwelling, granola-eating city slickers" who supported the environmentalists. Premier Harcourt tried to address the volatile gathering, saying he would not approve the CORE recommendations, only to be drowned out by the protestors.

The summer of protest in Clayoquot Sound did not for a moment stop the logging. As Tzeporah Berman put it in *This Crazy Time*, "MacMillan Bloedel was still logging Clayoquot as quickly as they could" through the summer of 1994. Now hired by Greenpeace as a campaigner, Berman asked that organization to send its mother ship to Clayoquot Sound to protest the continued logging at Bulson Creek. When it emerged that Nuu-chah-nulth leaders did not want Greenpeace protesting in the Sound because they valued the jobs provided by logging, long and difficult negotiations ensued. Moses Martin, chief councillor of the Tla-o-qui-aht, pointed out to Berman and her colleagues, "You have to understand you're concerned about the trees and the wildlife, and many of us share those concerns, but we're also carrying...the highest suicide rates in Canada, we have the highest unemployment rates in Canada, and our people are struggling so hard to survive that our culture and language are dying."

In May 1995, Dr. Fred Bunnell's nineteen-member scientific panel released its report, setting out new guidelines for forest practices in Clayoquot Sound and providing over 170 recommendations that would make forestry in this area "not only the best in the province, but the best in the world." The report emphasized that "the key to sustainable forest practices lies in maintaining functioning ecosystems and that planning must focus on these ecosystems rather than on resource extraction." It recommended that clear-cutting be replaced by variable retention forestry, an approach that would leave some trees standing in each area in order to protect the health of the forest ecosystem. The panel stated that the cultural values of the inhabitants of the Sound must be respected, and study of the scientific and ecological knowledge of Clayoquot Sound must continue. It also reduced the size of cutblocks, called for alternative harvesting measures, such as helicopter logging, and for sustainable forestry, with improved replanting and "greening" methods. The government could impose fines of up to a million dollars if the guidelines were not followed. Most of these measures had already been in place for months, many recommended a year earlier in Stephen Owen's CORE report. In July 1995, the government accepted most of the recommendations of the Clayoquot Scientific Panel.

By 1997, logging in Clayoquot Sound had been reduced to a tenth of what it was in 1991, with MacBlo recording losses of more than $350 million due to the limitations imposed by the Scientific Panel for Sustainable Forest Practices. In 1998, losses in sales of $1.1 billion forced the logging industry to cut jobs and close mills. Interfor closed its office in Tofino that year. The downturn forced MacMillan Bloedel, represented by Linda Coady, a Vancouver lobbyist who had been appointed vice-president of Environmental Affairs, to begin private talks with the Nuu-chah-nulth First Nations and five environmental organizations. The talks resulted in a Memorandum of Understanding (MOU) signed on June 16, 1999, establishing a joint venture between MacBlo and Ma-Mook Development Corporation, a Nuu-chah-nulth-owned company, to create Iisaak Forest Resources Ltd. ("Iisaak" means respect). Ma-Mook would control 51 percent of the new company and MacBlo 49 percent, with MacBlo handing over its Clayoquot Sound tree farm licences to Iisaak.

In accepting this mandate, Iisaak became the only company licensed to operate in the Sound, and it agreed to follow rigorous guidelines set out in the not-legally-binding MOU. The guidelines specified logging could only occur outside the intact old-growth valleys of the Sound, using only existing logging roads, and conducting what a MacBlo spokesman characterized as "boutique logging." All of the environmental groups save Friends of Clayoquot Sound, which had reservations about the compromise, promised to support Iisaak and help it look for new markets for its products. Twenty-four hours after signing this MOU, multinational giant Weyerhaeuser announced that it had bought MacBlo for $2.45 billion.

While all these protests and studies and discussions were taking place, the federal and provincial governments continued quietly working behind the scenes with the United Nations Educational Scientific and Cultural Organization (UNESCO) to have the United Nations declare Clayoquot Sound an international biosphere reserve. For many decades, scientists had recognized the unique biodiversity of the old-growth forests and the richness of marine life on the west coast, but much still needed to be learned. Between 1989 and 1991 a group of researchers, including Jim Darling, Kate Keogh, Josie Cleland, Karena Shaw, Mike Marrell, and Wendy Kotilla, worked in conjunction with the Nuu-chah-nulth of Clayoquot Sound to assemble "a scientifically acceptable pool of knowledge about the region that simply would not exist otherwise," according to Jim Darling. Their wide-ranging work addressed "what species are present and which areas are important to them and why...stream inventories, fish habitat mapping...amphibian surveys, dragonfly inventories, microclimate projects and more."

On May 5, 2000, Prime Minister Jean Chrétien and Premier Ujjal Dosanjh unveiled a plaque in Pacific Rim National Park declaring that the UN had designated Clayoquot Sound a UNESCO Biosphere Reserve, one of over 600 worldwide. This designation gave international recognition to Clayoquot Sound's biological diversity, "promoting and demonstrating a balanced relationship between people and nature." The designation did not mean the UN would exert any control over the Sound, nor did it mean an end to logging or mining in the region. As a biosphere reserve, all stakeholders would work to balance conservation with sustainable economic, social, and cultural development. First Nations would be allowed to continue logging in a sustainable manner within the reserve. Both the federal and provincial governments allocated funds to "support research, education and training in the Biosphere region," with the federal government contributing $12 million to establish the Clayoquot Biosphere Trust.

In the end, the "War in the Woods" of 1993 saw the environmental movement change the face of logging in British Columbia. It managed to shut down logging by multinational companies in Clayoquot Sound, paving the way for the Nuu-chah-nulth-owned Iisaak to become the only company working in the area. The activists' actions helped transform how forestry would be conducted in the province. The Forest Practices Code of 1995 brought immediate changes, and additional regulations have since refined that original legislation. Roads that once slid down mountainsides are now made to stay in place, fish-bearing creeks and wildlife habitat are better protected, clear-cuts are limited in size.

Yet although 60 percent of Clayoquot Sound now stands protected from logging, chainsaws are still at work there. In March 2007, a First Nations company, Ma-Mook Natural Resources Ltd., bought Interfor's 49,000-hectare tree farm licence in Clayoquot Sound. In order to finance the purchase, Ma-Mook entered into a joint venture with Coulson Forest Products, a logging company from Port Alberni, and soon lobbying began to allow logging in the intact watersheds of Clayoquot Sound. Although Ma-Mook's alliance with Coulson Forest Products lasted only three years, leaving Ma-Mook in sole charge of the company's timber holdings in the Sound, pressure to log areas of old growth still exists. Yet everyone involved in the forest industry knows that highly motivated individuals and vigilant environmental groups like Friends of Clayoquot Sound, Western Canada Wilderness Committee, and the recently formed Clayoquot Action group continue to keep a watchful eye on logging practices. No one in the business wants to attract the adverse publicity or reignite the bitter conflict of the early 1990s. For now, the unlogged, pristine valleys and watersheds that remain in Clayoquot Sound stand intact, but if one lesson has been learned from the events of the late twentieth century, it is that nothing here should ever be taken for granted.

In April 2014, on the thirtieth anniversary of the Meares Island Easter Festival and the Tla-o-qui-aht declaration of Meares as a Tribal Park, a group gathered in Tofino to commemorate this landmark event that kick-started so many years of protests against logging in Clayoquot Sound. Central to the celebration, Godfrey Stephens's five-metre-high carving *Weeping Cedar Woman* returned to Tofino after many years in his workshop in Victoria. Unveiled at her temporary location outside the Tofino Community Hall, *Weeping Cedar Woman* now stands fully restored, her tears flowing in cascades, one hand held out defensively, the other pointing at the earth.

The non-violent campaign conducted by protesters at the Kennedy River Bridge in 1993 became a template for environmental movements around the world. The Great Bear Rainforest campaign, Occupy Wall Street, Idle No More, the fight to stop the Enbridge Northern Gateway and Keystone XL pipelines have all been influenced and, in some fashion, inspired by the landmark protest in Clayoquot Sound. The events of 1993 also brought the Nuu-chah-nulth to the forefront of treaty nego-tiations, which the provincial government had been reluctant to begin. By signing an MOU with the Nuu-chah-nulth in March 1994, it took the first step in beginning the treaty-making process.

The protests of 1993 brought the quiet, rain-drenched town of Tofino

An arrest at the Kennedy River Bridge in 1993. Typically the protestors would lie on the road, offering no resistance as the RCMP carried them away. *Courtesy of Clayoquot Action*

onto the world stage in ways no one could have foreseen, initiating irreversible changes in the community. While media exposure during the protests put the devastation of clear-cut logging on the television screens of millions of viewers around the world, many reports juxtaposed shots of clear-cuts with stunning images of the pristine areas of the Sound. Displaying the wildlife, the beaches, the mountains, and the great forests of the west coast at their best, such coverage acted as a massive and immediate tourist magnet for the area. "Thank God for all the protests," said Gary Richards of Tofino Air, recalling the impact on his business. "Everyone wanted to hire us to fly them out to see the old-growth forest. They wanted to see the last big trees before they were cut down." Others wanted to see just the opposite. One German tourist reportedly arrived in Tofino and immediately ordered a float plane pilot to "Take me to a clear-cut!" Float planes flew many international journalists over clear-cuts, old-growth forests, glorious

During the protests at the Kennedy River Bridge during the summer of 1993, various groups would offer themselves to be arrested on designated days. Here young people await arrest, on a Kids' Day protest. Children as young as eleven were arrested. *Ron Shau photo, courtesy of Clayoquot Action*

beaches, glaciers, and then out to sea to spot grey whales, all in one flight.

Since that time, people have arrived in droves. In the scramble of development throughout the 1990s and early 2000s, Tofino has at times been overwhelmed by its own popularity, for preserving the beauty of the area, and sharing it with others, has come at a price. "One day all the West Coast territory will be opened up," declared Dorothy Abraham some sixty years ago in *Lone Cone*, "and one day it will be the greatest playground of the Pacific: people will swarm in, and the silence will be broken." She was absolutely right.

532

Chapter 22:

THE EMERGING SCENE

AS TOFINO SHIFTED FROM a resource-based to a tourist-based economy, the changes affected every person and every business in the town. The pilots of Tofino Air saw the change as clearly as anyone. In the 1980s, their business had been mostly connected with logging activity and fish farms; by the mid-1990s, Doug Banks, then co-owner of the airline, reckoned that 80 to 90 percent of their float plane charters catered to tourists.

Statistics concerning the numbers of visitors flocking into the area are notoriously difficult to come by, but as the *Westerly News* stated on February 2, 1994, "any way you count them, we do know that 1993 was a record year for visitation in this area." The article then quoted a Parks Canada estimate that in 1993 some 769,308 visitors entered the area. Although this may have included a good many locals, such a statistic at least gave an idea of the volume of traffic heading through the park, much of it ending up in Tofino. The sheer numbers of visitors, the long lineups in stores and restaurants, and the demands faced by locals left many in shock. In August 1994, *The Sound* magazine described what it termed Tofino's "schizophrenic" attitude to tourists: "They feed us, maybe even make us rich. But they crowd us, distract us, annoy us, repulse us...they make Tofino a town of strangers...It makes us want to run and hide until they all go away and we can again walk down the street and actually say hi to someone we know."

Many local people joined the rush to provide accommodation for the visitors, offering their homes as bed and breakfast establishments, and building suites and cabins for vacation rentals. As scores of such places began welcoming visitors, Tofino council faced one challenging decision after another about development, rezoning, and business licences, continually navigating a minefield of concerns about growth, the economy, the environment, and the very identity of the community.

Heated debates arose about setting limits on the numbers of certain businesses, the pros and cons of permitting helicopter tours, even whether quotas should be set to limit the numbers of tourists allowed in the area. Bars and coffee shops buzzed with discussions—was Tofino becoming another Banff or a "Whistler-on-the-beach"? And where on earth was the town heading if this deluge of tourists continued?

To complicate matters further, many of the tourists who arrived after 1993 had very different notions from the early campers and counterculture adventurers who made their way across Sutton Pass on the new road to the coast in the 1960s and '70s. These more affluent, often international, tourists required wilderness experiences on demand and had much higher expectations in terms of accommodation and amenities. Until now, services had been fairly limited and low-key. That began to change.

In the spring of 1993, Chris Le Fevre opened Middle Beach Lodge on MacKenzie Beach, an ambitiously designed structure with twenty-six rooms. Although Le Fevre initially envisioned a lodge with unassuming, family-friendly accommodation in a wilderness setting, providing neither phones nor television in the rooms, from the outset this new lodge attracted clients seeking something special. Among the first guests: Peter Garrett and his Midnight Oil bandmates, there to play their famous concert at the Black Hole; lawyer Robert Kennedy Jr.; a clutch of foreign media; and the first influx of the new ecotourists who began flocking to the west coast.

In surfing terms, Le Fevre caught the wave; his timing proved perfect. For the next few years he did not even bother advertising, benefiting from the rush of visitors who began arriving and who did his advertising for him by word of mouth. "People just kept coming," he marvelled. Following the success of his first lodge, and realizing the appetite for better-quality accommodation, in 1996 Le Fevre built a second lodge with additional amenities on the promontory at the north end of MacKenzie Beach.

The idea of offering more sophisticated accommodation in and around Tofino caught on. In 1996 the Wickaninnish Inn and Pointe Restaurant opened on the headland at the north end of Chesterman

Beach, fulfilling Howard McDiarmid's long-standing dream of building a spectacular resort there. His son Charles, who by then had worked many years in the high-end hotel trade, drew up the business plan and sought out interested investors, including a number of local people. Building this resort required a change in zoning from "forest rural" to "tourist commercial," a change bitterly opposed by many local residents. The McDiarmids found themselves vilified at public hearings in Tofino and saw a full-page ad denouncing their development in the local paper. After the zoning change had been approved by council, the group Friends of Chesterman Beach, having opposed the development proposal, appealed the new zoning in court. The judge upheld it.

Once it opened, the Wickaninnish Inn raised the bar dramatically for standards of accommodation and cuisine in the area. Other resorts followed suit. The ambitious Clayoquot Wilderness Resort opened at the mouth of the Bedwell (formerly Bear) River in 2000, near the site of the short-lived mining community of Port Hughes. Back in 1899, a fourteen-room hotel offered accommodation here, "which would not be out of place in any city," according to the *British Colonist*. The same location now presents a five-star resort offering wilderness experience with glamorous camping, or "glamping," in elaborate eco-safari tents, complete with world-class cuisine: to stay there can cost thousands of dollars a day. Next to enter the lists of high-quality resorts, Long Beach Lodge on Cox Bay opened in 2002, offering "luxury adventure travel."

Meanwhile, all around Tofino, standards rose in other hotels and restaurants, along with prices. Local people looked on in disbelief, bemused by the ever-increasing amenities, sometimes feeling unwelcome in these new places and astounded by the high prices. Some residents found lucrative employment in constructing the new resorts, and a significant handful of local artisans have had their work showcased in the top hotels. The skills of woodcarver Henry Nolla were integral in the design of the Wickaninnish Inn; his work there includes the massive adzed red cedar posts and beams that dominate the entranceways, the yellow cedar entrance doors inlaid with abalone, the twin eagles at the Pointe Restaurant, as well as the beam and detail work in all of the public spaces, and the fireplace mantels in each guest room.

Few new developments arrived without at least some controversy, as Chris Le Fevre discovered. Following his success in establishing Middle Beach Lodge in the mid-1990s, he went on to become Tofino's most ambitious developer. He is responsible for most townhouse and condominium developments in town, including the Eik Landing condominiums, the Fred Tibbs building, and Rosie Bay Estates. In 2008 he built the Cox Bay Beach Resort, and two years later he acquired and refurbished the well-known Weigh West Marine Resort, which he renamed Marina West.

The Eik Landing development stirred up a colourful local dispute surpassing most others, and bringing considerable media attention to Tofino. Le Fevre had purchased the waterfront property once owned by pioneer John Eik, known to old-timers as Eik's chicken ranch, and the site of one of the pre-war Japanese settlements in Tofino. On the property stood two massive red cedars, thought to be over 800 years old. Because of rot and the danger of the trees falling, insurers declared them hazardous and demanded they be cut down before the project proceeded. After one tree came down, some outraged citizens banded together to form the Tofino Natural Heritage Society to protect the other tree, which stood right beside the main road leading into downtown Tofino. The society began fundraising to save the massive "Eik Tree," the last example of old growth in Tofino. In full view of every tourist and passing car, two young people climbed twenty-four metres into the tree and spent twenty-eight days living up in the canopy to protect it from the chainsaw. They garnered nationwide media attention, with the press once again focusing on Tofino as the "Tree Hugging Capital of the World." Engineers and arborists worked to find some way to preserve the tree, and in the summer of 2002 engineers fitted the Eik Tree with a specially designed metal girdle, anchored into the bedrock.

That same year, Le Fevre purchased nearly six hectares of land adjacent to Tonquin Park, overlooking Tonquin Beach in Tofino. His plans to build forty-four condominiums and time-share properties there received approval from the municipality, but Tofinoites raised objections to a development so near the only wilderness park in town.

The famous Eik Tree caused a furore when arborists declared it unsafe and a developer sought permission to cut it down. Two protestors spent twenty-eight days living high in the tree to prevent its removal. In the summer of 2002, engineers fitted the tree with a specially designed metal girdle, anchored into the bedrock. *Ian Kennedy photo*

In November 2002, the municipal council tabled the development permit and held a public hearing, attended by over a hundred local residents. Le Fevre threatened to log his property if the municipality rescinded the approval it had already granted. This forced opponents of the project to form the Tonquin Nature Reserve Committee. In the end they purchased the land, using capital from Tofino Community Investments, a development company made up mostly of local people espousing sound environmental and business principles.

All developers in the area relied on the provision of one absolutely essential element—water. In 1995, following the outlay of $11.3 million in federal grant money to upgrade its water system, residents felt confident they had solved Tofino's nagging water problems. Not so. The construction of new resorts and new homes on the town's outskirts over the next decade strained the system to capacity, particularly in the summer months. This led the Tofino council to present a referendum in June 2004, proposing a $3.8-million upgrade of the system.

Fearing that if they passed this measure, even more development would ensue, Tofino voters rejected the proposal. The defeat forced the council to create a six-stage water-conservation plan. The plan imposed tight water restrictions during the summers of 2004 and 2005, but the following summer brought the water crisis to a head. Tofino once again hit the national and international headlines.

On August 29, 2006, after a two-month dry spell, Tofino mayor John Fraser announced that a severe water shortage forced him to impose Stage Five of the town's water conservation plan: a total ban on all water use, other than for firefighting. The edict required all hotels and lodgings, as well as food-service businesses, to shut down completely, closing their doors to potential guests just as the Labour Day weekend loomed, with some 10,000 visitors expected. This draconian move provided sensational copy for the media. After all, Tofino records an average of 3.3 metres, or ten feet, of rain annually and has measurable precipitation for 202 days a year. Given Tofino's renown as a moist tourist mecca in a rainforest, how could such a place be forced to shut its doors for lack of water? With phones ringing off the hook as concerned guests called about their reservations for the upcoming weekend, many hotels, as ordered, cancelled reservations, laid off staff, and phoned customers to tell them "Tofino is closed."

Not everyone agreed with this approach. Chris Le Fevre immediately secured a supply of water in Ucluelet, over forty kilometres down the road, and arranged for it to be carried to Middle Beach Lodge in tanker trucks. The municipality then tried to force all businesses, by law, to shut down, whether they had their own supply of water or not. This caused an uproar that precipitated an emergency council meeting on August 31—one of Tofino's more memorable civic events. With the meeting room packed, with people banging on the windows demanding to be let in, and with many reporters present, Le Fevre confronted the mayor about his decision to shut down business on one of the busiest weekends of the year. He stated that the mayor's decision had been premature and challenged him to seek solutions rather than proclaim edicts. "What it costs to truck the water into Tofino is a peppercorn compared to the amount of money and goodwill businesses could lose...

not to mention the trickle-down effect throughout the whole town," argued Le Fevre. "I have tanker trucks ready to begin pumping water into the municipal system right now and I'll put $50,000 on the table to set that plan in motion." He estimated that trucking water from Ucluelet would provide Tofino with nearly a million litres per day, which, along with the small amount of water still available from the reservoirs, would keep the town going—with usage restrictions—for up to two weeks. Council approved the plan and rescinded the order for businesses to shut down for the weekend.

Despite the procession of water-filled tanker trucks travelling up from Ucluelet, water use had to be carefully controlled. Restaurants used disposable plates and plastic cutlery, hotels provided guests with boiled water for drinking, use of hot tubs was banned, and surfers had to wash their wetsuits in a saltwater/vinegar combination instead of hosing them down with fresh water. Water restrictions remained in place until mid-September, when enough rain fell to replenish the reservoirs.

Following the water crisis, a joint federal, provincial, and municipal plan saw the town add a 4.5-million-litre reservoir at the Stump Dump near the airport, connecting it to the district's existing system. The plan also added Ginnard Creek, on Meares Island, to the water system, creating a 22.5-million-litre capacity at the new Ahkmahksis Reservoir. A new submarine line carried water from the reservoir, under Browning Passage, to a treatment plant on Sharp Road that removed the brownish colour and partially chlorinated the water. These new facilities were earmarked for use during summer months, when the water system was under greatest usage. Despite these improvements, municipal officials remain concerned for the future, anticipating ever greater demands on the water system. Tofino's manager of sustainability, Aaron Rodgers, believes the town must be open to creative and alternative solutions in the future: "Onsite storage of water is a possible solution, and we certainly should be looking at grey water recycling during the summer months."

Along with the water system, the question of sewage disposal has been a longstanding concern. Ever since 1999, Tofino has been considering an upgrade of its sewage system, last updated in 1984. With the provincial capital Victoria, Tofino shares the dubious distinction of being one of two major centres in the province still pumping untreated sewage into the Pacific Ocean. Tofino municipal staff and council made progress on a three-stage liquid waste management plan, but in 2006 balked at the cost of building a secondary treatment plant. By 2013, estimates for this stood at $18 million, a cost that would typically be shared by federal, provincial, and municipal governments. Given that the projected revenues for the Tofino District Council in 2014 are only $7.7 million, the expenditure on sewage treatment presents massive monetary and taxation problems. Yet the problem urgently needs to be addressed. "It's simply not acceptable anymore," said Tofino's mayor Josie Osborne, in an interview with the *Westerly News* on August 7, 2013. "Here we are in the UNESCO Biosphere Reserve and we have a moral obligation to make as little impact as possible on the natural environment, hence we should have sewage treatment." No plans for the new plant had been finalized as of spring 2014.

The question of sewage disposal received heightened attention with the construction of the new Tla-o-qui-aht Ty-Histanis village site in 2011. Located next to Esowista village, just north of Long Beach, Ty-Histanis stands on an 85-hectare parcel of land signed over by Parks Canada to the Tla-o-qui-ahts as an extension of the Esowista Reserve in 2007. The Tla-o-qui-ahts lobbied the Department of Aboriginal Affairs and Northern Development for funding to build a housing project on this newly acquired land, and in 2007 the department allocated $26.9 million to build a state-of-the-art aboriginal community. The plans for this new development, to be built in phases, feature 171 single-detached units, 32 duplexes, and a 12-unit elder complex, along with a community hall, school, health clinic, pharmacy, recreation centre, and centres for youth and elders. Planners insisted on geothermal energy to heat every building and the latest in green technology, intending this village to become a showpiece for First Nations development.

When the first phase of the development opened in 2011, it soon become apparent that Tofino Airport's old septic field did not have the capacity to handle the sewage from Ty-Histanis. The federal government then gave Parks Canada $3.3 million to connect the Green Point Campground and the Long Beach and Ty-Histanis water and sewage systems to the existing Tofino infrastructure. Funding for this also came from the Tla-o-qui-aht, through a 2009 government grant to fourteen First Nations for water and waste management projects. While this proposal pleased the staff of Parks Canada, who had long hoped for an upgrade to the park's water and sewage services, many Tofino residents did not wish to add more effluent to Tofino's sewers, increasing the amount being dumped raw and untreated into the ocean. The debate remains unresolved in 2014.

As tourism increased in Tofino and Clayoquot Sound through the 1990s and 2000s, everyone involved in the industry became part of a delicate balancing act, weighing commercial interests against the need to preserve the area. Many of the natural attractions eagerly marketed by local entrepreneurs and sought by tourists can suffer all too easily from exploitation and overexposure. One example among many is the concern, first arising in the early 1990s, about the multitude of whale-watching vessels approaching whales far too closely. As one whale-watching guide put it, "We're hugging the whales to death, great mobs of us—it can't be good for them." Over time, a variety of guidelines set out how boats should keep their distance. Concerns have also arisen about protecting tree roots and delicate mosses on hiking trails, about ensuring visitors do not remove sea stars and shells from the beaches, about the constant noise of float planes, and about tourists who foolishly approach bears and wolves in the hopes of a good photograph or, even worse, who try to entice them with food.

The Tofino mud flats present another case in point. Teeming with life, the nutrient-rich mud flats support the largest eelgrass beds on the west coast, offering safe breeding grounds for herring and other fish as well as for crabs and clams. They comprise 1,700 hectares around

Tofino, including Arukun and Duckling Flats on the southeast coast of
Meares Island, and the complex of mud flats along Browning Passage
on the east side of Esowista Peninsula. Hosts of migratory water birds
stop at this rich feeding ground as they follow the Pacific Flyway en
route from their Arctic breeding grounds to South America and back.
The mud flats also support a wide range of local bird species. Sea lions,
whales, and porpoises can often be found feeding in the shallows, while
bears and wolves roam the shorelines and intertidal zone. The numbers
of migratory birds are greatly reduced from earlier years, largely due
to disruption or destruction of feeding and resting places along their
migratory route. The Tofino mud flats offer an intensely valuable ecological area, beloved by bird watchers and duck hunters alike.

Early settlers marvelled when they saw the sky almost black with
birds flying over in untold numbers. Father Augustin Brabant wrote
of seeing "thousands of ducks and geese on the mud flats," as he made
his way along Tofino Inlet to Long Beach on his harrowing journey
southward with Bishop Seghers in 1874. Local people have always hunted ducks and geese on the flats, within gunshot sound of the village,

The mud flats bordering Meares Island and
Tofino have long been a favourite locale for
duck hunting. Two boys from Christie School,
identified on the photo as "James and Sennen,"
pose after a successful hunt in the early 1900s.
Mount Angel Abbey Library

and most boys learned to
hunt at a very young age.
An article in the *Colonist*
on December 6, 1911, noted
that "Harold Sloman, aged
14, of Clayoquot, had a great
day's shooting lately, the bag
consisting of 38 duck and 1
goose." When George Jack-
son lived at Long Beach in
the 1920s, he saw immense
flocks of ducks and geese
on the sloughs, in the mud
flats, and in his fields. On
January 3, 1928, he wrote
in his diary "Got six widgeon with two shells," and

ten days later, "Fired only two shots and got eight Widgeon. Could have got a hundred if wanted, the eight was enough." Haray Quisenberry and his wife, who homesteaded near the mud flats, relied on bird hunting for more than just food. Dorothy Abraham noted that "all of their pillows, cushions and eiderdowns, even the mattresses, were made from the down of ducks and geese they had shot." Most settlers would have done the same, especially those with a bevy of young boys who loved hunting and loved eating duck. Walter Guppy recalled that in his home, "When it came to feasting on the game, the rule was one duck per person, except for teal or butterballs; of these an adult or elder son might have two." Not to be outdone, Gordon Gibson, in *Bull of the Woods*, described eating three ducks at one meal on a particularly hungry day as a young man. As more visitors came to the area, duck hunting became an advertised attraction. In the 1950s, Betty Farmer's brochure for Clayoquot Hotel on Stubbs Island stated: "For the seasoned sportsman, there is unparalleled Salmon Fishing by Fly or Troll, Trout fishing in nearby lakes and for the man with the gun, such Geese, Duck and Brant as he has heretofore seen only in his dreams."

Early efforts to preserve the Tofino mud flats ended in a public relations fiasco in the mid-1970s. The BC government had formed the Ecological Reserves Committee in 1968 with the intention of preserving ecologically sensitive areas, and three years later an order-in-council set aside twenty-nine such areas in the province, including Cleland Island, just off Vargas Island. In 1973 the BC government's Fish and Wildlife Branch proposed establishing more reserves, and through another order-in-council set about creating a wildfowl refuge in the mud flats of Grice Bay and also at Matilda Inlet on Flores Island. The government failed to involve or consult with local people in this process. In response, a public meeting in the packed school gym in Tofino in December 1976 turned into a "hellfire occasion," according to Leona Taylor. Local duck hunters raised noisy objections, outraged that they could be banned from hunting on the mud flats, and others vociferously protested the high-handed tactics of the government. Archie Frank from Ahousat and Shortie Frank from Esowista both spoke out in defence of aboriginal rights to harvest crab and shellfish in the mud flats. The clamour rose to the point that government representatives feared violence might break out. "People were still bitter about the autocratic takeover of the Pacific Rim National Park land and the way those living within its boundaries had been forced out," Leona Taylor observed. "So by the time these provincial officials appeared with the 'good news' that an Order In Council would now make it unlawful for anyone to hunt in what had for long been our traditional bird-hunting territory, people were livid."

The storm over the wildlife reserve eventually blew over, but it made provincial officials cautious about pursuing further initiatives. After decades of consultation and debate, in 1993 the BC government created its first wilderness management areas (WMAs), recommending that the Tofino mud flats be a top priority for inclusion. In 1997, the flats, officially the Tofino Wah-nah-jus Hilth-hoo-is Mudflats, became a WMA. Under this designation, a local management committee, working with community groups, created a plan to protect the mud flats as a significant wildlife reserve while providing compatible recreational, commercial, and cultural activities in the area. Sport fishing and hunting are allowed in the Tofino WMA under limited conditions, the Tla-o-qui-aht retain the right to carry on traditional activities in the area, and commercial clam and crab harvesting is still permitted.

"The mudflats are like the womb of Clayoquot Sound," explained Josie Osborne, currently mayor of Tofino, who in her work as a marine biologist lobbied for the establishment of the WMA. "They give so much life. Baby Dungeness crab, rockfish, salmon—a lot of creatures get their start in the mudflats." Tla-o-qui-aht master canoe carver Joe Martin has described the flats as "one of the most important things in terms of ecology for the Sound. They have a huge influence on the First Nations that live around it."

Since 1997, an annual Shorebird Festival take place in Tofino every May, featuring talks, walks, and "Bird Brunches," and attracting great numbers of bird enthusiasts. While the WMA management committee supports such events, it is also acutely aware that there are limits to how much exposure the delicate mud flats can endure from an ever-increasing amount of tourist traffic.

On Chesterman Beach, with Frank Island in the background, young surfers run to catch the next wave. *Courtesy of Sarah Platenius*

Of all attractions on the west coast, the fastest-growing and most robust must be surfing. Every year more and more surfers flock to the beaches, and the fact that a number of star surfers have emerged from the area certainly helped raise the profile of the sport. Raph Bruhwiler, who grew up on Chesterman Beach, began taking surfing seriously from the age of twelve, when his parents sent him to California to attend a surf school. He won his first surf contest when he was thirteen, beating twenty- and thirty-year-olds, and in 2000 he became Canada's first surfing professional. By the late 1990s, Raph, Sepp, and Catherine Bruhwiler, as well as Peter DeVries, also raised on Chesterman Beach, had all won major competitions as they travelled the world surfing circuit. They made sure to be back in Tofino in 2000 to take part in Surf Jam, Canada's first pro-am surfing contest. Surf Jam began in 1988 as a small contest on Long Beach to showcase BC's top surfers. The 2000 competition took place at Cox Bay, with Peter DeVries, Raph, and Sepp Bruhwiler placing first, second, and third.

In the women's division, Tofino's Jenny Hudnall topped the field, with Catherine Bruhwiler second and Leah Oke third. In 2009, Peter DeVries became Canada's top surfer when he won the O'Neill Coldwater Classic right on his own North Chesterman Beach, beating 120 of the world's top surfers, to the delight of thousands of his hometown fans. In 2010 the editors of *Outside* magazine named Tofino the top surfing town in North America. The biggest surfing championship is now Rip Curl Pro, and at its eighth annual event in Tofino in 2014, over 150 surfers competed in front of an estimated 1,000 spectators.

Tofino stands out from most other surfing destinations because of the gender divide in the west coast waves. Girls and women make up anywhere from a third to a half of the surfing enthusiasts here, a phenomenon not seen elsewhere. Much of the credit for this goes to Surf Sister, a business founded in 1999 by Jenny Hudnall. Inspired by the Surf Divas of La Jolla, California, Jenny decided to encourage women to take up the sport in Tofino, and opened her surf school for women. Surf Sister began out of the back of Jenny's truck, soon moving into a small cabin she rented near Liz Zed's Live to Surf shop. Jenny hired only women to give lessons and found she had hit a niche market. Eventually her business expanded to the point she opened her shop in downtown Tofino, selling surf gear as well as operating the surf school. Surf Sister has proved hugely empowering, both for the instructors and for the women they teach. Today more women surf on the beaches of Canada's west coast than anywhere else in the world. "We still cater mostly to females," explained current owner Krissy Montgomery, "but we do give lessons to men too."

Most surfing competitions have women's divisions, but sensing a need for more female competition, Surf Sister and Tofino's Shelter Restaurant co-sponsored the first Queen of the Peak event, exclusively for women, in 2009. Since then Billabong sportswear and the Wickaninnish Inn have also come aboard as sponsors for the competition, held annually each October. "Not so long ago when I started surfing on Chesterman Beach with my brothers, I was the only girl," Catherine Bruhwiler recalled. "Now I am competing in a contest here in Tofino with fifty or sixty women. It's pretty special to be part of that, and to have seen such a dramatic change in the surfing scene in such a short time."

A keen group of young girls have taken to the waves, inspired by the women in Queen of the Peak. Chloe Platenius of Tofino, who donned her first wetsuit and started Boogie Boarding when she was two years old, took part in the new Princess of the Peak competition in 2012 at the age of six, as did six-year-old Sophia Bruhwiler. Aimed at girls under sixteen, the "Princess" event attracted some twenty young girls in 2013, with ten-year-old Matea Olin winning the title.

Surfing is central to the culture and economy of the west coast. Surfers inhabit the beaches year-round, no matter what the weather. Some nine surf schools operate in and around Tofino, and five surf shops brighten the area, with paddleboarding also on offer. Surfboards top every second car, and surfers ride to the nearby beaches with surfboards strapped to their bicycles. To honour the history and place of surfing on the west coast, local resident and surfer Devorah Reeves has opened the West Coast Surf Museum in Tofino.

Aaron Rodgers, Tofino's manager of sustainability, maintains that "the greatest asset for the town of Tofino has become surfing." Charles McDiarmid, owner of the Wickaninnish Inn, concurs: "Surfing is the new engine powering the future of tourism. Surfers may not be high end clients, but they are future high end clients and they bring with them friends, parents, grandparents to view surfing competitions." On competition weekends, not a room can be found in the town, campsites and parking lots are full, and cars line the highway by the beaches.

Importantly for the economy of Tofino, surfing tourism attracts a broad range of people beyond the core community of dedicated surfers. Many visitors who have never surfed in their lives will don the gear and brave the waves just to say they did. Family outings and reunions sometimes include cheerfully amateur efforts at surfing. When Mary Wilkie and her gang of ten relatives decided to get together to celebrate a fiftieth birthday, they chose to go surfing at Long Beach in November as part of the fun. Many of them from Port Alberni, all of them female, and ranging in age from three to eighty-three, every one rented surfing gear and took a board to the beach. Getting into the wetsuits provided half the entertainment, as every age, every size, geared up in gales of laughter. Once in the waves, only two succeeded in standing on their boards for a moment or two; the rest played in the waves, posed for photographs, and had the surfing experience of their lives.

In 1980, the Nuu-chah-nulth Tribal Council presented a land claim to the federal government for much of the land along the west coast of Vancouver Island, its adjacent islands, and surrounding waters. In 1983 the Canadian government accepted that claim as a starting point for negotiation, and since then First Nations land claims on the west coast have been working their way through various slow and complex processes. The Meares Island blockade of 1984, and the subsequent claim by the Tla-o-qui-aht and Ahousaht that they held aboriginal title to the island, "spurred on the creation of the British Columbia Treaty Commission, and gave new hope to First Nations in BC," according to Tla-o-qui-aht writer and band council member Eli Enns. The First Nations treaty process, which began in 1993, brings together representatives from the First Nations and the federal and provincial governments to determine the rights and obligations of all parties regarding land ownership and land use.

As an introduction to the treaty negotiation process, few voices from Clayoquot Sound carry more authority than that of Ahousaht hereditary chief Earl Maquinna George. In *Living on the Edge* he wrote:

> My ancestors have captured great whales, they and I have hunted the fur seal. I have fished and logged in many areas of First Nations territories. In the short period of a little more than a century, we have gone from using these things for our survival to being employed by large companies. We are now trying to regain some of what was ours so that we can survive with the food from the sea and also have work for our young people. Thus we sit at the treaty table and try to settle the issues of land and resources with the Crown.

Unlike most other regions of Canada, in British Columbia the government historically signed very few treaties with the First Nations. Between 1850 and 1854, Governor James Douglas, at the request of the British Crown, negotiated limited treaties with fourteen First Nations on Vancouver Island in order to purchase land for settlement. Eleven of these "Douglas Treaties" concerned land around Victoria, Sooke, and Saanich, with one at Nanaimo and two others at Fort Rupert (Port Hardy). These were the only land treaties in the province until 1899, when the federal government negotiated Treaty Number 8 with eight tribes in northeastern BC.

In 1973, Nisga'a chief Frank Calder, who served as an MLA in the BC legislature, launched a landmark case in the BC Supreme Court asserting that First Nations still held aboriginal title to their lands. The BC Supreme Court and later the provincial Court of Appeal upheld the province's claim that "Aboriginal title did not exist in BC. When this case reached the Supreme Court of Canada, the judges determined that the Nisga'a did indeed hold aboriginal title to their lands in northwest British Columbia prior to the arrival of British sovereignty, that this title had never been extinguished, and that it continued to exist. Despite making this all-important judgment, the Supreme Court of Canada dismissed Calder's appeal on a technicality. Still, its decision recognizing the Nisga'a's right to their land proved far-reaching, setting a precedent for all First Nations. This led to an immediate change in federal policy, with the Canadian government launching efforts to determine what rights aboriginal people had to land and resources, and also beginning negotiations with the Nisga'a over their land. Now First Nations in Canada do not have to prove aboriginal rights and title; these rights are recognized and protected by the Canadian Constitution. Furthermore, since the Supreme Court of Canada reached its decision in the case of *Delgamuukw v. British Columbia*, regarding a claim by the Gitksan/Wet'suwet'en people of northern British Columbia, First Nations' oral history has been recognized by the courts as admissible evidence in land claims.

In April 1993, the provincial and federal governments and the First Nations of BC established the BC Treaty Commission to begin discussions that would lead to treaty agreements with 111 bands in the province. They established a six-stage process for new treaty negotiations, with the Nisga'a already moving forward in a separate treaty process that would become the template for other negotiations. In 2000, the Nisga'a became the first aboriginal people in British Columbia to finalize a modern treaty with the provincial and federal governments.

In 1995, each of the fourteen Nuu-chah-nulth tribes chose a representative to participate in establishing the initial framework agreement of the treaty process. One tribe, the Ditidaht, chose to negotiate separately with Canada and the province. The negotiations began while a number of other contentious issues, including hunting rights, commercial fishing rights, and compensation for abuse in residential schools, continued to be pursued through both provincial and federal courts. With few guidelines and a multitude of issues to be considered, and with discussions taking place all over the province with scores of First Nations, negotiations proceeded slowly. In April 1997, Chief Earl Maquinna George, who represented the Ahousaht at the negotiation table, pinpointed one of the main problems preventing agreement: "We want to govern our own people, look after our own land, be our own stewards of what we have, what they've taken away. We want that back," he wrote. "We want to look after our own people and gain a sense of self-respect. It seems to me, based on the way the negotiators talk to us, that the government does not believe we can take care of ourselves and our resources. Thus, no real progress has been made toward a settlement."

In an attempt to speed up negotiations, the chief suggested that only six Nuu-chah-nulth negotiators, the Tripartite Standing Committee, sit at the negotiation table, instead of one negotiator for each tribe. This helped move proceedings along, and by March 2000 the negotiators for all parties initialled the Stage 4 agreement in principle (AIP) document, which then went to the various tribes for community consultation and approval. Only six of the Nuu-chah-nulth First Nations ratified this agreement in 2001, among them the Ahousaht and Hesquiaht. The Tla-o-qui-aht chose to leave the collective negotiating table, and in July 2008 began negotiating independently with the provincial and federal governments.

In November 2008, the Tla-o-qui-aht signed an incremental treaty agreement (ITA) with the provincial government, which awarded the nation approximately sixty-three hectares of land on the Esowista Peninsula, including a 12.1-hectare parcel on MacKenzie Beach next to the Tin Wis Indian Reserve, granted to the Tla-o-qui-aht in 1993 and now the site of Best Western Tin Wis Resort. An incremental grant of $600,000 accompanied this agreement as an advance by the province on a future treaty settlement package. In 2012, after the ITA's four-year term ended, the two parties renewed the agreement for another four years, as negotiations continued. While this took place, the Tla-o-qui-aht treaty negotiators presented their people with the Stage 4 AIP document for their endorsement. However, of the 269 ballots cast, only 42 percent of the voters supported the document, forcing the negotiators back to the treaty table.

For all First Nations in Clayoquot Sound, the treaty process has been long, slow, and often frustrating, and it remains unfinished. Working on the premise that aboriginal title to their traditional lands was never extinguished, the Tla-o-qui-aht, Ahousaht, and Hesquiaht all wish to control their territories, to implement their own visions for land use, and to expand their authority. They also wish to protect their resources and to have a controlling say in any future exploitation of these resources. Although land claims and treaty negotiations will not affect fee simple land, these processes have, over time, strongly influenced attitudes to and assumptions about land, both in Clayoquot Sound and elsewhere in Canada. They have also increased every citizen's understanding of the significance and strength of aboriginal title. In the early 1990s, Pacific Rim National Park became more widely known as Pacific Rim National Park Reserve, a public acknowledgement that aboriginal land claims to these park lands have not been concluded, and therefore potential rights are unsettled and remain open for negotiation. Along with seven other national park reserves formed in Canada since 1970, Pacific Rim continues to be managed under the Canada National Parks Act, pending the settlement of land claims.

The ongoing discussions about Nuu-chah-nulth control of their traditional territories carry great significance for future resource development in Clayoquot Sound. One example in Ahousaht territory is provided by Catface (Chitaapi) Mountain, thirteen kilometres north of Tofino, and three kilometres from Maaqtusiis on Flores Island. Mineral exploration on Catface dates back a long time; the rich copper deposits there have been known since the late nineteenth century. Mining recorder Walter Dawley reported in 1898: "Work has been done on the properties on this mountain [Catface], a 20 foot [6 metre] tunnel having just been completed on one claim. The ore carries a considerable percentage of copper." Dreams of striking it rich on Catface inspired many hopeful prospectors over the years, among them early settler Avery Rhodes. Shortly after Rhodes married Luella Stone at Ahousat in 1907, Daniel McDougall, the former police constable at Clayoquot, commented in a letter: "Well Luella is out of Harm Way now...Two Crazy People ought to have a Wise family. She need not fear...Avery is able to take care of her with his millions of gold and copper on Cat Face Mountain." Such unfulfilled dreams aside, no significant mining activity disturbed the potentially valuable rocks on Catface Mountain for many decades.

In 1960, Ontario-based Falconbridge Ltd. staked claims on Catface Mountain through Catface Copper Mines Ltd. Extensive exploration between 1960 and 1974, costing $10 million, determined that the Catface property potentially contained 300 million tons of copper ore that could best be extracted from an open-pit mine, with a life expectancy of twenty years. Walter Guppy, in *Wet Coast Ventures: Mine Finding on Vancouver Island*, speculated, "If it had been promoted earlier (in the late 1950s and '60s) it would have been another major open-pit operation, employing about eight hundred people. But, by the time the Catface deposit had come to the attention of Falconbridge...the era of bringing large open-pit base-metal mines into production was over. Costs had become too high and markets were soft."

From the late 1990s to the late 2000s, when world copper prices began to rise to record levels, Catface Copper Mines changed hands a couple of times. In April 2008, after Catface Copper had courted the Ahousaht for several years to win their approval for further exploration and perhaps a future mine, a small delegation of Ahousaht elders travelled to Vancouver to sign a three- to five-year Memorandum of

Understanding with the company. This agreement allowed Catface Copper to carry out test drilling in Ahousaht traditional lands to confirm Falconbridge's findings from the 1960s. For signing the MOU, the tribe received a signing bonus and an assurance that ten Ahousahts would be trained in diamond drilling and employed on site.

The Friends of Clayoquot Sound and other environmental groups immediately spoke out against any activity that could lead to an open-pit mine on Catface, fearing environmental degradation. The Tofino Chamber of Commerce also voiced its opposition to the project. In spite of this, the Ahousahts could sanction the mine if its people chose to move forward with the plan, given previous agreements with the government about resource management in the area. However, despite potentially large economic gains for the First Nation, protests have arisen among the Ahousaht about mining Catface. In 2013, representatives of Ancestral Pride Ahousaht Sovereign Territory travelled from Ahousat to Vancouver to express their opposition to the mine, gate-crashing the AGM of Imperial Metals (which acquired Catface Copper in 2009) at the Terminal Club. "We, as sovereign Indigenous people and nations, will continue to protect our waters and lands from industrial genocide," a spokesman declared. "Imperial Metals is not welcome on sovereign Ahousaht territory."

Meanwhile, Imperial Metals is also exploring the possibility of re-opening the old Fandora gold mine, located in Tla-o-qui-aht territory in the Tranquil River valley, about twenty kilometres northeast of Tofino. The company received a mineral exploration permit from the BC government in 2013, immediately drawing protests from the Tla-o-qui-aht, who claimed they'd been "blindsided" and that they were dissatisfied with the level of consultation by both the company and the provincial government. "Throughout those years of consultation, we have only sent the ministry letters of opposition and concern about the lack of process," Tla-o-qui-aht band councillor Saya Masso said in an interview with the *Globe and Mail*. "We are trying to encourage our hatcheries, our green energy projects...we are not against development, it is sustainable development that we want." Masso said that in correspondence with the government about the Fandora Mine, the Tla-o-qui-aht's "strength" of aboriginal title had been questioned, with "letter after letter challenging our connection to the land and very antagonistic letters of 'if you can't demonstrate a meaningful arrowhead in the ground then we're going ahead with this.'" As natural resource manager for the Tla-o-qui-aht, Masso devoted much of his energy to promoting run-of-the-river electricity-generating projects. The sustainable land use plan being developed by the Tla-o-qui-aht would be under serious threat if a mine were allowed in the area. As of early 2014, both the Fandora and Catface mining projects appeared to be on hold, with Imperial Metals declaring it had not decided whether to apply for mining permits. If it chose to proceed, environmental approval would be required from the provincial and federal governments.

In January 2014, five Nuu-chah-nulth First Nations won a highly significant case in the Supreme Court of Canada. Ending a decade-long court challenge, the court awarded the tribes, including the Hesquiaht, Ahousaht, and Tla-o-qui-aht, the right to catch and sell all species of fish in their territory. "The decision of the Supreme Court of Canada affirms what the Nuu-chah-nulth have always asserted," said Nuu-chah-nulth Tribal Council president Deb Foxcroft. "Nuu-chah-nulth are a fishing people, dependent on sea resources for our food and our economies."

In determining these First Nations' aboriginal rights to fish and to sell fish commercially, the court ensured the rights would be protected by law. No other First Nations in Canada have achieved such far-reaching rights to fish commercially in their territories; the lawyers for the Nuu-chah-nulth, Ratcliff and Company, stated that "this decision represents the broadest aboriginal rights success in Canadian history." The ruling will allow the tribes to conduct a modern commercial fishery, not just a fishery limited to "food, ceremonial and social" purposes, as earlier restrictions had stipulated.

The question of economic development for the First Nations underlies every discussion of resource management in Clayoquot Sound, be it fishing, mining, aquaculture, or logging. The high unemployment in the First Nations communities makes any prospective jobs in local resource industries potentially attractive. The *Westerly News* of May 13, 2010, quoted Tofino's mayor at the time, John Fraser, commenting on the Ahousaht chief and council's interest in the controversial Catface mine proposal: "Ahousaht is suffering with Third World conditions," said Fraser. "Unemployment is atrocious and the economic needs are desperate. So I can understand the huge pressure on the chief and council." Deputy Chief John Frank of the Ahousahts countered, "We looked after ourselves for thousands of years. We don't want the taxpayers to look after us."

In the face of grave social challenges, many Ahousaht leaders and elders have worked hard over the years to maintain the traditional values of the community and to counteract the negative pressures faced by their people. In the 1980s, Ahousaht hereditary chief Peter Webster became a leading spokesman, participating in workshops at Maaqtusiis against alcohol, drugs, and domestic and child abuse. In a column he wrote intermittently for the *Westerly News*, he spoke his mind, particularly about alcohol and its effects, sometimes risking censure from his own people for doing so. "Those of us that don't want to hear anything, it will be too bad for them...I know this [abuse] is caused by the great power of alcohol, and I also know somebody will give me hell for talking about alcohol." Having been an alcoholic himself, his voice carried authority. "The reason why I fight against alcohol is I have lost two of my sons and two of my grandsons within the period of nine years...I now understand and see what [alcohol] is and hear what I did not want to hear."

Webster also shared his heartfelt desire to revitalize the songs and the language of his people. As a child, he had been forbidden to speak his own language at the Ahousat residential school: "One time I was sent to bed without supper because I've said our word for 'where is it?'

And besides I didn't know a word of English." He never lost the language, and in the 1980s he assisted at the Ahousat school, teaching the Nuu-chah-nulth language and encouraging a resurgence of interest in the language, a movement that has grown stronger over time. "I know this linguistics will be something very good for every student that wants to learn," he wrote in March 1986. Now young children going to school in Ahousat all learn some of the Nuu-chah-nulth language, and even at Wickaninnish School in Tofino, everyone hears a Nuu-chah-nulth "word of the day" in the daily announcements. For some time, local Long Beach Radio also broadcast a "word of the day," thanks to Gisele Martin, daughter of the renowned Tla-o-qui-aht canoe carver Joe Martin.

In any way he could, Peter Webster, along with other elders, supported passing on traditional knowledge. He wrote with great pleasure of seeing an Ahousaht team participate in a "Bone Game Tournament" in Port Alberni, recalling how this traditional bone game, Lahal, accompanied by traditional songs, had been forbidden in his youth. "In my school days we were not allowed to do this game because we were singing Indian songs. Those Principals were crazy." Watching the Lahal tournament, Webster wrote: "I felt like crying in my heart overjoyed and we were about 150 people singing behind [the players] and after they won the game they sang the victory song."

The opening of the band-run Maaqtusiis School in Ahousat in September 1986 was hailed as a major step forward for the community. Nine years in the planning, the school welcomed students from Grades 1 to 12, and it attracted a number of Ahousahts, who had left to live elsewhere, to return to their native territory. The community of Maaqtusiis slowly expanded. An article in *The Sound* magazine in February 1992 began: "Ahousat is a fast growing town. There are 780 people living there...but there is a serious housing shortage...As in any expanding town, Ahousat is suffering some growing pain and sometimes these pains take the form of alcohol or drug abuse." The town by then had a Holistic Recovery Centre to deal with addictions. Just across from Maaqtusiis, on the other side of Matilda Creek, the facilities run by Hugh Clarke had slowly expanded ever since he purchased the old store, post office, and dock in 1959. A small motel and restaurant appeared next to the store, and with improved moorage and a fuel dock, fishing charters sometimes ran from there.

Since the mid-2000s, an ambitious expansion has been underway in Maaqtusiis, with some 200 homes slated to be built in a new subdivision, with many amenities provided. To serve the growing population, a high school opened at Maaqtusiis in 2011, operated by the Ahousaht Education Authority. This eased pressure on the older Maaqtusiis School, which by then was cramming some 215 students into its K–12 classrooms. The new high school had seventy students in its Grade 8–12 classrooms. At the opening ceremonies in September 2011, Ahousaht hereditary chief Shawn Atleo, at the time national chief of the Assembly of First Nations, addressed his community on the importance of education. "It's not always easy to accomplish something great like building a new school," he said, likening the creation of the school to the preparation for a whale hunt. Traditionally the entire community would work together preparing for the hunt, the fruits of which would sustain and nurture the community. "Education is the new whale," he said.

With thirteen fish farms operating in Ahousaht territory, some eighty Ahousahts are directly employed in the aquaculture industry and even more in support services for the industry, making this the biggest source of local year-round employment. In 2012 the Maaqutusiis Hahoulthee Stewardship Society was established to create and oversee future economic development projects for the Ahousaht people, its long-term goal to develop strategies for economic self-sufficiency. A year later the Maaqutusiis Hahoulthee Forestry Company was formed to involve more Ahousaht people in forestry activities. Currently the forestry company operates a cedar salvage operation, producing cedar shakes and shingles for a company in Abbotsford.

Ahousaht involvement in tourist-related activities, while not large, is on the increase. Since the establishment of the Ahousaht Wildside

Tla-o-qui-aht Tsimka Martin, wearing a cedar bark hat, steers a dugout canoe carved by her father Joe Martin. These excursions are among the attractions offered by her T'ashii Paddle School, welcoming visitors to experience Clayoquot Sound in a traditional manner. *Courtesy of T'ashii Paddle School*

Trail in 1996, a regular stream of hikers has tramped the twenty-two-kilometre trail through old-growth forest to the outer beaches on Flores Island and back to Maaqtusiis. A new Ahousaht-based company called Spirit Eagle Adventures offers cultural tours of the area, plans are in development to open a campsite, and in 2013 the twenty-four-bed Aauuknuk Lodge opened near Maaqtusiis to welcome visitors.

The First Nations of Clayoquot Sound have generally taken their time deciding how best to respond to tourists and adventurers wanting to visit their territories. Relatively few aboriginal-run tourist enterprises have developed, most of them in or near Tofino. For several years, Gisele Martin's Tla-ook Cultural Adventure Tours took visitors on cultural tours in traditional dugout canoes carved by her father, Joe Martin. Her sister, Tsimka Martin, transformed that business into her T'ashii Paddle School, offering paddleboarding and traditional canoe tours out of Tofino.

In more distant areas of Clayoquot Sound, like Hesquiat Harbour, the impact of tourism is so far negligible, although discussions have arisen about establishing and servicing hiking trails in that area. This heartland of Hesquiaht territory sees comparatively little traffic, for only highly motivated hikers venture this far afield. By contrast, countless boatloads and planeloads of people visit Hot Springs Cove, where the principal Hesquiaht village is located. The hot springs have become a major tourist attraction, drawing thousands of people a year.

Hesquiat Harbour features the Hooksum Outdoor School, housed in an immense cedar longhouse on the shore, an innovative and unusual facility that has welcomed groups of students since 1999. Initially students attended First Nations cultural "Rediscovery" camps, expanding on the camps that had been operating at Hesquiat since 1994. More recently, Hooksum has offered twenty-eight-day sessions of West Coast Outdoor Leadership Training as well as customized programs for school, university, youth, and adult groups. Owned and operated by Karen and Steve Charleson of the Hesquiaht First Nation, Hooksum applies traditional indigenous knowledge to outdoor education.

Building on the initiative of their first Tribal Park, established on Meares Island in 1984, the Tla-o-qui-aht have divided their entire territory into four different Tribal Parks. This designation allows for some low-impact tourist activities and limited resource development, while keeping the well-being of the ecosystem a priority. In 2008 the tribe created the Ha'uukmin—"like a great feast bowl"—Tribal Park, encompassing the entire Kennedy Lake watershed. Within Ha'uukmin, the Tla-o-qui-aht created the Clayoquot Valley Witness Trail, a hiking trail in the Clayoquot River valley. After entering into a partnership with West Coast Wild Adventures, they also set up a zipline to carry

This sign at the top of Sutton Pass on Highway 4 welcomes visitors into the territory of the Tla-o-qui-aht First Nation. *Ian Kennedy photo*

thrill-seekers high above the Kennedy River as it runs parallel to Highway 4 between Sutton Pass and the Tofino–Ucluelet junction. In 2013 the Tla-o-qui-aht created two more Tribal Parks, the Tranquil, which takes in the Tranquil River valley and the area surrounding Tofino Inlet, and the Esowista Tribal Park, encompassing the Esowista peninsula. Long-time Tofino resident Michael Mullin favours this move, suggesting, "The Tribal Parks present an opportunity that is different from having a casino and selling cigarettes. Someone once said that 'Enlightened native stewardship of the natural resources is our best long term option,' and I agree. It is their land and hopefully they will make better decisions than mining companies and Ottawa."

"We support any direction that will feed healthy homelands," said Saya Masso, natural resource manager for the Tla-o-qui-aht. "I see a one hundred year economy, a one thousand year economy...I want to support the sustainable [jobs]. I want fish in our rivers and tourism, campgrounds, trails, and a value-added forestry industry with a lower footprint—and everyone working together to recognize and achieve that."

The Tribal Parks designations put added pressure on the First Nations logging company Iisaak, by further limiting the areas it could access. By 2000, struggling with the debt incurred buying timber rights in Clayoquot Sound, the company began lobbying the provincial government for the right to log in the unprotected forested valleys of the Sound. In April 2011, Iisaak received permission to construct a logging road into the ancient forest on Flores Island, a move that flew in the face of its mandate to log in an environmentally sensitive manner. In 2012, following protests from environmental groups, Iisaak withdrew its application for a permit to log in Flores Island.

By the 1990s, former residential school students began to make themselves heard across Canada, giving public testimony about their experiences at the schools. Lisa Charleson, a Nuu-chah-nulth native crisis worker, attended a meeting in 1994 about the effects of these schools on her own people. Afterward, she wrote a letter to the editor of

The Sound, saying, "Up until the conference I hadn't heard anyone breathe a word about residential schools, good or bad, except the odd comment about the horrid oatmeal." Once they started, however, the revelations kept coming. In 1995, Arthur Plint, a former principal of the Alberni Indian Residential School, was found guilty of committing thousands of acts of sexual abuse against a group of eighteen former students at the school. This was the first case to appear before the courts alleging sexual abuse at a residential school on the west coast of Vancouver Island. It was not the last.

In 2001, the BC Supreme Court awarded substantial damages to an unnamed plaintiff who sued the Oblates of Mary Immaculate for "vicarious liability" in repeated incidents of alleged sexual abuse by a man employed at Christie School in the late 1950s/early 1960s. The alleged abuser had died in 1986. The BC Court of Appeal overturned this judgment in 2003, ruling that the Oblates could not be held responsible for the behaviour of an employee. The case then went to the Supreme Court of Canada, where once again it was overturned. In 2004, three former pupils of Christie School brought another case against the Oblates in which two employees of Christie School, one of them a brother, were named as perpetrators of sexual abuse in the school dormitories.

Over the years, more allegations of abuse at Christie School have surfaced, describing beatings, humiliation, and sexual abuse of students at the school. Some of these allegations have been made in statements by former students to the Truth and Reconciliation Commission (TRC), which began its work in 2008. At TRC hearings all across Canada, former students have shared publicly, and often for the first time, their memories of residential school, with the declared aim of revealing the truth of events in the past and working toward reconciliation. Some former students have alluded to the pain and abuse their parents, and even grandparents, suffered at residential schools. Several have named names.

"Brother Samson—he was a cruel man," Simon Lucas of Hesquiat recalled in his statement before the TRC in March 2012. At least three other former students of Christie School spoke of Brother Samson's cruelty; this is the brother whose photograph in a school publication from 1950 carries the caption "Disciplinarian." Simon Lucas attended Christie School for eight years during the 1950s. Like many others addressing the commission, he spoke of the pain of being punished for speaking his own language, and the grief of separation from his parents. He recalled leaving them at the cannery at Ceepeecee, his mother saying, "We don't want you to weep," and travelling by boat to the school with his brother, crying all the way.

Tom Curley also attended Christie School in the 1950s, from five years of age. He spoke before the TRC of staying awake at night, listening to other children crying in the dormitory. He described the confusion and fear of repeated sexual abuse, seeing a shadow by his bed at night in the dark dormitories, "and if he didn't get me he'd get someone else." He tried once to tell his parents, but they did not believe him, saying, "They're religious people, they don't do those things."

The theme of loss emerged most clearly from the testimony of former Christie School students. Loss of language, loss of identity, loss of pride in culture and family. Some spoke of anger, some of self-hatred, some of shame. Several related the current problems of their communities to their experiences in residential school; with no connection to their own families, they could not know how to be good parents themselves. At the end of twelve years in residential school, Pat Charleson asked himself "How do I learn to be native?" adding "My kids are still suffering from spinoffs of residential school."

In their TRC testimonies, while most former students shared comparable experiences, some people spoke of having gone through a healing process over many years, and they said they believed they could move on. "I can walk proudly now," Harold Lucas of Hesquiat commented. "On the healing journey I said to myself I am no longer the product of the system." Cliff Atleo of Ahousat asserted, "We have survived, we are gonna turn things around."

Following the closure of Christie School at Kakawis on Meares Island in 1971, the old buildings stood mostly silent for three years, occupied only by a few former staff and caretakers. Convinced that the facilities could be used to help their people, two former students, Louie Frank and Barney Williams Sr., joined in a campaign to establish an addiction treatment centre at Kakawis. The book *Healing Journeys: The Ka Ka Wis Experience, 1974-1994*, quotes Louie Frank talking of how a treatment centre would help people "come to grips with the alcohol problem... Some of us saw the potential at Christie and...somebody had to get the ball rolling." Barney Williams wrote letters to chiefs all along the coast, asking for support for what became known as the Ka Ka Wis Family and Community Development Project. A core community emerged to guide and support the centre, including representatives from the Oblates of Mary Immaculate and the Sisters of Saint Ann, from nearby First Nations, and from the wider community of counsellors and health care workers. The first residential facility of its type in North America, the centre offered support and living space for all members of its client families, not just for the addicted person. Families attended six-week-long sessions, working with staff and with other families to address addiction, health problems, unemployment, and domestic strife. Up to sixty-five people could be accommodated at a time, and on occasion the centre welcomed as many as seventeen children of their client families.

Later known as the Ka Ka Wis Family Treatment Centre, this facility operated on Meares Island for over thirty years, coming through many difficult times and perpetual financial challenges. It also survived a catastrophic fire in the summer of 1983, which saw the original Christie School buildings go up in flames. The immense blaze lit the sky for kilometres around. Macmillan Bloedel donated some fifty modular buildings from a disused logging camp up the Bedwell River so the centre could be operating again quickly. As time passed, the centre became a spiritual and therapeutic healing centre, with increased emphasis on First Nations spirituality and traditional ceremony as part of the "healing circle." From the late 1990s onward, it was clear that the facilities at Kakawis no longer served the needs of the centre, and a new and more convenient location was required. Finally, in 2009, the renamed Kackaamin Family Development Centre opened near Port

Alberni, where it currently offers seven six-week-long family sessions every year, and many other services for First Nations families.

At Kakawis, on the property where Christie School stood, wild daffodils bloom in the spring around the site of the former school. The large crucifix that once rose above the curving, south-facing beach has long since been removed; few traces remain of the large and domineering institution that operated here for so long. Some say the place is haunted yet by the spirits of children who attended the school during its seventy years of operation, and by the voices of parents still seeking their sons and daughters. Others believe the wounds of the past have begun to heal, that a time of reconciliation has come. Kakawis faces change and renewal in the hands of the Ahousaht people, for in January 2013 the Ahousaht band's economic development branch, the Maaqutusiis Hahoulthee Stewardship Society, purchased the 175-hectare property on Meares Island from the Oblates of Mary Immaculate. The elected chief and council hosted a celebration in honour of the acquisition and looked forward to developing tourism and business opportunities at this location, renamed Matsquiaht.

On June 11, 2008, Prime Minister Stephen Harper issued a formal apology to all former students of residential schools across Canada. "The government now recognizes that the consequences of the Indian Residential Schools policy were profoundly negative and that this policy has had a lasting and damaging impact on Aboriginal culture, heritage and language...The Government of Canada sincerely apologizes and asks the forgiveness of the Aboriginal peoples of this country for failing them so profoundly."

Another historic apology affecting the First Nations of Clayoquot Sound took place in July 2005. Over 200 years after the events of April 2, 1792, when the American trader Captain Robert Gray destroyed the village of Opitsat, setting fire to 200 homes, Gray's descendants made a public gesture of reconciliation. Along with several family members, William Twombly of Corvallis, Oregon, travelled to Tofino to apologize for the actions of his forefather. The party sailed up the coast aboard a replica of Gray's trading vessel, *Lady Washington*. Off MacKenzie Beach, several Tla-o-qui-aht chiefs pulled alongside in dugout canoes and heard Twombly's apology. "We are sorry for the abduction and insult to your chief and his great family and for the burning of Opitsat," said Twombly. "We have heard your words and accept," answered Barney Williams Jr., the band's chief councillor and beach keeper. Escorted by the canoes, the *Lady Washington* continued into Tofino Harbour, to be greeted by crowds of people. The Tla-o-qui-aht and Gray's descendants exchanged gifts and feasted, bringing together the five hereditary chiefs, a hundred band members, and hundreds of guests and dignitaries. Among the guests, William Kendrick Strong, of Glendale, Arizona, a descendant of American trader Captain John Kendrick, who traded on the West Coast aboard the *Columbia Rediviva*.

On November 17, 2012, the spirit of reconciliation for past wrongs again surfaced in a public event involving the Hesquiaht. Ida Chong, then the provincial minister of Aboriginal Relations and Reconciliation, expressed regret for the wrongful public hanging of John Anietsachist and Katkinna at Hesquiat, following the *John Bright* shipwreck of 1869. Many people had stoutly maintained their faith in the men's innocence over the years, believing the two had been shamefully treated. Anyone looking at court documents of the trial could see that faulty translations of the men's testimony likely contributed to the convictions of Anietsachist and Katkinna; anyone reading the inflammatory newspaper reports of 1869 could see they had been assumed guilty from the outset. At the time, both Bishop Charles Seghers, who attended the hanging, and Father Brabant, who lived many years at Hesquiat, publicly asserted their belief in the innocence of the men. Perhaps more importantly, stories and songs of their innocence had been handed down as part of the Hesquiaht oral narrative ever since the event. Hereditary Chief Victor Amos, a great-great-great grandson of Anietsachist, finally determined to clear his ancestor's name and approached the provincial government. In 2008, the Hesquiahts raised a carved memorial pole at Home-is near Estevan Point in honour of Anietsachist. Four years later, at a feast of reconciliation attended by hundreds, Ida Chong spoke on behalf of the provincial government, saying: "On this day, what took place was an offer from the province of regret, and an offer from the Hesquiaht of forgiveness."

In his book *Tsawalk: A Nuu-chah-nulth Worldview*, Ahousaht hereditary chief E. Richard Atleo explained the overarching principle of *heshook-ish tsawalk*, which translates as "everything is one." Expressing a continuum between the spiritual and physical worlds, *tsawalk* has guided the Nuu-chah-nulth way of life for millennia. "The nature of creation," Atleo wrote, "...demands constraint and respectful protocols rather than brute, barbaric and savage exploitation of resources." In this worldview, spiritual practices, hunting, fishing, family life are all profoundly connected, and all major decisions affecting the people and the land require careful deliberation and consensus.

The centuries following European contact with the First Nations on the west coast of Vancouver Island have seen more aggressive action than consensus, more division than unity. Different worldviews have collided along the coast, sometimes disastrously, as traders, missionaries, settlers, and resource seekers pursued their own agendas, all too often with no consideration for the indigenous people—or for the impact of their actions on the land, the water, the wildlife. One after another, invaluable resources were overharvested: sea otter, fur seal, salmon, herring, forests—to name only some. One after another, the aboriginal people along the coast faced grave losses, as their land, their health, their language, and their culture came under threat.

In more recent times, and very gradually, important changes have been taking place. The many fragmented and mutually exclusive worldviews of this area, its people, and its resources, have been slowly coming together as more people are listening more carefully to each other. It has become apparent that environmental concerns, tourism, and the economic health of the area are profoundly interconnected, as are the rights of First Nations and the interests of resource industries.

"We have a vision of land management that means sharing and

educating," Saya Masso of the Tla-o-qui-aht band council stated, "and we're expecting more banner years than broken years in managing our land and resources." As local resident Michael Mullin put it: "We can have a wholesome place and manage it without destroying it...People come back again and again because Clayoquot Sound isn't Disneyland. It's healthy, it's battery charging." And Tofino's mayor Josie Osborne pointed out how much the whole area had changed in recent years, making such statements possible. "When I first came here fifteen years ago I worked for the First Nations, I worked in all the various communities, I went to a lot of meetings and I've...[seen] a lot of fists pounded on tables and there was a lot of division. Today the way people relate to each other is changing...there is a new view and a new degree of empowerment."

Residents of Tofino and Clayoquot Sound are keenly aware that challenges and surprises lie ahead. They expect nothing less. After all, this is an area where people live with the knowledge that a tsunami could easily engulf them. This is where locals have seen the effects of a massive environmental protest radically change their economy, their image, their sense of community. People here know what it is to be scrutinized, damned, and praised by national and international media, and they truly know what it means to be one of the most popular destinations in Canada. None of this has come easily. Yet through it all, the people of Tofino and Clayoquot Sound have shared, and continue to share, a sense of being very fortunate to live where they are. Meanwhile, they ready themselves to catch the next wave of change, not knowing where it will take them. Here on the west coast, another wave is always about to break.

Sealing schooners like *Pathfinder* carried a dozen crewmen and up to twenty aboriginal harpooners. With the hunters' dugout canoes stacked on deck, from the mid-1880s onward the schooners sailed up to the seal rookeries in the Bering Sea, on voyages lasting several months. *Image B04177 courtesy of Royal BC Museum, BC Archives*

TIMELINE

National Gallery of Art, Washington DC

4,200 years ago Aboriginal people settle in Clayoquot Sound.

1774 Spaniard Juan Pérez makes contact with Hesquiahts off Perez Rocks near Estevan Point. He does not land.

1778 Captain James Cook lands at Nootka.

1786 Captain James Hanna becomes first European to enter Clayoquot Sound and trades for pelts at Ahousat.

Mount Angel Abbey Library

1787 Captain Charles William Barkley, accompanied by his wife, Frances, visits Chief Wickaninnish in Clayoquot Sound.

1788 Captain John Meares visits Chief Wickaninnish.

1788 "Boston Men" John Kendrick and Robert Gray arrive at Nootka.

1789 Spanish Captain Esteban José Martínez establishes fort at Nootka.

1789 Martínez seizes British ships at Nootka and imprisons their captains

and crews, precipitating the "Nootka Incident."

1791 Kendrick "buys" a portion of Clayoquot Sound from Chief Wickaninnish.

1791 Robert Gray builds Fort Defiance at Adventure Cove in Lemmens Inlet.

1792 Gray torches Opitsat village as he departs Clayoquot Sound.

1792 Captain George Vancouver arrives at Nootka to negotiate with the Spanish.

1793 Alexander Mackenzie arrives at the Pacific coast after crossing Canada by land.

1795 The Spanish withdraw from Nootka.

1803 Nuu-chah-nulth attack the trading vessel *Boston*. John Jewitt and one other crew member are taken captive and held for two years.

1811 Destruction of the trading vessel *Tonquin* near MacKenzie Beach. Scores of Tla-o-qui-aht and all but one of the crew are killed.

1843 Hudson's Bay Company establishes Fort Victoria.

1849 Vancouver Island established as a Crown Colony.

1854 William Banfield opens a seasonal trading post at Clayoquot on Stubbs Island.

1858 Fraser River gold rush brings tens of thousands of fortune seekers through Victoria.

1858 British Columbia established as a Crown Colony.

1860 Charles Barrett-Lennard and Napoleon Fitzstubbs circumnavigate Vancouver Island.

1861 Barrett-Lennard and Fitzstubbs briefly work at the Clayoquot trading post with Peter Francis.

1864 James Douglas Warren and the Boscowitz brothers take over the trading post at Clayoquot.

1864 *Kingfisher* attacked and sunk at Ahousat. Royal Navy gunships HMS *Sutlej* and HMS *Devastation* attack villages in Clayoquot Sound, killing 15 Ahousahts.

1866 Colonies of Vancouver Island and British Columbia unite.

1867 United States purchases Alaska from Russia for $7.2 million.

1868 The schooner *Favorite* launched at Sooke.

Mount Angel Abbey Library

1868 Pelagic fur seal hunting begins.

1869 *John Bright* founders near Hesquiat. Everyone aboard dies. Two Hesquiaht men are accused of murder, stand trial in Victoria in dubious proceedings, and are hanged at Hesquiat.

1871 British Columbia joins the confederation of Canada.

1874 Father Augustin Brabant and Bishop Charles Seghers make two trips to the west coast, seeking a site for a permanent Roman Catholic mission.

1874 Fred Thornberg installed as manager of J.D. Warren's trading post at Clayoquot on Stubbs Island.

1875 Father Brabant takes up residence at Hesquiat and builds the first Catholic church on the west coast.

Mount Angel Abbey Library

1876 Philadelphia Centennial Exhibition features west coast artifacts including an eighteen-metre-long dugout canoe made for Chief Maquinna of Nootka and sold for one hundred dollars.

1879 J.D. Warren pre-empts first land (25 hectares) in Clayoquot Sound on Stubbs Island.

1881 Harry Guillod becomes first Indian Agent for the West Coast Agency.

1884 Canadian government bans potlatch.

1886 Jacob Gutman and Alexander Frank purchase the Clayoquot store, retaining Thornberg as manager.

1886–89 Indian Reserve Commissioner Peter O'Reilly establishes Indian reserve lands for the Hesquiaht, Ahousaht and Tla-o-qui-aht people of Clayoquot Sound.

1886 SS *Maude* travels regularly from Victoria to Alberni. Advertisements appear for tourists to travel on the *Maude* up to Clayoquot.

1887 Sealing schooner *Active* sinks. Twenty-four Kelsemaht hunters and five white men die.

1889 Penney and Brown buy Clayoquot store.

Early 1890s The first handful of permanent settlers arrive on the Esowista Peninsula.

1890 Post office opens at Clayoquot, with John Penney as first postmaster.

1892 Saltery established at Clayoquot on Stubbs Island, salting down salmon in barrels.

1893 Thomas Earle purchases Clayoquot store from Penney. Filip Jacobsen appointed store manager and postmaster.

1893 John Grice pre-empts Lot 114 Clayoquot District, the site of modern-day Tofino.

1893/94 Thomas Stockham and Walter Dawley establish their store and trading post on Stockham Island.

1894 Norwegian settlers Jacob Arnet, Thomas Wingen, and Bernt Auseth pre-empt land in Mud Bay on Tofino Inlet. Jens Jensen pre-empts land in what is now Jensen's Bay.

1895 John Eik and Ole Jacobsen arrive in the area. The following year Eik pre-empts Lot 115 Clayoquot District, adjacent to the Grices' land.

1894-95 Stockham and Dawley open branch stores at Nootka and Ahousat.

1895 T.S. Gore surveys all of Esowista Peninsula.

Monks Collection, courtesy of Lois Warner

1895 Clayoquot cannery opens.

1896 First May Day celebration at Clayoquot on Stubbs Island to celebrate Queen Victoria's birthday.

D. Laval photo, Ken Gibson Collection

1896 SS *Tees* makes her first voyage on the west coast. This vessel became a regular on this run, sharing the route with other vessels until 1917.

1896 Rev. John Russell starts Presbyterian mission at Ahousat, shortly followed by a small day school.

1898 SS *Queen City* makes her first voyage on the west coast run, a route she would share for many years with SS *Tees*.

1898 Walter Dawley named mining recorder as mining exploration increases in Clayoquot Sound.

1898 Stockham and Dawley build a hotel on Stockham Island.

1898 Thomas Earle builds a hotel and a large dock at Clayoquot, on Stubbs Island.

1898 A one-room school opens at Schoolhouse Point in Browning Passage, built by local volunteers. Twelve children register in the first year.

1898 Methodist medical missionary, Dr. P.W. Rolston, arrives at Clayoquot.

1899 Port Hughes mining community is established at mouth of the Bedwell (Bear) River.

1899-1901 Gold rush for placer gold at Wreck Bay.

1899 The first attempt of many to build a road—in this case a trail—from Tofino to Ucluelet.

Mount Angel Abbey Library

1900 Christie School, the Roman Catholic residential school at Kakawis on Meares Island, opens. Father Maurus Snyder and Father Charles Moser arrive to work in the school and at the Catholic missions.

1900 "Clayoquot Townsite" is surveyed, where Tofino eventually would stand, on land owned by John Grice.

1900 *Hera* sinks in Tofino Harbour.

1900 Harlan Brewster appointed postmaster at Clayoquot.

1900-01 First store opens on the Esowista Peninsula, where Tofino now stands, owned by the Chinese gold seeker Sing Lee.

1902 Stockham and Dawley leave Stockham Island and take over Thomas Earle's establishment at Clayoquot on Stubbs Island.

1902 Telegraph office opens at Clayoquot, connecting to Alberni.

1904 Presbyterian residential school opens at Ahousat.

1904 Stockham and Dawley part company acrimoniously. Dawley remains in charge at Clayoquot.

1904 Louisiana Purchase Exposition World's Fair in St. Louis features exhibits from the west coast. Several Ahousaht people travel to Louisiana for the fair. Handwriting and fancy work from Christie School are displayed.

1904 Francis Garrard becomes the first lighthouse keeper at Lennard Island.

1905 The Sechart whaling station opens in Barkley Sound.

1906 A one-room schoolhouse is built in Tofino by volunteers. Twenty-eight children register in the first year.

1906 The Chinese trader Sing Lee dies. James Sloman and John McKenna purchase his store on the Esowista Peninsula, where Tofino now stands.

November 1906 The large sawmill at Mosquito Harbour on Meares Island begins operating.

1907 A small copper mine opens at Sydney Inlet, where prospectors had been at work for nearly ten years.

1907 The Cachalot whaling station opens in Kyuquot Sound.

1908 First government wharf built at Tofino.

1908 First lifeboat station built at Tofino. Early lifeboats were powered by oars.

1908 First church wedding of an aboriginal couple on the west coast.

Chief Napoleon Maquinna marries Josephine, both former Christie School students, at Yuquot.

1908 The Estevan Point lighthouse is built.

1909 First Tofino post office opens and E.B. Garrard is appointed postmaster.

1908 First Clayoquot Hotel burns down.

1910 The Kennedy Lake Hatchery opens.

1911 An international treaty ends pelagic sealing in the Bering Sea.

1911 Father Maurus Snyder leaves after 11 years as Christie School principal.

1911 Railroad connects Port Alberni to Nanaimo and the rest of Vancouver Island.

1911–13 British settlers arrive to take up land, sight unseen, on Vargas Island.

1912 Father Brabant dies in Victoria. Father Charles Moser placed in charge of the Hesquiat mission.

1913 First gas-powered lifeboat used at the Tofino Lifeboat Station.

1913 SS *Princess Maquinna* makes her maiden voyage up the west coast. The *Tees* shares the west coast route with the *Maquinna* until 1917.

1913 St. Columba Anglican church built at Tofino.

1913 Legislation passed making pot-latching a criminal act.

1914 The McKenna-McBride Commission conducts hearings to reassess boundaries of Indian Reserves throughout British Columbia. Nuu-chah-nulth leaders in Clayoquot Sound appeal for more land.

1914 Telegraph line is extended from Clayoquot to Nootka.

Monks collection, courtesy of Lois Warner

1914–18 Young men from the Tofino area sign up to serve in World War I, including most men who settled on Vargas Island.

1915 *Carelmapu* shipwreck off Long Beach.

1915 Ada Annie Rae-Arthur (Cougar Annie) arrives with her family at Boat Basin, in Hesquiat Harbour.

1916 A school opens on Vargas Island. Ten children register in the first year. The school lasts only two years.

1916 Results of McKenna-McBride Commission cede very small amounts of extra land to First Nations in Clayoquot Sound.

1917 Ahousat and Alberni residential schools both destroyed by fire; students who set the fires receive jail sentences. Similar attempts by students at Christie School fail to burn the school.

1919 The schooner *Favorite*, having served as part of a floating camp for salting pilchards and making bait at Pretty Girl Cove since 1917, sinks in a storm.

1922 School attendance becomes mandatory in British Columbia, for aboriginal and white children.

1923 Some ninety Japanese families have settled at Tofino, Clayoquot, and Ucluelet. Three Japanese settlements emerge in the Tofino area; at Clayoquot, Storm Bay, and on John Eik's property.

1923 A rough road now exists between Ucluelet and Long Beach.

1923 Tofino Community Hall opens, thanks to much volunteer labour.

1926 Sign erected at the government dock in Tofino: "Pacific Terminus of the Trans-Canada Highway." Thirty-three years later, the road finally connects Tofino to Alberni.

1927 At the height of the pilchard fishery, twenty-six pilchard reduction plants operated on the coast between Barkley Sound and Kyuquot.

1927 Tofino and Long Beach are connected by a rough road.

1927 First car drives on Long Beach.

1927 First motorcycle drives on Long Beach, reaching 145 kilometres (90 miles) per hour.

1929 *Princess Norah*, designed for the increasing tourist trade, makes her maiden voyage up the west coast.

Image D02715 courtesy of Royal BC Museum, BC Archives

1929 Veteran west coast mariner Captain Edward Gillam dies on board the *Princess Norah*.

1929 Tofino Board of Trade established.

1929 Wingen's shipyard opens on Tofino waterfront.

1931 Pageant commemorating the arrival of Captain Cook at Nootka is staged on Tonquin Beach in Tofino.

1932 Tofino incorporated as a municipality.

1935 Fish hatchery closes at Kennedy Lake.

1936 Tofino Hospital opens thanks to community fundraising efforts.

1937 Walter Dawley retires as Clayoquot postmaster after thirty-five years.

1930s Hazel and Jim Donahue begin to operate "Camp Maquinna" at Long Beach, welcoming visitors to camp or stay in cabins.

1936 Arthur and Helen Lovekin build their large "Lovekin Estate" on Long Beach, where they spent part of every year.

Courtesy of Fran Aitkens

1937 Peg and Dick Whittington build guest cabins near their home on Long Beach at what is now the Green Point Campground, calling their place "Singing Sands."

1939 The combined enrolment at Ahousat residential school and Christie School reaches nearly 200 pupils, from villages up and down the coast.

Tofino Municipality collection

1940 Ahousat residential school burns down, to be replaced by a day school.

1941 Estevan Point is shelled by a Japanese submarine.

1942 Betty Farmer purchases Stubbs Island, taking over the hotel, store, and bar at Clayoquot.

1942 All people of Japanese descent in Canada are declared enemy aliens and evacuated from the west coast; their fishboats are confiscated.

October 1942 RCAF Tofino air base officially opens.

1944 Speed limit of 15 miles per hour posted in Tofino Village.

1945 RCAF Canso plane #11007 crashes at the base of Radar Hill; all twelve passengers survive.

1946 Earthquake and tsunami hit the west coast.

1947 Resolution passed by the village of Tofino that "all orientals be excluded completely from the Municipality, and...prevented from owning property and carrying on business directly or indirectly within the Municipality."

1948 The Crab Dock starts business in Tofino, canning crab on site, and later salmon and clams. The business, Tofino Packing, continued until 1964.

Late 1940s The Wickaninnish Lodge

opens at the southern end of Long Beach, operated by Nellie and Joe Webb.

1952 Final voyage of the SS *Princess Maquinna*.

1952 Tofino Hospital burns down.

1953 Potlatch ban lifted.

1954 New Tofino Hospital opens.

1950s Combers Resort, operated by the Buckle family, opens at Long Beach. The Morae family build the resort called Long Beach Bungalows, next to the Wickaninnish Lodge.

1959 A gravel road connects Tofino and Ucluelet to Port Alberni. Locked gates at both ends restrict public access hours.

1959 Maquinna Hotel opens in Tofino.

1964 Alaska earthquake. Tsunami takes out Tofino's water line, does considerable damage at Hot Springs Cove and Port Alberni.

July 1964 Robin Fells and Jeff Crawford open the original Wickaninnish Inn on Long Beach.

1964 Post office at Clayoquot permanently closed.

1964 Betty Farmer sells Clayoquot Hotel and Stubbs Island.

1964 Locked gates are removed and travel restrictions lifted on the road to Alberni.

1966 First surfing competition held at Wickaninnish Beach.

1967 BC-based whaling ends. Last whale processed at Coal Harbour.

1968–69 "Hippies" establish themselves at Wreck Bay (Florencia Bay).

1970 Pacific Rim National Park officially established. A 20-mile-per-hour speed limit is set on Long Beach.

1970 Prime Minister Pierre Trudeau surfs at Long Beach.

1971 Pacific Rim National Park officially dedicated by Princess Anne. Two thousand people attend the ceremonies.

1971–75 Residences and commercial buildings removed from the new Pacific Rim National Park. Many homes and businesses are expropriated.

1971–76 Jim and Carolyn Hudnall operate sea lion and whale-watching tours from Long Beach.

1971 New Christie School Residence opens in Tofino. Christie School on Meares Island closes.

1971 Herring roe fishery frenzy starts on west coast with Japanese roe buyers throwing money around like confetti.

1972 Opening of Wickaninnish School in Tofino.

1972 Road paving completed between Port Alberni and the west coast.

1972 Herring processing plant opens in Tofino.

1973 People arrive by the thousands on the newly paved road. Easter weekend finds 1,700 groups camping on the beaches. May long weekend sees some 10,000 people camped on Long Beach.

1973 *I Heard the Owl Call My Name* filmed at Ahousat, starring Tom Courtenay.

1973 Jim Hudnall and Bruce Atkey begin renting surfboards at Long Beach.

1974 Ka Ka Wis Family Development Centre established at old Christie School on Meares Island.

1974–80 The Gust o' Wind Arts Centre and coffee shop provides space for young newcomers and artisans.

1975 All beaches within Pacific Rim National Park closed to camping and cars.

1976 Maureen Fraser opens the Common Loaf Bakery, famed for its cinnamon buns.

1979 The name "Nuu-chah-nulth Tribal Council" is adopted by the West Coast District Society of Indian Chiefs, formerly the West Coast Allied Tribes (est. 1958). The NTC represents fourteen First Nations on the coast, including the Ahousaht, Tla-o-qui-aht, and Hesquiaht.

1979 Friends of Clayoquot Sound formed.

1982 Jamie's Whaling Station begins offering whale-watching tours.

1982 Tofino Village becomes District of Tofino, with its boundaries extended.

1983 Dick Close opens Weigh West Marina catering to sport fishing enthusiasts.

April 1984 At the Meares Island Easter Festival, Tla-o-qui-aht chief councillor Moses Martin declares Meares Island a Tribal Park.

November 1984 Meares Island blockade at Heelboom Bay (C'is-a-quis Bay).

1984 Liz Zed opens Tofino's first surf shop, Live to Surf.

March 1985 The BC Court of Appeal issues an injunction freezing all logging on Meares Island.

1985 First fish farm opens in Clayoquot Sound, in Irving Cove, Tofino Inlet.

1986 Maaqtusiis School opens at Ahousat.

1988 Protests at Sulphur Passage attempt to stop Fletcher Challenge logging in Shelter Inlet. Of the thirty-five people arrested, twenty served jail sentences.

December 1989 Oil from the *Nestucca* oil spill off the Washington State coast arrives on beaches near Tofino, leading to a massive cleanup.

1991 Protests against logging in Clayoquot Sound escalate. Kennedy River Bridge is burned, throwing 210 loggers temporarily out of work.

1991 Bulson Creek logging protests lead to further arrests.

1993 Middle Beach Lodge opens.

April 1993 Premier Mike Harcourt announces the Clayoquot Land Use Decision. This pleases no one and protests continue to escalate.

July 1, 1993 Clayoquot Peace Camp opens at the "Black Hole" clear-cut near the highway. Daily blockades and arrests begin at the Kennedy River Bridge.

July 1993 Australian band Midnight Oil plays concert to 5,000 people at the "Black Hole."

August 9, 1993 Largest mass arrest in Canadian history, with 309 people arrested at the Kennedy River Bridge.

Courtesy of Clayoquot Action

August 1993 Mass trials of Clayoquot protesters begin in Victoria.

October 9, 1993 Peace Camp closes.

February 1994 Stephen Owen releases his CORE report protecting many wilderness areas from logging and recommending significant changes to forestry practices.

March 1994 Ten to twelve thousand forestry workers hold huge rally in Victoria protesting CORE report.

1996 Charles and Howard McDiarmid open the new Wickaninnish Inn on Chesterman Beach.

1997 Tofino Community Hall demolished.

1997 The Tofino Mudflats, officially named the Tofino Wah-nah-jus Hilth-hoo-is Mudflats, are designated a Wildlife Management Area.

1998 Iisaak Forest Resources Ltd. assumes the timber licences once held by MacMillan Bloedel in Clayoquot Sound.

Late 1990s Properties on Chesterman Beach reach the million-dollar mark.

1999 Surf Sister Surf School opens.

2000 Clayoquot Sound receives United Nations Biosphere Reserve status.

2000 Clayoquot Wilderness Resort opens at Bedwell River.

2001 In downtown Tofino, two protesters live for twenty-eight days in the 800-year-old "Eik Tree" to protest its removal. Saved from the chainsaw, the tree is now supported by a steel brace.

2002 Long Beach Lodge opens in Cox Bay.

Courtesy of Sarah Platenius

2004 Tofino voters turn down referendum to upgrade the town's water system.

2006 On Labour Day weekend, a water crisis forces the mayor to impose severe water restrictions, threatening closure of all hotels.

2008 Truth and Reconciliation Commission receives a five-year mandate to investigate abuses in residential schools.

2008 Prime Minister Stephen Harper issues a formal apology to students who attended residential schools across Canada.

2009 Ahousaht hereditary chief Shawn Atleo elected national chief of the Assembly of First Nations.

2009 Tofino's Peter DeVries wins the O'Neill Cold Water Classic surfing competition at North Chesterman beach.

2009 Surf Sister co-sponsors first "Queen of the Peak" surfing competition for women and girls.

2011 Ty-Histanis First Nations village is constructed near Long Beach.

2011 High school opens at Maaqtusiis, run by the Ahousaht Education Authority.

2012 Tla-o-qui-aht and Ahousaht reach an "Agreement in Principle," Stage 4 of treaty negotiations.

2014 The Supreme Court of Canada rules that the Tla-o-qui-aht and Ahousaht have the right to catch and sell all species of fish within their territory.

ACKNOWLEDGEMENTS

We could not have written this book without help from many sources. Leona Taylor stands out. Her dedicated volunteer efforts have provided access to many sources of west coast historical information. She catalogued Walter Dawley's papers in the BC Archives and transcribed, year after year, articles about the west coast from Victoria newspapers, as well as cataloguing many other west coast resources. Her work has been invaluable.

Adrienne Mason kindly shared her research, her notes, and the contents of her filing cabinet, bulging with west coast information, with unstinting generosity. We are greatly in her debt.

Over decades, Ken Gibson has collected a wealth of documents and photographs, leading the way in assembling a west coast archive. We are most grateful to him for his assistance, and for sharing the scrapbooks of his mother, Daphne Gibson.

Ronald MacLeod of White Rock has fielded more questions than he ever expected, and he kindly shared his memoirs. He checked many facts and has been a source of unfailing support. Along with Bob Wingen, he has been one of the best friends this book has had. Thank you both.

Dorothy Arnet has repeatedly provided material she and the late Edward Arnet collected over the years. Thank you, Dorothy. Our gratitude also to Roly Arnet for photographs, fact-checking, and much information.

The encyclopedic knowledge of Barry Campbell has come to our aid many times. His familiarity with the area, through many years working at Pacific Rim National Park Reserve, and his work assembling the impressive archives there, have been an enormous help. May his heroic battle against invasive species prevail.

Particular thanks to Sharon Keen for her expert research assistance, especially with land title information, and for insisting we pay attention to early survey maps and survey field books. We would never have managed that without her.

Abbot Gregory Duerr of Mount Angel Abbey generously allowed us to use photographs from the West Coast Collection of the Mount Angel

Abbey Archives, and to quote from documents in the archive. Thanks also to Suzanne McKenzie, archivist at Mount Angel Abbey Library.

At the Tofino Municipal Office, we thank Mayor Josie Osborne, Aaron Rodgers, and JoAnne Flasch. At the Alberni-Clayoquot Regional District, Charity Hallberg Dodds was exceptionally helpful.

We extend our thanks to the many people who have helped us at the following institutions: the Royal BC Museum and BC Archives, the Vancouver Island Regional Library, Vancouver Island University, and the Tofino-Clayoquot Heritage Society. Special thanks to Sarah Hurford at Library and Archives Canada in Ottawa; to Kirsten Smith and Jamie Morton at the Alberni Valley Museum; and to Judy Carlson at the Alberni District Historical Society.

For photographic help, thanks to Mark Kaarremaa, a good friend to several books about the west coast, to Bonny Glambeck and Dan Lewis of Clayoquot Action who came to our rescue with important photographs, and to Sander Jain and Adrian Dorst for their images. Carol and Robert Windley introduced us to Anthony Guppy's photographs, Lois Warner shared Harold Monks's collection, and Bob and Doris MacKenzie also provided photographs. Fran Aitkens has been most generous in sharing photographs and documents. Our gratitude also to Barb Gudbranson of the Ucluelet and Area Historical Society, Sandra Boutilier at the *Vancouver Sun*, Kelly-Anne Turkington at the BC Archives, Caron Olive of Pacific Rim National Park Reserve, Linda Reid at the Nikkei National Museum & Cultural Centre in Burnaby, and Elizabeth Yuriko Fujita and Theressa Takasaki at the Japanese Canadian Cultural Centre in Toronto. John Ford of the Pacific Biological Station in Nanaimo helped with techno-wizardry, and answered countless questions about marine mammals.

Carlos García González created the maps; we are most grateful for his patience, skill, and hard work.

At Harbour Publishing, we thank Anna Comfort O'Keeffe, Nicola Goshulak, and Annie Boyar.

Audrey McClellan, West Coast editor extraordinaire, has contributed an immense amount; her meticulous work frequently saved us from ourselves. We were most fortunate to work with her.

Many others come to mind; all have contributed more than they realize:

Arlene Armstrong (Pacific Rim National Park Reserve); Jack Arnet; Dorothy Baert; Doug Banks; Rick Beardsley; Warren "Whitey" Bernard; Ginty Bigwood; Susan Bloom; Bob Bossin; Randy Bouchard and Dorothy Kennedy; Mare Bruce, Peter Buckland; Dr. John Clague (SFU Earth Sciences); Dick Close; Cairn Crockford; Stephen Ellis; Bev Ford; Maureen Fraser; Masako Fukawa; Keith Gibson; Bonnie Glambeck and Dan Lewis (Clayoquot Action); Dr. Barry Gough; David Griffiths; Jacqui Hansen; Mary Hardy; Neil Havers; Mark Hobson; Thora Howell; Jim Hudnall; Peter Huestis (National Gallery of Art, Washington D.C.); Vicky Husband; Mildred Jeffrey; Dr. Melanie Kelman (Natural Resources Canada); Carolyn Khoury; Monseigneur Michael Lapierre (Diocese of Victoria); Suzanne Hare and Steve Lawson; Jim Lornie; Richard Mackie; Mary Mackinnon; Ronald MacLeod (Campbell River); Charles McDiarmid; Tsimka Martin and Emre Bosut; Janet Mason (BC Provincial Toponymist); Saya Masso; Ruby (Karatsu) Middeldorp; Jim Morgan (Pacific Rim National Park Reserve); Jeremy Mouat; Michael Mullin; Lorraine Murdoch; Linda Nichol (Pacific Biological Station); Joan and Colin Nicholson; Briony Penn; Alan and Dorothy Pineo; Dave Pettinger; Sarah, John, Reed and Chloe Platenius; Robert Punnett; Don Reksten; Janet and Marguerite Robertson; Ruth Sadler; Eve Savory; Brenda Silsbe; Joan Skogan; Cameron Smith (Statistics Canada, Vancouver); Godfrey Stephens; Lucas Stiefvater; Joanna Streetly; Jim Swartz; Ralph Tieleman; Denise Titian; Robert and Nancy Turner; Meg and Guido Van Rosendaal; Dean Wanless; Stephanie Warner; Sharon Whalen and Chris Taylor; Jan Wilson; Calvin Woelke (Surveyor General Division, Land Title and Survey Authority of BC); Tim Woodland and Chris Yorath.

From Ian, personal thanks to his dear wife, Judith, who never complained about being ignored for hours on end, and to Chris Le Fevre for his encouragement and generosity.

From Margaret, thanks to her daughter Emma, who has seen it all before and knew when not to call, and to Michael Taylor, who is so good at silence and never blinked.

SELECTED SOURCES

A complete bibliography and notes on sources are available on the Harbour Publishing website. The following is a selective list of the major sources for this book, not including newspaper and journal articles.

Private Collections and Archives

Many unpublished documents and memoirs, personal letters, scrapbooks, and private collections of material have been made available to us by various individuals. These have been central sources in several chapters.

Archival collections consulted include: Alberni District Historical Society and Alberni Valley Museum; Diocese of Victoria archives; BC Archives and Royal BC Museum; Library and Archives Canada; Mount Angel Abbey library; Pacific Rim National Park Reserve archives; Queen of Angels Monastery archives; Surveyor General Division, Land Title and Survey Authority of BC.

At the BC Archives certain collections stand out: Walter Dawley's papers, the Earl Marsh Accession, Crown Land Pre-emption Records, and annual reports and records of various provincial governmental departments.

At Mount Angel Abbey library: the diary of Father Charles Moser, and letters and papers of Father Maurus Snyder (including many letters from Father Brabant).

At Library and Archives Canada: correspondence and reports about the Christie and Ahousat residential schools from the RG 10 collection, particularly Volumes 6430, 6431, 6439, and 6441.

Journals and Newspapers

See the "Victoria's Victoria" website for access to the British Colonist (from 1859) and the *Victoria Daily Colonist* (from 1910): www.victoriasvictoria.ca

Ha-shilth-sa newspaper. http://www.hashilthsa.com/

Tofino Time magazine. http://www.tofinotime.com/magazine/

West Coast Journal, The Westerly, Westerly News. Weekly newspapers from Ucluelet and Tofino. Incomplete collection, 1983–99, courtesy of Adrienne Mason

West Coast Advocate. "Tofino News" columns and other articles about Tofino, 1939–57, courtesy of Adrienne Mason.

The Sound magazine from 1991–99, courtesy of Adrienne Mason.

We have consulted several municipal sources. These include documents concerning land transactions on Stubbs Island and Wickaninnish Island, from the Alberni-Clayoquot Regional District office, Port Alberni. From Tofino Municipal offices: Tofino Board of Trade minutes (1929 onward) and Tofino Village Council minutes (1932 onward).

Reports

Arbour, Daniel, Brenda Kuecks, and Danielle Edwards, eds. *Nuu-chah-nulth Central Region First Nations Governance Structures 2007/2008.* Vancouver: Ecotrust Canada, September 2008. See online at http://ecotrust.ca/sites/all/files/ECReport-FNGovernance.pdf.

Bouchard, Randy, and Dorothy Kennedy. *Clayoquot Sound Indian Land Use.* Prepared for MacMillan-Bloedel Limited, Fletcher Challenge, and the British Columbia Ministry of Forests. Victoria: BC Indian Language Project November 1990.

Scientific Panel for Sustainable Forest Practices in Clayoquot Sound. *First Nations' Perspectives Relating to Forest Practices Standards in Clayoquot Sound: Appendices V and VI.* Victoria: Cortex Consultants Inc., March 1995.

Books

Abraham, Dorothy. *Lone Cone: A Journal of Life on the West Coast of Vancouver Island, B.C.* Victoria: privately printed, 1945.

Adachi, Ken. *The Enemy that Never Was: A History of the Japanese Canadians.* Toronto: McClelland and Stewart, 1976.

Arima, E.Y. *The West Coast (Nootka) People.* Victoria: British Columbia Provincial Museum, 1983.

Arima, Eugene, and Alan Hoover. *The Whaling People of the West Coast of Vancouver Island and Cape Flattery.* Victoria: Royal BC Museum, 2011.

Atleo, E. Richard (Umeek). *Tsawalk: A Nuu-chah-nulth Worldview.* Vancouver: UBC Press, 2004.

Barrett-Lennard, Charles Edward. *Travels in British Columbia with the Narrative of a Yacht Voyage around Vancouver's Island.* London: Hurst and Blackett, 1862.

Banfill, Nurse B.J. *With the Indians of the Pacific.* Toronto: Ryerson Press, 1966.

Barman, Jean. *The West Beyond the West: A History of British Columbia.* 2nd ed. Toronto: University of Toronto Press, 1996.

Berman, Tzeporah, Christopher Hatch, Maurice Gibbons, Ronald B. Hatch, Gordon Brent Ingram, and Loys Maignon. *Clayoquot and Dissent.* Vancouver: Ronsdale Press, 1994.

Berman, Tzeporah, with Mark Leiren-Young. *This Crazy Time: Living our Environmental Challenge.* Toronto: Alfred A. Knopf Canada, 2011.

Bossin, Bob. *Settling Clayoquot.* Victoria: Provincial Archives of British Columbia, 1981.

Boyd, Robert. *The Coming of the Spirit of Pestilence: Introduced Infectious Diseases and Population Decline among Northwest Coast Indians 1774–1874*. Seattle: University of Washington Press, 1999.

Breen-Needham, Howard, Sandy Frances Duncan, and Deborah Ferens, eds. *Witness to Wilderness: The Clayoquot Sound Anthology*. Vancouver: Arsenal, 1994.

Bridge, Kathryn. *Extraordinary Accounts of Native Life on the West Coast: Words from Huu-Ay-Aht Ancestors*. Canmore: Altitude Publishing, 2004.

Busch, Briton Cooper. *The War Against the Seals: A History of the North American Seal Fishery*. Montreal: McGill-Queen's University Press, 1985.

Cail, Robert E. *Land, Man, and the Law: The Disposal of Crown Lands in British Columbia, 1871–1913*. Vancouver: UBC Press, 1974.

Campbell, K. Mack. *Cannery Village: Company Town: A History of British Columbia's Outlying Salmon Canneries*. Victoria: Trafford Publishing, 2004.

Cannings, Richard and Sydney Cannings. *British Columbia: A Natural History*. Vancouver: Greystone Books, 1996.

Clayton, Daniel W. *Islands of Truth: The Imperial Fashioning of Vancouver Island*. Vancouver: UBC Press, 2000.

Cole, Douglas, and Ira Chaikin. *An Iron Hand Upon the People: The Law Against the Potlatch on the Northwest Coast*. Vancouver: Douglas & McIntyre, 1990.

Cole, Douglas. *Captured Heritage: The Scramble for Northwest Coast Artifacts*. Vancouver: Douglas & McIntyre, 1985.

Coyle, Brendan. *War On Our Doorstep: The Unknown Campaign on North America's West Coast*. Surrey: Heritage House, 2002.

Crockford, Cairn Elizabeth. "Nuu-Chah-Nulth Relations in the Pelagic Sealing Industry, 1868–1911." MA thesis, University of Victoria, 1996.

Dorricott, Linda, and Deidre Cullon, eds. *The Private Journal of Captain G.H. Richards: The Vancouver Island Survey (1860–1862)*. Ronsdale Press: Vancouver, 2012.

Drucker, Philip. *Indians of the Northwest Coast*. Garden City, N.Y.: Natural History Press, 1963.

Drucker, Philip. *The Northern and Central Nootkan Tribes*. Washington: Smithsonian Institution Bureau of American Ethnology, 1951.

Duff, Wilson. *The Indian History of British Columbia Vol. 1: The Impact of the White Man*. Victoria: British Columbia Provincial Museum, 1965.

Efrat, Barbara S., and W.J. Langlois. *Nutka: The History and Survival of Nootkan Culture*. Victoria: Provincial Archives of British Columbia, 1978.

Faa, Eric. *Norwegians in the Northwest: Settlement in British Columbia, 1858-1918.* Victoria: Runestad, 1995.

Fisher, Robin. *Contact and Conflict: Indian-European Relations in British Columbia, 1774-1890.* Vancouver: UBC Press, 1977.

Ford, John K.B. *Marine Mammals of British Columbia.* Victoria: Royal BC Museum, 2014.

Francis, Daniel, ed. *Encyclopedia of British Columbia.* Madeira Park, BC: Harbour Publishing, 2000.

Fukawa, Masako, with Stanley Fukawa and the Nikkei Fishermen's History Book Committee. *Spirit of the Nikkei Fleet: BC's Japanese Canadian Fishermen.* Madeira Park, BC: Harbour Publishing, 2009.

Fukawa, Masako, ed. *Nikkei Fishermen on the BC Coast: Their Biographies and Photographs.* Madeira Park, B.C.: Harbour Publishing, 2007.

George, Chief Earl Maquinna. *Living on the Edge: Nuu-Chah-Nulth History from an Ahousaht Chief's Perspective.* Winlaw, BC: Sono Nis 2003.

Gibson, Gordon. *Bull of the Woods.* Vancouver: Douglas & McIntyre, 1980.

Gibson, James. *Otter Skins, Boston Ships, and China Goods: The Maritime Fur Trade of the Northwest Coast 1785-1841.* Montreal: McGill-Queens University Press, 2001.

Glavin, Terry. *The Last Great Sea: A Voyage through the Human and Natural History of the North Pacific Ocean.* Vancouver: Greystone Books, 2003.

Golden Jubilee of Christie Indian Residential School: 1900-1950. Victoria: Acme Press, 1950.

Gough, Barry M. *Gunboat Frontier: British Maritime Authority and Northwest Coast Indians 1846-1890.* Vancouver: UBC Press, 1984.

Gough, Barry. *Fortune's a River: The Collision of Empires in Northwest America.* Madeira Park: Harbour Publishing, 2007.

Gough, Barry. *The Northwest Coast: British Navigation, Trade and Discoveries to 1812.* Vancouver: UBC Press, 1992.

Guppy, Anthony. *The Tofino Kid: From India to this Wild West Coast.* Duncan, BC: Fir Grove Publishing, 2000.

Guppy, Walter. *Wet Coast Ventures: Mine-Finding on Vancouver Island.* Victoria: Cappis Press, 1988.

Guppy, Walter. *Clayoquot Soundings: A History of Clayoquot Sound 1880s-1980s.* Tofino, BC: Grassroots Publication, 1997.

Guppy, Walter. *Eighty Years in Tofino*. Duncan, BC: Fir Grove Publishing, 2002.

Hagelund, William A. *Whalers No More*. Madeira Park, BC: Harbour Publishing, 1986.

Harper, Frank. *Journeys: Stories from Clayoquot Sound*. Tofino, BC: Cherub Books, 2006.

Harris, R. Cole. *Making Native Space: Colonialism, Resistance, and Reserves in British Columbia*. Vancouver: UBC Press, 2002.

Harris, Douglas C. *Landing Native Fisheries: Indian Reserves and Fishing Rights in British Columbia 1849–1925*. Vancouver: UBC Press, 2008.

Hayman, John, Ed. *Robert Brown and the Vancouver Island Exploring Expedition*. Vancouver: UBC Press, 1989.

Hempsall, Leslie. *We Stand on Guard for Thee: A History of the War Years at the Royal Canadian Air Force Stations, Ucluelet and Tofino*. Surrey, BC: Coomber-Hempsall Publishing, 2003.

Horsfield, Margaret. *Voices from the Sound: Chronicles of Clayoquot Sound and Tofino 1899–1929*. Nanaimo, BC: Salal Books, 2008.

Hume, Stephen, Betty Keller, Otto Langer, Rosella M. Leslie, Alexandra Morton, and Don Staniford. *A Stain Upon the Sea: West Coast Salmon Farming*. Madeira Park, BC: Harbour Publishing, 2004.

Jewitt, John. *White Slaves of Maquinna: John R. Jewitt's Narrative of Capture and Confinement at Nootka*. Surrey, BC: Heritage House, 2000.

Johnson, Peter. *Glyphs and Gallows: The Rock Art of Clo-oose and the Wreck of the John Bright*. Surrey, BC: Heritage House, 1999.

Kelm, Mary-Ellen. *Colonizing Bodies: Aboriginal Health and Healing in British Columbia, 1900–1950*. Vancouver: UBC Press, 1999.

Layland, Michael. *The Land of Heart's Delight: Early Maps and Charts of Vancouver Island*. Victoria: TouchWood, 2013.

Lillard, Charles. *Seven Shillings a Year: The History of Vancouver Island*. Ganges, BC: Horsdal & Schubart, 1993.

Lillard, Charles, ed. *Mission to Nootka 1874–1900: Reminiscences of the West Coast of Vancouver Island*. Sidney, BC: Gray's Publishing, 1977.

Lowther, Christine, and Anita Sinner, editors and contributors. *Writing the West Coast: In Love with Place*. Vancouver: Ronsdale Press, 2008.

McDiarmid, Howard. Pacific Rim Park: *A Country Doctor's Role in Preserving Long Beach and Establishing the New Wickaninnish Inn*. Victoria: privately printed, 2009.

MacGillivray, Don. *Captain Alex MacLean: Jack London's Sea Wolf*. Vancouver: UBC Press, 2008.

MacIsaac, Ronald, and Anne Champagne, eds. *Clayoquot Mass Trials: Defending the Rainforest.* Gabriola Island, BC: New Society Publishers, 1994.

McKelvie, B.A. *Tales of Conflict: Indian-White Murders and Massacres in British Columbia.* Surrey, BC: Heritage House, 1985.

McKervill, Hugh W. *The Salmon People.* Sidney, BC: Gray's Publishing, 1967.

Mackie, Richard, and Graeme Wynn, eds. *Home Truths: Highlights from BC History.* Madeira Park, BC: Harbour Publishing, 2012.

Magnusson, Warren, and Karena Shaw, eds. *A Political Space: Reading the Global through Clayoquot Sound.* Montreal: McGill-Queen's University Press, 2002.

Mason, Adrienne. *Historic Tofino: A Walk in Time.* Tofino, BC: Postelsia Press, 2012.

Mason, Adrienne. *Long Beach Wild: A Celebration of People and Place on Canada's Rugged Western Shore.* Vancouver: Greystone Books, 2012.

Meggs, Geoff. *Salmon: The Decline of the British Columbia Fishery.* Vancouver: Douglas & McIntyre, 1991.

Milloy, John S. *A National Crime: The Canadian Government and the Residential School System, 1879 to 1986.* Winnipeg: University of Manitoba Press, 1999.

Miller, J.R. *Shingwauk's Vision: A History of Native Residential Schools.* Toronto: University of Toronto Press, 1996.

Muckle, Robert J. *The First Nations of British Columbia.* Vancouver: UBC Press, 1998.

Murray, Peter. *The Vagabond Fleet: A Chronicle of the North Pacific Sealing Schooner Trade.* Victoria: Sono Nis Press, 1988.

Newell, Dianne. *Tangled Webs of History: Indians and the Law in Canada's Pacific Coast Fisheries.* Toronto: University of Toronto Press, 1993.

Nicholson, George. *Vancouver Island's West Coast 1762–1962.* Victoria: privately printed, 1965.

Nuu-chah-nulth Tribal Council. *Indian Residential Schools: The Nuu-chah-nulth Experience: Report of the Nuu-chah-nulth Tribal Council Indian Residential School Study, 1992–1994,* Port Alberni, BC: Nuu-chah-nulth Tribal Council, 1996.

Ormsby, Margaret. *British Columbia: A History.* Vancouver: Macmillan, 1958.

Palmer, Tim. *Pacific High: Adventures in the Coast Ranges from Baja to Alaska.* Washington, D.C: Island Press, 2002.

Peterson, Jan. *Journeys: Down the Alberni Canal to Barkley Sound.* Lantzville, BC: Oolichan Books, 1999.

Pethick, Derek. *First Approaches to the Northwest Coast.* Vancouver: J.J. Douglas, 1976.

Pitt-Brooke, David. *Chasing Clayoquot: A Wilderness Almanac.* Vancouver: Raincoast Books, 2004.

Platenius, John. *Tofino Guide.* Tofino, BC: Wild Cedar Publishing, 2011.

Popp, Carol. *The Gumboot Navy: Memories of the Fishermen's Reserve.* Lantzville, BC: Oolichan Books, 1988.

Ridley, Scott. *Morning of Fire: John Kendrick's Daring American Odyssey in the Pacific.* New York: HarperCollins, 2010.

Robson, Peter A. *Salmon Farming: The Whole Story.* Vancouver: Heritage House, 2006.

Reksten, Terry. *The Illustrated History of British Columbia.* Vancouver: Douglas & McIntyre, 2001.

Scott, Andrew. *The Encyclopedia of Raincoast Place Names: A Complete Reference to Coastal British Columbia.* Madeira Park, BC: Harbour Publishing, 2009.

Shilling, Grant. *The Cedar Surf: An Informal History of Surfing in British Columbia.* Vancouver: New Star Books, 2003.

Sproat, Gilbert Malcolm. *The Nootka: Scenes and Studies of Savage Life.* Edited and annotated by Charles Lilliard. Victoria, BC: Sono Nis Press, 1987. First published 1868 by Smith, Elder & Co.

Stewart, Hilary. *Cedar.* Vancouver, BC: Douglas & McIntyre, 1984.

Streetly, Joanna, ed. *Salt In Our Blood: An Anthology of West Coast Moments.* Tofino, BC: Aquila Instincts, 2002.

Suttles, Wayne, ed. *Handbook of North American Indians, Volume 7: Northwest Coast.* Washington, D.C.: Smithsonian Institution Scholarly Press, 1990.

Tamm, Eric Enno. *Beyond the Outer Shores.* New York: Thunder's Mouth Press, 2004.

Thompson, Jerry. *Cascadia's Fault.* Toronto: HarperCollins, 2011.

Titley, Brian. *A Narrow Vision: Duncan Campbell Scott and the Administration of Indian Affairs in Canada.* Vancouver: UBC Press, 1986.

Turner, Nancy J., and Barbara S. Efrat. *Ethnobotany of the Hesquiaht Indians of Vancouver Island.* British Columbia Provincial Museum Cultural Recovery Papers, No. 2. Victoria: Royal BC Museum, 1982.

Twigg, Alan. *First Invaders: The Literary Origins of British Columbia.* Vancouver: Ronsdale Press, 2004.

Usukawa, Saeko, ed. *Sound Heritage: Voices from British Columbia,* Vancouver: Douglas & McIntyre, 1984.

Van der Heyden, Reverend Joseph. *Life and Letters of Father Brabant: A Flemish Missionary Hero.* Leuven, Belgium: J. Wouters-Ickx, 1920.

Webster, Peter S. *As Far as I Know: Reminiscences of an Ahousat Elder.* Campbell River, BC: Campbell River Museum and Archives, 1983.

Wilson, Jeremy. *Talk and Log: Wilderness Politics in British Columbia.* Vancouver: UBC Press, 1998.

Woolford, Andrew. *Between Justice and Certainty: Treaty Making in British Columbia.* Vancouver: UBC Press, 2005.

Yorath, C.J. *The Geology of Southern Vancouver Island: Revised Edition.* Madeira Park, BC: Harbour Publishing, 2005.

Online Material

Ahousaht First Nation. *Ahousaht First Nation.* http://www.ahousaht.ca.

Clayoquot Biosphere Trust. *Clayoquot Biosphere Trust.* http://clayoquotbiosphere.org.

Clayoquot Sound Research Group. *A Political Space: Reading the Global through Clayoquot Sound.* Archived online by the University of Victoria. http://web.uvic.ca/clayoquot/home.html.

Friends of Clayoquot Sound. *Friends of Clayoquot Sound.* http://focs.ca.

Government of Canada. "First Nation Profiles": *Aboriginal Affairs and Northern Development Canada.* http://pse5-esd5.ainc-inac.gc.ca/fnp/Main/index.aspx?lang=eng

Government of Canada. "Indian Affairs Annual Reports, 1864–1990." *Library and Archives Canada.* http://www.bac-lac.gc.ca/eng/discover/aboriginal-heritage/first-nations/indian-affairs-annual-reports/Pages/introduction.aspx.

Government of Canada. "Schedule of Indian Reserves in the Dominion of Canada Part 2 Reserves in the Province of British Columbia Recompiled and Corrected up to March 31, 1943." *Library and Archives Canada.* http://www.bac-lac.gc.ca/eng/discover/aboriginal-heritage/first-nations/indian-affairs-annual-reports/Pages/item.aspx?IdNumber=33572.

Nikkei National Museum & Cultural Centre. "Nikkei Images." *Nikkei National Museum & Cultural Centre.* http://centre.nikkeiplace.org/nikkei-images/.

Province of British Columbia. "Historic Crown Grant Search." *The Province of British Columbia.* http://apps.gov.bc.ca/pub/rd/html/index.html.

Tla-o-qui-aht First Nations. *Tla-o-qui-aht First Nations.* http://www.tla-o-qui-aht.org.

Tla-o-qui-aht First Nations. "Tla-o-qui-aht First Nations Newsletter." *Tla-o-qui-aht First Nations.* http://tla-o-qui-aht.org/newsletter/newsletter.htm.

Truth and Reconciliation Commission of Canada. *Truth and Reconciliation Commission of Canada.* http://www.trc.ca/websites/trcinstitution/.

Truth and Reconciliation Commission of Canada. "Truth and Reconciliation Commission of Canada Webcast." *Livestream.* http://www.livestream.com/trc_cvr. (For dates and locations of specific TRC testimony cited in this book, see the notes on sources available on the Harbour Publishing website.)

Union of BC Indian Chiefs. "Unpublished Material." *Union of BC Indian Chiefs.* http://www.ubcic.bc.ca/Resources/ourhomesare/resources/unpublished.htm.

United Church of Canada Archives. "Ahousaht Indian Residential School." *The Children Remembered.* http://thechildrenremembered.ca/school-locations/ahousaht/.

Clayoquot Sound Timelines

Friends of Clayoquot Sound. "History." *Friends of Clayoquot Sound.* http://focs.ca/about-us/history/.

Iisaak Forest Resources. "Timeline 1978–2008." *Iisaak Forest Resources.* http://www.iisaak.com/timeline.html.

Ross, Andrew. "Clayoquot Sound Chronology." *A Political Space: Reading the Global through Clayoquot Sound.* Archived online by the University of Victoria. http://web.uvic.ca/clayoquot/files/appedix/Appendix2.pdf.

Tla-o-qui-aht First Nations. "Towards Resolution of the Land Question for Tla-o-qui-aht." *Inside Tla-o-qui-aht* 10, no. 2 (September 2008): 12–17. http://tla-o-qui-aht.org/newsletter/2008/SeptNews08.pdf.

Union of BC Indian Chiefs. "Historical Timeline: From 1700s to the Present." *Union of BC Indian Chiefs.* http://www.ubcic.bc.ca/Resources/timeline.htm#axzz2pO99iF8w

United Church of Canada Archives. "Ahousaht IRS Timeline." *The Children Remembered.* http://thechildrenremembered.ca/wp-content/uploads/2010/06/Ahousaht-IRS-Timeline1.pdf.

INDEX

fisheries patrol, 376–77
Japanese evacuation and, 387, 388
in Legion, 299
marriage of, 216
Princess Maquinna captains and, 370
in school, 335
surgery for son Ronald, 316
in WWI, 237, 239, 240
MacLeod, Ronald
on aboriginals in tourism, 364
on anti-Japanese feelings, 387, 388
on Boat Days, 352–53
on boys fishing, 378
on Clayoquot Days, 288–89, 290
in Fishermen's Reserve, 381
on Japanese playmates, 336
on lifeboat, 374
on *Princess Maquinna*, 353, 354
at *Princess Norah's* inaugural run, 368
on Rowland Brinckman, 305, 322
on *sake*, 343
on Sundays, 340
surgery, 316
on Tofino-Alberni road, 304, 438
on tourists, 316
on Trollers' Co-op, 344–45
visiting pilchard boats, 374
on weddings, 359
working at post office, 355
MacMillan Bloedel
BC government shares in, 515
boycotts of, 524–25
donation to hospital, 435
donation to Ka Ka Wis Family Treatment
Centre, 563
Highway 4 and, 437, 498
impact of Clayoquot Scientific Panel on,
527–28
internal report on protests, 510
Kennedy River Bridge fire and, 512
legal action against activists, 518, 522
logging during protests, 526
logging in Clayoquot Sound, 498, 499
Meares Island protests, 469, 501–5
use of own crews by, 500
MacMillan Provincial Park, 497
Madokoro, Hiroshi, 389
Madokoro, Mary, *see* Kimoto, Mary
Madokoro, Yoshio (Johnny)
as fisherman, 342
head of family, 341–42

impression of Tofino, 329
on Japanese at South Beach, 330
on Japanese evacuation, 386, 388–89,
389–90, 420
marriage of, 344
relocation to Alberni, 421
on *sake,* 320
schooling at Cumberland, 341
in Trollers' Co-op, 344
on Yasumatsu Isozaki, 324
Mae, Olivia, 488–89
Maekawa, Larry, 343
Magee, Bernard, 67
Magnesen, Alfred, 165, 166, 168, 170
Maiden, Cecil, 360
Mainstream Canada, 292, 494
Makah Tribe, 28
Malahat, 375–76
Malaspina, 375
Malaspina, Alejandro, 147
Maldonado, Manuel Antonio Flores, 57
Malleville, 108–9
Malon, Helen, 230–31, 232–34, 237, 239, 303
Malon, Madeline, 298, 391
Malon, Pierre, 230, 298, 416, 417
Malon, Yvonne, 230
Maltby, George, 143, 151, 156, 206, 211–12,
214, 330, 377
Maltby Slough, 330
Ma-Mook Development Corporation, 528
Ma-Mook Natural Resources, 529–30
Manhattan I, 372
Manhattan II, 373
Manhousaht First Nation, 23, 24, 242, 249
maps, 43, 306. *See also* nautical charts
Maquinna (late eighteenth century;
Mowachaht chief), 44, 48, 49, 51–52,
59–60, 65, 68
Maquinna (mid-nineteenth century;
Mowachaht chief),136
Maquinna (late nineteenth century;
Mowachaht chief), 97, 104, 254
Maquinna, Napoleon
(Mowachaht chief), 245–46, 311, 572–73
Maquinna, Will, 269
Maquinna Hotel, 405, 408–9, *462,* 467, 468,
486, 500, 575
Maquinna Marine Provincial Park, 484
Marchand, Len, 486
Margaret C., 372
Margaret, HMCS, 381